The Ubiquitous Śiva

AMERICAN ACADEMY OF RELIGION

ARR RELIGION IN TRANSLATION

SERIES EDITOR
John Nemec, University of Virginia

A Publication Series of
The American Academy of Religion
and
Oxford University Press

THE SABBATH JOURNAL OF JUDITH LOMAX
Edited by Laura Hobgood-Oster
The Antichrist Legend
A Chapter in Jewish and Christian Folklore
Wilhelm Bousset
Translated by A. H. Keane
Introduction by David Frankfurter

LANGUAGE, TRUTH, AND RELIGIOUS BELIEF
Studies in Twentieth-Century Theory and Method in Religion
Edited by Nancy K. Frankenberry and Hans H. Penner

BETWEEN HEGEL AND KIERKEGAARD
Hans L. Martensen's Philosophy of Religion
Translations by Curtis L. Thompson and David J. Kangas
Introduction by Curtis L. Thompson

EXPLAINING RELIGION
Criticism and Theory from Bodin to Freud
J. Samuel Preus

DIALECTIC
or, The Art of Doing Philosophy
A Study Edition of the 1811 Notes
Friedrich D. E. Schleiermacher
Translated with Introduction and Notes by Terence N. Tice

RELIGION OF REASON
Out of the Sources of Judaism
Hermann Cohen
Translated, with an Introduction by Simon Kaplan
Introductory essays by Leo Strauss
Introductory essays for the second edition by Steven S. Schwarzchild and Kenneth Seeskin

DURKHEIM ON RELIGION
Émile Durkheim
Edited by W. S. F. Pickering

ON THE *GLAUBENSLEHRE*
Two Letters to Dr. Lücke
Friedrich D. E. Schleiermacher
Translated by James Duke and Francis Fiorenza

HERMENEUTICS
The Handwritten Manuscripts
Friedrich D. E. Schleiermacher
Edited by Heina Kimmerle
Translated by James Duke and Jack Forstman

THE STUDY OF STOLEN LOVE
Translated by David C. Buck and K. Paramasivam

THE DAOIST MONASTIC MANUAL
A Translation of the Fengdao Kejie
Livia Kohn

SACRED AND PROFANE BEAUTY
The Holy in Art
Garardus van der Leeuw
Preface by Mircea Eliade
Translated by David E. Green
With a new introduction and bibliography by Diane Apostolos-Cappadona

THE HISTORY OF THE BUDDHA'S RELIC SHRINE
A Translation of the Sinhala Thupavamsa
Stephen C. Berkwitz

DAMASCIUS' *PROBLEMS & SOLUTIONS CONCERNING FIRST PRINCIPLES*
Translated with Introduction and Notes by Sara Ahbel-Rappe

THE SECRET GARLAND
Āṇṭāḷ's Tiruppāvai and Nācciyār Tirumoḻi
Translated with Introduction and Commentary by Archana Venkatesan

PRELUDE TO THE MODERNIST CRISIS
The "Firmin" Articles of Alfred Loisy
Edited, with an Introduction by C. J. T. Talar
Translated by Christine Thirlway

DEBATING THE DASAM GRANTH
Robin Rinehart

THE FADING LIGHT OF ADVAITA ACARYA
Three Hagiographies
Rebecca J. Manring

THE UBIQUITOUS ŚIVA
Somānanda's Śivadṛṣṭi and His Tantric Interlocutors
John Nemec

PLACE AND DIALECTIC
Two Essays by Nishida Kitarō
Translated by John W.M. Krummel and Shigenori Nagatomo

THE PRISON NARRATIVES OF JEANNE GUYON
Ronney Mourad and Dianne Guenin-Lelle

DISORIENTING DHARMA
Ethics and the Aesthetics of Suffering in the Mahābhārata
Emily T. Hudson

THE TRANSMISSION OF SIN
Augustine and the Pre-Augustinian Sources
Pier Franco Beatrice
Translated by Adam Kamesar

FROM MOTHER TO SON
The Selected letter of Marie de l'Incarnation to Claude Martin
Translated and with Introduction and Notes by Mary Dunn

DRINKING FROM LOVE'S CUP
Surrender and Sacrifice in the Vārs *of Bhai Gurdas*
Selections and Translations with Introduction and Commentary by Rahuldeep Singh Gill

THE AMERICA'S FIRST THEOLOGIES
Early Sources of Post-Contact Indigenous Religion
Edited and translated by Garry Sparks, with Sergio Romero and Frauke Sachse

GODS, HEROES, AND ANCESTORS
An Interreligious Encounter in Eighteenth-Century Veitnam
Anh Q. Tran

THE SUBHEDAR'S SON
A Narrative of Brahmin-Christian Conversion from Nineteenth-century Maharashtra
Deepra Dandekar

POETRY AS PRAYER IN THE SANSKRIT HYMNS OF KASHMIR
Hamsa Stainton

THE UBIQUITOUS ŚIVA VOLUME II
Somānanda's Śivadṛṣṭi and His Philosophical Interlocutors
John Nemec

AAR
AMERICAN ACADEMY OF RELIGION

The Ubiquitous Śiva

SOMĀNANDA'S ŚIVADṚṢṬI AND HIS PHILOSOPHICAL INTERLOCUTORS
VOLUME II

John Nemec

OXFORD
UNIVERSITY PRESS

OXFORD
UNIVERSITY PRESS

Oxford University Press is a department of the University of Oxford. It furthers the University's objective of excellence in research, scholarship, and education by publishing worldwide. Oxford is a registered trade mark of Oxford University Press in the UK and in certain other countries.

Published in the United States of America by Oxford University Press
198 Madison Avenue, New York, NY 10016, United States of America.

Library of Congress Cataloging- in- Publication Data
Nemec, John.
The ubiquitous Siva Volume II : Somananda's Sivadrsti and his philosophical interlocutors/
John Nemec.
pages cm. —(AAR religions in translation)
In English and Sanskrit (romanized); includes translations from Sanskrit.
Includes bibliographical references.
ISBN 978-0-19-756672-5 (hardcover : alk. paper)—ISBN 978-0-19-756673-2 (pbk. : alk. paper)—
ISBN 978-0-19-756675-6 (ebook) 1. Kashmir Saivism—Doctrines. 2. Somananda. Sivadrsti I.
Somananda. Sivadrsti. English. Selections. II. Somananda. Sivadrsti. Sanskrit. Selections.
III. Title. IV. Series.
BL1281.1545.N46 2021
294.5—2.dc22 2010043392

DOI: 10.1093/oso/9780197566725.001.0001

Paperback printed by Marquis, Canada
Hardback printed by Bridgeport National Bindery, Inc., United States of America

for Carmen

{ CONTENTS }

{ ACKNOWLEDGMENTS }

The present volume is the product of more than three years of steady work, and its completion would not have been possible without the assistance, encouragement, and support of colleagues, friends, and family. I could hardly thank all those who helped to make this book possible.

At the University of Virginia I have been fortunate to work with excellent colleagues. Among them I thank Cindy Hoehler-Fatton for her constant thoughtfulness and intellectual curiosity and Kevin Hart for endless good conversation and his always sound advice. Shankar Nair, too, has been an encouraging conversation partner. I also thank Michael Allen for answering several of my queries regarding Somānanda's arguments against the Vedāntins, as well my colleagues who responded to parts of this work in the context of UVA's Religious Studies Colloquium in the spring of 2019. It is a pleasure to have colleagues like these, who are also friends. In the Department of English, I am grateful for numerous conversations with David Vander Meulen around critical editing and textual criticism, as I have learned a lot from his knowledge of the history and practices of these academic disciplines. I also thank my former Ph.D. students Jef Pierce and Adam Newman for their conversation around this book (and much more), and, from among our current doctoral students, Meghan Hartman, Matt Leveille, Eliot Davenport, Courtney Averkamp, and Sam Grimes for the same.

A number of colleagues were generous in answering queries I had in the course of preparing this book, which served to improve my understanding of various passages of text and the philosophical or other issues addressed therein. For this I thank in particular Vincenzo Vergiani, Alex Watson, Michael Slouber, and Matthew Kapstein. Dan Lusthaus is a tremendous conversation partner, whose encyclopedic knowledge and unending curiosity are inspiring. I also thank Larry McCrea for inviting me to the second Around Abhinavagupta Conference, held at Cornell University in the autumn of 2016, in which I presented some of the work appearing in the present volume, and also for his instructive response to the same at that conference. Peter Bisschop put what was the product of that conference through a very helpful peer review (published now as what is listed in the bibliography as Nemec 2019), for which I am most grateful. And I thank Shaman Hatley for looking over the critical edition and for helpful suggestions for improving the same.

Gerry Larson offered thoughtful replies to my queries about Sāṅkhya philosophy and looked at selected passages of the *Śivadṛṣṭivṛtti* where Utpaladeva takes on this school's philosophical positions. I deeply regret that he cannot be here to see this work in its completed state. I, like all who knew Gerry, will miss him. Another good colleague and dear friend passed, too, before I could thank her for her support, humor, and guidance in this (and all my work), and for her simple and profound friendship. I will miss Anne Monious and deeply wish I could share the occasion of the publication of this book with her.

Without the encouragement of Lyne Bansat-Boudon, I would not have completed this project. Not only did she (together with Matthew Kapstein) invite me to the École Pratique des Hautes Études to give lectures in the late spring and early summer of 2016, when some of the materials herein were first examined by me, but she also pressed me to continue working with the *Śivadṛṣṭi* in a moment when I was less inclined to do so. I thank her, and Eric, for their friendship and support.

Many others, too, have been constant sources of friendship and have helped to cultivate a sense of well-being, or they have been supportive of this project in ways big or small, among them Rosane Rocher, Tim and Jen Dobe, Michael Linderman and Johann Vento, Mike and Amy Miller, Dominick Mis, Luis Pillich and Kendra Rothmaier, Barbara Holdrege, Mark Juergensmeyer, Tom Carlson, Loriliai Biernacki, Glen Hayes, Florinda De Simini, Frank Clooney, Hamsa Stainton, Douglas Brooks, Liam and Heather Murphy, Elise Auerbach, Louisa and Thomas Matthews, Brad Moore, Ahmed al-Rahim, Jeff Roth and Maria Sanders, Ellen Posman, Jonah Arcade and Samantha Dunnion Arcade, Nina Mirnig, Peter and Vanessa Ochs, Archana Venkatesan, Elaine Fisher and Jason Schwartz, and Rachel McDermott. Thank you.

I thank also Emil Homerin, who has been a constant source of inspiration since he taught me in my undergraduate days at the University of Rochester. His sudden passing in December of 2020 was utterly tragic and remains difficult to fathom. I, like all who knew Emil, deeply feel his absence, particularly so around the occasion of publishing this volume.

Elements of this project were presented at the AOS National Meeting, and I thank my colleagues there for their responses to the same and for their shared interest in and camaraderie over the years around working with Indian religious and other texts, among them Patrick Olivelle, Stephanie Jamison, Don Davis, David Brick, Adheesh Sathaye, Mark McClish, David Buchta, Steven Lindquist, Lauren Bausch, Dolores Pizarro Minakakis, and Tim Lorndale.

A work of this kind requires an access to unpublished textual sources that is not always so easy to gain. I thank the University of Virginia for the Arts, Humanities, and Social Sciences grant that allowed me to travel to India in the summer of 2016 in order to examine such sources. Christopher Tompkins sent me, unsolicited, digital copies of all of the "S" manuscripts, which he had photographed in Srinagar. These have proven to be tremendously helpful to the current project, and I thank him for his generosity. In particular, I am indebted to my friends and colleagues, Bharati Jagannathan and Prabhat Basant, for their help in securing access to the two "D" manuscript witnesses of the National Archives of India, and I thank the National Archives for permitting the same. I also continue to be grateful to all the libraries and archives in India that allowed me access to their manuscript collections around the time of the publication of the first volume of *The Ubiquitous Śiva*, including the Adyar Library, the Bhandarkar Oriental Research Institute, Calcutta Sanskrit College, the Niedersächsische Staats- und Universitätsbibliothek in Göttingen, the Staatsbibliothek zu Berlin, the Raghunath Mandir Library, the Rajasthan Oriental Research Institute library at Jodhpur, and the manuscript library of Trivandrum University. In addition, I thank the staff at the Government Sanskrit College, Thripunithura (Cochin) for their openness and kindness during a visit I made there in the summer of 2018.

The present book is formatted with the use of XeLaTeX and in particular a "style" file written by Somadeva Vasudeva around the publication of the first volume of *The Ubiquitous Śiva*. I thank him, again, for just that.

My understanding of the work put into evidence here was nurtured in my years of study in India, first with B. N. Pandit in New Delhi, Jammu, and elsewhere, and subsequently with Hemen Chakravarty and Mark Dyczkowski in Benares. I am thankful for all my teachers and for these three in particular for those happy years, too long ago now, in India. I only wish Hemenji and Panditji were here, still, to share in the publication of this volume.

Two colleagues deserve particular mention. James Reich and Ben Williams agreed to read the entire fourth *āhnika* of the *Śivadṛṣṭi* with me. This we did via Skype in weekly meetings over the 2018–2019 academic year, which greatly aided in the development of my understanding of the materials here to hand. One could not ask for better colleagues than these two, or better companions in reading Sanskrit, and I am grateful to them for the consideration and time they gave to this project.

At Oxford University Press, I thank my editor, Cynthia Read, for her steady interest in this book and for putting the manuscript through the peer review. Needless to say, publication would not have been possible without her support. Harmony Denronden expertly copyedited the manuscript with true professionalism, for which I am truly grateful. I also thank Theo Calderara for writing the book contract, Rajesh Kathamuthu for leading the production team, and the two anonymous readers for their thoughtful reviews of the manuscript.

Closer to home I owe a debt of gratitude to my parents, Joe and Judy Nemec, for all their support over many years, and also my brothers and sisters in law, Joe and Jen and Mike and Alexandra, for the same. Most of all, I thank Carmen, my wife, and AJ, our child, for their patience, enthusiasm, love, and support throughout the writing of this book, and for much beyond this. I could not have done it without them.

{ ABBREVIATIONS }

A	*Aṣṭādhyāyī* of Pāṇini
ChUp	*Chāndogya Upaniṣad*
HB	*Hetubindu* of Dharmakīrti
ĪPK	*Īśvarapratyabhijñākārikā* of Utpaladeva
ĪPKVṛ	*Īśvarapratyabhijñākārikāvṛtti* of Utpaladeva
ĪPṬ	*Īśvarapratyabhijñāṭīkā*, a.k.a. *Īśvarapratyabhijñāvivṛti*, of Utpaladeva
ĪPV	*Īśvarapratyabhijñāvimarśinī* of Abhinavagupta
ĪPVV	*Īśvarapratyabhijñāvivṛtivimarśinī* of Abhinavagupta
IsMEO	Istituto Italiano per il Medio ed Estremo Oriente
JAOS	*Journal of the American Oriental Society*
JGJRI	*Journal of the Ganganath Jha Research Institute*
JM	*Jayamaṅgalā* ad *Sāṅkhyakārikā*, of Śrī Śaṃkara
KKGU	*Kriyākālaguṇottara*
KSTS	Kashmir Series of Texts and Studies
KT	*Kiraṇa Tantra*
KuSaṃ	*Kumārasaṃbhava* of Kālidāsa
KVṛ	*Kiraṇavṛtti* of Bhaṭṭa Rāmakaṇṭha
MaBhā	*Mahābhāṣya* of Patañjali
MāVṛ	*Māṭharavṛtti* ad *Sāṅkhyakārikā*, of Māṭharācārya
MīSū	*Mīmāṃsāsūtra* of Jaimini
MT	*Mṛgendratantra*
MTṬ	*Mṛgendratantraṭīkā* of Nārāyaṇakaṇṭha
NB	*Nyāyabindu* of Dharmakīrti
NBhūṣ	*Nyāyabhūṣaṇa* of Bhāsarvajña
NBṬ	*Nyāyabinduṭīkā* of Dharmottara
NGMPP	Nepal-German Manuscript Preservation Project

NK	*Nyāyakandalī* ad PDhSaṃ, of Śrīdhara
NM	*Nyāyamañjarī* of Jayanta Bhaṭṭa
NS	*Nyāyasūtra* of Gautama, a.k.a. Akṣapāda
NSBh	*Nyāyasūtrabhāṣya* of Vātsyāyana
PDhSaṃ	*Padārthadharmasaṃgraha* of Praśastapāda
PS	*Paramārthasāra* of Abhinavagupta
PSam	*Pramāṇasamuccaya* of Dignāga
PSSaṃVi	*Paramārthasārasaṃgrahavivṛti* of Yogarāja
PV	*Pramāṇavārttika* of Dharmakīrti
PVin	*Pramāṇaviniścaya* of Dharmakīrti
PVSV	*Pramāṇavārttikasvopajñavṛtti* of Dharmakīrti
PVV	*Pramāṇavārttikavṛtti* of Manorathanandin
SāṅKā	*Sāṅkhyakārikā* of Īśvarakṛṣṇa
ŚBh	*Śābarabhāṣya* ad *Mīmāṃsāsūtra*, of Śabarasvāmin
ŚD	*Śivadṛṣṭi* of Somānanda
ŚDVṛ	*Śivadṛṣṭivṛtti*, a.k.a. *Padasaṅgati*, of Utpaladeva
SP	*Saṃbandhaparīkṣā* of Dharmakīrti
SSi	*Sphoṭasiddhi* of Maṇḍana Miśra
ST	*Siddhitrayī* of Utpaladeva
ŚV	*Ślokavārttika* of Kumārila
ŚVNRĀ	*Ślokavārttikanyāyaratnākara* of Pārthasārathi Miśra
TĀ	*Tantrāloka* of Abhinavagupta
TĀV	*Tantrālokaviveka* of Jayaratha
TS	*Tattvasaṅgraha* of Śāntarakṣita
TSā	*Tantrasāra* of Abhinavagupta
TSP	*Tattvasaṅgrahapañjikā* of Kamalaśīla
VP	*Vākyapadīya* of Bhartṛhari
VPVṛ	*Vākyapadīyavṛtti* of one Harivṛṣabha
VS	*Vaiśeṣikasūtra* of Kaṇāda
VSVṛ	*Vaiśeṣikasūtravṛtti* of Candrānanda
WZKM	*Wiener Zeitschrift für die Kunde des Morgenlandes*
WZKS	*Wiener Zeitschrift für die Kunde Südasiens*
WZKSO	*Wiener Zeitschrift für die Kunde Süd- und Ostasiens*
YD	*Yuktidīpikā* commentary (anonymous) on the SāṅKā
YS	*Yogasūtra* of Patañjali

{ PART I }

Introduction to the Translation

Somānanda's Philosophical Interlocutors

Introduction

The present volume offers a critical edition and annotated translation of the fourth chapter, or *āhnika*, of the *Śivadṛṣṭi* (ŚD) of Somānanda (fl. ca. 900–950), along with the extant passages of the commentary thereon of his immediate disciple, Utpaladeva (fl. ca. 925–975), the *Śivadṛṣṭivṛtti* (ŚDVṛ). This is, of course, a sequel volume. Its predecessor, published with OUP in 2011,[1] included a critical edition and translation of the first three chapters of the ŚD and ŚDVṛ, along with an analytical introduction discussing Somānanda's biography, his lineage, the Pratyabhijñā ("Recognition") school of philosophical thought that he founded, and the intellectual and cultural milieu of the Kashmir Valley in which he lived and wrote. Relying on the contextual information elaborated in the first, the present volume more narrowly examines only the relevant passages of the ŚD and ŚDVṛ. In doing so it stands witness to a fundamental change of focus in Somānanda's *magnum opus*: the first chapters of the ŚD, while they offered a précis of his theological views (chapter one), were substantially comprised of the author's critiques of competing schools of thought, including a proximate, esoteric Śaiva school—that of the goddess-centered Śāktas (chapter three)—and the philosophy of the linguistic monism of the Grammarian Bhartṛhari that influenced it, which Somānanda famously and thoroughly attacked in ŚD chapter two.

The fourth *āhnika* offers a self-conscious shift in the focus of the ŚD in two senses. First, Somānanda here turns his attention away from the milieu of Śaiva esoteric traditions—his "tantric interlocutors," as they were labeled in the first

[1] John Nemec, 2011, *The Ubiquitous Śiva: Somānanda's Śivadṛṣṭi and His Tantric Interlocutors*, New York: Oxford University Press.

The Ubiquitous Śiva Volume II. John Nemec, Oxford University Press. © Oxford University Press 2021.
DOI: 10.1093/oso/9780197566725.003.0001

volume—in order directly to engage selected mainstream schools of Hindu and Buddhist philosophy. Second, as Utpaladeva indicates in his commentary on ŚD 4.1-2ab, Somānanda also shifts his mode of discourse from one of identifying the shortcomings in others' positions and anticipating opponents' criticisms of his own to one primarily of developing constructive arguments meant to illustrate positively (*vidhimukhena*) the logical necessity of his settled opinion (*siddhānta*) that everything is of the nature of Śiva.

These "positive" arguments regularly come in the form of interrogating the philosophical positions of others, with Somānanda arguing that a proper understanding thereof proves the logical necessity of his own. That is, Somānanda argues implicitly and explicitly that his opponents cannot formulate their own philosophical positions *unless they implicitly accept his Śaiva ontology of unity* in doing so.[2] Four philosophical schools are engaged extensively, each well established in the subcontinent in its premodernity and well-known outside tantric circles of practice and thought. These include: Buddhist Epistemology and the writings of Dharmakīrti in particular, and the Sāṅkhya, Nyāya-Vaiśeṣika, and Mīmāṃsā schools of Hindu philosophy. In what follows, I summarily review Somānanda's engagements with each, after first identifying what I argue he presents formally as his settled opinion or *siddhānta*.

1A. SOMĀNANDA'S *SIDDHĀNTA*

The view for which Somānanda advocates herein is fundamentally an ontological one.[3] And his proposition, that all things in the universe are in their very nature identical with the one and unitary Śiva,[4] who exists in the form of consciousness, is presented on the order of a formal syllogism that is structured as follows.

---

[2] As Somānanda says in his summary of the chapter, a thorough understanding of his interlocutors' views proves the oneness (in the form of their very Śiva-nature) of all entities in the universe. See ŚD 4.125cd-126ab: *paracittaparijñānāt tasmāj jñeyaikyatā tataḥ || sārthasenāvanādyātma jagaty aikyaṃ sphutaṃ sthitam |*. "Hence, oneness may be known from the thorough knowledge (that is furnished here in this chapter) of the (philosophical) thoughts of others. Unity, the nature of which is (similar to) that of a caravan, an army, a forest, or the like, clearly exists in the universe."

[3] The arguments for ontological unity take various forms in the present chapter, as we shall see, but of particular note are the passages in which Somānanda makes arguments regarding the ontological presuppositions necessary to validate the logic of his opponents' epistemological views. For example, at ŚD 4.93cd-98a he interrogates the *kṣaṇabhaṅga* theory of his Buddhist interlocutors, the notion that all phenomena exist only in instantaneous moments and no longer. In doing so, he challenges the very possibility that such a theory could, in the absence of the existence of a single unity underlying and constituting such momentary instants, account for the possibility of inferential knowledge. This is so whether it is inference for oneself (*svārthānumāna*) or inference for another (*parārthānumāna*) that is placed under question. Ontology, in a word, defines the limits of his opponents' epistemological view, as he argues that only Śaiva non-duality can guarantee the very logical coherence of the same.

[4] See ŚD 4.1ab: *athedānīṃ pravaktavyaṃ yathā sarvaṃ śivātmakam*. "Next, the manner in which everything is of the nature of Śiva is now to be explained (by me)."

1. All phenomena in the world are possessed of Śiva-nature,

2. because all phenomena in the world are possessed of causal efficacy.

3. Whatever has causal efficacy exists as a power or capacity that is controlled by an agent—what is Śiva-nature. This is so in the manner that a king directs those who serve him, for example, or the god of the dualist Śaivas deploys the power of illusion (*moha*) and karmic equanimity respectively to create the world and to grace some among those dwelling within it with liberation.[5]

4. Since all phenomena in the world are, indeed, possessed of causal efficacy, which is the mark of Śiva-nature (this inasmuch as the phenomena are identified ontologically with Śiva by virtue of being his very powers or *śaktis*),

5. therefore all phenomena in the world are powers or capacities of one who controls them—Śiva—, which is to say they are possessed of Śiva-nature.

While neither Somānanda nor Utpaladeva explicitly characterize them as such, I propose that the opening passages of the present *āhnika* communicate all these five standard components of the well-known syllogism of the Nyāya.[6] Thus:

The thesis or *pratijñā*, i.e., number (1) as listed, is offered at ŚD 4.1ab, where Somānanda says that everything is of the nature of Śiva (*sarvaṃ śivātmakam*).[7]

The reason or *hetu* (2) is furnished immediately following, at ŚD 4.1c-d, where Somānanda says that nothing found in the world is "incapable" or *aśakta*, and only a real thing (*vastu*) could be *śakta*.[8]

The example or *udāharaṇa* (3) is offered at ŚD 4.4, where Somānanda says that all things, although capable of producing their own effects, are dependent for their efficacy on the one who deploys them toward some end, like a king who directs those who serve him or like Īśvara, according to the Śaiva Siddhānta,

---

[5] On these positions of the dualist Śaiva Siddhānta school, see footnote 21 of the translation.

[6] These passages are consonant with what is presented at ŚD 1.2, where Utpaladeva in his ŚDVṛ glosses the verse in question by suggesting it encapsulates a logical argument: he there identifies a thesis or *pratijñā*, a reason or *hetu*, and a means of knowing them (*pramāṇa*). See Nemec 2011: 104–106 and 277–278. The relevant passage reads in part as follows (lines 34–36 of my edition of Utpaladeva's commentary on the first *āhnika*): *sarvabhāveṣu svātmaiva śiva iti vyavahartavyam iti pratijñā. nirvṛtacidityādiviśeṣaṇakalāpo hetuḥ. sphurann iti dharmiṇo hetoś ca svasaṃvedanapratyakṣaṃ pramāṇam.*

For the Nyāya syllogism see NS 1.1.32: *pratijñāhetūdāharaṇopanayanigamanāny avayavāḥ* | "The (five) members (of the syllogism) are: the thesis [*pratijñā*], the reason [*hetu*], the example [*udāharaṇa*], the application [*upanaya*], and the conclusion [*nigamana*]."

[7] ŚD 4.1ab is translated in footnote 4.

[8] ŚD 4.1c-d: *nāśakto vidyate kaścic chaktaṃ vastv eva* . . . "Nothing exists that is incapable (of causal efficacy); (and) that which is capable (of causal efficacy) definitely is a real thing. . . "

deploys powers to create the universe and liberate bound souls.[9] Somānanda also further elaborates his understanding of the particular relationship of a capacity for causal efficacy to the agent who controls it, after he identifies the *hetu* and prior to the *udāharaṇa*, viz., at ŚD 4.1d-3. We shall return to this key passage momentarily.

The "application" or *upanaya* (4) is proffered at ŚD 4.5: Somānanda there states that Śiva alone, who is absolutely one—unique—engages in various ways with his powers or capacities, which are by their very natures the many (capable) entities in the universe; and he does so, Somānanda suggests, because he is uniquely and fully identified with those powers or capacities.[10]

Finally, the conclusion or *nigamana* (5) is stated at ŚD 4.6-7ab: all entities in the world are existent inasmuch as all entities are capable, and as such they are real in the ultimate sense of being Śiva, who is fully identified with the capacities themselves.[11]

The warrant that justifies the formal structure of this syllogism is identified at ŚD 4.1d-3. It is this, namely, that the *very existence* of multiple capable entities in the world, what can be known ostensively, demands the existence of an organizing agent who commands and controls them, lest all things be themselves utterly independent.[12] This is so because action of any sort, on Somānanda's view, is predicated on intention: an agent of action must exist who wishes to perform the act or acts in question. And each capable entity must be understood to be kept to a discrete and designated sphere, a circumscribed scope of action, lest everything be capable of doing anything. Only the existence of a single and fully independent agent who controls these entities guarantees not only that the range of their respective capacities is circumscribed, but also that they may be mutually coordinated and set in motion.[13] All capable entities,

---

[9] ŚD 4.4: *nṛpādisādhanāpekṣā svakarmaphalatā bhavet | sarvaḥ śakto 'pi sāpekṣa īśavan mohasāmyayoḥ ||*. "The state of being of one who owns the rewards of one's own actions must depend on the means of the king, etc.(, whom one has served). Everything, although capable (of producing its own effect), is dependent, like the Lord on delusion and (karmic) equanimity."

[10] ŚD 4.5: *tasmād anekabhāvābhiḥ śaktibhis tadabhedataḥ | eka eva sthitaḥ śaktaḥ śiva eva tathā tathā ||*. "Therefore, Śiva alone is empowered, he being absolutely unique, one who remains occupied in various ways with the powers, whose natures are multiple, this because he is not different from them."

[11] ŚD 4.6-7ab: *tathā yatra sad ity evaṃ pratītis tad asat katham | yat sat tat paramārtho hi paramārthas tataḥ śivaḥ || sarvabhāveṣu cidvyakteḥ sthitaiva paramārthatā |*. For my translation of the present passage, see at footnote 20 of the present introduction. Or, perhaps it is better to view both the "application" and the conclusion of the syllogism to be expressed at ŚD 4.5, with ŚD 4.6-7ab expressing the implications of the same.

Let me note that, from this author's point of view, the following is a weak point in the syllogism: it could be argued that Somānanda presupposes the non-duality he claims to find in the Śiva-nature of all. That is, Somānanda may be said to argue in a valid manner for the need for a single, ultimately placed agent to command and control multiple capable entities, but one could argue he does not make a valid claim to the ontological identity of those entities—as powers or otherwise—with that single agent.

[12] See ŚD 4.1d-2ab: . . . *te 'pi no || iṣyante bahavaḥ śaktāḥ sarvasvātantryam āpatet |*. ". . . although we certainly do not accept that the many [entities in the world] are themselves (individually) capable: that would lead to everything being independent."

[13] See ŚD 4.2cd-3: *athaikasyādhikā śaktir nyūnaśaktinibandhinī || svakāryaviṣaye sarvaḥ śakta eva nibandhanam | śaktasya śakyate kartum evaṃ cen nānyaśaktatā ||*. "Rather, a superior power of one

in a word, must be understood to be placed in and partake of such a structural matrix, such that superior capacities bind or restrain subordinate ones, all in a unitary and controlled hierarchy. Otherwise, there would be no way *logically* to understand a plural number of powers or capacities to function in a coordinated manner.

This—what is a theological claim made by way of this logical claim—is in fact fundamental to the entire thread of arguments in the present chapter of the ŚD. The claim is, moreover, not only that multiplicity can *only* exist by way of unity, but also that the very evidence for unity is the readily apparent multiplicity in the universe, which one experiences—knows—habitually in quotidian experience! For the fact that everything that is knowable performs some action and effects some result—at the very least anything knowable in consciousness is capable of making itself thus known—suggests not only that all that can be experienced is real, but that all phenomena require a place in this structured hierarchy and must be associated with a single agent who orders and controls them. In a word, all must be identified with the one Śiva as his powers, Somānanda argues, for only this non-dual identification can explain the mutual interrelation and functioning of the multiple capable entities that ostensively may be said to exist.

This thesis and its syllogistic components are tested repeatedly in the fourth *āhnika* against the views of Somānanda's philosophical interlocutors and with respect to a range of philosophical issues. Thus he may be said to offer a positive account for his philosophical position by way of criticizing the limits of his opponents' views, illustrating how they must presuppose his Śaiva non-duality in order to justify their particular treatments of particular philosophical problems, including, among other concerns, the nature of language and its denotative capacity; a proper understanding of causality, mereology, and the nature of perception; and an examination of the grounds on which one can justify or explain inferential reasoning. It is to these particular arguments that we now turn.

1B. SOMĀNANDA'S ENGAGEMENT WITH BUDDHIST EPISTEMOLOGY

The language used in this introductory section of the *āhnika* is, *prima facie*, not only consonant with but evocative of Śaiva theological formulations. This is particularly evident inasmuch as Somānanda says that "real things" (*vastus*) in the world are "capable" or *śakta*, the latter term of course calling to mind the feminine power or *śakti* that is invoked across Śaiva literatures and in the ŚD

[capable agent] restrains a subordinate power (of the same). Everything(, however,) is fully capable within the domain of its own work; (for) the (only) restraining that can be effected belongs to the one [agent] who is capable. If this is the case, the others are not (individually) capable."

itself.[14] In fact, however, Somānanda here also cites the writings of the Buddhist epistemologist Dharmakīrti. For in suggesting that nothing found in the world is "incapable" (*aśakta*), ŚD 4.1 clearly draws a contrast with the *Pramāṇavārttika* (PV) regarding the nature of objects of cognition, which for Dharmakīrti may be divided into objects that are capable of causal efficacy (*arthakriyā*) and what are not real objects, such as the floating hair one might sense on the eye, which have no causal efficacy.[15] Utpaladeva in explaining Somānanda's reference to the non-existence of anything that is incapable (*nāśakto vidyate kaścit*, ŚD 4.1c) makes the reference more explicit by speaking explicitly in terms of the causal efficacy (*arthakriyā*) of such objects, which is of course a key concept of Dharmakīrtian thought, and he goes on to describe the nature of the *vastu* (ŚD 4.1d) by paraphrasing but reformulating Dharmakīrti's view of the same: the real thing, Utpaladeva explains, if it is capable, exists in the ultimate sense or is *paramārthasat*, what is Śiva-nature itself.[16] Indeed, though this statement again evokes Śaiva theological terminology precisely in referring to the *vastu* as *paramārthasat*, it is fundamentally a reworking of the formulation offered in the NB: "That [*svalakṣaṇa*] alone is what exists in the ultimate sense. This is so because that which is real [*vastu*] is defined by its capacity for causal efficacy."[17]

The argument, then, is crafted in opposition, first of all, to Dharmakīrti's twofold classification of reality, his distinction of what is the ultimate reality from what is merely conventionally real.[18] It is for this reason that Utpaladeva repeatedly explains Somānanda's verses by arguing that whatever is found in the world—whatever is sensible in any sense in consciousness, including the floating hair—is real in the ultimate sense, at the very least for making itself known in consciousness at all.[19] And, indeed, Somānanda, too, is explicit

---

[14] ŚD 4.5 (cited in footnote 10) explicitly refers to Śiva and his *śaktis*, and "power" was a major concern of ŚD 3. See, esp., ŚD 3.2cd-3: *na śivaḥ śaktirahito na śaktir vyatirekiṇī || śivaḥ śaktas tathā bhāvān icchayā kartum īdṛśān | śaktiśaktimator bhedaḥ śaive jātu na varṇyate ||*. "Śiva does not exist apart from *śakti*; *śakti* is not different (from Śiva). And Śiva is empowered [*śakta*] to create such entities at will. In Śaivism, no difference whatsoever between power and the one possessing the power is described."

[15] See PV (*pratyakṣapariccheda*) 3.1: *pramāṇaṃ dvividhaṃ meyadvaividhyāc chaktyaśaktitaḥ | arthakriyāyāṃ keśādir nārtho 'narthādhimokṣataḥ ||*. "The means of knowledge is two-fold because the object of knowledge is two-fold, this [i.e., the latter double-nature] inasmuch as it [i.e., the object] is capable or incapable of causal efficiency [*arthakriyā*]. The hair (one erroneously sees floating on one's eye), for example, is not a real object, because there is no determinate apprehension of it as such." The present rendering is a slight modification of that of Franco and Notake 2014: 29.

[16] See ŚDVṛ ad ŚD 4.1-2ab (lines 8–9 of the present edition): *śaktaṃ cet, tad vastv eva paramārthasad eva śivarūpam iti.*

[17] See NB 1.14-15: *tad eva paramārthasat. arthakriyāsāmarthyalakṣaṇatvād vastunah.*

[18] Dharmakīrti states this well-known position at, e.g., PV (*pratyakṣapariccheda*) 3.3 (with 3.3ab being identical to PVin 2.55ab): *arthakriyāsamarthaṃ yat tad atra paramārthasat | anyat saṃvṛtisat prokte te svasāmānyalakṣaṇe ||*. "What is capable of causal efficacy is real in the ultimate sense, here. The other is conventionally real. The two are (respectively) referred to as the *svalakṣaṇa* and the *sāmānyalakṣaṇa*."

[19] Somānanda's understanding of all as real in the ultimate sense is found at ŚD 4.1-2ab and is reinforced by Utpaladeva's commentary thereon, as cited in footnote 16. See also, e.g., ŚDVṛ ad ŚD 4.6-7ab (lines 40–41 of the edition of the present volume): *śaktaṃ vastv evety uktaṃ, vastu ca sad ucyate.*

in stating as much, in what I identify as the *nigamana* or conclusion to his syllogism:

> Thus, how could that [i.e., the *vastu*] be inexistent where it is perceived in this way as existing? Indeed, that which is existent is the ultimate reality; (and since) it is the ultimate reality, it follows from that that it is Śiva. The state of being the ultimate reality is fully present in all entities, because they are manifested in consciousness.[20]

There may be no binary classification of phenomena into qualitatively different classes or types of objects of knowledge on this view—particular, real entities (*svalakṣaṇas*), on the one hand, and conceptual forms, on the other (what, as is well known, Dharmakīrti suggests are apprehended respectively by two corresponding means of knowledge[21]). This is to say that Somānanda rejects the fundamental division of percept from concept that is favored by his Buddhist interlocutors. So much is articulated in a difficult passage of the *āhnika* (at ŚD 4.81cd-84ab) for which the commentary is lost. There, Somānanda argues (in consonance with the Mīmāṃsā, as we shall see) that the two types of objects of which the Buddhists conceive must be mutually integrated in a Śaiva matrix of non-duality if his opponent's position is logically to cohere. For there would otherwise be no way for conceptual forms to relate to perceptual phenomena.[22]

---

yac ca sat, tan nāsad iti sa eva paramārthaḥ. yasmāc ca paramārthas tataḥ sattvāt paramārthatvāc chivaḥ. "[Somānanda] has said that that which is capable (of causal efficacy) is definitely a real thing [*vastu*], and he (now) says that the *vastu* is existent. What is existent, moreover, is not inexistent; thus, it is itself the ultimate reality. And since it is the ultimate reality, it follows from that—i.e., from its being the ultimate reality, due to the fact that it is existent—that it is Śiva."

Utpaladeva also elaborated his argument that *everything* appearing in consciousness is real in this sense later in his commentary on ŚD 4.6-7ab. There, he entertains the objection of an opponent who asks how something in the world that is apparently insentient (*jaḍa*) could be counted as Śiva. Utpaladeva replies that, inasmuch as an entity is known in consciousness it is manifested in consciousness, and this alone establishes its very existence as what is the ultimate reality, namely, as the manifesting consciousness.

20 See ŚD 4.6-7ab, recorded at footnote 11.

21 See PV (*pratyakṣapariccheda*) 3.54cd: *tasya svapararūpābhyāṃ gater meyadvayaṃ matam* ||. "It is held (by Dignāga) that there is a pair of objects of cognition, because that [particular] is understood by its own form (via direct cognition) and by way of another form (via inference)." (Translation a modification of Franco and Notake 2014: 140.) The same was noted too, at PV (*pratyakṣapariccheda*) 3.1, cited in footnote 15.

22 Given Somānanda's well-known and vociferous rejection of Bhartṛhari's ontology, to which he devoted an entire *āhnika* of the ŚD, one may rightly question how, precisely, he comes to accept a concept that is evocative of—not at all to say identifiable with—a central tenet of the philosophy of the Grammarians, namely, the fact that all phenomena are imbued with a nature that is *śabda* or "speech." (That all is infused with *śabda* is of course expressed at VP 1.131ab, also cited at ŚD 2.10ab: *na so 'sti pratyayo loke yaḥ śabdānugamād ṛte* |. "There is no understanding in the world that is not connected with speech.") Somānanda's views on the matter will be examined in greater detail with our discussion of his engagement with the philosophical views of the Mīmāṃsā, but suffice it here to say he evidently follows Kumārila in understanding the nature of the object perceived to be imbued with linguisticality inasmuch as a universal or *sāmānya* is innately associated with it. This does not suggest, however, that

Also embedded in the logic of the syllogism that defines Somānanda's "settled opinion" is a challenge to Dharmakīrti's conception of error. Simply, if everything in the world is Śiva, inasmuch as everything is real, the latter because everything is capable, then even what are conventionally understood to be erroneous or illusory cognitions must be conceived in the same fashion: *everything* is real in the ultimate sense (*paramārthasat*). Thus, as I have indicated elsewhere,[23] it is in the fourth *āhnika* that Somānanda delivers an argument for the ultimate reality of apparent illusions, what he promised in the first *āhnika* to explain "later on," the promise coming in the form of an explicit rebuke of Dharmakīrti's own understanding of the matter.[24] Simply, the present chapter and its commentary suggest that *nothing* that appears in consciousness may be said to be erroneous, because, as stated, "the state of being the ultimate reality is fully present in all entities, because they are manifested in consciousness." The fact of appearing in consciousness renders any cognition real in just that sense—of being consciousness.

The present concern is discussed at length in the fourth *āhnika*, where two distinguishable, though philosophically related, analyses of the problem merit our attention. First, consider an interesting passage of Utpaladeva's commentary (found at ŚDVṛ ad ŚD 4.19-21ab) that deals with error by addressing the nature of dreaming sleep. There, Utpaladeva argues that even a cognition of something that does not exist in the everyday world, such as that of water in a dream, is capable of causal efficacy and therefore is real. This is so inasmuch as such cognitions can please the agent who knows them. Thus, the dreamer of the present example may delight in the satisfaction of drinking water in a dream, the delight being real even while the water is merely imagined.[25] For causal efficacy is not dependent on the external reality of a cognitive experience;

Somānanda denies the possibility of non-conceptual perception, as Kumārila also does not. See section 1c of the introduction, entitled "Somānanda's Interaction with His Mīmāṃsaka Interlocutors."

[23] See Nemec 2011: 8, fn. 16. Cf. Nemec 2012: 233.

[24] This is found at ŚD 1.45cd-46ab: *dṛśyante 'tra tadicchāto bhāvā bhītyādiyogataḥ* || *tatra mithyāsvarūpaṃ cet sthāpyāgre satyatedṛśām* |. "By his will, entities are seen here that are associated with fear, etc. If you argue that they have an erroneous nature, I will establish the reality of such entities later on." The passage, as is well known—see, e.g., Gnoli 1957: 22—, evokes the PV (*pratyakṣapariccheda*) 3.282: *kāmaśokabhayonmādacaurasvapnādyupaplutāḥ* | *abhūtān api paśyanti purato 'vasthitān iva* ||. "He who is blinded by intense desire, by sorrow, by fear, by drunkenness, by dreaming of thieves, etc., can see, as clearly as if they were before him, things that, in reality, do not exist." (Translation Gnoli's [*op. cit.*], also cited in Nemec 2011: 143–144, fn. 335, where, regrettably, the citation erroneously directs the reader to a [non-existent] p. 28 of Gnoli's article.)

[25] See ŚDVṛ ad ŚD 4.19-21ab, esp. lines 130–131: *abhrāntatvād vāstavasvapnajalasya pānādyarthakriyā bhrāntāpi syāt, tṛṇnivṛttyā tu tṛptiḥ svasaṃvedanasiddhā na visaṃvadati.* "A causal efficacy—that of drinking, for example—may exist (within the dream-state) for water that is real in a dream, because it [i.e., the water] is not unreal (in the dream), although it [i.e., the causal efficacy] is unreal (outside of the dream); and still, with the quenching of one's thirst (in the dream) there is a satisfaction that, having been established in self-awareness, does not deceive." The passage is not without text-critical difficulties, however, about which see the critical edition and footnote 103 of the translation. See also footnote 104 of the translation for an explanation of how and to what degree

it may be found even in phenomena that appear only to the internal sense organ.[26]

More generally—this is the second analysis of error—the ŚD details at length an argument for the reality of supposedly erroneous perceptions. Their reality, Somānanda again argues, consists in the very fact that such perceptions appear in consciousness. In making this case, Somānanda suggests that Dharmakīrti can draw a distinction between real and unreal objects of knowledge only conventionally, and only by first implicitly accepting the Śaiva view that all phenomena are real *qua* appearing in and as Śiva-as-consciousness. He says:

> Those [perceptions] that could be conceived of as erroneous cognitions are found to be capable of manifestation in consciousness. That constitutes reality; (and) that [reality] (in turn) is the Śiva-nature that exists here [in even these "erroneous" perceptions], as well.[27]

So much effectively claims what Utpaladeva's *Īśvarapratyabhijñākārikās* (ĪPK) and *Īśvarapratyabhijñākārikāvṛtti* (ĪPKVṛ) so famously stated, that all that is inexistent must be only that—totally beyond the realm of the knowable—while all that is existent need do nothing to obtain that existence.[28] *Anything* appearing in and as consciousness is real, existent *qua* appearing as such; nothing that cannot appear in consciousness may be countenanced at all.

Appearing or existing, to reiterate, is on this view always tied to an agent, a knower who wishes to know or do whatever it is that appears in consciousness.[29] All phenomena are possessed of existence in the ultimate sense, are *paramārthasat*—capable (*śakta*) of effecting some result wished for by the one

---

Utpaladeva here affirms Dharmottara's understanding of right or correct knowledge to make the claim that the water that is real in a dream is non-deceptive (*avisaṃvādaka*).

[26] On the pair of sense organs, internal and external, described in Utpaladeva's writings, see footnotes 237, 263, 276, 284, and, especially, 283 of the translation.

[27] See ŚD 4.7cd-8b: *mithyājñānavikalpyānāṃ sattvaṃ cidvyaktiśaktatā || vidyate tat tad atrāpi śivatvaṃ*. . . . The same is also cited in Nemec 2012: 228, fn. 9. On the textual variants found herein, see the critical edition and footnote 35 of the translation. On the word-order (*anvaya*) of the verse, see footnote 36 of the translation.

Cf. ŚDVṛ ad ŚD 4.7cd-9, lines 53–55 of the present edition (and note the parallels with ŚDVṛ ad ŚD 4.6-7ab, recorded in footnote 42 of this volume's translation): *mithyājñānavikalpanīyānāṃ rajatasarpādīnāṃ ghaṭādīnām iva cidvyaktiśaktatā prakāśamānatā nāma vidyate, tad eva sattvaṃ paramārthatvam ato 'pi tac chivatvam*. "Those [perceptions] that could be conceived of as erroneous cognitions—those of silver (for mother-of-pearl) or a snake (for a rope), for example—are, like (perceptions of) pots, etc., simply found to be capable of manifestation in consciousness, which is to say they are manifested in consciousness [*prakāśamānatā*]. That itself constitutes their reality, i.e., being the ultimate reality; (and) that, it also follows, is (their) Śiva-nature."

[28] I here refer to ĪPK 2.4.3a-d: *yad asat tad asad yuktā nāsataḥ satsvarūpatā | sato 'pi na punaḥ sattālābhenārtho* . . . "That which is non-existent is non-existent; it is not tenable that that which is non-existent has an existent nature. As for that which is existent, by contrast, there is no need for it to acquire existence." Note also the similarity of expression in ĪPK 2.4.3a and ŚD 4.6ab (*tathā yatra sad ity evaṃ pratītis tad asat katham*).

[29] See, e.g., ŚD 4.8b-9a: . . . *kena vāryate | iti ced eṣu satyatvaṃ sthitam eva cidudgamāt || tathā śivodayād eva* . . . "Objection: By what are they averted? (Reply:) Reality is fully established in these

agent in existence, Śiva. Cognitions are never unreal inasmuch as they are *always* what is wished for by the sovereign who deploys them, this being what makes them capable in the first place. This is so such that, for example and by way of analogy, a king may issue alloyed coins that are nevertheless valued in everyday transactions as if they were made of pure gold, simply because he wishes it to be thus.[30]

Endeavoring logically to guarantee this proposition—that no cognition is erroneous—Somānanda devotes considerable effort to proving that no cognition may be said to be invalidated, this—again—in an explicit dispute with Dharmakīrti. He argues that no cognition or any element of the experience thereof may be shown to have been false subsequent to the cognition thereof. None may be contradicted. This includes the moment of time in which a cognition appeared, the act of its production, the agent's experience thereof, the sense organ that knew it, the relation of the sense organ to the object of cognition in question, the activity of seeing erroneously, and the locus where such a cognition is said to have occurred.[31] It is not possible even for a subsequent cognition to contradict a previous one. This Somānanda argues by claiming that neither of the two types of contradiction identified by Dharmakīrti himself—mutual non-concomitancy (*sahānavasthiti*) and incompatibility (*parasparaparihāra*)—validly describes any subsequent cognition that might be posited as the invalidator of a preceding one.[32] Simply put, he argues that error cannot exist, because no cognition (*qua* appearing in and as consciousness) can be invalidated.

Not only does Somānanda argue that the fact of appearing in consciousness proves the real existence of any phenomenon thus appearing, but he also implies that his Buddhist opponents misunderstand the nature of what they deem to be the measure of reality—causal efficacy (*arthakriyā*). For every moment of cognition is at minimum capable of causing itself to be known. Indeed, according to Somānanda, the nature of causal efficacy is found only in the capacity of a cognition to delight the cognizer, which one must understand to be present in all cognitions.[33]

[supposedly 'erroneous' perceptions], because they arise in consciousness, this simply because Śiva arises in such a manner."

[30] See ŚD (and ŚDVṛ ad) 4.10-11ab.

[31] All of this is spelled out serially and in detail in ŚD, and ŚDVṛ ad, 4.15-22. See also Nemec 2012: 227–230.

[32] See ŚD and ŚDVṛ ad 4.23, 4.24, and 4.25-26. See also Nemec 2012: 230–232, esp. fns. 17, 18, 19, and 20.

[33] See, esp., ŚD 4.20cd-21ab, as well as ŚD 4.12cd-14 and the commentary thereon. ŚD 4.20cd-21ab reads as follows: *tāvatā vyavahāro vā yad ātmāhlādamātrakam* || *arthakriyāsamarthatvam etad evāsya vāstavam* |. "Alternatively, (one may understand the matter as follows:) the mundane activity [*vyavahāra*] exists (only) to the extent that the self is delighted; this alone is the true capacity for purposeful action belonging to this [object used in mundane activity]."

Still elsewhere (namely, at ŚD 4.68 and following), Somānanda challenges the notion that a universal or *sāmānya* may be established by mere convention, as his Buddhist opponents would have it. He argues that the consequence of such a position would be that language would lose its denotative capacity. Indeed, he claims that it is not possible for a theory of denotation to rely solely on convention (*saṃketa*), because the very establishment of the convention—that a word may properly be taken to refer to a particular thing in the world—could never occur in the absence of the existence of a prior and innate connection of word and thing. A theory of linguistic meaningfulness based in convention, that is, presumes the existence of the very possibility of the relation of word and thing that it seeks to explain, a connection that Somānanda, like his Mīmāṃsaka counterparts, evidently understands to be natural.[34] Yet again, then, Somānanda suggests that his interlocutors' philosophical position is tenable only by way of their implicit acceptance of his own.

The absence of a real—non-constructed, substantial—universal (*sāmānya*) in the philosophy of the Buddhist epistemologists, Somānanda further argues, would also render inferential reasoning impossible. For, he suggests, it is impossible for his Buddhist opponent to explain the possibility of inferring the presence of fire where smoke is visible (for example), this in the absence of a unity that could guarantee the very possibility of associating one *svalakṣaṇa* (e.g., that of smoke) with another (e.g., that of fire), even if the invariable concomitance of the two were apprehended.[35] The reason offered to justify this claim is the fact that each *svalakṣaṇa*, understood by the Buddhists to be absolutely unique, would be incapable of effecting a generalized and generalizable instance of inferential knowledge abstracted from the unique particulars in question. Somānanda further argues that no conventional, constructed understanding of the nature of the universal could serve to explain how the divide between a truly unique *svalakṣaṇa* and a general characteristic thereof (such as having the nature of "fire," or having the nature of "smoke") could be bridged, which is indispensably necessary for inferential reasoning. And Somānanda in fact reasons that it is *the Buddhists' own understanding of the universal* that proves that no instance of valid knowledge (*pramā*) could be produced thereby.[36] Not even a *sādṛśya* or "similarity" among perceptions of

---

[34] See ŚD 4.78-81ab. I examined these passages in some detail in Nemec 2019.

[35] See ŚD 4.84cd-85.

[36] See ŚD 4.86. Unfortunately left out of this argument is any sense of Dharmakīrti's (well-known) response to this concern, namely, that the product of one of the two means of valid knowledge—inference—is such that it is useful, even if it is the product of what ultimately is unreal and in this sense erroneous. To this position, an opponent of the Buddhists objects by asking how it is that a false apprehension can be a means of knowing. (See PV [*pratyakṣapariccheda*] 3.55: *ayathābhiniveśena dvitīyā bhrāntir iṣyate | gatiś cet pararūpeṇa na ca bhrānteḥ pramāṇatā* ||. "The second [apprehension, namely, that of the particular in another form] is considered to be false because it determines [the object] incorrectly. [Objection:] If [the second apprehension, namely, inference is] an apprehension [of

unique *svalakṣaṇas* could explain the same, Somānanda says, because the nature of the *sādṛśya* by definition cannot with any veridicality be associated with *svalakṣaṇas* when they are in fact unequivocally and utterly unique. Only by sharing a true, common nature, a real quality—what is impermissible on the Buddhist's own formulation—could perceptions of *svalakṣaṇas* be mutually identified or associated.[37] In a word, much in the manner of his critique of invalidation, Somānanda here exhibits a reliance on a critique of Buddhist ontology to suggest that the disparate *svalakṣaṇas* could never be properly mutually related such that one (utterly unique) *svalakṣaṇa* could lead to a valid inference regarding the presence of another. Indeed, he concludes, only the existence of a unity defining and underlying each could afford such a possibility.[38] The Buddhist opponents, that is, must implicitly assume the unity for which Somānanda argues in order logically to proffer the very position they claim as true. The division of entities into two types, ultimately real *svalakṣaṇas*, on the one hand, and merely constructed and therefore only conventionally real universals (*sāmānyas*), on the other,[39] is, on Somānanda's view, simply untenable.

A similar line of attack is prosecuted, as well, in response to the *kṣaṇabhaṅgavāda* (to which Somānanda explicitly refers at ŚD 4.93c), the doctrine of the instantaneous destruction of each momentary *svalakṣaṇa*. Somānanda argues that the utter uniqueness and momentariness of all

---

the particular] with another form, [it is false], but a false cognition is not a means of knowledge [just like an illusion]." Translation that of Franco and Notake 2014: 141.)

Dharmakīrti's reply is that even a false cognition can sometimes offer a valid means of knowledge, because it can lead one successfully to engage a causally efficacious action. (See PV [*pratyakṣapariccheda*] 3.56: *abhiprāyāvisaṃvādād api bhrānteḥ pramāṇatā | gatir apy anyathā dṛṣṭā pakṣaś cāyaṃ kṛtottaraḥ* ||. "(Reply:) Even an error is (sometimes) a means of knowledge, because the intention (of the one acting on the knowledge produced by the error) is not violated [*-avisaṃvāda*]. Even an apprehension [*gati*] that is at variance [*anyathā*] is seen (to lead to an object capable of causal efficacy), and this position (of the opponent, viz., that inference must apprehend something real) has been answered to." See also the rendering of Franco and Notake 2014: 142 and the notes thereon. The present translation is an adaptation of theirs.)

To exemplify as much Dharmakīrti offers the famous example of two errors, each involving a misperception leading to an awareness of the presence of a gem, only one of which leads one to grasp the gem. The light of a lamp, seen through a keyhole, could be mistaken for a jewel, as could the light of the jewel itself. The latter, if pursued, will lead one to acquire the gem, while the former will not. See PV (*pratyakṣaparicheda*) 3.57-58: *maṇipradīpaprabhayor maṇibuddhyābhidhāvatoḥ | mithyājñānāviśeṣe 'pi viśeṣo 'rthakriyāṃ prati || yathā tathāyathārthatve 'py anumānatadābhayoḥ | arthakriyānurodhena pramāṇatvaṃ vyavasthitam* ||. "When one person runs toward the light of a jewel and another person runs toward the light of a lamp (seen through a keyhole), both thinking that it is a jewel, they are both in error but there is a difference (for them) in the efficacy (of their respective cognitions). In the same way, even though both inference and pseudo-inference are false, efficacy determines which of the two is valid." (Translation a modification of that of Franco and Notake 2014: 144. See also ibid.: 22, fn. 53 for further explanation of the reference to the light of the lamp seen through a keyhole.)

[37] See ŚD 4.87ab.

[38] See ŚD 4.93ab.

[39] See PV (*pratyakṣaparicheda*) 3.3, cited in footnote 18.

phenomena would inhibit all inferentiality and even conceptuality.[40] This is so because the very stability of any instance of valid knowledge (*pramā*) must of necessity be, *on the Buddhists' own logic*, conceptually constructed and therefore self-contradictory in nature. That is, Somānanda argues that a *pramā* is deceptive (*visaṃvādaka*) on their own definition; for while it is understood to furnish valid knowledge, what it offers is a form that in its very capacity to perdure is false: it deceptively presents a stability (or non-momentariness) where none exists. This, then, constitutes Somānanda's critique of inference for oneself (*svārthānumāna*).[41] And in the absence of a unity of all phenomena, Somānanda concludes in a rhetorical flourish, the instantaneous destruction of all—including the instantaneous destruction even of the abstract concept or idea of "instantaneous destruction" itself—would render it impossible for the *kṣaṇabhaṅga* doctrine to be communicated to one by another.[42] So much, then, for the Buddhists' conception of inference for another (*parārthānumāna*).

The logic of Somānanda's *siddhānta*, in sum, implicitly and explicitly challenges the notion that causality could function in an impersonal manner and by being grounded in an ontology recognizing a multiplicity of phenomena only related by such (contingent) causal events. Indeed, the entire core ontology of the PV is challenged in that Somānanda and Utpaladeva reject the notion, expressed at PV (*pratyakṣapariccheda*) 3.44, that everything that is real necessarily ceases to exist.[43] Instead, Somānanda argues not only that disparate appearances, disparate capable phenomena, could not be coordinated and could not interact in the absence of the existence of an organizing matrix, directed by an agent who possesses and directs and orders capable phenomena as capacities, but also that everything is always and ever existent, if not always perceptible (for the reasons explained in the section entitled "Somānanda's

---

[40] See ŚD 4.93cd-94.

[41] See ŚD 4.95: *sthiratvaṃ kṣaṇikatvāc ca pramāṇāṃ cintayā sthitam | avisaṃvādirūpāc ca viruddhaṃ tat kathaṃ bhavet* ||. "Moreover, because the instances of valid knowledge [*pramā*] are (thus) momentary in nature, their stability is established (only) by way of intellectual reflection; and, given that (you maintain that) they are by nature reliable [*avisaṃvādi*], (we ask:) how can they be possessed of that [stability,] which is contrary (to their real nature)?" Note that I have twice emended the verse. I conjecture that we should read *kṣaṇikatvāt* where *kṣaṇikatvaṃ* (or an obvious corruption thereof) is attested by both extant manuscripts; and I emend with *avisaṃvādirūpāc ca* for the reading in K[ed.] of *apy asaṃvādarūpaṃ ca*. See the critical edition of the present volume and footnotes 380 and 381 of the translation. Note also that Somānanda might here be taken implicitly to critique what is said at PV (*pramāṇasiddhipariccheda*) 2.1ab, for which see also footnote 381 of the translation.

[42] See ŚD 4.96: *yāvan na sarvabhāvānām ekatvena vyavasthitiḥ | pareṇa kṣaṇabhaṅgasya parāmarśāgamaḥ kutaḥ* ||. "As long as there is no fixed existence of all entities (in the universe) as a unity, how could another bring one to reflect on the instantaneous destruction (at all)?"

[43] See PV (*pratyakṣapariccheda*) 3.44: *vastumātrānubandhitvād vināśasya na nityatā | asaṃbandhaś ca jātīnām akāryatvād arūpatā* ||. "Because [being] real is sufficient to entail cessation, [the universal, were it to be real, would] not be permanent. Moreover, it would follow from universals' not being effects, [that is to say, from the alternative view,] that they [would] have no connection [with individuals] and [would] have no [own] nature." Translation that of Franco and Notake 2014: 121.

Critique of the Sāṅkhya Theory of Causality"). Somānanda argues, in a word, that none of the philosophical positions of the Buddhists addressed by him is logically supportable unless a unity as mapped in the syllogism found at the beginning of the *āhnika*, a unity *embodied in the person of an ever-existent, power-wielding god, Śiva*, is implicitly assumed to exist.

1C. SOMĀNANDA'S INTERACTION WITH HIS MĪMĀṂSAKA INTERLOCUTORS

Engagement with the Mīmāṃsā in the present *āhnika* merits particular attention and remark. Similar to his treatment of the other major philosophical traditions with which he contends, Somānanda intimates that Mīmāṃsaka philosophical formulations implicitly rely on the existence of a Śaiva nondualism in order to cohere logically. Unlike his treatment of the other schools, however, he sometimes suggests as much not to counter their views but evidently to guarantee them. This is to say that Somānanda sometimes reads the Mīmāṃsā sympathetically, *particularly inasmuch as they insist on the reality of what may be known ostensively of the world; for reality conforms to the very manner in which it habitually appears*. Indeed, Somānanda implicitly welcomes the ostensive epistemological principle that suggests that, barring any invalidating cognition, what is perceived in and as the mundane, everyday world must be accepted as real and accounted for as such. And as we shall presently see, he adopts some of the philosophical positions of his Mīmāṃsaka interlocutors, though understanding them to be logically coherent, as is his wont, only by way of accepting the real existence of his Śaiva, non-dual ontology.

An echo of this positioning is in evidence in a passage bordered on both ends by Somānanda's arguments against the viability of his Buddhist opponent's understanding of inferential reasoning, wherein a possible appeal to the testimony of a reliable person (*āpta*) as a valid means of guaranteeing inferential knowledge is rejected in a manner that echoes Mīmāṃsaka arguments against the *āpta* as a *pramāṇa*.[44] But it is with Somānanda's criticism of his Buddhist

[44] See ŚD 4.91-93ab: *nāptavākyād athāstīha tatsatyatve 'dṛḍhā matiḥ | vārān śataṃ hi yo vaktā satyabhāṣī kadācana || so 'py anyathā pradarśyetākṣayato rāgadveṣayoḥ | pitrāder apy asatyatvaṃ tatrānyatra na niścayaḥ || tasmān na bhede bhāvānāṃ tadgrahādy api yujyate |*. "Now, it [i.e., knowledge of the fact that smoke is connected with fire] is not the product, here, of the testimony of a reliable person; the determination (one may obtain from that reliable person) is not firm (even) when he is truthful. For even the speaker who expresses what is true one hundred times can teach inaccurately at any time, because passion and aversion are undecaying. Even one's forefathers, among others, (sometimes) lack in veracity; one can have no conviction therein on another occasion [i.e., in the testimony of one less reliable than a revered ancestor]. Therefore, that [nature of inference (*anumānatva*)] which for its part involves the apprehension of that [relation] or the like is not possible if the entities (that populate the world) are (mutually) differentiated."

The context in which this critique is deployed is somewhat surprising. It is an interlude that emerges in the context of a thorough critique of the Buddhist opponent's understanding of inference. Given that there is no other school of thought that so vociferously argues against the validity of the

interlocutors' understanding of language that he makes plain his willingness implicitly to accept Mīmāṃsaka formulations. As I have detailed elsewhere,[45] and as intimated in the section "Somānanda's Engagement with Buddhist Epistemology," it is in the course of challenging his Buddhist opponent's notion that convention (*saṃketa*) may explain the denotative capacity of speech that Somānanda takes up with apparent approval particular Mīmāṃsaka ideas about the nature of language. So much is rendered in evidence in the form of two favorable citations of Mīmāṃsā authors and works.

The first is of a passage of the *Śābarabhāṣya* (ŚBh) ad *Mīmāṃsāsūtra* (MīSū) 1.1.5, wherein it is argued that the connection between word and thing denoted thereby is innate, never constructed:

> For the word is found in the mouth and the object (denoted by it) on the ground—where can there be a meeting (of the two)?[46]

This, which clearly cites ŚBh ad MīSū 1.1.5,[47] is articulated by Somānanda to defend his understanding of the denoter-denoted relationship, which he says can only be guaranteed by the existence of a singular nature of all phenomena. It is the unitary nature of all as Śiva that allows the mutually distinct entities, word (*śabda*) and object (*artha*), to be related (*saṃgama/saṃbandha*). Śaiva non-duality, in other words, guarantees a Mīmāṃsā view of the relation in question.

To wit, Somānanda argues that certain plainly observable capacities of language demand the existence of all as Śiva, as follows. First, language may be used effectively to refer to unseen or unreal entities,[48] the latter of which are particularly problematic if one understands the connection or *saṃbandha* of word and object to be real, the logical implication being that unreal objects denoted by speech would themselves have to be real in order to partake (as *saṃbandhins*) in their very relations with the words that denote them. A unity of all existence is therefore required to allow for such a possibility,

---

āpta as *pramāṇa* as does the Mīmāṃsā, however, it seems likely that it is to their position on the matter that Somānanda gestures. He does so, moreover in a manner that aligns him with that school. More than this, it seems Somānanda deploys the Mīmāṃsaka argument in opposition to a Naiyāyika's understanding of *āpta* as *pramāṇa*, using the position of the former school to criticize that of the latter. See footnote 371 of the translation, where relevant passages of the *Nyāyasūtra* (NS), *Mīmāṃsāsūtra* (MīSū), and the *Śābarabhāṣya* (ŚBh) commentary on the latter (at MīSū 1.1.5) are cited. Also cited there is Dharmakīrti at PV (*pramāṇasiddhiparicheda*) 2.1-7 (esp. at 2.1cd-2), for it is possible Somānanda here has in mind the notion that the words of another can serve as a means of knowledge according to his Buddhist opponent. Finally, note also that the passage in question is not without both text-critical and interpretive difficulties, about which see footnotes 372 and 375 of the translation, as well as the critical edition of the present volume at lines 495–499.

[45] See Nemec 2019.

[46] See ŚD 4.72cd: *mukhe hi śabdo bhūmau ca vidyate 'rthaḥ kva saṃgamaḥ* ||.

[47] There the following is said: *mukhe hi śabdam upalabhāmahe, bhūmāv artham.* "For we perceive the word in the mouth, the object on the ground." See footnote 332 of the translation.

[48] See ŚD 4.73cd-75. On the opponent here addressed, however, see footnote 335 of the translation. Cf. Nemec 2019: 246–250.

reality and unreality being comprehensible, one may implicitly understand Somānanda to argue, only on the outlined terms: a connection of a word to an unreal entity poses no problem when reality and existence are understood as the Śaivas understand them—viz., *qua* the fact of appearing in and as consciousness. Somānanda similarly suggests that the same eternally existent relation could not be countenanced in instances where novel associations of word and meaning are fashioned, as when naming a newborn child or applying the word "cow" to a newborn calf, for example. It is the ontological unity of such names and objects, Somānanda argues, that necessarily serves to guarantee the Mīmāṃsaka understanding of language as regards denotation in such instances.[49]

Thus guaranteed, moreover, the Mīmāṃsā view is implicitly accepted. It is only the implicit presupposition of the existence of just such a natural connection of word and object, Somānanda suggests, that may allow for an explanation of denotation based in convention (*saṃketa*).[50] As Śabara himself did, then, Somānanda treats the argument for the natural connection of word and object in the context of dealing with an opponent who cannot accept the same. In the ŚBh, the very possibility of such a connection is challenged by the opponent; Somānanda's ŚBh citation, that is, is uttered by the *pūrvapakṣin*. And the ŚD answers the objection in full: it is not merely the *fact* of the connection being ostensively in evidence that allows one to presume its real existence, but there *must* be such a connection because it is ontologically grounded, for the identity of all as Śiva guarantees just this.

Following this is the second direct quotation of the writings of his Mīmāṃsaka interlocutors. Somānanda favorably cites an adjacent philosophical formulation concerning the relationship of word to thing-in-the-world, this time drawing from Kumārila's *Ślokavārttika* (ŚV), at a part of the text where it tends to the section of the ŚBh already cited. Yet again, Somānanda invokes a Mīmāṃsaka argument that was itself deployed against a Buddhist opponent in order himself to counter a Buddhist opponent. The citation is found at ŚD 4.83ab, which is a close rephrasing of ŚV, *pratyakṣapariccheda*, verse 112cd:

> (After all:) Of what kind is the action (of perception) that is similar to the awareness of children, mute people, and the like?[51]

---

[49] See ŚD 4.76-77.

[50] Indeed, I suggest that Somānanda argues precisely as much at ŚD 4.78-81ab. See the translation and corresponding footnotes. See also Nemec 2019: 253–258.

[51] ŚD 4.83ab: *bālamūkādivijñānasadṛśī kīdṛśī kriyā* |. Compare with ŚV, *pratyakṣapariccheda*, v. 112: *asti hy ālocanājñānaṃ prathamaṃ nirvikalpakam* | *bālamūkādivijñānasadṛśaṃ śuddhavastujam* ||. See footnote 352 of the translation for a rendering of this verse (that of McCrea 2013), its context, and its significance in Kumārila's œuvre.

The argument of the present passage is this, that linguistic patterning is intrinsic to all acts of perception, because what is known by *pratyakṣa* is of necessity—by the very nature of the objects perceived—imbued with the capacity for expression in speech, this in turn because inherent in the object is a universal or *sāmānya*, on which speech is based. Like Kumārila before him, reference to the perception of children (presumably before they have acquired the ability effectively to use speech), "mutes" (*mūka*), and the like means to suggest that even those who have no robust access to language see in a manner that is patterned by the universal that defines the very possibility of language itself, because the object of perception cannot but be twofold, both individual and universal by nature. And like Kumārila before him, Somānanda articulates this view in the course of rejecting his Buddhist opponent's contention that percept may be separated absolutely from concept. Indeed, Somānanda argues that in the absence of just such an innate association of word and object, embodied by the innate co-presence of individual entity and universal or *sāmānya*, no apprehension of an object could be fruitfully associated with conception at all.[52]

Here, then, it is indisputable that Somānanda deploys Kumārila in opposition to his Buddhist opponent, and in doing so he puts to use an argument that the latter articulated in opposition to Dignāga and the same school of Buddhist thought as the one with which Somānanda is clearly engaged. In doing so, moreover, it is apparent—it is at the very least implied—that Somānanda accepts the Mīmāṃsaka's understanding of language as being innately associated with things in the world, but not in the sense of Bhartṛhari's linguistic monism, only in the sense of the ostensively verifiable invariability of connection, a sort of middle position between the philosophy of the Grammarians and the doctrine of the conventionality of speech articulated by their shared Buddhist opponent (so too Naiyāyikas and Vaiśeṣikas).[53]

It is certain, then, that Somānanda understands the philosophical positions of his Mīmāṃsaka interlocutors to require the existence of all as Śiva if they are to cohere logically; he also implies—at the least—that their views of language, thus grounded, are worthy of adoption. Somānanda's acceptance of their views, moreover, again serves to support the core argument he wishes to prosecute in the present chapter, in that they affirm the core thesis of his syllogistic argument, namely, that everything is equally of the nature of Śiva. For it is the Mīmāṃsaka's theory of meaningfulness that allows him not only to make sense of how language is demonstrably used in everyday experience but

---

[52] See ŚD 4.81cd-84ab.

[53] One may perhaps find this association with Mīmāṃsaka formulations regarding language unsurprising given Abhinavagupta's similar apparent alliance with the same school, so too his reluctance to accept the *sphoṭa* doctrine so regularly defended by the Grammarians (but rejected by Kumārila), about which see Torella 2004, esp. 173–174.

also logically to prove that the Buddhists' denial of its integrated presence in perceptual realities is untenable, which is essential if Somānanda is to defend his core claim that all phenomena uniformly are of a kind.

1D. SOMĀNANDA'S CRITIQUE OF THE SĀṄKHYA THEORY OF CAUSALITY

If the Mīmāṃsā gains such acceptance in the present *āhnika* (albeit only when, or at the least only inasmuch as, their views may be guaranteed by a Śaiva non-dual ontology), the same cannot be said of the philosophical views of the Sāṅkhya. For while the Sāṅkhyas articulate a theory of causality to which the authors of the Pratyabhijñā also subscribe—the *satkāryavāda* or doctrine that the effect is existent in its cause prior to the production of the former—Somānanda roundly rejects their understanding of the same. This he does in an extended critique, found at ŚD 4.33cd-60ab, beginning with an unequivocal statement of support for the *satkāryavāda* that offers another reason (*hetu*) to understand everything to be the nature of Śiva: Śiva alone exists as the cause, prior to the production of all the effects that constitute the multiple universe; and it is Śiva alone who arises *as* the effects, as everything that appears in the universe.[54]

Such a view of causality is vital to the articulation of the thesis of Somānanda's *siddhānta*, of course, because he cannot countenance the identity of everything in the universe as Śiva unless he understands all to have been prefigured in Śiva prior to their creation, or he would have to explain away the appearance of multiplicity by way of an appeal to illusionism or the like, something he is wont not to do. Indeed, he criticizes a series of Vedāntic philosophical formulations precisely for failing to establish any model of non-dualism that logically accounts for the multiple universe as real and existent.[55] But if both the Sāṅkhya and the Pratyabhijñā accept the *satkāryavāda*, what, on Somānanda's view, distinguishes their respective views of causality?

The ŚD plainly states the fault of the Sāṅkhya position: the materialism of their view renders their understanding of the *satkāryavāda* incoherent, because it cannot account for a world that appears as it does in quotidian experience.

---

[54] See ŚD 4.33cd-34: *ito 'pi sarvaśivatā sata utpattiyogataḥ || sa evāste purā tādṛkśaktirūpasvarūpakaḥ | sa eva kāryarūpeṇa bhagavān avakalpate ||*. "Everything is of the nature of Śiva for this reason, as well, because (only) that which is (already) existent can arise (as an effect). He alone is present at the beginning, his nature being in the form of such a potentiality [i.e., such a potential to be manifested as an effect]; (and) he alone, the Blessed One, is fit to exist in the form of the effect."

A detailed account of many of the arguments here reviewed is to be found in Ratié 2014a. Some of what is presented here of necessity goes over materials she has covered therein, though we differ in explaining some of the particulars.

[55] I have examined these arguments in detail in a forthcoming article that offers a critical edition and translation of the relevant passages of the ŚD, which are found at ŚD 6.1-24ab. See Nemec forthcoming.

Specifically, the Sāṅkhya *satkārya* theory cannot account for the fact that the effect that is unequivocally existent prior to its production may on occasion *not* be perceptible in quotidian experience prior to the same; the *absence* of a perceptible presence of what is, in fact, fully existent is inexplicable on the Sāṅkhya theory. The logic for this argument is as follows.

Somānanda, one may note first of all, states that the effect *must* exist prior to its production, because it must be present if it is to be connected to its causes, the factors of action or *kārakas*—agent, instrument, and so on—that fashion it. That is, the *asatkāryavāda* or the doctrine that the effect is inexistent prior to its production is rejected out of hand.[56] But, the Sāṅkhya *pūrvapakṣin* protests, he, too, accepts this position and therefore should not be called to account for a flawed causal theory,[57] Utpaladeva understanding his opponent's interpretation of *sat-kārya* on the terms expressed in the *Jayamaṅgalā* (JM) ad *Sāṅkhyakārikā* (SK) verse 9, if my interpretation (and emendation) of the ŚDVṛ is to be accepted.[58]

All that remains to be explained, then, is *not* how an effect comes into existence, for it is always existent, prefigured in its cause. Indeed, Somānanda's Sāṅkhya interlocutor suggests, the production of an already existent effect would, in fact, produce nothing: the effect that is prefigured in its cause is present both prior to and following its manifestation.[59] What must be explained is rather how an ever-existent cause may leave its effect sometimes *unmanifested*, at other times manifested and visible. The concern is one of manifestation, not production or creation.

Somānanda catalogs the possible explanations for manifestation in the form of an opponent's critique of the *satkāryavāda*. The opponent notes that the manifestation (*abhivyakti*) itself, like the effect (*kārya*) it makes manifest, must be either existent or non-existent prior to its manifestation. If the former, then the manifestation would be perceptible prior to its own production; if the latter, the *satkārya* doctrine is contradicted. And, finally, the appearance of the manifestation cannot be explained by an appeal to the notion that it cannot

---

[56] See ŚD 4.49cd-50a: *janmakāle ghaṭābhāvāt saṃbandho naiva kārakaiḥ || nāsaṃbandhasya karaṇam*. . . "(To sum up:) There simply is no relation (of what is to be produced) with the factors of action (in the *asatkāryavāda*), because (that which is to be produced,) the pot(, for example,) does not (yet) exist at the moment of its production; (and) there can be no production of that whose (causal) relation does not exist (with that which produces it)."

[57] See ŚD 4.50b: *satkāryāc cet sa vidyate* |. "Objection (of the Sāṅkhya *satkāryavādin*): That [relation] exists, (on our view,) because (we maintain that) the effect is existent (prior to its being produced)."

[58] See ŚDVṛ ad ŚD 4.49cd-51ab, especially at line 290 of the present edition. The rationale for my emendation is recorded in footnote 238 of the translation.

[59] See ŚD 4.35a-c: *satkāryaṃ nopapannaṃ cet sataḥ kiṃ karaṇena yat | abhivyaktir athāsyātra kriyate* . . . "If one argues that an effect that is existent (before the operation of its cause) is not supported by rational justification, since (one may ask:) 'what use is the production of that which is (already) existent?,' then one (who supports the *satkāryavāda*) may reply: A manifestation of this [effect] is produced, here."

appear without being itself manifested, for the postulation of a manifestation of the manifestation would lead to a *regressus* ad infinitum.[60]

It is in Somānanda's response to this objection that a distinction between his own understanding of the *satkāryavāda* and that of his Sāṅkhya interlocutor is made evident. He and Utpaladeva suggest that it is precisely because a manifestation is *not* evident before it is produced that the Sāṅkhya understanding of the *satkāryavāda* fails: inasmuch as an effect is inherent in its cause, the logic of the *satkāryavāda* would demand the non-existence of the very manifestor (*vyañjaka*) of an effect whenever the manifested (*vyaṅgya*) effect were absent, simply because the latter is always prefigured in the former.[61] For, since the threat of infinite regress proscribes any appeal to the notion that a manifestation must itself be manifested if it is to be known, the very absence of an awareness of the manifested entity logically signals the absence of the manifesting agent.[62] In effect, then, Somānanda and Utpaladeva argue that the Sāṅkhya understanding of the *satkāryavāda* might be deemed to cohere logically in its account of the causal process where it describes the production of a material object by a material cause, but it ultimately fails, because a theory of causality involving the devolution of a single and unitary materiality (*mūlaprakṛti* or *pradhāna*) into discretely discernible entities cannot explain the nature of one's *experiences* (or perceptions) of the manifestations of such entities.

---

[60] All of this is articulated at ŚD 4.35d-37ab.

[61] See ŚD 4.50cd-51: *sann apy asāv asaṃvedyo vyañjakasyāpy abhāvataḥ || tasmāt svayaṃ svabhāvena bhāvair bhāvī bhaved bhavaḥ |.* "Although (you maintain that) it [i.e., the effect] is existent (prior to its being produced), it cannot be known by consciousness (at that time); (and) because (it therefore logically follows that) that which manifests it, for its part, does not exist (at that time), therefore existence must be that which immanently exists of its own accord as (all) the entities (in existence), by its very nature."

[62] See ŚDVṛ ad ŚD 4.49cd-51ab (lines 290–296 of the present edition): *tad api na, yataḥ sann apy asau janyo ghaṭādir artho 'saṃvedyo 'saṃvedyatvāc ca saṃbandhino 'prakhyatvena saṃbandhāgamanaṃ vyañjakatvaṃ ca kumbhakārāder ghaṭaṃ prati nāsti yataḥ sarvathā pratītyagocare vastuni vyañjako na bhavati. siddha evārthe vyañjako mato yathā ghaṭādau dīpaḥ. tato vyañjakasyāpy abhāvataḥ kathaṃ saṃbandhaḥ. evaṃ hi kāraṇaṃ kāryātmanā sat tadā bhaved yady avyatirekas tayoḥ syāt. sa ca pratyakṣaviruddhaḥ.* "(Reply:) This, too, is not tenable, since the object that is to be produced—the pot, for example—, although it is existent (prior to its being produced, on your view), cannot be known by consciousness (at that time); and because this entity that is (causally) related (to the causes that effect it) is not directly perceptible (at that time), this inasmuch as it cannot be known by consciousness, the (causal) relation is not obtained (at that time); and, (consequently,) the potter, e.g., cannot be (properly understood to be) the agent who manifests the pot (at that time, viz., before the manifestation of the same), because, if a real thing lies entirely beyond the range of perception, there (by definition) can be no agent present who manifests it. It is (only) when an object is fully established (within the range of perceptibility) that one understands the agent who manifests it to exist, as (one understands) a lamp (to be the manifesting agent) with respect to a pot, for example. Hence, given that (logic therefore dictates that, on your view,) the agent who manifests (the manifestation), for its part, does not exist (prior to the manifestation), (we ask:) how can a relation exist (between it and the effect it is said to manifest)? For, if the cause (that is the manifesting agent) were thus existent in the form of the effect (that is the manifested entity) at that time [i.e., prior to the manifestation of the latter], the two would be indistinguishable(, which means the manifested entity would always be visible when the manifestor is present). And that is contradicted by (what is seen in) direct perception."

Now, Somānanda's critique, as it is elaborated and clarified by Utpaladeva, leans on an adaptation of Dharmakīrti's concept of *sahopalambhaniyama*, which Somānanda evokes at ŚD 4.41b-42ab. Indeed, Somānanda and Utpaladeva both suggest that the object and the perception of it are one and the same,[63] and Utpaladeva may be seen to closely paraphrase Dharmakīrti in explaining the very nature of the manifestation (*vyaṅgya*) and manifesting agent (*vyañjaka*), at ŚDVṛ ad ŚD 4.49cd-51ab,[64] where he explains the necessary existence of the manifesting agent where the manifested entity is present.[65] How, then, do Somānanda and Utpaladeva claim to escape the self-same problem, namely, that the presence of the manifestor requires the appearance of the manifestation on a *satkārya* theory of causality?

Their explanation of the possibility of *non*-cognition begins with a declaration, again, of their adherence to the core proposition of the *satkāryavāda*, what Utpaladeva describes as the doctrine that the effect is forever existent (*sadāsatkāryavāda*),[66] this being evidently how he would label the Śaiva position:

---

[63] See ŚD 4.41b-42ab: . . . *na ca vā vyatirekataḥ* | *vyaktiḥ sthitā padārthānāṃ ghaṭo vyakto 'bhidhīyate* || *tasmāt sa eva vyaktyātmā na vyakter vyatiriktatā* |. "And, alternatively, it is not the case that the manifestation exists by way of the things (manifested by it) being different (from it). The pot is said to have been manifested(, for example). Therefore, it is that [pot] that is the nature of the manifestation; the manifestation is not different (from it)."

That this passage constitutes a reference to *sahopalambhaniyama* is, as Ratié 2014a: 158 notes, made evident by Utpaladeva's commentary, which alludes to the very same. See the relevant passage of the corresponding ŚDVṛ commentary (lines 234–237 of the present edition): *tathābhivyaktis tāvan nārthād vyatirekeṇa sthitā tathānupalambhāt. abhedenaiva ca vyavahāraḥ. tathā hi ghaṭo vyakto 'bhidhīyate vyaktyabhedena. tasmāt padārtha eva vyaktyātmā. sa ca san kriyate, na tu vyakter vyatiriktāyā asatyāḥ karaṇam.* "Thus, the manifestation, first of all, does not exist apart from the (manifested) object, because it is not perceived as such. And one (also) speaks (of the two) without (making) any distinction whatever (between them). For instance: the pot is said to have been manifested, without being distinguished from the manifestation. Therefore, the thing itself is the (very) nature of the manifestation, and it is produced while (already) existing (prior to its manifestation); and it is not the case(, therefore,) that a manifestation that is different (from the real thing it makes manifest) is produced as that which is not existent (prior to its production)."

Note, finally, the need to emend both the text and commentary here (about which see footnotes 179 and 188 of the translation, as well as the notes in the critical edition).

[64] See footnote 62. The same passage is cited in Ratié 2014a: 153, fn. 93, but without noting Utpaladeva's reference to the PV therein.

[65] I propose, that is, that the ŚDVṛ ad ŚD 4.49cd-50ab (lines 293–294 of the present edition) offers a close paraphrase of PV (*svārthānumānapariccheda*) 1.263cd-264ab. Dharmakīrti's pair of half-verses read as follows: *svajñānenānyadhīhetuḥ siddhe 'rthe vyañjako mataḥ* || *yathā dīpo 'nyathā vāpi ko viśeṣo 'sya kārakāt* |. Utpaladeva's commentary (*op. cit.*) says the following: *siddha evārthe vyañjako mato yathā ghaṭādau dīpaḥ.* We may translate Dharmakīrti's pair of half-verses as follows: "We maintain that, as regards an object that is established, the manifestor [*vyañjaka*] (thereof) is that which causes an awareness of the other by way of a cognition of itself, just as a lamp (with regard to the object it illumines). Were it otherwise, on the other hand, what would differentiate it [i.e., the manifestor] from the producer (of the object)?" This is to say, then, that the manifestor must be present for the manifested entity to be made evident.

Note that the same passage of the PV is cited by Mahimabhaṭṭa, for which see Reich 2016: 291, fn. 123. My translation is a modification of his.

[66] See ŚDVṛ ad ŚD 4.51cd-52, lines 303–304 of the present edition.

the effect must be always and forever identical to the cause if the former is possibly to be produced.[67] Indeed, effects *are* their causes, even as superficial differences in their respective names (*nāma*) and configurations (*saṃsthāna*) may be countenanced; and the cause (i.e., Śiva) is not destroyed when the effect is destroyed, given the shared essential nature of both, just as gold is gold, notwithstanding the particular form it takes (such as a golden bracelet being fashioned out of a golden diadem, for example).[68]

So far, the Sāṅkhyas and the Śaivas may be said to agree on these essential points of their shared doctrine of causality. Yet, the view of the latter is distinguishable from that of the Sāṅkhya, Utpaladeva explains, inasmuch as *what it is* that is the cause is differently understood. Utpaladeva criticizes at length the Sāṅkhya understanding of the transformation of one material substance—the three *guṇas* taken together (*traiguṇya*)—into the many distinguishable entities in existence, and he does so precisely because the Sāṅkhyas postulate the existence of real differences of quality among some such entities. One must explain how an effect can truly exhibit difference with its original cause, he suggests, given that the effect is always already present in the cause. Only one kind of entity can permit as much—consciousness. Materiality cannot do so without contradiction. Only consciousness makes it possible to account for the manifestation of phenomena that show such similarity and difference simultaneously.[69]

But if destruction occurs, an opponent asks (at ŚD 4.55cd-56ab)—if, that is, entities come into existence and subsequently disappear—then, given that Śiva is everything in the universe, is he not destroyed when the given entity is destroyed? Or does Śiva fail to be omnipresent? Either horn of the dilemma (*vikalpa*), it would appear, will gore Śaiva non-duality.

Somānanda proposes the Śaivas escape this dilemma by arguing that no destruction (*vināśa*) of entities in the world occurs at all, because destruction in fact involves nothing other than the manifestation of another part of Śiva. Destruction, that is, does not involve any complete elision of the entity said to be destroyed.[70] What this means, Utpaladeva explains, is that destruction is nothing more than the manifestation of something new and the cessation

---

[67] See ŚD 4.51cd-52: *ito 'pi viddhi satkāryaṃ mṛtpiṇḍāt kiṃ ghaṭaḥ pṛthak || apṛthag vā pṛthaktvena paṭādeḥ karaṇaṃ na kim | anupādānataiva syād apṛthaktve sa eva saḥ ||*. "For this reason, as well, know the effect to be existent (prior to its being produced): is the pot different from the ball of clay, or is it not different? Why wouldn't a cloth, e.g., be produced (from the ball of clay) as a result of it being different (from its cause)? It [i.e., the cause] simply would not be the material cause (of its effect, if the latter is different from the former). (By contrast:) When it is not different, it is nothing but that [cause]."

[68] See ŚD 4.53-54ab.

[69] See ŚDVṛ ad ŚD 4.53-54ab. See also footnote 261 of the translation, which notes Ratié's similar treatment of this passage, as well a passage of Abhinavagupta's ĪPV that takes up the matter (one also cited by Ratié).

[70] See ŚD 4.56cd-57ab: *naivaṃ yato hi bhāvānāṃ vināśe 'smāsu neṣṭatā || aṃśābhivyaktitā nāśo na nāśaḥ sarvalopitā |*. "(Reply to the opponent's objection:) This is not so, since we do not maintain

of the manifestation of something that preceded it. "Destruction," in fact, is constituted only by the cessation of the *non*-manifestation of the new effect. As Utpaldeva explains the matter,[71] "For in our philosophy, at the moment when the bracelet (made of gold) is produced from the (golden) diadem, there occurs a manifestation of a part (that is the bracelet) that is nothing but gold; it is the manifestation of the preceding moment, that of the transformation of the diadem (into the bracelet), that is spoken of as destruction, but it is not the case that every part (of the gold) ceases to appear. Hence, there is no fault associated with the immediate destruction (of the diadem, in the present example); nor is the part [i.e., the bracelet] devoid of co-presence (with the diadem, in the present example), because only the non-manifestation (of the new effect, the bracelet) is destroyed."

This is to say that "destruction," exemplified by the production of a golden bracelet fashioned out of what had been a diadem made of gold, does not involve the total disappearance of the earlier entity. For in both the earlier entity and the newly fashioned one, nothing but the manifestation of the same article—gold, in the present exemplar—occurs. So too with Śiva-as-consciousness: everything in the universe is caused by, *is* itself, the same consciousness, the ever-existent effect-in-its-cause. This is so regardless of the particular names or configurations adopted. No part is in fact destroyed. And what is newly manifested is not incompatible with what had been manifested earlier. All that occurs, then, is a cessation or "destruction" of the *non*-manifestation of the "new" manifestation, namely, the bracelet in the present example.

Indeed, Somānanda argues that if a manifestation were destroyed, an infinite regress would ensue; and "destruction" is in fact nothing more than an incapacity of the sense organs (*indriya*).[72] As Utpaladeva explains it (and as I have illustrated before in a detailed study of the Pratyabhijñā theories of error[73]), it is one constituted not by a non-cognition of a discrete object but

---

that the entities are destroyed. For, destruction is (nothing more than) the fact that a part (of Śiva-nature) is manifested; it is not the case that destruction is a complete elision (of the 'destroyed' entity in question)."

[71] See ŚDVṛ ad ŚD 4.56cd-57ab (lines 347–350 of the present edition): *asmaddarśane hi mauleḥ kaṭakotpādakāle 'ṃśasya hemamātrasyābhivyaktiḥ prāktanasya mauliparināmakṣaṇasyeti nāśa ucyate na tu sarvāṃśādarśanam. tato na niranvayavināśadoṣaḥ, nāpy aṃśasya niranvayatānabhivyaktimātrasya nāśatvāt.*

[72] See ŚD 4.57cd-58: *abhivyakter vināśitve tatrāpy ānantyam āpatet || indriyāṇām asāmarthyamātram atra vināśitā | asāv evānabhivyaktiḥ sa pracchannas tadā sthitaḥ ||*. "If (you argue that) the manifestation is destroyed, (then we reply:) in that case, also, (there is a fault:) an infinite regress would arise. Here [in Śaivism], destruction is merely an incapacity of the *indriyas*. It is simply a non-manifestation; that which has been concealed remains existent at that time."

[73] See Nemec 2012. Others have subsequently noted the same strategy in Utpaladeva's writings. See footnote 293 of the translation.

by the absence of the non-cognition of the ubiquitous non-duality of Śiva-as-consciousness. This is to say, then, that the very production of perceptible objects in the universe consists in nothing other than the *non*-cognition of Śiva's non-duality (*śivābhedākhyāti*), and the "destruction" of such objects consists in nothing other than a return to a cognition of the unity of Śiva, which renders the objects in question no longer objects of a particular, discrete awareness, no longer what can be known by the internal and external sense organs.[74] There is no destruction at all, only an immersion again of awareness into the unity that is the nature of Śiva's consciousness.[75]

To sum up: only the Śaiva *satkāryavāda* theory can account for the co-presence of manifestor (*vyañjaka*) and manifested (*vyaṅgya*), on Somānanda's and Utpaladeva's view, because only it can logically account for the fact that both are *always* present, in the form of a unitary and ubiquitous Śiva-as-consciousness. In fact, as Utpaladeva explains, the perception of discrete entities—of a bracelet instead of a diadem, for example—involves a *non*-cognition of this non-duality (*abhedākhyāti*). The Śaivas, in other words (and, again, as I have argued elsewhere[76]) invert the structure of manifestation and non-manifestation in explaining each. The manifestor—Śiva—on the one hand, always manifests everything, an indiscriminate and omnipresent "all" in which every discrete entity is ever present but impossible to discern for being imbued with unity. One can always perceive this non-dual unity of all; the manifestor *always* makes evident the manifested. The appearance of discrete entities in the world, on the other hand—what one may colloquially refer to as "manifestation"—involves a failure to cognize this unity. It is an *absence* of the only awareness that is fully real. And the cessation of the same—the non-manifestation or "destruction" of a particular object—is nothing more than the

---

[74] See ŚDVṛ ad ŚD 4.57cd-58, lines 362–364 of the present edition: *evam asmaddarśana īśvarapratyabhijñoktanītyā yathobhayendriyavedyatvaṃ śivābhedākhyātimayam arthānāṃ karaṇam, tathā vināśa ubhayendriyavedyatvābhāvaḥ śivābhedaḥ śivatvena pracchādanam*. "In this way, in our philosophical system, as per the principle that has been articulated (by me) in the *Īśvarapratyabhijñā*, just as the production of objects, which consists of the non-cognition of the non-duality of Śiva, is their being objects of both (external and internal) sense organs, so also (their) destruction is non-difference with Śiva, the absence of the state of being an object of both (internal and external) sense organs; it is a concealment (of the objects) as Śiva."

[75] See ŚDVṛ ad ŚD 4.59-60ab, lines 373–377 of the present edition: *mahattvalohitatvocchritatvādisāmānyāntarasaṃparke 'ntaravasthita evendriyavedyo 'bhedākhyātimayaḥ kriyata iti pūrvam uktam. tasmād uktakrameṇa bhāvānāṃ śivatattvanimajjanarūpeṇa tadabhedākhyātivināśe 'pi śivatattvāvināśitā. evam utpattivināśānyathānupapattyā sarvaśivatā vyavasthitā*. "It was mentioned, earlier, that it is only when it exists internally (in consciousness), in association with the other (relevant) universals, (viz.,) being large, being of reddish color, being tall, etc., that it [i.e., the pot, for example] is produced as what is known by the sense organs, as that which consists of the non-cognition of (Śiva's) non-duality. Therefore, on the basis of the arguments just presented, there is no destruction of Śiva-nature, even when the non-cognition of the non-duality of that [Śiva-nature] is destroyed, this in the form of the immersion of the entities (that are "destroyed") in Śiva-nature. In this way, because production and destruction are not possible in any other way, the Śiva-nature of everything is firmly established."

[76] See footnote 73.

restoration of a full cognition of non-duality, a recognition again of what is ever present. Thus, Somānanda explains, there is only one reality, and nothing is created or destroyed, only perceived or not.[77]

The detailed account of the *satkāryavāda* in the ŚD, then, serves to support the thesis (*pratijñā*) of the syllogism that opens the present *āhnika* by offering another reason (*hetu*) for the same. It defines the very manner in which a causal process, a procedure for the manifestation of apparently multiple entities in the universe, can be accounted for in the context of an ontological non-dualism. The Sāṅkhya causal theory, even if it, like the Śaiva one, may properly be labeled a *satkārya* doctrine, fails to account for the appearance of the world *as it is experienced in quotidian life*, as a world where entities are "manifested" and "destroyed" and cannot always be seen to be present. Causality, then, must be grounded as much in explaining the non-manifestation of entities as in explaining how the multiple entities of the universe may be produced, for which, Somānanda and Utpaladeva argue, only a theory of all as Śiva-as-consciousness can account.

1E. SOMĀNANDA'S ENGAGEMENT WITH NYĀYA AND VAIŚEṢIKA AUTHORS AND WORKS

Perhaps the most challenging component of Somānanda's syllogism is what I refer to as the warrant by which he justifies his claim, for what is argued is counterintuitive. In essence, Somānanda claims that the very appearance of *multiple* entities in the universe of experience proves that an underlying *unity*, a oneness, is in fact present. Paradoxical as this might seem, I would suggest so much represents a core strategy of Brahmanical thought, of Hindu philosophy, at least from the time of the production of the Upaniṣads. And perhaps, then, it is no coincidence that the present *āhnika* leans on a metaphor, the aforementioned one of gold and the objects fashioned of it, that is present, *mutatis mutandis*, in early Upaniṣadic sources.[78] The world of multiplicity is real, as the Upaniṣads teach, *and* a real behind (or within, or existing as) the real must exist that orders and structures all of it. Somānanda's warrant, as I've identified it, establishes just such a claim.

While the particular context of this warrant and the syllogism it authorizes show a deep indebtedness with and concern for the philosophy of the Buddhist Epistemologists, this being evident also in Somānanda's engagement with the Mīmāṃsā and Sāṅkhya schools, the fundamental claim that parts require a

---

[77] See ŚD 4.59-60ab and Utpaladeva's commentary on the same.

[78] See, e.g., ChUp 6.1.5: *yathā somyaikena lohamaṇinā sarvaṃ lohamayaṃ vijñātaṃ syāt | vācārambhaṇaṃ vikāro nāmadheyaṃ loham ity eva satyam ||*. Olivelle (1996: 148) translates as follows: "It is like this, son. By means of just one copper trinket one would perceive everything made of copper—the transformation is a verbal handle, a name—while the reality is just this: 'it's copper.'" Cf. ChUp 6.1.4 and 6.1.6.

whole in which to be organized or with which to be identified finds fuller expression in ŚD 4 with Somānanda's treatment of his Nyāya and Vaiśeṣika interlocutors. Two sections of the ŚD deal explicitly and at some length with this opponent.

First, Somānanda argues that there could be no whole comprised of parts, *even on the Naiyāyika-Vaiśeṣika understanding thereof*, in the absence of a unity as Śiva.[79] In the absence of the existence of a unity-as-Śiva, parts could never be associated with a whole in the manner that Somānanda's realist, dualist interlocutors would have it,[80] their views of the same being used in an analogy for the unity Somānanda espouses, as we shall see, at the close of the *āhnika*.[81] He further argues that the problem persists when one considers the nature of a universal and the member instances of the same: for all the particulars of a class equally to share an identification with the same universal, one must allow for an entity to exist simultaneously as both particular *and* universal, which can only be explained by Śaiva non-dualism.[82] Nyāya-Vaiśeṣika mereology, in a word, presupposes a Śaiva non-duality.

Second, Somānanda comprehensively scrutinizes the Nyāya-Vaiśeṣika theory of cognition in two conceptually related passages of text.

In a first passage that deals with a particular technical problem, found at ŚD 4.64cd-66, Somānanda queries whether a Naiyāyika-Vaiśeṣika theory of cognition logically could explain how one set in deep sleep could awaken from it, a problem that of course was also dealt with elsewhere in Sanskrit

---

[79] See ŚD 4.60cd-63ab: *itaś ca sarvaśivatāvayavebhyo na kutracit* || *vyatireko 'vayavinas tad evedaṃ vicāryatām* | *bhinneṣv aikyam abhedaś ca yathā tatra vyavasthitaḥ* || *tathā tatra parijñeyaṃ patyuḥ sāmarthyam īdṛśam* | *abhinne bhedatā yena bhinneṣv apy asty abhedatā* || *yathāvayavagaṃ rūpaṃ tathā sarvapadārthagam* |. "It is for this (following) reason, as well, that everything is possessed of Śiva-nature: nowhere is there a distinction of the whole from its parts. This is the very item that must be considered(, as follows). Unity exists in the divisions, and since a non-duality is present there, one must therefore understand a kind of capacity of the Lord to be present there; it is by means of it that the multiplicity (of the parts) exists in the undivided [unity], and the non-duality exists in all the divisions. Just as a (single) form is present in the parts (of which an individual such as Devadatta is formed), so also a (single) form [i.e., Śiva-nature] is present in everything (in the universe)."

[80] See ŚD 4.63cd-64ab: *kva pāṇipādaṃ kva śiro yathaikyaṃ bhinnadeśagam* || *tadvat sarvapadārthānāṃ jagaty aikye sthitaḥ śivaḥ* |. "Where is hand and foot, where the head? Just as the unity (that is Devadatta) is present in these different places, so also Śiva exists in a unity of all real things in the universe." Cf. the corresponding passage of the ŚDVṛ (lines 397–398 of the present edition): *avayavabhedasyāpy abhinnāvayavirūpatā śivarūpatayaiveti pratipāditam īśvarapratyabhijñāyām. evaṃ jagaty aikye śivarūpatopapādikā sthitā.* "The division that is the parts is itself of the nature of the undivided whole, simply inasmuch as it is of the nature of Śiva—so much was explained (by me) in the *Īśvarapratyabhijñā*. In the same way, Śiva-nature, the producer (of the universe), exists in the unity (found) in the universe."

[81] This is expressed in the form of analogizing Śaiva non-duality with collective wholes, single entities made up of integrated parts. See ŚD 4.126ab, which is cited also at footnote 2 of the present introduction.

[82] See ŚD 4.67 and Utpaladeva's commentary on the same.

philosophical works, not least in the Nyāya literature itself.[83] Somānanda argues that it cannot, because their theory of cognition involves a two-step process of knowing, one involving both a first apprehension of a material object (*artha*) by way of a material sense organ (*indriya*) making contact (*sannikarṣa*) with it, the second step in the cognitive process involving the communication of the product of that contact to the knower, the *ātman*, by way of the *ātman* directing the *manas* to convey the same.

Such a complex cognitive process, Somānanda suggests, even were its two steps to occur simultaneously, simply cannot account for how it is that one may awaken from sleep. For if the knower, the *ātman*, were not aware already of the sound that is said to occasion the awakening, then the *manas* could not be directed by that knower to convey an awareness of the same. And if the knower, though asleep, *is* sufficiently aware of it to be able to direct the *manas* to convey the contents of the initial apprehension by *indriyārthasannikarṣa*, then the cognitive state in question would be indistinguishable from the waking state.[84] This is so, Somānanda argues, because the Nyāya-Vaiśeṣika theory of cognition requires agents to be active, to choose to act, in order for cognitions to register with them; and such intentional activity defines the nature of the waking state, deep sleep being understood by Somānanda's interlocutors to be a state of consciousness characterized by the knower's inactivity.[85]

This criticism having been articulated, Somānanda summarily concludes that everything is of the nature of Śiva (*sarvaṃ śivātmakam*, ŚD 4.66d). Utpaladeva explains what is meant by this by indicating that on the Śaiva view,

---

[83] See, e.g., Sharma 2004. Cf., esp., NSBh ad NS 2.1.26 and 2.1.29, cited in footnote 316 of the translation.

[84] See ŚD 4.64cd-66c: *śabdāder grahaṇaṃ nāsti pūrvāparasahoditaiḥ* || *manasaḥ preraṇaṃ kasmāt prāgjñānena vinā sthitā* | *sarvaikatāta evātra tathā sauṣuptabodhanam* || *ghaṭate kathaṃ nimittasya prāgyogāyogacoditaiḥ* | *yoge jāgradavasthaiva* . . . "One would not apprehend (the *tanmātras* or sensibilia, viz.,) sound, etc., by means of (either) sequential or simultaneously arisen [cognitions](, if consciousness and its object were mutually distinct). Why would the mind be impelled to act in the absence of a prior cognition? For this very reason, a unity exists in everything, here. And with what have been put forth as arguments [*-codita*] regarding whether the cause (of awakening one in deep sleep) is connected (to the one who is to be awoken) prior (to being awoken) or is not connected, (we ask:) how is it possible to awaken from deep sleep? If connected, this entails nothing other than the waking state."

[85] So much is implicit, at least, in the ŚDVṛ ad ŚD 4.64cd-66 (lines 413–417): *tathā hy uccaiḥśabdādijñānaṃ prabodhanimittaṃ tasya ca prāg yogo 'tha na yoga iti codyaiḥ kathaṃ ghaṭanam, tathā hi prāk śabdādijñānena yoge jāgradavasthaiva syāt tasyās tathālakṣaṇatvāt, prāk śabdādijñānasya nimittasya tu virahe kathaṃ prabodhaḥ*. "To explain: Awareness [*jñāna*] of loud sounds or the like is the cause that awakens one (from deep sleep), and with what have been put forward as arguments as to whether it [i.e., the cause] is joined prior (to the awakening), or is not (so) joined, (we ask:) how is this [cause of the awakening] possibly brought about? To explain (further), if one is joined to the awareness of the (loud) sound or the like prior (to awakening from deep sleep), this would entail nothing other than the waking state, because that is the very definition thereof. And yet, how can one be awoken if the cause—a prior awareness of the (loud) sound or the like—were found wanting?"

Note, however, that the NSBh offers an explanation that answers this problem, for which see footnote 316 of the translation.

when everything is one, awakening from sleep is constituted by the presence of an absence, the absence of the cognition of non-dual Śiva-nature. It is the waking state, that is to say, that involves a sort of passivity, a failure to act, on the part of the knower. And it is in the course of falling—and being—asleep that one engages activity: the agent actively and positively cognizes non-duality in deep sleep.[86] This inversion, what constitutes to my mind an ingenious philosophical move, solves the problem of sleep and sets as the standard a non-duality that is active, structured precisely in line with Somānanda's and Utpaladeva's explanations of "destruction" that were reviewed in the section "Somānanda's Critique of the Sāṅkhya Theory of Causality." It also requires one to understand multiplicity, the very possibility of subject-object distinctions and any awareness thereof, to be a function of unity, and not the other way around.

The second passage in which the Nyāya-Vaiśeṣika theory of cognition is engaged is rather more extended, it beginning at ŚD 4.100cd-101 and, I would argue, reaching nearly to the end of the fourth *āhnika*. Like the one just surveyed, it depends on a critique of the cognitive process as understood by the realist, dualist schools, as articulated, for example, in *Vaiśeṣikasūtra* (VS) 3.1.13:[87]

> What is produced from the contact of the *ātman*, the sense organ, the *manas*, and the object is other [i.e., is direct cognition].

Somānanda argues that this theory of cognition cannot cohere inasmuch as it relies on an ontological dualism, whereby the particular elements in the cognitive process are qualitatively different, some having a form or being *mūrta*, others being without a material form or *amūrta*. He argues, that is, that Nyāya-Vaiśeṣika ontology must logically presuppose the existence of an underlying unity of nature—a unity defined by qualitative identity—for it to cohere. Once again, then, Somānanda claims his opponent's philosophical system coheres only by implicitly accepting his non-dual Śaiva ontology.

The verses of the ŚD in which this argument is prosecuted fall exclusively in the portion of the fourth *āhnika* for which no commentary remains extant, and as such they may be understood only with close and slow reading. My interpretations of these passages, therefore, are perhaps best taken to be

---

[86] See ŚDVṛ ad ŚD 4.64cd-66 (lines 417–419): *tad etad eva syād vidyaikatve śivatvākhyātiprakriyāmātram etat syāt. tīvraśabdādikenājñātenāpy āvaraṇapreraṇe kṛte sauṣuptavinivṛttir iti ca paroktaṃ kutaḥ, pramāṇāt siddham iti ca na niścāyakaṃ katham.* "Thus, this alone must be the case: When knowledge is unitary, this [cause of the awakening] can be nothing but the procedure of the non-cognition of Śiva-nature; the state of deep sleep is interrupted when a severe noise, e.g., for its part unexpected, impels one to obscure (one's awareness of non-dual Śiva-nature). And therefore, (we ask:) this [mere procedure] could be contradicted, how? And since it is proven by a valid means of knowing, (we ask:) it is not conclusive, how?" Note the variant reading and emendation to the text, here, recorded in the notes to the edition and explained at footnotes 318 and 320 of the translation.

[87] VS 3.1.13: *ātmendriyamano'rthasannikarṣād yan niṣpadyate tad anyat.* Cf. NS 1.1.4, cited and translated in footnote 396 of the translation.

somewhat provisional given the difficulties of reading them without the aid of a commentary. And yet, I submit, they *are*, on the whole, comprehensible, and—indeed—they merit our sustained attention.

The argument, as noted, begins at ŚD 4.100cd-101, where Somānanda suggests (in his terse, telegraphic style) that a unity of all is required if his realist opponent is to be able to explain how it is that the *ātman* could occasion any activity in the sense organs (*indriyas*), the problem being that the latter have form or are *mūrta* while the former is *amūrta*, without a material form.[88] Nor, argues Somānanda, can the *manas* be understood to motivate the same array of sense organs, even if it, like the *indriya*, is held to be *mūrta* on his opponents' view, because, we must understand him to suggest, the Nyāya-Vaiśeṣika itself does not proffer such a role for it. Rather, only a unity of all can explain the connection of the immaterial *ātman* to the material *indriyas*.[89]

Next, the argument turns to the question of how the knower and object known could hook up in the dualist system in question, with Somānanda stating plainly that no apprehension (*grahaṇa*) or cognition (*jñāna*) of the object could occur at all if the entities cognized were (ontologically) distinct.[90] The mere contact of sense organ and object (*akṣārthasaṃyogamātra*) could not lead the knower to know the object (in the absence of the existence of a Śaiva non-dual ontology), Somānanda argues, because there is no way to explain how such contact would make the knower—the *ātman*—, who does not participate directly in the contact of *indriya* and *artha*, aware of their product.[91]

The Naiyāyika-Vaiśeṣika replies as one would expect, arguing that cognition must involve two steps, the phenomenon of memory, for example, being a mode of awareness that demands a knower that is not the sense organ, one informed by but distinct from the *manas*, which serves to establish the very necessity of such a complex, two-step cognitive process.[92] Somānanda, in reply, queries how the cognitive procedure may be understood to occur

---

[88] See ŚD 4.100cd-101a: *tathātmecchāvaśān nākṣagrāme ceṣṭopapadyate || mūrtacodakavaikalyān . . .* "And, (in the absence of the existence of unity,) no activity in the array of the organs of sense would be possible by dint of the will of the *ātman*, because there is a defect in (conceiving of the *ātman* as) the impeller of that which has a form."

[89] See ŚD 4.101b-d: . . . *manaś cet preritāsya no | ekatve punar īdṛk syāt sarvatraiva hi yuktatā ||*. "Objection: The *manas* is that which incites this [array] to act. (Reply:) This is simply not the case. If a unity exists, however, there could be such a condition; for a state of being connected would exist absolutely everywhere." See also the corresponding notes to the translation, especially footnote 392.

[90] See ŚD 4.102ab: *na cāpi bhede bhāvānāṃ grahaṇaṃ jñānam eva vā |*. "It also is not the case that one could apprehend the entities, or cognize them fully [*eva*], if dualism were to exist."

[91] See ŚD 4.102cd-103: *saṃyogenopapadyeta yadi dṛṣṭyādinā bhavet || naivam akṣārthasaṃyogamātrāt kiṃ boddhur udyamaḥ | saṃyoge 'nyasya sañjāte katham anyasya boddhṛtā ||*. "Objection: It [i.e., the apprehension, or cognition] is possible by way of a connection; it can come to be by way of the faculty of seeing, etc. (Reply:) So much is not the case. Why would the mere connection of the sense organ and object cause the knower to exert himself? How, when the connection has been produced of one entity, is another the knower?"

[92] See ŚD 4.104ab and, esp., footnote 399 of the translation.

sequentially. What, he asks, may explain how the *manas* conveys the product of the *indriyārthasannikarṣa* to the *amūrta* knower, the *ātman*?[93] Indeed, what, precisely, is conveyed thereto? It cannot be the state of the nature of the real object, Somānanda argues, because it has a form and thus cannot make contact with the *amūrta ātman*, the two being qualitatively mutually distinct in nature.[94] And if his dualist opponent wishes instead to argue that the form (*rūpa*) of the object is conveyed, Somānanda argues, this too cannot be so; for, he notes, a quality (*guṇa*) such as form can only inhere in a substance (*dravya*), on his opponent's view, and the substance in question must be *mūrta*, as this is all that could hold a quality like *rūpa*.[95]

Next, Somānanda queries how the mechanical cognitive process articulated by his opponent could account for cognitions distorted by the desire of the knower.[96] A cognition that is so distorted cannot be brought mechanically to the knower, he argues, because it is not possible that the *manas* could convey such a one, the *manas* being a mere instrument and insentient.[97] This is to say that, on his opponent's own cognitive theory, the *manas* is capable of reporting only what it witnesses; it cannot introduce distortions into what is produced as a result of the material and mechanical contact of *indriya* and *artha*.

Similarly, Somānanda further argues, the *ātman* cannot be understood to influence what is presented to itself, because one would have to explain what the *ātman* does, on such an understanding of the matter,[98] and Somānanda argues that no such explanation is logically tenable. On the one hand, if the opponent argues that the *ātman* triggers the presentation of the distorted

---

[93] See ŚD 4.104cd-106.

[94] See ŚD 4.106cd-107a: *manasā nīyate tasya kiṃ padārthasvarūpatā || sāśakyā mūrtarūpatvād* . . . "(So:) What of it is conveyed by the *manas* (to the *ātman*)? (Objection:) The state of the nature of the thing (apprehended by the *indriyārthasannikarṣa*). (Reply:) That [state] is not possible (to be conveyed to the *ātman*), due to the fact that it has a material form [*mūrtarūpatvāt*]."

[95] See ŚD 4.107b-c and footnote 406 of the translation: . . . *rūpaṃ cen na kathaṃ guṇaḥ | guṇino nīyate* . . . "Objection: The form (is brought by the *manas* to the knower). (Reply:) Not so. How could a quality belonging to the entity possessing such a quality be conveyed?" See also footnote 406 of the translation.

[96] See ŚD 4.107c-d: . . . *'nyatra tṛṣārtaiś cākṛtiṃ prati* |. "And how, as regards the particular configuration [*ākṛti*] (of that *guṇa*), is that [quality of the one possessing it] brought (to the *ātman* in a manner rendering it) otherwise (than its true nature) by those affected by desire?" As noted in footnote 407 of the translation, one must read both *nīyate* (4.107c) and *katham* (ŚD 4.107b) into the present sentence.

[97] See ŚD 4.108a-c: *atha jñānaṃ na manasas taj jñānam upapadyate | karaṇatvāj jaḍatvāc ca* . . . "Objection: A cognition (of the qualities of the object appearing in a manner distorted by the knower's desire is brought to the knower). (Reply:) Not so. It is not possible that that (is a type of) cognition (that) belongs to the *manas*, because (according to you) the latter is (merely) an instrument and is insentient."

[98] This is communicated in an incredibly terse passage that, on my reading, telegraphs two meanings in an overlapping syntax. See ŚD 4.108d: *tasya ced ātmanātra kim* ||. I read *ātmanā* twice, with what precedes and what follows it, to gather the following meaning from the *pāda*: "Objection: It is by means of the *ātman* that it [i.e., the distorted cognition] belongs to it [i.e., the *manas*]. (Reply:) What use is the *ātman*, here?" See also footnotes 410 and 411 of the translation.

cognition at its only point of contact in the two-step cognitive process—in the *manas*—then the cognition would be distorted only at the level of the *manas* and not at the prior stage in the process, when the *indriya* apprehends the *artha*, which would lead the *ātman* to cognize the distorted qualities of the object only at the level of the *manas* and not in the *artha* itself.[99] If, on the other hand, the opponent claims that it is the *ātman*'s consciousness that knows the object in its distorted form, then there would again remain a difference between the object first apprehended (by the *sannikarṣa* of *indriya* and *artha*) and the one ultimately present in the *ātman*'s consciousness.[100] Nor, Somānanda adds, can the *ātman* impute its state of consciousness on the *manas* such that the latter would be inclined to take in the product of the initial apprehension of *indriya* and *artha* in a similar fashion as it; for the *manas*, which is material and acts only mechanically, cannot be understood to have been "penetrated" by the immaterial *ātman*, such that the latter could implant its mode of awareness in the former.[101]

If the stepped cognitive procedure cannot introduce distortion mid-stream, at the levels either of the introduction of cognitive information to the *ātman* or to the *manas*, Somānanda's opponent argues next, then couldn't the distortion enter at the *conclusion* of the cognitive process?[102] No, Somānanda replies, because the *ātman* would no longer be set in a chain of contact with the object after the cognition of the latter is conveyed to it by the *manas*; thus, the awareness of the *ātman* could alter only its state of understanding, but not its cognition, of the object.[103]

Somānanda next ponders whether his opponent could argue that the distortion may be understood to be triggered by the object itself. Perhaps, that is, it is the object itself that impresses the *ātman* with a *saṃskāra*, such that

---

[99] See ŚD 4.109a-d: *karaṇe jñānasaṃbandhād bāhyārthe kiṃ na kalpyate | buddher guṇatvaṃ manasi prāpnuyād* . . . "If (you argue) it is the trigger [*karaṇa*], because of the connection of the cognition (to the *ātman*), (we reply by asking:) do you not conceive of it [i.e., the distorted cognition] with respect to the external object? The possession of the (distorted) qualities belonging to the cognition [*buddhi*] would be at hand in the *manas* (but not with respect to the external object)."

[100] See ŚD 4.109d-110: . . . *atha cetasā || evaṃvidho ghaṭo 'trāste ity ātmā pratibodhyate | tad evaṃ pūrvadṛṣṭasya varṇanāsadṛśaṃ bhavet* ||. "Objection: It is by dint of (the *ātman*'s) consciousness that the self [*ātman*] is informed that a pot of such a kind(, e.g.,) is present, here. Reply: In this way, that which was first seen (in the initial perception) would be different from the description (given of it by the awareness of the *ātman*)."

[101] See ŚD 4.111: *varṇanena ca caitanyam etāvan manaso yadi | svātmaśaktisamāveśād amūrtāveśatā katham* ||. "And if you argue that the *manas* is possessed of such a consciousness by way of the description, this because it is penetrated by the power of the self with which it is associated [*svātma-*], (then we reply:) how is there a state of penetration (effected) by that [*ātman*] which does not have a material form?"

[102] See ŚD 4.112a-b: *tena vā sampratīte 'rthe kriyate* . . . "Alternatively, (you might argue) it [i.e., the consciousness of the object as distorted] is produced by way of that [description] once the object has been thoroughly cognized."

[103] See ŚD 4.112b-113c. Cf., especially, footnote 426 of the translation.

the perspective of the *ātman* is distorted. The advantage to this proposition is this, that the distortion could pass through the staged cognitive process from the very beginning, such that no inconsistency could be identified in the presentation of the contents of the cognition in its various stages: the cognition would be distorted from the very initial moment of the *sannikarṣa* of *indriya* and *artha* and all the way to the *ātman*'s awareness of the object of cognition. Yet, Somānanda replies, this explanation of distortion is also untenable; for the object, which is *mūrta*, cannot impress what is *amūrta*, i.e., the *ātman*; nor can a form (*rūpa*) of the impression mark the *ātman*, because both the *rūpa* and the *ātman* (and the consciousness of the latter) are without a material form (*amūrta*) and thus incapable, Somānanda argues, of being mutually combined (this following the logic of his dualist interlocutors).[104]

Next, Somānanda queries how the form of the impression makes itself known. Does it do so itself, Somānanda asks? That is, if it is meant to impress on the *ātman* in such a manner that the latter sees the object in question in a distorted fashion, then one may fairly ask how it is that such an object may make itself known in just such a distorted form.[105] The very concept of a "distortion," after all, signals the presence of a quality or appearance that is not natural to the object itself. Somānanda's opponent replies by proffering, at ŚD 4.115d, that the very "excess" or difference from the object that constitutes the distortion allows the form of the impression to be known by the *ātman*, to which Somānanda replies by asking what role the *manas* plays in conveying the same to the *ātman*, just as he asks the same question of the sense organ, as well.[106] And when his opponent replies by reiterating that the *indriya* must be understood to stand as part of a sequential chain of cognition and is followed in that cognitive process by the contact of the *manas* with the *ātman*, Somānanda replies devastatingly by noting that, inasmuch as the cognitive process as the Naiyāyikas and Vaiśeṣikas understand it is mechanical (in no small part because largely material in nature), one can only therefore conclude that the present explanation of distorted cognition requires his opponent to understand the cognitive apparatus invariably to report "up the chain" to the *ātman* cognitive

---

[104] See ŚD 4.113d-115ab: . . . *yadi vā tatsvarūpataḥ* || *saṃskaroti tadātmānam amūrte saṃskṛtiḥ katham* | *tadrūpam ātmany etad yenāśleṣo yadi cocyate* || *caitanyenāpy amūrtena miśratānyasya kīdṛśī* |. "Alternatively, you might argue that, given its nature, it [i.e., the object] marks the *ātman* with an impression at that time. (Reply:) How can the formation (of an impression) [*saṃskṛti*] occur when it [i.e., the *ātman*] is without a form? And if you respond by saying that this, the form of that [impression] is (found) at the *ātman*, because of which they are connected, (then we reply:) what sort of a state of combination could the one [i.e., the form or *rūpa* of the *saṃskāra*] have even with (the) consciousness (belonging to the *ātman*), which is (also) without a form?"

[105] See ŚD 4.115c: *kiṃ svayaṃ tatprameyatvam.* "Does it [i.e., the form or *rūpa* of the impression or *saṃskāra*] make itself an object of knowledge of its own accord?"

[106] See ŚD 4.115d-116a: . . . *asya ced atirekataḥ* || *manasā kiṃ kim akṣeṇa* . . . "If you reply by arguing (that the form or *rūpa* of the *saṃskāra* can make itself known as an object of knowledge) as a result of its difference, (we reply:) of what use is the *manas* (in this process)? Of what use is the sense organ?"

information that is in fact false. It would convey *not* what is present or real in instances where a cognition is distorted by the desires of the *ātman*, but rather what is in fact *not* present, which is to say cognition as his opponents explain it is in such instances "blind" in its sequential chain (*andhapāramparyatvarūpa*), incapable, in such instances at least, of conveying reliable information.[107] What makes this reply so devastating is the fact that it suggests that the sequential procedure of cognition contradicts the definition of perception,[108] for the perceptual process would produce what is not a perception at all.

Having thus argued that his opponent's two-phased sequence of cognition is untenable for the reasons reviewed here, Somānanda turns to another concern in his critique of his opponents' theory of cognition, one that echoes what was said earlier in the *āhnika* about the problem of explaining how it is one can awaken from a deep sleep. Somānanda asks, that is, what functional use there is in the *ātman* impelling the *manas* to convey to it what is known from the contact of the *indriya* with the *artha*. For whether the object in question has been cognized or not, the impelling is logically untenable. If the object of cognition has been cognized, already, there is no need to impel the *manas* to act, because the *ātman* already knows the product of the *indriyārthasannikarṣa*; and, conversely, the *ātman* has no way to know of the existence of the object in question if it has not yet been cognized, nor, it therefore follows, does it have any possible way to know to tell the *manas* what to report to it. Indeed, Somānanda concludes, only a unity of the duality of thing impelled, act of impelling, and agent thereof could logically explain cognition on his opponents' model. Yet again, that is, Somānanda suggests a philosophical formulation of his *śāstric* interlocutor implicitly depends logically on his own non-dual Śaiva ontology. (All of this is expressed at ŚD 4.117-119ab.)

Somānanda next argues in a terse but fascinating passage that a similar unity is required if a memory is to transpire,[109] for only a unity of two distinct

[107] See ŚD 4.116b-d: . . . *tena cet tatparamparā | evaṃ tad andhapāramparyatvarūpam idaṃ sphuṭam* ||. "Objection: The latter is succeeded in a sequential chain (of the act of cognition) by the former. (Reply:) In this way, it [i.e., the *prameyatva* or 'state of being an object of knowledge' that belongs to the *rūpa* of the *saṃskāra*] has as its form of an uninterrupted sequence (of cognition) that is blind. This is clear."

[108] See NS 1.1.4, cited also at footnote 436 and translated at footnote 396 of the translation: *indriyārthasannikarṣotpannaṃ jñānam avyapadeśyam avyabhicāri vyavasāyātmakaṃ pratyakṣam.*

[109] See ŚD 4.119cd-123ab: *tathā smaraṇayogāc ca smaryate kiṃ tathāvidham || yādṛg dṛṣṭaṃ dṛṣṭatā syād athavā jñānam eva tat | dṛṣṭasaraṇayor aikye sthite tad upapadyate || tathā sā pratyabhijñānāt sa evāyam iti sthitiḥ | yujyate katham atraiva jñānayoḥ kālabhinnayoḥ || dvayor aikyam anaikyaṃ vā tadaikyaṃ bhinnayoḥ katham | anaikye na sa evāyam iti syād ghaṭadaṇḍayoḥ || tasmād aikyam iha spaṣṭaṃ saṃsāre samavasthitam* |. "And, it is thus (that one must understand the Śaiva reality, what is a complete unity, to have been proven) in consequence of (the cognition that is) memory(, as well). (For, we ask:) What is remembered (according to you)? (Opponent's Reply:) Just that of such qualities as what was perceived [*dṛṣṭa*] (in the initial cognition). (Somānanda:) The fact of having been seen must be present (in the memory-cognition), or perhaps it [i.e., the memory] is the (initial) cognition itself. That [i.e., the act of remembering] is possible (only) when a unity is established of that which was (first) perceived and the memory (thereof), and how is that condition possible here in this very instance [*atraiva*] as a result

cognitions can explain the awareness that "this entity in front of me is that very one I saw before." That is, Somānanda argues that memory involves just such a "recognition" or *pratyabhijñāna*, and so much is impossible in the absence of the unification of both cognitions, the earlier one of the initial cognition of an object, and the subsequent one that remembers the same as that which had been cognized, before. Once again, then, an analysis of his opponent's view proves the reality of Somānanda's own non-dual ontology. Indeed, acts of memory, properly understood, prove that all must be one—the unitary Śiva-as-consciousness—for short of the unification of the disparate pair of cognitions that allow for recognition (and with it a memory-cognition), one could have no experience of memory at all.

Now, this passage merits further comment not only because it deploys the term *pratyabhijñāna* for the first time in any work of the "Recognition" or Pratyabhijñā school, as other scholars have noted, already,[110] but also because it deploys an argument that is, I submit, best understood to apply particularly to a Naiyāyika (and, perhaps, Vaiśeṣika) opponent, and not to the problem of memory-cognitions as it is generally understood (by Buddhists or others, as well).[111] It would be in a sense unsurprising to understand the matter to involve a Naiyāyika opponent in particular, because, as is well known (but hardly noted in scholarship on Śaiva philosophy), the term *pratyabhijñāna* is used in the *Nyāyasūtras* and their commentaries precisely where an argument is offered for the existence of the *ātman* as the knower in whom cognitions are located as qualities thereof and which are therefore comparable (what on their view is indispensable to acts of memory)—a position that stands in contrast, implicitly and explicitly, with the formulations of their Buddhist opponents.[112] And Somānanda, who has taken up several lines of criticism against the Nyāya, could be expected to query in particular their understanding of the ways in which cognitions may be set in mutual relation—in a word, unified—because he is intensely concerned with defeating the momentariness doctrine of his Buddhist opponent and would therefore be intent on understanding the limits of his Naiyāyika counterpart's arguments for the existence of a permanent self or *ātman*.

---

of a recognition [*pratyabhijñānāt*] that 'this is that very one,' when the two cognitions are temporally divided? Either the two [cognitions] are unified, or they are not unified. (Opponent's Objection:) They are unified. (Somānanda's Reply:) How so for two (ontologically) distinct [cognitions]? If(, by contrast,) they are not unified, (then) there can be no (recognition that) 'this is that very one' for a pot and a stick. Therefore, unity is clearly established in *saṃsāra*, here."

110 Torella (1994: xx) and, before him, Kupetz (1972: 4–5) have both highlighted this passage for its use of the term. See footnote 447 of the translation.

111 Torella (ibid.), e.g., has suggested that the term is used "to demonstrate the essential unity, or possibility of unification, of cognitions (against Buddhists, etc.)." Kupetz (ibid.) merely associates the term with Śaiva philosophical formulations (as he understands them).

112 See NS 3.1.7, cited and translated (with the corresponding passage of the NSBh) in footnote 447 of the translation.

The question of the particular identity of Somānanda's opponent in the passage in question hinges on the particulars of the argument. According to the ŚD, the memory cognition must appear in a form that comports either a quality of its having been seen before, or it must be identical with the initial cognition that the memory cognition recalls.[113] So much can only be accomplished by a full, epistemological non-dualism, Somānanda argues, one that sees ultimate identity in the two cognitions of an act of memory, which is difficult to countenance even if an *ātman* stands as the locus for both. Indeed, Somānanda demands an answer of his opponent as to whether there is a unity (*aikya*) of the two cognitions or not, and—what is key—his opponent replies by claiming the existence of just such a unity of the two cognitions in question (viz., the initial one of an object and a subsequent memory of the same that leads to the recognition that the content of the memory-cognition is that of what was previously cognized) (ŚD 4.122). It is likely, I would therefore suggest, that Somānanda here gives voice to a realist opponent who allows for a "unification" of the two cognitions in the *ātman* and as qualities thereof, what is referred to in the Nyāya literature as a *pratisandhāna*. (Conversely, I suggest it is exceedingly unlikely he would put the same reply to his question in the mouth of his Buddhist Epistemologist interlocutor, who would not admit to such a oneness of ontologically distinct, instantaneous *jñāna*s and instead would explain memory as being possible as a result of the influence of an impression or *saṃskāra*.) And yet, what is meant by the *pratisandhāna* of cognitions in the *ātman* might amount to a mutual juxtaposition and not a full unification of what are discrete epistemic phenomena on the dualists' understanding, and Somānanda would want to press his Naiyāyika opponent to concede his epistemological non-dualism. This he in fact does, on my reading, by suggesting that no unity or *aikya* may be understood to exist for the two cognitions if they are mutually distinct.[114]

Further evidence, if circumstantial, also suggests a Naiyāyika interlocutor is here addressed. For the passage of text presently under discussion is bordered on both ends with arguments or allusions to that same philosophical opponent. We have already reviewed in detail what precedes it. Here, we note that following ŚD 4.119cd-123ab are the *āhnika*'s concluding remarks, wherein Somānanda sums up the chapter in a manner that apparently echoes his interest in Nyāya-Vaiśeṣika philosophy: at ŚD 4.123cd-126ab he reiterates that all entities may be joined or connected only by way of a unity, but he does

---

[113] See ŚD 4.120ab, cited in footnote 109. One can detect a similar concern in the ĪPK, as well, at, esp., ĪPK (and ĪPKVṛ ad) 1.3.1: *satyaṃ kiṃtu smṛtijñānaṃ pūrvānubhavasaṃskṛteḥ* | *jātam apy ātmaniṣṭhaṃ tan nādyānubhavavedakam* ||. ĪPKVṛ: *pūrvānubhavasaṃskāraprabodhajanmāpi smṛtir ātmamātraniṣṭhatvāt svarūpasaṃvedikaiva na tu pūrvānubhavāveśābhāvāt pūrvānubhūtārthavyavasthāpikā ghaṭate.*

[114] See ŚD 4.122b: *tadaikyaṃ bhinnayoḥ katham* |. See also notes 448 and 442 of the translation.

so in particular, and as noted,[115] by suggesting that the unity he has in mind is similar to that of a caravan, an army, or a forest, entities that are one but nevertheless are comprised of constituent entities or parts. All the disparate things in existence are of the nature of Śiva, he thus suggests with these analogies, because they in their aggregate *are Śiva*. But an irony may be found in this statement, in the fact that his realist and dualist interlocutors also refer to such composite entities, as may be seen, *mutatis mutandis*, in the NS—but not just this. For the examples of an army and a forest are deployed in the NS not to illustrate a true unity, but rather what they posit is only an apparent unity found in what are in fact disparate entities (about which see footnote 457 of the translation). Put differently, the conclusion, like Somānanda's interpretation of memory-cognitions and the recognitions (*pratyabhijñānas*) they constitute, suggests again that true unity exists where his dualist counterparts understand there to be multiplicity; and the very exemplars the Naiyāyika offers of false unities, of multiplicity where they say unity is only erroneously posited, furnish for Somānanda exemplars of the very ontological unity on which, he suggests, they must rely if their philosophical positions are to cohere logically. This is to say that the entire section of the ŚD (i.e., ŚD 4.101cd-4.123ab) is presented and appears to be a sustained treatment of a single opponent, much as the views of Buddhist Epistemology are dissected at length and essentially without interruption from ŚD 4.78-4.98a.

If the opponent of the *smṛti-jñāna* passage is indeed a Naiyāyika, then, recognizing that the argument by grounding the very possibility of memory on the unification of cognitions is precisely what is argued in ĪPK 1.3 and deployed against a Buddhist opponent, a certain irony lies in this fact. For, as Torella (1994: xxii–xxiii) has noted, Utpaladeva in his ĪPK and ĪPKVṛ deploys the logic of the Buddhist Epistemologists to defeat a Naiyāyika understanding of external objects and concepts such as relation only to go on logically to defeat the Buddhist himself. Here the opposite ordering of opponents is found. If the present interpretation of ŚD 4.119cd-123ab is correct, then Somānanda here refers to a *pratyabhijñāna* in the course of correcting the Naiyāyikas' understanding of the unification of cognitions, who, in turn, had deployed the concept of "recognition" (effectively, on Somānanda's view?) to challenge their Buddhist interlocutors in their denial of the existence of the *ātman*. Perhaps, then, we would be fully justified in understanding Somānanda here again to suggest that an opposing school's philosophical position is logically tenable—and therefore may only be successful in its challenge to Buddhist formulations—if a Śaiva unity is implicitly accepted as the real, underlying ontology of all.

---

115 See footnotes 2 and 81.

To sum up: Somānanda's extended treatment of Nyāya-Vaiśeṣika philosophical formulations clearly indicates he opposes their dualism precisely because it does not account for the manner in which individual entities can logically be understood to stand in mutual relation. And he understands the appearance of duality in precisely the inverse manner as does his realist interlocutor: apparent duality, on his understanding, proves unity. Unity is presupposed but may be subjected to a sort of (metaphorical) dissection by way of a witnessing of one or another of its aspects or parts (*aṃśas*). Reality is not built up from discrete entities into complex wholes but is a single unity that comes to be known in real and discrete parts. In a word, Somānanda's thorough critique of his dualist, realist interlocutors serves to support the warrant that justifies the core argument of the fourth *āhnika*, leading him logically to claim, as he does, that the appearance of multiplicity in fact serves to establish the very existence of the one, unitary Śiva.

1F. CONCLUSION

The preceding survey of the contents of the fourth *āhnika* equips one for further reflection on the structure of the ŚD as a whole, so too the arc of its philosophical narrative. We have noted, already, that the fourth *āhnika*—at least as Utpaladeva understands it—stands as a fulcrum, a moment of transition from the critique of others' views found among the opening chapters to the positive articulation of Somānanda's own. This may be said to be so notwithstanding the fact that the bulk of the *āhnika* serves to criticize the views of other schools, because those criticisms in fact illustrate the logical necessity of the existence of Somānanda's own ontological (and epistemological) non-dualism, as we have repeatedly seen.

Now, much remains to be deciphered and explained in the succeeding three chapters of Somānanda's master-work. And yet, a clearer synoptic vision of the ŚD in its overarching structure is more readily evident from our present vantage point, past the half-way point in the text and beyond the boundary where all commentarial works are lost to us. What we see is a book that opens and closes with particular sectarian concerns, the first *āhnika* outlining Somānanda's theological vision in clearly Śaiva terms, the last *āhnika* articulating the manner of practice that his philosophical vision demands.[116] Between these bookends are a series of *āhnika*s that deal with opponents' philosophical views.

Here, something of the trajectory of the philosophical concerns in the text becomes evident. Central to Somānanda's philosophical project is the notion that proof of the supremacy of his settled opinion (*siddhānta*) is found in a proper analysis of the appearance of multiple entities in the universe. Such

[116] These items were discussed in the introduction to Nemec 2011, esp. at pp. 25–31 and 44–50.

entities are *real* on Somānanda's view, to be sure; he never countenances their unreality. Indeed, his insistence on the real existence of the world *as it is experienced in quotidian life* not only explains his apparent sympathy for his Mīmāṃsaka counterparts but also justifies, on his view, his entire philosophical project: it is *only* Śaiva non-dualism that can account logically for the existence of the apparently multiple universe experienced in quotidian life. The warrant of the syllogism he offers at the opening of the *āhnika*, in other words, stands as the philosophical bedrock of his thought. Explain everyday reality in a manner that conforms to mundane experience, he intimates, or hang up your philosophical spurs.

This direction leads Somānanda to examine in detail the world of phenomena as powers. It explains, that is, his concern with the philosophy of the Śāktas, as is in evidence in the third *āhnika*, so too his detailed critique of Bhartṛhari in the second, he also being one who concerned himself with powers. It likewise explains his engagement with Buddhist epistemology as seen in the present *āhnika* (and elsewhere in the text, as well). In each case, Somānanda ponders how one might explain the mutual interaction of disparate forces—phenomena—in the universe, such that they may, indeed, be said to be real and, as important, to cohere as a (dynamic) system; he is intensely concerned, that is, with the explanation of the existence of multiple capable (*śakta*) entities that can perform various and varied activities, and yet can also stand in mutual relation, such that one does not unduly impinge on another's innate capacities. As we have seen, for Somānanda such a model demands the existence not only of a coherent whole, a system or order, but also one that must culminate in the unitary presence of a single controlling agent who exists as the powers or capacities.

The Śāktas could not account for such coherence, he argued, because they failed to countenance the existence of a supreme agent who would direct and order the powers and thus justify their mutual co-presence in the universe.[117] Neither could Bhartṛhari explain the same, Somānanda argued, for while Bhartṛhari acknowledged the existence of a supreme agent—*paśyantī*—it was one, on Somānanda's view, conceived in a manner that failed fully to embrace unity, *paśyantī* standing instead only at the ontological level of a subtle subject-object duality and thus unable fully to countenance the existence of a single, supreme agency that could coordinate and direct and embody the empowered entities.[118] Finally, Somānanda argues, implicitly at least, that the Buddhist Epistemologists cannot explain the co-presence of multiple forces or powers, because they fail to conceive of any manner by which they may logically be understood to interact systematically, as a complex whole. This

[117] See, esp. ŚD 3.1 and Nemec 2011: 72–76 and 350–351.
[118] See, esp., ŚD 2.1 and Nemec 2011: 62–64, 146–150, and 304–306.

failure, moreover, is rooted in an inability to understand the true power of *all* phenomena, viz., to make themselves known to a unitary agent who is identified with and cognizes them.

Now, Somānanda's concern for logically proving the existence of a unity in—or, rather, existing as—the many is in further evidence in the *āhnika*s of the ŚD subsequent to the present one, as mentioned.[119] And yet, to reiterate, much work remains to be completed in the effort to interpret these later chapters, what amounts, as it did in the present chapter (particularly after the commentary is lost), to a project of recovery that is grounded in a painstaking semantic decipherment of Somānanda's terse and telegraphic verses. With the edition and translation of the present *āhnika*, then, only a part of the project of understanding the ŚD in its full range of meaning has come to fruition, just as it can only be with a final engagement with Somānanda's ŚD that the total reach of his thought might be fully appreciated.

At present, however, one may already note what was not evident prior to the present study, namely that Somānanda was rather more intensely interested in the philosophy of Buddhist epistemology than was previously known. Indeed, Dharmakīrti absolutely pervades the fourth chapter of the ŚD and ŚDVṛ, looming as his thought does in nearly every corner of the *āhnika*, even in Somānanda's treatment of Sāṅkhya and Mīmāṃsaka philosophical formulations. More than this, Somānanda engages Dharmakīrti's philosophy in a manner that prefigures Utpaladeva's (more celebrated) treatment of the same. His understanding of memory and "recognition" (*pratyabhijñāna*), for example (and as we have seen), anticipates, in its essential contours, at least, Utpaladeva's very dispute with the same Buddhist school.[120] Even if Somānanda fronts theological vocabulary and concerns in the ŚD, precisely the opposite tack as the one in evidence in the ĪPK,[121] moreover, it is nevertheless the case that a deeper understanding of the middle and late chapters of the ŚD (perhaps minus the seventh, which, as noted, largely examines Śaiva practice) illustrates a degree of *consistency* in Pratyabhijñā thought that has not yet been noted or adequately appreciated, inasmuch as all the major authors of the tradition held Buddhist Epistemology close in mind and developed sometimes surprisingly consistent arguments against the same.

This is to say that the fourth *āhnika* sheds further light on precisely what was anticipated (perhaps uncontroversially) in the first volume of *The Ubiquitous Śiva*, namely, that it is to Bhartṛhari and the Buddhists that much intellectual debt is owed in the history of Śaiva philosophy in Kashmir.[122] Indeed, it is in the context of explaining the existence of a world of multiple capable entities

---

[119] See footnote 55.

[120] See also footnote 447 of the translation.

[121] See Nemec 2011: 15–16.

[122] See Nemec 2011: 76–78, esp., 77.

and with his insistence on the logical necessity of the existence of a single, unitary, and ultimate agent—Śiva, precisely the one who is promoted in Śaiva sectarian and esoteric works—that he engages these authors and their ideas, and those who follow them in their thinking. Simply put, the *Śivadṛṣṭi* offers a thoroughly complex instance of Hindu-Buddhist debate, one registering and critiquing the views of a range of esoteric and "orthodox" philosophical and sectarian traditions along the way.[123]

It is increasingly clear that, however challenging it is to read and interpret, Somānanda's *magnum opus* must be counted among the landmark works in the history of Indian *philosophy*. For the ŚD not only offers an important window into the intellectual history of the Valley of Kashmir around the turn of the second millennium, but—and we are now in a position to say so more clearly than ever before—it also boasts of a clear and substantial legacy, one often found in the writings of Utpaladeva and Abhinavagupta, which owe more to Somānanda's intellectual project than was previously known. As abstrusely as Somānanda's *philosophical* contributions might present themselves to contemporary scholars of Indian religion and philosophy, then (appearing as they do largely in the sections of the ŚD for which no commentaries remain extant), and even while their full scope remains yet to be recovered, the fact that their influence was and is felt across Indian intellectual history signals they merit a fuller integration into the scholarly account of the history of Śaiva—and Kashmiri, and Indian—intellectual history. One hopes the present contribution will serve to further that very endeavor.

About the Edition

2A. MANUSCRIPTS CONSULTED FOR THE CRITICAL EDITION

In addition to the readings of the KSTS edition ($K^{ed.}$) (including the corrected readings thereof, $K^{ed.p.c.}$, that are printed in a sometimes overlooked, four-page list of errata appended to the edition[124]), I have collated those of twelve manuscript witnesses of the ŚD and ŚDVṛ in the course of preparing the edition included in the present volume. Six of these witnesses were not consulted for the production of the first volume of *The Ubiquitous Śiva*, while the remaining six are the same as those collated in the edition of the first three *āhnika*s of Somānanda's text and its principal commentary. Four of the additional witnesses are drawn from among a group of five manuscripts housed in the Oriental Research Library, Srinagar, which were not available to me around the

[123]This is a debate, or a history of debate, with clear antecedents, moreover; in engaging Dharmakīrti so extensively in the ŚD, Somānanda debates an author whose predecessor, Dignāga, himself clearly had Bhartṛhari in mind in formulating various of his own philosophical positions (as is well known).

[124]See, e.g., footnote 195 of the translation.

time when I prepared the first volume.[125] These are here labeled S^2, S^3, S^4, and S^5. (The remaining Srinagar manuscript recently made available to me, what I have labeled S^1, records only the first *āhnika* of the ŚD and ŚDVṛ.) One among these witnesses, S^4, records only a small portion of the fourth chapter of the ŚD and ŚDVṛ, and its readings are of course incorporated into the present edition only where they are available. All of the additional manuscript sources—including S^1—witness both Somānanda's *mūla* and Utpaladeva's commentary, meaning that it remains the case, here, as with the first volume, that only two manuscripts examined by me, T and C, record only the ŚD without Utpaladeva's commentary.

Of particular note are the manuscript witnesses I have labeled D and D^a, the remaining two of the sources consulted for the present edition that were not available to me at the time of the production of the first volume of *The Ubiquitous Śiva*. These are currently housed in the National Archives, New Delhi, and they are, it is clear, witnesses to which Madhusudan Kaul had access in the production of $K^{ed.}$. (In fact, the preface to his edition suggests they were the only witnesses of the ŚDVṛ that were available to him in the production of the *editio princeps*.)[126] These are in fact two partial manuscripts of the text and commentary, which cover consecutive sections of the ŚD and ŚDVr, though with some overlap. They are written in different hands, their text sized differently to the manuscript pages, but they bound together in a single codex.

Further details regarding all the manuscript witnesses are noted, as follows, the sources appearing here in the order in which the manuscript readings are regularly recorded in the edition.

T

This is the manuscript of Trivandrum University, number 5854-H. Details regarding this witness are available in the first volume of *The Ubiquitous Śiva*.

C

This is the manuscript of the Calcutta Sanskrit College, CS 3, 153. Details regarding this witness are available in the first volume of *The Ubiquitous Śiva*.

D

This manuscript is housed in the National Archives, Delhi. It is a paper document written in *śāradā* script the dimensions of which I have not measured, as I was provided a digital copy of the manuscript (with full permissions) by way of the kind assistance of Dr. Prabhat Basant and, before him, Dr. Bharati

---

125 I thank Christopher Tompkins for sharing digital copies of these manuscripts with me.

126 See Kaul 1934: i–ii.

Jagannathan (two dear colleagues and friends), and I have not seen the original document. The witness is bound in a codex, Manuscripts Belonging to the Archaeology and Research Department, Jammu and Kashmir Government, Srinagar, no. 7, vol. II. It records both the *mūla* and the commentary, beginning from the opening of the first chapter and up to the ŚDVṛ ad ŚD 4.64cd-66 (precisely where manuscript S^5 breaks off, as well, and very close to the place where P, R, and S^4 break off a few words further into the ŚDVṛ). Folio 180r. is the last that records the work and its commentary, and the text of ŚD 4 begins on folio 142r. The manuscript regularly records nine lines of text per folio side with some 14 *akṣaras* recorded per line, all written in the center of a larger page with wide margins, which are often filled with marginal notes. Short notes glossing particular Sanskrit terms of the *mūla* and commentary are also often written between the lines of text. The ŚD and ŚDVṛ are preceded (prior to the beginning of the first lines of the first *āhnika*) with a *maṅgala* as follows: *oṃ śrīgaṇeśāya namaḥ oṃ namo gurave oṃ*. Folio sides are numbered on the bottom left corner of the verso sides. There can be no question that the present item is the one identified by Madhusudan Kaul, the editor of the KSTS edition, as the item "(a)" he accessed in preparing his edition of the ŚD and ŚDVṛ. He notes (Kaul 1934: i–ii) that the manuscript is numbered "7," dates to the last third of the nineteenth century, is 10" by 6.5" in its dimensions, contains 176 leaves, and is bound in a codex together "with the *Īśvarapratyabhijñāvimarśinī*, the *Parātrīśikā* and the *Paramādvayadvādaśikā*." One may confirm this to be the source "(a)" for $K^{ed.}$ by the fact that the present witness records in its marginalia *every* footnote printed in the KSTS edition (at least for *āhnika* 4), as well as a handful of additional marginal notes not printed by Kaul (but recorded in the footnotes to the present translation). Given that Kaul has suggested that the present item is the only witness to the commentary to which he had access in preparing his edition, D is an essential resource for identifying and evaluating the silent emendations that sometimes appear in $K^{ed.}$. Its readings are largely correct and have proven to be instrumental to the endeavor to establish the critical text.

D^a

This manuscript is housed in the National Archives, Delhi. It is bundled together with D and immediately follows it in the codex of which it is a part: immediately following D are preserved 12 folio sides that also are of the ŚD and ŚDVṛ. I label these as witness D^a. The dimensions of this manuscript are the same as those of D. These folia are, like D, numbered at the bottom left of the verso folio sides; the enumeration as we have it begins with folio 171r. and runs through to folio 176, with 176v. being the last folio side present in the codex (though it is not numbered, perhaps because the folio side is almost entirely blank, recording as it does only the last few *akṣaras* of the ŚDVṛ ad ŚD

4.73cd-75). D^a is also written in *śāradā* script, but in a different hand. It contains some marginal notes. The witness records 16 lines of text per folio side, some 18–20 letters per line. Beginning at the middle of ŚDVṛ ad ŚD 4.51cd-52 (at *mṛtpiṇḍād dhi ghaṭasya*, line 304 of the present edition), it ends at the end of the extant commentary on the ŚD, at ŚDVṛ ad ŚD 4.73cd-75 (line 464 of the present edition) with *jagataś ca pratibhāsamānaśabda*, followed by three dots level with the top, horizontal line of the *śāradā* script (precisely where G, J, and S^2 break off, as well). Note, then, that this witness—what is clearly only the last part of another manuscript witness than D that was appended to the same—overlaps in its readings with D from ŚD and ŚDVṛ ad 4.51cd-52 up to ŚD and ŚDVṛ ad 4.64cd-66. Its readings are largely correct and are incredibly valuable for establishing the text. Kaul clearly made use of this witness, but he does not note the fact that his source "(a)" is in fact comprised of two manuscript witnesses, D and D^a.

G

This is the Göttingen manuscript. Niedersächsische Staats- und Universitätsbibliothek, number: Cod.Ms.Sanscr.Vish 5 (11). Details regarding this witness are available in the first volume of *The Ubiquitous Śiva*.

J

This is the Jammu manuscript, owned by the Raghunāth Mandir Library, Jammu. Details regarding this witness are available in the first volume of *The Ubiquitous Śiva*.

S^2

This is a manuscript housed in the Oriental Research Library of Srinagar, MS. No. 1560.7-8. It is a manuscript recorded in *śāradā* script. The text includes the *mūla* and the commentary of the ŚDVṛ from the beginning of the first chapter up to the commentary on ŚD 4.75 (what is recorded as ŚD 4.74 in the KSTS edition, where two consecutive verses are recorded as ŚD 4.70), where the text of the commentary breaks off at precisely the place where it runs out in the KSTS edition. The verses of the *mūla* are highlighted in a yellowish hue. The scribe records the text on both sides of the folia, which are written in what appears to be a bound book. The dimensions of the text are unknown to me, as I have not seen the physical object but only have access to a PDF copy thereof. The manuscript regularly records 12 lines of text per folio side, and roughly 14–18 *akṣaras* per line of text. Folia are numbered toward the bottom left corner of every verso side, the numbering beginning with 1, written in *śāradā* script. The last folio side is 108v. The fourth chapter of the ŚD begins on folio 84v. The *maṅgala* that opens the manuscript reads: *oṃ śrīgaṇeśāya namaḥ. śrīr astu.* (Auspicious Symbol). The same auspicious symbol appears just prior to the *avataraṇikā* introducing ŚD 4.1, and *oṃ* is recorded just prior to the beginning of the same verse. The manuscript is written in a clear hand, includes numerous marginal corrections written by the hand of the scribe, and offers largely correct readings of the text and its commentary.

*S*³

This is a manuscript housed in the Oriental Research Library of Srinagar, MS. No. 1139. It is a manuscript recorded in *devanāgarī* script. The text includes the *mūla* and the commentary of the ŚDVṛ from the beginning of the first chapter up to the commentary on ŚD 4.74 (what is recorded as ŚD 4.73 in the KSTS edition, where two consecutive verses are recorded as ŚD 4.70), where the text of the commentary breaks off at precisely the place where it runs out in the KSTS edition. (The verses of the *mūla* are highlighted with reddish smearing.) The manuscript is 30 folia in length, and the scribe records the text on both sides of the folia, which are written on unbound leaves of country paper that are yellow in color and frayed at the edges, sometimes heavily so. I have not seen the physical object, having had access only to a PDF copy thereof. The Oriental Research Library listing records the dimensions of the leaves as being 19.5cm by 33cm. The manuscript regularly records 17 lines of text per folio side, and some 42–48 *akṣaras* per line of text. Folia are numbered toward the top left and bottom right corners of every verso side excepting 1v., which appears to be written entirely on a paper that is pasted onto the folio side in question. The fourth chapter of the ŚD begins on folio 23v. The *maṅgala* that opens the manuscript reads: *oṃ namo gurave. oṃ. Oṃ* also appears just prior to the *avataraṇikā* introducing ŚD 4.1. The manuscript is written in a clear hand, includes several marginal corrections written apparently by the hand of the scribe, and it offers largely correct readings of the text and its commentary, though sometimes it records obviously erroneous readings.

*S*⁴

This is a manuscript housed in the Oriental Research Library of Srinagar, MS. No. 1176. It is recorded in *śāradā* script. The work is written on yellowish paper and records both the *mūla* and Utpladeva's commentary. I have not seen the physical object, having had access only to a PDF copy thereof. The *maṅgala* that opens the manuscript reads: (Auspicious Symbol) *svasti śrīśivasvarūpāya gurave namaḥ. oṃ.* The pages of this manuscript are out of order, and while the Oriental Research Library listing suggests it is comprised of loose folia, the PDF images I have of the text appear to show the folia bound to one another. Many folia are missing. Only some of the fourth chapter of the ŚD, along with the majority of the first three chapters and commentary, are found recorded in this manuscript. There are 34 folia, and the scribe records text on both sides, with folios numbered on the bottom left of the verso sides in *śāradā* numbers. The scribe records 22 lines of text per folio side (or sometimes 23), with approximately 22–24 *akṣaras* per line. There is some fraying at the edges of the pages, but these do not interfere with the readings of the manuscript, as wide margins surround the text on all sides. The text of the commentary breaks off at ŚDVṛ ad ŚD 4.64cd-66, precisely where P and R end. The manuscript records many correct readings. There are five folio sides that record a portion of the fourth chapter of the ŚD and its commentary, from ŚDVṛ ad ŚD 4.49cd-51ab to the middle of the commentary at ŚDVṛ ad ŚD 4.64-66; they include what are lines 292 to line 405 of the present edition. These are those of folio 41r.-43r., which may be found, in order (at least as they appear in my digitally imaged copy of the MS), as follows: folio 41r. is found opposite folio 20v.; what should be numbered folio 41v. but is unnumbered is found opposite a blank verso side of text; folio 42r. is found opposite folio 10v.; finally, folia 42v. and 43r. are found opposite one another, with folio 42v. labeled as such. I have identified the numbers and sides of the remaining folia sides of chapter 4 by counting forward and backward from this, the only folio side from the chapter that the scribe numbers.

S[5]

This is a manuscript housed in the Oriental Research Library of Srinagar, MS. No. 1003. It is a manuscript recorded in *śāradā* script. The text includes the *mūla* and the commentary of the ŚDVṛ from the beginning of the first chapter up to the beginning of the commentary on ŚD 4.66. The text ends mid-sentence (and without the final r of the last recorded compound) at . . . *śabdasparśarūpāder viṣayasya sarvasya pūrvāparasahotpannai* . . . (precisely where D abruptly ends, as well). The manuscript is 68 folia in length, and the scribe records the text on both sides of the pages, which are loose folios of country paper that are yellow in color, and sometimes frayed at the edges. I have not seen the physical object, having had access only to a PDF copy thereof. The Oriental Research Library listing records the dimensions of the leaves as being 16cm by 28.5cm. The manuscript almost invariably records eight lines of text per folio side and approximately 36–42 *akṣaras* per line of text. Folia are numbered toward the bottom left corners of every recto side, with the occasional exception. The fourth chapter of the ŚD begins on folio 53v. The *maṅgala* that opens the manuscript reads: *oṃ namo gurave. Oṃ* also appears just prior to the *avataraṇikā* introducing ŚD 4.1. The manuscript is written in a clear hand, includes rare marginal corrections that were apparently written by the hand of the scribe, and it offers largely correct readings of the text and its commentary.

P

This is the Pune manuscript. Bhandarkar Oriental Research Institute, number: 805 of 1891–1895. Details regarding this witness are available in the first volume of *The Ubiquitous Śiva*.

R

This is the manuscript of the Rajasthan Oriental Research Institute, Jodhpur. Details regarding this witness are available in the first volume of *The Ubiquitous Śiva*.

2B. A MANUSCRIPT EXAMINED BUT NOT COLLATED

In addition to the six new witnesses examined for the present edition, there is one additional manuscript source of (a part of) the section of the ŚD and ŚDVṛ examined in this book, which was not available to me around the time of the production of the first volume of *The Ubiquitous Śiva* and which I have examined but have elected not to collate into the present edition. This is a *devanāgarī* manuscript held at the Raghunath Mandir Library (Shri Raghunatha Temple MSS. Library), Jammu, manuscript number 2332.[127] It is held by the library under the title "*Śivadṛṣṭivivṛti*" and said to be authored by "Śrī Utpaladevaḥ Rājānakaḥ." The manuscript consists of 54 folia, which record 20 lines of text per folio side (both the recto and verso sides are used), with some 17–20 *akṣara*s recorded per line of text. There are no marginal notes recorded in this manuscript. The scribe has numbered the folios at the top-left corner of the verso sides. The text includes the ŚD and the ŚDVṛ up to the end of the ŚDVṛ commentary ad ŚD 4.49cd-51ab, at line 299 of the present edition. This manuscript is very similar in appearance to that of the Pune manuscript (P), and it very often shares variants witnessed by manuscripts P and R, though it sometimes apparently shares readings with G and J.

2C. THE RELATIONSHIP OF THE MANUSCRIPTS

In the first volume of *The Ubiquitous Śiva* (Nemec 2011: 89) I proposed the mutual relationship of the six manuscripts examined for the edition of ŚD, *āhnika*s 1–3 to stand diagrammed in a *stemma codicum*, as below.

An examination of the additional witnesses made available to me in the preparation of the present, sequel volume confirms the overall structure of this *stemma*.[128] For one, consultation of these additional manuscript sources confirms the fact that T and C sometimes witness readings shared only among

---

127 I wish to thank Chetan Pandey for having sent me an electronic copy of this manuscript.

128 While I overstated the case in the first volume, claiming there to have been two full-blown recensions of the ŚD, a Northern and a Southern one (for which see Nemec 2011: 85–86), I maintain

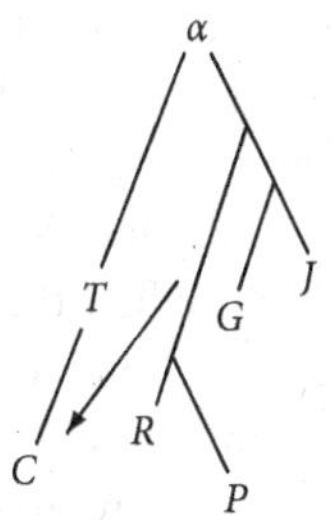

themselves but at variance with all the others manuscript sources.[129] All the six freshly examined manuscripts, that is, may be located in the right-hand side of the stemma.

If one considers the extent to which the respective manuscripts witness the ŚD and ŚDVṛ—if, that is, one takes into account the places where the manuscripts break off—then two groupings of the new witnesses become evident. On the one hand, D^a and S^2 share with G and J the fact that they end at ŚDVṛ ad ŚD 4.73cd-75; so too does S^3, though it ends a few lines earlier in the same passage of ŚDVṛ commentary. S^4, in turn, breaks off in its recording of the ŚDVṛ precisely where P and R do (at ŚDVṛ ad ŚD 4.64cd-66), and D and S^5 do so just a few *akṣaras* prior to these.

On the basis of this understanding of the distribution of manuscripts, one would expect to find places where S^4, S^5, and D agree with P and R against the readings of D^a, S^2, S^3, G, and J. Such a distribution is nowhere found in this precise formulation; there are, nevertheless, indications that this grouping of manuscripts is partially warranted, because so much is mostly reflected in the distribution of certain variant readings, particularly of the ŚDVṛ. Perhaps the closest we witness to a distribution of variant readings that reflects the grouping of manuscripts according to their endpoints is found at line 392 of the present edition, where S^2, S^3, and S^5 share readings with G and J, along with D^a, and over and against those of D, S^4, P, and R.[130]

---

that the *relationship* of the manuscripts as identified in the first volume of the *Ubiquitous Śiva* was soundly discerned.

[129] This is perhaps most evident in the fact that, excepting T and C, all the witnesses examined for the present edition (viz., D, G, J, S^2, S^3, S^5, P, and R) omit ŚD 4.25-31 (with D^a and S^4 not being witness to this part of the fourth *āhnika*, as noted). A similar distribution of manuscript readings may also be found, for example, at ŚD 4.54d, where T and C read *kuṇḍalādike* while all the other manuscript witnesses, along with $K^{ed.}$, read *kuṇḍalādinā*; ŚD 4.55d, where D, D^a, G, J, S^2, S^3, S^4, S^5, P, R, and $K^{ed.}$ read *abhidhīyatām* while T and C read *abhidhīyaṃtāṃ*; ŚD 4.56c, where T and C read *bhāvanā*, all the other witnesses and $K^{ed.}$ *bhāvānāṃ*; and ŚD 4.62c where T and C read *abhinnabhedatā*, all the other witnesses and $K^{ed.}$ *abhinne bhedatā*.

[130] See line 392: *yathā*] $K^{ed.p.c.}$; *tathā ca* $D^aGJS^2S^3S^5$, *tathā* $DS^4PRK^{ed.a.c.}$. See also, e.g., at line 294 of the edition, where D, S^4, P, and R share the same reading—they all are missing the particle *api*—against the readings of G, J, $S^{2p.c.}$, S^3, S^5, and $K^{ed.}$, which read *apy*. ($S^{2a.c.}$ reads *api*; D^a does not witness this passage.)

What is more common, however, is to see the "S" manuscripts accord in the readings they witness. And there are indeed a handful of places where G, J, P, and R accord over and against the readings of S^2, S^3, and S^5 (and, if we had its readings in such instances, we would guess S^4, as well).[131]

We continue to see, as we did in the first three *āhnika*s of the ŚD and ŚDVṛ, groupings of P and R against all the other readings.[132] Indeed, it is perhaps the most frequently appearing distribution of variants in the fourth *āhnika*, wherein P and R share a reading not witnessed in the other manuscripts examined for the present edition (apart from the recording of obviously erroneous readings unique to C).

G and J also commonly record readings not found in any of the other manuscript witnesses.[133]

It is not infrequently the case that D witnesses what is found in the "S" manuscripts, against J and G,[134] and sometimes, more importantly, also P and R.[135] D also occasionally diverges from all the other manuscript readings.[136] We also see at least one instance where D accords with P and R against the readings of the other manuscripts.[137] Finally, all the "S" manuscripts occasionally accord with D and D^a against the readings witnessed by G, J, P, and R.[138]

D^a on a rare occasion shows an affinity with G and/or J where they diverge from the other manuscripts.[139] And D^a sometimes witnesses unique readings.[140]

S^2 also occasionally witnesses readings not found among the other manuscripts examined for the present edition.[141]

---

[131] See, e.g., line 32 of the edition: *śaktisattā*] GJPR; *śaktimattā* DS^{2}S^{3}S^{5}K$^{ed.}$ Cf. line 33, which offers nearly the same, only D and J reversing places: °*śakta*°] JS^{2}S^{3}S^{5}K$^{ed.}$; °*śakti*° DGPR.

[132] This is so at, e.g., ŚDVṛ ad ŚD 4.49cd-51ab (line 296 of the present edition): there all the manuscripts witness *tayoḥ* excepting P and R, which erroneously read *tayo*. So too at line 298 of the edition: *bhāvābhāvaiḥ*] DGJS^{2}S^{3}S^{4}S^{5}K$^{ed.}$; *bhāvābhāvai* PR. Cf. the more substantial variant at ŚD 4.16d: *prabādhyate*] TCDGJS^{2}S^{3}S^{5}K$^{ed.}$; *prabudhyate* PR. Many other examples may be found in the apparatus.

[133] See, e.g., line 304: *kāryakāraṇatopapattiḥ*] DS^{2}S^{3}S^{4}S^{5}PRK$^{ed.}$; *kāryakāraṇatātpattiḥ* G, *kāryakāraṇatāpattiḥ* J. Cf. line 317: *paryālocya*] DD^{a}S^{2}S^{3}S^{4}S^{5}PRK$^{ed.}$; *paṭālocya* GJ. Line 328: °*paryālocanād anupapattir*] DD^{a}S$^{2p.c.}$S^{3}S^{4}S^{5}PRK$^{ed.}$; °*paryālocanānupapattir* GJ, °*paryālocanād anupapattir* S$^{2a.c.}$. Line 346: *noktadoṣaḥ*] DD^{a}S^{2}S^{3}S^{4}S^{5}PRK$^{ed.}$; *nokto doṣaḥ* GJ. Cf. a more substantial variant at line 82: *gaṇanāyām*] GJK$^{ed.}$; *kalanāyām* DS^{2}S^{3}S^{5}P$^{p.c.}$R, *kalamāyām* P$^{p.c.}$.

[134] See, e.g., line 43: *sattaiva*] DS^{2}S^{3}S^{5}PRK$^{ed.}$; *satteva* GJ.

[135] E.g., at line 35: *paṭacitā*] GJPRK$^{ed.}$; *ghaṭacitā* DS^{2}S^{3}S^5; line 140: °*kālo gataḥ*] DS^{2}S^{3}S^{5}K$^{ed.}$; °*kālāgataḥ* GJPR. See also at line 14, e.g., *virodha*] GJPRK$^{ed.}$; *om.* DS^{2}S^{3}S^5.

[136] E.g., at line 113: *saṃbandhābhāve*] GJS^{2}S^{3}S^{5}PR; *sambandhabhādhe* D, *saṃbandhabādhe* K$^{ed.}$. So also at line 362: *ukta*] D^{a}S^{4}PRK$^{ed.}$; *ādi* D, *udita* GJS^{2}S^{3}S^5.

[137] See line 268: *notpadyeta*] GJS^{2}S^{3}S^{5}K$^{ed.}$; *notpadyate* DPR.

[138] See line 391: *eva*] DD^{a}S^{2}S^{3}S^{4}S^{5}K$^{ed.}$; *om.* GJPR.

[139] See, e.g., line 331: *evaṃ*] DS^{2}S^{3}S^{4}S^{5}PRK$^{ed.}$; *om.* D^{a}G, eva J. See also, esp., footnote 153.

[140] See, e.g., line 355 of the present edition: *tasya*] DGJS^{2}S^{3}S^{4}S^{5}PRK$^{ed.}$; *arthasya* D^a. Cf. line 356: *arthotpādoktadoṣo*] DGJS^{2}S^{3}S^{4}S^{5}PRK$^{ed.}$; *pūrvoktadoṣo* D^a.

[141] See 4.73d: *yogitā*] TCD^{a}GJS^{3}K$^{ed.}$; *yogyatā* S^2; line 449: *ekacittattvātmatāṃ*] S^2; *ekacittvātmatāṃ* D^{a}GJS^{3}K$^{ed.}$.

S^3, in turn, appears to be rather close to G and J and sometimes records variants shared only by those two manuscripts,[142] though sometimes it concurs with P and R against G and J.[143] And sometimes it witnesses unique readings,[144] some of them being errors unique to S^3 that are not found in any of the other manuscripts.[145] So too, does S^2 sometimes witness unique errors.[146]

S^4 not infrequently shows itself to accord in its readings with R more than do other manuscripts.[147] More generally, it sometimes accords with the pair P and R, where the readings of these two witnesses diverge from the other manuscripts.[148] And it, too, occasionally introduces readings unique (among these witnesses) to it.[149]

If we are to read D^a, S^2, S^3, G, and J as of a kind, then we may be able to see a grouping thereof of D^a and S^2, on the one hand, and G, J, and S^3, on the other.[150] But sometimes D^a, S^2, and S^3 split from G and J.[151] And we not infrequently see not S^3 but S^2 join the readings of G and J, and this after being corrected to read in accordance with G and J.[152] This suggests that S^2 was read alongside a manuscript that held the readings recorded by G and J. Finally, on at least one occasion we see S^2 and S^3 share a reading against those of D^a, G, and J, at a point in the text (ŚDVṛ ad ŚD 4.64cd-66) where the readings of P, R, D, and S^5 are no longer available to us, nor those of S^4.[153]

---

142 See, e.g., line 322 of the edition, at ŚDVṛ ad ŚD 4.53-54ab: *avastutā*] $DD^aS^2S^{3p.c.}S^4S^5PRK^{ed.}$; *vastutā* $GJS^{3a.c.}$. See also line 385: *pratītiḥ*] $DD^aS^2S^{3p.c.}S^4S^5PRK^{ed.}$; *pratīti* $GJS^{3a.c.}$.

143 See line 147: *nivṛttyā nivṛtteḥ, nābhāvataḥ*] $K^{ed.}$; *nivṛttyā nivṛttenābhāvataḥ* $DGJS^2S^5$, *nivṛttānivṛttenābhāvataḥ* S^3PR.

144 See line 141: *kālabhedena*] $DGJS^2S^5PRK^{ed.}$; *kāle bhedena* S^3. Line 274: *jāyeta*] $DGJS^2S^5PRK^{ed.}$; *jāyate* S^3.

145 See line 267: *kartur*] $DGJS^2S^5PRK^{ed.}$; *kartu* S^3. Cf. line 268: *samūhaḥ*] $DGJS^2S^5PRK^{ed.}$; *samūha* S^3. Line 274: *ghaṭādiḥ*] $DGJS^2S^5PRK^{ed.}$; *ghaṭādi* S^3. Line 288: *satsu*] $DGJS^2S^5PRK^{ed.}$; *tatsu* S^3. And, e.g., line 358: *evābhivyakter*] $DD^aGJS^2S^4S^5PRK^{ed.}$; *evābhivyakte* S^3.

146 See, e.g., line 308 *apṛthaktve*] $DD^aGJS^3S^4S^5PRK^{ed.}$; *apṛktve* S^2. Cf. line 330: *eva*] $DD^aGJS^{2p.c.}S^3S^4S^5PRK^{ed.}$; *ava* $S^{2a.c.}$.

147 For example: ŚD 4.52b: *karaṇaṃ*] $TCDGJS^2S^3S^5PK^{ed.}$; *kāraṇaṃ* S^4R; line 322: *prakāśanaṃ*] $DD^aGJS^2S^3S^5PK^{ed.}$; *prakāśamānaṃ* S^4R. Cf. at line 335 of the present edition: *saṃsthānamātrabheda uktaḥ*] $DD^aGJS^2S^3S^5K^{ed.}$; *saṃsthānabhedamātra uktaḥ* S^4R, *saṃsthānabhedamātramuktam* $P^{p.c.}$, *saṃsthānabhedamātrayuktaḥ* $P^{a.c.}$.

148 At SDVṛ ad ŚD 4.49cd-51ab, for example (line 294 of the edition), one sees a reading of *arthe vyañjako* that is witnessed by D, G, J, S^2, S^3, S^5, and $K^{ed.}$, where S^4, P, and R read *arthavyañjako*. (D^a does not witness the passage in question.) See also, e.g., line 306: *parihāreṇa em.*; *aparihāreṇa* $DD^aGJS^2S^3S^5K^{ed.}$, *apahāreṇa* S^4PR. Cf. ŚD 4.59a: *ito 'pi nāśo* $TCDD^aGJS^2S^3S^5K^{ed.}$; *yato* nāśe (hypometric) S^4, *yato nāśe pi* P, *yato nāśo pi* R. And, e.g., line 365: *tathā* $DD^aGJS^2S^3S^5K^{ed.}$; *om.* S^4PR.

149 See, e.g., line 366: *ghaṭādiḥ śivatayā* $DD^aGJS^2S^3S^5PRK^{ed.}$; *ghaṭādiśivatayā* S^4.

150 See, e.g., line 422: *śāvaleyādīnāṃ*] $D^aS^2K^{ed.}$; *śāvalīyādīnāṃ* GJS^3.

151 See, e.g., line 434: *hematāmrayoḥ*] $D^aS^2S^3K^{ed.}$; *haimatāmrayoḥ* GJ.

152 See line 451: *bhinnatve*] $GJS^{2p.c.}$; *cittattve* $D^aS^{2a.c.}K^{ed.}$, *ciktattve* S^3; line 259: *tat tadā*] $GJS^{2p.c.}$; *tadā* $DS^{2a.c.}S^3S^5PRK^{ed.}$. See also line 266: *kāraṇatā kartṛtā*] $DS^{2a.c.}S^3S^5PRK^{ed.}$; *kāraṇakartṛtā* $GJS^{2p.c.}$.

153 See line 412: *abhedākhyātimayaṃ*] S^2S^3; *abhedābhidhāyimamayaṃ* D^aGJ, *abhedābhidhāyimayaṃ* $K^{ed.}$.

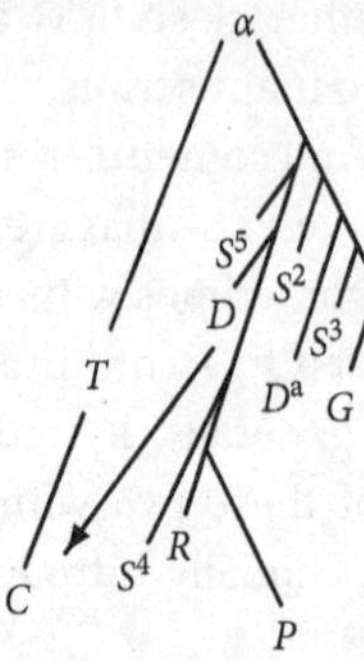

Taking all of this data together, one may again say, as we did in developing the stemma in the first volume of *The Ubiquitous Śiva,* that any of the manuscript readings may possibly be correct, because, apart from the transmission of readings from T to C (though with contamination), it appears that none of the manuscripts examined herein show a direct transmission, without intermediate stages, from one to another. Whatever the limitations of developing a stemma, then, it is nevertheless, on my view, of some utility at least in attempting to render the relationship of the manuscripts in some cogent form. In doing so, I suggest we can imagine three of the six manuscript witnesses that were freshly examined for this sequel volume stemming from the line of transmission drawn from the point where G and J diverge from P and R to the point where G diverges from J. S^3 would branch at a point closest to the divergence of G from J, D^a somewhat up the stemma chain from S^3, and S^2 above D^a. One may imagine the opposite line of transmission—the one drawn to P and R from where the line of transmission leading to them breaks from the one leading to G and J—also to show three manuscripts spurring off of it, first S^5 closest to the break from *α*, followed by D, and with S^4 closest to P. This may be diagrammed in a stemma as illustrated here above.

This diagram, though it offers a fuller representation of the relationship of the various manuscript witnesses than was available in the first volume of *The Ubiquitous Śiva*, given the addition of a half-dozen new witnesses for the present edition, comes with the following caveat. Unlike in the first volume of *The Ubiquitous Śiva*, the relative dating of these new manuscripts is less certain, such that the present diagram should not be taken, for example, to suggest that S^4 is particularly a more recent manuscript in its production than D. Indeed, it appears that all the freshly examined manuscripts (S^2, S^3, S^4, S^5, and D and D^a) are likely to have been produced in a relatively compact period of time, perhaps around the end of the nineteenth century. The present diagram as modified, then, should be taken to symbolize the development of the readings these witnesses preserve, not the dating of the materials on which such readings were recorded and transmitted.

2D. CONVENTIONS OF THE CRITICAL EDITION

Most of the conventions obeyed in the production of the present edition are the same as those that governed the production of the first volume of *The Ubiquitous Śiva*. The (relatively small) differences are noted in what follows.

As with the first volume, the apparatus for the present edition is a fully positive one: it explicitly identifies all the sources that record the text appearing above the line—the text, that is, that I judge to represent the form of the ŚD and ŚDVṛ as their authors intended them; and it also explicitly identifies any and all variant readings and their sources.

There are five registers of notes to the critical edition. The first and third registers record any comments, parallel passages, or the like that are related to the root text (*mūla*) and its commentary, respectively. The second and the fourth record the variant readings from the respective works, with the former recording the variants of the *mūla* by verse number and quarter-verse (*pāda*), respectively labeled a, b, c, and d, and the latter recording the variants found in the commentary by the line number of the present edition. The fifth, bottom register of notes records the folia on which the given passages of text are recorded, noting the turns of folio pages by first identifying the manuscript in question, followed by folio number and an indication of whether the following text appears on the front ("r" for recto) or back ("v" for verso) of the given folio side. Manuscripts that record text on only one side of course do not make this distinction, and I record only the folio number. Note, however, that when there is nothing to record in a given register on a given page, fewer than five registers of notes will appear on the page in question of the present edition. This often occurs, for example, on pages of the edition on which only the readings of a long passage of the commentary are reported. It is also always the case that no more than three, and sometimes only two, registers of footnotes may appear on the pages that, because the commentary is lost after ŚDVṛ ad ŚD 4.73cd-75, record only the *mūla*.

All variant readings are noted following the accepted reading, and I note the sources in which they appear. Variant readings are recorded precisely as they are witnessed in the manuscripts, while the accepted readings are silently corrected in order to standardize spelling for reasons of euphonic combination or *sandhi*, gemination and degemination (e.g., *sarva* ← *sarvva*), the replacement of *anusvāra* with the homorganic nasal (e.g., Sāṅkhya ← Sāṃkhya), and the like. The only exception to this is that I often add in square brackets the *avagrahas* that would have to be understood in the variant manuscript readings, e.g., *[']ntaravasthita*.

The variations in the punctuation of the commentary that are frequently found in the manuscripts are generally not recorded in the present edition (and the punctuation varies greatly from manuscript to manuscript, the conventions for punctuation and the recording of other "accidentals" varying greatly among them). Generally, I have preserved the punctuation of K$^{ed.}$, though I sometimes modify it for semantic reasons. When I do so I acknowledge the same in the notes to the edition and translation and sometimes make reference to the relevant manuscripts, if any, that punctuate in the manner I recommend.

When a manuscript records any correction in the readings it witnesses, I note both the reading *ante correctionem* ($^{a.c.}$) and the reading *post correctionem* ($^{p.c.}$). Any text that is absent from a manuscript is marked as such with *om.*, this of course being an abbreviation for "om(itted text)." Any reading in a manuscript that is missing due to damage to the physical manuscript, such as fraying at the ends of the folio in question, is marked with dashes: – – –. Unlike the edition of the first volume, however, I mark the number of *akṣaras* I see missing in the text, one dash-mark for each missing *akṣara*. Illegible text, in turn, is recorded with the following symbol: <?>, again one symbol for each illegible *akṣara*. When the text possibly can be made out, but the reading remains uncertain, I sometimes note the possible reading within the angled brackets, e.g., <e?> or, where one of two readings could be possible, <e/o?>.

Emendations are noted with *em.*, conjectural emendations with *conj.*, and textual corrections with *corr.* Where another scholar has proposed an emendation, I record his or her name in parentheses following the emendation proposed by her or him.

About the Translation

The present translation includes the entirety of the fourth chapter of the ŚD, along with all of the extant portions thereon of Utpaladeva's commentary.

The translation strategies pursued in this book largely match those deployed in preparing the first volume of *The Ubiquitous Śiva*. The translation offered is meant to be a literal one, but one that presents the material in idiomatic English. Needless to say, it is often difficult to conform to these two sometimes-conflicting standards, particularly given that the text in question is syntactically complex and sometimes elliptically written, as well as semantically rich. Somānanda's style, too, is notably difficult. It frequently offers a telegraphic and therefore laconic documentation of philosophical arguments. He furthermore assumes that the reader is familiar with the matters at hand, and his style is therefore declarative rather than explanatory: the implications of his arguments are rather left to the commentator (and the reader) to digest and elaborate. In short, the ŚD constitutes a highly complex, often telegraphic, regularly difficult, and sometimes awkward theological-cum-philosophical verse.

Utpaladeva's commentary is extremely helpful to our understanding of the ŚD. More than a simple word-by-word gloss of his teacher's *magnum opus*, it is rather more expanded and explanatory, and his comments are essential to our understanding of the ŚD, the root text (*mūla*) on which it comments. This is not to say that one must always translate according to the commentator's interpretation of the text: Utpaladeva can in some instances, at least, be seen to reinterpret Somānanda's text, as we also noted in the first volume of *The Ubiquitous Śiva*. The reader should also note, however, that sometimes an ambiguity resulting from Somānanda's laconic and telegraphic style is only fully clarified in the commentary, this giving the reader something of the experience of reading the original text and commentary, albeit in translation.

Though, as mentioned, Utpaladeva's commentary is much more than a word-by-word gloss of Somānanda's verses, one should not take this to suggest that he never glosses particular terms. He very often does, though he does so in a manner that is sometimes awkward to render in English translation: in many instances, Utpaladeva glosses a given term in the context of long and syntactically complicated sentences. And although I do not highlight the lemmas in the translation of the commentary, I attempt to make them easily identifiable by singling out the glosses provided for them. I do this regularly by introducing the glosses with "i.e.," sometimes with "that is," and sometimes by placing the gloss in em-dashes (— —) following the word Utpaladeva wishes to explain, all of this in an attempt to preserve something of the syntax of the commentary. It is not always possible, of course, perfectly to accomplish this goal, and I sometimes translate long sentences with a couple, or a number, of shorter ones. When I do so, I do so silently, without indicating that the syntax has been modified for reasons associated with the production of a fluid, readable translation.

In order to render the text in a comprehensible English, I often translate Sanskrit sentences written in the passive voice with English sentences in the active voice. Likewise, I freely translate Sanskrit participles with finite verbal constructions in English, just as I translate abstract constructions into idiomatic English. I regularly render nominal sentences in Sanskrit with verbal ones in English. I also translate the Sanskrit connective word "and" (*ca*) into idiomatic English, sometimes replacing it with "moreover," "in addition," or the like. I take equal liberty with the other Sanskrit connectives, *tu* ("but," "and," "however") and *vā* ("or," "and," "on the other hand"). Finally, I generally do not replicate in translation the gender of the various Sanskrit proper names and/or key terms.

Although both Somānanda and Utpaladeva use a great deal of technical language, I have endeavored to limit, as far as I thought possible, the use of untranslated Sanskrit words in the translation (though I do quote the Sanskrit when the terms in question are relatively well-known, technical ones of particular note, or when they are deployed in a manner less commonly attested in the corpus). I don't feel it is necessary, however, to develop new translations of relatively well-known Sanskrit terms just for the sake of avoiding the use of Sanskrit in the translation. Indeed, such a practice could easily create confusion when a well-known term is rendered with a new and therefore unfamiliar English-language term.

There is another reason for quoting Sanskrit terms in the translation: I sometimes do so in places where Utpaladeva analyzes a given word, or simply defines the term in question with a pure synonym. (This is one reason that I quote the Sanskrit verses of the ŚD prior to their translations: the presence of the verses beside the translations allows even those who do not read Sanskrit to understand from where Utpaladeva has taken a given term he subsequently glosses.) Virtually all of the Sanskrit terms that appear in the translation have been explained in the introduction, in the various notes to the translation, or in Utpaladeva's very explanations of the terms in question. I should add that I have also generally endeavored, though not without exception, to translate a single Sanskrit term with a single English equivalent, not because I believe that doing so is a practice indispensable to any sound theory of translation—I do not—but because I think it will simplify matters for the reader. (This translation practice is of course more difficult to sustain when rendering longer portions of a given work, as one inevitably encounters a greater variety of contexts and therefore a greater semantic range for certain lexical items, which must be presented to the reader with the appropriate emphasis and nuance in English.)

Whatever text I supply to—that is, read into—the translation is included in parentheses: (). I also place in square brackets— [] —any language that is used to explain that which immediately precedes what is thus bracketed. As these materials are added to, or offered in explanation of, what is found in the Sanskrit text, the translation has been composed in a manner that allows it to be read legibly even when excluding anything found in parentheses or brackets. This is so with only two types of exceptions: first, I also sometimes identify in square brackets the referent of a pronoun or the agent of an action who is signified obliquely by the conjugation of a given verb, in which case what is recorded in square brackets must be read into the sentence in question. (Note that I employ this same convention even when the action in question is conveyed through one of the many nominal constructions of Sanskrit.) The most common example of this is found repeatedly in passages of Utpaladeva's commentary that cite or refer to portions of the ŚD: "[Somānanda] says."

Second, particular problems are encountered with the passages of the ŚD for which there is no commentary available to us. In these places, the notes offered sometimes entertain the possibility of alternative interpretations, and they also frequently indicate what is absent by way of ellipsis and must be supplied by *anuvṛtti*, the standard rules of anaphora, in a given line of text. The telegraphic nature of Somānanda's style, then, sometimes leads me to incorporate into the translation a greater amount of text recorded in brackets or parentheses, which I have generally otherwise endeavored to keep to a minimum in order to preserve, as much as possible, a sort of "lightness" to the English rendering. (It must be admitted that I have not succeeded in this endeavor to the same degree as in the first volume of *The Ubiquitous Śiva*.)

As with the first volume, I frequently make reference to the ĪPK and ĪPKVṛ of Utpaladeva in the translation and notes thereto, and in doing so I regularly refer to the numbering of the verses found in Torella's edition of these texts. References to passages of the *Śivadṛṣṭi* and Utpaladeva's commentary thereon correspond with the numbering of verses found in my edition. I likewise very often refer to passages of the commentary by referring the reader to passages identified by the line numbers of my edition at which the given text is recorded.

The many notes accompanying the translation are meant to serve two (distinct) audiences. Some are purely technical notes, which explain philological problems, reveal textual problems or variants, explain my interpretations of the many compound words in the Sanskrit text, and address other, similar types of concerns. Others are rather meant for the general reader—or at least they are meant to speak only to semantic or philosophical concerns, to explain what I take Somānanda or Utpaladeva to *mean to say* in a given passage. They explain, that is, the flow of logic found in the text, or they elaborate on a given term, concept, or concern found in the text and its commentary. When an important term is translated, I often record in the notes the Sanskrit term that was translated (as mentioned, already). Wherever possible, I indicate the presence of parallel passages and identify any passages of text that are quoted elsewhere in the primary literature. Finally, I sometimes refer in my translation and notes to the various types of Sanskrit compounds—coordinative (*dvandva*), determinative (*tatpuruṣa*), descriptive (*karmadhāraya*), exocentric/possessive (*bahuvrīhi*), and so forth—this in no small part because Utpaladeva, like all good Sanskrit commentators, not infrequently discusses these grammatical forms in his commentary. Those who, being unfamiliar with such Sanskrit grammatical constructions, wish to know more about them are advised to consult the detailed and relatively speaking accessible, if compact and therefore somewhat laconic, explanations thereof that may be found in the readily available volume by Michael Coulson, *Teach Yourself Sanskrit*.[154]

Finally, it is my hope, as it was with the first volume of *The Ubiquitous Śiva*, that each reader will be able to choose how to use these various materials when reading the translation, and in particular I hope the non-specialist will be able comfortably to read my English rendering, with the aid of the relevant notes, without being confronted too often or too intrusively with the sort of minutiae, technical concerns, and jargon that would scare off all but the most stubbornly persistent reader.

---

[154] Michael Coulson, [1976] 1992, *Teach Yourself Sanskrit*, 2nd Edition, Chicago: NTC Publishing.

{ PART II }

The Translation

Chapter Four of the *Śivadṛṣṭi* and *Śivadṛṣṭivṛtti*

4.1-2ab

Having expelled the doubts regarding the (supposed) faults (in our non-dualism) that could be communicated by others,[1] [Somānanda] now says the following to state that in reality the true nature of everything[2] is that of Śiva (himself):

[1] The present expression (*parodbhāvanīyadūṣaṇaśaṅkānirākaraṇe kṛte*, line 1 of the present edition) refers to a series of possible faults that others suggest might mar the Śaiva position. These were addressed in the third chapter of the ŚD, and are found listed at ŚD 3.21-32. Somānanda opens his reply to these objections at ŚD 3.33ab and devotes most of the balance of the chapter to his responses. ŚD 3.33ab reads as follows: *ityākṣeparakṣanārtham atra pratividhīyate.* Utpaladeva, explaining both the compound and the meaning of *atra* in a couple of ways, glosses as follows (for which see Nemec 2011: 367, lines 216–218 of the edition): *īdṛśāt parakṛtān mahākṣepāt svadarśanasya rakṣaṇārtham asya vākṣepasya rakṣaṇārthaṃ nivāraṇārtham atrākṣepe sati svadarśane 'tra vā samarthanaṃ kriyate.* Note also that Utpaladeva concludes his commentary on chapter 3 of the ŚD by stating at ŚDVṛ ad ŚD 3.97cd-99 (for which see Nemec 2011: 396, lines 583–584) that all the faults (*dūṣaṇa*) in question are avoided when one understands everything to be of the nature of Śiva: *ataḥ sarvam eva bhāvajātaṃ śivātmakaṃ sthitaṃ tathābhāve sarvadūṣaṇaparihārād iti.* "Hence, absolutely everything, i.e., the (entire) mass of entities (that makes up the universe), is established as having Śiva as its nature, because every fault is avoided when this is the case. This is definitive."

[2] I here (line 1 of the present edition) accept a variant reading of D of *sarvaśivatattvam* (though there is degemination of *tt* of *-tattvam* in the manuscript's reading), where all the other manuscripts consulted, as well as K$^{ed.}$, read *sarvaśivatvam*. It is the *lectio difficilior*, and loss of *ta* can be explained by haplography. Note that it appears just such a transcription error is present in K$^{ed.}$, which, Kaul reports, had D as its sole witness of the commentary—this or Kaul silently emended the text (or accessed another manuscript thereof). Indeed, not only does D witness the reading of *sarvaśivatattvam* over and against *sarvaśivatvam*, but Kaul also records a note on this term (p. 143, fn. 2 of the KSTS edition) that replicates a marginal note of D, but with a similar error in transcription (or another silent emendation). The footnote in K$^{ed.}$ reads *sarvaṃ ca tacchivatvam*, but the marginal note in D (folio 142r.) reads *sarvaṃ ca tacchivatatvam* (with degemination of *tt* of *-tattvam*).

The Ubiquitous Śiva Volume II. John Nemec, Oxford University Press. © Oxford University Press 2021.
DOI: 10.1093/oso/9780197566725.003.0002

4.1 athedānīṃ pravaktavyaṃ yathā sarvaṃ śivātmakam
nāśakto vidyate kaścic chaktaṃ vastv eva te 'pi no
4.2 iṣyante bahavaḥ śaktāḥ sarvasvātantryam āpatet

Next, the manner in which everything is of the nature of Śiva is now to be explained (by me). Nothing exists that is incapable (of causal efficacy);[3] (and) that which is capable (of causal efficacy) definitely is a real thing, although we certainly do not[4] accept that the many [entities in the world] are themselves (individually) capable: that would lead to everything being independent.

Immediately after repudiating the (supposed) faults (identified by others regarding our non-dualism), this is now to be declared *affirmatively* by me, (namely,) the manner in which everything is proven to be of the nature of Śiva.[5] That is what [Somānanda] said (at ŚD 4.1ab).

That which is incapable of causal efficiency and (simultaneously) exists—there is no such thing, because so much [i.e., the nonexistence of such an entity] truly conforms with the instrument (of knowing)—(whether it is) perception or intellectual reflection.[6] If capable, then it definitely is a real thing,

---

[3] Here, Somānanda wishes to contrast his position with that of Dharmakīrti and the Buddhist Epistemologists. According to Dharmakīrti, there are two means of knowledge (*pramāṇa*) inasmuch as there are two types of objects (*prameya*), the latter being either capable or incapable as regards *arthakriyā*. See PV (*pratyakṣapariccheda*) 3.1: *pramāṇaṃ dvividhaṃ meyadvaividhyāc chaktyaśaktitaḥ | arthakriyāyāṃ keśādir nārtho 'narthādhimokṣataḥ ||*. "The means of knowledge is two-fold because the object of knowledge is two-fold, this [i.e., the latter double-nature] inasmuch as it [i.e., the object] is capable or incapable of causal efficiency [*arthakriyā*]. The hair (one erroneously sees floating on one's eye), for example, is not a real object, because there is no determinate apprehension of it as such." The present translation is a slight modification of that of Franco and Notake 2014: 29 (and about the meaning of *adhimokṣa* see ibid.: 32, fn. 8).

[4] *No* (ŚD 4.1d) should be understood to include the negative particle (*na*) in combination, by *sandhi*, with the emphatic particle *u*.

[5] In saying the present offers an argument in the affirmative (*vidhimukhenaiva*, line 6 of the present edition), Utpaladeva contrasts the contents of the present chapter with the counterarguments Somānanda offered in chapter 3 against opponents' possible objections (about which see footnote 1).

[6] In other words, it is invariably the case that anything that is found in existence is efficacious in some manner or another, whether it is known through perception (*prakhyā*) or intellectual reflection (*upākhyā*). The reasons for this are explained in what follows.

Utpaladeva here in part echoes PV (*pratyakṣapariccheda*) 3.1 (quoted in footnote 3) in paraphrasing Somānanda's criticism of it at ŚD 4.1cd, and the two terms here deployed, *prakhyā* and *upākhyā*, apparently used here to displace the terminology ubiquitously found in the writings of the Buddhist Epistemologists (*pratyakṣa* and *anumāna*), are also paired elsewhere in Utpaladeva's œuvre. See, e.g., the *Ajaḍapramātṛsiddhi*, verses 2 and 3. Lawrence (2009: 642) there translates the terms respectively with "basic knowledge" and "expressed knowledge" and notes (ibid., fn. 75) that Abhinavagupta also pairs the terms in his ĪPV commentary at verses 1.1 and 1.21, and in the first of his two benedictory verses to the *Dhvanyālokalocana* (about which see Ingalls, Masson, and Patwardhan 1990: 43, who translate, respectively, with "genius" and "speech," renderings that seem to have been influenced by the *Bālapriyā* subcommentary of Rāmaṣāraka, where the terms are respectively glossed with *kaveḥ pratibhā* and *vacanam*). The terms are also paired, e.g., at ĪPVV ad ĪPK 2.3.8 and in Yogarāja's commentary on the *Paramārthasāra* of Abhinavagupta at verse 44.

it definitely exists in the ultimate sense; (thus,) it has Śiva's nature. This is definitive.[7]

To explain: Agency is the capacity to produce action, what is the state of being composed of consciousness; it also is the (very) nature of Śiva, because it is impossible that agency belongs to a form of consciousness that is devoid of will.[8] (Thus:) If [a real thing,] a pot or a cloth, e.g., is capable of producing (an action), then it is independent, has consciousness as its nature; (and thus,) it must be of the nature of Śiva.[9] This is definitive.

But, we do not accept that the many [things], i.e., the pots, etc., are individually capable: everything, it would thus follow, would be possessed of independence.[10] And consequently, given the fact that the implication (in understanding everything to be individually independent) is (that each independence would be) distinct, one [independence] would suffer the unwanted consequence that its nature, (being both) new and old, would be (self-)contradictory, since it

---

[7] What Utpaladeva says here (at lines 8–9 of the present edition, viz., *śaktaṃ cet, tad vastv eva paramārthasad eva śivarūpam iti*) serves to echo but modify Dharmakīrti's NB 1.14 (*tad eva paramārthasat*) and 1.15 (*arthakriyāsāmarthyalakṣaṇatvād vastunah*): "That [*svalakṣaṇa*] alone is what exists in the ultimate sense. This is so because that which is real is defined by its capacity for causal efficacy." Cf. PV (*pratyakṣapariccheda*) 3.3ab (which is identical to PVin 2.55ab): *arthakriyāsamarthaṃ yat tad atra paramārthasat* |. It seems not unlikely that Somānanda would have had these passages in mind, as well, at ŚD 4.1d.

[8] Compare the present with ĪPKVṛ ad ĪPK 2.4.21: *cidvapuṣaḥ svatantrasya viśvātmanā sthātum icchaiva jagat prati kāraṇatā kartṛtārūpā saiva kriyāśaktiḥ. evaṃ cidrūpasyaikasya kartur eva cikīrṣākhyā kriyā mukhyā, nākartṛkaṃ karmāsti karmādīnāṃ kartṛmukhenopacārataḥ.* "The very will of him who has consciousness as his nature and is free to appear as the universe constitutes the fact that he is the cause of the universe; that alone, which has agency as its form, is the capacity for action. Thus, the primary [*mukhyā*] action is referred to as the desire to act; it belongs uniquely to the unitary agent, whose nature is consciousness. There is no object of action without an agent; action, in fact, is attributed to the object, etc., only in a figurative sense, through the agent." The translation is a slight modification of Torella's, for which see Torella 1994: 187–188. Emphasis on the "desire to act" (*cikīrṣākhyā kriyā mukhyā*) constitutes an oblique reference to the power of "eagerness" (*aunmukhya*), the first part of the power of will (*icchāśakti*), described by Somānanda in ŚD 1. See, esp., ŚD 1.7cd-8. Cf. ŚD 1.13cd-17.

[9] Here, Utpaladeva applies the general logic regarding agency, expressed in the previous sentence, to a particular *vastu* such as a pot or a cloth. Of course, reference to the *vastu* as *svatantra* also signals its agency on the well-known principle that the agent is the one who is independent (A 1.4.54: *svatantraḥ kartā*). On the agency of all phenomena, see, e.g., Nemec 2011: 25–31; Torella 1994: xv–xvi.

It is possible, at least, to read the present passage (line 11 of the present edition: *ghaṭapaṭādikaṃ karaṇaśaktaṃ cet, tat svatantraṃ cidrūpaṃ śivarūpam eveti*) as recording the objection of an opponent. On this interpretation, one could translate as follows: "Objection: The pot or the cloth, e.g., is capable of producing (an action); (thus, they are themselves volitional agents). Reply: (Yes;) it [i.e., the pot or the cloth, e.g.,] is independent, has consciousness as its form, and is the very form of Śiva."

[10] Utpaladeva's commentary clearly indicates that *sarvasvātantrya* (ŚD 4.2b) should be understood to be a genitive *tatpuruṣa* compound. Note also that the present passage—*bahavaś ca ghaṭādayaḥ pratyekaṃ śaktā neṣyante, sarveṣāṃ tathā svātantryaṃ prasajyate*—anticipates what is said at ŚDVṛ ad ŚD 4.2cd-3, especially at lines 20–22 of the present edition: *tad evaṃ yadi sarvaśaktitvam iṣyate, tato nānyeṣāṃ ghaṭādīnāṃ pratyekaṃ śaktatā svatantratā.*

would have to be new, but also old.[11] And it [i.e., the *svātantrya* or independence] is not perceived in this way.

4.2cd-3

athaikasyādhikā śaktir nyūnaśaktinibandhinī
4.3. svakāryaviṣaye sarvaḥ śakta eva nibandhanam
śaktasya śakyate kartum evaṃ cen nānyaśaktatā

Rather, a superior power of one [capable agent][12] restrains a subordinate power (of the same). Everything(, however,) is fully capable within the

---

[11] The argument is not entirely clear to me, but it seems to suggest that entities such as a pot or the like would be independent in two ways if one understood their independence to be self-contained, belonging to the given object alone, of itself. The reasoning is this: newly fashioned entities are clearly suborned in some important sense to the agent who crafts (and then wields) them, and thus their independence—their capacity to perform actions—is said to be fashioned by the one who creates them; yet, the independence must also be understood as belonging exclusively and individually to the new item, inasmuch as it is said to be a distinct entity that is individually independent. Thus, the former independence is counted as "old," endowed by the one who created the object, the latter "new," possessed of the object that did not exist prior to its production. Both must be accepted, but the two are mutually contradictory in nature, one being new, the other old. This anyhow is how the matter is explained in a marginal note on the left-hand side of manuscript D (folio 143v.), which is also recorded in K[ed.] (at Kaul 1934: 145, fn. 5, where the footnote is tied to the verb, *prasajyate*, of the previous sentence, but explains the reference to the independence being "new" and "old"): *yadi ca pratyekaṃ ghaṭādau svātantryaṃ svayam iṣyate ekapramātranadhīnatvād bhinnabhinna evābhisaṃdhiḥ sarvatra prasajyate, tathā ca ghaṭotpattau navaṃ svakīyam eva svātantryaṃ kiṃ kiṃ vā nirmātṛkṛtaṃ purāṇam ity ekasyaikatra niścayābhāvād ubhayam āpatati. tac cāniṣṭam. tata etat siddhaṃ tasyaiva śaktimataḥ śaktisvarūpaṃ sarvaṃ padārthajātaṃ śaktam eva na tu tasya svakīyaṃ leśamātreṇāpīty advayam eva phalitam.* "And if one maintains that independence innately is (found) individually in (every entity,) a pot, e.g., (then,) because they [i.e., the individual independences] do not depend on a single [i.e., unitary] agent of knowing, the implied sense that obtains as an unwanted consequence, in every case, is (that the entities in which the independence exists are) fully [*eva*] mutually distinct. Accordingly, when a pot (for example) is produced, one may ask whether it has a new independence that is entirely its own, or whether it has an old one that was fashioned by the one who produced it [i.e., the pot, e.g.]. Thus, since there is an absence of any determinate judgment regarding one [independence] in the same place [i.e., in the pot, e.g.], it follows that both (the 'new' and the 'old' forms of independence) stand. [In other words, the independence could rightly be considered both new and old.] And this is not what is desired. Consequently, this has been proven, that the entire mass of things is fully capable, it having as its nature [i.e., it is fully capable *because* it has as its nature] the (very) power of the (single agent of knowing, Śiva, the) possessor of power himself; and it is not the case that it [i.e., the mass of entities] has even a scrap of its own [distinct or separate independence]. Therefore, non-duality alone bears (philosophical) fruit." Cf. Kaul's note 4, p. 146, which records a marginal note found in the bottom margin of manuscript D (at folio 143v). Note also that Chaturvedi (1986: 124) understands the passage in a similar manner.

Finally, two items of marginalia are found in D that are not recorded in K[ed.]. First, *pratyekaṃ* is recorded above *bhinna* of *bhinnābhisandhitayā* (found at line 13 of the present edition) in D folio 143v., and *svakīyaṃ* is recorded in the right margin apparently to gloss *navam* of *navam idam astu* (line 13 of the present edition), also in D folio 143v.

[12] *Eka* contrasts with *bahu* (ŚD 4.2a). The referent of *eka* is somewhat unclear, but it probably should be understood to refer to one capable or empowered agent or entity, though it is conceivable, at least, that it could refer to one "independence" or *svātantrya*.

domain of its own work; (for) the (only) restraining that can be effected belongs to the one [agent] who is capable. If this is the case, the others are not (individually) capable.[13]

Rather, a power of one [capable agent][14] is superior, since it[15] restrains, i.e., holds back, the other power; and consequently the latter is a subordinate [power] of that [capable agent].[16]

Everything, however, is fully capable in its own work, which is the domain (of its action); for the restraining, i.e., the (act of) holding back, belongs exclusively to the one who is capable; but grains of sand do not contain the capacity to dispense sesame oil.[17]

Thus, if this is the case, i.e., if one maintains that everything is (the) power (of the one capable agent), then it follows that the others—pots, etc.—are not individually capable, i.e., are not independent.[18]

Note, therefore, the parallel use of *eka* at ŚD 4.5, where Śiva is described as the one and only capable or empowered entity: *tasmād anekabhāvābhiḥ śaktibhis tadabhedataḥ | eka eva sthitaḥ śaktaḥ śiva eva tathā tathā ||*.

[13]Thus, the model is not of competing entities, each fully capable and fully independent, but of a single independent and empowered entity—Śiva—who subordinates and elevates one or another of his powers, so as to effect various actions.

[14]See footnote 12.

[15]The demonstrative pronoun *asau* (line 18) may be masculine in gender, referring to "the one" (*eka*), or feminine, referring to the power (*śakti*). The latter interpretation is correct, for the present glosses *nyūnaśaktinibandhinī*.

[16]The demonstrative pronoun *tat* (line 19) must refer to *eka*, preceding.

[17]The present exemplar—that of drawing sesame oil from sand—is also deployed in the *Māṭharavṛtti* ad *Sāṃkhyakārikā*, p. 12, cited in Ratié 2014a: 142, fn. 61. The same is also found in the *Mahābhāṣya* (MaBhā) of Patañjali, at *Śivasūtra* 5.4 (edition of Kielhorn 1880, vol. 1: p. 31, lines 1–4), where an extended discussion of the meaningfulness of *varṇas* is engaged. The relevant excerpts of the MaBhā read as follows: . . . *ekaḥ ca tilaḥ tailadāne samarthaḥ tatsamudāyaḥ ca khārī api samarthā* . . . and . . . *ekā ca sikatā tailadāne asamarthā tatsamudāyaḥ ca khārīśatam api asamartham*. Here, Patañjali is addressing the question of whether *varṇas* are meaningful or not (for which see the edition of Kielhorn 1880, vol. 1: p. 30, line 1: *kim punaḥ ime varṇāḥ arthavanta āhosvit anarthakāḥ*). The present example serves to help to answer the question (in the affirmative—they are meaningful) by pointing out that if one of a group is capable of some action, then a collection of the same should be, as well. Similarly, if one item of a group is incapable, so too is every member of that group: no grain of sand yields sesame oil.

Thus, Utpaladeva may be understood in this passage to suggest that each entity is capable in its own domain of action, but cannot exceed it. Or, particularly if read in light of the example furnished in the following verses (at ŚD 4.4-5), perhaps the point is that the empowered agent is the only one capable of restraining the others, because the others are not of the same class as it. Or, finally, perhaps the point is that the superior and restraining power cannot render the other powers entirely incapable, all of them being of the same class of entity (i.e., all are "empowered"), even if one is superior in strength to the others.

[18]Utpaladeva here indicates (. . . *nānyeṣāṃ ghaṭādīnāṃ* . . . *śaktatā svatantratā*) that *anyaśaktatā* (ŚD 4.3d) is a genitive *tatpuruṣa* compound. Note also that the present passage (lines 20–22 of the present edition)—*tad evaṃ yadi sarvaśaktitvam iṣyate, tato nānyeṣāṃ ghaṭādīnāṃ pratyekaṃ śaktatā svatantratā*—echoes what was said at ŚDVṛ ad ŚD 4.1-2ab (lines 12–13): *bahavaś ca ghaṭādayaḥ pratyekaṃ śaktā neṣyante, sarveṣāṃ tathā svātantryaṃ prasajyate.*

4.4-5

For example:

4.4. nṛpādisādhanāpekṣā svakarmaphalatā bhavet
sarvaḥ śakto 'pi sāpekṣa īśavan mohasāmyayoḥ
4.5. tasmād anekabhāvābhiḥ śaktibhis tadabhedataḥ
eka eva sthitaḥ śaktaḥ śiva eva tathā tathā

The state of being of one who owns the rewards of one's own actions must depend on the means of the king, etc.(, whom one has served).[19] Everything, although capable (of producing its own effect), is dependent, like the Lord on delusion and (karmic) equanimity. Therefore, Śiva alone is empowered, he being absolutely unique, one who remains occupied in various ways with the powers, whose natures are multiple, this because he is not different from them.

The state of being of one who owns the rewards of one's own actions entirely depends on the means, i.e., the conduct, of the king, e.g., whom one has served. *Svakarmaphalatā* (ŚD 4.4b) refers to the condition of the one for whom the results of action are his own, *svakarmaphala* being an appositional possessive compound [i.e., a *samānādhikaraṇabahuvrīhi*], "one's own" [*sva*] meaning that the fruits of his actions are to be enjoyed by him.[20] For although innately capable, everything is employed (in activity) only while being dependent (on Śiva), as also (is the case) in the philosophy of the dualists: Īśvara (there) depends on delusion, i.e., the *māyātattva*, in order to engage in creation; and he depends on karmic equanimity (in order to engage) in grace, but he is neither incapable nor is he not sovereign.[21]

---

[19] My translation here follows the ŚDVṛ, which notes that *svakarmaphala* is a *bahuvrīhi* compound. A similar analogy is recorded, e.g., at VP 3.7.22-23: *yathā rājñā niyukteṣu yoddhṛtvaṃ yoddhṛṣu sthitam | teṣu vṛttau tu labhate rājā jayaparājayau || tathā kartrā niyukteṣu sarveṣv ekārthakāriṣu | kartṛtvaṃ karaṇatvāder uttaraṃ na virudhyate ||*.

So, too, e.g., in the *Yogasūtrabhāṣya* ad YS 2.18, where the following is said: *yathā vijayaḥ parājayo vā yoddhṛṣu vartamānaḥ svāmini vyapadiśyate, sa hi tatphalasya bhokteti, evaṃ bandhamokṣau buddhāv eva vartamānau puruṣe vyapadiśyete, sa hi tatphalasya bhokteti.* (I am grateful to Vincenzo Vergiani for bringing this latter passage to my attention.)

[20] *Karma-phala*, presumably, should be understood to mean *karmaṇāṃ phalāni*.

[21] Reference here is to a doctrine of the Śaiva Siddhānta that specifies that the descent of divine grace or *śaktipāta* can occur when the initiand is beset with a *karmasāmya*, an impasse resulting from "the balance of two equally powerful, simultaneously maturing actions. . . that blocks the soul's capacity to experience" (Goodall 1998: xxxiii). And, at *Kiraṇa Tantra* (KT) 5.6cd-8ab, *moha* is mentioned explicitly (at 5.7a), and it is explained by Bhaṭṭa Rāmakaṇṭha in his *Vṛtti* on the KT (the KVṛ) as the impurity (*mala*) that causes delusion. When it becomes incapable of performing its function of deluding bound souls, a moment is occasioned when Śiva awakens such individuals, this, we are told, in a manner similar to that of a *guru* who awakens with a stick only the sleeping students who are in fact able successfully to be taught.

Therefore, Śiva (alone), who is absolutely unique, is occupied in various ways[22] with the powers, whose natures [*svabhāva*] are multiple—are those of the pot and the cloth(, e.g.,)—because he is not different from them—those powers—,[23] which is to say (he is not different from them) because the (very) existence of the powers defines what it means to be Śiva;[24] (and he is occupied with them in various ways) because he consists in the many things, the capable pot, cloth, etc.[25]

There could be no synthesis [*anusaṃdhāna*] of the awareness of a pot with that of a cloth if the former, whose form is (only) of the same measure (as that of the pot), were independent.[26] Therefore, the true nature [*tattva*] of consciousness is absolutely unitary, the form of which is the endless universe. This is certain.

On the alternative explanations in the Śaiva Siddhānta of *śaktipāta*, and Bhaṭṭa Rāmakaṇṭha's exegetical adaptation of the KT to his own position, see Goodall 1998: xxxii–xxxvi and, esp., KT 1.20cd-22ab and the KVṛ on the same. Cf. Goodall 1998: 215–221, esp. 215–216, fn. 171; and KT 5.1 *ff.*, translated in Goodall 1998: 325 *ff.*

22 Utpaladeva here glosses *tathā tathā* (ŚD 4.5d) with *tena tena prakāreṇa*.

23 *Śakti* in *tacchaktyabhedataḥ* (line 32) glosses *tat* in *tadabhedataḥ* (ŚD 4.5b).

24 I understand *śaktisattālakṣaṇatvāc chivatvasya* (lines 32–33) to gloss *tadabhedataḥ* (ŚD 4.5b); but it is at least possible that the expression should be read with what follows rather than what precedes it. On this latter interpretation of the syntax, the passage could be rendered with ". . . Śiva, who is absolutely unique inasmuch as the existence of the powers defines what it means to be Śiva. . . ."

While K[ed.] reads *śaktimattā*, as do D, S[2], S[3], and S[5], I accept the variant reading of *śaktisattā* that is found in four manuscripts—G, J, P, and R—which is the *lectio difficilior.*

25 It is tempting to accept the variant reading of *śakti* for the reading of *śakta* found in K[ed.], this in the present expression (i.e., *anekaśaktaghaṭapaṭādipadārthātmakatvāt tasya*). The variant parallels both Somānanda's *mūla*, which reads *anekabhāvābhiḥ śaktibhis* (at ŚD 4.5ab), and Utpaladeva's comment on the same (i.e., *anekaghaṭapaṭasvabhāvābhiḥ śaktibhis*). A scribe could have changed the reading to *śakta* with the wish to reflect the repeated mention of everything as being capable (*śakta*) (for which see ŚD 4.1-3 along with the relevant passages of Utpaladeva's commentary, and note that the very same is stated here, at 4.4c: *sarvaḥ śakto 'pi*). It is also possible that a scribe inadvertently left off the final short *-i* of *śakti*, explaining thereby a change from *śakti* to *śakta*. Nevertheless, I (tentatively) preserve the reading of K[ed.] (= *śakta*), because it records the *lectio difficilior*; because this reading is confirmed by perhaps the oldest manuscript of the commentary available to me (= J), along with the other *śāradā* manuscripts excepting D and G; and because there is a certain semantic economy of the reading thus constituted: it states that Śiva, who is the one *śakta* entity, *is* the very *padārthas*, which therefore should also be described (as the *vastus* have been in several places, even if paradoxically so) as *śakta*.

26 The point made here is that one could not have awareness of a pot, e.g., together with an awareness of something else, a piece of cloth, e.g., if the former (or the latter, for that matter,) were entirely independent or isolated, the awareness being of a scope that *only* takes in, e.g., the pot. The awareness of the pot would be limited to the pot alone and would not lead to a composite awareness of the pot sitting upon a cloth, for example.

A parallel to the present statement may be found at ĪPK 1.3.6-7: *evam anyonyabhinnānām aparasparavedinām | jñānānām anusaṃdhānajanmā naśyej janasthitiḥ || na ced antaḥkṛtānantaviśvarūpo maheśvaraḥ | syād ekaś cidvapur jñānasmṛtyapohanaśaktimān ||*. (Cf. also ĪPKVṛ ad ĪPK 1.8.10: *tattadvibhinnasaṃvidanusaṃdhānena hi vyavahāraḥ. ekaś ca prakāśātmā tadanusaṃdhānarūpaḥ sa eva caikaḥ pramātā paramātmasaṃjñaḥ.*) See also Torella 1994: xvi, fn. 15, where the author cites the present passage of Utpaladeva's commentary ad ŚD 4.4-5, as follows: "If things were in themselves totally independent, the unification (*anusaṃdhāna*) of their cognitions would be impossible (ŚDVṛ p. 147)."

4.6-7ab

4.6. tathā yatra sad ity evaṃ pratītis tad asat katham
yat sat tat paramārtho hi paramārthas tataḥ śivaḥ
4.7. sarvabhāveṣu cidvyakteḥ sthitaiva paramārthatā

Thus, how could that [i.e., the *vastu*] be inexistent where it is perceived in this way as existing? Indeed, that which is existent is the ultimate reality; (and since) it is the ultimate reality, it follows from that that it is Śiva. The state of being the ultimate reality is fully present in all entities, because they are manifested in consciousness.

[Somānanda] has said that that which is capable (of causal efficacy) is definitely a real thing [*vastu*],[27] and he (now) says that the *vastu* is existent. What is existent, moreover, is not inexistent; thus, it is itself the ultimate reality. And since it is the ultimate reality, it follows from that—i.e., from its being the ultimate reality, due to the fact that it is existent—that it is Śiva.

Objection: How can Śiva exist as nothing but what is the ultimate reality? Is that which is insentient, for its part, not the ultimate reality?[28]

Reply: No. How could the very existence of that which is insentient have been attained without its being manifested in consciousness? For existence is the condition of having a form that shines forth [*sphuradrūpatā*],[29] and the condition of having a form that shines forth is the state of being manifested in consciousness [*prakāśamānatā*].[30] And it follows from this that insentience truly does not exist; for the state of being manifested in consciousness is an identity with the manifesting consciousness [*prakāśa*].[31] The manifesting

---

[27] ŚD 4.1d in part reads *śaktaṃ vastv eva*, precisely what is here cited.

[28] Or perhaps: "As for that which is insentient, how is it not the ultimate reality?" In other words, the opponent may be understood to presume that what is "insentient" (*jaḍa*) cannot be the ultimate reality. Thus, he questions how Śiva can be everything and only be what is *paramārtha*; for, the opponent objects, insentient entities exist, and what is *jaḍa* is not *paramārtha*, is not identifiable with *Śiva*.

[29] On the meaning and possible translations of *sphuradrūpatā*, see Bansat-Boudon 2014: 48–76, esp. 52–56.

[30] While Somānanda does not use the language of *prakāśa* and *vimarśa* in a technical sense to describe the functioning of the power of consciousness (about which see Torella 1994: xxiii–xxiv; cf. Nemec 2011: 34), Utpaladeva here invokes this nomenclature (with *prakāśamānatā*) in order to describe the manifestation in consciousness (*cidvyakti*) to which Somānanda refers at ŚD 4.7a. Compare the present passage of the ŚDVṛ with ĪPK 1.5.14: *sā sphurattā mahāsattā deśakālāviśeṣiṇī | saiṣā sāratayā proktā hṛdayaṃ parameṣṭhinaḥ ||*. Cf. the ĪPKVṛ on the same: *sphuradrūpatā sphuraṇakartṛtā abhāvāpratiyogiṇī abhāvavyāpinī sattā bhavattā bhavanakartṛtā nityā deśakālāsparśāt saiva pratyavamarśātmā citikriyāśaktiḥ. sā viśvātmanaḥ parameśvarasya svātmapratiṣṭhārūpā hṛdayam iti tatra tatrāgame nigadyate.*

[31] There is no distinction between the light and its illumination. Thus, to appear in consciousness is by definition to *be* the real light of consciousness, which is unequivocally understood not to be insentient. Cf., e.g., ĪPK 1.5.2cd: *na ca prakāśo bhinnaḥ syād ātmārthasya prakāśatā ||*. See also the ĪPKVṛ (ad loc.), which reads in part: *prakāśamānatā cārthasya prakāśaḥ svarūpabhūto na tu bhinnaḥ.*

consciousness, moreover, is incontrovertible,[32] is the foundation of all [entities], is the ultimate reality. And all [real entities], the pot, etc., partake of that unique manifesting consciousness [*ekaprakāśātmatā*] inasmuch as they are equally of the nature of the manifesting consciousness. For this very reason, they partake of that unique (principle that is) Śiva.

This has been explained at length (by me) in the *Īśvarapratyabhijñā*.[33]

4.7cd-9

mithyājñānavikalpyānāṃ sattvaṃ cidvyaktiśaktatā
4.8. vidyate tat tad atrāpi śivatvaṃ kena vāryate
iti ced eṣu satyatvaṃ sthitam eva cidudgamāt
4.9. tathā śivodayād eva bhedo mithyādikaḥ katham
vyavahārāya satyatvaṃ na ca vāvyavahāragam[34]

---

[32]The term translated with "incontrovertible" is *anapahnavanīya*. For a parallel use of the term, see, e.g., Yogarāja's commentary on Abhinavagupta's *Paramārthasāra*, ad PS 47 and PS 50. Bansat-Boudon and Tripathi translate with "undeniable" (2011: 26), "incontrovertible" (2011: 212), and "[the 'I'] that can never be denied" (2011: 215). See also the ĪPV ad ĪPK 1.2.3, p. 61, line 6.

[33]Kupetz (1972: 140) here refers the reader to ĪPK 1.5.3, which reads as follows: *bhinne prakāśe cābhinne saṃkaro viṣayasya tat | prakāśātmā prakāśyo 'rtho nāprakāśaś ca sidhyati ||*. "If light were undifferentiated (in itself) and differentiated (from objects), then objective reality would be confused. The object that is illuminated must itself be light; that which is not light cannot be established." (Translation Torella's.) It is also possible that Utpaladeva here has ĪPK 2.4 in mind, as well.

Kaul 1934: 148, fn. 2 reproduces (with silent, necessary corrections) a marginal note found in manuscript D at the bottom of folio 146v. in order also to refer the reader to ĪPK 1.5, but to 1.5.20 in particular, which is cited in the marginal note: *ghaṭo 'yam ity adhyavasā nāmarūpātirekiṇī | pareśaśaktir ātmeva bhāsate na tv idantayā ||*. "The determinate cognition [*adhyavasā*] 'this is a jar,' beyond the linguistic sign and the thing signified [*nāmarūpa°*], is the very power of the supreme Lord. It is manifested in the same way as the self and not in terms of 'this.'" (Translation Torella's.) This verse, as is evident, suggests that even a determinate cognition such as "this is a pot" appears not externally to the self, but within the self, despite reaching the level of *vikalpa* or conceptualization.

Other important parallel passages are also to be found in Bansat-Boudon and Tripathi 2011: 69, fn. 265, and PSSaṃVi ad PS 30, where Yogarāja quotes the famed dictum, *nāprakāśaḥ prakāśate*. See also ibid.: 164, fn. 703, where Bansat-Boudon cites Vāmanadatta's *Saṃvitprakāśa* 1.12 as the possible source thereof. (I thank Lyne Bansat-Boudon for having reviewed this passage of my translation and for referring me to this source.)

[34]The KSTS edition interprets the *sandhi* of the present passage differently than it is here represented.

I understand there to be no hiatus following *vā* (ŚD 4.9d), thereby understanding the negative prefix *a-* to precede *vyavahāraga* (= *avyavahāragam*); K$^{ed.}$ preserves the hiatus. Note that two manuscripts, G and J, support the interpretation that I favor. In these manuscripts, ŚD 4.9d reads as follows: *na caivāvyavahāragam*. Given the variant reading found in these manuscripts of *na caiva* for *na ca vā*, the alpha privative is rendered explicit in them (because *eva* ends in a short vowel *a* but is connected with what follows by the long vowel *ā*, which can only be accounted for by the presence of the alpha privative in *avyavahāragam*).

The same interpretive decision regarding the hiatus following *vā* is required in the commentary, as well, at line 58 of the present edition (at *vāsatyatvam*), and in that instance the same manuscripts support our preference for eliminating the hiatus: G and J explicitly mark (with *avagrahas*) the presence

Those [perceptions] that could be conceived of as erroneous cognitions[35] are found to be capable of manifestation in consciousness.[36] That constitutes reality; (and) that [reality] (in turn) is the Śiva-nature that exists here [in even these "erroneous" perceptions], as well.[37] Objection: By what are they averted? (Reply:) Reality is fully established in these [supposedly "erroneous" perceptions], because they arise in consciousness, this simply because Śiva arises in such a manner.[38] (Objection:) How can a distinction exist that is based on erroneousness, etc.?[39] (Reply:) That [type of distinction] serves mundane activity, and it is not the case, by contrast, that reality is not found in mundane activity.[40]

---

of the alpha privative prior to *satyatvam*. K[ed.], however, again records a hiatus between the two terms: *vā satyatvam*. See footnotes 40 and 45.

[35] Chaturvedi (1986: 128) reads *mithyājñānavikalpa* for *mithyājñānavikalpya* (as do all the manuscripts examined for this edition excepting D[p.c.], it must be added), and he understands it to be a *dvandva* compound referring to perceptual and conceptual errors, *mithyājñānas* and *mithyāvikalpas*, the former being exemplified by the cognition of silver for mother-of-pearl or of a snake for a rope, the latter, he suggests, by the erroneous idea of the existence of a son of a barren woman (*vandhyāputra*). This is certainly a possible interpretation of the verse passage, but it is one that is not supported by the commentary.

I had accepted the manuscript reading of *vikalpānāṃ* that was unanimously recorded in all the manuscripts that were available to me at the time, in Nemec 2012: 228, fn. 6. I did so with the suspicion that Kaul had silently emended the text, from *vikalpānāṃ* to *vikalpyānāṃ*. Seeing that in fact the scribe who recorded the marginal notes of D made the change I suspected had occurred by Kaul's hand, I am more comfortable accepting this reading, what is in fact the *lectio difficilior* and is supported by the reading of the ŚDVṛ. The present edition, of course, reflects this change in my thinking.

[36] The word order (*anvaya*) of the present passage is communicated in the commentary, where Utpaladeva suggests one should read ŚD 4.7cd-8ab as follows: *mithyājñānavikalpyānāṃ cidvyaktiśaktatā vidyate. tat sattvam, atrāpi tat śivatvam.* My translation reflects this word order.

[37] In D (folio 147r.), a marginal note written between the lines of text and above *tat tad atra* (ŚD 4.8a), which is not replicated in K[ed.], reads as follows: *paramārthas* (corr: *paramārtha*, D) *tarhi sattvaṃ*. (I add the gemination in *sattvaṃ*.) The manner in which this note is recorded is somewhat confusing, because *tarhi* is written below the rest of the text, with the horizontal line that runs across many of the *akṣaras* in Śāradā script penned above it and level with those of *paramārthas . . . sattvaṃ*, but not used. I think this anomaly can be explained, however, by the fact that the *r* of *tarhi* is recorded in Śāradā with a horizontal line. One may infer, then, that the scribe began to write the ligature *rhi* before having recorded the initial *ta* of *tarhi*. Realizing his mistake after having written the *r* but before recording *hi*, he changed tracks and attached below what would have been *r* the needed *ta*, leading *tarhi* to be recorded in a subscript. Interestingly, this suggests that the scribe penned the horizontal lines of the Śāradā *akṣaras* first, including *tarhi*, and then filled out the *akṣaras* below, which illustrates the sequence in which the penstrokes were applied in writing out the Śāradā text.

[38] That is, because Śiva arises in the form of such moments of consciousness.

[39] *Ādi* here refers to non-erroneousness: Utpaladeva's commentary refers to a *samyagmithyātvabheda*.

[40] As noted in footnote 34, I here interpret the *sandhi* differently than did Kaul in the Kashmiri edition. If one were here to read *vā vyavahāragam* (where I read *vāvyavahāragam*), then one could translate ŚD 4.9cd as follows: "(Reply:) That [type of distinction] serves mundane activity, and it is not the case, by contrast, that reality is found (fully, without qualification) in the mundane activity." Kupetz (1972: 141) understands the text in this manner, as he renders the line with "(Answer:) Reality is not a matter of everyday-reality or usage."

Those [perceptions] that could be conceived of as erroneous cognitions—those of silver (for mother-of-pearl) or a snake (for a rope), for example—are, like (perceptions of) pots, etc., simply found to be capable of manifestation in consciousness, which is to say they are manifested in consciousness [*prakāśamānatā*].[41] That itself constitutes reality, i.e., being the ultimate reality; (and) that, it also follows, is (their) Śiva-nature.[42]

We simply accept,[43] moreover, that this [Śiva-nature] cannot be averted: reality exists in these [supposedly "erroneous" perceptions] inasmuch as they are manifested in consciousness, since this is the (very) flow of Śiva as the various forms.[44]

(Objection:) But if both the cognition of a pot and the cognition of silver (for mother-of-pearl) are real, then how can they be differentiated, as being (respectively) correct and erroneous?

(Reply:) That [type of distinction] serves mundane activity, i.e., it has a use (only) in mundane activity; and it is not the case, by contrast, that the reality of the mundane activity becomes an unreality as a result of its being less than fully developed.[45]

---

[41] K[ed.] here records *prakāśamānatā nāma*, as do two additional manuscripts (G and J). (See the present edition, line 54). D, however, along with all the other manuscripts, omits *nāma*. It is tempting to take up this alternative reading—i.e., to omit *nāma* —inasmuch as the presence of this indeclinable could possibly be explained by dittography combined with metathesis, i.e., duplicating *māna* of *prakāśamānatā* but reversing the order of the letters. (Interestingly, Kaul 1934: i–ii notes that D was the only source of the commentary available for the production of the published edition [K[ed.]], meaning either he may have himself produced this transcription of *nāma* by error, or otherwise he had access to an additional manuscript copy of the commentary that witnessed this reading.)

[42] The passage here translated—*tad eva sattvaṃ paramārthatvam ato 'pi tac chivatvam*—parallels what is said at ŚDVṛ ad ŚD 4.6-7ab (lines 40–41 of the present edition): *yac ca sat, tan nāsad iti sa eva paramārthaḥ. yasmāc ca paramārthas tataḥ sattvāt paramārthatvāc chivaḥ.*

[43] The present passage serves to answer the query expressed at ŚD 4.8b-c: *kena vāryate iti cet.*

[44] The present passage—*anivāryaṃ caitad iṣyata evaiṣu satyatvaṃ cidabhivyakteḥ, tena tena rūpeṇa śivasya prasaro 'yaṃ yataḥ*—can be understood to echo a passage of ŚDVṛ ad ŚD 4.6-7ab: *prakāśaś cānapahnavanīyaḥ sarvapratiṣṭhārūpaḥ paramārthaḥ. sarveṣāṃ ca ghaṭādīnāṃ prakāśarūpatāyāṃ viśeṣābhāvād ekaprakāśātmatā, tata evaikaśivatvam.* Note also the parallel passage at ĪPK 4.12: *sarvo mamāyaṃ vibhava ity evaṃ parijānataḥ | viśvātmano vikalpānāṃ prasare 'pi maheśatā ||*. See also the corresponding passage of the ĪPKVṛ: *kṣetrajñasyāpīśvaraśaktyaiva vikalpārambha iti taddaśāyām api parijñāteśvarabhāvasya mamāyaṃ saṃsāramayo vibhava ity abhedena viśvam āviśataḥ parāmarśamātrān aśeṣān vikalpān saṃpādayato maheśvarataiva.*

[45] I here interpret the *sandhi*—and therefore the meaning of the passage in question—differently than Kaul does in the KSTS edition. There, Kaul reads *vā satyatvaṃ* where I read *vāsatyatvaṃ*. Two manuscripts, G and J, explicitly mark the *sandhi* here and prefer the interpretation I have selected, as both manuscripts insert an *avagraha* prior to *satyatvam*, following *vā*. Cf., supra, footnotes 34 and 40.

If one were rather to understand the text here to read *vā satyatvam*, one could translate the present passage as follows: ". . . but it is not the case, by contrast, that the reality of the mundane activity becomes reality (itself), because it is less than fully developed." Kupetz (1972: 141) has interpreted the passage in precisely this manner, translating as follows: "Because of its uncertainties, however, everyday reality is not truly real." He adds (ibid.): "Note: In saying that 'everyday-reality is not real', Utpala is not contending that the everyday-world is itself illusory or false, but rather that any distinctions of the everyday-world are false, i.e., invalid criteria of reality. Somānanda next provides an example of the vagaries of the ordinary world which is attested to today by our own use of paper money."

4.10-11ab

4.10. tathā ca deśe kvacana rājājñā jāyate yathā
vyavahāro 'stu dīnārair etair avyavahāragaiḥ
4.11. pravartate tathābhūtair anyatrāpi tathānyathā

Accordingly,[46] just as the dictate of the king is applicable in a given kingdom—(when he says, e.g.,) "trade [*vyavahāra*] must be conducted with these gold coins that are not (yet) circulating in trade"[47]—so elsewhere, as well: it [i.e., the *vyavahāra*] proceeds "falsely" [*anyathā*] by means of those [perceptions] that are of a similar nature (to the alloyed coins).[48]

Trade simply is conducted in accordance with the dictate of the king, even with alloyed gold coins.

So it is elsewhere, as well: Mundane activity [*vyavahāra*]—the initiation of temporal differences, etc.—exists as a result of nothing but (Śiva's power of) will, i.e., as stipulated (by him) [*yathāsaṃketaṃ*], entirely irrespective of the real.[49]

4.11cd-12ab

vyavahārasya satyatve sarvatrāsatyataiva te
4.12. satyatve tasya hāniḥ syāt pakṣe 'bhyupagate kila

(Objection:) If the mundane activity is real, you maintain that it is unreality that exists everywhere. (And thus:) If it [i.e., the universe] were

---

[46] A note that is not recorded in K^ed. appears in D (folio 148r.) above ŚD 4.10a, which reads as follows: *vyavahārasatyatvasyāsatyatvaṃ darśayati*. "[Somānanda] shows (with ŚD 4.10-11ab) the unreality of the reality of the everyday world." My understanding of 4.10-11ab and its commentary, as well what follows in the ŚD and ŚDVṛ, does not accord with the position articulated in this marginal note, however. (This is not the only place where I disagree with an interpretation offered by the author of these marginalia, moreover. See also footnote 71.)

[47] The term here rendered is *avyavahāragaiḥ*. An error of transcription appears in Nemec 2012: 235, fn. 32, where I wrongly recorded *vyavahāragaiḥ* (hypometric) for *avyavahāragaiḥ*. The error is regretted.

[48] The same analogy is deployed at ŚD 4.19-21ab.

[49] In other words, Śiva can manifest entities as they are or he can do so in "erroneous" cognitions, all according to his will, just as the king can command that transactions take place with fully weighted gold coins or with alloyed coins. Thus, I here concur with Chaturvedi's (1986: 129) interpretation of this passage over and against that of Kupetz, who suggests the present addresses the role of the king in the world. See Kupetz 1972: 142.

real, there would be a deficiency in the position you have admitted (as your own).[50]

(Objection:) But[51] if you maintain that the mundane activity, which is less than fully developed, is real, even though it is unreal,[52] then this entire universe, which (on your view) is real, would exist as the same class of entity; this means that, like the mundane activity, it would be one whose ultimate reality is an unreality.[53]

If (you maintain that) it, i.e., the universe, is real in the ultimate sense, this would be the nature of your error: the reality (of the universe) would resemble the mundane activity, and in this way there would be a deficiency in the position you have articulated, i.e., the one that has been expressed in the (Śaiva) *śāstras*, namely, the doctrine that everything is real.[54]

4.12cd-13ab

tasyāpi kiṃ śivāvāptiḥ katham uktā hy asatyatā
4.13. vyavahāratayaivāsti satyatvaṃ na nibandhanāt

(The objection continues:) Does it, for its part, obtain Śiva(-nature)? For, (if so, then) how could you say it is unreal?[55] **(Reply:) Its reality exists only inasmuch as it is a mundane activity; it does not exist causally.**

---

[50]The mundane activity or *vyavahāra* in question is described at ŚD 4.11ab. Thus, the opponent objects to the idea that Somānanda can say, as he does at ŚD 4.9cd (. . . *satyatvaṃ na ca vāvyavahāragam*), that reality extends to this *vyavahāra* but is not defined by its erroneousness.

Kupetz translates the present pair of half-verses as follows: "Your mistake arises in taking the position that everything is real. For if even the illusions of the world are real, then everything is unreal." He goes on to comment as follows: "The meaning of *ślokas* 11 and 12 is difficult to understand because the word *vyavahāra* is being used to represent both ordinary pot-perceptions and illusory perceptions of rope-snakes. The objector appears to be arguing that: 1. if pot-perceptions and illusions are equally real, then the world is reduced to the level of illusion, and 2. if the world, with all its uncertainty, is of the highest reality, then Śiva is reduced to being of the nature of that uncertain world. Utpala answers that the everyday-world is indeed real in terms of everyday-functioning, but that its uncertainty precludes its acting as an agent of sublation." (See Kupetz 1972: 142–143.)

[51]That is, the opponent suggests that it is not possible to maintain that apparently erroneous *vyavahāras* are real, as Somānanda suggested at ŚD 4.7cd-9 and 4.10-11ab.

[52]The language of the present passage, *yadi punar aprarūḍhasya vyavahārasyāsatyasyāpi satyateṣyate*, echoes that of ŚDVṛ ad ŚD 4.7cd-9 (line 58 of the present edition): *na cāprarūḍhatvād vyavahārasatyatvaṃ vāsatyatvaṃ bhavati.*

[53]I understand *asatyatāparamārtham* to be a *bahuvrīhi* compound describing *jagat*, "the universe."

[54]The opponent's argument presumes, then, that *vyavahāra* must be unreal in some important sense, meaning it would be impossible for the Śaivas to claim that everything is real.

[55]Somānanda's opponent disputed the claim that the mundane activity, the *vyavahāra*, could be real, this at ŚD 4.11cd-12ab. Here, the opponent denies Somānanda any occasion to claim the second of the pair of logical possibilities (i.e., the second of two *vikalpas*), namely, the possibility that Somānanda could understand the *vyavahāra* to be *unreal*, because, the opponent argues, Somānanda cannot claim it is unreal if it is possessed of Śiva-nature.

(Objection:) Do you maintain that it, i.e., the mundane activity, for its part, obtains Śiva(-nature)—is of the nature of Śiva—as a result of arising in consciousness, meaning that its Śiva-nature is effortlessly arrived at?[56] If this is the case, how can you say that this mundane activity is for its part unreal? This means that it can only be real, when this is the case.

(Reply:) True.[57] However, the reality of this mundane activity also exists only inasmuch as it is a mundane activity; it does not exist causally, however, i.e., as a result of its being a cause [*nibandhanatvāt*], meaning (it does not exist) by dint of being fully developed.[58]

4.13cd-14

vikalpādeḥ samutpattiḥ sata eva prajāyate
4.14. nābhāṣya vyavahārārtham evaṃ vastv iti niścitam
tathaivāstu śivāvasthā kenāsau vinivāritā

Having said[59] a *vikalpa*, e.g., does not give rise to that which is fully real,[60] (I add that) it is certain that the real exists in this way[61] for the purpose of the mundane activity. Its condition as Śiva must exist precisely in this manner. By what could it be opposed?

---

[56] The present translation of *anāyāsāgatā* partially echoes that of Kupetz (1972: 142): "If that everyday-world is obtained to be Śiva through the arising of consciousness, then its being of the nature of Śiva is easily arrived at."

[57] That is, Utpaladeva assents to the notion that *vyavahāra* must be real inasmuch as it is naturally possessed of Śiva-nature (*śivatā*).

[58] Kupetz translates the present passage as follows: "True. But the reality of the everyday-world is through its everyday usage, not because it is certain or because it serves to deny (illusion)." (See Kupetz 1972: 142.) Chaturvedi suggests that the present suggests the world is real insofar as it exists in the form of the everyday, but that in reality Śiva alone is real and nothing else. (See Chaturvedi 1986: 130.) I here do not accept the variant reading of *asatyatvaṃ* for K[ed.]'s *satyatvaṃ* (line 76). The variant is recorded in all eight of the witnesses of this passage that were examined for the present edition, including D (which Kaul reports is the only witness of the commentary used in the preparation of K[ed.]). It is therefore tempting to accept this reading for this reason if no other. But as the present passage of the ŚDVṛ explains ŚD 4.13ab and as *satyatvam* is a lemma, this would require one to emend *satyatvaṃ* at ŚD 4.13b to *asatyatvaṃ* (which requires crossing the *pāda* boundary). After much consideration, I have settled instead on the present interpretation: the reality of *vyavahāra* is mundane, not fully developed or fully causally efficacious. Nevertheless, it is real (about which, see the immediately following passage of commentary, at ŚDVṛ ad ŚD 4.13cd-14). Note, finally, that it is apparent that Kaul here silently emended the ŚDVṛ in the course of preparing the edition of K[ed.], to good effect.

[59] Here Somānanda refers to what was said at ŚD 4.13ab.

[60] One must read the negative particle (*na*) of ŚD 4.14a with the preceding half-verse. The *post correctionem* reading in the KSTS edition of the relevant passage of the ŚDVṛ suggests that Utpaladeva did just this, and my conjectural emendation of the text at line 81 of the present edition reflects the same. See footnote 63.

[61] "In this way" (*evam*) refers to the fact that some of what appears in consciousness may be counted, for conventional reasons or the functioning of mundane activity, as that which is erroneous or "unreal."

And it is not the case that a *vikalpa*, e.g.—an independent[62] cognition of, for example, silver (for mother-of-pearl)—results in the production of the arising of that which is fully real, i.e., of an object, as that which has been caused (by that *vikalpa*).[63] What then?

Having said as much, i.e., having stipulated as much, (Somānanda adds that) it is certain, i.e., definite,[64] that the real[65] exists in this way for the purpose of the mundane activity—i.e., a purchase may be made with alloyed gold coins, (or)

---

[62] Utpaladeva here describes *rajatādijñāna* as *svatantra* to indicate that such cognitions as that of silver where mother-of-pearl is in fact present are not connected to the object that was seen in direct perception. A similar use of the term is found in ĪPKVṛ ad ĪPK 1.8.2. The verse reads as follows: *viśeṣo 'rthāvabhāsasya sattāyāṃ na punaḥ kvacit | vikalpeṣu bhaved bhāvibhavadbhūtārthagāmiṣu ||*. "There can be no difference by any means, however, in the reality of the appearance of an object in the *vikalpas* regarding future, present, or past objects." The *Vṛtti* says the following: *smṛtyutprekṣārūpeṣu pratyakṣapṛṣṭhapātiṣu svatantreṣu vānyeṣu vikalpeṣu kālatrayaviṣayeṣv arthāvabhāso 'ntas tulya evāvasthitaḥ*. "In *vikalpas* following direct perception, the forms of which are memory and imagination, or in the others, which are independent (of direct perception), the scope of which are (all) the three moments of time, the appearance of the object is equally established as internal."

On the meaning of *utprekṣā*, see the helpful note of Ratié 2011a: 46, fn. 25.

[63] In other words, the misperception of silver where mother-of-pearl is present does not cause the mother-of-pearl in fact to come into being. Kaul had already recorded (*post correctionem*) the presence of the negative particle in the first sentence of the commentary: he locates it in the first position in the list of errata of K$^{ed.}$: *na vikalpādeḥ* . . . (line 80 of the present edition). I have conjectured that the negative particle appeared at the end of the sentence in question. This would leave us with an unusual word-order—the negative particle in the final position—but it can be explained by the fact that Utpaladeva not infrequently preserves the word-order of the *mūla* in his commentary. (See, e.g., the first lines of his commentary on ŚD 4.12cd-13ab, which closely reproduce the word-order of the half-verse on which he comments.) I propose that Utpaladeva placed the negative particle at the end of the sentence and not the beginning to match the word-order of the *mūla*, as follows: *vikalpādeḥ svatantrād rajatādijñānāc ca nibaddhatvena sata evārthasyotpattiḥ saṃpadyate na. kiṃ tarhi, tathābhāṣya*. . . . So much replicates the word order of the half-verse he glosses, excepting that Utpaladeva inverts the order of *samutpattiḥ* and *sata eva*. In accepting this emendation, one may readily understand why *na* was lost in all the manuscripts I have examined for the present edition: *saṃpadyate na* would easily have appeared to a copyist as an error (as, e.g., *saṃpadya tena*), and could have been corrected silently by the copyists in the transmission of the text. It is clear, regardless, and as Kaul's correction indicates and as Kupetz (1972: 143) also noted, that a negative particle is needed in the commentary if it is to accord with what is said in the *mūla*.

[64] I eliminate the period of K$^{ed.}$, which appears there following *iti* and prior to *niścitaṃ niścayaḥ*. Here, Utpaladvea indicates that *niścitam* should be read with *iti* to mean *iti niścayaḥ*. He also understands *vyavahārārtham* to be a part of the *iti*-clause and to be adverbial (or perhaps a *bahuvrīhi* compound describing *vastu*), serving thus to explain how the real (*vastu*) exists or why it exists as it does.

[65] I have offered a conjectural emendation of the text at line 83 of the edition, positing that one must supply *vastv* there following *vāstu* and prior to *iti niścitaṃ niścayaḥ*. The loss of the term in this case is explained by haplography. In offering this emendation, one can see a clear replication of the word-order of ŚD 4.14a-b in the commentary, as follows, with lemmas in bold: *tathā*-**ābhāṣya** *saṃketya* **vyavahārārtham evaṃ** *kūṭadīnāraiḥ krayo 'stu, adyārabhya kālagaṇanāyām ayaṃ saṃvatsaraḥ saṃvatsarārambho vāstu* **vastv iti niścitaṃ** *niścayaḥ*. One could alternatively consider accepting the reading of K$^{ed.p.c.}$ of *vāstu* for *vastu* at ŚD 4.14b. I have elected not to accept this reading, however, first of all because it is not attested to in any of the manuscripts examined for this volume, and secondly because *evaṃ vastu* appears in the next line of the ŚDVṛ, at line 83 of the present edition, where it is clearly a lemma.

the year, or the beginning of the year, may register in the calculation of time once it first has (been understood to have) commenced at a particular moment of time [*adyārabhya*].[66]

Alternatively, (reading the syntax differently, ŚD 4.14a-b means:) the real, for its part, exists in this way; i.e., although it is real (in the ultimate sense) [*satyam api*], it is temporal, etc.[67] Therefore, it [i.e., the real] is one whose purpose in mundane activity is ascertained.[68] And its abiding as the (very) nature of Śiva must exist precisely in this manner. By what could it be opposed, since its arising in consciousness is in consequence of its being possessed of Śiva-nature?

The mark [*nimittam*] has been declared, already,[69] regarding the divergence of views concerning whether a *vikalpa*, i.e., mundane activity, is real or unreal; it is the one (that Somānanda articulated) concerning the reality of that which is manifested in consciousness: it is definitely real.[70] And thus, at no time whatever should this be forgotten, since the reality (of the *vikalpa* or the *vyavahāra*) results from (their) being made up of the non-cognition of the non-duality of consciousness.[71]

---

[66] I here understand Utpaladeva to gloss, or rather explain, *evam* (ŚD 4.14b) with *kūṭadīnāraiḥ krayo 'stu, adyārabhya kālagaṇanāyām ayaṃ saṃvatsaraḥ saṃvatsarārambho vāstu.* (See footnote 65 for a reproduction of the passage with the lemmas in bold.) Note also the parallel with what is found at ŚDVṛ ad ŚD 4.10-11ab (lines 62–63 of the present edition): *rājājñayā kūṭadīnārair api vyavahāro 'sty eva. tathānyatrāpīcchāmātrād yathāsaṃketaṃ vastv anapekṣyaiva kālavyavasthārambhādivyavahāraḥ.*

[67] I understand *kālādi* to be a *bahuvrīhi* compound describing *vastu*.

[68] The present alternative understands *vyavahārārtham* (ŚD 4.14a) not to be in the *iti*-clause and to be a *bahuvrīhi* compound describing the *vastu*. On this latter interpretation of the syntax, Utpaladeva suggests that the word order (*anvaya*) at ŚD 4.14a-b should be construed as follows: *evaṃ vastv iti vyavahārārthaṃ niścitam*: "The real is thus [i.e., is imbued with the marks of mundane activity such as temporality]. Therefore, its purpose in mundane activity is (clearly) ascertained."

[69] D (folio 150v.) records a marginal note above *prāṅ nimittam* (line 86) and below *vyavahārasya* (line 85), which extends into the right margin and is not recorded in the KSTS edition. It reads, simply, *vyavahārasya satyatve ityādinā*. This evidently is a *pratīka* reference to ŚD 4.11cd-12ab and, one assumes, ŚD 12cd-13ab. It is in this pair of half-verses that the reality or unreality of *vyavahāra* are pondered in the form of an opponent's objection.

[70] That is, one may know the *vikalpa*, the *vyavahāra*, is real, for which see ŚD 4.13a-b, where Somānanda uses the term here cited, *satyatva*, to refer to the *vyavahāra*. Cf. ŚD 4.7cd-9 and, esp., the corresponding passage of the ŚDVṛ. Cf. ŚDVṛ ad ŚD 4.6-7ab.

[71] Kaul (1934: 151, fn. 3) records a note, which appears verbatim in the left-hand margin of D (at folio 150v.) that states that the present passage suggests that reality in no way is a result of the non-cognition of non-duality: *cidabhedākhyātimayatvena na kathañcanāpi satyatvam ity arthaḥ*. "This means that reality does not exist in any way as the non-cognition of the non-duality of consciousness." I think this view is mistaken. It is, more precisely, rather that the (so-called) "erroneous" perception is nothing more than an "error of omission," a non-perception of that which is truly present. This omission is an absence—it is nothing at all; for it is understood to be something that is in no way present. As such, error has no ontological status whatever, and it is precisely and only through the *non*-perception of unity—itself an absence or non-existence of awareness—that one comes to know anything about the world. See Nemec 2012 for more on this formulation as it appears in the ŚDVṛ (where it was first articulated), and for its legacy in the writings of Abhinavagupta.

This is not the only place where I disagree with an interpretation of the author of these marginalia. See also footnote 46.

4.15-16

4.15. mithyātvaṃ kriyate kasya kiṃ kāle yatra tad bhavet
kāla eva sa na bhaved iti cen naiva kutracit
4.16. akāle jananaṃ kiñcid bādhyate vā janikriyā
kṛtvā kāryaṃ kriyā yātā gatāyāṃ kiṃ prabādhyate

What is made to be erroneous? Is it that the very moment of time in which that [misperception][72] must arise cannot (properly) come to pass?[73] If you argue as much (we reply): It is not so.[74] No production whatsoever occurs anywhere outside of time.[75] Alternatively, (you might argue) it is the act of production (of the erroneous cognition) that is invalidated. (We reply:) An action, having produced its effect, elapses. What is invalidated when it has (already) gone?[76]

When an invalidating means of knowledge exists, moreover,[77] the erroneousness in a cognition must depend on (there being a) negation: "this is not silver"; "this is not silver, it is mother-of-pearl." The erroneousness must be effected by that invalidating means of knowledge. Therefore, (Somānanda asks:) of what is it [i.e., the erroneousness] made?[78]

---

[72] Utpaladeva glosses *tat* (ŚD 4.15b) with *rajatādi* (see the ŚDVṛ at line 95 of the present edition). One should note, however, that *rajatādi* is a variant reading—$K^{ed.}$ there records *rajatatā*—one attested in all the manuscripts consulted for the edition included in this volume, excepting D. It is likely that the text first read *rajatādi*, however, until *di* was left off by a scribe or scribes in the transcription of the text, leaving only *rajatā*, for this is precisely what is preserved in $D^{a.c.}$; that reading is susceptible to a subsequent and erroneous scribal "correction" to *rajatatā*.

[73] That is, does the opponent claim that erroneousness is caused by the fact that the moment when the cognition in question could properly have occurred cannot take place?

[74] Following Utpaladeva's commentary, I read *na* (ŚD 4.15d) twice, first as a reply to the objection and again with the substance of the reply to the objection.

[75] In a previous rendering of this passage (Nemec 2012: 229, fn. 10) I did not read *bādhyate* with what follows, as is more natural given the word-order of the verse, the disjunctive particle (*vā*) being enclitic. This interpretation is supported, moreover, by the *anvaya* telegraphed in the commentary.

[76] That is, what is invalidated when the act of producing the erroneous cognition is gone? Note that Utpaladeva understands *kim* (ŚD 4.16d) to mean both "what" and "why." See footnotes 80 and 82.

[77] *Ca* (line 93) is connective with the previous section of the ŚD and ŚDVṛ, where Somānanda has said (ŚD 4.14cd) that Śiva-nature is found even in apparently erroneous phenomena and cannot be averted, and where Utpaladeva has said (ŚDVṛ ad ŚD4.13cd-14) that one should not forget that the appearance of *vikalpas* and mundane activity or *vyavahāra* is the product of the non-cognition of the non-duality of consciousness.

[78] *Tat* in the present phrase (*tat kasya kriyate*, line 95 of the present edition) might not mean "therefore" and could be taken to refer to the erroneousness or *mithyātvam*, which is mentioned in the immediately preceding sentence (line 94).

N.B.: A marginal note of D folio 151r. is written above *tat kasya kriyate*, which is not recorded in the KSTS edition. It reads: *atra vikalpayati*.

Regarding that, do you accept that the erroneousness exists because the very moment of time in which that, i.e., the (cognition of) silver, e.g., could come into being does not occur?[79]

That cannot be so; for there is simply no production whatsoever of anything outside of time, i.e., in the absence of the moment of time (when it could occur). This means (that this cannot be so,) because it is impossible for an action to be atemporal.

Alternatively, if you argue that it is the act of production (of the erroneous cognition) that is invalidated, we reply: not so. An action, having produced its effect, (the cognition of) silver, for example, is completed. What is the purpose of the invalidation of that [action of the production] which no longer exists, given that it is voided entirely of its own accord?[80] And what invalidation could there be, given that the object of the invalidation[81] does not exist at that moment (when the invalidation is to take place)?[82]

4.17-18

4.17. athānubhavagā bādhā nānubhūto 'nyathā bhavet
athendriyasya bādhyatvaṃ tatkālaṃ yādṛg indriyam
4.18. tadāndhyaṃ janyate kena tasya kālāntarasthiteḥ
sarvaiḥ samatvaṃ bādho vā saṃbandhe jananaṃ katham

Objection: The invalidation is situated in the experience. (Reply:) That which has been experienced cannot become otherwise. Objection: The sense organ is susceptible to invalidation. (Reply: In that case:) The kind of sense organ that exists at that moment is rendered unable to convey sense data at that time.[83] How can all [cognitions] (produced by that sense organ) be (rendered) the same (as the erroneous cognition) as the result

[79] The KSTS edition punctuates prior to *sa kāla eva na bhavatīti mithyātvam ity abhyupagamaḥ*, but I have eliminated the period in the present edition.

[80] There is no need for any invalidation, because that which is meant to be invalidated ceases to exist of its own accord. In other words, Utpaladeva here understands *kim* (ŚD 4.16d) to mean "why."

[81] D folio 152r. records a marginal note above *bādhaviṣayasya* (line 99 of the present edition) that glosses the term with *rajatasya*. This note was not recorded by Kaul in K$^{ed.}$.

[82] In other words, Utpaladeva here understands *kim* (ŚD 4.16d) to mean "what."

[83] Literally, a "blindness" (*āndhya*) is produced for it. (On how to interpret *tadāndhyam*, see esp. footnote 85.)

A synonym of *āndhya* is used in a similar manner in PS 30 (quoted in Kupetz 1972: 61): *etad tad andhakāraṃ yad bhāveṣu prakāśamānatayā | ātmānatirikteṣv api bhavaty anātmābhimāno 'yam* ||. Yogarāja's commentary ad PS 30 reads as follows: *etat tad andhakāram ity eṣā sā samanantarapratipāditā viśvamohinī pūrṇatvākhyātirūpā bhrāntiḥ, yad bhāveṣu pramātṛprameyarūpeṣu viśvavartiṣu padártheṣu prakāśamānatayeti*.

of a state belonging to that [*indriya*] in a subsequent moment of time?[84] **Alternatively, (you might argue) the invalidation is of the relation (of sense organ with object of sense). (Reply:) Whence the production (of the cognition in question)?**

Now, if you maintain that the invalidation is situated in the experience of the silver (where mother-of-pearl is in fact present), we reply: not so. For it is not tenable that an object that has been experienced is one that has not been experienced.

Objection: The sense organ that causes the cognition of silver, of two moons, and the like is not a (valid) sense organ and therefore is invalidated.

Reply: Not so. For that which invalidates the sense organ is not able to make it unable to convey sense data [*āndhya*], i.e., to render it void [*abhāva*]; for the kind of sense organ that exists at that moment—i.e., at the moment of the cognition of silver (for mother-of-pearl), for example—perceives [*upalabdhi*] pots, etc., at that time.[85]

Objection: The invalidation (of the *indriya*) occurs when, in a subsequent moment of time, that which invalidates it arises, because it [i.e., the *indriya*] is unstable.[86]

(Reply:) When the invalidation is obtained as a result of (the emergence of) a state belonging to that [*indriya*] in a subsequent moment of time,[87] the invalidation (that mars the sense organ) suffers the fact that even the correct cognitions that occurred at that time are fully the same as the erroneous

---

[84] Note that Utpaladeva's commentary evidently reads *bādha* (ŚD 4.18c) twice, both with what precedes and what follows it. I have translated more simply, reading *bādha* only with what follows it.

[85] "At that time" (*tadānīm*) refers to the period of time around when the *indriya* is said to produce the erroneous cognition.

Utpaladeva's commentary signals two interpretations of *tadāndhyam* (ŚD 4.18a): it may be comprised either of the combination of *tadā* and *āndhyam* or of *tat* and *āndhyam*, the latter being understood as a genitive *tatpuruṣa* compound. The ŚDVṛ here reads as follows: *tasya tadānīṃ ghaṭādīnām upalabdheḥ*. *Tasya* glosses *tat* in *tadāndhyam* and *tadānīm* glosses *tadā*. Given this glossing of the compound, I considered emending *upalabdheḥ* (line 108) with *anupalabdheḥ* on the understanding that the term as emended would explain *āndhya*. But the commentary without the emendation makes better logical sense (because Utpaladeva declares in the immediately preceding that the *bādhaka* is *not* able to make the *indriya* "blind"), and all the manuscripts support reading *upalabdheḥ*.

[86] The argument is that the *indriya* sometimes sees correctly, but is also invalidated on certain occasions; it is only in a particular and subsequent moment that an *indriya* that produced an erroneous cognition in an earlier moment is shown to have been faulty. Otherwise, it functions properly.

[87] It is possible that *tat-* of *tatkālāntarasthiter* (lines 109–110 of the edition) does not refer to the *indriya*. Yet, the passage of the ŚD being glossed (ŚD 4.18b) reads *tasya kālāntarasthiteḥ*, and thus it is more likely that *tat* is compounded. If, however, it were understood not to be a part of the compound, *tat* could mark the reply to the objection stated immediately preceding, in which case it would be more plausible to read *kālāntarasthiteḥ* in apposition with *tasya* (at ŚD 4.18b), understanding it to be a *bahuvrīhi* compound. As should be clear from my translation, however, I read the compound in the ablative and understand it not to describe the *indriya*.

cognitions.[88] And this is not tenable, because cognitions of (entities such as) pots, etc., arising in the concurrent moment are produced as correct (cognitions).[89]

Objection: The invalidation is of the relation of the sense organ to the object, etc.[90] Reply: Not so. For how could the cognition be produced if the relation were non-existent?

Therefore, in as much as the production (of the "erroneous" cognition) occurs in conceptual construction, the invalidation has no purpose whatever, since there is nothing that can be negated in any respect in the cognition of, e.g., silver (for mother-of-pearl).[91] No invalidation, moreover, results from (the conceptual construction, that, e.g.,) "it is mother-of-pearl, it is not silver." For it is neither the case (that something is negated) as a result of the cognition "I have understood mother-of-pearl as silver," nor even in any way (as a result of the cognition) "(I have cognized silver) via a recourse to a locus that is the shell,"[92] because absolutely everything manifesting in consciousness has its own form and its own locus (in consciousness).[93] In every respect, what has been manifested is exactly that; it cannot be made to be otherwise. Therefore, it is definitely real; erroneousness therefore does not exist at all.

---

[88] That is, at the time of the cognition that is proven erroneous. If there is a fault in the *indriya*, then it is one that would affect *all* the cognitions that the sense organ produces in the same period of time.

[89] The point is that the *indriya* in question functions properly at the same time as (and subsequent to) the invalidation of the erroneous cognition(s), meaning the *bādha* cannot be of the *indriya* itself, even if it is incurred in a subsequent moment of time.

[90] It is not clear to me to what the term *ādi* ("etc.") of *indriyaviṣayādīnāṃ* (line 112) here refers. Perhaps it is best understood to refer to the awareness or cognition that is the product of the contact of the sense organ (*indriya*) with the object of sense (*viṣaya*).

[91] Compare what is said in the present passage (*tasmād yāvat saṃbhavaṃ vikalpane sarvathā rajatādipratītau na kiñcin niṣeddhuṃ śakyata iti na kaścid bādhārthaḥ*) with the standard Utpaladeva established for proving the existence of *mithyātva*, at ŚDVṛ ad ŚD 4.15-16, lines 93–94 of the present edition: *bādhake ca pramāṇe sati nedaṃ rajataṃ nedaṃ rajataṃ śuktiketi niṣedhaniṣṭhatayā pratītau mithyātvaṃ syāt*. Clearly, Utpaladeva here wishes to suggest that this standard cannot be met in instances when one perceives silver where mother-of-pearl is in fact present.

See footnote 95 for references to similar formulations in the ĪPK and ĪPKVṛ.

[92] A marginal note in D (folio 153v.) that is not recorded in K$^{ed.}$ is found written above *avaṣṭambhenety api* (line 116 of the present edition). It reads simply: *pūrvanyāyenaiva*.

[93] Here, I understand *svarūpadeśatvāt* to mean that that which is being manifested in consciousness has a nature such that it has its own form (*svarūpa*) and its own locus (*svadeśa*). On this interpretation, *na hi rajatatvena śuktikā pratipanneti vā pratīteḥ* (lines 115–116) refers to the fact that the *form* or *nature* of the supposedly erroneous cognition cannot be invalidated, and *śuktideśāvaṣṭambhenety api na kiñcit* (line 116) refers to the fact that the *locus* of the supposedly erroneous cognition cannot be invalidated in any way whatever.

A marginal note in D (folio 153v.) that is not recorded in K$^{ed.}$ is found written above *svarūpa°*; it reads: *nānyadeśatvam ity arthaḥ*. This suggests that the author of these notes thought that *svarūpadeśatva* was a *tatpuruṣa* compound referring to the fact that the nature of a particular entity was "located" in a particular place (in consciousness). My interpretation of the passage differs from this one in the ways just outlined here.

This, moreover, may be ascertained[94] from the *Īśvarapratyabhijñā*.[95]

4.19-21ab

4.19. vyavahārasya bādhā ced vyavahāre yatheṣṭatā
kvacit satyasuvarṇasya pratyante vyavahāritā
4.20. kūṭakārṣāpaṇādau vā vyavahāro 'pi dṛśyate
tāvatā vyavahāro vā yad ātmāhlādamātrakam
4.21. arthakriyāsamarthatvam etad evāsya vāstavam

Objection: The invalidation is of the mundane activity.[96] (Reply:) The mundane activity is as it is wished to be. Somewhere in a bordering

---

[94] A marginal note that is not recorded in K^ed. is found written above *avaseyam* (line 119 of the present edition) in D (folio 153v.); it says, simply: *samyaṅ niścetavyam.*

[95] See, e.g., ĪPK 1.7.12: *evaṃ rūpyavidābhāvarūpā śuktimatir bhavet | na tv ādyarajatajñapteḥ syād aprāmāṇyavedikā* ||. "In this way, the knowledge of mother-of-pearl arises in the form of the absence of knowledge of silver, but it cannot convey the invalidity of the initial cognition of silver." (Translation a modification of Torella's.) In particular, see the corresponding passage of the ĪPKVṛ: *śuktijñānam eva rajatajñānābhāvarūpaṃ sidhyati, tadānīntanaśuktijñānānubhavena na bhinnasyātītasya rūpyajñānasyāprāmāṇyam.* "The cognition of mother-of-pearl is itself established in the form of the absence of the cognition of silver; it is not the case that the experience of the cognition of mother-of-pearl at that time establishes the invalidity of the distinct cognition of silver that occurred earlier." (Translation a modification of Torella's.)

See also ĪPK 1.7.13: *dharmyasiddher api bhaved bādhā naivānumānataḥ | svasaṃvedanasiddhā tu yuktā saikapramātṛjā* ||. "Invalidation cannot take place even by inference, since the property possessor (of that invalidation) itself is not proved; however, it [i.e., the invalidation] is established in one's own awareness, what is suitably understood as being born in the unitary cognizer." (Translation a modification of Torella's.) The ĪPKVṛ ad ĪPK 1.7.13 reads as follows: *śuktikājñānakāle ca na pūrvaṃ rajatajñānam asti. tataḥ sa dharmī na siddha iti nānumānena bādhā, ekapramātṛmayasvasaṃvedane tv ekadeśāvaṣṭambhyubhayajñānamayasaṃbandhabhāsanāt sidhyati. paścātsaṃvādaḥ pratyakṣasvasaṃvedane pūrvasyāpi tasya bhāsanād ekaṃ pramāṇam itarad anyatheti bhavati. saṃvādo 'py ekapramātṛkṛtaḥ.* "Moreover, the earlier cognition of silver does not exist in the (subsequent) moment when one cognizes mother-of-pearl. Hence, the property possessor (of the invalidation, viz., the cognition of mother-of-pearl) is not established; therefore, there is no invalidation by way of inference. However, it [i.e., the invalidation] is established in the self-awareness that consists in the unitary agent of knowing, because the connection between the pair of cognitions [i.e., that of silver and that of mother-of-pearl] appears (there) inasmuch as they both resort to a single locus (in which they appear). The subsequent congruence, in the form of knowing that one is valid, while the other is not, occurs because there appears in the self-awareness of the (present) direct cognition (of mother-of-pearl) the earlier [cognition, i.e., that of silver], as well. (Thus:) The congruence, too, exists on account of the single agent of knowing." (Translation a modification of Torella's.)

Finally, ĪPK 1.7.14 (quoted in footnote 99) addresses the nature of *vyavahāra* or mundane activity, precisely what is taken up (yet again) by Somānanda at ŚD 4.19-21ab (although with a different emphasis), thus suggesting that Utpaladeva has these verses in mind when referring in the ŚDVṛ to the *Īśvarapratyabhijñā*, as well that he had the present passages of the ŚD in mind when composing ĪPK (and ĪPKVṛ ad) 1.7.

[96] The precise meaning of the term *vyavahāra* here can be somewhat difficult to pin down. As previously (ŚD 4.10-11ab, 4.11cd-12ab, 4.12cd-13ab, 4.13cd-14), the term may be understood to refer to the "mundane activity" that is erroneous cognition. Thus, Utpaladeva in the commentary for this verse refers to the *rajatavyavahāra*, the erroneous perception of silver for mother-of-pearl. It can also refer

country, real gold is the currency of trade; but trade [*vyavahāra*] also is seen in alloyed coins and the like.[97] Alternatively, (one may understand the matter as follows:) the mundane activity [*vyavahāra*] exists (only) to the extent that the self is delighted; this[98] alone is the true capacity for the purposeful action belonging to this [object used in mundane activity].[99]

Objection: The mundane activity itself is invalidated, which is to say that the mundane activity of the (perception of) silver (for mother-of-pearl) may not (properly) be performed. (Reply:) This, too, is not so, because the conduct is of a mundane activity that is wished for. There is no distinction of real from unreal on its account.

To explain (by way of analogy): Somewhere in a bordering country trade [*vyavahāra*] of pure gold occurs thus, i.e., of that sort of (precious) metal. And trade (also) is seen with alloyed coins and the like because the king wishes it to be so.[100]

Alternatively, (one may understand the matter as follows:) the mundane activity exists only to the extent that there is delight, and this[101] alone, the capacity of the object to produce delight, exists (only) when it [i.e., the object] is capable of producing causal efficacy, this by way of the fact that it has

---

to the way in which things are conventionally engaged, i.e., to custom, which conveys the sense of a quotidian interaction or engagement.

[97] The same example—of trade with alloyed coins—is also deployed at ŚD 4.10-11ab.

[98] *Etat* here refers to the *ātmāhlādamātraka*, literally "what has as its measure the delight of the self."

[99] A parallel to this passage is found at ĪPK (and ĪPKVṛ ad) 1.7.14, even if Utpaladeva's emphasis there is different than Somānanda's (the latter speaks in terms of the supposed erroneousness or non-erroneousness of *vyavahāra*, the former its relative purity or impurity): *ittham atyarthabhinnārthāvabhāsakhacite vibhau | samalo vimalo vāpi vyavahāro 'nubhūyate* ||. "Thus ordinary worldly activity, whether pure or impure, is experienced as resting on the Lord associated with the manifestation of greatly differentiated objective realities." (Translation Torella's.) See also the corresponding commentary of the ĪPKVṛ: *māyāśaktyā bhedaviṣayo 'yaṃ sarvo vyavahāras tathājñāninām śuddho 'jñānāndhānāṃ tu malinas tattadbhinnārthāvabhāsabhāji bhagavati saṃbhāvyate 'nubhavena.* "All practical activity, based on differentiation due to the power of *māyā*, is pure for those who possess such knowledge, impure for those who are blind because of nescience. It is possible to grasp, through direct experience, that all this daily practical activity is founded on the Blessed One, engaged in the manifestation of the various differentiated realities." (Translation Torella's.)

The *avataraṇikā* of Abhinavagupta's ĪPV (vol. 1: p. 312, lines 3–9) ad ĪPK 1.7.14 alludes to the concerns raised in ŚD 4.19-21ab: *na kevalam ete kāryakāraṇabhāvasmaraṇabādhāvyavahārāḥ sakalalokayātrāsāmānyavyavahārabhūtā ekapramātṛpratiṣṭhā, yāvad avāntaravyavahārā api ye krayavikrayādayaḥ samalāḥ, upadeśyopadeśabhāvādayaś ca nirmalāḥ, te 'py ekapramātṛniṣṭhā eva bhavanti— vyavhāro hi sarvaḥ samanvayaprāṇa ity upasaṃhārakrameṇa darśayati.*

[100] In neither case does the activity involved in the commerce, in the *vyavahāra*, suggest the relative purity or impurity of the gold in the coins that are put to use. To recognize the difference in the weighting of the coins demands a rather different analysis. So too, with a cognition: what one *does* when one sees silver is indistinguishable vis-à-vis *the activity* from that of mother-of-pearl. Another basis for error must be found.

[101] *Etat* here is a lemma and, as Utpaladeva explains, refers to *āhlādamātrakam*, literally "that which has delight as its measure."

been established in self-awareness.[102] (For example:) A causal efficacy—that of drinking, for example—may exist (within the dream-state) for water that is real in a dream, because it [i.e., the water] is not unreal (in the dream), although it [i.e., the causal efficacy] is unreal (outside of the dream);[103] and still, with the quenching of one's thirst (in the dream) there is a satisfaction that, having been established in self-awareness, does not deceive.[104] And that, for its part, is the delighting causal efficacy of which either the alloyed (coin), e.g., or the dream-water, e.g., may be possessed; (and) that,[105] too, is real and can be engaged

---

[102]The present explains *ātmāhlādamātraka* (ŚD 4.20d). The capacity of the object in question to produce delight, its *āhlādakāritva*, lies in the fact that it is able to effect purposeful action—its *arthakriyākāritva*. And this may occur because the object is established in one's self-awareness—due to its *svasaṃvedanasiddhatva*. This latter reference to this famous principle of Buddhist Epistemology (which also, of course, was adopted into the Pratyabhijñā) thus may be understood here to explain Somānanda's reference to the *ātman* in *ātmāhlādamātraka*.

[103]The water is real in the dream—no mirage, e.g., appears in the dream—and it can produce *arthakriyā* in the dream. And though the action in the dream does not produce any causal efficacy in the "real world" of the waking state, it does, however, have an effect inasmuch as it is established in one's self-awareness, is *svasaṃvedanasiddha*: it renders an experience of delight or satisfaction in the knower.

I here accept a variant reading of *abhrāntatvād*, which is attested in G, J, $S^{2a.c.}$, S^{3}, and S^{5}. D, $S^{2p.c.}$, P, R, and $K^{ed.}$ record *bhrāntatvād* (line 130 of the present edition), though D deletes a now illegible *akṣara* prior to *bhrāntatvād*. I suspect the presence of *bhrāntāpi* (line 130 of the present edition) influenced the copyists, some of whom may have intentionally changed *abhrāntatvād* to *bhrāntatvād* (as may well have happened in D).

Kupetz (1972: 145) interprets the compound *vāstavasvapnajala* differently than I have, understanding it to refer to both "real and/or dream water." I understand it to refer to "real water-in-a-dream."

[104]Thus, an "erroneous" dream of drinking water produces a real delight in the agent. Here, Utpaladeva is deploying Dharmottara's understanding of right or correct knowledge to make the claim that the water that is real in a dream is not deceptive. Dharmakīrti at NB 1.1 makes clear that actions that produce rewards are preceded by correct cognitions: *samyagjñānapūrvikā sarvapuruṣārthasiddhir iti tad vyutpādyate*. "The accomplishment of all human goals is preceded by correct knowledge [*samyagjñāna*]; therefore, this [correct knowledge] is discussed in detail (here in the *Nyāyabindu*)." Dharmottara comments on this passage by saying the following (see NBṬ, pp. 17–18): *avisaṃvādakaṃ jñānaṃ samyagjñānaṃ loke ca pūrvam upadarśitam arthaṃ prāpayan saṃvādaka ucyate. tadvaj jñānam api pradarśitam arthaṃ prāpayat saṃvādakam ucyate*. Ratié (2007: 351, fn. 78) translates the passage as follows: "'Right knowledge' is a knowledge which is not deceptive [*avisaṃvādaka*]. And in the world (as well), (someone) who makes (us) reach an object that (he) has first shown (to us) is called 'trustworthy' [*saṃvādaka*]. Accordingly, the knowledge also which makes (us) reach an object that (it has previously) shown to us is called 'trustworthy'." She concludes (ibid.), "Right knowledge is therefore defined as that which is not later contradicted by another cognition, and which effectively brings about the effect that we are expecting from it, i.e. which has 'causal efficacy' (*arthakriyā*)." (Cf. Ratié 2011a: 134, fn. 56.)

Utpaladeva's argument here in a sense stretches the limits of this definition by allowing something similar to what Dharmakīrti allows of inference: while inference on the latter's view may furnish information that can produce causal efficacy, what is offered in the inference, being conceptual and bound in language, is constructed and not truly real. Utpaladeva here offers a similar analysis of some types of perception, such that perceptions of objects that have no corresponding reality in the world of everyday transactions or activity (*vyavahāra*)—and in this sense are "erroneous"—may nevertheless be counted as non-deceptive. In this case, the real effect is satisfaction in the knower, even though the action is "illusory," which can be taken to illustrate precisely a "false" cognition that is wished for (*iṣṭa*) and has a real effect even while ultimately constituting a kind of *bhrānti*.

[105]*Tat* (line 132) here refers presumably to the *arthakriyāsamarthatva* of both the alloyed coin and the dream-water.

in activity [*vyavahārya*].[106] Therefore, the invalidating state is not found in the mundane activity, either.[107]

4.21cd-22

atha ced deśabādho vā taddeśe rajataṃ na hi
4.22. yatra kāle sarajato deśo 'bhūt sa gatas tadā
kālāntareṇa deśo 'sau kā bādhā bhinnakālayoḥ

Now, if you instead argue that the locus is invalidated, because silver does not exist in that locus (where it was erroneously perceived), (we reply:) the locus containing the silver existed in a moment of time that has then passed. The locus (of the invalidation) exists after an interval of time; what invalidation is there for the two, which exist in different moments of time?

Now, if you instead argue that the locus is invalidated because the silver of one locus has been perceived as having another locus, we reply: not so.

---

[106] Here (lines 132–133 of the present edition) Utpaladeva justifies Somānanda's description of *arthakriyāsamarthatvam* as *vāstavam* (ŚD 4.21ab).

Kupetz (1972: 144–145) has translated the present passage of the ŚDVṛ as follows: ". . . Mere pleasure is the extent of the everyday world. The pleasure-causing nature of the everyday-world is proven by one's own awareness of the causal efficacy of an object. Even the act of drinking may be illusory. Either dream-water or real water may be drunk, yet the satisfaction which results (in either case) is proven by one's own awareness of satisfaction and is irrefutable. The pleasure caused by false coins or dream-water, etc., is also reality of an everyday sort. Thus, there are no grounds for denial in the everyday-world."

[107] Utpaladeva's commentary is here reminiscent of what he says at ĪPK (and ĪPKVṛ ad) 2.3.12: *arthakriyāpi sahajā nārthānām īśvarecchayā | niyatā sā hi tenāsya nākriyāto 'nyathā bhavet* ||. "Causal efficiency itself is not intrinsic to things, since it is determined by the will of the Lord. Thus a thing may not be said to be different because it does not possess a certain efficiency." (Translation Torella's.)

The corresponding passage of the ĪPKVṛ, reads as follows: *ullekhaghaṭādīnāṃ bāhyārthakriyāvirahe 'pi ghaṭāditaiva, asvābhāvikatvāt tasyā īśvareṇa pratyābhāsaṃ niyamitāyāḥ* "Objects, such as the jar etc., when imagined do not lose their nature as a jar etc., even if they lack the ability to produce external effects, because this capacity is not intrinsic to their being (*asvābhāvikatvāt*), since it is determined by the Lord for every single manifestation." (Translation Torella's.)

See also Abhinavagupta's summary of both in his ĪPVV (vol. 3, p. 151, lines 5–9): *arthakriyāpīti sā tāvat svarūpaṃ na bhavatīty uktam, asvarūpabhūtāpi ca na sahajā ananyāpekṣā īśvarecchāniyatyapekṣaṇāt. tena tasyā akaraṇān nānyatvam ity avastutvaṃ, vastvantaratvaṃ vā bhavitum arhatīti sūtrārthaḥ. ullekhā eva ghaṭādayas teṣāṃ bāhyasya svalakṣaṇasya yā arthakriyā tayā virahe 'pīti vṛttyarthaḥ.* In these passages, the term *ullekha* should be understood to refer to a sort of mental image, much in the manner of *samullekha* at, e.g., ĪPK 1.6.11, about which see Ratié 2011a: 426, fn. 138: "Le *samullekha* est imagination au sens d'une activité de production d'images mentales: le substantif est formé à partir de la racine *likh*-, « dessiner »."

Clearly, then, the present verses and commentary wish to redefine the notion of causal efficacy or *arthakriyā* as defined by their Buddhist interlocutors. (Torella 1994: 170, fn. 26 also notes that the Buddhists would object to the Śaiva notion, articulated at ĪPK 2.3.10-11, that the internal and external nature of a manifestation is essentially the same.) As Somānanda himself said at ŚD 4.20cd-21ab, the true capacity for causal efficacy is measured by the degree to which the *ātman* is delighted. There must be an agent, in short, whose *arthas* or goals are served if there is to be *arthakriyā*.

The locus that is the resting place of the silver[108] existed in a moment of time that is no longer present at the moment when the silver that is to be invalidated is cognized.

Therefore, the invalidation is performed by an invalidating cognition.[109] And, in this way, it is not the case (that any invalidation of the locus occurs), because the two loci of silver exist in different moments of time.

To explain: The moment of the (cognition of) silver, which appears in one locus, has (already) passed at the moment when (the cognition of) silver for (what in fact is) mother-of-pearl (occurs); and, for that reason, (Somānanda asks:) what invalidation is there, since, given the temporal difference, there is no incompatibility of the difference of loci?[110]

4.23

4.23. jñānāntareṇa jñānaṃ tadvirodhād atha bādhyate
na bādho bhinnakālatvāt prāktanasyāpy abhāvataḥ

---

[108] K[ed.] reads *sa rajatāśrayo* at line 138 of the present edition, and all the manuscripts I have examined for the edition record the same *akṣaras* here (excepting D[a.c.], which reads *saṃrajatāśrayo*). I have conjectured that *sa* should be eliminated, it being likely to have been the silent addition of a scribe/copyist who wished to match the wording of the commentary to that of ŚD 4.22a. The appearance here of *sa* in the nominative appears to me to be highly unlikely, because its presence would muddle the syntax of Utpaladeva's commentary, given the use of the relative pronoun (*yasmin*, line 138 of the present edition) in the passage in question. Yet, to read *sarajatāśraya* (understanding *sarajata-* as a lemma) produces an awkward compound. Reading *rajatāśraya* alone suggests that Utpaladeva offered an elegant gloss of *sarajata*; and Utpaladeva has modified the language of the *mūla* in other ways, as well, in his explanation of ŚD 4.22ab. (Utpaladeva replaces *yatra kāle* with *yasmin kāle* and *gata* with *nāsti*, here, for example; and, indeed, this kind of rephrasing is not uncommon in the ŚDVṛ.) James Reich suggested to me that it is possible, too, that Utpaladeva had written . . . *sarajato rajatāśrayo* . . . , with the reading witnessed here being the result of haplography. While this is possible and a very intriguing suggestion, I in the end have judged it likelier that Utpaladeva would not have been so mechanical in recording his gloss and would rather have spoken in the manner suggested by my conjectural emendation.

[109] The argument is that the *deśa* (in consciousness—see the ŚDVṛ at footnote 93) of one cognition cannot be invalidated by way of a cognition in another, because they are temporally separated. Thus, it is not possible that the locus of an earlier cognition of silver may be invalidated by a subsequent cognition that silver is in fact mother-of-pearl, because a temporal difference separates the loci (in consciousness) of the two cognitions of silver. The appearance of the latter does not nullify the fact of the appearance of the former.

[110] Simply put, Utpaladeva and Somānanda reduce the question of the disparity of the loci (in consciousness) of silver to one of a difference in the temporal locations of the respective cognitions.

It is at least worth pondering whether *tathā hi śuktikārajatakāle 'nyadeśarajatakālo gataḥ* (line 140 of the present edition) has been interpolated into the text. It may once have been a marginal note that was inadvertently incorporated into the ŚDVṛ. For (a) it essentially (if somewhat awkwardly) replicates what was said earlier in the commentary, (b) it serves as an explanation for what Utpaladeva meant in the immediately preceding sentence, and (c) the commentary would cohere as a whole and would read as a comprehensive explanation of the *mūla* without it. We must note, however, that working somewhat against this proposition is the fact that all the manuscripts of the ŚDVṛ examined for the present edition include this passage of text.

Objection: The cognition is invalidated by a subsequent cognition, since they are (mutually) incompatible.[111] (Reply:) There is no invalidation (in this instance), because the preceding [cognition] itself occurs in a different [i.e., earlier] moment of time, (and there is no invalidation because the prior cognition disappears naturally,) not because it ceases to exist.[112]

Objection: The cognition of silver is invalidated, i.e., made to cease, by the cognition of mother-of-pearl, because they are incompatible, this in turn because it is with respect to the very same real thing that the cognition of silver and the cognition of mother-of-pearl occur.

Reply: Not so. It is not tenable that a difference (in the two cognitions) regarding the one real thing occurs simultaneously.[113] On the contrary, because there is a sequence (of the two cognitions), there is no incompatibility (thereof, just as there is not, e.g.,) of milk and thick, sour milk,[114] this because the preceding[115], which was seen (earlier), ceases by disappearing from sight naturally, not because it ceases to exist.[116]

---

[111] ŚD (and ŚDVṛ ad) 4.21cd-22 queried the disparity between two loci of two cognitions of silver. (See, esp., the ŚDVṛ at footnotes 109 and 110.) Somānanda's and Utpaladeva's reply was that a temporal difference precluded the possibility of invalidation on the basis of the apparent incompatibility of the two loci (in consciousness). The present passage records an opponent's objection that seeks to overcome the temporal problem by claiming that two cognitions, though appearing sequentially, may be said to be mutually incompatible.

[112] Following Utpaladeva, I here read the negative particle (*na*, ŚD 4.23c) twice, once with *bādha* and once with *abhāvataḥ*. (In fact, one could read it a third time, understanding it to reply to the opponent's objection with "not so.")

The present rendering of ŚD 4.23cd follows Utpaladeva's commentary and differs from one presented by me in Nemec 2012: 229, fn. 13. Particularly given what Somānanda says at ŚD 4.24ab, however, the rendering of Nemec 2012 is very possibly more true to Somānanda's intended meaning. In that earlier publication, I translated as follows: "Now, if you argue that the cognition (of silver) is invalidated by another cognition [i.e., by that of mother-of-pearl], since it is incompatible with it, (we reply:) there is no invalidation since the preceding [cognition] itself no longer exists given that it occurs in a different [i.e., earlier] moment of time." This interpretation does not invoke the *satkāryavāda* in the manner that Utpaladeva does and instead emphasizes the momentariness of cognitions in a manner that echoes Dharmakīrti's formulations, precisely what Somānanda addresses at ŚD 4.24 and following. Indeed, Utpaladeva may well be reading into Somānanda's text, here, with his interpretation of *abhāvataḥ* (4.23d).

[113] Thus, the present objection examines the problem of two incompatible cognitions that occur *in the same locus*.

A note recorded in Kaul's edition (1934: 157, fn. 1) explains *yugapadanyathātvam ayuktam*) (found in Utpaladeva's commentary at lines 145–146 of the present edition). The same note is recorded in the margin of D at the bottom of folio 156r. It reads as follows: *yugapadanyathātvam ayuktaṃ, na hi śuktikājñānena*(em.; *śuktijñānena* DK[ed.]) *rajatajñānaṃ bādhyate svasmin viṣaye ātmani ca svarūpe dvayor jñānayor niṣṭhitayor viśrāntayor anyonyaṃ virodhasyābhāvāt. atha parasparaparihāra eva viruddhayor yugapaddvayoḥ, tarhi sarveṣāṃ jñānānāṃ virodhād bādhyabādhakabhāvasya niṣṭhaiva na labhyeti sutarāṃ satyetaravibhāgasya vilopa āyātaḥ.*

[114] On the proper translation (into French) of the term *dadhi* see Ratié 2011a: 96, fns. 158 and 159.

[115] That is, the preceding entity (i.e., milk in the present analogy), or the preceding cognition (i.e., that of silver where only mother-of-pearl exists).

[116] This is to say, of course, that Utpaladeva makes use of a standard exemplar of the *satkāryavāda* in explaining the non-incompatibility of the pair of cognitions in question. See also, especially, ŚD (and ŚDVṛ ad) 4.56cd-57ab.

4.24

4.24. sahānavasthitir nāsti virodhaḥ prāgvināśataḥ
anyonyaparihāro vā jñānājñānātmakaḥ sthitaḥ

The incompatibility that is impossibility of (the) co-presence (of mutually distinct entities) [*sahānavasthiti*] does not exist (here), due to the destruction in an earlier moment (of the prior cognition, before the subsequent cognition arises); nor does a mutual exclusion exist, one of awareness and the absence of awareness.[117]

Even the incompatibility that is the impossibility of (the) co-presence (of mutually distinct entities) does not exist (here); for when it comes to the cognitions of silver and mother-of-pearl,[118] a cognition that on account of its being momentary has been destroyed in an earlier moment cannot be made to cease by another [cognition], as cold becomes arrested by heat.[119]

In addition, there is no incompatibility that is of the nature of mutual exclusion, one consisting of awareness and the absence of awareness . . . of existence and non-existence. . . .[120]

---

[117] One must read the negative particle (*na*) with the second half-verse as well as the first, and I have translated as such.

[118] I here emend the text (line 151 of the present edition) to *rajataśuktikā* from *rajataśukti*, the latter being the reading of K[ed.] and of every manuscript examined by me. We see elsewhere a slip from *śuktikā* to *śukti* in the transmission of the text, despite the clear distinction of the two in Utpaladeva's commentary (in one place, at least, viz., at ŚDVṛ ad ŚD 4.17-18, line 116 of the present edition). See, on the one hand, for example, manuscript D at line 144 of the present edition (which reads *śuktijñānaṃ* for *śuktikājñānaṃ*); or the marginal note of D (quoted at footnote 113), which is recorded at the bottom of folio 156r. of that manuscript and cited in K[ed.]. (Note, on the other hand, the use of the term *śukti* synonymously with *śuktikā* at, e.g., ĪPK and ĪPKVṛ ad 1.7.12, cited at footnote 95.)

[119] The distinction here enumerated is one that involves what Bandyopadhyay labels "factual contradiction," which Dharmakīrti distinguishes from what Bandyopadhyay labels "logical contradiction." See NB 3.74: *dvividho hi padārthānāṃ virodhaḥ.* "Opposition between objects is of a double kind." A "factual contradiction" is found, according to Dharmakīrti, in the impossibility of the co-presence of two things *(sahānavasthāna)*, as with heat and cold. See NB 3.75: *avikalakāraṇasya bhavato 'nyabhāve 'bhāvād virodhagatiḥ.* "When (one fact that) has duration (as long as) the sum-total of its causes remains unimpaired, and it (then) vanishes as soon as another, (the opposed,) fact appears, it follows that both are incompatible. . . . " The example Dharmakīrti furnishes is that of heat and cold, further indicating that Utpaladeva (so too Somānanda) has him in mind here. See NB 3.76: *śītoṣṇasparśavat* : ". . . just as the sensations of heat and cold." (The translations here quoted are Stcherbatsky's, for which see Stcherbatsky [1932] 1993, vol. 2: 187.)

I address this matter in Nemec 2012: 230–232. Cf. Bandyopadhyay 1988: 229–232 for a treatment of the categories of contradiction conceived by Dharmakīrti.

[120] The present refers to a second type of incompatibility conceived by Dharmakīrti, that of "logical contradiction," viz., the existence of mutually incompatible natures (*parasparaparihāra*) such as existence and non-existence (*bhāvābhāvavat*). See NB 3.77: *parasparaparihārasthitalakṣaṇatayā vā bhāvābhāvavat.* "There is also (opposition between two facts) when their own essence consists in mutual exclusion, as between the affirmation and negation (of the same thing)." The translation here quoted is Stcherbatsky's, for which see Stcherbatsky [1932] 1993, vol. 2: 192.

4.25-26

4.25. ajñānatve parijñāte tadā syāt svavirodhitā
ajñānatve svabhāvena virodhaḥ kena vāryate
4.26. naivam atra svabhāvatve virodho bādhanātmakaḥ
sa vivekadṛśā jñeyo na svabhāvena kutracit

If an absence of awareness (in the cognition) were observed, it would be incompatible with itself at that time.[121] If the absence of awareness (in the cognition) were to exist by its (very) nature, by what could the incompatibility be averted?[122] In this way, there is no invalidating incompatibility here in the fact that it has that nature (as cognition).[123] That [invalidating incompatibility] can be known by way of a discriminating knowledge (of distinction), nowhere by the nature (of the cognitions).[124]

The commentary breaks off at this point and is lost from this point up to Utpaladeva's treatment of verses 4.30cd and following. *Bhāvābhāvayoḥ* would probably have been read with what once followed it, and therefore I have translated it with surrounding ellipses.

[121] That is, the cognition would be incompatible with itself at the time when the absence of awareness were perceived of it. Thus, we should understand Somānanda here to explain his objection to the possibility, brought to question at ŚD 4.24cd, that a cognition has a double and mutually self-contradictory nature, one that is aware and not aware.

[122] Alternatively, *svabhāvena* could be read syntactically with both what precedes it *and* what follows it: if it is by its very nature that the cognition is possessed of *ajñānatva*, then the contradiction is with this nature, so by what could it be averted?

[123] Simply, there is no "logical contradiction" or *parasparaparihāra* in the nature of the *jñāna*.

[124] This apparently means that the *virodha* is known only intellectually, not by virtue of the nature of the phenomena in question. Yet, while here suggesting that the incompatibility may be known by way of some "discriminating knowledge" (*vivekadṛś*), Somānanda also explicitly states that all *vikalpa*s are real, this at ŚD 4.27ab and following. What must be meant is that such a knowledge, like the distinction of "erroneous" from correct cognitions (and as is suggested at ŚD 4.7cd-9), serves the purposes of the everyday world. Note also that Utpaladeva at ŚDVṛ ad ŚD 4.17-18 suggests that no conceptual understanding of an invalidation (of the sort exemplified for example by understanding "it is mother-of-pearl (I saw), it is not silver") creates any actual invalidation or contradiction of cognitions.

N.B.: K$^{ed.}$ records ŚD 4.25-31 in a single block quotation. The edition prepared for this volume does the same, due to the absence of any surviving commentary to separate the ŚD verses in question; but the present translation divides them into four groups based on the concerns they address and the apparent structure of the argument. First, ŚD 4.25-26 deal with the nature of "logical contradiction" as it relates to cognitions, as we have seen. Following this, ŚD 4.27-29ab address the nature of incompatibility as it relates to *vikalpas*, concluding that everything, all of it appearing in consciousness, is equally real. (ŚD 4.29ab presents itself as a concluding statement, one that has parallels at ŚD 4.5, 4.47, 4.51ab, 4.60ab, 4.77, 4.93ab, 4.100ab, 4.119ab, and 4.123ab.) I understand a new concern to be addressed beginning with ŚD 4.29cd, that of the unity of the cognition with its object. Finally, at 4.30cd-31 Somānanda's attention turns to addressing the theory of a realist opponent, a Naiyāyika-Vaiśeṣika, who understands the object of cognition to be of a composite nature and ontologically different from the consciousness that knows it.

4.27-29ab

4.27. tathā sarvavikalpānāṃ satyarūpatvadarśanāt
garuḍādiśarīreṣu viṣabhūtāpahārataḥ
4.28. pratiṣṭhādevakarmādidhyānādiphalayogataḥ
satye 'pi na phalaṃ dṛṣṭaṃ kvacid rājñātisevite
4.29. tasmād avasthitaṃ sarvaṃ sattvaṃ cidvyaktiyogitā

So too for all conceptions, because we observe that their nature is real;[125] for, (to argue by way of analogy,) poison is counteracted and evil spirits are concealed in the bodies of Garuḍa and others;[126] (and,) (again to argue by analogy, this is so) in consequence of the (fact that) results (are produced) in the (external rites, viz., the) installation (of an image in a temple), the worship of the gods, etc., and in (the internal practices, viz.,) visualization, etc.[127] (And yet:) No result is seen anywhere, even in what is real, when

---

[125] Incompatibility (*virodha*) was said at ŚD 4.26 to exist for cognitions only insofar as one has a discriminating knowledge (*vivekadṛś*) of the same. Here, Somānanda says that the same applies to all conceptions or *vikalpas*. This is to say that I understand ŚD 4.27a to mean the following: *tathā sarvavikalpānām api sa bādhanātmako virodho vivekadṛśā jñeyaḥ, na svabhāvena kutracit.*

[126] Just as Garuḍa's body may ingest (and counteract) poison, and just as possessing spirits may be contained in the bodies of others, so also may *vikalpas* be contained in Śiva, even if they convey what could be conceived of as erroneous, or "poisoned," information. Thus, any invalidating incompatibility among *vikalpas* must be known through an analysis of them, not by virtue of their very natures.

Note that *-apahārataḥ* here conveys two meanings, referring both to the neutralizing of poison and the concealment of spirits in the bodies in question. Reference to this pair of concerns, poison (*viṣa*) and demonic possession by a *bhūta*, is commonly attested and addressed in a pair of genres of tantric texts, the Bhūta and Gāruḍa Tantras, as is well known. In a personal communication (via email, January 3, 2017), Professor Michael Slouber tentatively confirmed my sense that Somānanda here is implicitly referring to the idea that Garuḍa can eat or consume poisons, handling them by digesting them, and he furnished the following references to the same.

Garuḍa is said to eat poison/snakes at KKGU 6.53 (for which see Slouber 2016: 159 and 228). Another reference to Garuḍa eating snakes may be found at *Saṃhitāsāra* 138, which Slouber edited in his M.Phil. thesis at Hamburg University, 2011 (pp. 47–48). I here quote that Prakrit verse, as emended by Slouber, his Sanskrit reconstruction of the verse, and the same author's translation of the same: *phaṇamaṇiṇaā visajalaṇadūsahā palaagajjaphukkārā | haraladdhamaṇūṇāseṇa kavaliā viagaṇāheṇa ||*. (*Chāyā*:) *phaṇamaṇināgā viṣajvalanaduḥsahāḥ pralayagarjaphūtkārāḥ | haralabdhamanunyāsena kavalitā vihaganāthena* || 138 ||. "Nāgas with jewels in their hoods, unbearable because of the burning of their venom, hissing like the thunder at the end of the cosmos, are devoured by the Lord of Birds whose installation (*nyāsa*) [was done] with formulas obtained from Hara."

A mantra following KKGU 31.59 (Slouber 2016: 273) indicates that Bhagīśvara (whom Slouber suggests is "probably a goddess even though this name is masculine," because the *mantra* also refers to her as Mahāśabarī) is told to eat poison. Finally, Khaḍgarāvaṇa (Bhairava) is said to eat evil beings at KKGU 11.27. (This citation is unpublished but may be found in NGMPP manuscript no. B25/32, folio 58r2: *grasate duṣṭasattvāni*). I am grateful for Michael Slouber's help in understanding this passage of the ŚD and for furnishing these parallel textual references.

[127] What apparently is meant is that these rituals and practices, which need not be performed by one who knows Śiva, nevertheless prove to be efficacious if engaged, and thus find use in the world. Analogously, *vikalpas*, too, are efficacious and are not unreal, even if they, like such rituals and practices, are only conventional in nature.

it [i.e., the real entity] is overindulged by (even) the king(, for example).[128] Therefore, everything exists as that which is real, what is the state of being associated with manifestation in consciousness.

4.29cd-30ab

yatra yatrāsti satyatvaṃ tatrāsti śivarūpatā
4.30. vyatireke na yujyeta vijñānaṃ hi ghaṭādiṣu

Śiva-nature(, in turn,) is present wherever reality is present;[129] for consciousness would not concentrate upon pots, etc., if there were a separation (of that which is real from Śiva-nature).[130]

On the conventional nature of such practices according to Somānanda, see Nemec 2011: 44–50; on his understanding of the nature of *vikalpas*—real, but less than fully developed—see ŚD 4.13cd-14. Cf. ŚDVṛ ad ŚD 4.19-21ab. Finally, see the introduction to the present volume.

[128] As I understand it, the point made here stands in contrast to what has been said about *vikalpas*, which in the immediately preceding half-verse were validated on an analogy with the fruitfulness of actions such as image installation and *dhyāna*. There, the point was that such in fact extraneous acts are nevertheless efficacious. Here, the inverse proposition is made: even what is "fully" real or substantial is of no use to those who foolishly engage with it. Thus, Somānanda suggests, one's understanding—discriminating insight—is determinative, not the supposed but ultimately unreal dualism that separates real entities from "unreal" ones.

The interpretation offered here depends on what I consider to be a very tentative conjectural emendation: I propose *rājñātisevite* (ŚD 4.28d) where K[ed.] reads *ajñānisevitāt*, T records *rājño [']tisevitāt*, and C (partially supporting T) reads *rajño visevitāt*. I had also considered the possibility of emending to *ajñānisevite*, "when it is tended to by one who is ignorant," but this relies too heavily on the reading of K[ed.], which may be the product of a silent emendation of Kaul.

[129] I accept the reading of ŚD 4.29cd as attested to in T, which reads *yatra yatrāsti satyatvaṃ tatrāsti śivarūpatā* for K[ed.]'s (unmetrical) *yatra yatra tatra tatra satyatvaṃ viśvarūpatā*. In particular, I accept the reading attested by T (and C) of *śivarūpatā* for K[ed.]'s *viśvarūpatā*, because I recognize a parallel in what is here stated with what has been said, already, at ŚD (and ŚDVṛ ad) 4.6-7ab and 4.7cd-9, especially 4.7cd-8ab. Utpaladeva's commentary clarifies that the latter of these ŚD passages declares that even what are conceived of as erroneous cognitions are able to be manifested in consciousness (i.e., they are possessed of *cidvyaktiśaktatā*), which in turn guarantees that they are real (*sattva*) and therefore are possessed of *śivatva*. Here, a similar pattern of thinking is in evidence, that of *satyatva* being conterminal with *śivarūpatā*, the former being a matter of the entities in question being associated with a manifestation in consciousness (*cidvyaktiyogitā*). This reading also allows for a more cogent interpretation of what follows, for which see below, especially footnote 130.

Note also that while the replacement of *śivarūpatā* with *viśvarūpatā* may be explained as a scribal error by metathesis, the manuscripts also record Utpaladeva referring to the *viśvarūpa* of Śiva-nature at ŚDVṛ ad ŚD 4.32-33ab, though I there emend to *śivarūpa*, as well. (See footnote 151.) Somānanda, however, would probably not object to the concept of *viśvarūpatā* being coupled with *satyatva*, for he says at ŚD 5.105 that all entities are omnipresent: *sarve bhāvāḥ svam ātmānaṃ jānantaḥ sarvataḥ sthitāḥ*. "All entities, being aware of their own nature, exist as all others." (See Nemec 2016: 345 for a more complete treatment of this passage.)

[130] The present passage suggests that an object perceived in consciousness, on the one hand, and the consciousness itself, on the other—what is Śiva's very nature as consciousness—cannot be (ontologically, or for that matter epistemologically) divided. This suggests, in turn, that *satyatva* and *śivarūpatā* might be understood to correspond respectively to the object cognized and the consciousness thereof, the two ultimately being mutually identified. An analysis of the perceptual process therefore

4.30cd-31

mūrtāmūrtadharmayogo ghaṭas tasya na gocaraḥ
4.31. amūrtā na ca vāṇūnām antar eva praveśitā
pratipattuḥ kathaṃ vetti ghaṭo 'yaṃ pratibhedataḥ

A pot that is endowed with (both) qualities of having a form and of not having a form would not be (able to be) an object of sense of that [consciousness](, on the one hand).[131] Neither is it the case, on the other hand, that (you may maintain that) those [objects] do not have a form.[132] The atoms (that make up pots, etc.,) enter fully into the one who perceives them.[133] How could a separation (of perceiver from object perceived) lead one to know, "this is a pot"?[134]

Mūrtāmūrtadharmayoga is a *bahuvrīhi* compound, describing a pot, e.g., as possessing a connection with qualities such as having a form and not having a form.[135] (On the one hand:) Being separated (from consciousness, ontologically and by dint of this qualitative difference in nature), it is not able to become an object of sense of that, the (very) consciousness of the pot. This is what was stated (by me) in the *Īśvarapratyabhijñā*: "the object would remain non-light as before. . ."[136] and so on.

---

proves the relationship between reality and Śiva, on this interpretation. Utpaladeva quotes a verse of the ĪPK that invokes the *sahopalambha* principle of the Vijñānavāda in the very next extant passage of the ŚDVṛ (which glosses ŚD 4.30cd-31), which also might be taken to support this interpretation. See footnote 136.

[131] The ŚDVṛ (line 168) and the standard rules of anaphora both indicate that *tasya* (ŚD 4.30d) refers to the consciousness (*vijñāna*) mentioned at ŚD 4.30b, here described by Utpaladeva as *ghaṭātman*, a consciousness of (literally "consisting in") the pot.

[132] The ŚDVṛ clarifies at line 172 of the present edition that *amūrtāḥ* (ŚD 4.31a) refers to pots, etc.: *na ca vā ghaṭādayaḥ paramāṇurūpatve 'mūrtāḥ*.

[133] As Utpaladeva explains it, this is to say that the two, knower and object known, must be mutually identified. (Note that *antar* commands the genitive, thus the declension of *pratipattṛ*.)

[134] The argument prosecuted at ŚD 4.30cd-31 engages a realist opponent, a follower of the Nyāya-Vaiśeṣika who understands objects to be of a composite nature, both having a form and not having a form. The crux of the argument is that entities that are possessed of both *mūrta* and *amūrta* qualities, as the Nyāya-Vaiśeṣika suggest of common objects in the world, could not be known by consciousness, which can only be *amūrta* and cannot make contact with what is *mūrta*. Somānanda also presses this line of argumentation at length, through an analysis of the process of cognition as his opponents understand it, at ŚD 4.100cd and following. (On the concept of *amūrtatva* in the writings of Somānanda, see Nemec 2016; Nemec 2018.)

[135] The compound analysis (*vigraha*) also suggests a *karmadhāraya* relationship for *mūrtāmūrta-dharma*.

[136] See ĪPK 1.5.2: *prāg ivārtho 'prakāśaḥ syāt prakāśātmatayā vinā | na ca prakāśo bhinnaḥ syād ātmārthasya prakāśatā ||*. "If it were not essentially light, the object would remain non-light as before; and the light is not differentiated (from the object); being light constitutes the very essence of the object." (Translation Torella's.) The relevant passage of the ĪPKVṛ reads as follows: *pramātṛsaṃjñaprakāśasvarūpatāṃ vinā yathādau ghaṭo 'sya nāvabhātas tathā jñānakāle 'pi syāt, prakāśamānatā cārthasya prakāśaḥ svarūpabhūto na tu bhinnaḥ*. As Torella (1994: 111, fn. 5) notes and

Neither is it the case, on the other hand, that (you may maintain that) pots, etc., inasmuch as they are formed of minute atoms [*paramāṇurūpatva*], do not have a form.[137] For, (on your view,) the measure of a non-ubiquitous substance,[138] or even a (simple) compatibility with (the occupying of) a physical place, is (what defines) that which has a form [*mūrti*].

Hence, (your view can only cohere if) those atoms (that make up the pots, etc.,) enter fully into the one who perceives them, (this perceiver being one) who is made of consciousness, his nature being that of Śiva. This means they are identical (with the one who perceives them). Otherwise, how could the separation (of the agent from the object he perceives) be the cause to lead him, the perceiver, to know "this is a pot"?[139] This means that he could not know it in any way at all (if perceiver and perceived were mutually distinct).

4.32-33ab

4.32. vinaikatvaṃ ca na bhavet kārakatvaṃ kadācana
śaśaśṛṅgādike nāpi syāt vibhaktyā samanvayaḥ
4.33. sarvathābhāvaśabdasya nāsty abhāvātmakaṃ kvacit

In the absence of unity, moreover, it[140] could never at any time be something that is instrumental to action, nor even could a word for that which is utterly non-existent be connected with a case-ending when

---

as is by now well known, the principle here stated has a Vijñānavāda pedigree, and is expressed in Prajñākaragupta's *Pramāṇavārttikālaṃkāra*. So, too, as Torella again notes, does the PVin declare the object and its cognition to be identical, since they are always perceived together (*sahopalambha*), as per PVin 1.55ab: *sahopalambhaniyamād abhedo nīlataddhiyoḥ*. Cf. PVV ad PV (*pratyakṣapariccheda*) 3.335 (p. 131): *tatra darśanena jñānenopādhinā viśeṣaṇena rahitasya nīlāder agrahāt tasya grahe ca nīlasya grahāt sahaiva nīladhiyor vedanād darśanaṃ nīlādinirbhāsaṃ nīlākāraṃ vyavasthitam. yat tāvan nīlādikaṃ bāhyam ity ucyate tad jñānena sahopalambhaniyamāt tadabhinnasvabhāvaṃ dvicandrādivat.*

137 In other words, in attempting to reconcile the difference between cognition and its object, it is not possible for the realist opponent to reduce an object that is understood *both* to have *mūrta and amūrta* qualities to one that is only without a form or *amūrta*, by claiming that the *mūrta* qualities thereof, being ultimately rooted in *paramāṇus*, are really *amūrta*.

138 Here, the terminology of the PDhSaṃ is used. At p. 308, lines 5–7, e.g., Praśastapāda says the following: *mūrtir asarvagatadravyaparimāṇaṃ tadanuvidhāyinī ca kriyā sā cākāśādiṣu nāsti tasmān na teṣāṃ kriyāsaṃbandho 'stīti*. "The measure of a non-ubiquitous substance [*asarvagatadravyaparimāṇa*] is that which has a form [*mūrti*], and action conforms to that; and since it [i.e., action] does not exist in ether and the rest, it follows that they are not connected to action." See Nemec 2016, especially pp. 352–354, for a discussion of this passage. The NK of Śrīdhara (p. 308, lines 14–17) explains this passage as follows: *caturṣu mahābhūteṣv ivākāśādiṣu kasmāt kriyotpattir na cintitety āha. ākāśakāladigātmanām iti. kriyātvaṃ mūrtatvena vyāptaṃ mūrtatvaṃ cākāśādiṣu nāsty ataḥ kriyāvattvam api na vidyate ity arthaḥ*. Cf., also, ŚD and ŚDVṛ ad 2.76cd.

139 The commentary indicates that the *tas* affix (A 5.3.7: *pañcamyās tasil*) of *pratibhedataḥ* is ablative in meaning and refers to what would cause the agent to know the pot as such.

140 The present refers to the pot, e.g., that could not be perceived in the absence of its identity with the consciousness that perceives it. See ŚD 4.30ab and 4.30cd-31.

referring to (an inexistent object such as) the horn of a hare, e.g.[141] **Nowhere does something non-existent exist.**[142]

What you accept, moreover, as this, the pot's performing its own function, e.g.,[143] could not exist in the absence of it being possessed of a nature that is unitary consciousness; for it is impossible for that which is insentient—that

---

[141] Cf. ĪPK 2.4.16: *ata eva vibhaktyarthaḥ pramātrekasamāśrayaḥ | kriyākārakabhāvākhyo yukto bhāvasamanvayaḥ* ||. "For this very reason, the meaning of the case endings, which has a unitary basis in the agent of knowing, is the (only) logically tenable relation that exists between things, it being referred to as the relation between action and the factors of action [*kārakas*]." (Translation an adaptation of Torella's.) See also the corresponding passage of the ĪPKVṛ: *ekapramātṛsaṃlagnas tu kriyākārakabhāvākhyo vibhaktyartho bhūmibījodakādīnāṃ samanvayo yukto na tu śuṣko 'nyaḥ kāryakāraṇabhāvaḥ*. "The connection between earth, seed, water and so on is correctly understood as the meaning of the case endings consisting in a relation between verbal action and the factors of action, depending on a single subject, and is not to be identified with some other type of 'dry' (*śuṣka*) connection such as that of cause and effect." (Translation Torella's.) Utpaladeva is likely to have referred to the same passage in his commentary on ŚD 4.42cd-44ab; see lines 248–251 of the Sanskrit edition.

Cf. also ĪPK 1.2.9-10 and the commentary thereon, as well as ĪPK 2.2.6. Note also that Kaul records a note (1934: 157–158, fn. 1) that refers the reader to ĪPK 1.7.2-3.

[142] Utpaladeva refers the reader to his ĪPK and its auto-commentaries in commenting on this passage, and in doing so probably has in mind places where he addresses Buddhist opponents. The vocabulary of his commentary here ad ŚD 4.32-33ab also evokes the thinking of Dharmakīrti and the Buddhist Epistemologists by referring (at line 182 of the present edition, e.g.) to *arthakriyākāritva*. (See the translation of the commentary and the notes thereon.) But it is very likely that Somānanda (also) had a realist opponent in mind here, possibly the same Naiyāyika or Vaiśeṣika opponent he addressed in ŚD 4.30cd-31 or possibly the work of Kumārila, given that the two passages are interwoven syntactically. To have both a Buddhist and a realist opponent simultaneously in mind, however, would not be unusual; Torella (1994: 112, fn. 6) notes that Utpaladeva was "implicitly critical particularly of the Buddhist and Kumārila theses" at ĪPK (and ĪPKVṛ ad) 1.5.2, which Utpaladeva cited in his commentary ad ŚD 4.30cd-31.

Given Somānanda's likely interlocutors in the present passage, then, it is perhaps useful to note that reference to *atyantāsattva* in Utpaladeva's commentary (line 183) echoes the language of Kumārila's ŚV (*abhāva* section) verse 4, which refers to *atyantābhāva* or total non-existence, an *abhāva* exemplified by the absence on the head of a rabbit of any low appendages that are extended and solid, these being in the form of the horns of a rabbit: *śiraso 'vayavā nimnā vṛddhikāṭhinyavarjitāḥ | śaśaśṛṅgādirūpeṇa so 'tyantābhāva ucyate* ||. (Cf. the ŚVNRĀ commentary of Pārthasārathi Miśra on the same verse: *śaśaśṛṅgādirūpeṇeti. śṛṅgasya yad asadrūpaṃ śaśamūrddhāvayavasamavetaṃ so 'tyantābhāva ity arthaḥ*.) The same term (*atyantābhāva*) is used in Bhaṭṭa Jayanta's NM, as well, in the first *āhnika*, section on *abhāva*, around verses 208*ff.* (Here, well-known Nyāya classifications of types of non-existence are discussed.) See NM (vol. 1: p. 166, lines 7–8 of the Mysore edition): sa ca *dvividhaḥ—prāgabhāvaḥ, pradhvaṃsābhāvaś ceti. caturvidha ity anye—itaretarābhāvaḥ, atyantābhāvaḥ, tau ca dvāv iti*.. . . More is said of *atyantābhāva* at verse 210ab: *sa evāvadhiśūnyatvād atyantābhāvatāṃ gataḥ* |.

Finally, note that the arguments here considered are similar to those found in ŚD 4.73cd-75 inasmuch as both deal with the possibility of speaking of unreal entities. The opponent there is a Mīmāṃsaka, and the grounds for Somānanda's objections are different there: he interrogates the problem while understanding there to be an eternal connection between word and thing (which is a Mīmāṃsaka doctrine), suggesting that the existence of such a connection is tenable only if the thing so connected is real. See below, especially footnotes 336 and 338.

[143] Reference here to the *svakāryakaraṇa* of the pot echoes what was said at ŚD 4.3ab: *svakāryaviṣaye sarvaḥ śakta eva*. The pot's "performing its own function" involves the carrying of water, for example.

which is devoid of intention—to perform (its own function).[144] This, too, has been stated (by me) in the *Īśvarapratyabhijñā* itself.[145] Therefore, everything that is real by dint of being capable of producing purposeful action has Śiva as its nature.[146]

As for that which you suppose to be utterly non-existent [*atyantāsattvena*]—the horn of a hare, for example—a word that is understood to express (such) an utter absence of existence, being used with reference to that (sort of) object, could not be connected to a case-ending(, this if the object in question were truly non-existent). This is so because, since "a horn of a hare" is understood and named (when one uses a word to refer to it),[147] (it is clear that the case-endings are used; and) the case-endings require the factors of action [*kārakas*] (in order to be deployed), and because, since the factor of action [*kāraka*] (of the *karman* or object named) is an instrumental cause of the (real) action

---

[144] This is a view expressed elsewhere by Utpaladeva. See, e.g., ĪPK 2.4.14, where he suggests something similar, namely, that that which is insentient cannot "expect," or have motivation toward, another entity: *asmin satīdam astīti kāryakāraṇatāpi yā | sāpy apekṣāvihīnānāṃ jaḍānāṃ nopapadyate ||*. "Also the relation of cause and effect conceived as 'there being this, this other is produced' (*asmin satīdam asti*) is not admissible for realities that are insentient and as such incapable of 'requiring' (*apekṣā*)." (Translation Torella's.) Cf. the corresponding passage of Utpaladeva's *Vṛtti: asmin satīdaṃ bhavatīti niyataṃ paurvāparyaṃ kṛttikārohinyudayayor akāryakāraṇayor apy astīti pūrvasya sāmarthye parasya satteti syāt kāryakāraṇabhāvaḥ, tac cāpekṣārahitānāṃ jaḍānāṃ na yuktam. etāvad etat syāt pūrvasya sāmarthyaṃ parasya sattā na caivaṃ kiñcid uktaṃ syān na ca pūrvasya sāmarthyalakṣaṇaḥ svabhāvaḥ parasattārūpaḥ.* Finally, see Torella 1994: 183, fn. 26.

[145] See ĪPK 2.4 for a discussion of the limited powers of insentient entities, in particular 2.4.14 (quoted in footnote 144). See also: ĪPK 2.4.2: *jaḍasya tu na sā śaktiḥ sattā yad asataḥ sataḥ | kartṛkarmatvatattvaiva kāryakāraṇatā tataḥ ||*. "But an insentient reality does not have this power—namely, to confer existence on something that is not. Therefore, the relation of cause and effect is essentially reduced to that of agent and object of the action" (translation Torella's); ĪPK 2.4.16 (quoted in footnote 141); and Torella 1994: 184, fn. 28.

Finally, note also that Somānanda expresses a sympathetic idea at ŚD 5.16-17ab (discussed in Nemec 2016: 348–350): *jānan kartāram ātmānaṃ ghaṭaḥ kuryāt svakāṃ kriyām | ajñāte svātmakartṛtve na ghaṭaḥ sampravartate || svakarmaṇi mamaitat tad ity ajñānān na ceṣṭanam |*. "Cognizing itself as the agent, the pot may perform its own action. If it were not aware of its own agency, the pot would not undertake an action. There would be no performance of its own action if it were not aware that it was its own."

[146] I understand *śivarūpa* to be a *bahuvrīhi* compound.

[147] Reference here is to the principle, perhaps articulated first of all in Praśastapāda's PDhSaṃ, that the *padārthas* are existent, can be named, and can be known. See PDhSaṃ (p. 16, lines 1–2): *ṣaṇṇām api padārthānām astitvābhidheyatvajñeyatvāni.* See also the NK on the same passage (p. 16, lines 3–8): *yady api dharmāḥ ṣaṭpadārthebhyo na vyatiricyante kiṃ tu ta evānyonyāpekṣayā dharmā dharmiṇaś ca bhavantīti. tathāpi teṣāṃ dharmirūpatayā parijñānārthaṃ pṛthaguddeśaṃ karoti. ṣaṇṇām apīti. astitvaṃ svarūpavattvaṃ ṣaṇṇām api sādharmyaṃ yasya vastuno yat svarūpaṃ tad eva tasyāstitvam. abhidheyatvam apy abhidhānapratipādanayogyatvaṃ tac ca vastunaḥ svarūpam eva bhāvarūpam evāvasthābhedena jñeyatvam abhidheyatvaṃ cocyate.* Jha [1915] 1982: 37 translates as follows: "Though the properties are nothing beyond the six categories, and it is these themselves that become objects and properties with reference to another,—yet, in order to show the categories in the character of *objects*, that the text refers to them as 'to all the six categories.' '*Being-ness*'—i.e., the property of existing in a particular form—is common to all the six categories; as it is the natural form of an object that constitutes its '*being*.' '*Predicatability*'—capability of being predicated or spoken of also is a form of the thing itself; as it is only the positive form of an object that, under certain circumstances, is known as 'cognisability,' and under others as 'predicatability."'

(of naming that object), it is not possible that that which is inexistent [i.e., the object or *karman*] is a factor of action (in the act of referring to said object). Therefore, existence itself, the appearance of Siva-nature, is (found) there, as well, because of the (necessary presence of a) connection (of a word) with the case-ending(, which is necessarily present) when the state of being a factor of action is present (in the form of the object that is being named, i.e., the *karman*, the "horn of a hare").[148] In reality, moreover, the very perception [*avabodha*] that a pot performs a purposeful action such as carrying water is itself what is possessed of that very nature [i.e., that of being the pot]; and a pot, e.g., if it were different from that [perception], could not succeed in acting in the manner in question.[149] This is shown (by me) in

---

[148]The argument, then, is that the *śaśaśṛṅga* itself, being the object of the action of the naming of or reference to it and therefore one of the *kārakas* of this verbal action, serves a real role in the same. This cannot be done by that which is unreal. It is evident, then, that Utpaladeva here is pursuing a sort of argument that echoes what Johannes Bronkhorst has referred to as the "correspondence principle," namely, the notion that if there is a word for a thing then a corresponding thing, which is named by the word, also must exist. (See Bronkhorst 2011, and on Utpaladeva's adoption of this principle, see especially pp. 68–70.)

What Utpladeva means by the reality of the "horn of a rabbit," however, is this, that it is a phenomenon appearing in consciousness as a form of consciousness—it is real inasmuch as everything is equally real *qua* appearing in consciousness. Its reality can lead to purposeful action and "real-world" results, for example a sense of joy in imagining the appearance of such a thing. (Indeed, as we see in what follows—at *abhāvo 'pi jñāyamāno* . . . , lines 190–191 of the present edition—Utpaladeva argues that the reality of such "non-existent" entities is confirmed by the very fact that their "non-existence" can only consist of consciousness, which is fully real.) Utpaladeva's point thus is not to say that the horn of a hare is as real as, e.g., the spots on a cow. Rather, it is that inasmuch as it is made of consciousness it is not different from any entity appearing in the world. (See footnote 150.) Compare this idea, then, with that of the water imagined in a dream, which is treated at ŚDVṛ ad ŚD 4.19-21ab. See also ĪPK 2.4.3-4.

On the *kārakas* in Pāṇini (on which this argument appears to be based), see Cardona 1974. Compare also the present passage with ĪPKVṛ ad ĪPK 2.4.16, quoted in footnote 141.

[149]As a note found at the bottom of folio 159v. of manuscript D suggests (what is transcribed into K[ed.] at footnote 4, p. 159 of that edition), the present passage is added to argue that it is not possible to dismiss the reality of "the horn of a hare" or the like on the basis of the fact that such an entity is not a real thing at all but rather is only an idea, a semantic meaning devoid of a physical or real referent. This interpretation is not possible, the note suggests, because such a position presumes that the existence of something appearing in the world is qualitatively different from the consciousness that knows it. The note reads as follows: *nanu ca śaśaśṛṅgaṃ jñāyate 'bhidīyate iti kathaṃ kriyāyogo 'tra prātipadikamātre hi vidhir ayam. na hi karmādikārakayogo 'tra saṃbhavatīti, vyavahāraś ca karmādikārakādhīna eveti kathaṃ kriyānimittatvam ity āśaṅkya vyavahāre ca yad bhāvarūpāṇāṃ kārakāṇāṃ bījabhūtaṃ tattvaṃ tat samarthayati yena bhāvābhāvarūpaṃ sarvaṃ samānam evādhyavasīyata ity āha vastutaś ceti.* "And one might object: The horn of the hare is (merely) known, named. So, how is there here a relation (of it) to an action, for this grammatical rule (regarding the use of case-endings) only concerns the nominal base (to which the case-ending is appended) [*prātipadika*] (and not a real object). Indeed, no relation to the *kāraka* of the object of an action, etc., is possible here. And, thus, the mundane activity (of speaking of the 'horn of a hare') is entirely devoid of the *kāraka* of the object of an action, etc., ('out there' in the world,) so how is this [i.e., 'object'] an instrument of an action? Having considered this doubt, moreover, one contemplates the reality in the mundane activity (of speaking of the 'horn of a hare'), which is the source of the factors of action that are the (very) natures of entities (found in the world); it is that by which everything, whether of an existent or an inexistent nature, is ascertained to be entirely alike. [Utpaladeva] says 'in reality, moreover' to express just this." (Cf. also footnote 147.)

the *Pratyabhijñā* itself, when I consider (the expression:) "there is one named Himālaya."[150]

(Thus:) Even that which is being cognized as a non-existence consists in nothing but consciousness, and since it has that nature, it is fully possessed of Śiva-nature.[151] Therefore, nowhere does something non-existent, i.e., something that is not possessed of Śiva's nature, exist in the universe.

4.33cd-34

ito 'pi sarvaśivatā sata utpattiyogataḥ
4.34. sa evāste purā tādṛkśaktirūpasvarūpakaḥ
sa eva kāryarūpeṇa bhagavān avakalpate

Everything is of the nature of Śiva for this reason, as well, because (only) that which is (already) existent can arise (as an effect). He alone is present

---

150The reference here might properly be understood to be to ĪPKVṛ ad ĪPK 2.4.20, where Utpaladeva refers to Himācala, arguing that even existence itself is a volitional action and therefore cannot be engaged by what is insentient: *jaḍasyāpy asti bhavatīty asyām api sattākriyāyāṃ bubhūṣāyogena svātantryābhāvād akartṛtvam, tena pramātaiva taṃ bhāvayati tena tena vā himācalādinā rūpeṇa sa bhavatīty atra paramārthaḥ.* "That which is insentient, for its part, cannot be the agent as regards even this action of existing—'it exists,' 'it is'—because it cannot be associated with the desire to exist, because it is devoid of (all) independence. Therefore, it is the knowing agent who causes that to exist; or, he (alone) exists in various forms such as the Himācala mountain or the like. This is what is the ultimate reality, here." (On the meaning of the compound *bubhūṣāyoga*, see ĪPVV, vol. 3, p. 252: *iyatā vṛttir ubhayathā gamitā: bubhūṣāyogena yat svātantryam, tasyābhāvāt; ayogena ca yaḥ svātantryābhāvas tata iti.* The same is cited in Ratié 2011a: 684, fn. 91. She there translates as follows: "De ce fait, la *Vṛtti* doit être comprise de deux manières à la fois—[comme signifiant, d'une part,] '[l'inerte n'est pas l'agent de l'action d'être], à cause de [son] absence de liberté, car [l'action d'être] comporte un désir d'être (*bubhūṣā-yogena*)', et [d'autre part,] '[l'inerte n'est pas l'agent de l'action d'être], à cause de [son] absence de liberté, du fait qu'[il] ne possède pas [de désir d'être] (*bubhūṣā-a-yogena*).")

It is also possible, however, that Utpaladeva here refers to his long auto-commentary on the ĪPK, the *Īśvarapratyabhijñā-vivṛti* or *-ṭīkā* (ĪPṬ), for the ŚDVṛ here precisely reads *himālayo nāmāsti* and does not refer to (what is a synonym, viz.,) *himācala*. That the term *himālaya* might have appeared in the *Ṭīkā* is perhaps suggested by Abhinavagupta's reference to the same phrase in his ĪPVV ad 2.4.20 (KSTS edition, vol. 3, p. 248, ll. 20*ff.*), where he quotes the source of this expression, the first half-verse of Kālidāsa's *Kumārasaṃbhava* (KuSaṃ), which reads as follows: *asty uttarasyāṃ diśi devatātmā himālayo nāma nagādhirājaḥ.* It therefore seems not unlikely that Utpaladeva in the ŚDVṛ here refers to a citation or allusion of his own to the same half-verse of the KuSaṃ, one that appeared in this part of the ĪPṬ; and Abhinavagupta addressed the matter as he did in the ĪPVV because of what was said in that long auto-commentary on the ĪPK. (I thank James Reich for his comments on this passage of text, which clarified my understanding of the same.)

151 *Śivarūpa* is here a *bahuvrīhi* compound. Note that I here emend to *śivarūpa eva* (line 190 of the present edition) where K$^{ed.}$ and all the manuscripts examined by me read *viśvarūpa eva.* There is some confusion elsewhere in the text of *viśvarūpa* for *śivarūpa*, specifically at ŚD 4.29d. Here, it is possible that the use of the term *viśva* in *viśvamadhye* (line 191) influenced a scribe in the course of copying the text, but it seems more likely that, as at ŚD 4.29d, the error is the result simply of metathesis. The idea here expressed is one that is repeated several times in this chapter of the ŚD and its commentary, namely, that whatever exists, inasmuch as it is manifested in/as consciousness, is Śiva. See also footnote 129.

at the beginning,[152] his nature being in the form of such a potentiality [i.e., such a potential to be manifested as an effect]; (and) he alone, the Blessed One, is fit to exist in the form of the effect.[153]

For this reason, as well, everything is of the nature of Śiva, because the collection of entities that come into existence arises only as that which is existent (prior to being produced), because it is not possible that that which has that nature (of being that which arises), what consists in an effect, is associated with unreality even prior (to its being produced) [*prāg api*], it [i.e., unreality] being incompatible (with that which is existent). And it is that [effect], in the form of a sprout, (for example,) that must be existent even prior (to being produced); (for) if, prior to being effected [*pūrvam*], the sprout is endowed with a nature that is existence, (and if it exists) in the form of a potentiality (for being effected), it will again come to exist in the form of an effect: as the sprout (itself).[154]

4.35-37ab

4.35. satkāryaṃ nopapannaṃ cet sataḥ kiṃ karaṇena yat
abhivyaktir athāsyātra kriyate sāpi kiṃ satī
4.36. kriyate hy asatī vātha satyāḥ kiṃ nopalabdhatā
vyaktyabhāvād athānantyam asatyā hānisaṃbhavaḥ
4.37. svayam evāśrite pakṣe tadvad vā vastv asad bhavet

If one argues that an effect that is existent (before the operation of its cause) is not supported by rational justification,[155] since (one may ask:) "what use is the production of that which is (already) existent?," then one (who supports the *satkāryavāda*) may reply: A manifestation

---

[152] This is to say that Śiva alone is present prior to the manifestation of the already existent effect.

[153] Ratié 2014a: 150, fn. 83 also records a translation of ŚD 4.33cd-34: "For this [following reason] as well, [namely,] because [only an already] existing [entity] can arise [as an effect,] everything is Śiva: it is [Śiva] who continuously exists (*āste*) up to now, [since he] has as his nature the form of such a power; only the Lord is fit (*avakalpate*) [for existing] in the form of the effect."

[154] In a word, this is an unmistakable articulation of the *satkāryavāda*, the doctrine, espoused by the Sāṅkhya and other schools (including the Śaiva authors of the Pratyabhijñā), that the effect is inherent in the cause.

Compare the present translation of ŚDVṛ ad ŚD 4.33cd-34 with that of Ratié (2014a: 150, fn. 83): "For this reason as well, [namely], because all the entities that arise arise only while [already] existing, due to the impossibility for that which has this nature [of arising and] which consists in an effect of being in contact with nonexistence, which is contradictory [with existence,] even before [it arises], everything is Śiva. And this very [effect] must have the form of an [already] existing sprout even before [it arises as such], if the sprout, which has as its reality existence [and] takes the form of a potentiality, exists before [and] then exists in the form of the effect consisting of a sprout."

[155] The response to this criticism—that the *satkāryavāda* is not rationally justifiable—is found at ŚD 4.37cd-43c.

of this [effect] is produced, here. (Opponent's Objection:) Is it, for its part, produced as that which (already) is existent, or as that which is not existent?[156] Now, (if you, the *satkāryavādin*, argue that it is the former, one may ask:) why is this (already) existing [manifestation] not perceived? Objection (of the *satkāryavādin*): This is the result of there being no (prior) manifestation (of this already existing manifestation). (Reply:) There is (therefore) an infinite regress.[157] (Conversely:) A (previously) non-existent [manifestation] occasions the demise of the (very) thesis on which you [the *satkāryavādin*] yourself rely. Or, in the same way,[158] the real thing (that is understood as the effect) must be non-existent (prior to its production).[159]

Now, if[160] one argues that an effect that is existent (before the operation of its cause) is not supported by rational justification,[161] since the production of that which is (already) existent is useless, then one [i.e., the *satkāryavādin*] could reply: it is not the nature of the existing [effect], but rather the manifestation of it, that is produced.

---

[156] I understand *hi* here (at ŚD 4.36a) to serve simply to fill out the meter (*pādapūraṇa*).

[157] The manifestation would not be perceived because of the fact that it had not yet been manifested; but if it needs a manifestation to be manifested, then so too does the manifestation of the manifestation, and so on ad infinitum.

[158] That is, just as the *abhivyakti* is held to be *asat*, so the same fault in the *satkāryavādins*' position could be produced if they understand the *vastu*, for its part, to be non-existent prior to its production.

[159] Utpaladeva interprets the meaning of ŚD 4.37ab in two ways. The present translation renders the first of the two. Following the second interpretation and reading *svayam evāśrite pakṣe* with what follows it (rather than what precedes it, as it is here rendered), one could translate the half-verse as follows: "Or, having resorted to the [*asatkārya*] position of your own accord (you might argue that), in the same way (as the *abhivyakti* is *asat*), the real thing (that is understood as the effect also) must be non-existent (prior to its production)." See also footnote 168.

Ratié 2014a: 146 also offers a translation of ŚD 4.35-37ab, as follows: "[Let us] consider [the following objection] (*cet*) [to the *satkāryavāda*]. The effect cannot exist [before the operation of its cause], because there is no point in the production of [that which already] exists. [If the Sāṃkhya answers]: 'But what is produced in this case is [merely] the manifestation (*abhivyakti*) of this [effect],' this [manifestation] itself, is it produced while [already] existing or while being nonexistent? If [the Sāṃkhya replies that it already exists], how is it that this [already] existing [manifestation] is not perceived? If [the Sāṃkhya opponent replies]: 'because there is no manifestation [of this already existing manifestation],' there is an infinite regress; alternatively, [if he had rather reply that this manifestation is produced while being nonexistent], this nonexistent [manifestation] is capable of destroying the thesis on which [he] himself relies: in the same way, the thing [regarded as the effect] should be [admitted to be] nonexistent [before its production]."

[160] A marginal note in D (folio 161r.) is recorded above *yadi sadrūpaṃ* (line 204 of the present edition), which is not replicated in the notes to the KSTS edition. It reads, simply: *naivam ity atra sambandhaḥ*.

[161] Utpaladeva here indicates that *satkārya* (ŚD 4.35a) is a *karmadhāraya* compound: *sadrūpaṃ kāryam*.

(Response of the opponent of the *satkāryavāda*:) That, too, is not tenable, since one may ask whether that [manifestation], for its part, is produced as something that is (already) existent or is not (already) existent.[162]

Regarding the former, if one [i.e., the proponent of the *satkāryavāda*] argues that the manifestation is existent (prior to its production), then (the one arguing against the *satkāryavāda* may ask:) what is produced (by the cause)? Why is it that the effect is not perceived (prior to its production)?[163]

Objection (of the proponent of the *satkāryavāda*): Although the manifestation exists (prior to being manifested), the effect (of it) is not perceived because there is no manifestation of the manifestation (at that time).[164]

Reply (of the opponent of the *satkāryavāda*): A manifestation (therefore) is (necessarily) produced of the (second) manifestation, as well. Thus, since the aforementioned fault applies there [with the second manifestation], as well, there is an infinite regress.[165] And, hence, the perception of the effect that has (here) been put into discussion cannot be completed.[166]

If (the proponent of the *satkāryavāda* instead argues that) a (previously) non-existent manifestation is produced,[167] then (the opponent of the *satkāryavāda*

[162] A parallel argument was already put forward in the *Nyāyabhūṣaṇa* of Bhāsarvajña, for which see NBhūṣ, p. 459: *kāryasyābhivyaktiḥ kāraṇena kriyata iti cet, sā yady asatī kriyate, tato 'sat kāryaṃ syāt. satī ced abhivyaktis tadavasthaṃ kārakānarthakyam. abhivyakter apy abhivyaktiḥ kriyata iti cet, sāpi satī syād asatī vety aparyavasānam.* The same was cited in Ratié 2014a: 145, fn. 68 and translated by her as follows: "If [the Sāṃkhya opponent explains] that [it is] the manifestation (*abhivyakti*) of the effect [that] is produced by the cause, [we answer the following:] if this [manifestation] is produced while being nonexistent, then let [us] admit that the effect is nonexistent [before the operation of the cause]. [But] if the manifestation [already] exists [before the operation of the cause], the same uselessness of the factors of action ensues. If [the opponent replies] that this manifestation is produced by another manifestation, might this other [manifestation] be existing [before the operation of its cause] or not?—[thus there is] an infinite regress."

[163] If the effect (*kārya*) exists prior to its manifestation, then why is the *abhivyakti* not apparent prior to the application of its cause?

[164] I here understand *abhivyakter* (line 207) to be read twice, with both what precedes and what follows it.

Ratié (2014a: 147) records *abhivyaktrabhāvāt* for what is found in K$^{ed.}$, viz., *abhivyaktyabhāvāt*. All the manuscripts examined for this edition support the reading of K$^{ed.}$. Ratié does not explain the difference between the reading she records and what is printed in the published edition, even while she normally does so when proposing to emend the text. Apparently the change is the result of a mistranscription. Anyhow, she translates as follows: "If [the Sāṃkhya opponent replies that] although this manifestation [already] exists, because there is no manifesting agent (*abhivyaktṛ*) [in the form of a cause, we] do not perceive the effect [that is this manifestation], then it is through [another] manifestation that this manifestation is produced;. . ."

[165] Utpaladeva here glosses *ānantya* (ŚD 4.36c) with a synonym, *anavasthā*.

[166] Or, perhaps, "And, hence, the perception of the effect that has (here) been commenced (to be produced). . ." Because the manifestation of the pre-existent effect is the product of a manifestation that, in turn, is the product of another manifestation, and so on ad infinitum, the first effect cannot reach its completion and be seen.

[167] This is to say that the proponent of the *satkāryavāda* suggests that the manifestation or *abhivyakti* is *not* existent prior to its production. What is implied is that he does so by understanding the manifestation to be an exception to the rule; for (it is implied), he simultaneously argues that the *kārya* or effect *is* existent prior to its production, even while the *abhivyakti* is not. In what follows,

may reply): when a (previously) non-existent [manifestation] is produced, the fault arises that this destroys the view upon which you, yourselves, rely.

Or,[168] in resorting to the (view that there is a) production of that which is non-existent in order to overcome the *regressus* ad infinitum that exists with respect to the manifestation, (you, the supporter of the *satkāryavāda*, might argue that) the real thing—the sprout, for example—like the manifestation, is also fully non-existent (before it is manifested).[169] (If so, the opponent may ask:) What(, then,) is the point of this (maxim of a) half-aged woman [*ardhajaratīya*][170]—the effect is existent (prior to its manifestation)?[171]

Utpaladeva (following Somānanda) will consider the possibility that for the *satkāryavādin* it is not only the *abhivyakti* but also the real thing (*vastu*) that is to be effected that is inexistent before its production. See also, especially, footnote 170.

N.B.: A footnote appearing in K[ed.] (p. 162, fn. 4) reads as follows: *ekatra sad anyatrāsad iti hāniḥ, sā ca na sarvathā bhāva evety arthaḥ*. This is a verbatim transcription of a marginal note appearing in D (folio 161v.), with the exception that Kaul's transcription adds the connective particle (*ca*), which is not found in D.

[168] Utpaladeva identifies two ways in which the *satkāryavāda* might fail. The first was articulated in the immediately preceding passage, where it was suggested that the *satkāryavādin* might argue that the manifestation or *abhivyakti* is produced without being existent prior to its manifestation (that is, it is *asatī*). On that interpretation, Utpaladeva suggested that *svayam evāśrite pakṣe* (ŚD 4.37a) should be read with *hānisaṃbhavaḥ* (ŚD 4.36d).

In the present passage, Utpaladeva understands ŚD 4.37a to be read with what follows it: he suggests that the *satkāryavādin* might himself (unintentionally or thoughtlessly?!) resort to the *asatkārya* view, that not just the manifestation, but also the effect, is inexistent prior to being produced. The advantage of doing so is that there would not have to be a manifestation of a manifestation, and hence no infinite regress, because the entity produced would not exist at all until manifested, and therefore there would be no need to explain the fact that it was not visible prior to its manifestation. Of course, as noted the cost is steep: it requires abandoning the *satkāryavāda*.

[169] I here punctuate following *asad eva* (line 212); K[ed.] does not, but a pair of manuscripts does, for which see the notes in the present edition.

[170] The term here used, *ardhajaratīya*, refers to the maxim of a "half-aged woman" (*ardhajaratīya-nyāya*), old in some respects, young in others. By analogy, the argument used here is thought to be half-committed to one point of view, half to another, incompatible one. See Ratié 2014a: 147, fn. 72, where she translates with "half-senile" and traces the analogy, via Apte's gloss of the term (Apte [1890] 1959: Appendix E, s.v. *ardhajaratīyanyāyaḥ*), to Vardhamāna's *Gaṇaratnamahodadhi* 3.195: *yathā strī na taruṇī ślathastanatvāt kṛṣṇakeśatvān na jaratī vaktuṃ śakyate tadvat siddhāsiddhaṃ prayojanam*. "Just as a woman cannot be said to be young because her breasts are flaccid and cannot be said to be old [either] because her hair is black, so also the signification is that of what is (both) accomplished and unaccomplished" (translation Ratié's, with minor modifications).

What this means in the present context is that Utpaladeva here understands the opponent of the *satkāryavāda* to accuse the *satkāryavādin* of having given up on his partial adaptation of the *asatkārya* position (applying it only to the *abhivyakti* or manifestation and not the *vastu* or real thing that is manifested). See footnote 167; cf. footnote 168.

[171] Ratié (2014a: 147) has translated ŚDVṛ ad ŚD 4.35-37ab as follows: "But let us consider (*yadi*) [the following objection]. The effect cannot have an [already] existing nature [before the operation of its cause], because the production of an [already] existing [thing] is useless (*viphala*). If [the Sāṃkhya replies that] it is not the [very] nature of the existing [effect] that is produced, but rather, the [mere] manifestation of this [effect], this is not correct either for the [following] reason: should this [manifestation] be produced while [already] existing or while being nonexistent? Among these [two options,] if [the Sāṃkhya replies that this manifestation is produced] while [already] existing, then what is produced [by the cause]? [And] how is it that the effect [which is this manifestation] is not

4.37cd-42ab

naivaṃ yasmāt tāṃ vihāya sarvatrānyatra satkriyā
4.38. ity abhyupagamo 'smākaṃ naikenānyatra tulyatā
kalpyā vaiśeṣikāṇāṃ hi kartṛtaiveśvare sthitā
4.39. tadvan na kiṃ pṛthivyāder bauddhe jñānam avasthitam
svānyaprakāśakaṃ nānyat tadvad anyan na kiṃ bhavet
4.40. bāhyaṃ rūpādi jalpanti pramāṇaṃ codanaiva te
niyamād dharmaviṣaye tasmān naikena tulyatā
4.41. bahūnāṃ kalpanīyātra na ca vā vyatirekataḥ
vyaktiḥ sthitā padārthānāṃ ghaṭo vyakto 'bhidhīyate
4.42 tasmāt sa eva vyaktyātmā na vyakter vyatiriktatā

(Reply:) It is not so,[172] since we exclude (only) that[173] and accept that an existing [effect] is otherwise produced in every case. No (global) conformity to one [principle] is imagined elsewhere.[174] Indeed, according to the Vaiśeṣikas (the) agency (for creating the universe) is established in Īśvara alone.[175] Why is it not the same for (*dravyas*, or substances, such as) the earth, etc.? In Buddhist [doctrine], a cognition is established to be that which illumines both itself and another [i.e., the object]; another does

perceived? If [the Sāṃkhya opponent replies that] although this manifestation [already] exists, because there is no manifesting agent (*abhivyaktṛ*) [in the form of a cause, we] do not perceive the effect [that is this manifestation], then it is through [another] manifestation that this manifestation is produced; so because the previously mentioned fault occurs here again, there is an infinite regress (*ānantya* = *anavasthā*), and therefore the perception of the effect, which is the topic of this discussion, cannot occur. But [if the Sāṃkhya opponent had rather reply that] this manifestation is produced while being nonexistent, then since [according to him] there is a production of [that which is] nonexistent, there follows the refutation of the thesis on which [he] himself relies. [That is to say:] alternatively, if, in order to get rid of the infinite regress regarding this manifestation, [the opponent had rather] rely on [the thesis that the manifestation] is produced [while being] nonexistent, [then] just as this manifestation, the thing too [that is manifested]—a sprout for instance—is necessarily nonexistent; [therefore] what is the point of this [maxim of] a half-senile woman (*ardhajaratīya*): 'one must admit that the effect is [already] existing'?"

172 That is, it is not the case that *satkāryavādin* destroys his own position by understanding the *abhivyakti* or manifestation to be inexistent prior to its manifestation, because he does not claim that the real thing, or *vastu*, is thus. He adopts, in other words, the position Utpaladeva has described immediately above as that of the maxim of the half-aged woman (*ardhajaratīya-nyāya*), or one leaving him open to the criticism of incompatibility in argument. It is to counter this claim to incompatibility that Somānanda has the *satkāryavādin* now speak.

173 Here, *tām* in *tāṃ vihāya* refers to the manifestation or *abhivyakti*.

174 *Anyatra*, "elsewhere," (ŚD 4.38b) refers to other philosophical systems.

175 I read the emphatic particle (*eva*) out of the regular word-order (*bhinnakrama*), understanding it to modify *īśvara* and not *kartṛtā*, this following Utpaladeva's commentary (line 225 of the present edition): *tathā hi vaiśeṣikeṣv īśvara eva viśvakartā.*

On the well-known Vaiśeṣika doctrine of Īśvara as the cause of the ordered universe, see, e.g., Candrānanda's commentary ad VS 1.1.3: *īśvaraś ca sādhitaḥ tanubhuvanādīnāṃ kāryatayā, ghaṭādivad, buddhimatkartṛkatvānumānena.*

not. Why doesn't another [entity] that is external (to consciousness)—a visible object, for example—do the same? They [i.e., the Mīmāṃsakas] speak about[176] the injunction being of necessity the only valid means of knowing the *dharma*.[177] Therefore, one should not imagine that a (global) conformity of the many [means and objects of knowledge] to one [principle] exists here [in our system](, either).[178] And, alternatively, it is not the case that the manifestation exists by way of the things (manifested by it) being different (from it). The pot is said to have been manifested(, for example). Therefore, it is that [pot] that is the nature of the manifestation;[179] the manifestation is not different (from it).[180]

---

[176]The verb here used, *jalpanti*, can communicate a somewhat negative sense, suggesting a "prattling on." It does not seem, however, that Somānanda here wishes to condescend to his Mīmāṃsaka counterparts. Note, too, that several manuscripts (D, $S^{2a.c.}$, S^3, and S^5) here read *kalpanti*.

[177]One must understand an implied *iti* to encase what is said by the Mīmāṃsakas, for reference to *codanā* as a *pramāṇa* cannot be taken to be the object of the verb.

[178]Ratié (2014a: 156) has translated ŚD 4.37cd-41a as follows: "It is not so, because we acknowledge that with the exception of this [manifestation], in all other [cases], there is [only] a production of an [already] existing [effect]. [And] in other [systems,] one does not have to postulate that one [given principle] must equal[ly apply to everything]. For according to the Vaiśeṣikas, agency is established with respect to the Lord [only, but] why is it not so for the earth and other [substances]? In the Buddhist [system], cognition is established to be that which manifests itself and [something] else, [but] why is it that no other [entity] external [to consciousness], such as visible thing, can be so? [And] the [Mīmāṃsakas] claim that necessarily, the only means of [valid] knowledge as regards *dharma* is [Vedic] injunction[, and not perception for instance.] Therefore in this [system of ours as well,] one does not have to postulate that one [given principle] equal[ly applies] to the various [means and objects of knowledge]."

[179]I here emend the text, proposing *vyaktyātmā* for *vyaktātmā* (ŚD 4.42a). Only one manuscript supports this emendation, and it does so only partially as the reading therein is corrupt: C erroneously reads *vyaktyātā* where all the other manuscripts and the KSTS edition read *vyaktātmā*. Nevertheless, it is not difficult to imagine a scribe recording *ktā* for *ktyā*: they are somewhat similarly written in both *devanāgarī* and *śāradā* scripts and, more importantly, one can imagine a scribe influenced by the presence of other, surrounding occurrences of *kta* (*vyakto* at 4.41d; *vyakter* at 4.42b). Not only is it more logical to understand C's erroneous reading to derive from *vyaktyātmā* than from *vyaktātmā*, but the meaning of the text also is better comprehended if read as emended. For the point Somānanda here is making is not that the nature of the object—the pot, in this instance—is manifested (*vyaktātmā*), what was said already at ŚD 4.41d; rather, Somānanda here wishes to say that the object itself is identical with, is the nature of, the manifestation, i.e., is *vyaktyātmā*. (Note that it is also possible to understand the term to be a *bahuvrīhi* compound, meaning it would suggest that the thing itself has as its very nature the manifestation.) The point is that what is here said identifies the pot and the manifestation; it does not suggest merely that the latter makes the former evident. I apply the same conjectural emendation to the lemma recorded in the commentary (line 236), as well, for which see footnote 188.

[180]While it is possible to read *vyakteḥ* (ŚD 4.42b) in the ablative, Utpaladeva understands it to be in the genitive: he glosses (at lines 236–237 of the present edition) with *na tu vyakter vyatiriktāyā asatyāḥ karaṇam*.

Ratié (2014a: 157) has translated ŚD 4.41b-42ab as follows (reading *vyaktātmā* where I conjecture *vyaktyātmā* and understanding *vyakteḥ* at SD 4.42b to be declined in the ablative, though she understands its gloss to suggest it is declined in the genitive, for which see footnote 190): "And this manifestation (*vyakti*) does not exist apart (*vyatirekataḥ*) from things: [it is] the pot [that] is said to be 'manifested'; therefore it is the very [pot] that has its nature manifested, [and it] is not distinct from manifestation." Finally, note that Ratié conjectures that one should read *sā* for *vā* at ŚD 4.41b, an emendation that, on the one hand, is plausible. On the other hand, Somānanda repeatedly uses the

(Reply:) It is what you have said that is not tenable, since we accept only this much, that any other effect is fully existent (prior to being manifested) apart from that—i.e., apart from the manifestation. Indeed, not all ideas [*artha*] in a (given) philosophical system are in every case equal (in their application).

For instance, the Lord alone is the creator of the universe according to the Vaiśeṣikas, while a substance such as the earth is not. In Buddhist philosophy, the cognition alone illumines itself and the other [i.e., the object of cognition], while a visible object, for example, does not. They, i.e., the Jaiminīyas [= the Mīmāṃsakas], say the injunction alone is of necessity the means of knowing *dharma*:[181]

"*Dharma* is an aim that is defined by injunction (alone)"; (MīSū 1.1.2.)

by contrast, direct perception, e.g.,[182] is not.

Therefore, even as regards another [school of thought](, let alone our own), one should not commit the fault of engendering a (global) conformity for the many means of knowledge or objects of knowledge, which share a common characteristic (such that they are respectively able to be classed together as means or objects of knowledge), to a single [principle] that is conceived of as a distinct characteristic (belonging not in common to all such entities equally, but to one among them uniquely).

Thus, all objects are effects that are fully existent;[183] yet, the manifestation is an effect that emphatically is not existent (prior to its production), just as (the Mīmāṃsakas maintain that), unlike the injunction, none of the other *pramāṇas* are means of knowing *dharma*; (or) just as, (according to the Vaiśeṣikas,) unlike the substance that is the Lord, no (other) substance at all, the earth, etc., is the cause (of the creation) of the universe.[184]

---

same formulation (i.e., *na ca vā*), elsewhere. For example, he does so at ŚD 2.55d, 3.88c, 4.9d (which, the commentary suggests, cannot be emended away), 4.31a, 4.43d, 4.87c (= 4.86c in K[ed.]), and at 6.96c. A marginal note of D (folio 164v.), recorded in K[ed.] at p. 164, fn. 3, also attests to the same.

[181] See footnote 177.

[182] *Ādi* here of course refers to the other *pramāṇas* accepted by the Mīmāṃsā.

[183] All objects are effects that are existent prior to their production, with the exception of the kind of effect that is the manifestation (*abhivyakti*), as Utpaladeva says next.

[184] Compare the present translation of the commentary with that of Ratié (2014a: 156–157), who has rendered ŚDVṛ ad ŚD 4.37cd-42ab to this point as follows: "That which you have stated cannot be legitimately held, because first of all, with the exception of this manifestation, we admit that [any] other effect is indeed [already] existing. For in each system, every point does not have to be equal[ly valid with respect to everything]. To explain: among Vaiśeṣikas [it is admitted that] only the Lord is the creator of the universe, whereas a substance such as earth and so on is not [admitted to be such an agent]. In the Buddhist system it is cognition that manifests itself and [something] else, [namely its object], whereas a visible thing for instance is not [considered to be capable of thus manifesting itself and something else]. The Mīmāṃsakas claim that necessarily, only [Vedic] injunction is a means of [valid] knowledge with regard to *dharma*, [when stating] '*dharma* is whatever beneficial matter known through [Vedic] injunction [alone]', whereas [they do not consider] perception and so on as [valid means of knowledge regarding *dharma*]. Therefore for [any] other [system] as well as [for ours,] one should not commit the fault of equal[ly applying] to the various means and objects of knowledge, which have one [particular]

And there is also a rational justification to this; it is not a mere opinion.[185] Thus, the manifestation, first of all, does not exist apart from the (manifested) object, because it is not perceived as such.[186] And one (also) speaks (of the two) without (making) any distinction whatever (between them).[187] For instance: the pot is said to have been manifested, without being distinguished from the manifestation.

Therefore, the thing itself is the (very) nature of the manifestation,[188] and it is produced while (already) existing[189] (prior to its manifestation); and it is not the case(, therefore,) that a manifestation that is different (from the real thing it makes manifest) is produced as that which is not existent (prior to its production).[190]

---

characteristic, one single [principle] regarded as having a different characteristic. Therefore [we can rightly state that] all things are effects while existing [before the causal operation, and that] nonetheless manifestation is an effect that does not exist [before the causal operation], just as [in the Mīmāṃsakas' system, the fact that Vedic] injunction is [a means of valid knowledge] with respect to *dharma* does not [entail that] the other means of knowledge [should also be valid with respect to *dharma*, or] just as, [in the Vaiśeṣikas' system, the fact that] the substance that is the Lord [is the cause of the universe] does not [entail that] a substance such as the earth should [also] be the cause of the universe."

[185] The translation here offered of *upapattir api cātrāsti, nābhyupagamamātram* is that of Ratié 2014a: 157, fn. 102. In other words, as Ratié there summarizes it: ". . . the argument does not amount to some arbitrary opinion, since Somānanda endeavours to justify it by explaining that the *abhivyakti* of the pot does not exist apart from the pot: *one cannot consider it as an effect distinct from the effect that it manifests*, because when a pot is produced, there is no production of a manifestation of the pot that would be nonexistent before the operation of the pot's cause and distinct from the pot, so that the opponent cannot ask whether the manifestation, regarded as an effect, is in turn existing or not before the operation of the cause, for the simple reason that there is no such effect as a 'manifestation of the pot' that would exist independently of the effect 'pot'" (emphasis Ratié's).

[186] Here, then, reference is made to Dharmakīrti's famed argument that the invariable co-presence of the perception of an entity and the appearance of the same indicates that the two are identical. See PV (*pratyakṣapariccheda*) 3.335: *darśanopādhirahitasyāgrahāt tadgrahe grahāt | darśanaṃ nīlanirbhāsaṃ nārtho bāhyo 'sti kevalam* ||. "Because there is no apprehension of an [object that would be] devoid of the particularity that is perception; and because there is an apprehension [of an object] when there is an apprehension of its [perception, one must conclude that] it is perception that bears the aspect 'blue'; there is no external object that would exist independently [of its cognition]." (Translation Ratié's). See Ratié 2010a: 439–446 (esp. pp. 443–444). Cf. Ratié 2011a: 345–366 and Ratié 2014a: 158, fn. 105.

[187] An appeal to how one normally speaks about the entity in question thus serves to justify an understanding of the same.

[188] I here emend the text (line 236), conjecturing one should read *vyaktyātmā* where all the manuscripts and K$^{ed.}$ read *vyaktātmā* (with the exception of S^2, which reads *vyaktātmāt*). About this emendation, which is of a lemma, see footnote 179. Note, also, that it is possible to understand the term in question not to be a *tatpuruṣa* compound (as here translated) but a *bahuvrīhi* compound: the thing itself "has as its nature the manifestation."

[189] D (folio 164r.) records a gloss that is not reproduced in the notes of the KSTS edition: it reads *vyaktiḥ* (presumably meant to be synonymous with *abhivyakti*) and is written above *san kriyate* (line 236 of the present edition). A problem arises with this note, however, if it is understood, as it must be, to gloss the subject of the present clause (*sa ca san kriyate*): *vyakti* is feminine in gender, while both *sa* and the present participle *san* are masculine in gender and therefore must be understood to refer to the *padārtha*, the "object" or "thing," and not the manifestation.

[190] Thus, I understand Somānanda and Utpaladeva here to explain the theory that the *abhivyakti* is *asatī* (what is an exception to the *satkāryavāda*) by simultaneously identifying it with the *padārtha* it

4.42cd-44ab

dīpena kriyate vyaktir ghaṭādeḥ sata eva vā
4.43. yathā sataḥ kriyā vyaktir vyakteḥ sattve tathā kṛtiḥ
ekenāparatulyatvān na ca vāsata udbhavaḥ
4.44. kim āśritya pravartante tadabhāvasvarūpataḥ

Alternatively,[191] a lamp produces the manifestation of a pot, for example, that is fully existent (prior to its manifestation). Just as there is an action that is the manifestation of that which is existent (prior to its being illumined), so also a manifestation is produced (only) when it is existent (prior to its production),[192] because the one is the same as the other.[193] And, by contrast, it is not the case that something arises that is not existent (prior to its production). (For, we may ask:) Do they [i.e., the factors of action or *kārakas*] act having first resorted (to some object)?

---

manifests, which is existent prior to its being manifested. If the object is not yet manifested, the nature of the manifestation (as not-yet-existent) stands as an exception to the *satkāryavāda*, inasmuch as it is not existent until it is manifested; yet, inasmuch as the manifestation *is* the object—the pot, e.g.—it *is* existent prior to its manifestation, because the object that is seen is itself thus existent.

See also Ratié 2014a: 155–160, who has reviewed this argument at some length, and note that she has there translated this final passage of ŚDVṛ ad ŚD 4.37cd-42ab, as follows (reading *vyaktātmā* where I emend with *vyaktyātmā*): "For sure, such a manifestation [of e.g. the pot] does not exist apart from the object, because it is not perceived thus [i.e. apart from the object]. And [we] talk and act (*vyavahāra*) without [making] any distinction [between them]. To explain: the pot is said to be manifested, without being distinguished from manifestation. Therefore it is the thing itself that has its nature manifested. And this [thing] is 'produced' while already existing, but there is no production of a manifestation that would be nonexistent [before the operation of the cause and] distinct [from the object]."

191 The alternative is one of offering a different way of explaining the *satkāryavāda*. In the previous, the manifestation was said to be new, but identical with the object it manifests, the *padārtha*, and therefore existent prior to its production. Here, the manifestation is explained by way of an analogy with light that illuminates an already-present and existent object, which suggests that manifestation is comprised of an action that makes apparent an entity that existed prior to said action. The two explanations are thus compatible, according to Somānanda and Utpaladeva.

192 Kaul (1934: 164, fn. 2) records a note that suggests that the present passage argues that the basis of existence and manifestation is the same, because they have the same nature: *tena nātra sattvavyaktyor bhinnam adhikaraṇaṃ samānasvarūpatvāt*. The same note appears verbatim in the top margin of manuscript D, folio 164v.

193 This is to say that the manifestation is the same as the entity that is manifested. Alternatively, one could render *ekenāparatulyatvāt with*, "because the other [i.e., the manifestation] accords with the one [principle, viz., that of the *satkāryavāda*]" and read it with what follows it. (Ratié 2014a: 158 offers this interpretation, for which see footnote 195.) Utpaladeva apparently authorizes this interpretation when he says the following (line 245): . . . *iti sarvatra tulyaḥ satkāryavādaḥ*. My rendering interprets the passage differently in that I read ŚD 4.43c with 4.43a-b, because Utpaladeva's ŚDVṛ also explains the passage in this manner, at lines 245–246 of the present edition: *yataḥ padārthena satā kāryeṇa vyakter api tadabhinnāyās tulyatvam*. Thus, Utpaladeva indicates that as he understands it Somānanda intended both meanings.

For the nature of that [object that they are to effect][194] would be one of non-existence.[195]

This is absolutely not new;[196] for a lamp produces the manifestation of, e.g., a pot that is fully existent (prior to its manifestation).[197] Thus, it is the thing that is acted upon.[198] And, hence, just as the action is referred to as the manifestation of, e.g., the pot that is existent (prior to the production thereof), so also the manifestation, for its part—which, being the (very) form of the thing, is fully existent (prior to its production)—is produced by, in the present example, the lamp; or, (one may understand the phenomenon per the following analogy:) the form of the sprout (that is existent prior to its manifestation, is produced) by the seed, for example. Therefore, the doctrine that the effect

---

[194] See the commentary below, where the referent of *tat* in *tadabhāvasvarūpataḥ* is explained (line 253): *viṣayasya ca kāryasya tadānīm abhāvasvarūpatvāt.*

[195] A note furnished by Kaul (1934: 164, fn. 1) suggests the present passage is meant to show that the appearance is not different from the entity itself and to entertain an objection to the same. The note is also recorded in the bottom margin of manuscript D, folio 164r.: *tad evaṃ ". . . na ca vā vyatirekataḥ | vyaktiḥ sthitā padārthānāṃ . . ." ity uktam. athedānīm anayoḥ sāmānādhikaraṇyam eva sādhayati dīpeneti. nanu ca yadi sann eva, tarhi tasyābhivyaktir nāma kim. athābhivyaktyā svarūpalābhas tarhy abhivyaktir evāstu, kṛtaṃ satkāryavādenety*(K^ed.^; *satkāryavedetya* D) *ata āha dīpeneti.* "Thus, in this way [Somānanda] has (already) said the following [ŚD 4.41b-c]: '. . . And, alternatively, it is not the case that the manifestation exists by way of the things (manifested by it) being different (from it). . .' Next, he now establishes, at ŚD 4.42cd-44ab [referred to by quoting the *pratīka*], that the two [i.e., the object and the manifestation thereof] have precisely the same substrate [*sāmānādhikaraṇya*]. Moreover, he says what he does at ŚD 4.42cd-44ab [again referred to by quoting the *pratīka*] to respond to the following objection: 'If it [i.e., the object] definitely is existent (prior to its manifestation), then, why, pray tell, the manifestation of it? (And:) If (you argue that) it [i.e., the object] acquires its nature by means of the manifestation, then it can be nothing other than the (non-preexistent) manifestation (and therefore only comes to exist when it is manifested), so be done with the *satkāryavāda*."'

Ratié 2014a: 158 has translated ŚD 4.42cd-44ab as follows: "Alternatively, [let us consider that] a lamp produces the manifestation of e.g. a pot that [already] exists; [in such a case,] just as [one can say that] there is a production that is a manifestation of the existing [pot,] in the same way, [one can also say that] there is a production of [its] manifestation, while [this manifestation already] exists. And [thus] since [in fact] the single [principle of the *satkāryavāda*] equal[ly applies not only to the effect but also] to another [thing, namely manifestation,] there is no arising whatsoever of a nonexistent [effect in any case. Otherwise,] with respect to what would [the causes] occur, since their [very] nature [of causes] could not exist [when they are supposed to act]?" Ratié 2014a: 158, fn. 106 further indicates that Eli Franco suggested the (sensible) emendation of *vyakteḥ* for *vyakte* (ŚD 4.43b) and that the same is confirmed in one manuscript examined by her (apparently the one cited as manuscript J in the present edition). Yet, one must note that the same reading was recorded in the errata of K^ed.^, at p. 3 of the *śuddhyaśuddhipattram*, which is appended to the published edition. Finally, Ratié also proposes to read *na caivāsata* for *na ca vāsata* at ŚD 4.43d. On the reading *na ca vā* see footnote 180.

[196] That is, the production (*karaṇa*) of the manifestation, mentioned in the last line of the ŚDVṛ ad ŚD 4.37cd-42ab (at lines 236–237 of the present edition, which reads in part: *sa [padārthaś] ca san kriyate, na tu vyakter vyatiriktāyā asatyāḥ karaṇam*), is not new (*apūrva*). On the meaning of this sentence, see also Ratié 2014a: 159, fn. 107.

[197] Just as a lamp illumines a pot that exists prior to the light reaching it, so too does the manifestation (*abhivyakti*) make perceivable an entity that existed prior to its manifestation.

[198] In other words, to produce the *abhivyakti* is to produce the *padārtha*. They are one and the same, and thus the principle that the effect is existent prior to its manifestation is preserved.

is existent (prior to the operation of its cause) applies equally everywhere.[199] This is so because the manifestation, for its part, not being different from it, is identical with the effect—the object that is existent (prior to being produced).[200]

The manifestation, moreover, is (nothing other than) the fact of (the thing in question) being manifested in consciousness, what is identity with the manifesting consciousness (itself);[201] it is the presence in various forms of the manifesting light of consciousness [*citprakāśa*], which is fully existent (prior to its manifestation), is beginningless and endless, (and) is the sprout, for example.[202] Thus has the proponent of the doctrine of manifestations come to express the doctrine of the (pre-)existent effect.[203]

If, moreover,[204] an effect that is not existent (prior to its manifestation) were to arise, then (we would ask:) the factors of action [*kārakas*]—do they act, i.e., are they employed, they having first resorted (to), i.e., having first aimed at (some

---

[199] See footnote 193.

[200] Chaturvedi has suggested that the present passage expresses the idea that the cause is identical with the effect in the Śaiva system. See Chaturvedi 1986: 143. Kaul 1934: 165, fn. 1 transcribes a marginal note of D (folio 165r.) that suggests the present argument is similar to what is expressed at ĪPK 1.7.1: *yā caiṣā pratibhā tattatpadārthakramarūṣitā | akramānantacidrūpaḥ pramātā sa maheśvaraḥ ||*.

[201] Compare the present passage to what appears at ŚDVṛ ad ŚD 4.6-7ab, which reads in part as follows (at lines 43–45 of the present edition): *sphuradrūpatā hi sattā. sphuradrūpatā ca prakāśamānatā. tataś ca jaḍatā tāvan nāsti. prakāśamānatā hi prakāśābhedaḥ. prakāśaś cānapahnavanīyaḥ sarvapratiṣṭhārūpaḥ paramārthaḥ*. In particular *prakāśamānatā hi prakāśābhedaḥ* offers a parallel to what is here said, viz. *prakāśamānatā prakāśātmatā*.

Finally, a footnote recorded in K^ed.^ (p. 165, fn. 1) that transcribes a marginal note of D (folio 165r.) adds into its transcription the term "*ata(s)*" in the following: *nanu ca yadi sad eva kāraṇe kāryaṃ tarhi keyaṃ vyaktir nāmety ata āha*. The term does not appear in D. Also, *de* of *sad eva* is on my reading illegible in D.

[202] Ratié reads *aṅkurādi* (line 247) with what precedes it (for which, see footnote 203). I read it with what follows it, if somewhat tentatively, on the basis of interpreting the passage in light of a parallel expression found in the ŚDVṛ ad ŚD 4.6-7ab, for which see footnote 201.

[203] Ratié (2014a: 159–160) has translated the present passage of the ŚDVṛ as follows: "[In fact] this [production of the manifestation] is not new at all. For [when we say] 'the lamp produces the manifestation of e.g. an already existing pot,' [in fact] it is the thing itself[, i.e. the pot,] that is acted upon [and therefore constitutes the effect of the action]. And so just as [one can say that] there is a production called the 'manifestation' of an existing [effect] such as the pot, in the same way, [one can say] that there is a production by a lamp for instance of the manifestation itself, which[, insofar as it is regarded as an effect, merely] consists in the thing [itself, so that just as the thing itself, it] already exists; or [one can say that there is a production] by a seed for instance of [a manifestation] consisting in a sprout. Therefore the thesis that the effect exists [before the operation of its cause] is equal[ly applied] to everything, since even manifestation, insofar as it is not distinct from the [object that it manifests], is equivalent with the [already] existing effect that is the thing. And manifestation is the fact that the sprout for instance is manifest, [i.e.] the fact that [it] consists in the manifesting [agent] (*prakāśa*); it is the existence (*avasthāna*) in this or that form of the manifesting [agent] that is consciousness, [a manifesting agent] that is devoid of beginning or end (*anādinidhana*), [i.e.] that [always] already exists—this is how the proponent of manifestation (*abhivyakti*) expresses the thesis that the effect exists [before the operation of its cause]."

[204] A footnote in K^ed.^ (p. 165, fn. 2) reproduces a marginal note of D (folio 165v.). K^ed.^, however, includes an error of transcription: it reads *dhūmābhāsa iti* where D records *dhūmāvabhāsa iti*. In addition, K^ed.^ does not witness the following, which appears at the conclusion of the same marginal note in D: *atra ca praśūdhījaṃ (= praśuddhijaṃ (?))pūrvoktaṃ tena tenāvasthānam iti*.

object)?[205] (For:) The cause-effect relation is brought about [*pravartana*],[206] (as I have explained it) in the *Īśvarapratyabhijñā*, by virtue of consisting in the (mutual) connecting of the factors of action of the action (in question),[207] just as an object [*rūpam*] is acted upon [*codita*] at the beginning of (the act of) cooking, for example.[208]

Alternatively,[209] "do they act having first aimed at (some object)" means with respect to which object would they [i.e., the *kārakas*] have a capacity (to act)? For if the object does not exist (prior to its manifestation), the capacity (of the *kārakas* to act) would be inapplicable, because it [i.e., the capacity] depends on (the existence of) an object (on which to act); and (he asks with respect to which object the *kārakas* would be able to act) because the object—which is the effect—would be one whose nature is non-existent at that time.[210]

4.44cd-45ab

ghaṭāntaraṃ pūrvadṛṣṭam ākalayyātha ceṣṭanam
4.45. *anyenānyasya kalanāsaṃbhavād aticitratā*

Objection (of the *asatkāryavādin*): There is an effort made (on the part of the *kārakas*), after they first take hold of that which is different from the pot (that they will produce), (and) which is seen (to exist) prior (to the production of that pot). (Reply:) The one [object, i.e., the effect] is utterly

---

[205] Here, I understand Utpaladeva to suggest that *kim* (ŚD 4.44a) is an indeclinable particle of interrogation that marks a question. In what follows, he will interpret *kim* as the accusative singular of the interrogative pronoun and the object of the absolutive. See footnote 209.

The problem is that the *kārakas* could not be connected to anything on which they could act, this in order to create the effect in question when that entity is, at the point of the act in question, utterly inexistent. A parallel argument was given by Utpaladeva at ŚDVṛ ad ŚD 4.32 (lines 183–187 of the present edition): *yad apy atyantāsattvenābhimataṃ śaśaśṛṅgādi tatrārthe vartamānasya sarvathaivābhāvavācitvena matasya śabdasya vibhaktyā yogo na syāt. śaśaśṛṅgaṃ jñāyate 'bhidhīyate ceti kārakāśritatvād vibhaktīnām asataś ca kārakatvāyogāt kriyānimittatvāt kārakasya. tasmāt tatrāpi vibhaktiyogena kārakatve sati sattaiva śivatākhyā*. There, the claim *in nuce* is that there must be something real (*qua* the fact of its appearing in consciousness) that is associated with even an unreal entity such as the horn of a rabbit.

[206] The verbal noun here used, *pravartana*, echoes the present active verb (*pravartante*) used in ŚD 4.44a.

[207] A footnote in K[ed.] (p. 165, fn. 3) reproduces a long marginal note of D (folio 165v., left-hand margin). K[ed.], however, witnesses a variant in its transcription from D. K[ed.] reads in part . . . *tadā bhaved bhavadukter avasaro 'sataḥ kāryotpāde*, where D records the following: . . . *tadā bhaved bhavadukter avasaro 'sataḥ kāryetyādeḥ*.

[208] What is said here at lines 250–251 of the present edition—. . . *kāryakāraṇabhāvasya kriyākārakasaṃbandhamānatveneśvarapratyabhijñāyāṃ pravartanaṃ pākādyārambhe rūpam iva coditam*—is similar to what is expressed at ĪPK 2.4.16 and, in particular, the corresponding passage of the ĪPKVṛ. Renderings of these passages are offered at footnote 141.

[209] Here, Utpaladeva understands *kim* (ŚD 4.44a) to be the neuter interrogative pronoun declined in the accusative and the grammatical object of the absolutive *āśritya*. Previously, he understood it to be an indeclinable particle of interrogation that marks a question, for which see footnote 205.

[210] Here, *tadānīm* refers to the moment of the production of the effect in question.

amazing, because it is impossible for it to be made with the other [i.e., with that which is different from the pot].[211]

Objection: There is an effort made—work, or a capacity—belonging to the factors of action [*kārakas*], this with their making of a sprout, (e.g.,) which is seen (to exist) prior (to the production of that new effect), i.e., which was produced prior (to the production of the effect, in the form of that which is different from the effect and on which the *kārakas* act in order to produce that effect, the seed that is acted upon to make the sprout in the present example).

Reply: That [effort made, i.e., work or capacity] is not suited to seeds or the like, because, since they are not sentient, they are devoid of (any capacity of) taking hold (of anything).[212] Even where there is a sentient cause,[213] a potter for

---

[211]The logic of this argument is this, that if the effect is inexistent prior to its production, then whatever is accessed in the production of the effect is utterly different therefrom. The one cannot result materially from the other, then, in that they are held to be mutually utterly distinct.

The present pair of half-verses responds directly to the concern raised by Somānanda at ŚD 4.44ab, namely, the question of how an *asatkāryavādin* can claim that the *kārakas* may act when that which they are to produce is not yet existent. Here, it is the nature of the entities that produce the effect that is examined. The nature of the role of the object to be effected will be examined in the immediately following passage of the ŚD.

It is possible, in ways outlined in the notes to the translation of Utpaladeva's commentary (especially at footnote 214), that a paronomasia (*śleṣa*) may here be intended. At the least, Utpaladeva elicits a double-meaning from the present ŚD passage.

Finally, Kaul (1934: 166, fn. 4) records a marginal note found in D (folio 166r.), which explains the present verse in the following manner: *nanu kim idam ucyate viṣayasya tadānīm asattvāt kasmin viṣaye teṣāṃ sāmarthyam iti. yadi ceyanmātram evātra sādhyaṃ yat pūrvam api sāpekṣatvam iti, tadā siddham etat, yataḥ pūrvotpannam apy aṅkurādy asti tat sāpekṣatvena sarvaṃ siddhyatīty āśaṅkyāha ghaṭāntaram ityādi.* "[Somānanda] says what he does at ŚD 4.44cd-45ab [referred to by quoting the *pratīka*] after having considered the following objection (of the *asatkāryavādin*): what are you saying when you enquire as to with respect to which object they [i.e., the *kārakas*] would have a capacity (to act), because the object (as you understand it) is not (yet) existent at that moment (when it is about to be produced)? If, moreover, only this much is to be proven here, namely, that they [i.e., the *kārakas*] are dependent (on, or in other words related to, an object that is actually present) even prior (to the production of the effect in question), then (we object by pointing out that) so much has been established (already). For the sprout, for example, exists, it also having been produced (in the form of something else, i.e., the seed) prior (to the action that results in its production); thus, everything is proven (to be produced), because of the dependence (of the *kārakas* on entities different from but capable of leading to the production of the *asat* effect)."

[212]The *asatkāryavādin* opponent makes the claim that factors of action (*kārakas*) may produce results even as that which they will effect is not yet existent, because by working on or with what is present but different from the effect, they may bring about the intended result. Utpaladeva's response is to argue that this requires an intentionality on behalf of some maker of the effect. Causality cannot be intrinsic to the entities in question, because the effect is not innately associable with what causes it, effect and causes being mutually utterly distinct. In what follows, Utpaladeva considers the viability of the *asatkāryavādin's* position in relation to sentient causes, a potter producing a pot, for example. In doing so, he evidently elicits a *śleṣa* meaning from the pair of half-verses on which he comments, about which see footnote 214.

N.B.: I understand *tat* (line 257) to be polysemic: it marks the response to the objection in question, and it also serves as a neuter pronoun referring to *ceṣṭana*. I thus render the term twice in the present translation.

[213]A footnote in the KSTS edition (Kaul 1934: 166, fn. 5) that transcribes a marginal note of D (folio 166v.) explains the matter as follows: *idam atra tātparyam. idaṃ hi vaktavyaṃ kiṃ kumbakāro*

example, (there is a problem)—even there, if what is a different pot that exists prior (to the production of the new pot) were taken into consideration (by that potter), then (we ask,) what has been attained (by the potter) for the other pot—the one that is to be produced at that time—because of which it is produced? [Somānanda] derisively says that such an object is utterly amazing, because it comes into existence even without being produced.[214]

'pi ghaṭakartā dehādirūpaḥ, utasvit tadvyatiriktaḥ kaścana cetano 'pi. yadi ca dehādir jaḍarūpaḥ, tad atra vaktavyaṃ bījādibhyo 'cetanebhyaḥ(D; 'cetanemyaḥ K[ed.]*) ko 'sya viśeṣaḥ teṣām api jaḍapakṣīkṛtatvād ākalanāsaṃbhavāt. atha tadvyatiriktaś cetanas tathāpi kim ity āha yatrāpi sacetanam iti, kim āyātam iti. na hi tasya tat kāraṇaṃ saṃpannaṃ yena sāpekṣatvam api tv antaḥ kumbhakārasaṃvidi sphurann eva bahir nirgacchatīti.* "The following is what is essentially meant, here. This, indeed, is what you [the proponent of the *asatkāryavāda*] must explain: is the potter himself the maker of the pot, he being composed of the (material and insentient) body, etc.? Or, is it someone different from that [body, etc.], who is for his part sentient(, who makes the pot, e.g.)? If, moreover, (you maintain that) it is the body, etc., (of the potter,) which is insentient in form, (that is the maker of the pot,) then this must be explained, here [as regards this position]: what special property is there that belongs to this [insentient, material potter], that is different from the insentient seeds, etc.? For, since you have accepted the view that they all [*api*] are insentient, they(, like the body of the potter,) are not capable of (intentionally) taking hold (of anything). If you argue that there is a sentient one [i.e., the maker of the pot, e.g.,] who is different from that [material body of the potter, e.g.], then, even then, (one must ask,) 'why (is the effect produced)'? Thus, [Utpaladeva] says, 'even where there is a sentient [cause],' (and) 'what has been attained?' For that (supposed) cause of that [material and *asat* effect] is not (thus) brought about, one by which a dependence (on an object or *karman*) is established (for the capacities that are to produce such an utterly inexistent or *asat* effect). Rather, [the sentient causal agent] being fully active (only) inside the consciousness of the potter, emerges externally." The existence of an (immaterial) intentional agent who causes the production of the effect, in other words, cannot explain the source of the production of that which is utterly inexistent (*asat*) prior to its being effected. The effect has to come from something, and the something from which it comes is inherent in that effect: the *satkāryavāda* alone can explain the production of an effect. The present note may also be said to offer a partial parallel to what is said in the ĪPV ad ĪPK 2.4.4 (vol. 2: p. 140, lines 5–9): *kumbhakārahṛdaye antarmanogocaratvāt pūrvam api svasaṃvidekātmatayā vicitratvena viśvasya bhedābhedātmanā parivartamānasya spandanena sphurato yat antaḥkaraṇabahiṣkaraṇadvayavedyatvam ābhāsyate, eṣaiva sā kāryakāraṇatā.*

[214] In other words, the *asatkāryavādin* must still explain from where the previously non-existent effect has come. A sentient agent producing a pot cannot produce it out of thin air, even if that agent had the intention to fashion a pot, had seen another similar effect made prior to the production in question, and therefore had an understanding of what could be fashioned in the new object in question.

Reading in light of the present passage of Utpaladeva's commentary, one may understand ŚD 4.44cd-45ab to offer a second meaning via *śleṣa* or paronomasia. If this were intended, it would result from Somānanda exploiting two possible senses of the verbal root *kal* (viz., "to know" or "to make"), as Utpaladeva here clearly does by understanding forms of *ākal* either to mean "to take hold" or "to consider." On this possible second interpretation of ŚD 4.44cd-45ab, one would there understand Somānanda also to address the activity of a sentient agent, as follows: "Objection: Having considered another pot that had been seen previously, (the potter, e.g., knowing how to make pots, exerts) the effort (of the *kārakas* in the production of, in the present example, a new pot). (Reply:) The one [pot, i.e., the new one] is utterly amazing, because it is impossible for it to be made (by the potter) with the other one [i.e., the previously seen pot]."

Abhinavagupta, too, recognizes a polysemy in the root *kal*, for he cites Bhūtirāja, a guru and author of the Krama, for his analysis of the name Kālī, which appeals to two meanings in explaining it, "to project" and "to know," this at *Tantrasāra*, p. 30, lines 15–17: *yad āhuḥ śrībhūtirājaguravaḥ "kṣepāj jñānāc ca kālī kalanavaśatayātha. . ." iti.* (Reference to the same is found in Sanderson 2007: 362, fn. 432).

4.45cd-47

aṅkuro jāyata iti na bhavet kārakātmatā
4.46. asattve kārakāṇāṃ hi samūho na bhavet tadā
karmākhyasya hy asatyatvāt tatsaṃbandho 'satā katham
4.47. tasmāt sa eva bhagavān svayam eva prakalpate
tathātathābhāvarūpaiḥ sann eva parameśvaraḥ

Consider that the sprout comes into existence. It cannot be a factor of action (in its own production) if it is not existent (prior to its being produced). Indeed, the (entire) collection of factors of action cannot be activated at that time, because what is referred to as the object is not (yet) existent (to be acted upon). How can they[215] be connected with that which is not existent? Therefore, it is he (alone), the Blessed One, Parameśvara, who, fully existent, prospers as the forms of the various entities, entirely of his own accord.[216]

Consider that the sprout comes into existence in the place where the seed is found. In this, the sprout that is not existent (prior to its being produced) cannot be a cause, i.e., it cannot be an agent (of the act of its own production).

Alternatively, consider that a potter produces a pot.[217] What relation (in this) do either the other *kāraka*s (than that which is the *karman* or object) or the agent have to the non-existent object? (There is none.) Thus, how is there a collection of *kāraka*s (operative, here)? (There is not.) Hence, the action (of the production of the object) cannot occur.[218]

---

[215] While I here render *tat-* of *tatsaṃbandha* (ŚD 4.46d) with "they," Utpaladeva suggests that *tat-* may be understood in two ways, either to refer to the "*kāraka*s (other than the object or *karman*)" (*kārakāntarāṇām*) or to the agent (*kartṛ*).

[216] As noted (see footnote 211), the present passage of the ŚD addresses the *asatkāryavādin*'s understanding of causality by critiquing any possible manner in which they could conceive of the nature of the object, or effect, of the causal process in question. ŚD 4.44cd-45ab offered a criticism of their understanding of the cause or *kāraṇa* in causal processes as conceivable by the *asatkāryavādin*. As Utpaladeva understands it, Somānanda entertains here two possible ways of understanding the effect. The first involves an effect or object (*karman*) that is created in a process that occurs naturally, given the nature of the effect; the second suggests that the effect is the product of an extrinsic cause (with the aid of other concomitant causes like instruments, etc.), an external agent, a potter creating a pot, for example. So much constitutes a perfect parallel with the examination of two categories of causes found at ŚD 4.44cd-45ab. See Utpaladeva's commentary on the present passage of the ŚD.

[217] The previous criticized the possibility that the *asatkāryavādin* might explain the production of the effect by way of it being itself causally efficacious or having an agentive role in its own creation, which is impossible inasmuch as it is inexistent at the time. Here, the possibility of an effect produced by an extrinsic cause is weighed.

[218] That is, it cannot occur in accordance with the *asatkāryavāda*, even if the cause is extrinsic to the object effected.

Parallel concerns are also addressed at ĪPVV ad ĪPK 2.4.2 (vol. 3, p. 186, lines 15–19): *aṅkurasya sato vāsato vā yat paridṛśyate sattvaṃ, tatra na bījasya śaktir nāṅkurasya. aṅkuro jāyate iti hy aṅkuravṛttānto 'nyasya bījasya kathaṃ śaktiḥ, aṅkuraś ca na kaścana tadā. tasmāt kriyāśaktyā bhāsyamānaṃ karmaiva*

Therefore, Parameśvara, who has consciousness as his nature, prospers—comes into being—as the forms of the various entities, entirely of his own accord. And he is *eternally* existent; so, how can one object that the nature of the effect is not existent (prior to its being produced)?

4.48-49ab

4.48. svayaṃ ca na prajāyeta kenānyena prajanyate
vyatiriktena kartrādyā yadi syus te tadātmakāḥ
4.49. tat tasya janmitā yuktā vyatiriktaiḥ kathaṃ bhavet

And (since) it cannot be produced of its own accord, (therefore, we ask:) by what other[219] that is different (from that object) is it produced? If you argue it is those [causes] beginning with the agent (that produce it), (we reply: in that case) they would be of the nature of that [object].[220] So, how could it be tenable that it is produced by those [causes] that are (utterly) different (from it)?[221]

And since one may ask how the pot, e.g., could be produced of its own accord, given that it is not existent (prior to its production)—since, that is, one may ask how it could be the agent of (its own) production—therefore, (we must also ask:) by what capacity, even one, such as the potter, that is different (from the object effected), could it be produced? How, that is, could that which is not existent be produced, it being devoid of any nature that could render it fit for production, since it is no different than the horn of a hare?[222]

---

kāryaṃ, bhāsayitā ca kartaiva kāraṇam. Cf. ĪPV ad ĪPK 2.4.2 (vol. 2., p. 137, line 8 to p. 138, line 6), and ĪPK 2.4.2: *jaḍasya tu na sā śaktiḥ sattā yad asataḥ sataḥ | kartṛkarmatvatattvaiva kāryakāraṇatā tataḥ ||.*

[219] A marginal note in D (folio 168v.) appears above *kena* (ŚD 4.48b), which is not transcribed into K[ed.]. It reads, simply: *hetunā.* Utpaladeva, however, rather more explicitly understands the question to be one of what capacity or *sāmarthya* could produce the effect. See footnote 221 and Utpaladeva's commentary on the present ŚD passage.

[220] In other words, an effect that does not exist prior to its production by definition cannot be of the nature of its causes. It is only effected by them, but is not of their nature. And yet the effect must come from somewhere, so if it is not at all of the nature of its causes, on the one hand, Somānanda argues that it therefore cannot be created at all. If, on the other hand, it is of the nature of its causes, then the *satkāryavāda* is articulated, even if inadvertently.

[221] The present seems to replicate what was offered in ŚD 4.45cd-47, where Somānanda criticized the *asatkāryavādin*'s understanding of the nature of the object that is effected in a causal process. Here, however, it is the *capacity* of some cause or causes to produce an object, under the *asatkāryavādin*'s understanding of causality, that is scrutinized.

[222] I understand *aviśiṣṭam* (line 276 of the present edition), of course read with *śaśaśṛṅgāt*, to be a *hetugarbhaviśeṣaṇa*, an adjective of cause: the effect in question is void of any nature that could render it fit to be produced, this *because* it is no different (in its ontological status) than the horn of a rabbit.

Note also that I read *janyeta* (line 276 of the present edition) twice in the present passage, with both *tadā kena sāmarthyenānyenāpi kumbhakārādinā* (line 275) and with *katham asaj janmayogyatālakṣaṇasvabhāvarahitaṃ śaśaśṛṅgād aviśiṣṭaṃ* (lines 275–276). In both instances, the verb serves to explain *prajanyate* (ŚD 4.48b), and Utpaladeva here seems to understand *kena* in ŚD 4.48b to mean

Even if that which produces it is existent (prior to the production of this object), nevertheless that which is to be produced[223] (by it) could never come to share in its reality (according to the very logic of the *asatkāryavāda*),[224] this because it [i.e., that which is to be produced] is (by definition) different (from that which is to produce it). Hence, it[225] does not become fit (to be produced as an existent effect) even by means of that [reality belonging to that which supposedly produces it].[226] For if it[227] could be employed in this way to make (that which is to be produced) fit for production—if,[228] that is, it were tenable that it[229] could produce that [previously inexistent entity that is to be produced][230]—then (both) the producer, i.e., the agent, and the concomitant causes consisting of the instrument, etc., would be of the nature of that which is to be produced. But, (you do not accept that they are of the nature of that which they produce, so:) how can those [causes], which, while they are existent (prior to the production of the object in question that is to be produced) are (utterly) different (from what is to be produced), come to produce that which is not existent (prior to its being produced)?

---

both "by what" (with *kena* of the first passage here cited) and "how" (glossed with *katham* in the second passage here cited).

[223] Kaul records a note (1932: 168, fn. 4) that reflects the contents of two marginal notes in D (folio 168r.). D glosses *tatsattā* (line 277 of the present edition) simply with *janayitṛsattā*. K^ed. adds to this another marginal note from D, recording the following: *janayitṛsattā. janyasya asata iti śeṣaḥ*. See footnote 224.

[224] D records the following gloss (folio 168r.) above *janyasya* (line 277 of the present edition), which is combined with another in a footnote in K^ed.: *asata iti śeṣaḥ*. See footnote 223.

[225] A marginal note in D (folio 168r.) is recorded above that manuscript's *post correctionem* reading of *tasya* (line 278 of the present edition), one which simply glosses with *janyasya*. This gloss is transcribed into a footnote in K^ed. in combination with another marginal note, about which see footnote 226.

[226] The reality of the producer cannot account for the reality of the produced when one maintains that the latter is not-existent prior to the activity of the former and is entirely different from the same. There would be nothing to connect the former to the latter, the latter being entirely *new*, according to the *asatkāryavāda*. Utpaladeva goes on to express the very same.

A marginal note in D (folio 168r.) is recorded above *tayāpi* (line 277 of the present edition), which reads *janayitṛsattayā*. K^ed. p. 168, fn. 5 records this gloss with an added explanation thereof, as follows: *janayitṛsattayā, tasya janyasya, yogyatāpattiḥ sattvayogyatā*. See, also, footnote 225, as Kaul's note as here recorded incorporates text from the marginal note recorded there.

[227] Kaul 1934: 168, fn. 6 notes that one should understand *sā* (line 278 of the present edition) to refer to *janayitṛsattā*, "the reality of that which produces (the effect)." A marginal note written above *sā* in D (folio 168r.) records precisely the same gloss.

[228] A footnote found in K^ed. (p. 168, fn. 7) glosses *yadi* (line 278 of the present edition) with *yujyetety uktaṃ, tām evopapattim āha yadīti*. This is a transcription of a marginal note that appears in the left margin of D (folio 168v.).

[229] "It" refers to the reality (*sattā*) of the producer.

[230] A gloss appears in a note of D (folio 168v.) that is written above *tasya* (line 278 of the present edition): *janyasya*. This gloss is evidently not transcribed into the footnotes of K^ed..

4.49cd-51ab

janmakāle ghaṭābhāvāt saṃbandho naiva kārakaiḥ
4.50. nāsaṃbandhasya karaṇaṃ satkāryāc cet sa vidyate
sann apy asāv asaṃvedyo vyañjakasyāpy abhāvataḥ
4.51. tasmāt svayaṃ svabhāvena bhāvair bhāvī bhaved bhavaḥ

(To sum up:) There simply is no relation (of what is to be produced) with the factors of action (in the *asatkāryavāda*), because (that which is to be produced,) the pot(, for example,) does not (yet) exist at the moment of its production;[231] (and) there can be no production of that whose (causal) relation does not exist (with that which produces it).[232] Objection (of the Sāṅkhya *satkāryavādin*): That [relation] exists, (on our view,) because (we maintain that) the effect is existent (prior to its being produced). (Reply:) Although (you maintain that) it is existent (prior to its being produced), it cannot be known by consciousness (at that time); (and) because (it therefore logically follows that) that which manifests it, for its part, does not exist (at that time), therefore existence must be that which immanently exists of its own accord as (all) the entities (in existence), this by its very nature.[233]

---

[231] As Ratié 2014a: 152, fn. 91 notes, the present argument was accepted even in certain Śaiva circles. See e.g., MT 1.9.17: *anyathā kārakavrātapravṛttyanupapattitaḥ | śrutir ādānam arthaś ca vyapaitīty api tad dhatam ||*. Cf. MTṬ ad. 1.9.17: *saty asadutpattyabhyupagame kārakavrātasyaiva pravṛttir nopapadyate. asato hi kāryasya vandhyāsutāder ivotpattaye kiṃ kila kārakāṇi kuryuḥ. kārakapravṛttyanupapatteś ca ghaṭādicikīrṣor mṛtpiṇḍādy ānayetyādikā śrutiḥ, teṣāṃ ca kārakāṇām ādānaṃ grahaṇam, arthaś ca tadvyāpāralakṣaṇā kriyā vyapaiti vighaṭate. tasmiṃś ca vyapete sarvaceṣṭāvyāghātaḥ, pratyuta yuṣmatpakṣe jagadvyāhataṃ syāt.* See Ratié *op. cit.* for renderings of these passages.

[232] I emend to *nāsaṃbandhasya* at ŚD 4.50a. The reading published in K$^{ed.}$ is *nāsaṃbaddhasya*, which is also attested in D$^{p.c.}$, G, J, S^2, S$^{5p.c.}$, and P$^{p.c.}$. Note, however, that the commentary glosses (line 286 of the present edition) with *na cāvidyamānasaṃbandhasya*, and T and C, though corrupt, each offer support to the emendation I propose: T reads *nāsaṃnandhasya* and C reads *na saṃbaṃdhsya*. P$^{a.c.}$ and R also support this emendation: they read *nāsaṃvaṃddhaṃsya*, which is also a corrupted reading but one that witnesses the presence of an *anusvāra* before *dha*. The reading of the ŚDVṛ, which is better understood to gloss the *mūla* as emended, combined with a sense of what underlies the readings of T and C, together suggest the text first read as emended. As for what caused the germane variations in readings, I propose that it is likely that the relevant *anusvāra* of *nāsaṃbaṃdhasya* was accidentally dropped somewhere in the transmission of the text, leaving witnessed the grammatically incorrect *nāsaṃbadhasya* and thus occasioning a "correction" (erroneously so) by a scribe to *nāsaṃbaddhasya*.

[233] I understand ŚD 4.49cd-50a to sum up Somānanda's critique of the *asatkāryavāda*, which he prosecuted at ŚD 4.44ab, 4.44cd-45ab, 4.45cd-47, and 4.48-49ab. Ratié's (2014a: 153, fn. 92) translation of ŚD 4.49cd-51ab reads as follows: "If the pot does not exist at the time of [its] production, [it] has no relation whatsoever with the factors of action[, and] there is no production of what is not related [to the factors of action]. If [the Sāṃkhya explains that] because the effect is existing, this [relation] exists (*vidyate*), [we answer that in the Sāṃkhya system,] although the [pot] exists [before its so-called production, at that time] it is not an object for consciousness (*asaṃvedya*), and because [therefore] there is no manifesting agent either, as a consequence, Bhava [i.e., the all-encompassing consciousness] must be (*bhavet*) that which constantly exists (*bhāvin*) by itself, due its own nature (*svabhāva*), as [all] the entities (*bhāva*)." Note also that while I translate *bhavaḥ* (4.51b) with "existence," Somānanda could also here be punning, since *bhava* is also a name for Śiva.

(To sum up:) There is no relation(, if one accepts the *asatkāryavāda*,) of the pot that is to be produced with the potter, the ball of clay, or the like (that would produce it), because it does not (yet) exist at the moment when its production is begun; there can be no production, moreover, of that whose relation (with what produces it) is not (yet) existent, for want of a connection (of the non-existing thing that is to be produced with that which produces it) whether prior (to the moment when the production is begun) or otherwise.[234]

(Objection of the Naiyāyika-Vaiśeṣika:) Even while there is no (prior) connection to that which is to be produced,[235] the producers themselves possess a special property [*viśeṣa*] of their capacity [*sāmarthya*] as regards that [theretofore non-existent entity] in particular [*eva*]; because of it, given that those [producers] are existent (prior to the production in question), that [which is to be produced], having been made to be only of a particular kind [*viśiṣṭa*] (that conforms to the particular quality of the capacity of those producers), is [i.e., comes to be] possessed of the reality in them. Yet, it [i.e., the to-be-produced entity] is nothing at all [i.e., it does not exist at all] (prior to its production).[236]

(Utpaladeva's Reply): This doctrine of the effect that is not existent (prior to its production) has been refuted (by me) in the *Īśvarapratyabhijñā* and elsewhere.[237]

Note that the *Yuktidīpikā* has anticipated this objection and responds to it as follows (see YD, p. 117, line 12 to p. 118, line 7, also cited and translated in Ratié 2014a: 151, fn. 85): *etac cānupapannam. kasmāt? saty asati vā sambandhe doṣaprasaṅgāt. tad dhi kriyamāṇaṃ sati vā sambandhe kārakaiḥ kriyate 'sati vā. sambandhaś cāsya bhavan pravṛttikāle vā kārakāṇāṃ syān nivṛttikāle vā. kiṃ cātaḥ. tan na tāvat pravṛttikāle sambandho yuktaḥ. kasmāt? adravyatvāt. pravṛttikāle kartrādīnāṃ kriyāguṇavyapadeśābhāvād avastubhūtaṃ śaśaviṣāṇasthānīyaṃ vaḥ kāryaṃ na cāsti tathābhūtasya vastubhūtena sambandhaḥ. atha nivṛttikāle 'bhisambadhyate yad uktaṃ sato niṣpannatvāt kriyānutpattir iti tasya vyāghātaḥ. atha matam asaty api sambandhe niṣpattir bhavatīti tena kārakavyāpāravaiyarthyaprasaṅgaḥ. prāg api ca kārakopādānāt kāryaniṣpattiprasaṅga iti. uktaṃ ca: asattvān nāsti sambandhaḥ kārakaiḥ sattvasaṅgibhiḥ. asambandhasya cotpattim icchato na vyavasthitiḥ. iti.*

234 While K^ed.^ (p. 169, line 9) records a hiatus following *vā* (= *vā prasaṅgāt*), I understand the text to read *aprasaṅgāt* and thus erase the hiatus (at line 287 of the present edition).

235 A marginal note in D (folio 169r.) glosses *janya* (line 287 of the present edition) with *kārya*, what is not transcribed into K^ed.^.

236 The present passage—lines 287–289: *janyāsaṃbandhe 'pi tadapekṣayaiva janakānām eva sa sāmarthyasya viśeṣo yena teṣu satsu tasya viśiṣṭasyaiva sattā, na tu yasya kasyacid ity eṣo 'satkāryavāda īśvarapratyabhijñādau nirākṛtaḥ.*—parallels what was said at ŚDVr ad ŚD 4.48-49ab (lines 276–280): *janayitā yady api saṃs tathāpi tatsattā janyasya na kadācid bhavati vyatiriktatvāt, tatas tayāpi na tasya yogyatāpattiḥ. evaṃ hi sā janmayogyatāyāṃ vyāpriyeta yadi tayā tasya janmitā yujyeta yadi janayitā kartā sahakāriṇaś ca karaṇādirūpā janyātmakāḥ syuḥ.*

237 The term "etcetera" (°*ādi*) here may refer to the ĪPKVṛ and the ĪPṬ, but Utpaladeva normally does not use the term *ādi* when referring to his *Īśvarapratyabhijñā* works.

Here, it is possible Utpaladeva has ĪPK 2.4.2 and 2.4.3-4 in mind.

ĪPK 2.4.2 reads as follows: *jaḍasya tu na sā śaktiḥ sattā yad asataḥ sataḥ | kartṛkarmatvatattvaiva kāryakāraṇatā tataḥ ||*. "That power, because of which an existent or not-existent [effect] acquires existence, does not belong to that which is inert, however. Hence, the relation of cause and effect has as its reality nothing but the natures of the agent and the object of action."

ĪPK 2.4.3-4: *yad asat tad asad yuktā nāsataḥ satsvarūpatā | sato 'pi na punaḥ sattālābhenārtho 'tha cocyate || kāryakāraṇatā loke sāntarviparivartinaḥ | ubhayendriyavedyatvaṃ tasya kasyāpi śaktitaḥ ||*. "That

Objection (of the Sāṅkhya opponent): That, i.e., the relation, exists, (in our view,) because the cause, which is existent (prior to the production of the effect), is of the nature of the effect (even prior to the latter's production).[238]

---

which is non-existent is non-existent; it is not tenable that that which is non-existent has an existent nature. As for that which is existent, on the other hand, there is no need for it to acquire existence. If one objects that (cause and effect must exist, because) the relation of cause and effect is spoken of among people in the world, (we reply:) that [cause-effect relationship] is the fact that what is active internally becomes an object of awareness for both [internal and external] sense organs, through the power of that indefinable [being]." (See footnote 263 for ĪPKVṛ ad ĪPK 2.4.3-4.) Cf. the corresponding passage of the ĪPVV, which reads in part as follows (vol. 3, p. 187, lines 3–6): *sad vāsad vā kāryaṃ sambhāvyate dvyātmakam, anubhayarūpam anivācyam iti tu svavācaiva virudhyate | tatra yady asattā ghaṭasya rūpaṃ, tarhi svarūpaviruddhāṃ sattāṃ kathaṅkāram aṅgīkurutāṃ pādapatanair api rājoparodhair api vā nīlam iva pītatām |*.

Ratié notes that Utpaladeva may here have ĪPK (and ĪPKVṛ ad) 2.4.19 in mind: *na ca yuktaṃ jaḍasyaivaṃ bhedābhedavirodhataḥ | ābhāsabhedād ekatra cidātmani tu yujyate ||*. ĪPKVṛ: *jaḍasyābhinnātmano bhedenāvasthiter virodhād ayuktam, svacche cidātmany ekasminn evam anekapratibimbadhāraṇenāvirodhād yujyate.*

I wonder whether there is a passage now lost of the ĪPṬ that dealt with this particular argument, namely the existence of a special quality of the capacity of the producers to impart a new existence to the entity that is produced.

[238] I here emend the text (at line 290 of the present edition), proposing we read *sataḥ kāryātmakatvāt kāraṇasya* where K$^{ed.}$, supported by all the manuscripts examined for this edition, records *sataḥ kāryātmakatvāt kāryasya*. It does not seem likely that Utpaladeva would have understood the lemma being glossed, *satkāryāt* (ŚD 4.50b), to suggest that the effect (*kārya*) is existent inasmuch as it is of the nature of an effect. Rather, one would expect him to suggest that it is existent prior to its production inasmuch as it is of the nature of the cause, or, rather, that it is existent prior to its production because the pre-existent cause is of the nature of that effect. And, indeed, this is precisely what is said just below the present, in the same section of commentary of the ŚDVṛ, at line 295 of the present edition: *evaṃ hi kāraṇaṃ kāryātmanā sat tadā bhaved yadi. . . .*

I propose that the passage here under review conceptually paralleled the one that follows at line 295 but was changed by a scribe who saw *sataḥ* and *kāraṇasya* (of *sataḥ kāryātmakatvāt kāraṇasya*) both declined in the genitive and changed the latter to *kāryasya* in order to make it parallel the lemma (*satkārya*). A clue to this silent scribal change is also found in the word order of the commentary, which is slightly unusual, or at the least is distinctively patterned; we here see Utpaladeva twice append terms to the end of lemmas to explain ŚD 4.50b, which reads *satkāryāc cet sa vidyate* (what is not his habitual, default practice, though the present is not a unique passage of the ŚDVṛ for offering this pattern). The present passage of commentary, as emended and with lemmas placed in bold, reads as follows: *atha* **sa vidyate** *saṃbandhaḥ* **sataḥ kāryā***tmakatvā***t** *kāraṇasya* (with *atha* glossing *cet* and *sataḥ* standing for *sat* of *satkāryāt*, this by being taken out of the compound and declined). The ablative sense of the compound that is found in the *mūla* is recorded in the ablative ending of *kāryātmakatvāt*, further suggesting the last word of the sentence is appended by Utpaladeva syntactically at the end of this sentence (as *saṃbandhaḥ* was added by Utpaladeva following that which it explains). Thus, because the reading of *kāraṇasya* in fact mirrors precisely what is said at line 295 and is semantically more coherent; because the term is placed at the end, following the gloss of the ablative meaning of the compound being explained (meaning that *kārya* of *satkāryāt* was already quoted in *kāryātmakatvāt*), this in a passage of commentary that appends terms to the ends of items that are explained; and, finally, given the fact that a scribe is likely intentionally to have changed *kāraṇasya* to *kāryasya*, I therefore emend to *kāraṇasya*.

Note also the parallel with SāṅKā 9: *asadakaraṇād upādānagrahaṇāt sarvasambhavābhāvāt | śaktasya śakyakaraṇāt kāraṇabhāvāc ca sat kāryam ||*. "The effect is existent (prior to its production) because: there is no production of that which is not existent; one accepts (the necessary existence of) a material cause; it is not possible for everything to come into being (from anything else); because something is capable only of the production of that of which it is capable; and because of the nature of the cause/because the cause is existent (prior to the production of the effect)."

(Reply:) This, too, is not tenable, since the object that is to be produced—the pot, for example—although it is existent (prior to its being produced, on your view), cannot be known by consciousness (at that time); and because this entity that is (causally) related (to the causes that effect it) is not directly perceptible (at that time), inasmuch as it cannot be known by consciousness, the (causal) relation is not obtained (at that time); and, (consequently,) the potter, e.g., cannot be (properly understood to be) the agent who manifests the pot (at that time, viz., before the manifestation of the same), because, if a real thing lies entirely beyond the range of perception, there (by definition) can be no agent present who manifests it. It is (only) when an object is fully established (within

---

The *Jayamaṅgalā* (JM) interprets *kāraṇabhāvāt* in a manner similar to what I propose Utpaladeva understands his opponent here to argue (a formulation of the matter that Utpaladeva expresses, again, at line 295 of the present edition), and it is very possible Utpaladeva, glossing Somānanda, has this interpretation here in mind. The JM (p. 74, lines 14–17) reads as follows: *kāraṇabhāvāc ceti. kāraṇasya sattvād ity arthaḥ. yady asat kāryam utpadyate kim iti kāraṇād eva na kāryasya bhāvo bhavati. bhavati ca. tasmāc chaktirūpeṇāvasthitam iti gamyate.* "*kāraṇabhāvāc ca* (SāṅKā 9d) means (that the effect is existent prior to its production) because the cause is real. If an effect that is inexistent (prior to its production) were produced, then what would be the result? The coming into being of the effect(, in that case,) would come not to be the result only of the cause (of that effect). And (yet) it comes into being. Therefore, it [i.e., the effect] is present (in the cause) in the form of a capacity. This is how it [i.e., Sāṅkā 9d] is understood." See also Bronkhorst 2000 for a similar rendering, on which my understanding of the present passage is based.

Note, however, that the *Jayamaṅgalā* also considers the alternative that *kāraṇabhāvāt* should be understood to mean *karaṇasvabhāvāt*, for which see ibid., p. 74., lines 17–20: *athavā kāraṇabhāvād iti kāraṇasvabhāvāt. yatsvabhāvaṃ kāraṇaṃ* (corr.; *kāraṇa*, ed.) *tatsvabhāvaṃ kāryaṃ yathā snigdhasvabhāvebhyas tilebhyaḥ snigdham eva tailam, mṛdo mṛtsvabhāvo ghaṭaḥ. yady asatkāryaṃ syāt asatsvabhāvebhyo hy utpadyetety evaṃ sāṃkhyānāṃ sad evotpadyate iti siddhāntaḥ.* "Alternatively, *kāraṇabhāvāt* (SāṅKā 9d) means 'due to the nature of the cause.' A cause has a particular nature; the effect has the same nature, just as only the oil of the red castor-oil plant (is produced) from red castor-oil seeds, (or) a pot that is made of clay (is produced) from clay. For if the effect were not existent (prior to its production), it could arise from those the natures of which are not existent. It is in this way that the final position of the followers of the Sāṅkhya is established, viz., that only that which is existent (prior to its production) is produced." (A similar explanation of SāṅKā 9d is offered in the MāVṛ (p. 13, lines 10–11): *kiṃ ca kāraṇabhāvāc ca. kāryaṃ sad eva syāt. iha loke yallakṣaṇaṃ kāraṇaṃ tallakṣaṇaṃ kāryaṃ syāt. yathā kodravebhyaḥ kodravāḥ, vrīhibhyo vṛīhayaḥ syuḥ.* "Moreover, (we now analyze) SāṅKā 9d [quoted directly with *kāraṇabhāvāc ca*]. It is only an existent effect that may exist. Here in the world, a cause has a particular characteristic, (and) an effect (of it) must be that the characteristic of which is that (of its cause). Just as *kodrava* grains (are produced) from *kodrava* grains, (or) grains of rice must be (produced) from grains of rice."

Finally, as Ratié 2014a: 154, fn. 94 notes, Abhinavagupta anticipates this reply of the Sāṅkhya in the *avataraṇikās* to ĪPK 2.4.19 of both the ĪPV and ĪPVV, as follows: ĪPV, vol. 2: p. 176: *nanu pradhānaṃ pariṇāmakriyāyāṃ kartṛrūpam iyatā samarthitam iti ko doṣo, na hi puruṣavad asyākartṛtvam iṣyata iti.* "But through the [arguments expounded] so far, [you] have demonstrated that matter (*pradhāna*) consists in the agent of the action of transformation; therefore what is the fault [in the Sāṃkhya theory of causality]? For [the Sāṃkhyas] do not consider that this [matter] has no agency, contrary to the Person (*puruṣa*) [who remains inactive]" (translation Ratié's). ĪPVV, vol. 3, p. 234: *nanv iyatoktena pradhānasya kartṛtvaṃ samarthitaṃ bhavet, na cidrūpasya; tac ca nāniṣṭaṃ parasyeti.* "But through [the arguments] expounded so far, [you] may have demonstrated the agency of matter, but not that of what consists in consciousness; and the [Sāṃkhya] opponent does not deny this [agency of matter]" (translation again Ratié's).

the range of perceptibility) that one understands the agent who manifests it to exist, as (one understands) a lamp (to be the manifesting agent) with respect to a pot, for example.[239] Hence, given that (logic therefore dictates that, on your view,) the agent who manifests (the manifestation), for its part, does not exist (prior to the manifestation), (we ask:) how can a relation exist (between it and the effect it is said to manifest)?[240] For if the cause (that is the manifesting agent) were thus existent in the form of the effect (that is the manifested entity) at that time [i.e., prior to the manifestation of the latter], the two would be indistinguishable(, which means the manifested entity would always be visible when the manifestor is present). And that is contradicted by (what is seen in) direct perception.[241]

---

[239]I propose that the present passage of the ŚDVṛ (found at lines 293–294 of the present edition: *siddha evārthe vyañjako mato yathā ghaṭādau dīpaḥ*) is a close paraphrase of PV (*svārthānumānapariccheda*) 1.263cd-264ab: *svajñānenānyadhīhetuḥ siddhe 'rthe vyañjako mataḥ* || 3.263 || *yathā dīpo 'nyathā vāpi ko viśeṣo 'sya kārakāt* |.

[240]Thus, according to Somānanda and Utpaladeva, while the *asatkāryavādin* could not explain causality due to the absence of the effect (*kārya*) prior to its production, the *satkāryavāda* as understood by the Sāṅkhya cannot explain causality due to the absence of the cause (*kāraṇa*) of the manifestation of the effect. As Utpaladeva will go on to suggest, only the Śaiva position accounts for both sides of the causal relation, that of *kāraṇa* and *kārya*.

Ratié (2014a: 153) offers the following rendering of the present passage of the ŚDVṛ (reading *sataḥ kāryātmakatvāt kāryasya* where I emend to *sataḥ kāryātmakatvāt kāraṇasya*): "If [a Sāṃkhya were to say that] the relation [between the effect and the factors of action] exists (*vidyate*) since the effect, which exists [before its so-called production, already] consists in an effect [at that time and is therefore related to a cause], this too would not be [correct], because [in the Sāṃkhya system,] although this object to be produced—e.g. a pot—exists [before its so-called production, at that time] it is not an object for consciousness (*asaṃvedya*), and because due to the fact that it is not an object for consciousness, since this related [entity] is not perceptible, there can be no understanding of the relation [between the thing to be manifested and the manifesting entity,] and [as a consequence] the potter and [any other cause of the pot] cannot be the manifesting agent (*vyañjaka*) with respect to the pot, since there is no manifesting agent at all with respect to a reality [that supposedly exists] beyond the range of perception. [For] it is only when the object is established [i.e. manifested] that one considers [something] as a manifesting agent [of this manifestation]—for instance, a lamp with respect to [a manifested thing] such as a pot. Therefore, since there is no manifesting agent as well [as no manifested entity], how could there be any relation [between a manifesting cause and a manifested effect]?"

[241]Conceding that the follower of the Sāṅkhya, being a *satkāryavādin*, accepts the existence of the effect or *kārya* prior to its production, Utpaladeva, following Somānanda, challenges their understanding of the nature of the cause or *kāraṇa*, particularly the capacity of the cause, *as the followers of the Sāṅkhya understand it*, to produce its effect. Since the effect is not perceivable prior to its manifestation, Utpaladeva argues that by definition the manifesting agent or *vyañjaka*, what is the *kāraṇa*, cannot exist at that time, either. If the *vyañjaka* is understood to pre-exist the *vyaṅgya*, that is, then the latter *should* be visible whenever the former is present, the two being not different (*avyatireka*) inasmuch as the latter is inherent in the former. Thus, the Sāṅkhya understanding of the *satkāryavāda*, Utpaladeva argues, cannot account for phenomena as they are experienced.

The Śaivas, Utpaladeva has argued, may be said to avoid this problem: Śiva exists ever as the effects, but their visibility as discrete entities is only explicable as a non-cognition (*akhyāti*), as the failure to cognize the unity that is Śiva (as everything). The *abhedākhyāti* doctrine, then, which is first articulated in the ŚDVṛ, allows for Śiva to stand innately and permanently as all of existence, with *vyaṅgya*/*kārya* prefigured in the *vyañjaka*/*kāraṇa* at all times and therefore present at all times. It is only a *failure* to see this unity that accounts for the perception of individual entities in the world; yet, this

Therefore, Parameśvara—existence itself that is, of its own accord, the uncontradicted, unitary being of all entities—exists as the nature of such conditions. Being that which immanently exists as those existent and non-existent entities that reside in *saṃsāra*, he does not come into being for any other reason, i.e., by way of any other cause, because he is perpetually the (very) nature of those [entities]. Alternatively,[242] ("immanently exists" [*bhāvin*, ŚD 4.51b] means) the one who is permanently connected to the entities. Therefore, the doctrine that the effect is existent (prior to its production) is valid (only) inasmuch as Śiva is the cause.

4.51cd-52

ito 'pi viddhi satkāryaṃ mṛtpiṇḍāt kiṃ ghaṭaḥ pṛthak
4.52. apṛthag vā pṛthaktvena paṭādeḥ karaṇaṃ na kim
anupādānataiva syād apṛthaktve sa eva saḥ.

For this reason, as well, know the effect to be existent (prior to its being produced):[243] is the pot different from the ball of clay, or is it not different? Why wouldn't a cloth, e.g., be produced (from the ball of clay) as a result of it being different (from its cause)? It [i.e., the cause] simply would not be the material cause (of its effect, if the latter is different from the former). (By contrast:) When it is not different, it is nothing but that [cause].

---

failure or absence of cognition allows for an explanation of causality, of existence, and of the mundane perceptual process, such that *all* phenomena may be said to be present at all times, but only perceptible in instances when they are manifested, what in essence amounts to a failure to see any of the other entities equally (and always) present. On *abhedākhyāti* see Nemec 2012, footnote 293 of the present chapter, and the introduction to the present volume.

[242] Kaul notes that *athavā* offers a second explanation for the meaning of *bhāvī* (ŚD 4.51b), in K^ed. at p. 170, fn. 2: *bhāvīty asyārthāntaram āha athaveti. nityayoge matvarthīya inipratyayaḥ.* The two sentences recorded in this note are transcribed from D, where each is recorded surrounding that manuscript's reading of *athavā nityaṃ* (line 299 of the present edition), the former sentence appearing above, the latter below, *athavā*.

Another marginal note in D appears at the bottom of the same folio side, beneath what is written in the immediately preceding of Utpaladeva's commentary, viz., *bhavaty abhīkṣṇaṃ tatsvabhāvatvāt* (lines 298–299 of the present edition). This marginal note, which is not recorded in K^ed., reads as follows: *tācchīlye ṇinipratyayaḥ* (though *tya* of *pratyayaḥ* appears in a blotched hand). This appears to be a reference to Pāṇini (at A 3.2.78: *supy ajātau ṇinis tācchīlye*), a rule that allows for the affix *ṇini* when a habit is expressed and the word that is affixed with a case-ending in composition with it does not make reference to a class or genus (*jāti*). This, then, is meant to justify and explain the ending of *bhāvī*.

[243] A note in Kaul's edition suggests that Somānanda established, above—undoubtedly he means at ŚD 4.49cd-51ab—that the *satkāryavāda* is proven by an analysis of the nature of the cause; and now, the note adds, he will prove (here at ŚD 4.51cd-52) the soundness of the *satkāryavāda* by analyzing the nature of the effect. See Kaul 1934: 170, fn. 3: *itthaṃ kāraṇabhāvena satkāryavādaṃ samarthyedānīṃ kāryabhāvenāpi satkāryavādaṃ samarthayatīto 'pītyādinā.* This footnote in K^ed. is only a partial transcription of a longer marginal note in D (folio 170v.), which goes on to read as follows: *tatra sarvaṃ vākyaṃ dṛṣṭāntabhāvena kathitam api dārṣṭāntikasamarthanārtham ity āha ito 'pi śivātmateti.*

For this reason, as well, i.e., by dint of the fact that the objects (that are produced) are possessed of Śiva-nature,[244] know there is a rational justification for the doctrine that the effect is existent (prior to its production); for if the doctrine for the ball of clay and the pot is, for its part, that the effect is forever existent [*sadāsatkāryavāda*], there is a rational justification for the cause-effect relationship of the same.

Indeed, if (the effect,) the pot(, e.g.,) were different from (its cause,) the ball of clay, and thus were not existent (prior to its production), the production[245] even of a cloth or the horn of a rabbit could result (from the same cause), because they would not be different (from the pot) vis-à-vis their (prior) non-existence. And that does not occur, because, if the object were not existent (prior to its production), it would not be (logically) possible for the next step (in the causal chain) to be accepted as an effect that excludes other (possible effects);[246] (the cause,) the ball of clay, e.g., simply would not be the material cause (of its effect, the pot, e.g.). What this means is that it would not be the nature [*prakṛtirūpatā*] (of its effect) at all.

(By contrast:) When it is not different, it, i.e., the pot, is nothing other than the ball of clay, and it (thus) is not something new [*apūrva*]. It follows from this that the ball must be the pot, even prior (to the production of the latter).[247]

4.53-54ab

4.53. nāmasaṃsthānabhedaś ced dhaste muṣṭyādyabheditā
sthitam eva hi satkāryam ata evāvināśitā
4.54. śivasya bhāvanāśe 'pi maulināśe 'pi hemavat

---

[244] The present explains *ito 'pi* by suggesting that the effects have Śiva-nature (*śivātmatayārthānāṃ*, line 303 of the present edition); in the previous passage of the ŚD and ŚDVṛ (where Utpaladeva concluded at line 299 of the present edition by saying . . . *iti śivakāraṇatayā satkāryavādaḥ*) it was argued that Śiva is the cause. See footnote 243.

[245] Dª (folio 171r.) records a gloss in the line-space above *karaṇam* that simply reads *mṛtpiṇḍam*.

[246] I here propose to emend the text, suggesting one should read *anyaparihāreṇa* where Kᵉᵈ·, along with seven manuscripts (D, Dª, G, J, S², S³, and S⁵) read *anyāparihāreṇa* (and where S⁴, P, and R read *anyāpahāreṇa*). The presence of the long *ā* that I propose should be read as a short *a* can be explained as an addition by dittography: Kᵉᵈ· and the manuscripts that agree with it read *padabandhasyānyāparihāreṇa*, and a copyist could very easily have reproduced the *yā* found at the juncture of *padabandhasya* and *anya* at the juncture of *anya* and what follows it.

An alternative intervention would involve not making the emendation here proposed and instead emending from *aśakyatvāt* to *śakyatvāt*, thereby understanding the present to offer a contrary-to-fact understanding of the consequence of accepting the *asatkāryavāda*, namely, that it *would* be possible to accept as an effect a next step in the causal process that would *not* exclude other possible next steps. Indeed, a note appearing in the line-space above *aparihāreṇa* in Dª (folio 171r.) seems to support this interpretation of the clause, for it glosses its reading of *aparihāreṇa* with *doṣeṇa*. (N.B.: Yet another marginal note, in the right-hand margin of the same manuscript, explains Dª's reading of *paṇabandhana* (for *padabandha*) as follows: *padabandhanaṃ* (em.: *paṇabandhanaṃ* Dª) *hi śapathavad alaṅghyam* (em.: *alaṅgyam* Dª).)

[247] A gloss appearing above *tataḥ* ("It follows from this"; line 308 of the present edition) in Dª (folio 171r.) reads as follows: *yataḥ piṇḍa eva ghaṭaḥ*.

Objection: There is a difference in the name and configuration (of the cause and its effect).[248] (Reply:) There is no difference in (the nature of) the hand(, e.g.,) due to (its being clenched in) a fist, etc.[249] For it is firmly established (in such an example) that the effect is existent (prior to being produced). For this very reason, Śiva is not destroyed even when an entity is destroyed, just as gold (is not destroyed) even when a diadem (made of gold) is destroyed.[250]

Objection: A difference must exist, because there is a difference in the (respective) names and forms [*nāmasanniveśabhedāt*] of the ball of clay and the pot; so, how is the effect existent (prior to its production)?

Reply: No. The difference, here, is exclusively one of name and configuration, while there is none in the fact that they (both) are of the nature of clay,[251] just as (no difference is found) in (the nature of) a hand due to being (clenched into) a fist, or being stretched out and hollowed, for example. For both are one and the same hand, here [in this latter example], and both of these have a nature that is existent (prior to their production).[252] [Somānanda] has mentioned this, which is (an) extraordinarily well-known (example), moreover, to offer instruction regarding this [nature].[253]

---

[248]The objection is made to the notion, articulated in ŚD 4.52d (*apṛthaktve sa eva saḥ*), that the effect is forever identical to the cause (and, as Utpaladeva's commentary states, that nothing new is produced with the effect).

The scribe of D[a] (folio 171r.) glosses *saṃsthāna* with *racanā*. In addition the following is written on the same folio side in the right margin: *nanv e-*(four(?) *akṣaras* deleted and now illegible)*kādhikaraṇe katham cānayor nāmabhedaḥ. saṃsthānabhedād iti cet tathā ca saṃsthānabheda evānayor bhedahetur iti katham anyor apṛthaktvaṃ* (corr.: *apṛthaktva*) *tataś ca na satkāryatvam ity āśaṅkyāha*. I remain somewhat uncertain of the meaning of the argument presented in this marginal note, however, and present the following only as a tentative translation: "Objection (of the *pūrvapakṣin*): If, moreover, there is a (single?)... substratum (for the two), how can there be a difference in the names of the two? If one [i.e., the *uttarapakṣin*,] objects that this is the result of the difference of (their respective) configuration(s), and it thus follows the cause of the difference of the two lies exclusively in the difference of configuration, then (the *pūrvapakṣin* replies:) how are the two not (in actual fact) different? And hence, there is no *satkāryavāda*. Having considered this doubt, he [i.e., the *uttarapakṣin*] replies:. . ."

[249]As Utpaladeva indicates, *ādi* here refers to the hand being stretched out and hollowed, as if to hold water (*prasṛta*), or the like.

[250]The gold metaphor is explored repeatedly in ŚD 3, for which see ŚD 3.7cd-8, 3.18cd-20, 3.42cd-47, 3.84-85ab, and esp. 3.49cd-51ab; cf., e.g., ŚD 3.36cd-39 for other, similar metaphors, comparing the same with ŚD 4.126ab.

[251]A marginal note in D[a] (folio 171r.) explains the matter as follows: *yathā mṛdrūpatā mṛtpiṇḍe tathā ghaṭe 'pīty arthaḥ*. "What this means is that (this is so inasmuch as) just as the state of being clay is found in the ball of clay, so also is it found in the pot."

[252]A marginal note in D[a] (folio 171r.) understands "both of these" (*anayoḥ*, line 316) to refer to both configurations of the hand. It glosses with *saṃsthānabhedayor ity arthaḥ*.

[253]This example is also deployed at ŚD 1.13cd-17, for which see Nemec 2011: 27 and 118–121.

A note in D[a] (folio 171r.) seeks to explain the fame of the example in question by glossing with the following: *sāmānyalokaprasiddham apy etad ity arthaḥ*. "What this means is that this [example] is even well known by common people (*sāmānyaloka*)."

In reality, (your Sāṅkhya position may be summed up as follows:) the clay, for its part, consisting of the sensibilia [*tanmātras*]—sound, tactile form, etc.—of which one is aware (when one has contact with it), is different from water, etc., (but this is so only) as long as the three *guṇas* (of which it is made up) remain in the same condition (as being "clay"). Thus, even if it[254] is possessed of such a condition, (all) the effects, which begin with "the great" [i.e., *buddhi*] and end with the earth (-*tattva*), or (even may be said to) end with (particular manifestations, viz.,) pots and the like, (equally) have as their nature nothing but the (same) three *guṇas*, because the (entire) universe enters into a state of unity (in *mūlaprakṛti*).[255]

Yet, (you also maintain the following:) when there is a preponderance of (one or some among) them,[256] there is (made) a constituent part [i.e., a distinguishable and discrete entity]: this, which is made of the *tanmātra* of sound, is the ether; this is the earth; this is a pot; this is a cloth. And the constituent part, is, for its part, entirely real, because of its identity with that.[257] It is not possible, moreover, that what is being manifested in consciousness (as a constituent part) is unreal, since the three *guṇas* taken together would thus acquire the same [unreality], as well. The manifestation, in addition, must be a state of (the manifested entity) being understood by direct cognition, or by inference—it (thus) must in every respect be a state of (what is being manifested) possessing a real nature.[258]

---

[254] That is, the *traiguṇya* or the three *guṇas* taken together.

[255] This is to say, then, that even if the three *guṇas* taken together might have a particular configuration, such that one may recognize them as "clay," nevertheless *all* entities consist of nothing other than the same three *guṇas*. Reference here, then, is of course to the Sāṅkhya doctrine that the entire universe of manifested entities exists only in the form of the devolution of the singular *mūlaprakṛti* into such forms, and the same realities or *tattvas* that make up material existence can revert back to that configuration of the *guṇas*, which are universally present in materiality, what defines the second *tattva: prakṛti*. Material existence therefore, is in the end unitary, is one, even if the configurations of it (based on the particular conditions of the *guṇas*) are varied. See, e.g., SāṅKā 11: *triguṇam aviveki viṣayaḥ sāmānyam acetanaṃ prasavadharmi | vyaktaṃ tathā pradhānaṃ tadviparītas tathā ca pumān* ||. "The manifested, so too the primordial [= *mūlaprakṛti*], consists of the three *guṇas*, is undiscriminating, an object of knowledge, common, insentient, productive. And the *puruṣa* [*pumān*] is the opposite of this." (This translation is a modification of Larson 1969: 259.) To this point, then, the Sāṅkhya and Śaiva positions may be said to appear to be consonant in the sense that in each system all of creation is comprised of one "material," though they are not without differences even at this point of the comparison. (No non-dual Śaiva would allow the universe to be *acetana*, e.g., and so on). In what immediately follows, however, Utpaladeva will point out a flaw in Sāṅkhya theory of materiality and causality, as he sees it: not all the manifested entities are qualitatively mutually comparable.

[256] That is, of the three *guṇas* of which all effects consist.

[257] That is, the constituent part or *vibhāga* is real because it is identified with that *traiguṇya*, the three *guṇas* taken together.

[258] In other words, it is not possible to state that the differences found in the various entities are unreal or insubstantial, on the Sāṅkhya view, because the differences are the real product of a real change in the configuration of the *guṇas*, which themselves are said to be real. Such a real change cannot be deemed to be insubstantial, because it is seen and experienced, and what is seen and experienced

And, in this way, (causality, on your view, involves the production of real and substantial distinctions:) a pot comes into being when a ball of clay that is entirely different (from it) is existent (prior to its manifestation). The pot, moreover, is different (from the ball of clay); the clay, for its part, is different (in the following manner): it has entered into all those [entities] that are made up of clay, but the pot has not entered (into another entity comprised of it). And a unity of that which has (so) entered and that which has not (so) entered is impossible; and, for that reason, there is a fault (in your understanding of the *satkāryavāda*), namely, "why wouldn't a cloth, e.g., be produced (from the ball of clay)?"[259] Even if one accepts that, like a mirror, the three *guṇas* taken together bear the reflection of the universe, the cause (of manifestation) can only be that by the force of which such a reflection is borne;[260] (and) even as regards that [cause, i.e., the materiality of the *traiguṇya*, on your view], there is no rational justification, because one perceives differences and non-differences (in the reflection, or effects, in question).[261] Hence, all effects

---

is, according to the Sāṅkhya, nothing but the (material) *guṇas*. To say the changes are insubstantial or unreal, then, would require one to say that the *guṇas* themselves acquire such an unreality.

N.B.: A marginal note in D[a] (folio 171v.) reads as follows: *svamatena sarvasya sadrūpatve sati anyathā nopapadyate iti.* "When, according to one's own thinking, everything is possessed of a real nature, it is not logically possible for (one to claim) it to be otherwise."

[259]That is, the fault is precisely what is here cited, the argument expressed at ŚD 4.52b. If a cause can produce an effect that is qualitatively different from it, then why, Utpaladeva asks, isn't it the case that anything can be produced by anything else? The point is that the Sāṅkhya theory of the *satkāryavāda* establishes real differences in the manifested entities, which cannot be mutually reconciled. A difference in name and configuration (*nāmasaṃsthānabheda*), in other words, constitutes a real difference if one accepts the Sāṅkhya theory of the *satkāryavāda*. And, indeed, the SāṅKā allows for what is manifested to be different in its capacity to create. See SāṅKā 3: *mūlaprakṛtir avikṛtir mahadādayaḥ prakṛtivikṛtayaḥ sapta | ṣoḍaśakas tu vikāro na prakṛtir na vikṛtiḥ puruṣaḥ ||*. "*Mūlaprakṛti* is uncreated. The seven—'the great' [i.e., *buddhi*], etc., [i.e., *ahaṃkāra*, and the five *tanmātras*]—are created and creative, while the sixteen, on the other hand [i.e., *manas*, the five *buddhīndriyas*, the five *karmendriyas*, and the five *mahābhūtas*], are (only) created. *Puruṣa* is neither created nor creative." (This translation is based on that of Larson 1969: 256.)

Note, however, that the question of the production of *tattvas* after the last of them was engaged at ŚDVṛ ad ŚD 1.29cd-33, where an explanation is offered for the possibility that the last of the 36 *tattvas* is different insofar as it does not emanate realities below it in the hierarchy. See Nemec 2011: 130–135 and 293–295.

[260]That is, even if the Śaivas could accept that the Sāṅkhyas can argue that, because they maintain that everything in the universe is made of the *guṇas*, they understand an underlying non-difference to exist that unifies all the apparently mutually distinct entities in manifestation, it nevertheless is the case that this explanation if it is to cohere logically must also be able to account for what causes such a universe, so unified, to appear as it does. As Utpaladeva goes on to say, a problem arises in the Sāṅkhya account inasmuch as it cannot explain how forms may be "reflected" that are both mutually similar and dissimilar. Materiality, he argues, is unable to account for this level of ontological subtlety, as it were. See footnote 261.

[261]The point is that only the Śaiva view of the universe as Śiva-as-consciousness can logically account for the apparent differences in the universe, and for change to occur without a single reality being altered fundamentally. Utpaladeva has argued elsewhere, as well, that such a view cannot be countenanced in any system that fails to see the entire universe as consciousness, for which see, e.g., ĪPK 2.4.19: *na ca yuktaṃ jaḍasyaivaṃ bhedābhedavirodhataḥ | ābhāsabhedād ekatra cidātmani tu yujyate ||*.

exclusively consist in Śiva, who is made up of consciousness, this after the manner articulated in the *Īśvarapratyabhijñā*;[262] (and) [Somānanda] says as much at ŚD 4.53c: "For it is firmly established that the effect is existent (prior to being produced)."

For this very reason—i.e., because they are of the nature of Śiva inasmuch as they [i.e., the effects] are existent (prior to their being produced),—there is no destruction (of those effects); for Śiva, whose nature is that of self-aware consciousness, who is existent (prior to the production of effects), is (simply) not destroyed. And I have said as much in the *Īśvarapratyabhijñā*.[263]

See also the *Vṛtti* thereon: *jaḍasyābhinnātmano bhedenāvasthiter virodhād ayuktam, svacche cidātmany ekasminn evam anekapratibimbadhāraṇenāvirodhād yujyate.* (These passages were also cited in Ratié 2014a: 154, fn. 95.)

This is so, Abhinavagupta explains, because insentient entities cannot change form without being transformed fundamentally. See, e.g., ĪPV, vol. 2: pp. 176, line 10–177, line 2 (cited and translated in Ratié 2014a: 154, fn. 96): *evam ity abhinnarūpasya dharmiṇaḥ satatapravahadbahutaradharmabhedasaṃbhedasvātantryalakṣaṇaṃ pariṇamanakriyākartṛkatvaṃ yad uktaṃ tat pradhānāder na yuktaṃ jaḍatvāt. jaḍo hi nāma pariniṣṭhitasvabhāvaḥ prameyapadapatitaḥ; sa ca rūpabhedād bhinno vyavasthāpanīyo nīlapītādivat; ekasvabhāvatvāc cābhinno nīlavat. na tu sa eva svabhāvo bhinnaś cābhinnaś ca bhavitum arhati vidhiniṣedhayor ekatraikadā virodhāt.* (Ratié accepts the reading of *ekasvabhāvatvāc* from four manuscripts, this over and against the reading of the published edition of *ekasvabhāvavattvāc.*) Her translation is as follows: "Such [an agency means the following.] The agency in the action that is transformation (*pariṇamana*)—which [Utpaladeva] has described [earlier] as characterized by the freedom (*svātantrya*) to divide and unite numerous, constantly flowing properties [and] as belonging to a property-bearer having an undivided nature—is not possible for [something] such as matter, because [matter] is insentient. For what [we] call insentient has a [self-]confined (*pariniṣṭhita*) nature, it has fallen into the state of object of knowledge; and [if we assume it to be such an agent, we] must declare that it is differentiated (*bhinna*) due to the difference between the [various] forms [that it supposedly assumes,] such as blue and yellow, etc.; and [yet], since it has a unitary nature, [it must be] undifferentiated, as the blue is. But the same nature cannot bear to be both differentiated and undifferentiated, because [this would entail] a contradiction between an affirmation and [its] negation with regard to the same [thing] at the same time."

A gloss in D^a (folio 172r.) above *tatrāpi* (line 328 of the present edition) is written: *pratibimbe* ("in the reflection").

[262] Ratié (2014a: 154, fn. 95) translates the present as follows: "Even if [we] admit that [matter defined] as the three constituents (*traiguṇya*) bears the reflection of the universe, like a mirror, the cause can only be that thanks to which [it] bears such a reflection; and since [we] perceive that [bearing such a reflection] involves both difference and identity, [matter] cannot be [the cause]. Therefore all effects [are indeed mere manifestations of the cause but] exclusively consist in Śiva, who is nothing but consciousness, according to the principle [stated in] the *Īśvarapratyabhijñā* [treatise]."

Reference here is possibly to ĪPK 2.4.19, for which see footnote 261.

[263] It is not entirely clear to what Utpaladeva here refers his readers. The notion that what is non-existent is always non-existent carries implicit in it the notion that what is existent is always such, however, and so much is articulated at ĪPK 2.4.3-4 (cited and translated at footnote 237). See also the corresponding passage of the ĪPKVṛ: *asataḥ satsvabhāvatā viruddhā sataś ca siddhā. siddhasyaivāntarbāhyāntaḥkaraṇadvayīvedyatāpādanam īśvareṇotpādanam.* "A nature that is existent is contradictory for that which is not existent, and it is established for that which is existent. It is for the established [existent] alone that the Lord's act of producing occurs, which is the production (of that existent entity) as an object of knowledge for the pair of sense faculties, internal and external."

"As gold (is not destroyed) even when a diadem (made of gold) is destroyed," (ŚD 4.54b,) is an illustration that, as before,[264] is (offered) due to its currency among all people.[265]

4.54cd-55ab

nāśaḥ kaṭakarūpeṇa sadbhāvaḥ kuṇḍalādinā
4.55. *suvarṇatve 'pi na bhraṃśaḥ saṃsthāne 'pi vicāryatām*

The destruction is by way of the (non-manifestation of the) form of the bracelet, the real coming into existence is by way of (the production of the form of) an earring, or the like—no loss transpires as regards the nature of the gold itself (from which they are formed).[266] (Yet:) That must be considered even as regards the configuration (of that gold).[267]

[Somānanda] says that difference is one merely of (the) configuration (of a single reality), by way of a mundane illustration—of a bracelet, an earring, or the like (made of gold). (Yet:) That difference, even as regards (merely) the configuration, must be considered.

---

[264] Reference here is made by Utpaladeva to the fact that the exemplar was used earlier, at, e.g., ŚD 3.18cd-20. Alternatively, Utpaladeva points to the fact that Somānanda used another famous example, that of the hand and the fist, at ŚD 4.53b (an exemplar also deployed at ŚD 1.14cd, for which see Nemec 2011: 27, 118–121, and 286–288).

[265] To offer a commonly understood phenomenon as an example is a requirement for logical dispute, according to the Nyāya. See NS 1.1.25: *laukikaparīkṣakāṇām yasmin arthe buddhisāmyaṃ so dṛṣṭāntaḥ*. "That meaning/object that is understood in the same way by common people and those who are (well) studied is (the very definition of what constitutes) an example [*dṛṣṭānta*]."

[266] A marginal note in D^a (folio 172r.) introduces ŚD 4.54cd-55ab as follows: *athedānīṃ nāśasatattvam eva samarthayati nāśa iti. yathā hi kaṭakarūpanāśe kuṇḍalādisadbhāvane na suvarṇasya svarūpacyutiḥ, tathā tattadāvirbhāvatirobhāvādiṣu na śivatattvasya kācanāpi svarūpahāniḥ*. "Next, [Somānanda] now considers the very nature of the destruction with ŚD 4.54cd-55ab [quoted with the *pratīka*]. For just as there is no loss in the nature of gold when the bracelet is destroyed in the real production of the earring or the like, so in the same way there is no loss at all of the nature of the Śiva-*tattva* in the (various) appearances or disappearances of this or that [entity in the universe]."

[267] The standard rules of anaphora suggest it is the loss or *bhraṃśa* that must be considered, but Utpaladeva understands the passage to refer to the difference (*bheda*) between the various configurations of the gold and, by analogy, of consciousness.

A marginal note in D^a (folio 172r.) explains ŚD 4.55b as follows: *nanu cāstu śivatvam avasthitam eva tathāpi nāmasaṃsthānabhedas tāvat kathaṃ tadavasthitatvam ity ata āha saṃsthāne 'pītyādi*. "And one may object that while Śiva-nature may be fully established, it nevertheless is the case that a difference exists in its name and configuration; so, how is that established? For this reason, [Somānanda] says: '(Yet, that must be considered) even as regards the configuration."'

4.55cd-56ab

And by considering that, concluding it is Śiva alone who is the cause, [Somānanda] says:[268]

kiṃ śivatvena tad vyāptam avyāptaṃ vābhidhīyatām
4.56. vyāpitve tadvināśitvam avyāptau syāt pradeśitā

(Objection:) Is that [effect] pervaded by Śiva-nature or not pervaded by the same? That must be addressed. If it is pervaded, then he is destroyed (when the effect is destroyed); if there is no pervasion, he must be spatially limited.

(Objection:) If(, on the one hand,) Śiva-nature pervades the diadem, Śiva is destroyed when the diadem is destroyed. On the other hand, if it is not pervaded by Śiva(-nature), then Śiva exists (only) in a limited place: when he takes his place by precluding (from it) the places where are found the natures of the diadem, the pot, the cloth, etc., the place where his nature is present is interrupted, and it follows from this that he is not omnipresent. Therefore, a fault in the configuration (of Śiva-nature) is identified (by us) in both cases.

4.56cd-57ab

naivaṃ yato hi bhāvānāṃ vināśe 'smāsu neṣṭatā
4.57. aṃśābhivyaktitā nāśo na nāśaḥ sarvalopitā

(Reply:) This is not so, since we do not maintain that the entities are destroyed. For,[269] destruction is (nothing more than) the fact that a part (of Śiva-nature) is manifested; it is not the case that destruction is a complete elision (of the "destroyed" entity in question).

(Reply:) No fault (in our view) has been articulated (by you), since, as for us—we do not maintain that destruction of the entities is a topic to be explained [*viṣaya*]; what this means is we maintain that the entities are not susceptible to destruction (at all).

---

[268] Somānanda will here articulate an objection centered around the question raised at ŚD 4.54cd-55ab, and he will respond to the objection at ŚD 4.56cd-57ab.

A gloss in D^a (folio 172r.) explains the *avataraṇikā* to ŚD 4.55cd-56ab as follows: *uttaratra tatparyavasānaṃ tadarthaṃ tāvan nyāyam āha.*

[269] I read *hi* out of the regular word order (*bhinnakrama*). This is justified by Utpaladeva's commentary, which records both *yatas* (ŚD 4.56c) and *hi* (ŚD 4.56c) but distributes them in the manner reflected in the present translation.

For in our philosophy,[270] at the moment when the bracelet (made of gold) is produced from the (golden) diadem, there occurs a manifestation of a part (that is the bracelet) that is nothing but gold; it is the manifestation of the preceding moment, that of the transformation of the diadem (into the bracelet), that is spoken of as destruction,[271] but it is not the case that every part (of the gold) ceases to appear.

Hence, there is no fault associated with the immediate destruction (of the diadem, in the present example);[272] nor is the part [i.e., the bracelet] devoid of co-presence (with the diadem, in the present example), because only the non-manifestation (of the new effect, the bracelet) is destroyed.[273]

---

[270] A marginal note of D[a] (folio 172v.) explains the present passage as follows: *tena svarūpeṇa sthitasyaiva hemno 'bhivyaktāṃśasyotpattiḥ. anabhivyaktyā vināśaḥ, na tu svarūpeṇotpattināśāv ity arthaḥ.* "What this means is that the production of the manifested part that is gold fully exists as that very nature (as gold). The destruction is of a non-manifestation, but it is not the case that the production or the destruction occur by way of (the creation or elimination of) the (very) nature (of the objects in question)."

[271] I here read *abhivyakti* (line 348) twice, with what precedes it and with what follows it. In the latter case, I understand the term to appear in an *iti*-clause, as follows: . . . *abhivyaktiḥ prāktanasya mauliparināmakṣaṇasyeti nāśa ucyate*. . . .

[272] With *niranvayavināśa*, Utpaladeva refers to the total destruction of the entity in question. This does not occur, he argues, meaning such a destruction cannot stand as grounds for understanding Śiva, who is identical with the effect (*kārya*), to be destroyed when the effect is destroyed.

The same term appears in the PVV of Manorathanandin (p. 413, 16–414, 1): *na hy asata utpattimattvaṃ sataś ca niranvayavināśo 'nityatvaṃ hetuḥ sāṃkhyasiddhaḥ. bauddhasya punar āgamāt siddhaḥ.* "Indeed, the reason—viz., that something nonexistent comes into being or that an existent immediately is destroyed [and] is impermanent—is not established for the Sāṅkhya. For the Buddhist, however, it is established from scripture." See Tillemans 2000: 10, fn. 30. The translation is his.

[273] In other words, it cannot even be argued that there is a contradiction between the one object and the other, both made of gold (in the present example). Such a mutual contradiction could imply a sort of destruction, the one necessarily disappearing when the other appears. But, according to Utpaladeva, this does not occur at all; the two entities (the diadem and the bracelet made of gold, in the present example) can be co-present. For the transformation of one into the other is not understood as involving the destruction of the earlier-existing entity, the diadem, but rather what is understood as destroyed is the *non*-manifestation or *anabhivyakti* of the golden bracelet (again in the present example). As such, the crown is not understood to have been destroyed, and therefore it may not be said not to be co-present with the bracelet.

The description of the *aṃśa* as *anabhivyaktimātra* is apt, because the nature of a "non-manifestation" is precisely what will be examined in ŚD (and ŚDVṛ ad) 4.57cd-58.

Finally, note that Manorathanandin also uses the terminology here deployed, namely that of *niranvayatā* or "lack of co-presence." See PVV 427, 9–12: *tatra ca niranvayaviruddhate kathite. tathā hy abhivyaktacaitanyadehalakṣaṇapuruṣena sadvitīyatvaṃ sādhyam. tena ca kuḍye 'nvayo na dṛṣṭa iti niranvayatā. ghaṭasya tu kuḍye 'nvayo dṛṣṭa iti tena sadvitīyatvasādhanāt viruddhatā syāt.* "Now, here the lack of co-presence and the contradictoriness [of the reason] have been pointed out. As follows: 'having a companion in the form of a person characterized as a body with a manifested consciousness' is the *sādhya*. And thus co-presence [of the reason and this *sādhya*] in [the example,] the wall, is not observed: hence there is a lack of co-presence (*niranvayatā*). For the vase, however, the copresence in [the example,] the wall, is observed: thus, because [the reason] would prove 'having a companion in the form of the latter [i.e., the vase]' it would be contradictory." This is quoted at Tillemans 2000: 60, fn. 213. The translation is his.

4.57cd-58

abhivyakter vināśitve tatrāpy ānantyam āpatet
4.58. indriyāṇām asāmarthyamātram atra vināśitā
asāv evānabhivyaktiḥ sa pracchannas tadā sthitaḥ

If (you argue that) the manifestation is destroyed, (then we reply:) in that case, also, (there is a fault:) an infinite regress would arise. Here [in Śaivism], destruction is merely an incapacity of the *indriyas*. It is simply a non-manifestation; that which has been concealed remains existent at that time.[274]

Objection: Since the production is of nothing but the manifestation of the objects that fully exist (prior to their production), therefore, the destruction, too, is only of that [mere manifestation of the same].[275] It is in this sense [*iti*] that you [Śaivas] have said that destruction is the non-manifestation of nothing but an earlier part (of the nature of the entity that was manifested).[276]

(Reply:) This is not the case, because just as we have articulated a fault regarding the production of the object—viz., that the production is of a manifestation that, for its part, is either non-existent (prior to its production), or existent (prior to the same)—and (just as we argued) there is an infinite regress(, there, if the object can only be seen as the result of the manifestation

---

[274]That is, that which was supposedly "destroyed" is in fact merely concealed and remains existent after the so-called "destruction" has taken place.

[275]Note that *tasya* (line 355) is neuter in gender because grammatically it refers not to the feminine term *abhivyakti* ("manifestation") but to the neuter compound *abhivyaktimātra*, the "mere manifestation." D[a] (folio 172v.) records a marginal gloss that suggests that what is destroyed is the form of the manifestation (of the existent objects in question) and nothing else. The gloss simply is: *abhivyaktimātrarūpasya*.

[276]Here (at lines 354–355 of the present edition), Utpaladeva understands his opponent to suggest that, when he and Somānanda say that destruction entails nothing other than the non-manifestation of a part (*aṃśa*) that appeared in an earlier moment in time—*prāktanāṃśamātrasyānabhivyaktir vināśa ukta iti*—they in fact argue that the manifestation or *abhivyakti* is both created and destroyed: . . . *yathābhivyaktimātrasyotpādas tathā vināśo 'pi tasyaiveti*. The Śaivas' reply to this criticism follows hereafter; it suggests that what the opponent argues, here, in fact misrepresents what Somānanda and Utpaladeva have said. To wit, reference to destruction being a non-manifestation is also made at ŚDVṛ ad ŚD 4.56cd-57ab (line 350): . . . *anabhivyaktimātrasya nāśatvāt*. This, in turn, serves to explain what Somānanda said at ŚD 4.57ab: *aṃśābhivyaktitā nāśo na nāśaḥ sarvalopitā*. For Somānanda and Utpaladeva, then, destruction (*nāśa*) is *not* the cessation or "destruction" of a *manifestation* but rather is the manifestation of a moment of transformation of one and the same consciousness. Thus, Utpaladeva said (lines 348–349 of the present edition) the following about *nāśa: abhivyaktiḥ prāktanasya mauliparināmakṣaṇasyeti nāśa ucyate na tu sarvāṃśādarśanam*. The non-manifestation or *anabhivyakti* is not of the entity that is "destroyed"; rather, as Utpaladeva goes on to explain in the present passage of commentary, the non-manifestation is the incapacity of the *indriyas* (both "internal and external") to cognize an individual object, this incapacity itself being the absence of the non-cognition of non-duality or, more simply, a concealment of the *aṃśas* as Śiva. To fail to be manifested, in other words, is in fact *to appear* in the form of the undivided Śiva. There is, in a word, no real destruction at all.

of the manifestation of the object),[277] so in the very same way, (we here argue that) the destruction of the object is not logically justified, because it is not possible that that which is existent (prior to its production) is destroyed; and the same goes for the manifestation, as well.

Objection: It is the manifestation of the manifestation that is destroyed, not the reality (of the manifestation).

Reply: Therefore,[278] (you must argue by the same logic that) it is not the reality even of that manifestation of the manifestation that is destroyed, but rather it is the manifestation (of the manifestation of the manifestation that is destroyed). Hence, an infinite regress (again) ensues.[279]

Alternatively, (we may ask:) does the destruction of the manifestation, for its part, arise as that which is not existent (prior to its production), or as that which is existent (prior to the same)? If it is not existent, then the doctrine that the effect is existent (prior to its production) would be compromised, and there is no logical justification (for the production of that which is not existent before it is produced). If it is existent, then the destruction would have to occur *prior* (to the production of the manifestation).

Objection: The manifestation of the destruction is produced by a(nother) cause.[280] Reply: The aforementioned *regressus* ad infinitum (applies to the cause, as well); thus, there is an infinite regress (as regards the manifestation of the destruction).[281]

---

[277] The argument here cited appears at ŚD 4.35-37ab.

I have here accepted a variant reading of five manuscripts (D^a, S^2, S^3, S^5, and P$^{p.c.}$) at line 356 of the present edition (*asatyā utpattir* for K$^{ed.}$'s *asatyotpattir*) and have accepted another variant—again at line 356, but this time of manuscripts D and D^a—of *satyā ity* where K$^{ed.}$ and all the other manuscripts I have examined for the present edition record *satyety*. Clearly, the selection of these variants is called for, because otherwise the text here would have Utpaladeva referring to the question of whether the *production* (*utpatti*) is either false (*asatyā*) or not (*satyā*), while what is truly at question is whether the *abhivyakti* is existent (*satī*, declined in the genitive: *satyāḥ*) prior to its production or not, this being the matter to hand both here and at ŚDVṛ ad ŚD 4.35-37ab. The application of double-*sandhi* explains the variants in both cases, and undoing the double-*sandhi* justifies the changes to the KSTS edition.

N.B.: Manuscript D^a (folio 173r.) offers a marginal note to expand on what is here said, which reads as follows: *asatpakṣaś ca svayam eva nivṛtta iti punar nopāttam iti bodhyam.* "One must understand that, since the argument regarding the non-existent [manifestation] is intrinsically self-defeating, it is not spelled out again [here]."

[278] Here (line 358), *tat* is polysemous, indicating that the reply to the objection is offered and also meaning *tasmāt*, "therefore."

[279] D^a records a note that seeks to explain the present, but its meaning is unclear to me. It reads: *ekasya evābhivyakter vaḍatvam(?) iti.*

[280] In other words, one may claim that a real *vināśa* transpires. It may be understood to exist prior to its being effected, but it does not take effect until another cause (*kāraṇa*) triggers it. The problem with this position is explained in the reply.

[281] If the opponent claims that a cause (*kāraṇa*) activates, as it were, the destruction (*vināśa*), then that *kāraṇa* must either exist before it is put into action, or not. The same problems regarding the creation and destruction of this extrinsic cause therefore must be negotiated, leading either to the dissolution of the *satkāryavāda* or to an infinite regress of causes.

In this way,[282] in our philosophical system, as per the principle that has been articulated (by me) in the *Īśvarapratyabhijñā*,[283] just as the production of objects, which consists of the non-cognition of the non-duality of Śiva, is their being objects of both (external and internal) sense organs, so also (their) destruction is non-difference with Śiva, the absence of the state of being an object of both (internal and external) sense organs; it is a concealment (of the objects) as Śiva.[284] This is precisely what [Somānanda] said (at ŚD 4.58a-b): "(destruction is merely) an incapacity of the *indriyas*"; and (at ŚD 4.58c:) "it is simply a non-manifestation"; (and at 4.58d:) "that which has been concealed" as Śiva, i.e., the pot, e.g., "remains existent at that time."[285]

4.59-60ab

4.59. ito 'pi nāśo nāsty asya ghaṭasya karaṇāt punaḥ
nābhāvaprāptarūpasya karaṇaṃ yujyate punaḥ
4.60. tasmād bhāvavināśe 'pi śivatattvāvināśitā

---

[282] Dª (folio 173r.) adds to *evam* with a gloss of *sati*, suggesting it could be rendered with "this being so."

[283] See, first of all, ĪPK 2.4.3-4, cited and translated at footnote 237, and the corresponding passage of the ĪPKVṛ cited and translated at footnote 263. Cf. ĪPKVṛ ad ĪPK 1.8.8: *vikalpe ghaṭādyullekhaś cakṣurādyagocaro 'pi pṛthagābhāsād bāhya eva. ahaṃvimarśo hy antaratvam, idam iti tu bāhyatā. evaṃ ca ghaṭādīnām ubhayī bāhyatā bāhyāntaḥkaraṇadvayīvedyatā, sukhādes tv ekāntaḥkaraṇavedyataiva.* "The representation of a pot, etc., in conceptualization, although not within the range of the (organs of sense,) the eye, etc., is fully external, because of its appearance as what is separate. Indeed, the reflective awareness 'I' is internality (itself), while externality is (the awareness,) 'this.' In this way, moreover, both kinds of externality exist for pots, etc., viz., the state of being the object of cognition of the pair of senses, (both) internal and external. By contrast, pleasure, etc., are the object of one sense, the internal one." Finally, see ĪPK and ĪPKVṛ ad 2.2.2, where Utpaladeva suggests that there are two objects of knowledge, internal and external, what (we know from the overall structure of his system) may be cognized by corresponding internal and external senses. ĪPK 2.2.2: *tatraikam āntaraṃ tattvaṃ tad evendriyavedyatām | saṃprāpyānekatāṃ yāti deśakālasvabhāvataḥ ||.* "In this, there is one internal reality; this alone becomes multiple after having become perceptible to the senses, according to (its) spatial and temporal locations and (its) nature." (On the meaning of *tatra* see Torella 1994: 158, fn. 5.) ĪPKVṛ: *abhinnam eva tattvam antarbahirābhāsabhedād ekānekam, bahirdeśakālasvabhāvabhedābhāsasaṃbhedamayaikaikasvalakṣaṇābhāsānām anekatvāt.* "Reality is fully non-dual; it is one-and-many as a result of being divided into internal and external appearances, this as a result of the multiplicity of the appearances, what are the various individual *svalakṣaṇas* consisting of the divisions in the different external appearances, viz., space, time, and nature."

[284] Ratié (2014a: 162, fn. 113) has translated the present passage as follows: "Thus in our system, according to the principle that [I have already] stated in the *Īśvarapratyabhijñā* [treatise], just as the production of objects is [nothing but the property of] being an object of knowledge for both [external and internal] sense organs, [a property that] consists in the [mere] nonapprehension of the non-difference with Śiva (*śivābhedākhyāti*), in the same way, the destruction [of objects] is the [mere property of] not being an object for both [internal and external] sense organs, [a property that is] not distinct from Śiva [either and that is] the concealment (*pracchādana*) [of Śiva's nature] as being Śiva."

[285] The final *iti* (line 366) serves to mark the quotations of Somānanda's verse, but it also evokes the meaning "this is conclusive."

It is for this (following) reason, as well, that this[286] pot(, e.g.,) is not destroyed, (viz.,) because it is produced again. That the form of which has arrived at non-existence cannot possibly be produced again. Therefore, Śiva-nature is not destroyed even when the entity is destroyed.

It is for this (following) reason, as well,[287] that this[288] pot, e.g., is not destroyed, (viz.,) because it is produced, again. For an object whose form has arrived in every respect at non-existence—what is the equivalent of the horn of a hare—does not again acquire existence.[289]

Objection: It is an earlier pot that exists (at first) and (subsequently) acquires the very state of being (similar to) the horn of a hare [i.e., it truly becomes non-existent]; and it is an entirely different one that is (subsequently) produced (again).[290]

Reply: This is not so. For there can be no other pot than the (first) pot. It was mentioned, earlier,[291] that it is only when it exists internally (in consciousness), in association with the other (relevant) universals, (viz.,) being large, being of reddish color, being tall, etc., that it [i.e., the pot, e.g.,] is produced as what is known by the sense organs, as that which consists of the non-cognition of (Śiva's) non-duality.[292]

---

286 "This" (*asya*, ŚD 4.59a) refers to the entity that is said, at ŚD 4.58d, to have been concealed: *sa pracchannas tadā sthitaḥ*. The pronoun *sa* is explicitly associated with a pot, e.g., at ŚDVṛ ad ŚD 4.57cd-58, lines 365–366 of the present edition: *sa ghaṭādiḥ śivatayā pracchannas tadā sthita iti*.

287 Utpaladeva here glosses *ito 'pi* with *hetoḥ*.

288 See footnote 286.

289 Despite the somewhat unusual word order for a *vigraha* analysis, I think Utpaladeva nevertheless indicates that *abhāvaprāptarūpa* (ŚD 4.59c) is a *bahuvrīhi* compound, as I have translated it in Somānanda's verse. (In Utpaladeva's commentary *yasya* precedes instead of follows his enumeration of the relationship of the terms of the compound, at lines 370–371 of the present edition.)

290 In other words, the opponent objects by claiming that each entity that is experienced is newly manifested (in consciousness) in each instance. This allows the entity in question to be created and subsequently destroyed, for it needn't be recreated, but only replicated.

291 See ŚDVṛ ad ŚD 4.57cd-58 (beginning at line 362), which reads in part as follows: *evam asmaddarśana īśvarapratyabhijñoktanītyā yathobhayendriyavedyatvaṃ śivābhedākhyātimayam arthānāṃ karaṇam, tathā vināśa ubhayendriyavedyatvābhāvaḥ śivābhedaḥ śivatvena pracchādanam*. . . .

292 In other words, the object is not really destroyed. The particular qualities it possesses are conjured within consciousness, and, most importantly, there is therefore only one "source," as it were, from where "an entirely different pot" could come, viz., the one and the same non-dual Śiva. In a word, there can be no other "pot."

Ratié 2014a: 162, fn. 113 offers a translation of a part of the present passage, as follows (erroneously recording *antarasthita* for *antaravasthita* [at line 374 of the present edition]): "Cf. e.g. ŚDV, p. 174: *antarasthita evendriyavedyo 'bhedākhyātimayaḥ kriyata iti pūrvam uktam*. '[We] have already explained that [the pot] is produced [insofar as it becomes] an object for the sense organs, which is nothing but a nonapprehension of the non-difference [with consciousness], only if [this pot] exists within [consciousness]'." On the term *abhedākhyāti* and the study of it, see footnote 293. Compare, also, the present passage to ĪPK (and ĪPKVṛ ad) 2.3.4-5.

Finally, while K^ed.^ does not punctuate following *anyo ghaṭaḥ syāt* (line 373 of the present edition), I add a period in order to clarify the syntax of the present sentence.

Therefore, on the basis of the arguments just presented, there is no destruction of Śiva-nature, even when the non-cognition of the non-duality of that [Śiva-nature] is destroyed, this in the form of the immersion of the entities (that are "destroyed") in Śiva-nature.[293] In this way, because production and destruction are not possible in any other way, the Śiva-nature of everything is firmly established.[294]

4.60cd-63ab

itaś ca sarvaśivatāvayavebhyo na kutracit
4.61. vyatireko 'vayavinas tad evedaṃ vicāryatām
bhinneṣv aikyam abhedaś ca yathā tatra vyavasthitaḥ
4.62. tathā tatra parijñeyaṃ patyuḥ sāmarthyam īdṛśam
abhinne bhedatā yena bhinneṣv apy asty abhedhatā
4.63. yathāvayavagaṃ rūpaṃ tathā sarvapadārthagam

It is for this (following) reason, as well, that everything is possessed of Śiva-nature: nowhere is there a distinction of the whole from its parts. This is the very item that must be considered(, as follows). Unity exists in the divisions, and since a non-duality is present there, one must therefore understand a kind of capacity of the Lord to be present there; it is by means of it that the multiplicity (of the parts) exists in the undivided [unity], and the non-duality exists in all the divisions. Just as a (single) form is present in the parts (of which an individual such as Devadatta is formed), so also a (single) form [i.e., Śiva-nature] is present in everything (in the universe).[295]

It is for this (following) reason, as well,[296] that everything is possessed of Śiva-nature: the whole nowhere appears as different from its parts in either

---

[293] Destruction or *vināśa* involves nothing more than the cessation of the non-cognition of non-duality. It involves a unity with Śiva-nature; for it is a non-cognition of unity that causes entities to appear; and therefore it is a destruction of that non-cognition that renders the entities that had been caused by this non-cognition to be immersed, once again, in the unity of Śiva-as-consciousness. (See also above, at the ŚDVṛ at footnote 276).

One must note in particular that what is "destroyed," the non-cognition of non-duality, is in fact nothing at all; for it is an absence, which is (repeatedly) said to have no nature whatsoever: it is often said in Utpaladeva's ŚDVṛ to be *akiñcidrūpa*. What is implicated is not a true error or *bhrānti*, but an absence of non-cognition. About this, see Nemec 2012, which is the very first scholarly publication to identify the *abhedākhyāti* doctrine and which traced its development in the Pratyabhijñā's treatment of error. Cf. Ratié 2014a: 161–162, which makes use of this concept as unearthed in Nemec 2012, and compare, esp., her footnotes 112 and 113 therein.

[294] Or, perhaps better: "In this way, because there otherwise is no rational justification for the production and destruction (of entities), the Śiva-nature of everything is firmly established."

[295] Here I read *rūpa* (ŚD 4.63a) with what precedes and what follows it. On another possible interpretation of ŚD 4.63ab, see footnote 305.

[296] Utpaladeva here glosses *itaś ca* (ŚD 4.60c) with *ito 'pi ca hetoḥ*.

sensory or mental cognition.[297] Even those [Naiyāyikas and Vaiśeṣikas] who propose[298] that it is different (from its parts) maintain that the cognition (of that whole) occurs in a fully undifferentiated manner, by virtue of the inherence (of the whole in its parts).[299] And this is the item that must be considered.

Even though (the Naiyāyikas and Vaiśeṣikas maintain that) the divisions that are the parts are present in an extended appearance—indeed, this because (they maintain that only) an absence of extension is found (only) in what has no division, the measure of which is the *paramāṇu*[300]—nevertheless, it is a unitary object named Devadatta that appears as a single mass that is tightly connected [*niḥsandhibandha*]. Thus, a unity appears in those very divisions, i.e., parts.[301]

Since there is a unity there,[302] therefore there is a capacity there for that [unity], which has been mentioned (by me) in the *Īśvarapratyabhijñā*,[303] one

---

[297] This distinction of sensory from mental cognition is present, as well, in the ĪPK, for which see, e.g., *āhnika* eight of the first *adhikāra* of the ĪPK and ĪPKVṛ.

[298] A marginal note in D[a] (folio 173v.) glosses *pratijñātas* (line 385 of the present edition) with *pratijñayā sthāpitaḥ*.

[299] See, e.g., NS 2.1.32-36, esp. 2.1.34 (2.1.35 in Jha's translation): *sarvāgrahaṇam avayavyasiddheḥ*. "From the whole (*avayavi-*) not being established, one would not apprehend anything." Cf. NSBh ad NS 2.1.34: *yady avayavī nāsti sarvasya grahaṇaṃ nopapadyate. kiṃ tat sarvam. dravyaguṇakarmasāmānyaviśeṣasamavāyāḥ. kathaṃ kṛtvā. paramāṇusamavasthānaṃ tāvad darśanaviṣayo na bhavaty atīndriyatvād aṇūnām, dravyāntarañ cāvayavibhūtaṃ darśanaviṣayo nāsti, darśanaviṣayasthāś ceme dravyādayo gṛhante te niradhiṣṭhānā na gṛhyeran. gṛhyante tu kumbho 'yaṃ śyāma eko mahān saṃyuktaḥ spandate 'sti mṛnmayaś ceti, santi ceme guṇādayo dharmā iti. tena sarvasya grahaṇāt paśyāmo 'sti dravyāntarabhūto 'vayavīti.* "If the whole does not exist, it would not be possible to apprehend anything. What is this 'anything'? Substance [*dravya*], quality [*guṇa*], action [*karma*], universal [*sāmānya*], particular [*viśeṣa*], and inherence [*samavāya*]. How so? The state of the *paramāṇu*, first of all, is not one that is an object of perception, because the *aṇus* lie beyond the (reach of the) sense organs. Any other substance, moreover, is a whole; it would not be an object of perception (if one accepts the opponent's view, that wholes do not exist). These [entities], substance, etc., are found to be established as objects of perception; without a substratum, they would not be apprehended. Yet, they are apprehended: 'this is a pot, which is black, singular, large, intact/joined (to something else); it moves, and it is made of clay.' These, moreover, the qualities, etc., are properties (of the pot). Therefore, since one apprehends all (of them), we (can) see that the whole, being different from substance, exists."

A note in D[a] (folio 173v.) glosses *pratītiḥ* (line 385) with *avayavipratītiḥ*.

[300] In Nyāya-Vaiśeṣika ontology, it is the *paramāṇu* alone that is partless, as is well known. Therefore, the appearance of any extended entity of necessity involves the appearance of a complex of parts appearing as one. See footnote 299.

[301] Utpaladeva here (line 389) clearly makes reference to what is said at ŚD 4.61c: *bhinneṣv aikyam*, and I understand him to gloss *bhinneṣu* with *avayaveṣu*, but it is also possible that *bhinna* should be read adjectivally, as it is evidently used at line 391–392: . . . *avayaveṣu ca bhinneṣv ekaiva devadattatā yujyate.*

[302] I understand Utpaladeva to place *tatra* in the first position in the word-order of the present sentence (beginning at line 389 of the present edition) in order to capture Somānanda's use of two *tatras* in the *mūla* (at ŚD 4.61d and 4.62a), one in each part of the relative-correlative (*yathā-tathā*) clause. By placing it outside the structure of the same relative-correlative construction in the ŚDVṛ, that is, I understand Utpaladeva to suggest both halves of this construction stand in relation to the same "there."

[303] Of the various places where one could look for this idea in the ĪPK and ĪPKVṛ, perhaps 2.1.8 is the first to consider: *kintu nirmāṇaśaktiḥ sāpy evaṃviduṣa īśituḥ | tathā vijñātṛvijñeyabhedo yad avabhāsyate* ||. "Nevertheless, that manifestation of such a differentiation between subject and object of knowledge is the very creative power of the Lord, who knows thus" (translationTorella's). The

that belongs to the Lord—to Śiva, who is made up of consciousness;[304] it is by means of it—i.e., by means of this capacity—that the dualistic nature of the parts is (present) in Devadatta, who is undivided, and the fully unitary nature as Devadatta (simultaneously) is joined to the divisions that are (mutually) differentiated. Just as a single form is present in the divisions that are the parts (of "Devadatta"), (so also) in this (same) way, Śiva-nature is present in absolutely every object abiding in the entire triple world.[305]

4.63cd-64ab

This is precisely what he indicates:[306]

---

corresponding passage of the ĪPKVṛ reads as follows: *evaṃ pūrṇatayā prakāśamānasyāpi parameśvarasya saiṣā sṛṣṭiśaktir yajjñātṛjñeyasvabhāvā bhāvāḥ svato 'nyonyaṃ ca vibhāgenāvasīyante, na ca tathāvasāyena tasya svarūpasthitis tirodhīyate.* "The fact that the various entities existing as subject and object of knowledge are determined as differentiated from each other and from Parameśvara (or from the self), is [due to] the creative power of Parameśvara, who, yet, thus shines in absolute fullness, neither does his own permanent form ever in any way cease to exist as a consequence of this determination" (translation Torella's).

[304] The implication in describing Śiva as *cinmaya* is that his nature as consciousness endows him with the capacity in question. It is likely a *hetugarbhaviśeṣaṇa*, an adjective of cause: the capacity in question is Śiva's *because* he is made up of consciousness, which is the only supple entity that simultaneously could appear as what is both many and one (about which see above at ŚD, and ŚDVṛ ad, 4.53-54ab).

[305] My interpretation of this sentence, and of ŚD 4.63ab, depends on my understanding of the punctuation. One can interpret the verse (and the commentary) to present a "just as. . . so also. . ." construction (*yathā . . . tathā* . . . in the verse; "as. . . in this (same) way. . ." or *yathā . . . evam* . . . in the commentary), as I have done. And yet, one could also understand *yathā* to mean "since" and read the clause introduced by it with what precedes it, in both the verse and the commentary. On this latter interpretation, the period would come following *rūpam* (again in both the verse and the commentary, at the cæsura following ŚD 4.63a in the *mūla* and in the commentary at line 363 of the present edition); and a stand-alone sentence introduced by *tathā* (ŚD 4.63b) or *evam* (in the commentary, line 392) would offer a concluding, declarative, simple sentence. On this interpretation one would translate ŚD 4.63ab with ". . . , since a (single) form [i.e., Devadatta] is present in the parts. Thus, the (same) form [i.e., Śiva-nature] is present in everything." Similarly, one could translate the present passage of the commentary with ". . . , since a single form is present in the different parts. In this way, Śiva-nature is present in absolutely every object abiding in the triple world." Given the preference I have for the former interpretation, I have modified the punctuation of the ŚDVṛ as it is found in the KSTS edition, by recording a full stop after *yujyate* (line 392) and a comma after *ekaṃ rūpam* (on the same line of the present edition). K$^{ed.}$ records precisely the opposite punctuation (i.e., it records a comma after *yujyate* and a full stop after *ekaṃ rūpam*).

Utpaladeva here makes clear that it is existence as *both* one and many, as a whole including of multiple parts, that is explained by Śiva's capacity or *sāmarthya*. This discussion of such a capacity echoes one Utpaladeva articulated at ŚDVṛ ad ŚD 4.49cd-51ab, where he suggested no capacity of the causes could impart existence to an *asat* effect or *kārya*. There, no capacity of distinct entities in active combination could cause a new effect to come to be. Here, only Śiva's capacity (as consciousness) can allow multiple distinct entities in fact to exist *as a whole*.

[306] Utpaladeva here indicates that Somānanda explicitly draws the analogy telegraphed at ŚD 4.63ab, namely, that just as the one Devadatta inheres as a unity in the parts that make up that individual, so too does Śiva-nature inhere as a unity found in all the parts or entities that make up the universe.

kva pāṇipādaṃ kva śiro yathaikyaṃ bhinnadeśagam
4.64. tadvat sarvapadārthānāṃ jagaty aikye sthitaḥ śivaḥ

Where is hand and foot, where the head? Just as the unity (that is Devadatta) is present in these different places, so also Śiva exists in a unity of all real things in the universe.

The division that is the parts is itself of the nature of the undivided whole, simply inasmuch as it is of the nature of Śiva—so much was explained (by me) in the *Īśvarapratyabhijñā*.[307] In the same way,[308] Śiva-nature, the producer (of the universe), exists in the unity (found) in the universe.

4.64cd-66

śabdāder grahaṇaṃ nāsti pūrvāparasahoditaiḥ
4.65. manasaḥ preraṇaṃ kasmāt prāgjñānena vinā sthitā
sarvaikatāta evātra tathā sauṣuptabodhanam
4.66. ghaṭate kathaṃ nimittasya prāgyogāyogacoditaiḥ
yoge jāgradavasthaiva tasmāt sarvaṃ śivātmakam

One would not apprehend (the *tanmātras* or sensibilia, viz.,) sound, etc., by means of (either) sequential or simultaneously arisen [cognitions](, if consciousness and its object were mutually distinct). Why would the mind be impelled to act in the absence of a prior cognition? For this very reason, a unity exists in everything, here. And with what have been put forward as arguments [-*codita*] regarding whether the cause (of awakening one in deep sleep) is connected (to the one who is to be awoken) prior (to being awoken) or is not connected, (we ask:) how is it possible to be awoken from deep sleep? If connected, this entails nothing other than the waking state. Therefore, everything is of the nature of Śiva.

And it is for this reason that a unity exists in everything here in the universe, because there could be no cognition of any object [*viṣaya*], be it one

---

[307]This is a matter dealt with at ĪPK 2.2. See in particular ĪPK (and ĪPKVṛ ad) 2.2.5: *jātidravyāvabhāsānāṃ bahir apy ekarūpatām | vyaktyekadeśabhedaṃ cāpy ālambante vikalpanāḥ* ||. "Conceptions of the appearances that are universals or substances rest externally, as well, on a unitary nature, as well as on the differentiation of the (individual) manifestation and (its) parts." ĪPKVṛ: *gāvaś caitra iti ca matayo bahir api gomātraikaghanapuruṣaviśeṣākārābhāsaikyaṃ svalakṣaṇāvayavābhāsabahutvaṃ ca parāmṛśanti*. "Thoughts such as 'the cows, (or) Caitra,' moreover, although external, point to a unity—what is the appearance of a form: a single mass of cows, or a particular person—and to multiplicity, the appearances of the (relevant) *svalakṣaṇas* that are the parts (that make up the wholes)."

[308]I here accept the reading of K$^{ed.p.c.}$ at line 398 of the present edition, of *evam* for *eva* (which, given that manuscripts D/D^{a} were evidently the only ones available to Kaul of the SDVṛ, one may understand to be a silent emendation appearing in the *editio princeps*). On accepting this reading, I punctuate with a period following *īśvarapratyabhijñāyām*, a punctuation absent from K$^{ed.}$. The translation reflects these editorial decisions.

of sound, tactile form, visual form, or the like,[309] by means of sequential or simultaneously arisen cognitions, if they [i.e., the cognitions and their object] were (mutually) distinct.

To explain: How, to begin, could there be an initial cognition without the object?[310] And how could the two,[311] each fixed in its own (respective) nature, stand in a relation of that which apprehends and that which is apprehended, following (the initial cognition), or even conjointly (with it)?[312]

And why, in the absence of a cognition that is intent on the object, would the *ātman* impel the mind to act?[313]

Objection: That [impelling of the *manas* to act] has as its purpose the apprehension of the external object.

(Reply:) The initial cognition (has as its purpose the apprehension of the external object, on your view; so in that case), what use is there in impelling the *manas* to act? And it (simply) is not the case (on your view) that the object that is external (to consciousness) is perceived by a(ny) cognition that is (itself)

---

[309] Here, "or the like" (*ādi*) refers to the remaining two *tanmātras*, namely, taste (*rasa*) and smell (*gandha*).

[310] That is, on the dualists' theory, cognition begins with an initial perceptual act on the part of an *indriya*, which only occurs when a sense-object (*viṣaya*) is within the ken. (Each *indriya* can make contact with only one class of object, viz., the ear with sound, the skin with that which is tangible, etc.) Utpaladeva thus here signals that the realist Naiyāyikas and Vaiśeṣikas, the opponents whose views are here placed under question, understand this action to be brought about by the contact of a material sense organ (*indriya*) with an ontologically distinct, material object or *viṣaya*. What is particularly in question in the present explanation of Utpaladeva, then, is the very definition of *pratyakṣa* according to Naiyāyikas and Vaiśeṣikas, for which see NS 1.1.4: *indriyārthasannikarṣotpannaṃ jñānam avyapadeśyam avyabhicāri vyavasāyātmakaṃ pratyakṣam*. (See footnote 396 for my translation of the same.) Cf. VS 3.1.13 (also cited and translated in footnote 396.) On the well-known doctrine of the Nyāya that the *indriyas* are material, see NS 1.1.12, cited in footnote 391.

[311] This refers, by standard rules of anaphora, to the cognition (*jñāna*) and its object (*viṣaya*). Given the emphasis on the *tanmātras* in the previous sentence, however, as well reference to the objects of sense (*viṣaya*), it is also perhaps the *indriya* and the object (*viṣaya* = *artha*) more specifically that are implicitly in question.

[312] The question here, then, ultimately is one of how contact of sense organ and object (*indriya-artha-sannikarṣa*) can produce an awareness in the knower, the *ātman*, of the object in question, this, of course, on the dualists' understanding of the matter.

[313] The initial apprehension of an object by the organs of sense, the *indriyas*, cannot be known unless the *manas* "organizes" one's apprehensions, such that they can be cognized by the knower, the *ātman*. Indeed, it is entirely possible under the Nyāya-Vaśeṣika theory of cognition for a sense-organ to apprehend an object without the knower, the *ātman*, being aware of it. For, a second cognition, on their view, is required to recognize the content and nature of a first apprehension. Thus, Utpaladeva asks how the *manas* is impelled by the cognizer, the *ātman*, to select and highlight, as it were, that particular, initial apprehension from among many such mechanical apprehensions, produced as they are by the mutually distinct, material *indriyas*, which furnish awareness of mutually distinct phenomena, when the *ātman* is not yet aware of it or intent on knowing it. Put simply, the cause of knowing must be presumed to explain the resultant knowing that is being accounted for; because the initial act of apprehension is mechanical and not driven by a particular desire of an agent to see an object, there is nothing in it that signals to the knower such that that knower might wish to cognize it. On the role of the *ātman* as impeller of the *manas* see, e.g., NS 2.1.26 and esp. the NSBh thereon, cited in footnote 316.

intent (upon the object), on account of which the mind would not have to be impelled to act.[314]

Therefore, (you must understand matters as follows:) when awareness [*saṃvedana*] exists at all times in the unity of Siva, who has consciousness as his nature, this is the extent of the procedure (of cognition), viz., it is made by the power of limitation, as it was described (by me) in the *Īśvarapratyabhijñā*;[315] it is to be regarded as consisting of the non-cognition of non-duality.

And, (analyzing this cognitive procedure, we ask:) how in the absence of a unitary nature could one who is lodged in a deep sleep be awoken by the issuing forth of loud sounds, or the like? To explain: Awareness [*jñāna*] of loud sounds or the like is the cause that awakens one (from the deep sleep), and with what have been put forward as arguments as to whether it [i.e., the cause] is joined prior (to the awakening), or is not (so) joined, (we ask:) how is this [cause of the awakening] possibly brought about?[316] To explain (further), if one is joined

---

[314]Will or desire is a mark of the *ātman* in the Nyāya, for which see NS 1.1.10: *icchādveṣaprayatnasukhaduḥkhajñānāni ātmanaḥ liṅgam iti*. "Desire, aversion, effort, pleasure, pain, and cognition are the mark of (the existence of) the *ātman*." The NSBh on this passage reads in part as follows: *yajjātīyasyārthasya sannikarṣāt sukham ātmopalabdhavān, tajjātīyam evārthaṃ paśyann upādātum icchati, seyam ādātum icchā ekasyānekārthadarśino darśanapratisandhānād bhavati liṅgam ātmanaḥ*. See also footnote 313.

[315]It is perhaps to ĪPK (and ĪPKVṛ ad) 2.3.6 that Utpaladeva here refers his readers: *ābhāsabhedād vastūnāṃ niyatārthakriyā punaḥ | sāmānādhikaraṇyena pratibhāsād abhedinām ||*. The corresponding passage of the ĪPKVṛ reads as follows: *ekasminn eva svalakṣaṇe pratyābhāsaṃ niyatiśaktyā kāryaṃ niyamitaṃ tathābhūtānekakāryakṛdābhāsabhedādhikaraṇam ekaṃ ca. sāmānādhikaraṇyābhāsavaśād vastu. anekasyaikatā hi sāmānādhikaraṇyam*. It is, of course, also possible Utpaladeva here had in mind a passage from the ĪPṬ to which we no longer have access.

[316]The problem addressed here is that the realist opponent understands awareness of objects (such as the loud sounds that are said to awaken a person in deep sleep) to require not merely contact of the sense organs (*indriyas*) with the objects in question but also the engagement with those sense data by a second cognition, which is intentionally directed by the *ātman*. The question here asked, then, is how the sleeping person can be actively aware of the object while remaining in deep sleep. Note that the same example—that of a person awoken from deep sleep—was explicitly invoked by Vātsyāyana to explain why it is that perception is defined by the contact of *indriya* and *artha* and not that of the *ātman* and the *manas*, viz., because when asleep or distracted (as the NS states) the *ātman* is not present to direct the perceptual act, which nevertheless occurs. See NS 2.1.26: *suptavyāsaktamanasāṃ cendriyārthayoḥ sannikarṣanimittatvāt*. "And (NS 1.1.4 defines *pratyakṣa* as involving *indriyārthasannikarṣa* for this reason, too:) because it [i.e., perception] is caused by the contact of the sense organ and the object for those whose mind is asleep or preoccupied." Cf. the NSBh thereon, which reads in part as follows: *indriyārthasannikarṣasya grahaṇaṃ nātmamanasoḥ sannikarṣasyeti. ekadā khalv ayaṃ prabodhakālaṃ praṇidhāya suptaḥ praṇidhānavaśāt prabudhyate. yadā tu tīvrau dhvanisparśau prabodhakāraṇaṃ bhavatas tadā prasuptasyendriyasannikarṣanimittaṃ prabodhajñānam utpadyate. tatra na jñātur manasaś ca sannikarṣasya prādhānyaṃ bhavati. kiṃ tarhi? indriyārthayoḥ sannikarṣasya. na hy ātmā jijñāsamānaḥ prayatnena manas tadā prerayatīti*. "There is mention (in NS 1.1.4) of the contact of sense organ and object, (and) not the contact of the *ātman* and the *manas*, for this (following) reason: sometimes, one who having resolved to awaken at a particular hour has fallen asleep awakens by the force of that resolution. But when a loud sound or forcible touch is what causes one to awaken, then the awakening awareness [*prabodha-jñāna*] that arises for the one who had fallen asleep is caused by the contact of the sense organ [i.e., either the ear or the skin] (with the object, i.e., either the loud sound or the forcible shaking). And in such an instance the contact of the cognizer [i.e., the *ātman*] and the

to the awareness of the (loud) sound or the like prior (to awakening from deep sleep), this would entail nothing other than the waking state, because that is the very definition thereof.[317] And yet, how can one be awoken if the cause—a prior awareness of the (loud) sound or the like—were found wanting?

Thus, this alone must be the case: When knowledge is unitary, this [cause of the awakening] can be nothing but the procedure of the non-cognition of Śiva-nature; the state of deep sleep is interrupted when a severe noise, e.g.,

---

manas is not primary. What is then? The contact of the *indriya* and the *artha*. For it is not the case that the *ātman* desires to know (in such an instance), such that by its effort it would impel the *manas* to act at that time." (For NS 1.1.4 see footnote 396.) Jha 1939: 142 (on the rendering of which the present one is based, though there it is counted as NS 2.1.27) parenthetically adds an explanation of the significance of reference to the sleeping person's resolve to awaken at a certain hour, stating that it is this that ". . . gives rise to the effort necessary for bringing about the requisite Mind-Soul contact." It is against this very supposition that the present passage of the ŚDVṛ militates, Utpaladeva suggesting it is impossible for the *ātman* to effect such a resolve when the body (and mind) is asleep, because there would be no way for the *ātman* to know of the first step in the two-step cognitive process, that of *indriyārthasannikarṣa*. Nothing would allow it to initiate the necessary *ātmamanaḥsannikarṣa* to know an unexpected *artha*, such as a loud (but unexpected) sound.

Note, however, that Vātsyāyana offers an explanation for just this problem at NSBh ad NS 2.1.29 (NS 2.1.30 in Jha's translation): *asati praṇidhāne saṅkalpe cāsati suptavyāsaktamanasāṃ yad indriyārthasannikarṣād utpadyate jñānam, tatra manaḥsaṃyogo 'pi kāraṇam iti manasi kriyākāraṇaṃ vācyam iti. yathaiva jñātuḥ khalv ayam icchājanitaḥ prayatno manasaḥ preraka ātmaguṇaḥ, evam ātmani guṇāntaraṃ sarvasya sādhakaṃ pravṛttidoṣajanitam asti, yena preritaṃ mana indriyeṇa sambadhyate. tena hy apreryamāṇe manasi saṃyogābhāvāj jñānānutpattau sarvārthatāsya nivarttate. eṣitavyaṃ cāsya guṇāntarasya dravyaguṇakarmakāraṇatvam, anyathā hi caturvidhānām aṇūnāṃ bhūtasūkṣmāṇāṃ manasāṃ ca tato 'nyasya kriyāhetor asambhavāt śarīrendriyaviṣayāṇām anutpattiprasaṅgaḥ.* "(Objection:) Though there is no effort and there is no desire on the part of those whose minds are asleep or preoccupied, a cognition (nevertheless) arises from the contact of sense-organ and object. In such instances [*tatra*], the cause (of the cognition) is [i.e., must be] also the contact of the *manas*. Thus, the cause of the action as regards the *manas* (must be explained). This is what is said (by the opponent). (Reply:) In the very same way as (in the case of ordinary cognition) an effort that is a quality of the *ātman*, what is produced by the desire of the knower, is what impels the *manas*, so in the same way that which brings about the accomplishment of all [experience] in the *ātman* is another quality found therein, which is produced by a fault in the activity (of that knower, this in the form of *adṛṣṭa* or the non-visible karmic force). Because of it the *manas*, (thus) impelled, is connected to the sense-organ. For if the *manas* were not impelled by that [other quality in the *ātman*], then, because there would be no contact (of the *manas* with the *indriya*), no cognition would arise, and this being so, this [other quality] would then cease to be universally effective [*sarvārthatā*]. And (yet), one must approve of the fact that this other quality is the cause as regards substances, qualities, and actions; for otherwise, since no other cause than it would come to be for the actions of the four types of *aṇus*, which are (only) subtly material, nor for minds, the fault would arise that the body, sense-organs, and sense-objects would not be produced." See also Jha 1939: 144–145 (on which the present translation is based). It would have been interesting to know Utpaladeva's reply to the doctrine of *adṛṣṭa* as the cause for awakening one in deep sleep by an unexpected stimulus. On *adṛṣṭa* (though mostly in the Vaiśeṣika), see Wezler 1983; cf. Merkrebs 1977. See also Halbfass 1980b.

[317] This is so because to know the object, the *ātman* would have to be able to direct the *manas* to inform it of what was discovered through the initial contact of sense organ and objects of sense. This step in cognition, Utpaladeva here says, is precisely what defines a fully volitional, waking state of consciousness.

for its part unexpected,[318] impels one to obscure (one's awareness of non-dual Śiva-nature).[319]

And therefore, (we ask:) this [mere procedure] could be contradicted, how? And since it is proven by a valid means of knowing, (we ask:) it is not conclusive, how?[320]

4.67

4.67. sāmānyarūpatā vāsti sā cābhinnā viśeṣataḥ
bhinnābhinnātmakaḥ kvāpi padārthas tādṛg iṣyate

Alternatively,[321] a universal nature exists, and it is not different from the particular (of its class). Sometimes, (proponents of opposing schools maintain that) a real thing is composed of the distinct [particular] and the generic [universal or genus]; we accept just such a one.

Alternatively, a universal nature exists, which is a unitary nature belonging to all the particulars (of a class of entities), the brindled cow, etc., and it is not different from those particulars (of the class). For just as a real thing that is composed of the distinct [particular] and the generic [universal or genus] is

---

318 Perhaps one should accept the reading offered in K$^{ed.}$ of *ajñāna* for what I accept as the correct reading here (at line 418 of the present edition), viz., *ajñāta*, the latter being attested in all the five manuscripts examined for this passage for the present edition. Accepting *ajñāna*, one would understand the passage to mean that the "severe noise," e.g., is a form of not knowing, by which would be meant the lack of knowing the unity of Śiva-as-consciousness, the *abhedākhyāti* that is so often mentioned in the ŚDVṛ. I have not adopted this textual reading, however, because it has no support in the manuscripts examined by me (including D^{a}, which informed the edition of K$^{ed.}$), and because *ajñāta* presents itself as the *lectio difficilior*. One may tentatively conclude, therefore, that the reading of K$^{ed.}$ resulted from a silent emendation of the text by M. Kaul.

319 Thus, deep sleep involves an active involvement or awareness of Śiva-nature, while the waking state involves an inactivity, a non-awareness of the same. Thus, Utpaladeva inverts the locus of volition, finding it in deep sleep and not in the waking state, what amounts to a quite brilliant solution to the question of agency and the transition from deep sleep to the waking state: one fails to act in awaking, and one acts in falling or being asleep. (On the same, see the introduction to the present volume.) One may also compare the present analysis with that offered of deep sleep in the ĪPK and ĪPKVṛ, esp. at 3.2.13 and 3.2.15.

320 I conjecture the text should here be emended. K$^{ed.}$, prior to emendation, read as follows (line 419 of the present edition): *pramāṇāt siddham iti ca na niścāyakaṃ*. I suggest *pramāṇāt siddham iti ca na niścāyakaṃ katham*. The reading of K$^{ed.}$ is supported verbatim by D^{a}, G, J, S^{2}, and S$^{3p.c.}$. S$^{3a.c.}$ offers *niścāya katham*. I conjecture that the text originally read *niścāyakaṃ katham*, but lost *kaṃ* (*ka* with *anusvāra*) by haplography. Subsequent to this, I posit, a scribe eliminated *tha* to regularize to *niścāyakam*. Note there is a symmetry in the syntax of the text as I present it with what immediately precedes it: the immediately preceding clause also asks a rhetorical question following an *iti*-clause and ending in an interrogative; it reads (lines 418–419): *iti ca paroktaṃ kutaḥ*.

321 Somānanda argued in the immediately preceding passage of text (ŚD 4.64cd-66) that only a unity of consciousness could explain cognition. Here, he proffers an alternative proof, namely, that the existence of class universals proves the ontological unity for which he advocates.

recognized in the philosophy of the Sāṅkhyas, the Jains, etc.,[322] we (also) accept just such a one—i.e., just such a real thing [*vāstava*]. That [real thing], moreover, could not exist in the absence of the unity of reality. Thus the connection with what is about to be said.[323]

4.68-70

4.68. bauddhasya cen na sāmānyam anumānaṃ nivartate
yathā suvarṇabhāṇḍeṣu na tathā hematāmrayoḥ
4.69. suvarṇam ānayety ukte śūnyatā kiṃ pratīyate
viśeṣasparśavirahāt kadācid api yujyate
4.70. tattvasyaikyaṃ vinā na syād ekasyaiva viruddhatā
sāmānyena viśeṣeṇa katham ekasya yogitā

If for the Buddhist there is no universal, (then) inference ceases to occur.[324] (When one says "bring the gold,") (an awareness based on verbal

---

[322] It is notable that Utpaladeva associates this view first of all with the systems of the Sāṅkhyas and the Jainas, rather than those of the Naiyāyikas (and Vaiśeṣikas) as one might expect in the present context. After all, the NS, e.g., defines the universal in a manner that is innocuous enough and should be generally acceptable to the Śaivas: NS 2.2.70 (NS 2.2.69 in Jha's translation): *samānaprasavātmikā jātiḥ*. "The universal is of a nature that produces what is common." Cf. the corresponding passage of the NSBh: *yā samānaṃ buddhiṃ prasūte bhinneṣv adhikaraṇeṣu, yayā bahūnītaretarato na vyāvartante yo 'rtho 'nekatra pratyayānuvṛttinimittaṃ tat sāmānyam. yac ca keṣāñcid abhedaṃ kutaścid bhedaṃ karoti tat sāmānyaviśeṣo jātir iti.* (Cf. Praśastapāda's understanding of the universal at PDhSaṃ 10.0[311.13 *ff.*] and on universals in the Nyāya and Vaiśeṣika schools see also Chakrabarti 1975.) Why insist on a comparison with the Sāṅkhyas and the Jains over and against the views of Naiyāyikas and Vaiśeṣikas, then? The reason, it seems evident enough, is that the *sāmānya* in the Nyāya and Vaiśeṣika schools is understood to be ontologically different from the (non-repeatable) particular (*viśeṣa*), though they are intimately associated by way of *samavāya*. (So much is implicit and explicit in, e.g., Praśastapāda's PDhSaṃ, as is well known: *dravyaguṇakarmasāmānyaviśeṣasamavāyānām ṣaṇṇām padārthānām sādharmyavaidharmyatattvajñānam.*)

This stands in contrast to the Jaina view found, e.g., in the *Parīkṣāmukhasūtra* of Māṇikyanandī 4.1: *sāmānyaviśeṣātmā tadartho viṣayaḥ*. Here, the one and same object is of the nature of both the particular and the universal. (The same is quoted in Dravid [1972] 2001: 111, fn. 1.) Similarly, SāṅKā 11 (for which see footnote 255) suggests that all entities that are *vyakta* (i.e., manifested from the *avyakta* or unmanifested *mūlaprakṛti*) are *sāmānya*, as is the *pradhāna* itself. In a word, the Śaiva position as Utpaladeva here describes it is one that understands *sāmānya* and *viśeṣa* to be mutually identified, rather than intimately related but distinct as per the Nyāya-Vaiśeṣika.

[323] In what immediately follows, Somānanda and, in particular, Utpaladeva will suggest that there must exist a real universal, such that the nature of an object is both distinct and non-distinct. This they do in contrast to the position held by the Buddhist Epistemologists, who claim that the universal or *sāmānya* is a constructed and relational category. They also claim, with a realist opponent in mind, that this justifies their view that everything is made up of consciousness: only consciousness can be both individual and universal simultaneously. See in particular the ŚDVṛ ad ŚD 4.68-70, at lines 441–443 of the present edition, where Utpaladeva says the following: *acidrūpasya bāhyasyaitan na ghaṭate, tad vyanakti sāmānyenety abhedena, viśeṣeṇeti bhedena. cittattvasya punaḥ svacchandatvān naiva virodhaḥ...*.

[324] Perhaps Somānanda here has PV (*pratyakṣapariccheda*) 3.30 in mind when he suggests that his Buddhist interlocutor accepts no (real) universal: *arthānāṃ yac ca sāmānyam anyavyāvṛttilakṣaṇam | yanniṣṭhās ta ime śabdā na rūpaṃ tasya kiṃcana ||*. "That which is the universal [*sāmānya*] of things,

knowledge rooted in the universal does) not (arise) with respect to (mixed) gold and copper as (it arises) with respect to (pure) gold ornaments. Is it absence [*śūnyatā*] that is perceived when one says, "bring the gold," as a result of the absence of contact with a particular (that is not gold)? Is that appropriate somewhere?[325] It could not be so in the absence of the unity of reality: (for,) the one [object, e.g., a gold bracelet] itself would be (self-)contradictory. How could the one [object] be connected with the universal, (and) with the particular?

If there is no universal for the Buddhist, then he abandons the inference he lays claim to, which has the universal as its object. And without the universal, when one says "bring the gold" the awareness [*pratīti*] (that "this is gold" that arises for someone looking for gold) with respect to golden objects such as a bracelet or an upper-arm bracelet would not occur as it does with respect to (entities consisting of alloyed metal of both) gold and copper, because the awareness of gold only [*eva*] (in the context of both gold and copper) results from the absence of any contact with copper, while nothing at all is left out of (the awareness of those entities that are made only of gold,) the *kaṭaka* and *keyūra* bracelets, for example.[326]

---

moreover, what is characterized by the exclusion of others, (and) on which those words (for the things in question) are based—it has no nature [*rūpa*] whatever." See also the translation of Franco and Notake 2014: 92, on which the present one is based. Cf. PV (*pratyakṣapariccheda*) 3.43ab: *tasmāt samānatayaivāsmin sāmānye 'vastulakṣaṇam* |. "[Thus, because of its being common, a universal cannot have any relation with individuals.] Therefore, the common nature in this universal is the mark of [its being] unreal." Translation is that of Franco and Notake 2014: 119. Cf. also PV (*pratyakṣapariccheda*) 3.50: *jñānamātrārthakaraṇe 'py ayogyam ata eva tat | tad ayogyatayārūpaṃ tad dhy avastuṣu lakṣaṇam* ||. "It is for this reason that that [universal] is incapable even of producing an object that is the mere cognition (of itself). Since that [universal] is (thus) incapable, it has no nature [*arūpa*] (of its own); for that [failure to produce an object that is a cognition of itself] is the (very) characteristic (found) in unreal things." (Translation a modification of that of Franco and Notake 2014: 129.) Finally, see PV (*pratyakṣapariccheda*) 3.45: *yac ca vastubalāj jñānaṃ jāyate tad apekṣate | na saṃketaṃ na sāmānyabuddhiṣv etad vibhāvyate* ||. "A cognition, moreover, that is produced by the power of a real thing does not depend on verbal convention [*saṃketa*]. This [lack of dependence] is not manifested in the cognitions of universals." (Translation a modification of Franco and Notake 2014: 123.)

Note also that D^a (folio 175r.) glosses with *tarhi* ("therefore"), written above *anumānaṃ* (ŚD 4.68b) between the lines of text.

325 D^a (folio 175r.) records *kākvā* ("in a certain voice") above *yujyate* (ŚD 4.69d).

326 Here, Utpaladeva suggests that the cognition of gold alloyed with copper would, if one accepts the Buddhist understanding of the universal as a purely relational category, be impossible. For one could have an awareness of nothing but gold only by way of making no contact with the copper, which would not be possible in the instance in question, meaning Somānanda argues that one could not be aware of "gold" under such circumstances at all!

The problem of the inferential nature of language and its dependence on the universal is of course well known in the Buddhist epistemological tradition. See, e.g., PSam 5.1 (cited in TSP ad TS 1514, p. 539): *na pramāṇāntaraṃ śābdam anumānāt tathā hi tat | kṛtakatvādivat svārtham anyāpohena bhāṣate* ||. "Cognition based on the word [*śābda*] is not different from inference, for just as (an inferential mark or *liṅga* such as) the quality of having been produced [*kṛtakatva*] (proves the probandum, or *sādhya*, through the exclusion of others [*anyāpoha*]), it [i.e., the cognition based on the word] expresses its own object through the exclusion of others." (The translation, excepting very minor modifications, is that of

When one [i.e., the Buddhist] accepts the exclusion of the other [*anyāpoha*], for its part, as the universal, (then one may ask:) is it an absence the form of which is a pure negation [i.e., the total absence of that which is non-gold] that is cognized when one says "bring the gold," the cause being that there is no contact with a particular (that is non-gold)? Or, (to put the matter in terms of that with which one positively does have contact,) is it those particulars alone that are (mentally) excluded from that which is not made of gold, that (are cognized,) produce the judgment of gold, (and thereby) receive a unity (as a single class of entities—as "golden")?[327] [Somānanda] says in a certain tone of

---

Hattori, for which see Hattori 2000: 139; cf. Hattori 2006b: 56. Compare, also, with the translation of Jha 1937–1939, vol. 2: 754–755, noting that Jha counts TS 1514 as TS 1515.)

It also is not surprising that Somānanda appeals to Kumārila in dealing with this philosophical opponent, as we shall see; for not only is it plainly evident that Kumārila addressed the Buddhists' views on *apoha* in his ŚV, but his treatment of the views of his Buddhist counterparts are frequently cited in works that address the various issues related to the same. This includes not only Jayanta Bhaṭṭa's NM (about which see footnote 328) but also the present passage of the TS(P): PSam 5.1 is cited in the TSP under a verse (1514, numbered verse 1515 by Jha, this following the edition of Krishnamacharya) that serves to explain the capacity for a word to serve as a valid means of knowledge of the object of which it speaks. The reason it may convey knowledge of such an object, it is explained at TS 1514*ff.*, involves the fact that speech is inferential in nature; it is not to be understood as a valid *pramāṇa* in its own right that is different from *pratyakṣa* and *anumāna*. This explanation, in turn, is offered in the TS to reply to an objection expressed in the immediately preceding pair of TS verses (i.e., 1512–1513, numbered 1513–1514 by Jha), where it is asked what can connect a word to the external object it is meant to denote: *vacasāṃ pratibandho vā ko bāhyeṣv asti vastuṣu | pratipādayatāṃ tāni yenaiṣāṃ syāt pramāṇatā* || 1512 || *bhinnākṣagrahaṇādibhyo naikātmyaṃ na tadudbhavaḥ | vyabhicārān na cānyasya yujyate 'vyabhicāritā* || 1513 ||. "Now, what connection exists of words to real, external things, because of which these [words], in communicating those [real things], would be authoritative means of knowledge? It [i.e., the connection] cannot be one of identity, because they are apprehended by different sense organs, and for other reasons; it cannot be one of causality, because of the fallacious reasoning so involved. And no other [connection] is possible."

Kamalaśīla in glossing *pratibandha* makes explicit the reference to Dharmakīrti's twofold *svabhāvapratibandha* that is clearly also referred to in Śāntarakṣita's text, mentioning both a *pratibandha* characterized by causality (*tadutpattilakṣaṇa*) and one characterized by identity (*tādātmyalakṣaṇa*). (See TSP, p. 538, lines 11–13: *na hi vācyair vastubhiḥ saha kaścit tādātmyalakṣaṇaḥ tadutpattilakṣaṇo vā pratibandho vacasām asti, yena tāni vastūni pratipādayatām eṣāṃ vacasāṃ prāmāṇyaṃ syāt.* "For it is not the case that any connection exists, be it one of identity (*tādātmyalakṣaṇa*) or one of causality (*tadutpattilakṣaṇa*), of words with those real things that are to be denoted by words, because of which these words, in communicating those real things, would be authoritative.") Along the way, he cites an argument of Kumārila's (at *pratyakṣapariccheda*, verses 156–157) offered against the possibility of basing an understanding of difference on the fact that a given object is perceived by different sense organs, Kumārila being, in the *Pañjikā*, the *pūrvapakṣin* whose position is to be defeated. See also the translations of the present passages of the TS and TSP in Jha 1937–1939, vol. 2: 753–754.

327 On the term (*eka-*)*pratyavamarśa* see Eltschinger, et al. 2018: 6–7.

As I understand it, two problems are here addressed. The first problem is as follows: if gold, e.g., consists of nothing but not non-gold—if the universal is only a relational category built on what it is not—then awareness of gold amounts to the *absence* of an awareness of not-gold. Therefore, Utpaladeva suggests, the absence of contact with a particular that is not gold (such as copper, e.g.), what is in fact an *absence* of an awareness of that which is not gold, could lead one to have an awareness of gold. This is of course absurd. Second, Utpaladeva queries the nature of exclusion when one cognizes the particulars the nature of which is to produce an understanding not non-x. He asks whether it is appropriate for these (unique) particulars, consisting only in the exclusion of what is not gold, to lead

voice [i.e., with contemptuous irony] that it is this that must be explained (by his Buddhist opponent), viz., whether so much is somewhere appropriate; (and so much is not possible, for) this is never appropriate—that absence, for its part, appears.[328] Thus, this [view of the *sāmānya*] is not possible in the absence of a unity of the reality of consciousness in (all) things, because (in its absence) there would be a mutual contradiction in the nature of one and the same object.[329]

So much (also) is not possible for the external object, which is not made up of consciousness. [Somānanda] expresses that with "with the universal," i.e., with that which is nondifferentiated, (and) with "with the particular," i.e., with that which is differentiated.[330] By contrast, because the true nature of consciousness is free, there is no (self-)contradiction (of the *abheda* form that is the *sāmānya* and the *bheda* form that is the *viśeṣa* of the object of cognition), as has been stated (by me) in the Pratyabhijñā (corpus) itself.[331]

---

uniformly to the judgment "gold" and thus acquire a unity. This is to say that he argues that it is difficult for the Buddhists to explain how the particulars themselves that are seen (as not non-x) can lead to an awareness of a particular category of entities negatively so defined. Put differently, the previous instance involved the production of an awareness of a void, a total absence or *prasajyapratiṣedha*; the second instance understands a cognition of something that is present only inasmuch as what one does contact in the cognition is that which excludes what it is not, or in other words is another kind of absence.

[328]This general line of criticism is not unknown elsewhere, of course. The *Nyāyamañjarī* (NM), for example, understands *apoha* to require an *āśraya*, this because it is itself constituted as an absence. See Kataoka 2008: 19, 21, which reads (p. 19): [0 *upodghātaḥ*] *nanv apohaśabdārthapakṣe mahatīṃ dūṣaṇavṛṣṭim utsasarja bhaṭṭaḥ* | [1 *apohasyāśrayaḥ*] *tathā hy apoho nāma vyāvṛttir abhāva ucyate* | *na cābhāvaḥ svatantratayā ghaṭādivad avagamyate* | *tad ayam anyāśrito grahītavyaḥ* | *kaś ca tasyāśraya iti cintyam* |. . . (p. 21:) [1.5 *upasaṃhāraḥ*] *tasmāt sarvasādhāraṇaṃ pratipiṇḍaṃ parisamāptaṃ kimapi nūnam agonivṛtter adhikaraṇam abhidhātavyam* | *tac ca gotvam eva* | *tasminn aṅgīkṛte vā kim agovyāvṛttikalpanāyāsena* |. As Kataoka (2008: 1, 3) indicates, the passage of the NM in question itself summarizes the views of Kumārila on *apoha*. See also Hattori 2006b (cited in Kataoka 2008: 1), which offers a thorough summary of these arguments.

[329]This is so, evidently, because one and the same object would not be able to have the two contradictory aspects, i.e., universal and particular. The expression here used (*parasparaviruddhatva*, line 441 of the present edition), moreover, suggests that Utpaladeva here has in mind the second of two types of contradiction defined by Dharmakīrti, what Bandyopadhyay labels "logical contradiction," which is exemplified by the mutual contradiction of existence and non-existence. Reference to this type of contradiction is found at ŚD 4.24 and in Utpaladeva's commentary thereon. See also, esp., fn. 120, where NB 3.77 is quoted in reference to Dharmakīrti's definition of this type of contradiction.

[330]This is to say that an external entity that is *acidrūpa* could not appear as both and not be self-contradictory, this due to the absence of a unity of reality. Here, Utpaladeva, following Somānanda, turns the reader's attention to the position of a realist opponent, namely, a Mīmāṃsaka. (See below.) Note, also, that Somānanda argued for precisely this view of objects as both differentiated and unified at ŚD 4.67, where he stated his acceptance of a *padārtha* that is *bhinnābhinnātmaka*. Utpaladeva noted in his ŚDVṛ ad 4.67 (line 425 of the present edition), moreover, that it is in the present passage (4.68-70) that that position would be shown to be the appropriate one. See above, especially at footnote 323.

[331]See, esp., ĪPK 2.3.14: *guṇaiḥ śabdādibhir bhedo jātyādibhir abhinnatā* | *bhāvānām ittham ekatra pramātary upapadyate* ||. "In this manner, it is possible in one and the same agent of knowing for entities to be (simultaneously) possessed of difference, this by way of the qualities such as sound, and unity, this by way of universals, etc." See also the corresponding passage of the ĪPKVṛ: *bhāvānāṃ śabdarūpasaṃsthānādinā bhedākṣepo jātyādinā ca ekatākṣepo 'nubhūyamānaḥ pramātraikye ghaṭate. anyonyabhedavyavasthāpy anusaṃdhānāyattā.* "A difference is suggested for entities by way of

4.71-73ab

4.71. ekatattvaṃ vinaitac ca vyavahāro na jāyate
śabdārthayor na saṃbandho bhinnayor bhinnadeśayoḥ
4.72. viruddharūpayor bhinnakaraṇagrāhyayor api
mukhe hi śabdo bhūmau ca vidyate 'rthaḥ kva saṃgamaḥ
4.73. amūrta eko mūrtaś ca dvitīyo yogitā katham

Moreover, (human) discourse [*vyavahāra*] could not be produced in the absence of this single reality: there could be no connection of speech and object, which are (mutually) distinct, situated in different places, of (mutually) contradictory forms, and apprehended by different instruments. For the word is found in the mouth and the object (denoted by it) on the ground—where can there be a meeting (of the two)?[332] One is

---

sound, visible form, configuration, and the like, and unity is suggested by way of universals, etc.; that [i.e., each of the pair of suggestions] can be experienced (only) in the unity of the agent of knowing." Cf. also the renderings of these passages found at Torella 1994: 172 (and see there, esp., fn. 30, which explains the use of the term *ākṣepa*). Cf. ĪPK (and ĪPKVṛ) 2.2, and 2.2.1 in particular. ĪPK 2.2.1 reads as follows: *kriyāsaṃbandhasāmānyadravyadikkālabuddhayaḥ | satyāḥ sthairyopayogābhyām ekānekāśrayā matāḥ* ||. The corresponding passage of the ĪPKVṛ reads as follows: *kriyāvad anye 'pi saṃbandhādaya ekānekaviṣayā api satyābhāsāḥ, sarvadopayoginām eṣām arthavattvenāpariharaṇīyatvāt.* Also see ĪPK 2.1.1, which responds to a Buddhist's objection, found at ĪPK 1.2.9, that it is not possible for action (*kriyā*) to be both unitary and successive. ĪPK 2.1.1 reads as follows: *ata eva yad apy uktaṃ kriyā naikasya sakramā | eketyādi pratikṣiptaṃ tad ekasya samarthanāt* ||. The corresponding passage of the ĪPKVṛ reads as follows: *ekacittattvasamarthanād ekasaṃbandhī vyāpāra eka eveti kriyāpy apakṛtadūṣaṇā.*

Note that the translations of ŚD and ŚDVṛ ad 4.68-70 were improved in several places on the suggestions of an anonymous reviewer of Nemec 2019, for which see ibid.: 233, fn. 11 and 236, fns. 20 and 21. See the same article also for further discussion of the present passages of the ŚD and its commentary.

[332] Clear reference is here made to Śabara's *Bhāṣya* (ŚBh) on MīSū 1.5, which records what is nearly identical to what is said here: *mukhe hi śabdam upalabhāmahe, bhūmāv artham.* The statement is uttered by a *pūrvapakṣin* who argues that speech cannot be linked innately to its object, because the connection of the one to the other has to be cultivated, and anything cultivated is created or fabricated and therefore not eternal. The passage in question is introduced as follows: *syād etad evam. naiva śabdasya arthenāsti saṃbandhaḥ, kuto 'sya pauruṣeyatā apauruṣeyatā vā iti. katham? syāc ced arthena saṃbandhaḥ, kṣuramodakaśabdoccāraṇe mukhasya pāṭanapūraṇe syātām, yadi saṃśleṣalakṣaṇaṃ saṃbandham abhipretya ucyate.* "(Opponent's Objection:) The following must be the case: there simply is no connection of speech with the object. How could it [i.e., the connection] be (either) of human origin or not be of human origin? Why (is this a problem)? If a connection did exist with the object, the mouth would (respectively) be torn up and/or filled upon one's uttering of the words 'razor' [*kṣura*] or 'sweetmeat' [*modaka*], (this) if one intends the connection to be one of close contact [*saṃśleṣalakṣaṇaṃ saṃbandham*]." It continues as follows: *yadi prathamaśruto na pratyāyayati, kṛtakas tarhi śabdasya arthena saṃbandhaḥ. kutaḥ? svabhāvato hy asaṃbandhāv etau śabdārthau. mukhe hi śabdam upalabhāmahe, bhūmāv artham. śabdo 'yaṃ na tv arthaḥ, artho 'yaṃ na śabda iti ca vyapadiśanti. rūpabhedo 'pi bhavati. gaur itīmaṃ śabdam uccārayanti, sāsnādimantam artham avabudhyante. pṛthagbhūtayoś ca yaḥ saṃbandhaḥ, sa kṛtako dṛṣṭo, yathā rajjughaṭayor iti.* "(Opponent's Objection:) If it does not denote meaning on first being heard, then it follows that the connection of the word with the object (to which it refers) is artificial [*kṛtaka*] (and not eternal). Why? Because [*hi*] these two, word and object, are by nature unconnected. **For we perceive the word in the mouth, the object on the ground.** Moreover, [people] make the distinction: 'this is the word and not the object; this is the object, not the word.' So too is there a difference in (their respective) forms: [people] utter this word—'cow'—; they understand the object

without a form, and the second has a form—how can they be related (one with the other)?[333]

And it is for this (following) reason that a oneness exists, because (human) discourse could not be produced in the absence of the fact that a unitary nature of consciousness exists (of speech and its object). For how (else) could that connection of speech and object exist, it consisting of a single apprehension (of both *śabda* and *artha* simultaneously) [*ekaparāmarśamaya*] (and) taking the form of that which is denoted by speech and the denotative speech, when they [i.e., speech and its object] are (mutually) distinct;[334] situated in different

---

(to which it refers) to be (an actual cow, which is) possessed of a dewlap and the rest of it. And the connection between two (mutually) distinct entities, one can observe, is created/artificial, as is that of a rope and the pot (to which it is tied)." (Emphasis mine.)

See also Nemec 2019: 237–246.

[333]The verse numbering of the present critical edition and translation is at variance with that of the KSTS edition, because ŚD 4.70 is counted twice there, once at verse 4.70, and a second time for what is in fact ŚD 4.71. This discrepancy persists in the KSTS edition for the remainder of the fourth chapter of the ŚD. Such misnumbering is also replicated occasionally in the secondary literature, for example at Torella 1994: xx, where reference is made to the use of the term *pratyabhijñāna* at, Torella reports, ŚD 4.120a. The term in fact appears at 4.121a. See also Torella 1994: xxii, fn. 28, where reference is made to the appearance of a technical term of the Buddhist Pramāṇa Tradition at ŚD 4.71a: ". . . *svalakṣaṇa* (IV.71a)." One suspects that Torella meant to refer to the first *pāda* of what the KSTS edition numbers as verse 4.81, but what is in fact verse 4.82. (The term *svalakṣaṇa* does not appear in what is numbered verse 4.71 in the KSTS edition, but in what is numbered verse 4.81 in that edition.)

[334]I here select the variant reading of *bhinnatve* (line 451 of the present edition), which is attested in three manuscripts (G, J, and $S^{2p.c.}$), over and against the reading of the KSTS edition and those of three other manuscripts (where $K^{ed.}$, along with D^{a} and $S^{2a.c.}$, witnesses *cittattve*, and S^{3} records *ciktattve*). This is justified first and foremost by the fact that *bhinnatve* is demanded by the context. The passage of the ŚD (at 4.71cd-72ab) lists four concerns regarding the possibility that a connection of speech and object could exist. This is impossible, the argument goes, because (1) they are mutually distinct entities (they are described at ŚD 4.71d, in a *hetugarbhaviśeṣaṇa*, as *bhinnayoḥ*); (2) they are located in mutually distinct places (*bhinnadeśayoḥ*); (3) they are mutually contradictory in form or nature (*viruddharūpayoḥ*); and (4) they are apprehended by different instruments (*bhinnakaraṇagrāhyayoḥ*). It is clear that Utpaladeva's commentary glosses these in order: (1) *bhinnatve* (the variant reading accepted by me) in Utpaladeva's commentary glosses *bhinnayoḥ*; (2) *bhinnadeśatve* glosses *bhinnadeśayoḥ*; (3) *bhinnamūrtāmūrtatvādisvabhāvatve* glosses *viruddharūpayoḥ*; and (4) *bhinnendriyagrāhyatve* glosses *bhinnakaraṇagrāhyayoḥ*. Thus, the reading of *cittattve* (or its obviously erroneous variant of *ciktattve*) is on my view inferior, and possibly resulted from an intentional change of the term on the part of a scribe, under the influence of the apparent similarity of *bhinnatve* with *bhinnadeśatve*. Also, in *devanāgarī* script, at least (though not, in any significant manner, in *śāradā* script), *ca* and *bha*, when handwritten, often can be mistaken one for the other.

Note, however, that Utpaladeva refers at the end of the present passage to Somānanda expressing "the fact that they are (situated) in different loci, etc." [*bhinnadeśatādi*], which suggests a list beginning with the second of the four mentioned qualifications of *śabda* and *artha*. The first of the four, *bhinnatva*, is mentioned in the very last sentence of Utpaladeva's commentary. This could imply that *cittattve* is the correct reading, because it suggests Utpaladeva has in mind a list that begins with the second of the four items in question. Yet, he includes the first in the immediately following sentence, as just noted, which suggests that Utpaladeva understands the last three items to be referred to by Somānanda with ŚD 4.72c-d, and the first of the four with mention of the *saṃgama* at ŚD 4.72d, this being of course a synonym for *saṃbandha*, what can only exist when there are two distinct items to set in relation. There is, of course, no way to understand Somānanda not to have recorded *bhinnayoḥ* in the *mūla*. And so, for these negative reasons, too—namely that the arguments for *cittattve* that I can see are not on my view

places; of distinct natures, one having a form (in the case of the object) and the other not having a form (in the case of speech); and apprehended by different *indriyas*? [Somānanda] expresses just this, the fact that they are (situated) in different loci, etc., at ŚD 4.72cd [*mukhe hīti*, quoting with the *pratīka*]. That they are related (one with the other) is the fact that they are connected, and that is a single apprehension of the two real [entities], (which occurs as a single apprehension) even though they are (mutually) distinct.

4.73cd-75

tathātmāder adṛṣṭasya tacchabdair yogitā katham
4.74. asataḥ śaśaśṛṅgādeḥ śaśaśabdādinānvayaḥ
ghaṭate jātucin naivam asatāṃ vyavahāryatā
4.75. śabdena cet tad evaṃ hi sarvasaṃsāranāśatā
asatyavyavahāreṇa tādṛg eva jagad bhavet

(Somānanda's Objection:) And how can the unseen—the self, for example—be related to the words for them?[335] **(In addition:) No relation**

---

dispositive—and also because I have dismissed the possibility that the commentary originally recorded both readings (viz., *cittattve bhinnatve*), I select the reading of *bhinnatve* in the ŚDVṛ.

[335] The operative distinction here is of the *dṛṣṭārtha* and the *adṛṣṭārtha*, what is found, to be sure, in the Mīmāṃsā literature itself, at, e.g., ŚBh ad *Mīmāṃsāsūtra* 1.1.1. The distinction is more significantly treated in the Nyāya-Vaiśeṣika, however, for example in the *Nyāyasūtrabhāṣya* of Vātsyāyana. See, e.g., NS 1.1.7-8 and NSBh ad 1.1.8: *āptopadeśaḥ śabdaḥ* (1.1.7). *sa dvividho dṛṣṭādṛṣṭārthatvāt* (1.1.8). "Speech is (that valid means of knowledge or *pramāṇa* defined as) what is taught by a reliable person. It [i.e., the speech] is twofold inasmuch as the object thereof is (twofold, being either) of the nature of what is seen or what is not seen." NSBh ad 1.1.8: *yasyeha dṛśyate 'rthaḥ sa dṛṣṭārthaḥ. yasyāmutra pratīyate so 'dṛṣṭārthaḥ. evam ṛṣilaukikavākyānāṃ vibhāga iti. kimarthaṃ punar idam ucyate? sa na manyeta dṛṣṭārtha evāptopadeśaḥ pramāṇam, arthasyāvadhāraṇād iti, adṛṣṭārtho 'pi pramāṇam arthasyānumānād iti.* "That [speech] for which an object is seen here (in the world) is one whose object is seen; that for which it is known elsewhere is one [i.e., a word] whose object is unseen. In this way, one (rightly) may draw a distinction between the utterances of *Ṛṣis* and worldly utterances. But, for what purpose is this said (here)? So that not only the teaching of a reliable person whose object is seen is understood as a valid means of knowledge, on the premise that (only) an object/meaning (of this kind) may be accurately ascertained therefrom; (the teaching of) one [i.e., a reliable person] whose object is unseen also is a valid means of knowledge, on the premise that the [unseen] object/meaning (in question) may be inferred."

Also, (and as is well known) note that Vātsyāyana's commentary on NS 2.1.52 invoked the question of how one can speak of unseen entities, such as heaven or the like. There, the fact that one can speak of them allows one to distinguish the *pramāṇa* of speech from that of inference, for the former requires the words spoken to come from a reliable person (an *āpta*) in order to be counted as valid knowledge, while the latter *pramāṇa* operates independently of any consideration of the reliability of a speaker. See NS and NSBh ad 2.1.52: NS 2.1.52: *āptopadeśasāmarthyāt śabdād arthasaṃpratyayaḥ*. "The right cognition of an object arises from speech on the strength of the instruction of a reliable person." NSBh ad 2.1.52: *svargaḥ apsarasaḥ uttarāḥ kuravaḥ sapta dvīpāḥ samudro lokasaṃniveśa ityevamāder apratyakṣasyārthasya na śabdamātrāt pratyayaḥ. kiṃ tarhi? āptair ayam uktaḥ śabda ity ataḥ saṃpratyayaḥ, viparyayeṇa saṃpratyayābhāvāt na tv evam anumānam iti.* "Heaven, female nymphs, Uttara Kuru, the (form of the world being that of) seven continents, the (breadth of the) ocean, (and) the form of the world—it is not from any speech that objects such as these, which cannot be seen, are known. What then (causes one to know them)? The right cognition that arises is from speech that is uttered by reliable people; but because that right cognition is not produced (by speech) under other circumstances [i.e.,

of an unreal entity such as the horn of a hare could ever be possible with the word(s) "(the horn of) a hare," for example.[336] If you argue that this is not so [i.e., that this is not a problem], (because) one can speak about the unreal [entities] with language [*śabdena*],[337] then (we reply): (not so.) For, in this way all of *saṃsāra* is destroyed—because of the unreal discourse just such an (unreal) world would come to be.[338]

(Somānanda's Objection:) How could that which cannot be directly cognized, such as the self [*ātman*], and that which is unreal, such as the horn

---

when someone less than reliable is speaking], inference is not similarly situated [meaning it does not depend on the reliability of the one who speaks]."

Note that the Mīmāṃsā considers the *ātman* to be perceptible, but the Nyāya-Vaiśeṣika understand it to be inferred. It is well possible that Somānanda here deploys a Vaiśeṣika argument against the Mīmāṃsā in order to present the challenge to the latter's theory of denotation, one that, he suggests, is resolved by an acceptance of the ontological unity of all as Śiva-as-consciousness—including, particularly, speech and object. See Nemec 2019: 246–250 for a more detailed treatment of the identity of Somānanda's opponent in the present passage of the ŚD.

336 If the connection or *saṃbandha* is eternal, one linking (the eternal) word and thing, *śabda* and *artha*, then a word for an unreal thing must be connected to it. This is a problem if all is not consciousness, for it would require a real object—the unreal thing—to be connected to the word for it, this because the connection is, on this view, eternal and real.

The *Vaiśeṣikasūtra* and Candrānanda's commentary thereon, the *Vaiśeṣikasūtravṛtti* (VSVṛ), also dealt with the question of denoting unreal objects. There, the argument is made that the fact that one can use words for unreal things proves that in fact no connection (*saṃyoga*) of *śabda* and *artha* exists. See VS (and VSVṛ) ad 7.2.18: *asati nāstīti ca prayogāt.* "And (word and object are not connected,) because one says 'it does not exist' with reference to that which is inexistent." VSVṛ: *arthasaṃyoge sati śabdaḥ 'asati' abhāve 'nāsti' iti na prayujyeta. na hy asatā saṃyogaḥ.* "If a connection (of a word) to the object were to exist, (then) a word could not be used in relation to that which is inexistent, i.e., which does not exist, to say 'it does not exist.' For, no connection exists with that which is inexistent." Given that no innate *saṃyoga* of *śabda* and *artha* is possible, on this view, the argument is that the two are related by convention.

It is possible that Somānanda had this type of argument, offered from the point of view of a Vaiśeṣika, in mind when formulating the argument of the present ŚD passage. (See also footnote 335.)

On the dating of Candrānanda and the possibility that he hailed from (or was active in) Kashmir, see Nemec 2016: 347–348, esp. fns. 15 and 17.

337 I read the negative particle (*na*) twice, with both what precedes and what follows it.

It is also possible that Somānanda intended the verse to be understood differently than Utpaladeva's interpretation. ŚD 4.74cd–75ab may alternatively be taken as follows: "In this way, it is totally impossible that one can speak about the unreal entities. For, if (you say that) so much (is possible) by means of language, then all of *saṃsāra* would be destroyed." I thank an anonymous reviewer of Nemec 2019 (also mentioned therein at ibid.: 246, fn. 37) for pointing out this alternative interpretation of the syntax of this passage.

Note also that the objection suits a Mīmāṃsaka opponent, who would comfortably raise an objection on ostensive grounds, namely, that the very fact that one witnesses individuals using speech to refer to things we know to be unreal proves that it can be done and is fit and proper in the world.

338 The reply suggests that the ostensive argument proposed by the opponent (likely a Mīmāṃsaka, about which see also footnote 337) fails to answer to the question at hand: it cannot be the case that the mere observation of one speaking of unreal things explains it.

The arguments here considered are similar to those found in ŚD 4.32-33ab inasmuch as both deal with the possibility of speaking of unreal entities. The opponent there is a follower of the Nyāya-Vaiśeṣika, and the grounds for Somānanda's objections are different: there he queries the nature of the *kārakas* when the object is non-existent; here, it is implied, the problem involves not the *kārakas* but the connection of word to thing. See above, especially around footnotes 142 and 147.

of a hare, be joined with the word "*ātman*," or the like, and the word(s) "the horn of the hare," or the like, or even a (non-existent) sky-flower with the word "sky-flower"?[339]

(Opponent's) Objection: No fault thus ensues. For one can speak about just such unreal [entities] with language, because (we see in mundane experience that) words (for unreal entities) have what is unreal as their objects.

(Somānanda's) Reply: (In that case, we reply: not so;) for, in this way you have managed to destroy all that is *saṃsāra*.[340] [Somānanda] expresses that (view as follows): because of the unreal speaking and acting with language, just such an entirely unreal world would come to be.[341] And, of the world. . . *pratibhāsamānaśabda* . . .[342]

4.76-77

4.76. tathābhinavajātasya tannāmnā saṃgamaḥ katham
tatsaṃgamasyāsatyatve yantravaśyādikaṃ katham
4.77. tasmād aikyena tattvasya sarvaṃ tad api yujyate
vyatiriktena śabdena mantreṇānatirekiṇā

(Somānanda's Objection:) And how (if the connection is eternal, but is not based in the unity of all as Śiva) could a newborn be connected with its/his name?[343] (It can only be so if everything exists as Śiva-as-consciousness.) How, if the association of those [i.e., the name and the

---

[339] Both concerns seem to link back to what was said previously, at ŚD 4.71-73ab, namely, that there is no way to connect speech and object when the two are mutually distinct and qualitatively different entities. Both existing in a unified manner *qua* existing, ultimately, as the one self-luminous consciousness, however, solves this problem.

[340] Utpaladeva's commentary indicates that *sarvasaṃsāranāśatā* (ŚD 4.75b) is a genitive *tatpuruṣa* compound.

[341] See footnote 339.

[342] The ŚDVṛ is no longer extant from this point to the end of the ŚD. Since *pratibhāsamānaśabda*° is likely to have been construed with what followed it, I leave it untranslated and surrounded by ellipses.

[343] The "newborn" (*abhinavajāta*) may be a calf, its name being "ox," or perhaps it is a human male (*abhinavajāta* here being masculine in gender), "Devadatta" for example.

Regarding the former, see ŚBh on *Mīmāṃsāsūtra* 1.3.33, which reads in part as follows: *yadi yatra prayogo dṛṣṭaḥ, tatra vṛttiḥ, adyajātāyāṃ gavi prathamaprayogo na prāpnoti tatrādṛṣṭatvāt* | "If the use (of a word) is seen only with respect to that to which it has been applied, (then) there could be no first use (of the word 'cow') for a newborn calf, because one would not have seen it (applied) there (before, this for having no occasion for the same)." (I thank an anonymous reviewer of Nemec 2019—see at p. 251, fn. 46—for this reference.) Regarding the latter, see ŚV (*pratyakṣapariccheda*) 223: *devadattādiśabde tu saṃbandhādyatvadarśanāt* | *arthasyānityatāyāṃ ca tādrūpyasyāpy anityatā* ||. "(Objection:) But in a word such as 'Devadatta' one witnesses the origination of the connection (of the word, i.e., the name, to the object, i.e., the person so named); and as a consequence, given that the object is not eternal, the conformity (of that object) to the word also is not eternal." (Compare also with the translation of Jha [1900] 1983: 108.) Evidently, Somānanda does not accept as sufficient the reply to this objection, viz., ŚV (*pratyakṣapariccheda*) 224: *tatrāpy autpattikī śaktis tadrūpapratyayaṃ prati* | *grāhyagrāhakayor iṣṭā niyogasya tv anityatā* ||. "(Reply:) Even there, we accept as eternal the capacity of that which is signified [i.e., the object] and that which signifies [i.e., the word] to produce a cognition that is of the same quality (for the object as is signified by the word); the application (of the signifier to the signified, of the name to

one named, word and referent] were not real, could subjugation (of an individual) with (the ritual use of) a *yantra* occur, for example?[344] Therefore, it is due to the unity of reality that all that [world of things bearing names] without exception is joined (either) with (mundane) speech that is differentiated (from the object it denotes), (or) with *mantra*(-speech) that is not different (from the object it denotes).[345]

4.78-81ab

4.78. kathaṃ na devadattasya yajñadattavad ākhyayā
atra saṃketitatvāc cet saṃketenātra kiṃ kṛtam
4.79. saṃyogaś cen na dūreṣu mūrtāmūrteṣu yujyate
śabdasyoccāritadhvaṃsān naṣṭānaṣṭadvaye na ca
4.80. vācyavācakarūpaś cet sa eva niyamaḥ kutaḥ
uktasya vācakatvaṃ hi vācyatvam aparasya tu
4.81. vācyavācakarūpatve vācyavācakatānvayaḥ

---

the object), however, is not eternal." The proper answer to such a query, Somānanda seems to suggest, is to define on ontological terms how so much could be the case.

[344] *Yantravaśya* stands as an apparent reference to *vaśīkaraṇa* or subjugation by magic, one of what ultimately is a typology of six types of magic.

Note that I had considered the possibility that what should be read here is *mantravaśya* for *yantravaśya*, or subjugation by *mantra*. For this apparently is the point, namely, that *mantras* used to name the target of subjugation would not work if they did not properly refer to—if they were not in fact connected with—that target. And yet, performing the act in question not only with *mantras* but also with a *yantra* would not be unusual, and mention of the same would not vitiate the core meaning of the argument. I have preserved the reading recorded in the manuscripts available to me, therefore, because there are no variants at all therein, and if there were, *yantra* would anyhow have been the *lectio difficilior*.

On the "six acts" of magic, see, e.g., Goudriaan 1978: 251–412, esp. 310–332. Mention of *vaśīkaraṇa* and the use of *yantras* to accomplish the subjugation in question is also known in Buddhist works (as is generally known). See, e.g., Kuranishi 2013, esp. p. 269.

[345] *Mantra*-speech is said to be "not different," by which is cited the notion that this type of language is not primarily meant to convey an expressed meaning (*vācya*) beyond itself, as, most notably, *bījamantras* do not. The latter—mundane or *laukika* speech, as it is labeled in Jayaratha's *Tantrālokaviveka* (TĀV), where reference also is made to this distinction—by contrast, Somānanda refers to only obliquely.

The terms here used and the dichotomy of speech here noted are found, e.g., at TĀV ad *Tantrāloka* (TĀ) 5.134. The *avataraṇikā* to this TĀ passage reads as follows: *na kevalaṃ vācyārthāvyatirekiṇo lokottarā māntrā varṇā evaṃ yāval laukikā api, ity āha. . .* See also TĀ (and TĀV ad) 5.140-141 (vol. 3, p. 454–456): *tad evaṃ laukikānāṃ ghaṭādīnāṃ śabdānāṃ evam uccāraṇāt smaraṇād vā yatra saṃvidaikātmyāvāptāv upāyatvaṃ tatra sṛṣṭibījādīnāṃ kā vārtā ity āha: kiṃ punaḥ samayāpekṣāṃ vinā ye bījapiṇḍakāḥ | saṃvidaṃ spandayanty ete neyuḥ saṃvidupāyatām ||* 5.140 *|| ete saṃvidupāyatāṃ neyur iti kākvā vyākhyeyam. nanu samayānapekṣam eva katham evam ete kurvantīty āśaṅkyāha: vācyābhāvād udāsīnasaṃvitspandāt svadhāmataḥ | prānollāsanirodhābhyāṃ bījapiṇḍeṣu pūrṇatā ||* 5.141 *|| saṃvidaikātmyena sphuraṇāt vyatiriktasya vācyasyābhāvāt, tathā "udāsīnaḥ" svātmamātraviśrānter abahirmukho yo 'sau saṃvitspandas tadrūpāt "svadhāmataḥ" svaspharāt, tathā pramāṇātmanaḥ "prāṇasyollāsāt" prameyonmukhaṃ prasaraṇāt, tathā "nirodhāt" antarmukharūpe viśramāt sṛṣṭisaṃhārakāritvāt sṛṣṭibījādirūpeṣu "bījapiṇḍeṣu pūrṇatā" ananyonmukhatvān nairākāṅkṣyam ity arthaḥ. ghaṭādiṣu laukikeṣu punaḥ śabdeṣu vācyasadbhāvāder apūrṇatvāt samayādyapekṣatvam ity arthasiddham.*

How is one like Yajñadatta not (designated) by Devadatta's name? (The Buddhist opponent's) Objection: Because of the fact that there is agreement here (regarding the one denoted by the name). (Somānanda's Reply:) What service is done here by the agreement? (The Buddhist's) Objection: A connection (of the name with the person named). (Somānanda's Reply:) That [i.e., the connection or *saṃyoga*] is not possible with respect to those [entities, i.e., what are denoted and the words that denote them,] which are (mutually) distant, which (respectively) have a form and do not have a form;[346] nor, given that speech expires after it is uttered, is it (possible) with respect to the pair (in question), which (respectively) have perished [viz., the name "Devadatta," after it is uttered] and not-perished [viz., the perduring Devadatta himself]. (The Buddhist's) Objection: It [i.e., the *saṃyoga*] exists in the form of designatum and designator. (Somānanda's Reply:) Wherefrom this necessity? For what is uttered [i.e., speech, the name] is that which designates, while that which is designated is something different. If (you argue:) it [i.e., the *niyama* or necessity] is (found in) the (very) nature of the designatum and designator, (we reply:) there is(, in that case,) a definite link of the nature of the designatum to that of the designator.[347]

---

[346]The use of the plural is at least somewhat curious, given that what is probably being described here is the connection of a (single) name to a thing named. Nevertheless, the meaning is clear. Note, also, that reference to having a form and not having a form echoes the problem articulated earlier, at ŚD 4.71-73ab (esp. 4.73ab). This further implies, then, that the dual could reasonably have been expected in the present passage, as does what immediately follows (ŚD 4.79d): *naṣṭānaṣṭadvaye na ca.*

[347]The argument, it is clear, turns on Somānanda applying the very line of questioning that was prosecuted by the *pūrvapakṣin* of the *Śābarabhāṣya* to the view of his Buddhist opponents. (See footnote 332.) He asks how one can account for a connection or relation of speech, which denotes meaning, to the object it denotes, when the two are mutually distinct entities situated in mutually differing locations and are of distinct natures, the one (i.e., what is denoted; Devadatta, e.g.) having a form and being a perduring entity, the other (i.e., the name; "Devadatta," e.g.) not having form and perishing immediately after it is uttered. Somānanda objects to the possibility that the connection is ad hoc, constructed by convention, because, he argues, there would be no way to account for any necessary connection of designatum and designator, unless, that is, the designatum and designator are intrinsically connected, are connected inasmuch as it is their very nature to be thus (there must be a *vācyavācakatānvaya*). Put in other words—and as the Vṛttikāra in the ŚBh argued against the *pūrvapakṣin*, above, and as Kumārila, following on the ŚBh, did as well in his ŚV—the relation between *vācya* and *vācaka* (which are explicitly dealt with in the ŚV) cannot be fabricated; it must always have existed. See, esp., ŚV (*saṃbandhākṣepaparihāra*) vv. 5*ff.* It is at verse 12 of the *saṃbandhākṣepaparihāra* section that an opponent objects to the Mīmāṃsā view of the *saṃbandha* as permanent, arguing instead that it exists as a matter of convention: *svato naivāsti śaktatvaṃ vācyavācakayor mithaḥ | pratītiḥ samayāt puṃsāṃ bhaved akṣinikocavat* ||. "(Objection:) It is not of themselves that denoter and the denoted are together capable of expressing meaning; (rather,) comprehension [*pratīti*] can only arise from human [*puṃsām*] convention, like the (meaning of a) wink of an eye (may be understood by human convention)." See also Arnold 2006: 461–467 for a treatment of the issues here at hand, and see esp. p. 462 for Arnold's translation of *saṃbandhākṣepaparihāra*, v. 12. This may also be compared to that of Jha [1900] 1983: 349. Note, however, that while it seems likely the opponent is a Buddhist, it is at least possible that Somānanda here has a Naiyāyika or Vaiśeṣika opponent in

4.81cd-83ab

itaś cāsti jagaty aikyaṃ pratyakṣāgrahaṇād api
4.82. svalakṣaṇena yogitvād vyavahārasya sarvataḥ
loke cānupapatteś ca pramā vā vyavahāragā
4.83. bālamūkādivijñānasadṛśī kīdṛśī kriyā

---

mind, for they, too, hold that speech is conventional. On the notion that speech is denotative on the basis of convention according to the Naiyāyika Vātsyāyana, see NS and NSBh ad 2.1.55-56, esp., NSBh ad 2.1.56: *sāmāyikaḥ śabdād arthasampratyayo na svābhāvikaḥ. ṛṣyāryamlecchānāṃ yathākāmaṃ śabdaviniyogo 'rthapratyāyanāya pravartate. svābhāvike hi śabdasyārthapratyāyakatve yathākāmaṃ na syād yathā taijasasya prakāśasya rūpapratyayahetutvaṃ na jātiviśeṣe vyabhicaratīti.* "The right conception of a meaning from a word is based in convention; it is not natural. *Ṛṣis*, *Āryas*, and Barbarians [*mleccha*] use speech as they wish [i.e., without restrictions], this in order to cause one properly to understand an object. Indeed, if the nature of the capacity of speech to lead one properly to understand an object were natural (and not conventionally formed), it [i.e., the use of speech] would not be as they wish [i.e., without restrictions], just as the light of fire does not vary in causing one to know (the golden) color (of the fire) on the basis of the group (of people who know it)."

See also, e.g., VS 7.2.15*ff*., along with Candrānanda's commentary thereon, for a treatment of the conventional nature of denotation according to Vaiśeṣikas, esp. at VS 7.2.24: *sāmayikaḥ śabdād arthapratyayaḥ.* "The understanding of an object from speech is by convention." Candrānanda's VSVṛ on this passage reads as follows: *tasmāt saṃketanimittaḥ śabdād arthe pratyayo na saṃbandhāt.* "Therefore, the understanding as regards an object (one acquires) from speech has a convention as its cause; it is not the product of a (real, natural, and permanent) connection (of speech and object)."

One must also note that Dharmakīrti grounds his understanding of *saṃketa* in his theory of *apoha*, which in turn is based in an understanding of causality as that which establishes difference, what is not found in Dignāga's understanding. See PVSV ad PV 1.72cd (Gnoli 1960: 40): *yasya pratyāyanārthaṃ saṃketaḥ kriyate, abhinnasādhyān bhāvān atatsādhyebhyo bhedena jñātvā tatparihāreṇa pravarteteti.* "[A convention is established] so that, when one knows that [certain] entities having the same effects are *different* from [those] which do not have those effects, one may act [toward the former] by excluding the [latter]." The same passage is quoted in Arnold 2006: 441, fn. 64. The present translation, however, is that of Eltschinger, et al. 2018: 84. Compare also the translation of Dunne 2004: 343–344, cited also in Arnold (op. cit.).

For Dharmakīrti, convention is formed on the basis of identifying *bhāvas* that have common effects; yet, as above, the classification of such entities is based on a relative basis (measuring the entities in relation to others) and involves identification by way of exclusion. The convention, moreover, is precisely that, on Dharmakīrti's view. See PV (*pratyakṣapariccheda*) 3.171 (note that the edition of Sāṅkṛtyāyana 1953: 264, lines 8–9 reads *nirdṛṣṭārthena* for *nirdiṣṭārthena*; Sāṅkṛtyāyana 1938 records what here follows, excepting it reads *śrutāṃ* for *śrutau*): *tasmāt saṃketakāle 'pi nirdiṣṭārthena saṃyutaḥ | svapratītiphalenānyāpohaḥ sambadhyate śrutau ||.* "Therefore, it is also at the moment of (the applicability of) the convention [*saṃketakāle*] that exclusion of the other [*anyāpoha*], which is connected with an object that is indicated (by the *saṃketa*), one that itself results in knowledge of itself, is joined to what is communicated." (The same is cited in Arnold 2006: 444, fn. 70.)

Prajñākaragupta, commenting on PV 3.171 (edition of Sāṅkṛtyāyana, p. 264, lines 10–11), says the following: *saṃketayann api na vidhimukhena saṃketakāraḥ saṃketaṃ karoti, api tv anyāpohamukhenaiva yataḥ saṃketakāle 'py anyāpoha eva śrutau sambadhyate, na vastu.* "Although forming the convention, the convention-maker does not form the convention positively [*vidhimukhena*]. Rather, he does so only by way of exclusion of the other; for, even at the moment of (the formation of) the convention, it is only exclusion of the other that is joined to what is communicated; the real thing is not." The same passage is cited in Arnold 2006: 445. On ŚD 4.78-81ab, see also Nemec 2019: 253–258.

And,[348] it is (also) for this (following) reason that there is unity in the universe, because there would (otherwise) be no apprehension (of that universe) by means of direct cognition, either;[349] (this is so) because discourse/mundane activity [*vyavahāra*] is everywhere connected with the unique particular in the world, and because it[350] is not (otherwise) possible; or,[351] (this is so because) valid knowledge deals with discourse/mundane activity. (After all:) Of what kind is the action (of perception) that is similar to the awareness of children, mute people, and the like?[352]

---

[348] Having explored the problems associated with how the Buddhist Epistemologists could account for the fact that language can denote meaning, Somānanda here turns to the task of mapping the problems associated with their understanding of direct cognition or *pratyakṣa*, arguing that they must accept the existence of a (Śaiva) unity of all (as consciousness) in order for their position to cohere. In the present passage (ŚD 4.81cd-83ab) Somānanda deals with *nirvikalpaka* cognitions; in the next (ŚD 4.83cd-84ab) he deals with *savikalpa* cognition. Following that, beginning at ŚD 4.84cd, he will describe the problems the Buddhists have, as he understands them, in explaining how inference (*anumāna*) could function in the absence of the same unity. See below at footnotes 354 and 355.

[349] In a previous rendering of this passage, I paired ŚD 4.81c with what precedes it and accepted a variant reading of ŚD 4.81d, namely the reading of C of *pratyakṣād grahaṇād api for pratyakṣāgrahaṇād api* (attested to by T and K$^{ed.}$). Both interpretations are possible, but given that Somānanda repeatedly begins new arguments in the present chapter of the ŚD with *itaś ca* or the like, it seems better to read 4.81c with what follows it. For my previous interpretation of this passage, see Nemec 2017: 64–66.

[350] That is, the *vyavahāra*.

[351] I here propose a conjectural emendation of *vā vyavahāragā* where K$^{ed.}$, along with T, reads *ca vyavahāragā* and C witnesses *vācyavahārataḥ*. The close similarity of *cya* and *vya* in *devanāgarī* suggests that the corrupted reading of C has precisely this reading underlying it.

[352] The translation offered here differs somewhat from a rendering found in Nemec 2017: 65–66. An anonymous reviewer for Nemec 2019 made several suggestions that improved my understanding of this passage, for which I thank that reviewer. (See Nemec 2019: 258–259, esp. at footnote 58.)

Clear reference here is made to ŚV (*pratyakṣapariccheda*) vv. 112–113: *asti hy ālocanājñānaṃ prathamaṃ nirvikalpakam | bālamūkādivijñānasadṛśaṃ śuddhavastujam || na viśeṣo na sāmānyaṃ tadānīm anubhūyate | tayor ādhārabhūtā tu vyaktir evāvasīyate ||*. McCrea 2013: 135 translates as follows: "First there is an initial perception (*ālocanā*)—a non-conceptual awareness, similar to the awareness of children, mutes, and the like, and arising purely from the object. At that time, neither particular nor universal is experienced, but, rather, the individual (*vyakti*), which is the basis (*ādhāra*) of both, is apprehended." (Cf. the ŚVNRĀ on v. 112: *bālānām ivāvyutpannānām asmākam api cakṣuḥsannipātānantaraṃ savikalpāt prathamam asti nirvikalpakaṃ pratītisiddham ālocanavijñānaṃ śuddhavastuviṣayam, tadabhāve hi nirnimittaṃ na śabdasmaraṇaṃ syāt, asmṛtaśabdasya ca na śabdānuviddho vikalpaḥ sambhavatīti.* Finally, see also the translation, explanation, and notes to these verses in Taber 2005: 94 and 202–205.)

Here, Kumārila explicitly and directly challenges a core assumption of the Buddhist Epistemologists, namely, that a clear and absolute distinction exists between the object of direct cognition or *pratyakṣa*, on the one hand, which they claim is purely perceptual in nature, and the product of inference or *anumāna*, on the other hand, which they understand to be entirely conceptual in nature. Kumārila admits that an initial perception does occur as the Buddhists claim, without the presence of some conceptual coloring or content. But the second one is not. The object of cognition is not and cannot be a mere percept, but must be one that inherently also is comprised of a universal class of which it is a member (the *vyakti* cognized in the initial, *nirvikalpaka* cognition is the very basis of the *sāmānya*). The initial moment of cognition exists at a moment when the explicit idea or concept of the object's identity is missing—the judgment that "this entity before me is a pot," for example. What is perceived in the initial moment is only the pure *vyakti* or individual entity. But the subsequent conceptual cognition,

4.83cd-84ab

savikalpasya yogitvād yathāvastu grahaḥ katham
4.84. tena jñeyam ekam eva vastu bhinne grahaḥ kutaḥ

How(, moreover,) could a conceptual cognition accurately apprehend (a *svalakṣaṇa*, the object of cognition) as a result of it being connected (with it,) (if perception and conception were utterly divided)? (It cannot.) Thus, one should know the real thing to be absolutely one;[353] if it were divided, how could one apprehend it?[354]

---

which Kumārila claims to be conceptual perception, can grasp the object as a pot (*ghaṭa*)—the fact of being a pot or the class "pot-ness" (*ghaṭatva*)—the latter necessarily involving conceptuality.

As McCrea (ibid.) says of this passage, "By introducing as the content of our initial moment of perceptual awareness the entire object, undifferentiated but comprising both individuality and universality in its 'dual nature', Kumārila aims to defuse Dignāga's critique of universals as something introduced only in subsequent moments of awareness, and therefore not truly a perception of the object at all." So much is found at ŚV (*pratyakṣapariccheda*) vv. 118–120: *nirvikalpakabodhe 'pi dvyātmakasyāpi vastunaḥ | grahaṇaṃ lakṣaṇākhyeyaṃ jñātrā śuddhaṃ tu gṛhyate || na cāsādhāraṇatvena paravyāvṛttyakalpanāt | viśeṣānugamāklpteḥ sāmānyam iti nāpi tat || tataḥ paraṃ punar vastu dharmair jātyādibhir yayā | buddhyāvasīyate sāpi pratyakṣatvena saṃmatā ||*. "Even in non-conceptual awareness, there is apprehension of a thing with a dual nature (*dvyātmaka*): it can be explained via definitions, but it is grasped in its pure form by the knower—not as something unique, since it does not conceptualize the exclusion of others, nor as 'a universal' since it does not conceptualize recurrence across (a range of) individuals. After that, however, the awareness which determines the thing by way of its properties, such as its class character (*jātyādi*), is likewise regarded as perception" (translation McCrea's). Compare also with the rendering of Taber 2005: 98. Note also that, according to Pārthasārathi Miśra, the "dual nature" is that of the *sāmānya* and the *viśeṣa*. See his ŚVNRĀ on the passage in question: *dvyātmakasya sāmānyaviśeṣātmakasyety arthaḥ*. He goes on immediately to offer the following—fascinating and pellucid—explanation of Kumārila's position: *sāmānyāvabhāso 'pi pratītisiddha eva. na hi nirvikalpakenāgṛhītasya savikalpakenāpi grahaṇaṃ sambhavati, na vā agṛhīte sāmānye vyaktyantare pratyabhijñā sambhavati. tasmāt sāmānyaṃ viśeṣaś ca nirvikalpake 'pi prakāśata eva.* "The appearance of the universal is for its part fully established by the cognition. For, it is not the case that that which has not been apprehended by non-conceptual [awareness] can be apprehended by conceptual [awareness], for its part, nor is it the case that a recognition can arise as regards a universal that has not been apprehended, it being another individual entity. Therefore, (both) the universal and the particular fully are manifested even in the non-conceptual [awareness]."

To sum up, Somānanda here deploys Kumārila's conception of perception against that of his Buddhist opponents, to suggest that the nature and location, as it were, of the universal or *sāmānya* cannot be ontologically separated from the nature of the object with which it is related. See also Nemec 2019: 258–261. Finally, see Taber 2005: 1–43 for a thorough treatment of the nature of conceptualized and nonconceptual perception in Kumārila's thought.

[353] By "one" is meant both the particular and the universal, knowable both by perceptual and conceptual cognition.

[354] At ŚD 4.81cd-83ab, Somānanda dealt with non-conceptual cognition, arguing that the *sāmānya* must inhere in the object perceived in an initial perception thereof, even if only latently. Here, he deals with *savikalpa* cognition, what follows *nirvikalpaka* cognition according to the Mīmāṃsā. The opponent here, however, remains the Buddhist. Somānanda argues that not only would linguistic forms of knowing (and with them all inferential forms of knowing more generally) be impossible to guarantee in their veridicality if the *sāmānya* and *viśeṣa* were not, as McCrea 2013: 135 put it, "leveled," but the same would be true of conceptually imbued instances of perception, as well. There simply could be no correspondence of a conceptually imbued cognition to the real particular without accepting the real

4.84cd-85

tathānumānaṃ na bhaved dhūmāgnyor anvaye kvacit
4.85. apūrvayor gṛhīte 'pi tatkālaṃ gatayor dvayoḥ
agṛhīte na gṛhītaḥ saṃbandho 'gniḥ pratīyate

And,[355] no inference could arise anywhere (from a direct cognition, in the absence of the existence of a real universal), even if the invariable concomitance of smoke and fire(, for example,) were apprehended, the two being unique entities that are no longer existent at that time (of the inference).[356] If(, moreover,) that [invariable concomitance] has not been apprehended, the relation (between the perception of smoke and the presence of fire) is (also) not apprehended; (thus,) the fire is not cognized (by way of an inference based in seeing the appearance of smoke).[357]

4.86-87

4.86. sāmānyam aviśeṣaṃ ced aviśeṣāt kutaḥ pramā
viśeṣasyāpy apūrvatvāt kathaṃ cāsti samanvayaḥ
4.87. sādṛśyād atha cen nāsti yāthātmyena samāgamaḥ
na ca vātrānumānatvaṃ dhūmataḥ kevalād bhavet

---

presence of a real universal coterminous with that particular, not even the kind of ultimately erroneous but useful conceptions (useful for pointing fruitfully to particular causally efficacious *svalakṣaṇas*) imagined by Dharmakīrti (about which see, e.g. PV [*pratyakṣapariccheda*] 3.57-58, cited in footnote 378 and rendered in footnote 36 of the introduction). See also, e.g., Dunne 2004: 113–144, esp. 141–143.

Finally, note that the translation I here offer, still somewhat tentative as it was in Nemec 2019: 261, differs slightly in its interpretation of the syntax from the one there presented. (Most particularly, I here understand *savikalpasya* to be a subjective genitive.)

355 Here, Somānanda begins to consider the problems associated with the viability of inferential knowledge (*anumāna*) as it is understood by the Buddhist Epistemologists. Previously, at ŚD 4.81cd-84ab, Somānanda considered similar problems with their understanding of direct perception (*pratyakṣa*). Thus, both means of knowledge (*pramāṇa*) that are recognized by his Buddhist interlocutors are interrogated. The present discussion finds its conclusion at ŚD 4.93ab.

Note that Kumārila himself made a similar argument, as Taber 2005: 29 indicates. That is, he suggested that the viability of inference is directly implicated by the question of whether or not conceptual cognition is possible: if the latter is not possible, then inference is also not possible. See ŚV (*pratyakṣapariccheda*) 248cd-249ab: *sarvaṃ cāpy anumānādi pratyakṣe nirvikalpake || na pravartata ity etad anumāne 'bhidhāsyate* |. "And it will be stated in regard to inference that if perception is nonconceptualized, then all the other *pramāṇas* inference, and so forth, cannot function." (Translation that of Taber 2005: 146.)

356 Even if one did apprehend the invariable concomitance of probans and probandum, no logical connection could be made between the utterly unique *svalakṣaṇas*. Only the unity of *sāmānya* and *viśeṣa* could explain the very possibility of inferential knowledge.

357 The only relation recognized by Dharmakīrti is that of cause and effect, what can be established by a series of two perceptions and three non-perceptions, about which see footnote 369. (And even this relation is ultimately called into question as such, about which see SP 7*ff.*)

Note that I here read *na* (ŚD 4.85c) twice, with both *gṛhītaḥ saṃbandhaḥ* and with *agniḥ pratīyate*. Alternatively, one could read *agniḥ pratīyate* (ŚD 4.85d) with what follows it, understanding the passage to be a part of an opponent's objection, as follows: "Objection: The fire is cognized. (For:) There is a universal; it is the non-particular."

Objection (of the Buddhist opponent): There is a universal; it is the non-particular.[358] (Reply:) How (on your view) is valid knowledge the product of a non-particular?[359] And how, since the particular (according to you) is, for its part, unprecedented, could a connection exist (of that unique particular with the *aviśeṣa* or universal)?[360] Now, (on the one hand,) if you argue it [i.e., the connection (*samanvaya*)] is the result of similarity [*sādṛśya*], (we reply:) there is no conjunction [*samāgama*] (of the *sādṛśya* and the conceptions it conveys) with the real nature (of the particular).[361]

---

[358]The *sāmānya* may be said to be related to but different from the unique particulars, the *svalakṣaṇas*. It may be defined by the similarity of effect of the *svalakṣaṇas* in question, which therefore may be referred to by a common term. See, e.g., PVSV ad PV 1.137-142 (p. 239 of Pandeya's edition): *evaṃjātīyāś ca sarve samūhasantānāvasthāviśeṣaśabdā ye samastāḥ kiṃcid ekaṃ kāryaṃ kurvanti teṣāṃ tatra viśeṣābhāvād apārthikā viśeṣacodaneti sakṛt sarveṣāṃ niyojanārtham ekam ayaṃ lokaḥ śabaṃ teṣu niyuṅkte ghaṭa iti. te 'pi sajātīyād anyataś ca bhedāviśeṣe 'pi tatprayojanāṅgatayā tadanyebhyo bhidyanta ity abhedāt tato 'viśeṣeṇa pratīyante.* The purpose of this passage, then, is to record the *pūrvapakṣin*'s response to Somānanda's argument at ŚD 4.84cd-85. A single word may be used to refer to multiple unique things that function in a similar manner to effect a single result. A perception (of smoke, e.g.,) can lead to a (verbally based) conception that gives knowledge of another real phenomenon (fire, e.g.). In a word, Somānanda's Buddhist opponent claims a cogent explanation for the existence of a constructed, conventional universal that can effect the kinds of inferential knowledge here in question.

[359]How, if there is no truly shared nature belonging to multiple *svalakṣaṇas*, can valid knowledge come from what is not the particular? What does the *aviśeṣa* convey when the object is unique and by definition not intrinsically associable with a universal?

[360]Note that it is also possible to read 4.86b-c together, as follows: "How (on your view) is valid knowledge the product of a non-particular, since the particular, for its part, is unprecedented/unique?"

[361]I do not think reference to *sādṛśya* here is simply to the similarity of the perceptual image to the empirical object. Rather, Somānanda here suggests that his Buddhist opponent cannot argue that similarity (*sādṛśya*) may guarantee that a particular that is unique may be related to a general, universalized (and therefore conceptual) understanding of the same. He wishes to argue that to thus guarantee knowledge of a unique object—in relation to other objects like it or in relation to a previous experience of what may conventionally be conceived of as one and the same object—there must be something categorically real about the object itself that encompasses or guarantees the possibility of such similarity. Simply, a real *sāmānya* must properly be associated with the particular if any similarity is to be recognized at all.

Utpaladeva (and Abhinavagupta in explaining the same) also somewhat similarly argues that no *samanvaya* or connection is possible in the absence of a unifying capacity, what the universal here is understood by Somānanda to facilitate. See ĪPK 1.7.3: *deśakālakramajuṣām arthānāṃ svasamāpinām | sakṛdābhāsasādhyo 'sāv anyathā kaḥ samanvayaḥ ||*. "A connection between objects having a spatio-temporal succession and being self-contained is established by their manifestation in terms of unification. Otherwise, no connection at all is possible." (Translation Torella's.) ĪPKVṛ: *svarūpam avabhāsaṃ ca bhāvānāṃ svātmaparinisṭhitam eva. yugapadekābhāsanibandhanaś caiṣāṃ samanvayaḥ. so 'bhinnaḥ pramātṛlīnatayā kalpate.* "Things, both in their own nature and manifestation, are self-contained. A connection between them depends on their simultaneous and unitary manifestation (*yugapadekābhāsa°*). This undivided [manifestation, i.e., connection] is possible only if absorbed into the knowing subject." (Translation Torella's.) See also the corresponding passage of the ĪPV, which reads in part as follows (vol. 1: p. 283, also cited in Ratié 2011a: 146): *arthānāṃ jaḍānām, tadjñānānāṃ tadvikalpānāṃ tanniścayānāṃ ca deśakramaṃ kālakramaṃ cātyajatāṃ svasamāpinām svarūpamātrapratiṣṭhānāṃ kaḥ samanvayaḥ. na kaścid ity arthaḥ. yato hy asau samanvayaḥ sakṛdābhāsena deśakālākāramiśrīkaraṇātmanā yojanābhāsena sādhayituṃ śakyo nānyathā, na hi pṛthakpṛthak parikṣīneṣu srotaḥsu taduhyamānās tṛṇolapādayaḥ samanvayaṃ kaṃcid yāntīti.* Finally, see also ĪPK and, esp., ĪPKVṛ ad 1.3.2, where Utpaladeva suggests that memory cannot be explained by the power of a

Nor, on the other hand, could a legitimate inference (of the fire) arise, here, from (a cognition of) the (*svalakṣaṇa* of) smoke alone.[362]

4.88

4.88. tatsaṃbandhād athocyeta saṃbandhe dviṣṭhatā na ca dviniṣṭhatvād ekataragrahaṇān nāpi tadgrahaḥ

Objection: It[363] **may be said to result from the connection [*saṃbandha*] of that [smoke] (to fire).**[364] **(Reply:) If there is a connection, there must be a bilocation [*dviṣṭhatā*],**[365] **and the quality (belonging to the *saṃbandha*) of being bilocated cannot lead one to apprehend that [connection], nor could even the apprehension of (only) one of the two [relata].**[366]

---

latent impression or *saṃskāra*, because while so much can explain the similarity of the memory-cognition to the initial experience, it cannot explain the knower's experience of the memory-cognition as similar to the previous experience: *dṛk svābhāsaiva nānyena vedyā rūpadṛśeva dṛk | rase saṃskārajatvaṃ tu tattulyatvaṃ na tadgatiḥ ||*. "A cognition is only self-revealing; it cannot be known by another cognition, just as the cognition of taste is not known by that of shape. And the fact that [memory] arises from latent impressions implies its similarity to that [former perception], but not its cognition of the same." (Translation a modification of Torella's.) The corresponding passage of the ĪPKVṛ: *sarvā hi jñaptiḥ svasaṃvedanaikarūpānanyasaṃvidvedyā, rūparasajñānayor anyonyavedane 'nyonyaviṣayavedanam api syāt tataś cendriyaniyamābhāvaḥ. pūrvānubhavasaṃskārajatvena tatsādṛśyamātraṃ na tu pūrvānubhavāvagatiḥ, tadabhāvāt tatsādṛśyam api nāvaseyam.* "Every cognitive act is by nature only aware of itself and cannot be known by another awareness. If the cognition of shape could grasp the cognition of taste and vice versa, then each would equally perceive the object of the other, and in this way no restriction on the individual senses would exist. Since [memory] arises from the latent impression left by the former perception it only bears a similarity to that previous experience but does not have direct cognition of the same; (and) since that [direct cognition of the previous experience] is absent, not even the similarity to it can be ascertained." (Translation a modification of Torella's.)

About this passage see also Torella 1994: 99–100, esp. fn. 4, and consult also Ratié 2011a: 127–129, and especially her footnote 43, which seeks to clarify Torella's footnote 4 and his interpretation of these passages of the ĪPK and ĪPKVṛ.

362 One cannot establish the connection (*saṃbandha*, referred to at ŚD 4.85d) of "smoke" to "fire" from the cognition of the former, when the *svalakṣaṇas* in question are momentary and unique.

363 That is, that *anumānatvam* or legitimate inference that may arise from the cognition of smoke alone.

364 There are several ways to read this passage that differ from what is here offered. First, it is also possible to read *ucyeta* with what follows, taking *dviṣṭhatā* as the subject of the verb. This would require one *not* to punctuate at the cæsura, but such punctuation is not uncommon in the ŚD. Second, it is possible that *tatsaṃbandha* is not a compound, in which case *tat* could be taken to be the subject of the verb (reading *ucyeta* with what precedes it) and referring to *anumānatva* (ŚD 4.87c). In this case, however, one would have to supply references to the smoke and the fire (what stand in relation one to the other), and so semantically this would change little in interpreting the present passage.

365 It appears that Somānanda here has in mind Dharmakīrti's discussion of relations at, perhaps, SP 11ab: *dviṣṭho hi kaścit saṃbandho nāto 'nyat tasya lakṣaṇam |*. Cf. Prabhācandra ad SP 11: *na yena kenacid ekena saṃbandhāt seṣyate. kiṃ tarhi. saṃbandhalakṣaṇenaiveti cet tan na, dviṣṭho hi kaścit padārthaḥ saṃbandhaḥ, nāto 'rthadvayābhisaṃbandhād anyat tasya lakṣaṇam yenāsya saṃkhyāder viśeṣo vyavasthāpyeta.* The same passage of the SP, among others, is also alluded to at ĪPK 1.2.11, for which see footnote 366. Cf. Torella 1994: 95–97, esp. fns. 21–24 and 26; Ratié 2011a: 298–299, fn. 85.

366 No relation may be cognized (in the absence of a unity of consciousness in Śiva), because to do so one would have to cognize both relata to recognize it; but this is impossible given the mutually

4.89-90

4.89. dhūmadṛṣṭyātha kalpyeta vahnis tadyogitāpi ca
itaretaradoṣo 'tra durnivāraḥ prasajyate
4.90. yāvan na vahnikalanā na yogakalanā bhavet
yāvad vā yogakalanā na vahnikalanākṣamā

(The Buddhist's) Objection: Fire may be conceived of by way of the cognition of the smoke, as may its connection (to the smoke).[367] (Reply:)

---

distinct moments of awareness that make up cognition and reality. Given the duality of the *saṃbandha*, moreover, even a cognition of one relatum would not lead one to know the bilocation (*dviniṣṭhatva*), this being a matter also examined in more detail in what follows. Thus, Somānanda argues, the cognition, e.g., of smoke alone cannot lead one to know the causal connection of smoke to fire, this on the understanding of the matter put forward by his Buddhist interlocutors.

Utpaladeva engages this issue at ĪPK 1.2.11, where his *pūrvapakṣin* states that no entity can stand in two places at once, because this would require it to have a multiplicity of form. That very multiplicity, the implication is clear, would contradict the nature of the *svalakṣaṇas*, which are said to exist as singular, momentary, and unique phenomena. ĪPK 1.2.11: *dviṣṭhasyānekarūpatvāt siddhasyānyānapekṣaṇāt | pāratantryādyayogāc ca tena kartāpi kalpitaḥ* ||. "(The relation is unreal,) because the bilocated [relation] does not have a unitary nature; because that which is established [as existent] does not depend on another; and because dependence, etc., are impossible. Therefore, the agent, too, is (merely) conceived." Cf. the corresponding passage of the IPKVṛ: *saṃbandho dviṣṭho na caikenātmanobhayatrāvasthitir yuktā na ca dvayoḥ siddhayor anyonyāpekṣātmā nāpi svātmamātraniṣṭhayoḥ pāratantryarūpaḥ saṃbandhaḥ. tato yathā jñātṛtvaṃ kalpitaṃ tathā kartṛtvam apīti katham ātmā sarveśvara iti.* "A relation is bilocated, and it is not possible that a single nature may be present in both, nor is it [i.e., the relation] of the nature of the mutual dependence of a pair established [as existent], nor is it even the case that a relation is of the form of a dependence of two fully self-contained entities. Hence, just as the state of being an agent of knowing is (merely) conceptualized, so also is the state of being the agent of action. Hence, how is the Self the Lord of all?" (Cf. with SP 1: *pāratantryaṃ hi saṃbandhaḥ siddhe kā paratantratā | tasmāt sarvasya bhāvasya saṃbandho nāsti tattvataḥ* ||.) As a consequence, the relation is nothing other than a *vikalpa*. Indeed, Dharmakīrti recognizes no relation other than that of cause and effect, and even that is called into question (SP 7*ff.*), thus one should more specifically understand Somānanda here to argue that there would be no way of knowing even the concept of "relation" in the absence of an ontological (and epistemological) unity of all as Śiva. (See also footnote 365.)

Cf. SP 5 (also cited and translated in Ratié 2011a: 298, fn. 85): *tau ca bhāvau tadanyaś ca sarve te svātmani sthitāḥ | ity amiśrāḥ svayaṃ bhāvās tān miśrayati kalpanā* ||. "Both these two things, and that which is different from them [i.e., the *saṃbandha* itself]—all these abide only in themselves. Hence [*iti*], entities in themselves are not interrelated. (However,) it is the conceptual construction [*kalpanā*] (of a relation or merger) that causes them to be interrelated." (Prabhācandra glosses this verse as follows: *tau ca bhāvau saṃbandhinau tābhyām anyaś ca saṃbandhaḥ, sarve te svātmani svasvarūpe sthitāḥ. tenāmiśrā vyāvṛttasvarūpāḥ svayaṃ bhāvāḥ, tathāpi tān miśrayati yojayati kalpanā.*) Note also that SP 5cd-6 is quoted in the ĪPVV (vol. 1: p. 200, lines 16–18) at the commentary ad ĪPK 1.2.10; it is also quoted in the *Saṃbandhasiddhi* (edition of M. Kaul), p. 3, line 23. See also Frauwallner 1934; Torella 1994: 95–96, esp. fns. 21 and 22.

[367]The opponent's argument here is that cognition of smoke also yields knowledge of the connection of the same to fire, thus vitiating the need to explain the cognition of the two relata at once. Somānanda's reply to this objection immediately follows. It seems to me that the principal opponent remains the Buddhist, but note also that the necessity of seeing both the probans (or *liṅga*) and the connection of the same to the probandum (or *liṅgin*) is well known in various Indian systems of inferential logic, as at, e.g., NSBh ad NS 1.1.5, which reads in part as follows: *tatpūrvakam ity anena liṅgaliṅginoḥ saṃbandhadarśanaṃ liṅgadarśanaṃ cābhisambadhyate. liṅgaliṅginoḥ saṃbaddhayor*

The error of mutual dependence [*itaretaradoṣa*], which is difficult to overcome, applies here: as long as one does not conceive of (the fact that) the fire (is present), (on the one hand,) one cannot conceive of the connection (of the fire to the smoke). As long as one does not conceive of the connection, on the other hand, it[368] is not fit for (the furnishing of) the conception of (the presence of) fire.[369]

---

darśanena liṅgasmṛtir abhisaṃbadhyate. smṛtyā liṅgadarśanena cāpratyakṣo 'rtho 'numīyate. "'Preceded by that [i.e., perception]' (NS 1.1.5); by this is meant the perception of the relation of probans(, smoke, e.g.,) and probandum(, fire, e.g.), and perception of the probans. The memory of the probans is connected with the perception of the two related entities, probans and probandum. It is by means of the memory and the perception of the probans that the unperceived object [i.e., the probandum, fire, e.g.] is inferred." (Cf. the translation of Jha 1939: 25.)

368 That is, the conception of the connection (*yogakalanā*).

369 One should probably understand *na* in ŚD 4.90d to be read with what precedes it *and* what follows it (interpreting the compound at 4.90d to read *vahnikalanā-kṣamā).* It is also possible to interpret the *sandhi* in ŚD 4.90c in a manner that allows one to read a negative prefix (*-a*) into the passage, this by understanding there to be no hiatus following *vā: vā-ayogakalanā.* In this case, one would read *na* only with what follows it. Finally, it is possible to read an alpha privative into the compound *vahnikalanākṣamā* (viz., *vahnikalanā-akṣamā*, or even to read as two separate words: *vahnikalanā akṣamā*), in which case the negative particle would only be read with what precedes it.

The present argument essentially anticipates Utpaladeva's and Abhinavagupta's similar claim, that a unified knower must connect discrete perceptions, inasmuch as both depend on the notion that the cognitions in question are utterly momentary. See, esp., ĪPK 1.2.10, where the Buddhist position is articulated: *tatra tatra sthite tat tad bhavatīty eva dṛśyate | nānyan nānyo 'sti saṃbandhaḥ kāryakāraṇabhāvataḥ* ||. "This is what is seen and nothing else: where one or another entity is present another entity comes into being. There is no other relation [*saṃbandha*] than that of the relation of cause and effect." (This translation is based on the renderings of Torella 1994: 95 and Ratié 2011a: 298, fn. 85.) The necessity of a single knowing agent to establish such a relation is articulated at, e.g., ĪPK 1.7.4: *pratyakṣānupalambhānāṃ tattadbhinnāṃśapātinām | kāryakāraṇatāsiddhihetutaikapramātṛjā* ||. "Perceptions and non-perceptions, which concern this or that distinct part (of the cause-effect relation), may cause the establishment of the cause-effect relation (only) by being produced by a single agent of knowing." (The present translation is based on those of Torella 1994: 137 and Ratié 2011a: 147.) The perceptions and non-perceptions in question are five, two perceptions and three non-perceptions that prove the causal relationship between, e.g., smoke and fire. (Cf. for example the *Hetubindu* [HB] of Dharmakīrti, p. 4: *idam asyopalambha upalabdhilakṣaṇaprāptaṃ prāg anupalabdham upalabhyate, satsv apy anyeṣu hetuṣv asyābhāve na bhavatīti yas tadbhāve bhāvas tadabhāve 'bhāvaś ca pratyakṣānupalambhasādhanaḥ kāryakāraṇabhāvas tasya siddhiḥ.* "The relation of cause and effect [between A and B], that is, the presence [of B] when A is present, and the absence [of B] when A is absent, the establishment of which is made thanks to perception and non-perception (*pratyakṣānupalambha*), is established thus: when there is a perception of A, B, for which the conditions of perception are fulfilled, [and] which was not perceived until then, is perceived; [whereas] even when some other causes [of B] are present, when A is absent, [B] is not present [either]." Translation that of Ratié 2011b: 484, fn. 17. See also Ratié 2011a: 148, fn. 89. Cf. also, e.g., SP 13.) So much is discussed by Abhinavagupta in the ĪPV, in a passage that corresponds with ĪPK 1.7.4 (KSTS edition, vol. 1: pp. 284–285, also cited in Ratié 2011a: 147): *ihāgnau pratyakṣe dhūmaṃ nopalabhate, tato dhūmaṃ pratyakṣeṇa paśyaty agniṃ tu yadi nopalabhate dhūmaṃ api nopalabhata iti pratyakṣābhyāṃ anupalambhaiś ceti pañcakāt kāryakāraṇabhāvo dhūmāgnyoḥ siddhyatīti yad uktaṃ tat katham?* "How can what has been said be the case? Namely, that the cause-effect relation of smoke and fire is established by these five—two perceptions and (three) non-perceptions, viz., when one sees fire here, one does not see the smoke; after this one sees the smoke via direct cognition; and if one does not see fire, one does not see smoke, either." Abhinavagupta, echoing Utpaladeva's verse, goes on to explain that the correlation of the knowledge produced by

4.91-93ab

4.91. nāptavākyād athāstīha tatsatyatve 'dṛḍhā matiḥ
vārān śataṃ hi yo vaktā satyabhāṣī kadācana
4.92. so 'py anyathā pradarśyetākṣayato rāgadveṣayoḥ
pitrāder apy asatyatvaṃ tatrānyatra na niścayaḥ
4.93. tasmān na bhede bhāvānāṃ tadgrahādy api yujyate

Now, it[370] is not the product, here, of the testimony of a reliable person;[371] the determination (one may obtain from that reliable person) is not firm (even) when he is truthful. For even the speaker who expresses what is true one hundred times can teach inaccurately at any time, because passion and aversion are undecaying.[372] Even one's forefathers, among

---

these cognitions, each fixed only in itself, demands the existence of a single agent of knowing. (These arguments are surveyed in some detail in Ratié 2011a: 145–152. Cf. Torella 1994: 137, fn. 6.)

[370] That is, an understanding of the fact that smoke is connected to fire.

[371] Alternatively, one could understand the present to express the clear objection of the opponent: "Objection [*atha*]: This is not the case [*na*]; it is due to the testimony of a reliable person (that one knows fire from smoke, as this reliable person explains that the sight of smoke indicates a connection with fire, and with it a knowledge of fire from the sight of smoke)."

The argument calls to mind one deployed by the Mīmāṃsā against the Nyāya, the latter school accepting testimony as a *pramāṇa*. See, e.g., NS 2.1.68 (2.1.69 in Jha's translation): *mantrāyurvedaprāmāṇyavac ca tatprāmāṇyam āptaprāmāṇyāt.* "The validity of that [Veda], moreover, like the validity of *mantras* or Āyurveda, is derived from the validity of the reliable person." Cf. MīSū 1.1.27-28 and Śabara's commentary thereon. More importantly, see ŚBh ad MīSū 1.1.5: *tathā ca codanālakṣaṇaḥ samyakpratyaya iti. pauruṣeye hi sati saṃbandhe yaḥ pratyayaḥ, tasya mithyābhāva āśaṅkyeta. parapratyayo hi tadā syāt.* "Accordingly, proper understanding is characterized by injunction. For, if one relies on a human being (for some knowledge), one may question whether the understanding (so acquired) is erroneous. For, in that case, the understanding must be (derived) from another." It is not the view of the Naiyāyika, however, that inference is a means of knowledge that must be guaranteed by the testimony of a reliable informant, nor is this the position of Somānanda's Buddhist opponent. Why, then, Somānanda wishes to raise this issue here is somewhat unclear. Perhaps the argument is simply that no tradition of instruction could rescue his opponent's (or his opponents' [?]) position, be the opponent a Buddhist, a Naiyāyika, etc., that they can, in the absence of the unity of all as Śiva, explain how the sight of smoke can lead to an awareness of the presence of fire. Or, it is just perhaps possible that Somānanda here has in mind the definition(s) of *pramāṇa* offered by Dharmakīrti at PV (*pramāṇasiddhipariccheda*) 2.1-7 (esp. at 2.1cd-2): *pramāṇam avisaṃvādi jñānam arthakriyāsthitiḥ | avisaṃvādanaṃ śabde 'py abhiprāyanivedanād || vaktṛvyāpāraviṣayo yo 'rtho buddhau prakāśate | prāmāṇyaṃ tatra śabdasya nārthatattvanibandhanam || gṛhītagrahaṇān neṣṭaṃ sāṃvṛtaṃ dhīpramāṇatā | pravṛttes tatpradhānatvād heyopādeyavastuni || viṣayākārabhedāc ca dhiyo 'dhigamabhedataḥ | bhāvād evāsya tadbhāve svarūpasya svato gatiḥ || prāmāṇyaṃ vyavahāreṇa śāstraṃ mohanivartanam | ajñātārthaprakāśo vā svarūpādhigateḥ paraṃ || prāptaṃ sāmānyavijñānam avijñāte svalakṣaṇe | yaj jñānam ity abhiprāyāt svalakṣaṇavicārataḥ || tadvat pramāṇaṃ bhagavān abhūtavinivṛttaye | bhūtoktiḥ sādhanāpekṣā tato yuktā pramāṇatā ||*. On the meaning of this passage, see the renderings, e.g., of Nagatomi 1957: 5–7; and Katsura 1984. Cf. Lindtner 1991; Krasser 2001.

[372] Note the text is unstable at ŚD 4.91c. The *editio princeps*, K$^{ed.}$, understands the relevant half-verse to read *na rājate hy ayovaktā satyabhāṣī kadācana*, which may be rendered as follows: "For, it is never the case that a truth-teller who utters (the word) 'metal' shines (as does the metal itself)." Chaturvedi (1986: 161), in turn, has proposed to emend *hy ayovaktā* to *dvayor vaktā*, and on his reading, the *satyabhāṣī āpta* is nowhere one who can speak "for the two," i.e., for the smoke and the fire (and their relation). I have adopted the reading of T. This requires one to read *kadācana* (ŚD 4.91d) with

others, (sometimes) lack in veracity; one can have no conviction therein[373] on another occasion.[374] Therefore, that [nature of inference (*anumānatva*)] which for its part involves the apprehension of that [relation] or the like is not possible if the entities (that populate the world) are (mutually) differentiated.[375]

4.93cd-94

kṣaṇabhaṅgaparāmarśād apy etad upapadyate
4.94. śaktāśaktavikalpair hi dīpajvālādyudāhṛtaiḥ
sthiratā nopapannā te pratyakṣenāpi ca sthitā

This[376] can be rationally justified by a consideration of (your doctrine of the) instantaneous destruction (of all phenomena), as well. For, according to you, (real) permanence [*sthiratā*] is not obtained by way of conceptual constructions—which are exemplified by the (apparently perduring) flame of a lamp, for example[377]—whether they are capable or incapable,[378] nor is it established by direct cognition, either.[379]

---

the half-verse that follows it (and, somewhat irregularly, without the negative particle *na*); but it is not uncommon for Somānanda *not* to punctuate at the end of a half-verse or verse.

[373]That is, in testimony.

[374]If one cannot invariably trust the word of one's forefathers, then testimony offered by others (of lesser status) is all the less reliable. See footnote 371.

[375]It appears that *tadgrahādi* (ŚD 4.93b) should be understood to refer to what is said at ŚD 4.88 (. . . *nāpi tadgrahaḥ*). As we have seen, Somānanda there argues that, under the system of the Buddhist Epistemologists, one could not explain the nature of inference (*anumānatva*, mentioned at ŚD 4.87c) by way of an appeal to an apprehension of the connection or *saṃbandha* between the probans and the probandum, this for the fact that the connection involves a bi-location or *dviṣṭhatā*. "Etcetera" (-*ādi*), then, can here be taken to refer to *anumānatva* being explicable by way of one knowing the same *saṃbandha* in the manners explained at ŚD 4.89-90 (i.e., involving the cognition of both the probans and the relation of the same to the probandum by way of a single perception of the probans) and at ŚD 4.91-92, viz., the explanation involving the testimony of a reliable person (*āptavākya*).

[376]"This" (*etat*) here should be taken to refer to the fact that *anumānatva* (referred to with *tadgrahādi*, a *bahuvrīhi* compound, at ŚD 4.93b) is impossible (*na*. . . *yujyate*, ŚD 4.93a-b) in the absence of the existence of a unity of all entities. As before, then, the present carries on an analysis of the nature of inferentially derived instances of valid knowledge and whether they could be logically possible under the ontology of Somānanda's Buddhist opponents.

[377]The flame from a lamp, like all phenomena, is forever changing in every instant; it is no single phenomenon and it is not possessed of a "stability" or permanence. See also footnote 358.

[378]Chaturvedi (1986: 162) suggests that *śaktāśaktavikalpa* refers to two types of conceptual construction, one that has the capacity to lead to purposeful action and one that does not. Indeed, Dharmakīrti accounts for both types, the former as represented by the well-known example of the mistaken perception of the reflection of a jewel for the jewel itself, the latter by that of the light of a lamp seen through a keyhole (and understood to be the light of a gem). The conceptual form of the former, though erroneous, can lead to acquiring the jewel, but the latter example is of a conceptual form that will not accomplish the purpose in question. See PV (*pratyakṣapariccheda*) 3.57-58: *maṇipradīpaprabhayor maṇibuddhyābhidhāvataḥ* | *mithyājñānāviśeṣe 'pi viśeṣo 'rthakriyāṃ prati* || *yathā tathāyathārthatve 'py anumānatadābhayoḥ* | *arthakriyānurodhena pramāṇatvaṃ vyavasthitam* ||. (See footnote 36 of the introduction to the present volume for a translation of this pair of verses.)

[379]I here read the negative particle twice, with both *sthiratā* . . . *upapannā* and *pratyakṣenāpi ca sthitā*. One could alternatively consider emending the text here to *cāsthitā*. K[ed.] here records *ca sthitā*, T witnesses *ca sthitaiḥ*, and C reads *cāsthitaḥ*.

4.95

4.95. sthiratvaṃ kṣaṇikatvāc ca pramāṇāṃ cintayā sthitam
avisaṃvādirūpāc ca viruddhaṃ tat kathaṃ bhavet

Moreover, because the instances of valid knowledge [*pramā*] are (thus) momentary in nature, their stability is established (only) by way of intellectual reflection;[380] and, given that (you maintain that) they are by

---

The argument of ŚD 4.94, then, is that the fact that a concept perdures beyond a single instant cannot be explained by the proponent of the *kṣaṇabhaṅgavāda*. What would allow any phenomenon to perdure if all is utterly momentary in nature? Only a non-duality of the entities that make up existence could account for such *sthiratā*. Therefore, inasmuch as his opponents cannot account for the perduring nature of conceptual forms, they cannot account for inference, which depends on the same, not unless they presuppose the existence of a unity of all as Śiva.

One imagines that the kind of stability Somānanda has in mind is akin to that to which Dharmakīrti himself refers (with the term *dhrauvya*) at, e.g., PV (*svārthānumānaparicchedа*) and PVSV ad 1.75. PV 1.75 reads as follows (edition of Gnoli 1960: 41–42): *aviśeṣān na sāmānyam aviśeṣaprasaṅgataḥ | tāsāṃ kṣetrādibhede 'pi dhrauvyāc cānupakārataḥ* ||. Arnold 2012: 135 translates as follows: "Since there is no distinction [between occurrences of a universal], there is no universal [present in these herbs to explain their common effect], because [otherwise there would be] the unwanted consequence of non-distinction, even given the differences in the fields [from which they were harvested], etc.—and because [a universal is] not the performer of any function, owing to its permanence." Cf. Dunne 2004: 345–346. The relevant passage of the PVSV, as printed in Gnoli (ibid.), glosses 1.75 as follows (with the *mūla* here recorded in bold print): **aviśeṣād** *sāmānyasya* **na sāmānyam** *tatkāryakṛt. tasyāpi* **aviśeṣaprasaṅgataḥ. tāsāṃ kṣetrādibhede 'pi** *yadi hi sāmānyāj jvarādiśamanaṃ kāryaṃ syāt. tasyāviśeṣād vyaktīnāṃ kṣetrādibhede 'pi ciraśīghrapraśamanādayo [na(?)] viśeṣā guṇatāratamyaṃ ca na syāt. viśeṣe vā sāmānyasya svabhāvabhedāt svarūpahānam.* **dhrauvyāc ca** *sāmānyasya* **anupakārataḥ**. I offer the following translation of the verse and interspersed commentary, this rendering being a modification of that of Dunne (ibid.): "Because the universal is not possessed of difference, the universal is not that which makes that effect, this due to the unwanted consequence that there would be no difference for that [effect], either, even while there is difference—of fields (where planted), etc.—for those [medicines]. Indeed, if the effect, the calming of a fever, e.g., were the result of the universal, there would be (no) differences [*viśeṣāḥ*]—a slow or a quick calming (of the fever), for example—belonging to the individuals [*vyaktīnām*], nor would there be any qualitative difference thereof, because they would own no difference (in the nature) of that [universal], even despite the difference in the fields, etc., (where they were cultivated). Yet, if there were a difference belonging to the universal, then it would lose its (very) nature (as a single universal), because its nature would be divided. And (the universal is not that which produces the effect for this reason, as well,) because the universal does not perform any function, this because of its permanence." Note that a negative particle is wished for where marked in the text, above. It is perhaps possible that one could supply the same by reading not *na* there, but the alpha-privative (in a *nañ-samāsa*), which is allowed by a different interpretation of the *sandhi* and on the understanding that *avagrahas* are often dropped in manuscript transmission: *ciraśīghrapraśamanādayo 'viśeṣāḥ*.

380 I here conjecture that the text should read *kṣaṇikatvāt* where T and K[ed.] read *kṣaṇikatvaṃ* and C reads (hypometrically) *kṣaṇitvaṃ*. It seems possible that degemination led to the presentation of an apparently errant form (*kṣaṇikatvā*, losing the final *c* before *ca*), and a scribe, seeing the connective *ca* took both *sthiratvam* and (he supposed) *kṣaṇikatvam* to be joined thereby, whereas I understand *ca* to be connective with the previous verse.

nature reliable [*avisaṃvādi*],[381] (we ask:) how can they be possessed of that [stability,] which is contrary (to their real nature)?[382]

4.96-97ab

4.96. yāvan na sarvabhāvānām ekatvena vyavasthitiḥ
pareṇa kṣaṇabhaṅgasya parāmarśāgamaḥ kutaḥ
4.97. tato 'py etac chivātmatvaṃ bhāvānām upapadyate

As long as there is no fixed existence of all entities (in the universe) as a unity, how could another bring one to reflect on the instantaneous destruction (at all)?[383] It is also for that reason that this, the Śiva-nature of (all) entities, is rationally justified.

4.97cd-98a

tathārthāvagatir vākyāt padād vā nopapadyate
4.98. kṣaṇikatvena śabdānām. . .

And, on account of their momentariness, no understanding of the meaning of instances of speech would be obtained from a sentence or a word.[384]

---

[381] I here propose a conjectural emendation of *avisaṃvādirūpāc ca* where K$^{ed.}$ reads *apy asaṃvādarūpaṃ ca*, T witnesses *api saṃvādirūpāc ca*, and C *atisaṃvādarūpā ca*. T witnesses the very reading I conjecture, apart from recording *api* where I conjecture *avi-*, and *pi* and *vi* are exceedingly similar in the Malayalam script in which T is recorded.

Cf., e.g., PV (*pramāṇasiddhipariccheda*) 2.1ab: *pramāṇam avisaṃvādi jñānam arthakriyāsthitiḥ* |. (PV 2.1-7 is also cited in footnote 371.) See also Dharmottara's NBṬ, p. 17–18, on correct cognition as *avisaṃvādaka*, which is cited at footnote 104.

Given that Somānanda addresses problems with inference for another (*parārthānumāna*) in what follows (ŚD 4.96-97ab), it is best to understand ŚD 4.95, probably along with ŚD 4.93cd-94, to be intended to deal in particular with inference for oneself (*svārthānumāna*).

[382] That which is (falsely) experienced as or implicitly understood to be permanent or perduring cannot, by the Buddhist opponent's own definition, be a valid means of knowledge; thus, the valid knowledge [*pramā*], inasmuch as it is expressed in universals, is not valid, even if it conduces to a useful action or *arthakriyā*. Presumably, then, ŚD 4.95 deals particularly with *śakta-vikalpas* or those that are (indirectly) capable of causal efficacy. So much is of course an intricate concern of Buddhist epistemology, about which see, e.g., Franco and Notake 2014: 4–9, 31 fn. 4.

[383] It simply would not be possible, Somānanda argues with a touch of humor, for someone to communicate the very notion of momentariness to another if everything were truly momentary. So much echoes, *mutatis mutandis*, the arguments of Utpaladeva and Abhinavagupta for the necessary existence of a unifying agent who can facilitate a synthesis or *anusaṃdhāna* of cognitions. See, e.g., ĪPK 1.3.6-7; ĪPKVṛ ad ĪPK 1.8.10. See also ŚDVṛ ad ŚD 4.4-5, esp. at footnote 26, where the aforementioned passages are cited. Cf. ĪPK 1.7.3 and the ĪPV thereon (cited at footnote 361).

[384] Utter momentariness would prohibit any unification of cognitions, what is needed to conceive of the meaning represented by the combination of multiple sounds into words or sentences. See also footnote 383.

4.98b-100ab

. . . anabhivyaktito 'pi vā
sphoṭābhivyaṅgyapakṣe tu tatrāpi kramatā katham
4.99. nirbhāgatvāt sphoṭatattve sphoṭatattvātmakāt katham
ābhāsarūpavastūnāṃ śābdikānāṃ bhaved grahaḥ
4.100. tasmād evaṃvidhe 'rthe 'pi yuktatā syād ihaikyataḥ

Or also, (no understanding of the meaning would be obtained) on account of the non-manifestation (of that meaning).[385] And if one supposes that it[386] may be manifested as *sphoṭa*—with regard to that, too(we ask): how could there exist a sequentiality (of the *śabdas* or instances of sound/speech that manifest the meaning), since it [i.e., the meaning] is undivided at the level of the *sphoṭa*?[387] (Objection:) This results from (those instances of speech) consisting of the level of the *sphoṭa*. (Reply:)

---

[385]This raises a second potential problem with speech, following on the one noted at ŚD 4.97cd-98a. While the former objection, directed at the Buddhists, addressed a problem of explaining the unification of discrete cognitions, here the problem is one of explaining the devolution or deunification of a single, unitary meaning into elements that, taken together, manifest it. Somānanda's criticism is here conceptually similar to his arguments against non-dualist Vedāntins in the sixth *āhnika* of the ŚD in that he questions the logical coherence of his opponent's position on the grounds that it cannot logically justify the nature of a true unity that simultaneously is able to appear in the form of multiplicity. (Cf. ŚD 6.1-24ab, edited, translated, and explained in Nemec forthcoming. See also footnote 387.) The opponent here addressed is very likely to be Bhartṛhari or, in addition, Maṇḍana Miśra and his *Sphoṭasiddhi* (SSi).

Kumārila, as is well known, also argued against the proponents of *sphoṭa*, but not by challenging the capacity for the devolved manifestation of the same but by arguing that the sounds of speech combined with impressions left thereby directly communicate meaning. See, esp., ŚV (*sphoṭavādādhikaraṇa*) 131–132 (ed. of Śāstrī 1978: 383): *varṇā vā dhvanayo vāpi sphoṭaṃ na padavākyayoḥ | vyañjanti vyañjakatvena yathā dīpaprabhādayaḥ || sattvād ghaṭādivac ceti sādhanāni yathāruci | laukikavyatirekeṇa kalpite 'rthe bhavanti hi* ||. "Neither the letters nor the sounds of a word or a sentence manifest *sphoṭa* as that which manifests (meaning), just as the lights of lamps, e.g.(, do not manifest an intervening manifestor of the objects it illumines). And (the letters and the sounds are the manifestors for this reason): because, like a pot, e.g., they have existence. These proofs, as one might wish, may come up as regards an object imagined in a manner that is dissonant with the everyday world." (Translation a modification of that of Jha 1907: 280.) Cf. the corresponding passage of the ŚVNRĀ of Pārthasārathi Miśra (ed. of Śāstrī 1978: 383): *dhvanimātropādāne śaṅkhādidhvanīnāṃ sphoṭābhivyañjakatvasya parair aniṣṭatvād aṃśe siddhasādhyatvaṃ syāt, tan mā bhūd iti padavākyayor iti viśeṣaṇam. padavākyayor vartamānā varṇā dhvanayo vā sphoṭaṃ nābhivyañjantīty anvayaḥ*. See also, e.g., SSi (ed. and trans. of Iyer 1966: 9): *nanu ca varṇā evābhidheyādhigamanimittaṃ svābhidheyāvabodhāvadhilabdhaparicchedāḥ padaparikalpanābhājaḥ?*

[386]That is, the meaning (*artha*).

[387]The meaning is unitary, as is the *sphoṭa*, so how can a multiplicity manifest the same? For though the *sphoṭa* and the meaning with which it is identified are untouched by temporal distinction, they are said to be manifested by the same multiple entities, by way of the sounds. See, e.g., VP 1.76-78 (edition of Rau): *sphoṭasyābhinnakālasya dhvanikālānupātinaḥ | grahaṇopādhibhedena vṛttibhedaṃ pracakṣate || svabhāvabhedān nityatve hrasvadīrghaplutādiṣu | prākṛtasya dhvaneḥ kālaḥ śabdasyety upacaryate || śabdasya grahaṇe hetuḥ prākṛto dhvanir iṣyate | sthitibhedanimittatvaṃ vaikṛtaḥ pratipadyate* ||.

How could one come to apprehend what are ephemeral things as those that are of a linguistic nature [*śābdika*]?[388] Therefore, even an object [*artha*] of this kind (such that it is both "ephemeral" and linguistic) is viable, here,[389] (only) as a result of (the) unity (that is Śiva).[390]

4.100cd-101

tathātmecchāvaśān nākṣagrāme ceṣṭopapadyate
4.101. mūrtacodakavaikalyān manaś cet preritāsya no
ekatve punar īdṛk syāt sarvatraiva hi yuktatā

And, (in the absence of the existence of unity,) no activity in the array of the organs of sense would be possible by dint of the will of the *ātman*, because there is a defect in (conceiving of the *ātman* as) the impeller of that which has a form.[391] Objection: The *manas* is that which incites this

---

It is not evident to me how Somānanda would weigh in, if at all, on the argument between Kumārila and Maṇḍana Miśra regarding the manner in which disparate elements of speech-acts convey meaning, whether directly upon hearing the last phoneme in a meaningful string (with the help of an impression that reminds one of the previous phonemes of the same), as Kumārila would have it, or by way of the manifestation of something over and above those phonemes, namely, the *sphoṭa*, that is directly cognized, as Maṇḍana Miśra would explain the matter. On this matter as addressed in the Pratyabhijñā see Torella 2004; Nemec 2019, especially at p. 229, fn. 5; p. 246, fn. 35; and p. 263, fn. 67.

[388] Chaturvedi (1986: 164) understands the present to suggest that there can be no understanding of the *śabdatattva* through the appearances, the *vivartas*, because the latter are momentary and the former is one and unchanging.

It is possible to read *sphoṭatattvātmakāt* (ŚD 4.99b) twice, with what both precedes it and follows it. Doing so, one could translate as follows: "(Reply:) How could one come to apprehend what are ephemeral things as pertaining to language, (merely) as a result of (those ephemeral things) consisting of the nature of *sphoṭa*?"

Finally, for other arguments authored by Somānanda against the *sphoṭavāda*, see ŚD 2.58-61ab and 2.77 (translated and edited at Nemec 2011: 191–193, 203–204, 334–336, and 343–344).

[389] *Iha* (ŚD 4.100b) means either "here [in the world]" or "here [in your system]."

[390] Or, understanding *artha* (ŚD 4.100a) to mean "meaning" rather than "object": "Therefore, even meaning that is of this kind [i.e., such that it is made known by *sphoṭa*] is viable, here, (only) as a result of (the) unity (that is Śiva)."

[391] Or, it is possible, though less likely, that one could understand *mūrtacodakavaikalyāt* as follows: ". . . because there is a defect in (conceiving of the *ātman*, which is without form or *amūrta*, as) an impeller that has a form." The opponent is a Naiyāyika/Vaiśeṣika. The present concern is this, that while the *ātman* is *amūrta* in the Nyāya-Vaiśeṣika, the *indriyas* (and the *manas*) are *mūrta*. How the one impels the others to act is therefore in question, the two being on this view qualitatively different in their respective natures.

On the well-known doctrine of the Nyāya that the *indriyas* are material, see NS 1.1.12: *ghrāṇarasanacakṣustvakśrotrāṇīndriyāṇi bhūtebhyaḥ.* "The sense organs, the nose, tongue, eyes, skin, and ears, are (produced) from the elements." Cf. the corresponding passage of the NSBh of Vātsyāyana, which reads in part as follows: *bhūtebhya iti. nānāprakṛtīnām eṣāṃ satāṃ viṣayaniyamaḥ, naikaprakṛtīnām. sati ca viṣayaniyame svaviṣayagrahaṇalakṣaṇatvaṃ bhavatīti.* "As for 'from the elements,' (this means that) there is a limitation as regards the object for these, what are real [sense organs], whose constitutions are (mutually) varied, not unitary in their constitution. And there being a limitation as regards the objects, they are characterized by their apprehension (only) of their

[array] to act.[392] (Reply:) This is simply not the case.[393] If a unity exists, however, there could be such a condition; for a state of being connected would exist absolutely everywhere.[394]

4.102-103

4.102. na cāpi bhede bhāvānāṃ grahaṇaṃ jñānam eva vā
saṃyogenopapadyeta yadi dṛṣṭyādinā bhavet
4.103. naivam akṣārthasaṃyogamātrāt kiṃ boddhur udyamaḥ
saṃyoge 'nyasya sañjāte katham anyasya boddhṛtā

It also is not the case that one could apprehend the entities, or cognize them fully [*eva*], if dualism were to exist.[395] Objection: It [i.e., the apprehension, or cognition] is possible by way of a connection; it can come to be by way of the faculty of seeing, etc.[396] (Reply:) So much is not the case.

---

own (respective) objects." On the *amūrtatva* of the *ātman* see, e.g., PDhSaṃ (p. 308, lines 3–5): *ākāśakāladigātmanām saty api dravyabhāve niṣkriyatvaṃ sāmānyādivad amūrtatvāt.*

[392] If it is not the *ātman* but the *manas* that impels the *indriyas* to act, then the Naiyāyika or Vaiśeṣika can claim to have responded effectively to Somānanda's objection, for the *manas* is counted as *mūrta* in the realists' system. See, e.g., PDhSaṃ (p. 21, lines 21–22): *kṣitijalajyotiranilamanasām kriyāvattvamūrtatvaparatvāparatvavegavattvāni.* Note that *preritā* is in fact masculine in gender, while *manas* is neuter. It is possible to decline agent nouns in *-tṛ* in the neuter gender, on the model of *śuci*, but such forms are exceedingly rare. While there are variants recorded in the manuscripts that are perhaps worth pondering further (C and K$^{ed.a.c.}$ read *preryatāsya*, T reads *preryatātsya*), I think it most likely that the masculine form of the agent noun was simply used here in apposition with the neuter *manas*.

[393] The *ātman*, on the Naiyāyika's own view, has a role in impelling the act of cognition to take place, but the *manas* is merely an instrument in that process. That the *ātman* has experience in a body (and directs actions, etc., there) is noted at NS 1.1.11: *ceṣṭendriyarthāśrayaḥ śarīram.* Cf. NSBh ad NS 2.1.26, cited in footnote 316, which reads in part: . . . *ātmā jijñāsamānaḥ prayatnena manas tadā prerayatīti.* In other words and simply put, it is just not the case [*no*] that Somānanda's realist opponent understands the *manas* to impel the *indriyas* to act.

[394] Here, the Naiyāyika's view is said possibly to be confirmed—the *ātman* could cause the *indriyas* to make contact with the object of cognition—if, that is, one accepts the unity of reality for which Somānanda argues. This oneness would allow what is *amūrta* to have contact with what is *mūrta*. Note also that a similar argument (regarding *mūrtatva* and *amūrtatva*, though in relation to the Mīmāṃsā) was offered at ŚD 4.71-73ab.

[395] In the previous passage (ŚD 4.100cd-101), Somānanda criticized the process by which cognition is said to be initiated, according to the Nyāya-Vaiśeṣika. Here, he objects to the possibility that that cognitive process as they understand it could in fact lead the *ātman* to know the object apprehended by the *indriyas*. Note that I understand *bhede* (ŚD 4.102a) to be a locative absolute, what is a parallel to the other of the contrasting pair, *ekatve*, expressed in a locative absolute at ŚD 4.101c. It is also possible, however, to read it with *bhāvānām*: "It also is not the case that one could apprehend the entities, or cognize them fully [*eva*], if they [i.e., the entities] were different (from the knower)."

[396] In other words, a connection (by which I understand Somānanda to refer primarily to the contact or *sannikarṣa* of the *artha/bhāva* or entity perceived with the *indriya* or sense organ that perceives it and, secondarily, to the contact of the *manas* with the *ātman*) leads to the apprehension and, subsequent to this, the full cognition of the entities. "Etcetera" here very probably refers to the sense organs other than that of sight. It is also possible it refers to the subsequent stage in the cognitive

Why would the mere connection of the sense organ and object cause the knower to exert himself?[397] How, when the connection has been produced of one entity, is another the knower?[398]

4.104-107a

4.104. manaso bhinnakālatvāt smṛtijñānam athocyate
prārabdhaś cāsamāptaś ca vartamānaḥ kriyām anu
4.105. prakriyāmātram evaitad yataḥ pūrvāparātmatā
kriyāyāḥ kārakāṇāṃ hi kramo 'sty eva svakarmaṇi
4.106. yatra pūrvāparau śabdau kālaikyaṃ tatra yujyate
manasā nīyate tasya kiṃ padārthasvarūpatā
4.107. sāśakyā mūrtarūpatvād. . .

---

process, namely, the *jñāna* produced when the *ātman* knows the result of the *sannikarṣa* in question (via the *manas*).

Somānanda here works against the definition of *pratyakṣa* offered in the *Vaiśeṣikasūtras* of Kaṇāda. See VS 3.1.13: *ātmendriyamano'rthasannikarṣād yan niṣpadyate tad anyat.* "What is produced from the contact of the *ātman*, the sense organ, the *manas*, and the object is other [i.e., is direct cognition]." The same is referred to and explained in the NM of Jayanta Bhaṭṭa, p. 100, lines 11–12: *yad api kaiścit pratyakṣalakṣaṇam uktam, ātmendriyamano'rthasannikarśād yad utpadyate jñānaṃ tad anyad anumānādibhyaḥ pratyakṣam iti.* (The same is cited in Hattori 1968: 135, fn. 4.3.) Cf., also, NS 1.1.4: *indriyārthasannikarṣotpannaṃ jñānam avyapadeśyam avyabhicāri vyavasāyātmakaṃ pratyakṣam.* "A cognition that is produced by contact of sense organ and object, which is indescribable, inerrant, and definite in nature is *pratyakṣa*."

[397] That is, why would the *ātman* exert any effort in the cognitive process if the only impetus were the connection (*saṃyoga*), or contact (*sannikarṣa*), of the material *indriya* with the material *artha* (*akṣārthasaṃyogamātrāt*, ŚD 4.103a-b)?

[398] Put differently, how could knowledge (in the *manas*) produced via a connection of an *indriya* to an *artha* render the *ātman* the knower of the same? The entities involved are, on Somānanda's view, simply too far separated (as *mūrta*, *amūrta*, etc.) to be mutually related—unless, of course, one accepts the existence of the unity of reality for which he argues. On the establishment of this cognitive process and for a statement of the difference between the knower and that which contacts the object seen, see NS and NSBh ad 1.1.30: *yatsiddhāv anyaprakaraṇasiddhiḥ so 'dhikaraṇasiddhāntaḥ* || 1.1.30 || *yasyārthasya siddhāv anye 'rthā anuṣajyante, na tair vinā so 'rthaḥ sidhyati te 'rthā yadadhiṣṭhānāḥ so 'dhikaraṇasiddhāntaḥ, yathādehendriyavyatirikto jñātā darśanasparśanābhyām ekārthagrahaṇād iti atrānuṣaṅgiṇo 'rthā indriyanānātvaṃ niyataviṣayāṇīndriyāṇi svaviṣayagrahaṇaliṅgāni jñātur jñānasādhanāni, gandhādiguṇavyatiriktaṃ dravyaṃ guṇādhikaraṇam aniyataviṣayāś cetanā iti pūrvārthasiddhāv ete 'rthāḥ sidhyanti na tair vinā so 'rthaḥ sambhavatīti* |. "When something is proven another matter is proved. That is the *adhikaraṇasiddhānta*." NSBh: "When some fact is established, other facts are associated with it, (and) without those [other facts] that fact (that has been proven) is not proven; the (associated) facts are (thus) founded on the first one—this is the *adhikaraṇasiddhānta*. For example [*yathā*], the knower is (proven to be) different than the body and the sense organs because one object is apprehended by both (the sense organ of) seeing and (the sense organ of) touching. Thus, the associated facts in the present example [*atra*] are: (1) there exists a variety of sense organs; (2) the sense organs have particular objects of sense; (3) they are characterized by their respective (distinct) apprehensions of (particular) objects, (and) (4) are the means of cognition for the (distinct) cognizer; (5) a substance [*dravya*] is the locus of the qualities [*guṇādhikaraṇa*], other than the qualities of smell, etc.; (and, finally, unlike the *indriyas*,) (6) sentient beings do not have (only) a (single) particular (class of) object (of perception of which they are aware). Thus, these facts are proved when the prior fact is proven, (and) without them that (prior) fact would be impossible."

Objection: We speak of the cognition that is memory as being the result of the fact that the *manas* is present in different moments of time.[399] (Reply:) In regard to the action (of the cognitive process), there exists a moment of subsisting in time [*vartamāna*], one that has both commenced and has not been completed. This is simply the procedure (of the act of cognition), since action is sequential;[400] indeed, there must be a sequence of the

---

[399]The objection serves as the Naiyāyika's response to the question asked in the immediately preceding passage (at ŚD 4.103, esp. 4.103cd), namely, how it is that one entity, i.e., the *ātman*, can be the knower when the contact with the external object in the initial act of perception belongs to another entity, i.e., the *indriya* or sense organ. The argument is that because it is the *manas* that is present at both the moment of the initial cognition of some entity and at the moment of the memory of the same, the Naiyāyika's understanding of the *ātman* as the true knower is justifiable; for while the *indriyas* make contact with the objects, the absence of the objects in the cognition that is memory requires the existence of an *ātman* to know the awareness produced in the *manas* on that occasion, as on the occasion of the initial cognition. (This is stated in the NSBh explicitly in the commentary on NS 3.1.14, for which see footnote 442.) Otherwise, the experience of the two cognitions could not be accounted for, and the very possibility of the memory-cognition in particular would be inexplicable. Here, then, Somānanda will enquire after how the sequential nature of cognition, as understood in the Nyāya-Vaiśeṣika, might be understood to take place. He asks, that is, how the procedure may be understood to work if, indeed, there is a contact of one entity (i.e., the *indriya*, with the *artha*) that leads another entity (i.e., the *ātman*) to be the knower (as stated at ŚD 4.103).

On memory in the Nyāya-Vaiśeṣika, see VS 9.2.6: *ātmamanasoḥ saṃyogaviśeṣāt saṃskārāc ca smṛtiḥ*. "Memory is the result of the particular connection of the *ātman* and the *manas*, and the *saṃskāra* (from the prior experience that is remembered)." Cf. NS 1.1.16: *yugapajjñānānutpattir manaso liṅgam*. "The mark proving the existence of the *manas* is the non-appearance of simultaneous cognitions." That is, there must be a helper in cognition such that different sense organs can communicate what they know to the *ātman*, because it is not possible to know more than one object of sense at a time, even as many sense organs can be associated with a single object in a single moment of time. Cf. NSBh ad NS 1.1.16: *anindriyanimittāḥ smṛtyādayaḥ karaṇāntaranimittā bhavitum arhantīti. yugapac ca khalu ghrāṇādīnāṃ gandhādīnāṃ ca sannikarṣeṣu satsu yugapaj jñānāni notpadyante, tenānumīyate, asti tat tad indriyasaṃyogi sahakāri nimittāntaram avyāpi, yasyāsannidher notpadyate jñānaṃ sannidheś cotpadyata iti. manaḥsaṃyogānapekṣasya hīndriyārthasannikarṣasya jñānahetutve yugapad utpadyeran jñānānīti.*

Cf. VS 3.1.18, a *sūtra* commonly accepted by Naiyāyikas, which indicates that it is the contact(s) (occurring in a sequence) of the *ātman*, *indriya*, and *artha* that leads to correct knowledge: *ātmendriyārthasannikarṣād yad niṣpadyate tad anyat*. "What is produced from the contact of the *ātman*, the sense organ, and the object is different (than false knowledge, i.e., is knowledge)." VS 3.2.1, moreover, indicates the particular role of the *manas* in the cognitive process: *ātmendriyārthasannikarṣe jñānasya bhāvo 'bhāvaś ca manaso liṅgam*. "The presence and non-presence of knowledge, when there is contact of the *ātman* with the sense organs and objects is the mark that proves (the existence of) the *manas*."

On the need for there to be a cognizer (i.e., the *ātman*) that is different from the *manas* see NS 3.1.1-16, esp. 3.1.14-16 (treated in part at footnote 442). Cf. NSBh ad NS 3.2.19, which reads in part as follows: *yugapaj jñeyānupalabdhir antaḥkaraṇasya liṅgam, tatra yugapaj jñeyānupalabdhyā yad anumīyate antaḥkaraṇam, na tasya guṇo jñānam. kasya tarhi? jñasya vaśitvāt.*

Note: I here accept the readings of T and C of *bhinnakālatvāt* (ŚD 4.104a) for K[ed.]'s *abhinnakālatvāt*, by assuming no *avagraha* should be understood to be present. The reasons for preferring this reading are entirely semantic; as is well known, *avagrahas* are often not recorded in the manuscripts, meaning their presence or absence in the manuscript witnesses is regularly only presumed and thus is based entirely on the judgment—what is based in the semantics—of the reader.

[400]More literally, "since action is by nature possessed of prior and posterior [phases]" (*yataḥ pūrvāparātmatā kriyāyāḥ*). Reference is made here, then, to the well-known and widely accepted notion that action involves a series of steps over time. Such definitions of action are represented, of

factors of action in (the performance of) their own work. A temporal unity is (similarly) fitted where speech is sequential.[401] (So:) What of it[402] is conveyed by the *manas* (to the *ātman*)?[403] (Objection:) The state of the nature of the thing (apprehended by the *indriyārthasannikarṣa*).[404] (Reply:) That [state] is not possible (to be conveyed to the *ātman*), due to the fact that it has a material form [*mūrtarūpatvāt*].[405]

4.107b-d

. . . rūpaṃ cen na kathaṃ guṇaḥ
guṇino nīyate 'nyatra tṛṣārtaiś cākṛtiṃ prati

---

course, in the grammatical literature. See, e.g., MaBhā (edition of Kielhorn, vol. 1: p. 258): *kārakāṇāṃ pravṛttiviśeṣaḥ kriyā.* Cf. the *kriyāsamuddeśa* of Bhartṛhari's *Vākyapadīya*, VP 3.8.4: *guṇabhūtair avayavaiḥ samūhaḥ kramajanmanām | buddhyā prakalpitābhedaḥ kriyeti vyapadiśyate ||*. Allusion to such an understanding of action is also found at ĪPKVṛ ad ĪPK 1.2.9: *kriyāpi pūrvāparībhūtāvayavaikā kārakavyāpārarūpā na yuktā kramikasyānekakālaspṛśaḥ svātmaikyāyogāt, nāpi kālakramavyāpī caikasvabhāvaś ca tasyā āśrayo yuktaḥ, kevalaṃ gamanapariṇāmādirūpā sā kriyā. kāyādīnāṃ tu tattadbhinnadeśakālagatāpūrvasattāmātram etadatiriktasyānyasyānupalambhāt.*

As for Somānanda's opponent, here, there can be no doubt that the Naiyāyikas maintain that knowledge involves activity. See NS 1.1.17: *pravṛttir vāgbuddhiśarīrārambhaḥ.* "Activity is the undertaking of speech, mind, and body." Cf. the corresponding passage of the NSBh: *mano 'tra buddhir ity abhipretam, budhyate 'neneti buddhiḥ. so 'yam ārambhaḥ śarīreṇa vācā manasā ca puṇyaḥ pāpaś ca daśavidhaḥ. tad etat kṛtabhāṣyaṃ dvitīyasūtra iti.* "Here [at NS 1.1.17], *buddhi* means *manas*, the *buddhi* being that by which [something] is cognized. An undertaking by means of the body, speech, or mind is either meritorious or deleterious (and) of ten kinds. This has already been explained in (the commentary on) the second *sūtra*."

401 More literally, "where two moments of speech exist, one earlier, the other subsequent." Why Somānanda refers to a temporal unity around speech is at least somewhat unclear to me. Could it be he wishes to suggest that action (*kriyā*) is like speech in that each involves what is or can be conceived of as a single event—the making of a statement (which is comprehended by the listener in a single moment), or the performance of an act such as cooking rice—despite the fact that each involves a sequential procedure of many stages (uttering multiple syllables; or lighting wood, placing a pot on the fire, boiling water, etc.) that must be enacted over time? In what follows, Somānanda will interrogate in detail how the sequence of his opponents' epistemological act may be understood to function. This he does by probing the products of the various stages therein, including principally those of (a) the contact of the *indriya* and the *artha* and (b) the contact of the *manas* and the *ātman*. In all cases, Somānanda will note the ways in which his opponents' theory cannot account for the types of cognitions one knows to occur in quotidian experience. These arguments extend from the present passage to ŚD 4.116.

402 That is, what is it of that "other" that is possessed of the connection (*anya*, ŚD 4.103c, referring to the *indriya*) that is brought by the *manas* to the *ātman*?

403 What does the *manas* convey that is the result of the prior *indriyārthasannikarṣa*?

404 I had thought perhaps that what is meant is that the nature of the categories, the *padārthas*, that make up the object (or *artha*) is conveyed, but I think the interpretation as translated is more fitting of the argument.

405 The problem is that the *padārtha*—so too the *indriya* (and for that matter the *manas*)—is *mūrta*, while the *ātman* is *amūrta*. How, Somānanda asks, can something that has a material form be conveyed to what does not (short of accepting the ontological non-dualism of the Śaivas)? See also footnote 391.

Objection: The form (is brought by the *manas* to the knower). (Reply:) Not so. How could a quality belonging to the entity possessing such a quality be conveyed?[406] And how, as regards the particular configuration [*ākṛti*] (of that *guṇa*), is that [quality of the one possessing it] brought (to the *ātman* in a manner rendering it) otherwise (than its true nature) by those affected by desire?[407]

4.108-110

4.108. atha jñānaṃ na manasas taj jñānam upapadyate
karaṇatvāj jaḍatvāc ca tasya ced ātmanātra kim
4.109. karaṇe jñānasaṃbandhād bāhyārthe kiṃ na kalpyate
buddher guṇatvaṃ manasi prāpnuyād atha cetasā
4.110. evaṃvidho ghaṭo 'trāste ity ātmā pratibodhyate
tad evaṃ pūrvadṛṣṭasya varṇanāsadṛśaṃ bhavet

Objection: A cognition (of the qualities of the object appearing in a manner distorted by the knower's desire is brought to the knower). (Reply:) Not so. It is not possible that that (is a type of) cognition (that) belongs to the *manas*,[408] because (according to you) the latter is (merely)

---

[406] All *guṇas*, on the realists' view, must inhere in a *dravya*, but not all *dravyas* can hold or contain all *guṇas*. See, e.g., NSBh ad NS 1.1.5: *guṇāś ca dravyasaṃsthānāḥ*. (This is stated where Vātsyāyana explains how the existence of the *ātman* is proved by way of *sāmānyatodṛṣṭa* inference, because desire (*icchā*), which is a *guṇa*, must inhere in a *dravya*. The inference in question involves the inference of the probandum on the basis of a similarity with some object, where the relation between the two is imperceptible. See NSBh ad NS 1.1.5: *sāmānyatodṛṣṭaṃ nāma—yatrāpratyaṣe liṅgaliṅginoḥ saṃbandhe kenacid arthena liṅgasya sāmānyād apratyakṣo liṅgī gamyate, yathecchādibhir ātmā.*) Cf. PDhSaṃ (p. 186, lines 19–21): *rūparasagandhasparśeṣv anekadravyasamavāyāt svagataviśeṣāt svāśrayasannikarṣān niyatendriya-nimittam utpadyate. tenaivopalabdhiḥ*. Cf. also PDhSaṃ (p. 94, lines 6–7): *rūpādīnāṃ guṇānāṃ sarveṣāṃ guṇatvābhisambandho dravyāśritatvaṃ nirguṇatvaṃ niṣkriyatvam*. On the different types of *guṇas* see PDhSaṃ (p. 95, line 3): *rūparasagandhasparśaparatvāparatvagurutvadravatvasnehavegā mūrtaguṇāḥ*. And: PDhSaṃ (p. 95, lines 9–10): *buddhisukhaduḥkhecchādveṣaprayatnadharmādharmabhāvanāśabdā amūrtaguṇāḥ*. In a word, the (non-repeatable) *guṇas* inhere particularly in their particular *dravyas*; and what is at stake here is the cognition of material or *mūrta* entities in which particular qualities inhere, and which cannot inhere in what is *amūrta*. This is to say then that the *guṇas* in question must be conveyed in a *mūrta* substance or *dravya*. For the Naiyāyika/Vaiśeṣika to claim such a thing were conveyed to the *ātman*, therefore, would lead this opponent to confront anew the same problem as the one enumerated at ŚD 4.106cd-107a, namely, that the nature of the quality of the external entity (such as its form or *rūpa*), because it must be located in the entity (*artha*) itself, cannot be conveyed to the *ātman* for being perceivable only in a *mūrta* entity, since the *ātman* is *amūrta* and incompatible therewith.

[407] The concern, then, is to challenge the opponent to account for the way in which the emotions or impressions of the knower might possibly distort a cognition, such that the *ātman* is brought to a knowledge of an external entity that in fact differs from what could be correctly apprehended by the *indriyas*.

N.B.: I read *nīyate* twice, both here and in rendering 4.107b-c. I also read *katham* twice, also both here and in the previous.

[408] I read *na* (ŚD 4.108a) twice, once as the reply to the objection and a second time to negate the verb (*upapadyate*).

an instrument and is insentient.[409] Objection: It is by means of the *ātman* that it [i.e., the distorted cognition] belongs to it [i.e., the *manas*].[410] (Reply:) What use is the *ātman*, here?[411] If (you argue) it is the trigger [*karaṇa*], because of the connection of the cognition (to the *ātman*),[412] (we reply by asking:) do you not conceive of it [i.e., the distorted cognition] with respect to the external object?[413] The possession of the (distorted) qualities belonging to the cognition [*buddhi*] would be at hand in the *manas* (but not with respect to the external object).[414] Objection: It is by dint of (the *ātman*'s) consciousness that the self [*ātman*] is informed that a pot of such a kind(, e.g.,)[415] is present, here.[416] Reply: In this way, that which was first seen (in the initial perception) would be different from the description (given of it by the consciousness of the *ātman*).[417]

---

[409] In other words, it is not possible for the *manas* to introduce distortion into an apprehension that is the product of the *indriyārthasannikarṣa*; the *manas* can only convey the product of the *indriārthasannikarṣa*. On the instrumental nature of the *manas*, see, e.g., Śrīdhara's NK ad PDhSaṃ, p. 175, line 6: *manaś cetanaṃ na bhavati, karaṇatvād ghaṭādivad iti.* It must be noted, however, that this commentary might postdate Somānanda and may not have been known to him.

[410] If the *manas* itself cannot introduce a distortion in the cognition, then perhaps the *ātman* can play a role such that it influences, changes, what the *manas* registers. The reply to this possible objection follows.

[411] I here read *ātmanā* (ŚD 4.108d) twice, in both the opponent's reply and Somānanda's retort. If this interpretation is correct, then it must be added that this is a remarkably and unusually compacted style of verse.

[412] The opponent might argue that the *ātman* triggers a distortion of the *jñāna* in the *manas*, because the *ātman* is involved in the cognition through its own connection with it via the *ātmamanaḥsannikarṣa*. The reply to this hypothetical follows.

[413] That is, if the *ātman* triggers the distortion by way of its contact with the cognition (in the *manas*), then this could possibly account for the distortion of the cognition at the level of the *ātman*'s experience thereof upon its contact with the *manas*, but not at the level of what is reported to the *manas* as a result of the contact of the external object with the *indriya* that apprehended it. (The triggering occurs at too late of a stage in the procedure of the cognitive act.) There would thus be an inconsistency of the contents of a cognition in one and the same act of cognition. See also footnote 414.

[414] The *ātman* would know the distortions as belonging to the *manas* and not the external objects, that is. The *manas*, evidently, would be understood to be the *āśraya* or the *guṇin* for the *guṇa* that is conveyed to the *ātman*. See also footnotes 409, 410, 412, and 413. Note also that I understand Somānanda here to use the term *buddhi* in a manner that would be accepted by the Nyāya, viz., as referring to cognition. See NS 1.1.15: *buddhir upalabdhir jñānam ity anarthāntaram.* Vātsyāyana's NSBh: *nācetanasya karaṇasya buddher jñānaṃ bhavitum arhati, tad dhi cetanaṃ syāt, ekaś cāyaṃ cetano dehendriyasaṃghātavyatirikta iti. prameyalakṣaṇārthasya vākyasyānyārthaprakāśanam upapattisāmarthyād iti.*

[415] That is, a pot appearing to one as otherwise than it really is, under the influence of the desire of the knower.

[416] The argument is not entirely clear to me, but what is apparently suggested is that, despite the discrepancy between what is produced by the *indriyārthasannikarṣa*, on the one hand, and the awareness the *ātman* has of the contents of the *manas*, on the other, the consciousness or *cetas* of the *ātman* leads that *ātman* to understand the cognition as it appears in distorted fashion in the *manas* also to represent what is present in the external object itself.

[417] The cognitive process, in a word, cannot simply shed the products of the stages of which it is comprised. While the *cetas* of the *ātman* might describe an appearance that is different from what was known via the contact of the *indriya* and the *artha*, nevertheless the cognitive process still includes

4.111

4.111. varṇanena ca caitanyam etāvan manaso yadi
svātmaśaktisamāveśād amūrtāveśatā katham

And if you argue that the *manas* is possessed of such a consciousness by way of the description, because it is penetrated by the power of the self with which it is associated [*svātma-*],[418] (then we reply:) how is there a state of penetration (effected) by that [*ātman*] which does not have a material form?[419]

4.112-113c

4.112. tena vā sampratīte 'rthe kriyate kiṃ tadātmanā
tatsvarūpātmasaṃyogaḥ na yogo bhinnadeśayoḥ
4.113. manasāveditārthasya taddeśitvam athocyate
varṇite yogitā kasya...

Alternatively, (you might argue) it[420] is produced by way of that [description] once the object has been thoroughly cognized.[421] (Reply:) Of what use is the *ātman* at that time?[422] (Objection:) There is a connection of the *ātman* with the nature of that [object] (at that time).[423] (Reply:) No.

---

stages that offered different information. There is a *procedure* to cognition, precisely what Somānanda announced he would examine, at ŚD 4.104cd-106ab (see, especially, footnote 400.) Information is still delivered to the *manas* via the *sannikarṣa* of *indriya* and *artha*, such that it differs from what the *ātman* triggers itself to understand to be presented to it by that *manas*.

[418] Somānanda here considers the possibility that the consciousness of the *ātman* might affect not just it, but also the *manas*, such that the latter would witness the product of the *indriyārthasannikarṣa* in a manner similar to the experience of the *ātman*. This would eliminate the discrepancy between the product of the contact of the *indriya* and *artha* that appears to the *manas*, on the one hand, and the product of the contact of the *ātman* with the *manas*, on the other. To this the following reply is offered.

[419] Again, appeal is made to the nature of the *ātman* as *amūrta*: how could the *ātman* "penetrate" the *manas*, the *ātman* being *amūrta*, without a material form? Thus, whatever consciousness "infects" the *ātman* cannot be transferred to the *manas* such that the latter sees the product of the *indriyārthasannikarṣa* in a manner that matches what the *ātman* sees as a result of the *ātmamanaḥsannikarṣa*.

[420] That is, the consciousness or *caitanya*.

[421] Here, Somānanda considers the possible objection that a cognition reaches all the way to the *ātman* without alteration, and it is only after reaching the *ātman* that its contents are distorted by the consciousness of the *ātman*. His reply to this possible objection follows.

[422] That is, what role does the *ātman* play in this moment, *after* the conclusion of the cognitive process, such that the *ātman*'s understanding of the external object is distorted in its consciousness thereof? For cognition is supposed to involve contact of *ātman* and *manas*, and *indriya* and *artha*. See VS 3.1.13 and NS 1.1.4, cited in footnote 396; cf. VS 3.1.18, cited in footnote 399.

[423] In other words, the *ātman* through *sannikarṣa* makes contact with the (true) nature of the object that is (subsequently) conceived and known in a manner other than it is.

There can be no connection of the two entities whose loci are disjoined.[424] Objection: The object that is communicated (to the *ātman*) by the *manas* may be said to have the same locus as it.[425] (Reply:) What is connected (to the *ātman*) when it [i.e., the object] is described?[426]

4.113d-115ab

. . . yadi vā tatsvarūpataḥ
4.114. saṃskaroti tadātmānam amūrte saṃskṛtiḥ katham
tadrūpam ātmany etad yenāśleṣo yadi cocyate
4.115. caitanyenāpy amūrtena miśratānyasya kīdṛśī

Alternatively, you might argue that, given its nature, it [i.e., the object] marks the *ātman* with an impression at that time.[427] (Reply:) How can

---

[424] I read *na* twice, once as the reply to the opponent's objection, and again with the following reply to the objection. I also read *bhinnadeśayoḥ* for *abhinnadeśayoḥ*. (K$^{ed.}$ explicitly marks the presence of the *avagraha*, while the manuscripts almost never record *avagrahas* and so could be interpreted as witnessing either reading.) Finally, I also accept the variant reading shared by T and C, of *na yogo* for the reading in K$^{ed.}$ of *saṃyogo*. If one were to accept the reading of K$^{ed.}$, however, the argument would not be fundamentally changed.

What is meant, then, is evidently this, that the cognition, after having been conveyed to the *ātman*, cannot be held to be in contact with the *ātman*, because it is only what the *manas* brings to the *ātman* that comes into contact with it. Once this process is complete—that is, once the object has been thoroughly or completely cognized (*sampratīte 'rthe*)—it may no longer be said to be in contact with the *ātman*, which in Nyāya-Vaiśeṣika ontology is omnipresent but *amūrta* and so gaining of contact with external stimuli only through the *manas*. This explanation, then, that the *ātman* colors the cognition *after* the entire cognitive sequence is complete, requires a *second* moment of contact with the object of the cognition, which is not allowed for in their epistemology, despite the fact of the *ātman* 's omnipresence (about which see PDhSaṃ [p. 22, lines 11–12]: *ākāśakāladigātmanāṃ sarvagatatvaṃ paramamahattvaṃ sarvasamyogisamānadeśatvaṃ ca*). Again, then, a discrepancy in the knower's experience would occur: the process of the act of cognition as here understood would deliver a cognition of the object as it is but a consciousness of the object that is distorted.

[425] As, that is, the *ātman*. The implication is that the *ātman* may be put in contact with the *artha* by way of the *manas*, in the course of the process of cognition, so why can it not be in contact with the *ātman* under the theory here considered, as well? Somānanda will reply that this objection cannot explain the distortion, since it takes place only subsequent to the cognitive procedure. See footnotes 424 and 426.

[426] That is, the *caitanya* would "describe" an object that in no way remains connected to the *ātman*. The distorted description of the object would be divorced from the object it describes. The *caitanya*, in a word, could perhaps offer an abstracted "state of mind" regarding the object cognized, not an altered cognition of the same.

[427] That is, at the time after the object has been "thoroughly cognized." The point of the passage is to argue that it is not the *ātman* that, through its *cetas* or *caitanya*, "describes" the object or the cognition in such a manner that it is distorted, once the object is "thoroughly cognized" (*saṃpratīte 'rthe*) (ŚD 4.112a), but rather it is the *ātman* that is *itself* distorted, marked by a *saṃskāra*. The direction of the distortion is thus the opposite of what was considered, above. Note also that the subject of the verb could potentially have been taken to be *tat* (ŚD 4.114a), if one understands the text there to read *tad ātmānam*; and in this case *tat* would have to refer to the *manas*. This seems unlikely, however, given what is said of the *manas* at ŚD 4.108c, namely, that it is a mere instrument and is insentient

the formation (of an impression) [*saṃskṛti*] occur when it [i.e., the *ātman*] is without a form?[428] And if you respond by saying that this, the form of that [impression][429] is (found) at the *ātman*, because of which they are connected,[430] (then we reply:) what sort of a state of combination could the one [i.e., the form or *rūpa* of the *saṃskāra*] have even with (the) consciousness (belonging to the *ātman*), which is (also) without a form?[431]

4.115cd-116

kiṃ svayaṃ tatprameyatvam asya ced atirekataḥ
4.116. manasā kiṃ kim akṣeṇa tena cet tatparamparā
evaṃ tad andhapāramparyatvarūpam idaṃ sphuṭam

Does it[432] make itself an object of knowledge of its own accord? If you reply by arguing (that the form or *rūpa* of the *saṃskāra* can make itself known as an object of knowledge) as a result of its difference,[433] (we reply:) of what use is the *manas* (in this process)? Of what use is the sense

---

and therefore cannot but convey the product of the *sannikarṣa* of the *indriya* and the *artha*. I therefore understand the subject to be the implied *āveditārtha* (ŚD 4.113a), brought to the *ātman* by the *manas*.

428 The criticism offered here is simply this, that it is not possible for an entity without a form (*amūrta*) to "take on" such impressions or impurities *as they are situated in an external, material entity that has a form*. And yet the realists do understand the *ātman* to attract qualities. See, e.g., footnote 406, where desire and the like are associated (as qualities) with the *ātman*, at NSBh ad NS 1.1.5. Also noted there is a catalog of both *mūrta* and *amūrta guṇas* as recorded in the PDhSaṃ.

429 Note the parallelism of argumentation here with ŚD 4.106cd-107. There, Somānanda considered the possibility that his opponent would first argue that the *manas* brings to the *ātman* the state of the nature of the material object (*padārthasvarūpatā*), and, following this, when Somānanda objects that such a *mūrta* entity cannot be conveyed to the *amūrta ātman*, that the *rūpa* of the same is conveyed. Here, Somānanda considers the possibility that his opponent will first argue that a *saṃskāra* is impressed on the *ātman* by the object brought to him by the *manas*, and after Somānanda points out that so much cannot mark up the *ātman* given that the latter is *amūrta*, he imagines his opponent will suggest that the form or *rūpa* of the *saṃskāra* will impress the *ātman* by way of making a close association with it. In both cases, then, the procedure of cognition involves an attempt to bridge, as it were, the divide between the *mūrta* and the *amūrta*.

430 That is, because of which the *ātman* and the *saṃskāra* in question, the latter through the form (*rūpa*) by which it may be conveyed, are connected.

431 Or, perhaps: ". . . (then we reply:) what sort of a state of combination could the one [i.e., the *ātman*] have even with a consciousness (of that form [*rūpa*] of the *saṃskāra*) that is (also) without a form?" The argument is simply that two *amūrta* entities cannot make mutual contact, according to the realists' own ontology. Note also that while so much is not represented in this translation, it is nevertheless possible to read *api* (ŚD 4.115a) out of the word-order offered in the verse (*bhinnakrama*), understanding it to modify *amūrta* and not *caitanya*. Finally, note that a half-verse is found in T and C that is not witnessed in K$^{ed.}$, which follows what is numbered ŚD 4.115ab in the present edition. It reads as follows: *tayā prakriyayā vātha jñānam asyopajāyate*. For a rendering of the same see footnote 451.

432 That is to say, the form (*rūpa*) of the *saṃskāra*, which is brought to the *ātman*.

433 That is, if the opponent argues that the *rūpa* of the *saṃskāra* that is brought to the *ātman* is known as an object of knowledge by the latter because it contains something in excess of what is, in fact, present in the object, then Somānanda will reply as follows.

organ?[434] Objection: The latter is succeeded in a sequential chain (of the act of cognition) by the former. (Reply:) In this way, it[435] has as its form an uninterrupted sequence (of cognition) that is blind.[436] This is clear.

4.117-119ab

4.117. kim ātmapreraṇenātra jñāte 'jñāte 'thavā bahiḥ
jñāte tu jñānarūpatvāt preraṇaṃ kena hetunā
4.118. ajñāte 'mutra yāhīti preryate kena mānasam
preryapreraṇatatkartṛdvayaikyād upapadyate
4.119. tasmāj jñeyaṃ samagraikyavastu śaivaṃ vyavasthitam

Of what use is the impelling done on the part of the *ātman*, here [in the cognitive process], whether it [i.e., the object] has been cognized externally or not?[437] As regards [*tu*] (the instance) when it has been cognized, what causes the impelling, given the nature of the cognition?[438] If it has not been cognized, then how is the mind [*mānasa*] impelled (by the *ātman*) to act: "(now) go there"?[439] This[440] is possible (only) as a result of the unity of the duality of thing to be impelled, the act of impelling, and the agent thereof. Therefore, one must know the Śaiva reality of complete unity to have been (properly) established.[441]

---

[434] That is, what role in the sequence (*krama*) of the procedure (*prakriyā*) that is the action of cognizing an object in a distorted manner do the *manas* and the sense-organ play?

[435] That is, the fact of being an object of knowledge (*prameyatva*, ŚD 4.115c), which Somānanda questions for the *saṃskāra*, or rather, the *rūpa* of the *saṃskāra*.

[436] In other words, the sequence of the cognitive procedure conveys what is not, in fact present. The Naiyāyikas and Vaiśeṣikas thus explain direct cognition (*pratyakṣa*) in a manner that contradicts their very definition thereof (for which see, e.g., NS 1.1.4, also cited and translated at footnote 396: *indriyārthasannikarṣotpannaṃ jñānam avyapadeśyam avyabhicāri vyavasāyātmakaṃ pratyakṣam*). Somānanda apparently wishes, this is to say, to distinguish a properly functioning cognitive procedure, on the one hand, into which is introduced an element that leads the knower to make a judgment about an object in a manner that distorts that knower's understanding of the same, from a cognitive procedure, on the other hand, that in its very functioning delivers the knower a direct cognition of an object that is distorted.

[437] Note that it is likely that what is being said here concerns cognition in general and not merely the question of the nature of the cognition of an object under the influence of the knower's desire. See footnote 441.

[438] Why would the *ātman* need to impel the *manas* to inform it of the product of the *indriyārthasannikarṣa* if the *artha* in question has already been cognized?

[439] If the *ātman* has not yet cognized the object and therefore is unaware of it, what could lead it to impel the *manas* to inform it of the product of the contact of one or another *indrya* with that object (*artha*)? For the *ātman* would be unaware of the very existence of such an object and incapable therefore of any intention to see it.

[440] That is, the impelling.

[441] Again, then, Somānanda argues that his opponents' position can only be explained logically if they accept his ontological non-dualism. Note that I have grouped ŚD 4.117-119ab together on the understanding that the passage addresses a general concern Somānanda has with the theory of

4.119cd-123ab

tathā smaraṇayogāc ca smaryate kiṃ tathāvidham
4.120. *yādṛg dṛṣṭaṃ dṛṣṭatā syād athavā jñānam eva tat*
dṛṣṭasmaraṇayor aikye sthite tad upapadyate
4.121. *tathā sā pratyabhijñānāt sa evāyam iti sthitiḥ*
yujyate katham atraiva jñānayoḥ kālabhinnayoḥ
4.122. *dvayor aikyam anaikyaṃ vā tadaikyaṃ bhinnayoḥ katham*
anaikye na sa evāyam iti syād ghaṭadaṇḍayoḥ
4.123. *tasmād aikyam iha spaṣṭaṃ saṃsāre samavasthitam*

And, it is thus (that one must understand the Śaiva reality, what is a complete unity, to have been proven) in consequence of (the cognition that is) memory(, as well).[442] **(For, we ask:) What is remembered**

---

cognition of the Nyāya-Vaiśeṣika. It is also possible, at least, that the passage is meant to conclude the particular discussion of ŚD 4.115cd-116 regarding the cognition involved with *saṃskāras* (or the *rūpas* of *saṃskāras*). Of course, the presence of a commentary could have been helpful in clarifying any such ambiguities in our understanding of the *mūla*.

442The present passage is thoroughly difficult to interpret. I here understand Somānanda to return to the comment made at ŚD 4.104ab, where his realist opponent claimed that the cognition that is memory proves the necessity of a two-step process of cognition: one entity (i.e., the *indriya* in relation to an *artha*) is connected, but another entity (i.e., the *ātman*, via the *manas*) is the knower. There (about which see footnote 399), Somānanda's opponent suggested that the fact that the *manas* is present in distinct moments of time allows it to facilitate the recognition of two distinct cognitions, allowing for memory thereby. I propose that Somānanda here suggests that in consequence of memory, if it is properly understood, one must understand all reality to be properly understood only as a unity, i.e., precisely what was stated in the immediately preceding passage at ŚD 4.119ab. The argument attacks the notion that a unification of distinct cognitions occurs only by virtue of a common locus for those cognitions; rather, there must be a unification of the cognitions themselves in an epistemological non-dualism. On this reading, then, one may detect a certain rhetorical flourish in Somānanda's argument, for in debating the significance of memory he deploys against the Naiyāyikas what is a—perhaps *the*—key argument in their system for the existence of the *ātman* as knower distinct from the *manas* and *indriyas*. On memory proving the *manas* (as separate from a distinct knower, the *ātman*), see, e.g., VS 9.2.6; NS and NSBh ad 1.1.16 (quoted in footnote 399); and NS 3.1.1-16, esp. 3.1.14-16. Cf., e.g., Candrānanda's commentary on VS 9.2.6: *agnyarthino dhūmadarśanaṃ yad utpannaṃ, tadapekṣād ātmāntaḥkaraṇasaṃyogād, viśiṣṭāc ca bhāvanākhyasaṃskārād yatra dhūmas, tatrāgnir ity utpadyate.*

NS and NSBh ad 3.1.14 argue the dependence of memory on the existence of a permanent *ātman*. The argument responds to a *pūrvapakṣin* at NS 3.1.13 who claims that memory involves a quality caused by that on which it is focused, namely the object remembered, not the *ātman*. (See NS 3.1.13: *na smṛteḥ smartavyaviṣayatvāt.* NSBh ad 3.1.13: *smṛtir nāma dharmo nimittād utpadyate, tasyāḥ smartavyo viṣayaḥ, tatkṛta indriyāntaravikāro nātmakṛta iti.*) NS 3.1.14: *tadātmaguṇasadbhāvād apratiṣedhaḥ.* "There can be no denial (of the existence of the *ātman*), because it [i.e., memory] exists (only) as a quality of the *ātman*." The NSBh here reads in part as follows: *tasyā ātmaguṇatve sati sadbhāvād apratiṣedha ātmanaḥ. yadi smṛtir ātmaguṇaḥ, evaṃ sati smṛtir upapadyate nānyadṛṣṭam* (corr.; *nānyad dṛṣṭam*) *anyaḥ smaratīti. indriyacaitanye tu nānākartṛkāṇāṃ viṣayagrahaṇānām apratisandhānam, pratisandhāne vā viṣayavyavasthānupapattiḥ. ekas tu cetano 'nekārthadarśī bhinnanimittaḥ pūrvadṛṣṭam artham smaratīti ekasyānekārthadarśino darśanapratisandhānāt smṛter ātmaguṇatve sati sadbhāvaḥ viparyaye cānupapattiḥ.* "The (existence of the) *ātman* cannot be denied, because the existence of that [i.e., of memory] is dependent on it being a quality of the *ātman*. If memory is a quality of the *ātman*, then memory exists (only) when it [i.e., the *ātman*] exists; one cannot remember what another has perceived. And if the sense

(according to you)? (Opponent's Reply:) Just that of such qualities as what was perceived [*dṛṣṭa*] (in the initial cognition).[443] (Somānanda:) The fact of having been seen must be present (in the memory-cognition),[444] or perhaps it [i.e., the memory] is the (initial) cognition itself.[445] That [i.e., the act of remembering] is possible (only) when a unity is established of that which was (first) perceived and the memory (thereof),[446] and how

---

organs were conscious there would be no synthesis of the apprehensions of an object [i.e., one and the same object] that were produced by various agents [i.e., each conscious sense organ individually], or if there were a synthesis there would be no possibility of restricting (the cognitions) as regards the objects [i.e., any *indriya* could see in the manner of any other]. On the contrary, there is one conscious one who sees multiple objects via distinct causes (of perception) [literally: 'whose causes (of perception) are (mutually) distinct'], who remembers an object (that he himself has) seen before. Thus, memory exists when it is a quality of the *ātman*, because there can be a synthesis of perceptions belonging to a single perceiver of many objects, and it is not possible in the contrary formulation of the matter."

On my interpretation of ŚD 4.119cd-123ab, Somānanda challenges the sufficiency of a unitary, sentient agent—the *ātman*—to explain memory. What is needed in addition is a unification of cognitions as a single consciousness. Put differently, I suggest that Somānanda understands the *pratisandhāna* of the NSBh not to be synonymous with *anusandhāna*, as Utpaladeva and Abhinavagupta take it to be (in what is perhaps properly understood as, in part at least, an effort to avoid an argument with the Nyāya). See also Ratié 2011a: 66, esp. fns. 73, 74, and 75.

443 What is remembered can only be precisely what was seen by an agent in an initial cognition, period. Indeed, this is explicitly stated in the NSBh, e.g., ad NS 3.1.14, cited in footnote 442.

444 That is, the memory must carry with it the notion that what is seen there had been seen before. Thus, the cognition that is remembered is united in some way with the initial cognition.

445 The point made here is somewhat unclear to me. Is it that memory can be explained by a re-cognition of the initial cognition that is recalled to mind? It is true that the present passage reflects in part Utpaladeva's argument around memory in opposition to the position of the Buddhists, in particular at ĪPK and ĪPKVṛ ad 1.3.2. Utpaladeva there suggests that his Buddhist opponent cannot explain memory as resulting from the influence of a latent impression or *saṃskāra*, because while so much can explain the similarity of a memory-cognition to an initial experience, it cannot explain the knower's *experience* of the memory-cognition as similar to the previous experience. Put differently, the ŚD here may be taken to suggest not only that the knower of a memory must have awareness of a memory-cognition *as having been experienced before* (what is said just above), but also that so much might be accomplished by that knower directly perceiving such a previous cognition, which could only be possible with the existence of a unitary agent of knowing. On ĪPK 1.3.2 and the arguments involved therein, see footnote 361.

Two facts militate against understanding the present passage as an argument of Somānanda against the Buddhists, however. First, the issue of memory as per the understanding of his realist opponents, raised at ŚD 4.104ab, has not yet been treated in the ŚD, and this is a likely place to locate Somānanda's engagement with the same. Second and more importantly, Somānanda will have his opponent claim that the cognitions (the initial one and the memory thereof) are unified, which is not the Buddhist position, and about which see footnote 447.

446 I suggest that what is said here essentially anticipates Utpaladeva's objection in the ĪPK, put forward in opposition to the views of the Buddhist Epistemologists, which states that memory requires the existence of an eternal *ātman* to be explicable, because two cognitions must be compared. See ĪPK (and ĪPKVṛ ad) 1.2.3: *athānubhavavidhvaṃse smṛtis tadanurodhinī | kathaṃ bhaven na nityaḥ syād ātmā yady anubhāvakaḥ* ||. "Objection (of Utpaladeva, contra the Buddhist): How, if no eternal self-as-experiencer existed, could a memory arise, it being that which complies with that, a (previous) experience at a time when it has been destroyed?" ĪPKVṛ: *smṛtikāle pūrvānubhavanāśāt kathaṃ pūrvānubhavāvaṣṭambhadharmā smṛtir jāyeta yadi tadāpi tadanubhavabodho nānuvarteta, yaś ca anekakālasthāyī bodhaḥ sa evātmānubhavitā*. "How, given that at the time of the memory the earlier experience (that is remembered) is no longer extant, could a memory arise, its essential quality being

is that condition possible here in this very instance [*atraiva*] as a result of a recognition [*pratyabhijñānāt*] that "this is that very one,"[447] when the two cognitions are temporally divided? Either the two [cognitions] are unified, or they are not unified. (Opponent's Objection:) They are unified. (Somānanda's Reply:) How so for two (ontologically) distinct [cognitions]?[448] If(, by contrast,) they are not unified, (then) there can

---

its dependence on that prior experience, if at that time, itself, no awareness of that [prior] experience were operative; moreover, that awareness that is present persistently in multiple moments of time is no other than the self that is the experiencer?" The difference here is that Somānanda, if my interpretation is correct, takes issue with the Nyāya interpretation of this kind of unification, about which see footnotes 442, 445, and 447.

[447] Kupetz 1972: 4–5 suggests that the present passage addresses the concept of *pratyabhijñā* in Śaivism, noting it is a concept that deals with the nature of a cognition that requires one to have seen something in one cognition that is remembered in a second: "In [the ŚD] he [=Somānanda] defines *pratyabhijñā* as the realization of the immanence of Supreme Reality (Śiva) in this world consisting of multiple objects, sentient and insentient. This realization occurs by means of the perception and direct experience (*dṛṣṭa*) of one of reality's aspects and the simultaneous remembrance (*smaraṇa*) of its other aspects." Torella 1994: xx, in turn, points to ŚD 4.121a as the only place where Somānanda uses the term *pratyabhijñāna* (cited, however, as appearing at verse 4.120a, about which see footnote 333), noting that it there has "no pregnant meaning," by which he means it is not used in a manner that defines the school of thought of which Somānanda is counted as the founding author. He further suggests that the term ". . . is used as an argument to demonstrate the essential unity, or possibility of unification, of cognitions (against Buddhists, etc.)."

I argue that the matter addressed here relates to the understanding of recognition particularly as understood by the Naiyāyikas. Recognition is treated, in particular, at NS 3.1.7: *savyadṛṣṭasyetareṇa pratyabhijñānāt.* "Because there is recognition by the other [i.e., right eye] of what was seen by the left." Cf. the NSBh thereon: *pūrvāparayor vijñānayor ekaviṣaye pratisandhijñānaṃ pratyabhijñānam—tam evaitarhi paśyāmi yam ajñāsiṣam sa evāyam artha iti savyena cakṣuṣā dṛṣṭasyetareṇāpi cakṣuṣā pratyabhijñānād yam adrākṣaṃ tam evaitarhi paśyāmīti. indriyacaitanye tu nānyadṛṣṭam anyaḥ pratyabhijānātīti pratyabhijñānupapattiḥ. asti tv idaṃ pratyabhijñānam tasmād indriyavyatiriktaś cetanaḥ.* "Recognition is the cognition that brings together two cognitions applied to a single object, the two cognitions occurring one after the other (at different moments in time). 'I see now that very item that I saw (before); this is that very object.' (And,) (such an awareness, such that one may say) 'I see now that very one, which I saw before' is the result of a recognition by the other[, i.e., right] eye of that [object] that was seen with the left eye. If the sense organ were conscious (of this recognition), however, it would not be the case that what had been seen by the one would be recognized by the other, meaning that recognition would be impossible. Yet, such recognition does occur. Therefore, the one who is conscious is another than the sense organ." But here the problem Somānanda identifies is the lack of unification—of identification, in fact—of the two cognitions in question. If my interpretation is correct, Somānanda here wishes to argue that the locus of both cognitions in the *ātman* is insufficient to explain recognition. What is needed is a full epistemological unification of the two. See also footnotes 442, 445, and 446.

[448] This is to say, that is, that the epistemological dualism of Somānanda's realist opponents does not allow them to recognize a proper unification of the two cognitions in question. As noted (see footnote 442), Somānanda suggests that the *pratisandhāna* of his opponents cannot be taken to be synonymous with *anusandhāna*; the presence of two cognitions in a single locus—the *ātman* —cannot explain the mutual relation of those two cognitions.

Note that, if one breaks the *sandhi* differently, one may understand the text at ŚD 4.122b as follows: *tadā aikyam.* "(Opponent's Objection:) There is a unity (of those two cognitions) at that time [i.e., at the time of the memory]. (Somānanda's Reply:) How so for two (ontologically) distinct [cognitions]?"

be no (recognition that) "this is that very one" for a pot and a stick.[449] **Therefore, unity is clearly established in *saṃsāra*, here.**[450]

4.123cd-126ab

eṣaiva vārtā saṃyoge vasturūpatayā sthite
4.124. paraspareṇa cāpy atra teṣāṃ rūpeṇa vānyathā
tasmāt samastabhāvānām aikyenaivāsti saṃgamaḥ
4.125. śivikodvāhakānāṃ ca nyāya eṣo 'nuvartatām
paracittaparijñānāt tasmāj jñeyaikyatā tataḥ
4.126. sārthasenāvanādyātma jagaty aikyaṃ sphutaṃ sthitam[451]

This alone is the path [*vārtā*][452] **here [in *saṃsāra*] when connection exists by the fact of its being a real thing, so too (when it exists) as a reciprocal form belonging to those [real things in the world], or otherwise.**[453] **Therefore, connection exists exclusively by way of the unity of all entities.**[454]

---

[449] That is, without unity, one could not make an act of recognition. What is meant by referring to a pot and a stick? I would think, given that it expresses a contrary-to-fact statement, it is to make (a somewhat oblique) reference to a pot that, at some earlier time, was formed of clay and sat on the potter's wheel, which was spun by a potter with a stick. Mention of the stick thus signals a reference to a pot seen on an earlier occasion, namely the occasion of its production. The absence of any unity of the two cognitions—of the completed pot, and of the pot in the moment of its production—would preclude the possibility of knowing the pot seen on these two occasions to be one and the same object.

[450] I understand *iha* (ŚD 4.123a) to mean "here [in our analysis and repair of your arguments regarding memory]." It could also possibly be taken more simply to mean "here [in our Śaiva philosophy]."

[451] The chapter ends with a half-verse, what is a suggestion of a lacuna in the text. Perhaps the half-verse recorded in both manuscripts T and C following what is counted in the present edition as ŚD 4.115ab should be incorporated into the text. That half-verse reads as follows: *tayā prakriyayā vātha jñānam asyopajāyate*. This may be taken to introduce the argument Somānanda makes at what is labeled in the present edition as ŚD 4.115cd-116 by conceding for the sake of argument that his opponent can explain the manner in which a *saṃskāra* impresses the *ātman* by way of recourse to the form or *rūpa* of that *saṃskāra* marking the *ātman*. That is, Somānanda here suggests that the "procedure" (*prakriyā*) of the action (*kriyā*) that is cognition, which Somānanda began to examine at ŚD 4.104cd-106c-d, may possibly be explained in the manner just suggested by his opponent (though the following criticisms thereof doom his opponent to having to accept a Śaiva nondualism). The half-verse may be translated as follows: "Alternatively, if (we concede for the sake of argument that) that procedure (which you have just proposed regarding the *rūpa* of the *saṃskāra*) produces the cognition of this [object seen in a distorted fashion](, then we ask the following in objection)."

[452] That is, there is a unity in *saṃsāra* on the Śaiva model, as stated at ŚD 4.123ab.

[453] I am at least somewhat unsure of the present interpretation of ŚD 4.124ab. I read *vā* out of the normal word order (*bhinnakrama*), understanding instead *anyathā vā*, and the fact that the inversion of the word-order serves to allow conformity with the strictures of meter supports this understanding. On the present interpretation, two different ways of understanding connection or conjunction are explicitly noted, viz., when it exists as a real thing itself, as in, perhaps, the *samavāya padārtha*; or when connection exists as a form shared between entities, as in a *saṃbandha* linking two discrete *saṃbandhins*. Finally, Somānanda adds that any other conception of *saṃyoga* would require the existence of the same Śaiva non-dual ontology (*anyathā vā*).

[454] Or: "Therefore, (any) connection for (any and) all entities exists exclusively by way of unity."

And this is the principle for (causally linked stages of manifestation; for example,) the *śibika*, the lifting up (of the clay in forming a pot on the potter's wheel)(, etc.), that follow (one after another).[455] Hence, oneness may be known from the thorough knowledge (that is furnished here in this chapter) of the (philosophical) thoughts of others.[456] Unity, the nature of which is (similar to) that of a caravan, an army, a forest, or the like,[457] clearly exists in the universe.

Thus is concluded the fourth chapter of the Venerable *Śivadṛṣṭi*, which is characterized by the reproof for the inconclusive argumentation (of our opponents' philosophical positions).[458]

---

[455] Reference here, as I understand it, is to the stages of the development of a pot from a mass of clay. The *śibika* (and like it the *stūpaka*) is a stage in the development of a pot from an amorphous ball of clay. The point here, then, is to suggest that causality is sequenced only inasmuch as all entities, all stages of causality, are unified—one—in their very nature.

Note that I understand *śivikodvāhakānāṃ* implicitly to mean *śivikodvāhakādīnāṃ*.

[456] The two manuscripts (T and C) of this passage that were examined for this edition suggest that one should read the alpha privative (*a-*) prior to *parijñānāt*. (T reads *paracittāparijñānāt*, and C reads *paracitāparijñātā*.) If one were to accept the reading of T, the text could be rendered as follows: "Hence, oneness should be known as a result of the absence of a thorough knowledge in the thinking of others."

[457] The idea, then, is that the unity simultaneously consists of multiple parts. The metaphor of the army was also used in ŚD 3.36cd-39. Somānanda here might have in mind NS 2.1.36 (2.1.37 in Jha's translation): *senāvanavat grahaṇam iti cen nātīndriyatvād aṇūnām*. "If (the opponent of the Nyāya argues:) 'the apprehension (of entities made up of a collection of atoms) is similar to that of an army or a forest,' (then we, the Naiyāyikas, reply:) No. For (unlike the components of the army or the trees that make up the forest), the atoms are imperceptible by the sense organs." With this passage, the Nyāya conceives of an opponent who would argue against the real existence of a composite whole, by suggesting that the atoms that make up composite entities do so by forming conglomerations that, while consisting of many elements (i.e., the atoms), are not themselves constitutive of a real, single (composite) entity apart from the conception of it as just that. The example of such things are the forest and the army, both of which are made up of many elements but, at a distance, are seen as singular wholes, not because each is, in fact, unitary, but because each is seen at a sufficient distance to occlude the visibility of the many parts that make it appear to be one.

Somānanda, however, cites the examples of the army and the forest positively or favorably. That is, he suggests (against the Naiyāyika's use of the exemplars, placed as they are there in the voice of a *pūrvapakṣin*) that these are, in fact, themselves examples of single entities made of many distinct parts, the parts in fact depending on the existence of an underlying unity. There is irony, then, in this quotation, Somānanda using a bit of humor by presenting his view in a way that implicitly needles his Naiyāyika counterpart.

[458] On the meaning of *anupapatticodanā* compare with Prajñākaragupta's definition of a *vārttika* commentary in his *Pramāṇavārttikālaṅkārabhāṣya* (ed. Sāṅkṛtyāyana 1953, p. 521): *sūtrāṇām anupapatticodanā tatparihāro viśeṣābhidhānaṃ ceti vārttikalakṣaṇam*.

{ PART III }

The Edition

Chapter Four of the *Śivadṛṣṭi* and *Śivadṛṣṭivṛtti*

parodbhāvanīyadūṣaṇaśaṅkānirākaraṇe kṛte sarvaśivatattvam idānīṃ svarūpeṇopapādayitum āha

athedānīṃ pravaktavyaṃ yathā sarvaṃ śivātmakam
nāśakto vidyate kaścic chaktaṃ vastv eva te 'pi no 1

1a Note that T is badly frayed both at the bottom of folio 6r and at the top of folio 6v. Much of the text is here completely broken off from the manuscript and is entirely missing. 1a ŚD 1.45cd-46ab (*dṛśyante 'tra tadicchāto bhāvā bhītyādiyogataḥ* | *tatra mithyāsvarūpaṃ cet sthāpyāgre satyedṛśām* ||) anticipates ŚD 4.1*ff*.; Cf. PV (*pratyakṣapariccheda*) 3.282: *kāmaśokabhayonmādacaurasvapnādyupaplutāḥ* | *abhūtān api paśyanti purato 'vasthitān iva* || 1d The present remark stands in contrast to Dharmakīrti's understanding of the object. Compare the present, then, with PV (*pratyakṣapariccheda*) 3.1: *pramāṇaṃ dvividhaṃ meyadvaividhyāc chaktyaśaktitaḥ* | *arthakriyāyāṃ keśādir nārtho 'narthādhimokṣataḥ* || 1d T is damaged at *te 'pi no* but appears there to offer a correct reading.

1a athedānīṃ] DGJS²S³S⁵PRK^ed.; - - - T, athedānī C 1c vidyate] CDGJS²S³S⁵RK^ed.; - - te T, bhidyate P 1c kaścic] TDGJS²S³S⁵PRK^ed.; kaści C 1d chaktaṃ] TCDGJS²S³S⁵P^p.c.RK^ed.; chiktaṃ P^a.c.

---

1 G, J, S², S³ and S⁵ record a *maṅgala* of *oṃ* prior to their respective readings of the *avataraṇikā* to ŚD 4.1.

---

1 °dūṣaṇa°] DGJS²S³S⁵P^p.c.K^ed.; °dūṣa° P^a.c.R 1 sarvaśivatattvam] D; sarvaśivatvam GJS²S³S⁵PRK^ed. 2 upapādayitum] DGJS²S³S⁵K^ed.; upapadayitum PR

---

1 J folio 55r. 1 S⁵ folio 54r. 2 D folio 142v. 3 T folio 6v. 4 P folio 45.

The Ubiquitous Śiva Volume II. John Nemec, Oxford University Press. © Oxford University Press 2021.
DOI: 10.1093/oso/9780197566725.003.0003

iṣyante bahavaḥ śaktāḥ sarvasvātantryam āpatet

dūṣananirākaraṇād anantaraṃ vidhimukhenaiva saṃprati tad vaktavyam asmābhir yathā sarvaṃ śivātmakaṃ sidhyati tad ucyate. aśaktaś cārthakriyāyāṃ vidyate ca, ity etāvan nāsti prakhyopākhyākaraṇena tāvad avyabhicārāt. śaktaṃ cet, tad vastv eva paramārthasad eva śivarūpam iti. tathā hi kriyākaraṇaśaktiḥ kartṛtā cidrūpatā śivarūpatvam api cidrūpasyecchārahitasya kartṛtvāyogāt. ghaṭapaṭādikaṃ karaṇaśaktaṃ cet, tat svatantraṃ cidrūpaṃ śivarūpam eveti.

2a bahavaḥ] DGJ$S^{2}S^{3}S^{5}$PR$K^{ed.}$; - - - T, bahataḥ C 2a śaktāḥ] DGJ$S^{2}S^{3}S^{5}$PR$K^{ed.}$; śaktā - T, śaktā C 2b sarvasvātantryam] DGJ$S^{2}S^{3}S^{5}$PR$K^{ed.}$; - - - - - T, sarvaṃ svātaṃ amaṃ C 2b āpatet] DGJ$S^{2}S^{3}S^{5}K^{ed.}$; - - - T, āpatat C, āpayet PR

---

8 A gap following *e* in *etāvat* appears in S^{2}, apparently due to a flaw in the paper manuscript on which it is written. 8 *Khyo* in the reading of D (i.e., *prakhyopākaraṇena*) where the other manuscripts read *prakhyopākhyākaraṇena* is partially blurred, but nevertheless is legible. 8 A footnote in $K^{ed.}$ (p. 144) suggests a reading of *prākhyopākara°* for *prakhyopākhyākara°*. D does not record this reading, however, and Kaul suggests in his introduction that this was his only source for the edition of Utpaladeva's commentary. 9 Compare with Dharmakīrti's *Nyāyabindu* 1.14-15: *tad eva paramārthasat. arthakriyāsāmarthyalakṣaṇatvād vastunah.* Cf. PV (*pratyakṣapariccheda*) 3.3: *arthakriyāsamarthaṃ yat tad atra paramārthasat | anyat saṃvṛtisat prokte te svasāmānyalakṣaṇe ||* 9 $P^{a.c.}$ can be interpreted to read *śivarūyem*, $P^{p.c.}$ *śivarūyam.* 9 Compare *tathā hi...* with ĪPKVṛ ad ĪPK 2.4.21: *cidvapuṣaḥ svatantrasya viśvātmanā sthātum icchaiva jagat prati kāraṇatā kartṛtārūpā saiva kriyāśaktiḥ. evaṃ cidrūpasyaikasya kartur eva cikīrṣākhyā kriyā mukhyā, nākartṛkaṃ karmāsti karmādīnāṃ kartṛmukhopacārataḥ.* 10 P inserts a comma after *api.* 10 J can be interpreted to read *cidrūpe syecchārahitasya*, but I rather think it reads as recorded in the text above the line.

---

7 sidhyati] DGJ$S^{2}S^{3}S^{5}$R$K^{ed.}$; siddhaṃ P 7 ucyate] DGJ$S^{2}S^{3}S^{5}K^{ed.}$; ucyeta PR 8 vidyate] DGJ$S^{2}S^{3}S^{5}P^{p.c.}$R$K^{ed.}$; vidyato $P^{a.c.}$ 8 etāvan] DGS^{2}PR$K^{ed.}$; etat tāvan J$S^{3}S^{5}$ 8 prakhyopākhyākaraṇena] GJ$S^{2}S^{3}S^{5}$PR$K^{ed.}$; prakhyopākaraṇena D 8 tāvad avyabhicārāt] DGJ$S^{2}S^{3}S^{5}$ $K^{ed.}$; tadavyabhicārāt $P^{p.c.}$, tādavyabhicārāt $P^{a.c.}$R 9 cet] DGJ$S^{2}S^{3}S^{5}P^{p.c.}$R$K^{ed.}$; ce $P^{a.c.}$ 9 śivarūpam] DGJ$S^{2}S^{3}S^{5}P^{p.c.}$R$K^{ed.}$; śivarūpem $P^{a.c.}$ 9 kriyākaraṇaśaktiḥ kartṛtā] DGJ$S^{2}S^{5}$PR$K^{ed.}$; kriyākaraṇaśaktikartṛtā S^{3} 10 cidrūpasya] $D^{p.c.}$GJ$S^{2}S^{3}S^{5}$PR$K^{ed.}$; ced rūpasya $D^{a.c.}$ 10 icchārahitasya] $D^{p.c.}$GJ$S^{2}S^{3}S^{5}$PR $K^{ed.}$; icchārahitarasya $D^{a.c.}$ 11 cet] DGJ$S^{2}S^{3}S^{5}P^{p.c.}$R$K^{ed.}$; ce $P^{a.c.}$ 11 tat] DJ$S^{2}S^{3}S^{5}$PR$K^{ed.}$; *om.* G 11 eveti] DGJ$S^{2p.c.}S^{3}S^{5}$PR$K^{ed.}$; eti $S^{2a.c.}$

---

7 D folio 143r. 8 S^{3} folio 24r. 8 S^{2} folio 85r. 11 G folio 58v.

bahavaś ca ghaṭādayaḥ pratyekaṃ śaktā neṣyante, sarveṣāṃ tathā svātantryaṃ prasajyate. tataś ca bhinnābhisandhitayā navam idam astu purāṇam athāstv ity ekasya navapurāṇabhāvavirodhaprasaṅgaḥ. na caivaṃ dṛśyate.

athaikasyādhikā śaktir nyūnaśaktinibandhinī 2
svakāryaviṣaye sarvaḥ śakta eva nibandhanam
śaktasya śakyate kartum evaṃ cen nānyaśaktatā 3

athaikasyādhikā śaktir yasmād anyaśaktim asau nibadhnāti niyamayati, tataś ca tasya nyūnā. svakārye viṣayabhūte tu sarvaḥ śakta eva. nibandhanaṃ niyamanaṃ hi śaktasyaiva, na tu tailadānaśaktiḥ sikatāsu śakyakriyā. tad evaṃ

2d The vertical stroke of the second short *i* of °*nibandhinī* is inserted by the scribe into the reading of G. 3a S^5 notes that it has reversed the order of *śakta* and *sarva* by marking the the latter with a *śāradā* "1", the former with "2". 3b A later hand inserts a double *daṇḍa* at the end of the half-verse in P.

2c athaikasya] DGJS^{2}S^{3}S^{5}PRK$^{ed.}$; - - - - T, athekasya C 2c śaktir] DGJS^{2}S^{3}S^{5}PRK$^{ed.}$; - - T, śakti C 2d nyūna] CD$^{p.c.}$GJS^{2}S^{3}S^{5}K$^{ed.}$; - - T, nūna D$^{a.c.}$, nūnaṃ PR 2d °śakti°] CDJS^{2}S^{3}S^{5}PRK$^{ed.}$; - - T, °śaktir G 2d °nibandhinī] CDG$^{p.c.}$JS^{2}S^{3}S^{5}K$^{ed.}$; - b - ndh - n - T, °nibandhanī G$^{a.c.}$, °bindhanī (hypometric) P, °vindhanī (hypometric) R 3a svakārya°] CDGJS^{2}S^{3}S^{5}PRK$^{ed.}$; svakā<?>° T 3a sarvaḥ] DGJS^{2}S^{3}PRK$^{ed.}$; sarva<?> T, sarvaṃ C, śaktaḥ S^5 3b śakta] TDJS^{2}PRK$^{ed.}$; śakti C; śaktir G, sarva S^{3}S^5 3d cen] CDGJS^{2}S^{3}S^{5}PRK$^{ed.}$; ce T 3d nānyaśaktatā] TDGJS^{2}S^{3}S^{5}PRK$^{ed.}$; nāsya śaktitā C

---

18 S^2 deletes an illegible *akṣara* following *niba* of *nibadhnāti*. 18 A later hand inserts a comma after *niyamayati* in P. 19 In K$^{ed.}$, Kaul's edition first punctuates following *nibandhanam*, but this is corrected in the errata, where Kaul suggests one should punctuate prior to the same term, or in other words in the manner presented here. 20 A later hand inserts a comma after °*kriyā* in P.

---

13 °abhisandhitayā] DS^{2}S^{3}S^{5}PRK$^{ed.}$; °abhisaṃdhānatayā GJ 14 °virodha°] GJPRK$^{ed.}$; *om.* DS^{2}S^{3}S^5 18 nibadhnāti] DGJS^{2}S^{3}S^{5}P$^{p.c.}$RK$^{ed.}$; nibaprāti P$^{a.c.}$ 20 hi] DGJS^{2}S^{3}S$^{5p.c.}$PRK$^{ed.}$; *om.* S$^{5a.c.}$ 20 tailadāna°] DGJS^{2}S^{3}S^{5}P$^{p.c.}$RK$^{ed.}$; tailaśadāna° P$^{a.c.}$ 20 sikatāsu] D$^{p.c.}$GJS^{2}S^{3}S^{5}PRK$^{ed.}$; sikatā D$^{a.c.}$ 20 śakyakriyā] DGJS^{2}S^{3}S^{5}RK$^{ed.}$; aśakyakriyā P

---

12 D folio 143v. 14 R folio 37r. 14 J folio 55v. 15 S^5 folio 54v. 17 D folio 144r. 17 S^2 folio 85v.

yadi sarvaśaktitvam iṣyate, tato nānyeṣāṃ ghaṭādīnāṃ pratyekaṃ śaktatā svatantratā.

tathā hi
nṛpādisādhanāpekṣā svakarmaphalatā bhavet
sarvaḥ śakto 'pi sāpekṣa īśavan mohasāmyayoḥ 4
tasmād anekabhāvābhiḥ śaktibhis tadabhedataḥ
eka eva sthitaḥ śaktaḥ śiva eva tathā tathā 5

4a The scribe of D notes explicitly that he understands *āpekṣā* not to be compounded with what precedes it. 4b T is worm-eaten and therefore partially illegible (as noted in the variants) at °*phalatā bhavet*. 4b Compare ŚD 4.4ab with VP 3.7.22-23: *yathā rājñā niyukteṣu yoddhṛtvaṃ yoddhṛṣu sthitam | teṣu vṛttau tu labhate rājā jayaparājayau || tathā kartrā niyukteṣu sarveṣv ekārthakāriṣu | kartṛtvaṃ karaṇatvāder uttaraṃ na virudhyate ||* Cf. *Yogasūtrabhāṣya* ad YS 2.18: *yathā vijayaḥ parājayo vā yoddhṛṣu vartamānaḥ svāmini vyapadiśyate, sa hi tatphalasya bhokteti, evaṃ bandhamokṣau buddhāv eva vartamānau puruṣe vyapadiśyete, sa hi tatphalasya bhokteti.* 4c D records *tathā* in a small hand above *sarvaḥ*, what is not mentioned in the notes of $K^{ed.}$.

4b °phalatā bhavet] $DGJS^2S^3S^5P^{a.c.}RK^{ed.}$; °phalatā bha<?>et T, °phalatām eva ta (hypermetric) C; °phalatā bhaveta (hypermetric) $P^{p.c.}$ 4c sarvaḥ] $TDGJS^2S^3S^5PRK^{ed.}$; sarva C 4c sāpekṣa] $TDGJS^2S^3S^5P^{p.c.}RK^{ed.}$; sākṣām C, sāpekṣā $P^{a.c.}$ 4d īśavan] $CDGJS^2S^3S^5PRK^{ed.}$; īva - (hypometric) T 4d moha°] $CDGJS^2S^3S^5P^{p.c.}RK^{ed.}$; mo - T, soha° $P^{a.c.}$ 4d °sāmyayoḥ] $DGJS^2S^3S^5PRK^{ed.}$; °- - yo - T, °sāmyaho C 5a tasmād] $CDGJS^2S^3S^5PRK^{ed.}$; - smād T 5c sthitaḥ] $TDGJS^2S^3S^5PRK^{ed.}$; sthitā C 5c śaktaḥ] $TDGJS^2S^3S^5PRK^{ed.}$; śaktiḥ C 5d śiva eva] $TDGJS^2S^3S^5PRK^{ed.}$; śiyeva (hypometric) C

---

21 In S^2, *yadi* appears to have been added to the text after having first been omitted: the first *akṣara* appears added to the end of one line of text, the second to the beginning of the next line of text. 21 In S^2, *śaktatā* appears to have been corrected by a later hand, and the missing *akṣara* appears in the left margin.

---

21 śaktatā] $DGJS^{2p.c.}S^3S^5PRK^{ed.}$; śakta° $S^{2a.c.}$ 23 tathā hi] $DGJS^2S^3S^5P^{p.c.}RK^{ed.}$; tāthā hi $P^{a.c.}$

---

22 D folio 144v. 27 G folio 59r.

sevitanṛpādisādhanakāryāpekṣaiva svakarmaphalatā syāt. svāni bhogyāni karmaphalāni yasya tasya bhāvaḥ. yataḥ sarvaḥ svayaṃ śakto 'pi sāpekṣa eva vyāpriyate. yathā dvaitadarśane 'pīśvaro mohaṃ māyātattvaṁ apekṣya sarge pravartate, karmasāmyaṃ cāpekṣyānugrahe, na cāśakto 'nīśvaraḥ. tasmād anekaghaṭapaṭasvabhāvābhiḥ śaktibhis tacchaktyabhedataḥ śaktisattā lakṣaṇatvāc chivatvasyaika eva śivaḥ sthitas tena tena prakāreṇānekaśakta-

---

28 The scribe of D notes explicitly that *āpekṣā* is not compounded with what precedes it. Note also the variant in D of °*sādhanā* for °*sādhana*°, suggesting again the scribe here understood the term as the final member of the compound. 28 A footnote in K$^{ed.}$ (p. 147) suggests that one source examined for the KSTS edition (*kha*) reads °*sādhanā kāryā*° for °*sādhanakāryā*°. It turns out that this source is manuscript D. 28 In S^2, *t* of *syāt* is written in the bottom margin, and this is the last *akṣara* recorded on the side of the folio in question. 28 Prior to *svāni bhogyāni...yasya tasya bhāvaḥ*, D records the following, which is highlighted in yellow (indicating its deletion): *svāni bhogyāni karmaphalatā syāt*. 29 P could be interpreted to read *śarvaḥ* for *sarvaḥ*. 29 S^5 deletes a final *anusvāra* following *sarvaḥ*. 30 S^5 appears to black out a mark below *pri* of *vyāpriyate*. 30 In S^2, °*tattvam* appears initially to have been left out by the copyist, as the first two *akṣaras* appear extended past the margin at the end of one line of text, and the final *m* appears extended into the left margin at the beginning of the next line of text. 31 The negative particle, *na*, is blotched in G. 31 In S^2, a gap appears prior to *'nīśvaraḥ*, apparently a space left there due to a flaw in the paper manuscript itself. 32 S^2 marks the absence of a final *visarga* at °*svabhāvābhi* with a short double-underline.

---

28 sevitanṛpādi°] DGJS^{2}S^{3}S^{5}K$^{ed.}$; sevinṛpādi° P$^{a.c.}$R, sevyanṛpādi° P$^{p.c.}$ 28 °sādhana°] GJS^{2}S^{3}S^{5}PRK$^{ed.}$; °sādhanā D 28 °kāryāpekṣā] DGJS^{2}S^{3}S^{5}P$^{p.c.}$K$^{ed.}$; °kāryapekṣā P$^{a.c.}$R 30 vyāpriyate] DS^{2}S^{3}S^{5}PRK$^{ed.}$; vyāpṛyate GJ 30 yathā] DS$^{2p.c.}$S^{3}S^{5}PRK$^{ed.}$; yad vā GJ, tathā S$^{2a.c.}$ 30 apekṣya] D$^{p.c.}$GJS^{2}S^{3}S^{5}PRK$^{ed.}$; apīkṣya D$^{a.c.}$ 31 cāpekṣya] DGJS^{2}S$^{3p.c.}$S^{5}PRK$^{ed.}$; copekṣya S$^{3a.c.}$ 32 anekaghaṭapaṭa°] DGJS^{2}S^{3}S^{5}PR$^{p.c.}$K$^{ed.}$; anekaghaṭapaṭādi° P$^{a.c.}$ 32 °svabhāvābhiḥ] DGJS^{3}S^{5}PRK$^{ed.}$; °svabhāvābhi S$^{2p.c.}$, °svabhābhi S$^{2a.c.}$ 32 tacchakty°] DGJS^{2}S^{3}S^{5}RK$^{ed.}$; tacchaky° P 32 śaktisattā°] GJPR; śaktimattā° DS^{2}S^{3}S^{5}K$^{ed.}$ 33 °śakta°] JS^{2}S^{3}S^{5}K$^{ed.}$; °śakti° DGPR

---

28 S^2 folio 86r. 28 D folio 145r. 31 J folio 56r. 32 S^5 folio 55r. 33 D folio 145v.

ghaṭapaṭādipadārthātmakatvāt tasya. ghaṭacitas tāvanmātrarūpāyāḥ svātantrye paṭacitā sahānusaṃdhānaṃ na syāt. tasmād ekam eva cittattvam anantaviśvarūpam iti.

tathā yatra sad ity evaṃ pratītis tad asat katham
yat sat tat paramārtho hi paramārthas tataḥ śivaḥ 6
sarvabhāveṣu cidvyakteḥ sthitaiva paramārthatā

6b The writing of C is occluded in two places where it reads *vipratityes* for *pratītis*: *vi* is partially smeared, and a line appears to delete what might be an *anusvāra* following *ti*. 6d A double *daṇḍa* is inserted following ŚD 4.6 in P. 7b There is a blotch of ink above *tai* of *sthitaiva* in C.

6a tathā] CDGJ$S^2S^3S^5$PRK$^{ed.}$; yathā T 6a yatra] TDGJ$S^2S^3S^5$PRK$^{ed.}$; ya C 6a evaṃ] TDGJ$S^2S^3S^5$PRK$^{ed.}$; eva C 6b pratītis tad] TDGJS^3S^5PRK$^{ed.}$; vipratityes C, pratīti tad S^2 6b asat] TDGJ$S^2S^3S^5$PRK$^{ed.}$; *om.* C 6c sat] TDGJ$S^2S^3S^5$PRK$^{ed.}$; tat C 6c tat] TDJ$S^2S^3S^5$PRK$^{ed.}$; satya C; ta G 6c paramārtho hi] TDGJ$S^2S^3S^5$PRK$^{ed.}$; ramārtho hi C 6d śivaḥ] TDGJ$S^2S^3S^5$PRK$^{ed.}$; *om.* (hypometric) C 7a cidvyakteḥ] DG$S^2S^3S^5$PRK$^{ed.}$; cidvyak - e - T, vichakteḥ C, <?>id<?>kteḥ J 7b sthitaiva] CDGJ$S^2S^3S^5$PRK$^{ed.}$; - taiva T

---

34 Compare *ghaṭacitas...sahānusaṃdhānaṃ na syāt* with ĪPK 1.3.6-7: *evam anyonyabhinnānām aparasparavedinām | jñānānām anusaṃdhānajanmā naśyej janasthitiḥ || na ced antaḥkṛtānantaviśvarūpo maheśvaraḥ | syād ekaś cidvapur jñānasmṛtyapohanaśaktimān ||* Cf. also ĪPKVṛ ad ĪPK 1.8.10: *tattadvibhinnasaṃvidanusaṃdhānena hi vyavahāraḥ. ekaś ca prakāśātmā tadanusaṃdhānarūpaḥ sa eva caikaḥ pramātā paramātmasaṃjñaḥ.* 34 In D, *yadi* is written above its reading of *svātantryaṃ* for K$^{ed.}$'s reading of *svātantrye*. (Here, it seems K$^{ed.}$ was silently emended, as D is the only witness of the commentary for the *editio princeps.*) 35 An unidentified mark appears below *hā* of *sahānusaṃdhānaṃ* in S^2.

---

34 °ātmakatvāt tasya] D$S^2S^3S^5$PRK$^{ed.}$; °ātmakatvā tasya G, °ātmakatvād asya J 34 svātantrye] K$^{ed.}$; svātantryaṃ DGJ$S^2S^3S^5$, svātantrya° PR 35 paṭacitā] GJPRK$^{ed.}$; ghaṭacitā D$S^2S^3S^5$ 35 ekam] DGJ$S^2S^3S^5$K$^{ed.}$; anekam PR

---

37 S^2 folio 86v. 38 P folio 46. 38 D folio 146r. 39 R folio 37v.

śaktaṃ vastv evety uktaṃ, vastu ca sad ucyate. yac ca sat, tan nāsad iti sa eva paramārthaḥ. yasmāc ca paramārthas tataḥ sattvāt paramārthatvāc chivaḥ. nanu kathaṃ paramārthamātratvena śivaḥ, jaḍo 'pi kathaṃ na paramārthaḥ, tan na. jaḍasya sattaiva kathaṃ cidvyaktiṃ vinā siddhā. sphuradrūpatā hi sattā. sphuradrūpatā ca prakāśamānatā. tataś ca jaḍatā tāvan nāsti. prakāśamānatā hi prakāśābhedaḥ. prakāśaś cānapahnavanīyaḥ sarvapratiṣṭhārūpaḥ paramārthaḥ. sarveṣāṃ ca ghaṭādīnāṃ prakāśarūpatāyāṃ viśeṣābhāvād ekaprakāśātmatā, tata evaikaśivatvam. etad īśvarapratyabhijñāyāṃ vistāritam.

---

40 S^{2} highlights *śaktaṃ vastv evety uktaṃ vastu ca sad*, suggesting thereby—and of course erroneously—that the passage in question is part of the *mūla*. 40 S^{5} appears to black out a long *ā* following *ca* at *yac ca sat*. 41 S^{2} deletes an illegible *akṣara* following *paramārthaḥ*. 43 S^{5} records an *avagraha* prior to *siddhā* at its reading of *vināsiddhā*. 43 Compare *sphuradrūpatā*... with ĪPK 1.5.14: *sā sphurattā mahāsattā deśakālāviśeṣiṇī | saiṣā sāratayā proktā hṛdayaṃ parameṣṭhinaḥ ||* Cf. the ĪPKVṛ on the same: *sphuradrūpatā sphuraṇakartṛtā abhāvāpratiyoginī abhāvavyāpinī sattā bhavattā bhavanakartṛtā nityā deśakālāsparśāt saiva pratyavamarśātmā citikriyāśaktiḥ. sā viśvātmanaḥ parameśvarasya svātmapratiṣṭhārūpā hṛdayam iti tatra tatrāgame nigadyate.* 44 Compare *prakāśamānatā*... with ĪPK 1.5.2cd: *na ca prakāśo bhinnaḥ syād ātmārthasya prakāśatā. Vṛtti: ...prakāśamānatā cārthasya prakāśaḥ svarūpabhūto na tu bhinnaḥ.* 47 Reference to the *Īśvarapratyabhijñā* may refer in part to ĪPK 1.5.3: *bhinne prakāśe cābhinne saṃkaro viṣayasya tat | prakāśātmā prakāśyo 'rtho nāprakāśaś ca sidhyati || Vṛtti: prakāśamātraṃ cārthād bhinnaṃ sarvārthasādhāraṇaṃ tasya ghaṭasya prakāśo 'yam ayaṃ paṭasyaiveti viṣayaniyamo nirnibandhanaḥ. tasmād arthasya siddhiḥ prakāśātmatāyattā.* 47 It appears that S^{3} deletes a long *-ā* following *pra* of *īśvarapratyabhijñāyāṃ*.

---

40 ucyate] DGJ$S^{3}S^{5}$PR$K^{ed.}$; <?>cyte S^{2} 40 yac] DGJ$S^{2}S^{3}S^{5}P^{p.c.}K^{ed.}$; yaś $P^{a.c.}$R 41 yasmāc] DGJ$S^{2}S^{3}S^{5}P^{p.c.}K^{ed.}$; yasmāś $P^{a.c.}$R 41 sattvāt] DGJ$S^{2}S^{3}S^{5}K^{ed.}$; tattvāt PR 42 paramārthamātratvena śivaḥ, jaḍo 'pi kathaṃ na] DGJ$S^{2}S^{3}S^{5}K^{ed.}$; *om.* PR 43 sattaiva] D$S^{2}S^{3}S^{5}$PR$K^{ed.}$; satteva GJ 44 prakāśamānatā tataś ca jaḍatā tāvan nāsti] DGJ$S^{2}S^{3}S^{5}K^{ed.}$; *om.* PR 45 prakāśābhedaḥ] $D^{p.c.}$GJ$S^{2}S^{3}S^{5}$PR$K^{ed.}$; prakāśabhedaḥ $D^{a.c.}$ 45 anapahnavanīyaḥ] DGJ$S^{2p.c.}$PR$K^{ed.}$; anapahnanīyaḥ $S^{2a.c.}S^{3p.c.}S^{5}$, anapahnīnīyaḥ $S^{3a.c.}$ 45 °pratiṣṭhā°] DGJ$S^{2}S^{3}S^{5}$P$K^{ed.}$; °pratiṣṭā° R 46 prakāśarūpatāyāṃ] PR; prakāśarūpatāyā GJ$S^{2}S^{3}S^{5}$, prakāśarūpatayā D$K^{ed.}$ 46 eka°] D$G^{a.c.}$J$S^{2}S^{3}S^{5}$PR$K^{ed.}$; aika° $G^{p.c.}$ 47 eka°] DGJ$S^{2}S^{3}S^{5p.c.}$PR$K^{ed.}$; eva° $S^{5a.c.}$ 47 īśvarapratyabhijñāyāṃ] DGJ$S^{3}S^{5}$PR$K^{ed.}$; īśvarapratyabhijñāyāyāṃ S^{2}

---

40 G folio 59v. 43 D folio 146v. 45 S^{3} folio 24v. 46 S^{2} folio 87r. 46 J folio 56v. 47 S^{5} folio 55v.

mithyājñānavikalpyānāṃ sattvaṃ cidvyaktiśaktatā 7
vidyate tat tad atrāpi śivatvaṃ kena vāryate
iti ced eṣu satyatvaṃ sthitam eva cidudgamāt 8
tathā śivodayād eva bhedo mithyādikaḥ katham
vyavahārāya satyatvaṃ na ca vāvyavahāragam 9

mithyājñānavikalpanīyānāṃ rajatasarpādīnāṃ ghaṭādīnām iva cidvyaktiśaktatā prakāśamānatā nāma vidyate, tad eva sattvaṃ paramārthatvam ato 'pi tac chivatvam. anivāryaṃ caitad iṣyata evaiṣu satyatvaṃ cidabhivyakteḥ, tena tena

---

7c Something of a parallel passage to ŚD 4.7cd is found at ĪPK 4.12: *sarvo mamāyaṃ vibhava ity evaṃ parijānataḥ | viśvātmano vikalpānāṃ prasare 'pi maheśatā ||* Use of the term *prasara* is echoed, as well, in the ŚDVṛ ad ŚD 4.7cd*ff.* (line 56), below. 8c In S^2, ŚD 4.8c is not highlighted, suggesting it is not part of the *mūla*. Also, ŚD 4.8d-9 were initially left out and are recorded in the top margin in a smaller and perhaps later hand; though not highlighted, they are there marked as part of the "*mūlā.*" 9d $K^{ed.}$ preserves a hiatus after *vā* and understands the text here to read *vā vyavahāragam*, not *vā avyavahāragam*. G and J read *na caivāvyavahāragam* for *na ca vāvyavahāragam*, rendering explicit the presence of the alpha-privative. D, on the other hand, does *not* record the presence of an alpha-privative, something it commonly does at other *sandhi* boundaries. 9d A double *daṇḍa* is inserted by a later hand following ŚD 4.9cd in P.

7c mithyā°] TCDG$S^2S^3S^5$PR$K^{ed.}$; mathyā° J 7c °vikalpyānāṃ] $D^{p.c.}K^{ed.}$; °vikalpānām TC$D^{a.c.}$GJ$S^2S^3S^5$PR 7d sattvaṃ] CDGJ$S^2S^3S^5$PR$K^{ed.}$; śaktasat<?> (hypermetric) T 7d cidvyaktiśaktatā] CDGJ$S^2S^3S^5$PR$K^{ed.}$; cidvyaktaśaktatā T 8a tat tad] DGJ$S^2S^3S^5$PR$K^{ed.}$; tad d (hypometric) T, tadvad C 8b vāryate] TCDGJ$S^2S^3S^5K^{ed.}$; vāryatām $P^{p.c.}$, vāryato $P^{a.c.}$, vāryatā R 8d eva] TDGJ$S^2S^3S^5$PR$K^{ed.}$; evac C 9a śivodayād] TCDGJ$S^2S^3S^5K^{ed.}$; śivedayād PR 9b bhedo] CDGJ$S^2S^3S^5$PR$K^{ed.}$; bhe - o T 9b mithyādikaḥ] TDGJ$S^2S^3S^5$PR$K^{ed.}$; bhithādike C 9b katham] TCDGJ$S^{2p.c.}S^3S^5$PR$K^{ed.}$; kathaṃm $S^{2a.c.}$ 9c satyatvaṃ] TCDGJ$S^2S^3S^5K^{ed.}$; satyatva PR 9d ca] TDGJ$S^2S^3S^5$PR$K^{ed.}$; - C 9d vāvyavahāragam] TD$S^2S^3S^5$PR$K^{ed.}$; - pādyavahā- ragam (hypometric) C, evāvyavahāragam GJ

---

53 °śaktatā] GJ$S^2S^3S^5$PR$K^{ed.}$; °śaktitā D 54 prakāśamānatā nāma] GJ$K^{ed.}$; prakāśamānatā D$S^2S^3S^{5p.c.}$PR, prakāśamānatā na $S^{5a.c.}$ 54 eva] GJ$S^2S^3S^5$PR$K^{ed.}$; evaṃ D 54 sattvaṃ] DGJ$S^2S^3S^5K^{ed.}$; satva PR 54 paramārthatvam] $D^{p.c.}$GJ$S^2S^3S^5$PR$K^{ed.}$; paramārtham $D^{a.c.}$ 55 chivatvam] DGJ$S^2S^3S^5$P$K^{ed.}$; chivam R 55 caitad] D$S^2S^3S^5$PR$K^{ed.}$; cetad GJ 55 cidabhivyakteḥ] DGJ$S^2S^3S^5P^{p.c.}K^{ed.}$; cidabhirvyaktes $P^{a.c.}$R

---

48 D folio 147r. 53 D folio 147v. 54 G folio 60r.

rūpeṇa śivasya prasaro 'yaṃ yataḥ. ghaṭajñānarajatajñānayoś ca dvayor api satyatve samyagmithyātvabhedas tarhi katham. vyavahārāya vyavahāraprayojano 'sau. na cāprarūḍhatvād vyavahārasatyatvaṃ vāsatyatvaṃ bhavati.

tathā ca deśe kvacana rājājñā jāyate yathā
vyavahāro 'stu dīnārair etair avyavahāragaiḥ 10
pravartate tathābhūtair anyatrāpi tathānyathā

rājājñayā kūṭadīnārair api vyavahāro 'sty eva. tathānyatrāpīcchāmātrād yathāsaṃketaṃ vastv anapekṣyaiva kālavyavasthārambhādivyavahāraḥ.

10d An unidentified mark, perhaps a smudged or crossed-out *anusvāra*, appears above *r* of *etair* in S^3. 11a An *akṣara* is blacked out prior to *pravartate* in C.

10a deśe] TDGJ$S^2S^3S^5$PR$K^{ed.}$; deśaḥ C 10a kvacana] DGJ$S^2S^3S^5$PR$K^{ed.}$; śakte ca na T, kvacatā C 10b jāyate] CDGJ$S^2S^3S^5$PR$K^{ed.}$; yate T 10b yathā] CDGJ$S^2S^3S^5$PR$K^{ed.}$; tathā T 10c vyavahāro 'stu] $K^{ed. p.c.}$; vyavāhāro 'stu T, vyavahāro skta C, vyavahāras tu DGJ$S^2S^3S^5K^{ed. a.c.}$, vyavahārais tu PR 10c dīnārair] TDGJ$S^2S^3S^5$PR$K^{ed.}$; dīnāder C 10d etair] TDGJ$S^2S^3S^5$P$K^{ed.}$; atair C, eter R 10d avyavahāragaiḥ] TDGJ$S^2S^3S^5$PR$K^{ed.}$; avyavahārigai C 11a pravartate] CDGJ$S^2S^3S^5$PR$K^{ed.}$; pra - rttate T 11a tathābhūtair] TDGJ$S^2S^3S^5$PR$K^{ed.}$; tathābhūtaur C 11b anyatrāpi] TDGJ$S^2S^3S^5$PR$K^{ed.}$; anyātrāpi C 11b tathānyathā] TDGJ$S^2S^3S^5$PR$K^{ed.}$; yathānyāthā C

---

56 Note a passage parallel to what is here said (at *tena tena rūpeṇa...*) may be found at ĪPK 4.12: *sarvo mamāyaṃ vibhava ity evaṃ parijānataḥ* | *viśvātmano vikalpānāṃ prasare 'pi maheśatā* || See also the corresponding passage of the ĪPKVṛ: *kṣetrajñasyāpīśvaraśaktyaiva vikalpārambha iti taddaśāyām api parijñāteśvarbhāvasya mamāyaṃ saṃsāramayo vibhava ity abhedena viśvam āviśataḥ parāmarśamātrān aśeṣān vikalpān saṃpādayato maheśvarataiva.* 58 S^5 deletes *satyatvā* following *na cāprarūḍha°*. 58 $K^{ed.}$ reads *vā satyatvaṃ*. By contrast, two manuscripts, G & J, explicitly mark the presence (with *avagrahas*) of the alpha-privative and understand the passage to read *vā asatyatvaṃ*.

---

57 tarhi] DGJS^3S^5PR$K^{ed.}$; tahi S^2 62 vyavahāro] DGJS^2S^5PR$K^{ed.}$; vyahāro S^3 62 eva] $D^{p.c.}$GJS^2S^5PR$K^{ed.}$; aiva $D^{a.c.}S^3$ 62 °mātrād] DGJ$S^2S^3S^5P^{p.c.}K^{ed.}$; °mātrā $P^{a.c.}$R 63 yathāsaṃketaṃ] DGJ$S^{2p.c.}S^3S^5$P$K^{ed.}$; yathasaṃketaṃ $S^{2a.c.}$, yathāsaṃkataṃ R

---

57 S^2 folio 87v. 59 D folio 148r. 60 J folio 57r. 63 R folio 38r. 63 S^5 folio 56r.

vyavahārasya satyatve sarvatrāsatyataiva te 11
satyatve tasya hāniḥ syāt pakṣe 'bhyupagate kila

yadi punar aprarūḍhasya vyavahārasyāsatyasyāpi satyateṣyate, tad evaṃjātīyatayā sarvam idaṃ jagat satyaṃ syād asatyatāparamārthaṃ vyavahāravad ity arthaḥ. tasya jagataḥ paramārthataḥ satyatve saty ayaṃ doṣo vyavahārasadṛśasatyatātmakaḥ syāt tava. evaṃ ca sarvasatyatāvādapakṣe 'bhyudite śāstrodite hāniḥ syāt.

tasyāpi kiṃ śivāvāptiḥ katham uktā hy asatyatā 12
vyavahāratayaivāsti satyatvaṃ na nibandhanāt

11c The final syllable of *satyatve* is blotched in C. 11d While R reads *sarvatrāsatya°*, a gap and a slight blotch appear following *sarvatrā°*, and it is possible the scribe hesitated before or after having begun to record there what could be interpreted as a *p*, presumably of *sarvatrāpi* (viz., what appears in $P^{a.c.}$). 11d A mark appears in blue ink following *sarvatrā* of *sarvatrāsatyataiva te* in T. It appears to have been added by a late hand, the same one that numbered the folios of the manuscript (in Arabic numerals) at the right string-holes of the manuscript. 12b It is possible that C reads *'bhyuyagate* for *'bhyupagate*, rather than *'bhyupagame*. 12d Though the manuscript is frayed at T, a reading of *uktā* is almost legible, though the last ligature is mostly broken off, it being at the end of the line of text. 12d The double *daṇḍa* following ŚD 4.12 is inserted into the text of P. 13b D could at least be interpreted to read *satyatve* for *satyatvaṃ*, because the *anusvāra* is drawn in a way that is extended somewhat horizontally. But this is not uncommon in the hand of this manuscript, and it is better interpreted as an *anusvāra*.

11d sarvatrāsatya°] $TCDGJS^2S^3S^5P^{p.c.}RK^{ed.}$; sarvatrāpi satya° (hypermetric) $P^{a.c.}$ 12a tasya hāniḥ] $TDGJS^2S^3S^5PRK^{ed.}$; satyahāniḥ C 12b 'bhyupagate] $TDGJS^3S^5PRK^{ed.}$; 'bhyupagame C, [']bhyupagete S^2 12b kila] $TDGJS^2S^3S^5PRK^{ed.}$; kula C 12c tasyāpi] $TDGJS^2S^3S^5PRK^{ed.}$; tāsyāpi C 12c śivāvāptiḥ] $TDGJS^3S^5PRK^{ed.}$; śivāvāpi C, śivāptiḥ (hypometric) S^2 12d katham] $TCD^{p.c.}GJS^2S^3S^5PRK^{ed.}$; kathaṃm $D^{a.c.}$ 12d uktā] $DGJS^2S^3S^5PRK^{ed.}$; ukt<?> T, maṃktā C 12d hy asatyatā] $CD^{p.c.}GJS^2S^3S^5K^{ed.}$; - satyatā T, hi satyatā $D^{a.c.}$PR 13a vyavahāratayaivāsti] $TDGJS^2S^3S^5PRK^{ed.}$; vyavahāratayaisti (hypometric) C 13b satyatvaṃ] $TDGJS^2S^3S^5PRK^{ed.}$, satyatve C

---

68 saty ayaṃ] $DJS^2S^3S^5PRK^{ed.}$; *om.* G 69 °satyatātmakaḥ] $GJS^2S^3S^5PRK^{ed.}$; °satyātmakaḥ D 69 °vādapakṣe] $DGJS^2S^3S^5K^{ed.}$; °vad apekṣe PR

---

64 D folio 148v. 67 S^2 folio 88r. 68 G folio 60v. 69 D folio 149r.

tasyāpi vyavahārasya kiṃ cidudgamāc chivāvāptiḥ śivarūpateṣyate 'nāyāsāgatāsya śivatety arthaḥ. evaṃ cet katham asya vyavahārasyāpy asatyatoktā, satya evāyam evaṃ sati syād ity arthaḥ. satyaṃ, kintu vyavahāratayaivāpy asya vyavahārasya satyatvaṃ na tu nibandhanād nibandhanatvāt prarūḍhatvād ity arthaḥ.

vikalpādeḥ samutpattiḥ sata eva prajāyate 13
nābhāṣya vyavahārārtham evaṃ vastv iti niścitam
tathaivāstu śivāvasthā kenāsau vinivāritā 14

13c A single *akṣara*, apparently *sva*, is deleted prior to *samutpattiḥ* in S^2. 13d What appears to be a *visarga* is crossed out following C's erroneous reading of *prajāyetai* for *prajāyate*. 13d A double *daṇḍa* following ŚD 4.13 is inserted into the line of text in P. 14a The reading of R is blurred at *nābhāṣya* (apparently from water damage to the MS) but is nevertheless legible. 14b In C, the following *akṣaras* are crossed out in a light hand: *vaṃ vastv it*. 14c A short vertical line above *the* appears to mark the erroneous reading of *tathevāsu* for *tathaivāstu* in C. 14c The reading of R is blurred at *tathaivāstu śi°* (apparently from water damage to the MS), but is nevertheless legible.

13c vikalpādeḥ] TCDGJ$S^2S^3S^5P^{p.c.}$RK$^{ed.}$; vikālpādaiḥ $P^{a.c.}$ 13d sata] TCDGJS^2S^5PRK$^{ed.}$; sa (hypometric) S^3 13d prajāyate] TDGJ$S^2S^3S^5$PRK$^{ed.}$; prajāyetai C 14a nābhāṣya] CDGJ$S^2S^3S^5$K$^{ed.}$; nābhā (hypometric) T, na bhāṣya PR 14a vyavahārārtham] TDGJ$S^2S^3S^5$PRK$^{ed.}$; vahārārtha (hypometric) C 14b evaṃ] TDGJ$S^2S^3S^5$PRK$^{ed.}$; vaṃ (hypometric) C 14b vastv] TCDGJ$S^2S^3S^5$PRK$^{ed.a.c.}$; vāstv K$^{ed.p.c.}$ 14c tathaivāstu] TDGJ$S^2S^3S^5$PRK$^{ed.}$; tathevāsu C 14d kenāsau] CDGJ$S^2S^3S^5$PRK$^{ed.}$; ke - - T 14d vinivāritā] TDGJ$S^2S^3S^5$PRK$^{ed.}$; vinitānivā C

---

76 A gap in G appears before the final *ṃ* of its reading of *asatyatvaṃ*. The same appears in S^2, where a now-illegible *akṣara* is deleted prior to °*tvaṃ*.

---

73 vyavahārasya] DGJ$S^2S^3S^5P^{p.c.}$RK$^{ed.}$; vyavahārasyā $P^{a.c.}$ 73 'nāyāsāgatā] $D^{p.c.}$GJ$S^2S^3S^5$PRK$^{ed.}$; 'nāyaisāgatā $D^{a.c.}$ 74 asatyatoktā] D$G^{p.c.}$J$S^2S^3S^5$RK$^{ed.}$; asatyatotya $G^{a.c.}$, asatyatokta P 76 satyatvaṃ] K$^{ed.}$; asatyatvaṃ DGJ$S^2S^3S^5$PR 76 nibandhanād] DK$^{ed.}$; nibandhanā° GJ$S^2S^3S^5$PR

---

73 P folio 47. 73 J folio 57v. 74 D folio 149v. 77 S^2 folio 88v. 77 C folio 9r. 79 S^5 folio 56v.

vikalpādeḥ svatantrād rajatādijñānāc ca nibaddhatvena sata evārthasyotpattiḥ saṃpadyate na. kiṃ tarhi, tathābhāṣya saṃketya vyavahārārtham evaṃ kūṭadīnāraiḥ krayo 'stu, adyārabhya kālagaṇanāyām ayaṃ saṃvatsaraḥ saṃvatsarārambho vāstu vastv iti niścitaṃ niścayaḥ. athavaivaṃ vastv api satyam api kālādīti niścitavyavahārārtham. tasya ca tathaivāstu śivatattvenāvasthitiḥ, kena vinivāritā cidudgamāt śivatvalakṣaṇayogāt. vikalpasya vyavahārasya satyatvāsatyatvapakṣabhede prāṅ nimittam uktaṃ yat prakāśamānasya satyatve, satyatvam eva. cidabhedākhyātimayatvāt satyatvam ity evaṃ ca sarvatraiva na vismaraṇīyam.

---

80 It is possible that R reads *vikasyādeḥ* for *vikalpādeḥ*, as the writing is there blurred (apparently from water damage to the MS). 80 The reading of R is blurred at °*ārthasyot*° (apparently from water damage to the MS), but is nevertheless legible. 81 An *akṣara* is deleted following *evaṃ* in S^{3}, perhaps an ill-written *kū*, or perhaps *ke*. 82 P's *post correctionem* reading of *adyārambhya* (for the *ante correctionem* reading of *athārambhya*) is the modification of a later hand. 82 P's reading of *kālakalanāyām* for *kālagaṇanāyām* is corrected by a later hand. 83 I eliminate the full stop of K$^{ed.}$, which appears there following *iti* and prior to *niścitaṃ niścayaḥ*. 84 The reading of R is blurred at °*āvasthi*° but is nevertheless legible. 84 P records the vertical line of *va* in *avasthitiḥ* with a markedly thick line, appearing thereby to correct what could have been a prior reading of *avāsthitiḥ*. 85 S^{2} deletes a now illegible *akṣara* following *kena*. 85 A comma following *vinivāritā* is added by a later hand in P. 85 G deletes *vi* just prior to its correct reading of *vinivāritā*, perhaps because the deleted *akṣara* is blotched.

---

80 vikalpādeḥ] DGJS^{2}S^{3}S^{5}PRK$^{ed.a.c.}$; na vikalpādeḥ K$^{ed.p.c.}$ 80 °jñānāc ca] DGJS^{2}S^{3}S^{5}P$^{p.c.}$RK$^{ed.}$; °jñānāś ca P$^{a.c.}$ 80 nibaddhatvena] DS$^{2p.c.}$S^{5}K$^{ed.}$; nivandhanatvena G, nibandhatvena JS$^{2a.c.}$S^{3}PR 81 saṃpadyate na] *conj.*; saṃpadyate DGJS^{2}S^{3}S^{5}PRK$^{ed.}$ 82 krayo] DGJS^{2}S^{5}PRK$^{ed.}$; kriyo S^{3} 82 adyārabhya] DGJS^{2}S^{3}S^{5}K$^{ed.}$; adyārambhya P$^{p.c.}$R; athārambhya P$^{a.c.}$ 82 °gaṇanāyām] GJK$^{ed.}$; °kalanāyām DS^{2}S^{3}S^{5}P$^{p.c.}$R, °kalamāyām P$^{a.c.}$ 82 saṃvatsaraḥ] DGJS^{2}S^{5}PK$^{ed.}$; *om.* S^{3}, saṃvaṃtsaraḥ R 83 vāstu vastv] *conj.*; vāstv DGJS^{2}S^{3}S^{5}PRK$^{ed.}$ 84 śivatattvena] DGJS^{2}S^{3}S^{5}; śivatvena PRK$^{ed.}$ 85 vinivāritā] GJS^{2}S^{3}S^{5}PRK$^{ed.}$; nivāritā D 86 satyatvāsatyatvapakṣabhede] DS^{3}S^{5}K$^{ed.}$; satyatvāsatyatvapakṣabhedo GJS^{2}, satyatvāpakṣabhede PR 86 prakāśamānasya satyatve] DGJS^{2}S^{3}S^{5}K$^{ed.}$; prakāśamānasatyatve PR 87 °abhedākhyātimayatvāt] DGJS^{2}S^{3}S^{5}K$^{ed.}$; °abhedākhyāmayatvāt PR 87 ity evaṃ] DGJS^{2}S^{3}S$^{5p.c.}$PRK$^{ed.}$; ivaṃ S$^{5a.c.}$ 87 na] GJS^{2}S^{3}S^{5}PRK$^{ed.}$; *om.* D

---

80 D folio 150r. 81 S^{3} folio 25r. 82 G folio 61r. 84 D folio 150v. 85 R folio 38v. 86 S^{2} folio 89r. 87 J folio 58r.

mithyātvaṃ kriyate kasya kiṃ kāle yatra tad bhavet
kāla eva sa na bhaved iti cen naiva kutracit 15
akāle jananaṃ kiñcid bādhyate vā janikriyā
kṛtvā kāryaṃ kriyā yātā gatāyāṃ kiṃ prabādhyate 16

bādhake ca pramāṇe sati nedaṃ rajataṃ nedaṃ rajataṃ śuktiketi niṣedhaniṣṭhatayā pratītau mithyātvaṃ syāt. tena bādhakena pramāṇena mithyātvaṃ kāryam. tat kasya kriyate, tatra kiṃ yasmin kāle tad rajatādi bhavet sa kāla eva

---

15d One should consider reading *kasyacit* at ŚD 4.15d for *kutracit*, given the reading of the ŚDVṛ (lines 96-97): *naiva hy akāle kālābhāve kasyacij jananaṃ nāma kiñcit kālarahitāyāḥ kriyāyā ayogād ity arthaḥ.* 15d A double *daṇḍa* is inserted into the line of text after ŚD 4.15cd in P. 16b The vertical line marking the *i* vowel of °*kriyā* is missing in P.

15a kasya] TCDGJ$S^2S^3S^5K^{ed.}$; tasya PR 15b kiṃ kāle] CDGJ$S^2S^3S^5$PR$K^{ed.}$; kiṃ kāla T 15c eva] TDGJ$S^2S^3S^5$PR$K^{ed.}$; evaṃ C 15c sa na bhaved] DGJ$S^2S^3S^5K^{ed.}$; na saṃbhāvet T, na sa bhaved C, mana bhaved PR 15d cen] TCDGJ$S^2S^{3\,p.c.}S^5$PR$K^{ed.}$; cain $S^{3\,a.c.}$ 16a jananaṃ kiñcid] TDGJ$S^2S^3S^5$PR$K^{ed.}$; janaṃnaṃ kicit C 16b janikriyā] TDJ$S^2S^3S^5$PR$K^{ed.}$; janakriyā CG 16c kāryaṃ] DGJ$S^2S^3S^5$PR$K^{ed.}$; kā - T, varṇaṃ C 16c kriyā] DGJ$S^2S^3S^5$PR$K^{ed.}$; - yā T, kṣayaṃ C 16c yātā] TCD$S^2S^3S^5$PR$K^{ed.}$; yatā GJ 16d gatāyāṃ] TCDGJ$S^2S^3S^5$R$K^{ed.}$; gatāyaṃ P 16d prabādhyate] TCDGJ$S^2S^3S^5K^{ed.}$; prabudhyate PR

---

95 S^2 deletes a now illegible *akṣara* following *kriya* of *kriyate.* 95 A single vertical line follows *kiṃ* in G. It cannot be understood to be a single *daṇḍa*, because these are recorded in an ink of a different color in G, while the present mark is made in the same black ink of all the manuscript's *akṣaras*. Note, on the other hand, that J punctuates here, and the two manuscripts often punctuate in the same manner. 95 $K^{ed.}$ punctuates prior to *sa kāla eva na bhavatīti mithyātvam ity abhyupagamaḥ*, but I have eliminated the full stop in the present edition.

---

93 bādhake] DGJ$S^2S^3S^5K^{ed.}$; vāyake PR 93 ca] D$S^2S^3S^5$PR$K^{ed.}$; ka GJ 93 rajataṃ] DGJ$S^2S^3S^5P^{p.c.}$R$K^{ed.}$; rajateṃ $P^{a.c.}$ 93 nedaṃ rajataṃ] D$S^2S^3S^5K^{ed.}$; *om.* GJPR 95 rajatādi] GJ$S^2S^3S^5$PR; rajatatā $D^{p.c.}K^{ed.}$, rajatā $D^{a.c.}$

---

89 D folio 151r. 94 S^5 folio 57r. 95 G folio 61v. 95 D folio 151v.

na bhavatīti mithyātvam ity abhyupagamaḥ. tan na. naiva hy akāle kālābhāve kasyacij jananaṃ nāma kiñcit kālarahitāyāḥ kriyāyā ayogād ity arthaḥ. janikriyā vā yadi bādhyate, tan na. rajatādikāryaṃ kṛtvā kriyā samāptā. tasyā asatyāḥ ko bādhārthaḥ svayam eva tasyā abhāvāt. idānīṃ ca bādhaviṣayasyābhāvāt ko bādhaḥ.

athānubhavagā bādhā nānubhūto 'nyathā bhavet
athendriyasya bādhyatvaṃ tatkālaṃ yādṛg indriyam 17
tadāndhyaṃ janyate kena tasya kālāntarasthiteḥ
sarvaiḥ samatvaṃ bādho vā saṃbandhe jananaṃ katham 18

17b There is a crowding in the recording of the *akṣaras* in T that suggests the scribe initially wrote *nānubhūtā* for *nānubhūto*. 18b S^5 rewrites *ta* of *tasya* above the line, clarifying what was written below, what is the same *akṣara*, one that, while blotched in appearance, is nevertheless legible. 18d G appears to cover over a reading of *saṃbandaṃ* with its reading of *saṃbandhe* at ŚD 4.18d.

17a bādhā] TDGJ$S^2S^3S^5$PR$K^{ed.}$; bhovo C 17b 'nyathā] TDGJ$S^2S^3S^5$PR$K^{ed.}$; sya tathā (hypermetric) C 17c athendriyasya] TCDGJ$S^2S^3S^5K^{ed.}$; athaiṃdriyasya P, athaidriyasya R 17d tatkālaṃ] TDGJ$S^2S^3S^5$PR$K^{ed.}$; tātkālaṃ C 17d yādṛg indriyam] TDGJ$S^2S^3S^5$PR$K^{ed.}$; yādṛg īṃdriyaṃ C 18a tadāndhyaṃ] TDGJ$S^2S^3S^5$PR$K^{ed.}$; tadādyaṃ C 18b kālāntarasthiteḥ] DGJ$S^2S^3S^5$PR$K^{ed.}$; kālāṃtare sthiteḥ TC 18c samatvaṃ] DGJ$S^2S^3S^5$PR$K^{ed.}$; sa - - T, samastaṃ C 18d jananaṃ] TCDGJ$S^2S^3S^5K^{ed.}$; jana (hypometric) PR

---

96 S^3 is obscured at *hy a°* of *hy akāle*, but it appears to offer the correct reading. 98 S^5 records a gap the width of a single *akṣara* following *bādhya* of *bādhyate*. 99 D records *ko* but appears to cover over a prior reading of *kaṃ* in doing so. 99 S^3 appears perhaps to have first recorded *yabhāvāt* for *abhāvāt*. 99 The initial *akṣara* of *idānīṃ* is covered by a piece of tape in J.

---

96 mithyātvam] DGJ$S^2S^3S^5$P$K^{ed.}$; mathyātvam R 96 abhyupagamaḥ] DGJ$S^3S^5K^{ed.}$; abhyumagamaḥ S^2, atyupagamaḥ PR 96 tan na] $D^{p.c.}$GJ$S^{2p.c.}S^3S^{5a.c.}$PR$K^{ed.}$; tatra $D^{a.c.}S^{2a.c.}S^{5p.c.}$ 96 kālābhāve] DGJ$S^2S^3S^5K^{ed.}$; kābhāve PR 97 janikriyā] DGJ$S^2S^3S^5K^{ed.}$; janakriyā PR 98 rajatādikāryaṃ] DJ$S^2S^3S^5$PR$K^{ed.}$; rajatādikaṃ G 99 bādhārthaḥ] DGJ$S^{2p.c.}S^3S^5$PR$K^{ed.}$; badhārthaḥ $S^{2a.c.}$ 99 idānīṃ] DG$S^2S^3S^5$PR$K^{ed.}$; <?>dānīṃ J

---

96 S^2 folio 89v. 99 D folio 152r. 104 J folio 58v.

atha yadi rajatānubhavagatā bādheṣyate, tan na. na hy anubhūto viṣayo 'nanubhūto yuktaḥ. atha rajatadvicandrādijñānakāraṇam indriyam anindriyam iti bādhyate. tan na. na hi bādhakenendriyasyāndhyam abhāvaḥ kartuṃ śakyaṃ, tadrajatādijñānakāle yādṛg indriyaṃ tasya tadānīṃ ghaṭādīnām upalabdheḥ. atha kālāntare yadā bādhakotpattiḥ, tadā tasyānavasthānād bādhaḥ. tatkālāntarasthiter bādhopagame tadānīntanasamyagjñānair api mithyājñānānāṃ samatvaṃ nāma bādhaḥ prāpnoti. na caivaṃ yuktaṃ, vartamānakālabhāvināṃ ghaṭādijñānānāṃ samyaktvena saṃbhavāt. athendriyaviṣayādīnāṃ saṃbandhe bādhaḥ. tan na. saṃbandhābhāve hi kathaṃ jñānajananaṃ. tasmād yāvat saṃbhavaṃ vikalpane sarvathā rajatādipratītau na kiñcin niṣeddhuṃ śakyata iti na kaścid bādhārthaḥ. śuktikā rajataṃ na bhavatīti ca na bādhaḥ. na hi rajatatvena śuktikā pratipanneti vā pratīteḥ, śuktideśāvaṣṭambhenety api na kiñcit sarvasyaiva prakāśamānasya svarūpadeśatvāt. sarvathā yathā yat

---

105 The initial *akṣara* (*ra*) of the reading of R of *rajatānubhāvagatā* (for *rajatānubhavagatā*) appears as if it were a subsequent insertion (by the same hand) into the line of text. 111 S^{2} appears to correct its reading of *samatvaṃ* from what was *samyatvaṃ*. 113 D marks the final syllable of its reading of *sambandhabhādhe* as erroneous (by coloring it with a yellow mark), but no correction is offered. 114 In S^{2}, *e* of *niṣeddhuṃ* is heavily blotched, probably in order to cover a now-corrected reading of the text. 116 In S^{2} the final *akṣara* of *rajatatvena* is heavily blotched but appears to offer the correct reading.

---

105 °bhavagatā] DGJS$^{2p.c.}$S^{3}S^{5}K$^{ed.}$; °bhavatā S$^{2a.c.}$, °bhāvagatā PR 105 bādheṣyate] DGJS^{5}PRK$^{ed.}$; bā<?>eṣyate S^{2}, bādhyeṣyate S^{3} 105 tan na] DGJS^{2}S^{3}S^{5}K$^{ed.}$; na tan PR 106 'nanubhūto] D$^{p.c.}$GJS^{2}S^{3}S^{5}PR K$^{ed.}$; anubhūto D$^{a.c.}$ 106 anindriyam] DGJS^{2}S^{3}S^{5}P$^{p.c.}$RK$^{ed.}$; niṃdriyam P$^{a.c.}$ 108 tadānīṃ] DGS^{2}S^{3}S^{5}PRK$^{ed.}$; <?>dānīṃ J 109 tasyānavasthānād] D$^{p.c.}$K$^{ed.}$; tasyāśavasthānād D$^{a.c.}$, tasyāvasthānād GJ, tasyām avasthānād S^{2}S^{3}S^{5}PR 110 tadānīntana°] DS^{2}S^{3}S^{5}PRK$^{ed.}$; tadānīnttana° GJ 110 °samyagjñānair] DGJS^{2}S^{3}S^{5}PRK$^{ed.p.c.}$; °samyagjñānar K$^{ed.a.c.}$ 111 caivaṃ] DGJS^{2}S^{3}S^{5}PRK$^{ed.p.c.}$; cavam K$^{ed.a.c.}$ 111 °bhāvināṃ] S^{2}PRK$^{ed.p.c.}$; °bhavināṃ DGJS^{3}S^{5}, °bhāvinā K$^{ed.a.c.}$ 113 saṃbandhābhāve] GJS^{2}S^{3}S^{5}PR; sambandhabhādhe D, saṃbandhabādhe K$^{ed.}$ 114 vikalpane] DGJS^{2}S^{3}S^{5}K$^{ed.}$; vikalpena PR 114 sarvathā] DGJS^{2}S^{3}S^{5}PRK$^{ed.p.c.}$; savathā K$^{ed.a.c.}$ 114 °pratītau] D$^{p.c.}$GJS^{2}S^{3}S^{5}PRK$^{ed.}$; °pratau D$^{a.c.}$ 114 na] D$^{p.c.}$GJS^{2}S^{3}S^{5}PRK$^{ed.}$; *om.* D$^{a.c.}$ 115 kaścid] DS$^{2a.c.}$S^{5}PK$^{ed.}$; kiñcid GJS$^{2p.c.}$S^{3}, kaści R 116 pratipanneti vā] DGJS^{2}S^{5}PRK$^{ed.}$; pratipanne vā S^{3}

---

105 S^{2} folio 90r. 106 D folio 152v. 107 P folio 48. 108 R folio 39r. 108 G folio 62r. 109 S^{5} folio 57v. 110 D folio 153r. 113 S^{2} folio 90v. 114 S^{3} folio 25v. 115 D folio 153v. 116 J folio 59r.

pratibhātaṃ, tathaiva tat, nānyathā kartuṃ śakyata iti satyam eveti na kiñcin mithyātvam. etac ceśvarapratyabhijñāto 'vaseyam.

vyavahārasya bādhā ced vyavahāre yatheṣṭatā
kvacit satyasuvarṇasya pratyante vyavahāritā 19
kūṭakārṣāpaṇādau vā vyavahāro 'pi dṛśyate
tāvatā vyavahāro vā yad ātmāhlādamātrakam 20
arthakriyāsamarthatvam etad evāsya vāstavam

19a P records *ce* of its corrected reading (*ced*) in the right margin. 19d S^3 deletes *pra* prior to its correct reading of *pratyante*. 21a ŚD 4.21ab is omitted from G. 21b A parallel to ŚD 4.19-21ab is found at ĪPK 1.7.14: *ittham atyarthabhinnārthāvabhāsakhacite vibhau | samalo vimalo vāpi vyavahāro 'nubhūyate* || ĪPKVṛ: *māyāśaktyā bhedaviṣayo 'yaṃ sarvo vyavahāras tathājñāninām śuddho 'jñānāndhānāṃ tu malinas tattadbhinnārthāvabhāsabhāji bhagavati saṃbhāvyate 'nubhavena*. See, esp., the *avataraṇikā* of Abhinavagupta's ĪPV (vol. 1, p. 312, lines 3-9) ad ĪPK 1.7.14, which more clearly alludes to the concerns raised in ŚD 4.19-21ab: *na kevalam ete kāryakāraṇabhāvasmaraṇabādhāvyavahārāḥ sakalalokayātrāsāmānyavyavahārabhūtā ekapramātṛpratiṣṭhā, yāvad avāntaravyavahārā api ye krayavikrayādayaḥ samalāḥ, upadeśyopadeśabhāvādayaś ca nirmalāḥ, te 'py ekapramātṛniṣṭhā eva bhavanti – vyavhāro hi sarvaḥ samanvayaprāṇa ity upasaṃhārakrameṇa darśayati.*

19a ced] TCDGJ$S^2S^3S^5P^{p.c.}K^{ed.}$; dedhe $P^{a.c.}$, dhed R 20a kūṭakārṣāpaṇādau] DGJ$S^2S^3S^5$PR$K^{ed.}$; kūṭakarṣapaṇādau T, kūṭakarṣāpaṇādai C 20c vyavahāro] CDGJ$S^2S^3S^5$PR$K^{ed.}$; - - hāro T 20d ātmāhlādamātrakam] DGJ$S^2S^3S^5$PR$K^{ed.}$; ātmahlādamātrakaṃ T, ātmāhlādam ātmakam C 21a °samarthatvam] TDJ$S^2S^3S^5$PR$K^{ed.}$; °sarthatvam (hypometric) C, *om.* G 21b etad] TDJ$S^2S^3S^5$PR$K^{ed.}$; atad C, *om.* G 21b evāsya] TCDJS^2S^5PR$K^{ed.}$; vāsya (hypometric) S^3, *om.* G

---

119 The likely reference is to ĪPK 1.7.12: *evaṃ rūpyavidābhāvarūpā śuktimatir bhavet | na tv ādyarajatajñapteḥ syād aprāmāṇyavedikā* || ĪPKVṛ ad ĪPK 1.7.12: *śuktijñānam eva rajatajñānābhāvarūpaṃ sidhyati, tadānīntanaśuktijñānānubhavena na bhinnasyātītasya rūpyajñānasyāprāmāṇyam*. Cf. also ĪPK 1.7.13: *dharmyasiddher api bhaved bādhā naivānumānataḥ | svasaṃvedanasiddhā tu yuktā saikapramātṛjā* || ĪPKVṛ ad ĪPK 1.7.13: *śuktikājñānakāle ca na pūrvaṃ rajatajñānam asti. tataḥ sa dharmī na siddha iti nānumānena bādhā, ekapramātṛmayasvasaṃvedane tv ekadeśāvaṣṭambhyubhayajñānamayasaṃbandhabhāsanāt sidhyati. paścātsaṃvādaḥ pratyakṣasvasaṃvedane pūrvasyāpi tasya bhāsanād ekaṃ pramāṇam itarad anyatheti bhavati. saṃvādo 'py ekapramātṛkṛtaḥ.*

---

118 eveti] DGJ$S^2S^3S^5$PR; eva $K^{ed.}$ 119 etac] DGJ$S^2S^3S^5K^{ed.}$; etaś PR

---

119 G folio 62v. 120 D folio 154r. 122 S^2 folio 91r. 124 S^5 folio 58r.

vyavahāro 'pi yadi bādhyate rajatavyavahāro na kartavya iti. tad api na vyavahārasyeṣṭasya pravṛtteḥ. na tadvaśena satyāsatyavibhāgaḥ. tathā hi pratyantadeśe kvacit satyasuvarṇasya tathā vyavahāro, yādṛgayasaḥ. kūṭakārṣāpaṇādinā ca rājña iṣṭatvād dṛśyate vyavahāraḥ. athavā yad āhlādamātrakaṃ, tāvataiva vyavahāraḥ. etad eva cāhlādakāritvam arthasyārthakriyākāritve svasaṃvedanasiddhatvena, abhrāntatvād vāstavasvapnajalasya pānādyarthakriyā bhrāntāpi syāt, tṛṇnivṛttyā tu tṛptiḥ svasaṃvedanasiddhā na visaṃvadati. sāpi cāhlādikārthakriyā kūṭādeḥ svapnajalāder vā syāt, tad api satyaṃ vyavahāryaṃ ceti vyavahāre 'pi na bādhasthitiḥ.

---

126 A later hand might have added the second *y* of *vyavahārasya* in S^5. 126 S^2 deletes *eṣṭasya* prior to *pravṛtteḥ*. 127 R inserts a space following *satyasuvarṇasya tathā*. 127 P's reading of *yādṛg°* is corrected by a later hand. 130 D deletes an *akṣara*, now illegible, prior to *bhrāntatvād*. 130 The vertical stroke in J that marks the long *ā* that stands as the final and initial *akaras* of *°siddhatvena* and *abhrāntatvād*, respectively, is recorded in a manner that is longer than usual, but of a length shorter than a single *daṇḍa*. 130 S^5 deletes a now illegible *akṣara* prior to *bhrāntāpi*. 131 P's reading of *tṛṇnivṛttyā* is corrected by a later hand. 132 What is said here in Utpaladeva's commentary echoes ĪPK 2.3.12: *arthakriyāpi sahajā nārthānām īśvarecchayā* | *niyatā sā hi tenāsya nākriyāto 'nyathā bhavet* || The ĪPKVṛ there reads as follows: *ullekhaghaṭādīnāṃ bāhyārthakriyāvirahe 'pi ghaṭāditaiva, asvābhāvikatvāt tasyā īśvareṇa pratyābhāsaṃ niyamitāyāḥ*. Cf. ĪPVV (vol. 3, p. 151, lines 5-9): *arthakriyāpīti sā tāvat svarūpaṃ na bhavatīty uktam, asvarūpabhūtāpi ca na sahajā ananyāpekṣā īśvarecchāniyatyapekṣaṇāt. tena tasyā akaraṇān nānyatvam ity avastutvaṃ, vastvantaratvaṃ vā bhavitum arhatīti sūtrārthaḥ. ullekhā eva ghaṭādayas teṣāṃ bāhyasya svalakṣaṇasya yā arthakriyā tayā virahe 'pīti vṛttyarthaḥ*. 132 It is also possible that S^5 reads *kūṭadeḥ* for *kūṭādeḥ*. The hand is blotched there.

---

126 vyavahārasya] DGJ$S^{2p.c.}S^3S^5$PR$K^{ed.}$; vyavahāsya $S^{2a.c.}$ 126 iṣṭasya] DGJ$S^2S^3K^{ed.}$; iṣṭatāsyeṣṭasya S^5, iṣṭatāsya PR 127 yādṛg°] DGJ$S^2S^3S^5P^{p.c.}K^{ed.}$; yadṛg° $P^{a.c.}$R 127 kūṭakārṣāpaṇādinā] DG$S^2S^3S^5$PR$K^{ed.}$; kūṭakārṣāpaṇā - di<?>ā J 129 athavā yad āhlādamātrakaṃ, tāvataiva vyavahāraḥ. etad eva ca] D$S^2S^3S^5K^{ed.}$; athavā yad PR, etad eva ca GJ 130 abhrāntatvād] GJ$S^{2a.c.}S^3S^5$; bhrāntatvād D$S^{2p.c.}$PR$K^{ed.}$ 131 tṛṇnivṛttyā] DGJ$S^{2p.c.}S^3S^5P^{p.c.}K^{ed.}$; tṛnivṛttyā $S^{2a.c.}$, tpaṇnivṛttyā $P^{a.c.}$, tyaṇnivṛtyā R 131 tṛptiḥ] DGJ$S^2S^3S^5K^{ed.}$; tṛttiḥ PR 131 svasaṃvedanasiddhā] D$S^2S^3S^5$PR$K^{ed.}$; svasaṃvedasiddhā GJ 131 visaṃvadati] D$G^{p.c.}$J$S^2S^3S^5$P$K^{ed.}$; saṃvivadati $G^{a.c.}$, saṃvadati R 132 kūṭādeḥ] DGJS^2S^5PR$K^{ed.}$; kūṭadeḥ S^3 132 vyavahāryaṃ] DGJ$S^2S^3S^{5p.c.}$PR$K^{ed.}$; vyavavahāryaṃ $S^{5a.c.}$

---

126 D folio 154v. 129 R folio 39v. 130 D folio 155r. 131 S^2 folio 91v. 131 J folio 59v. 133 G folio 63r. G records *śrīgurubhyo namaḥ* at the top of the folio in question, centered at the top of the page.

atha ced deśabādho vā taddeśe rajataṃ na hi 21
yatra kāle sarajato deśo 'bhūt sa gatas tadā
kālāntareṇa deśo 'sau kā bādhā bhinnakālayoḥ 22

athānyadeśaṃ rajatam anyadeśam upalabdham iti yadi vā deśabādhaḥ. tan na. yasmin kāle rajatāśrayo deśo 'bhūt, sa kālo bādhyarajatajñānakāle nāstīti bādhakajñānena bādhaḥ kriyate. na caivaṃ rajatadeśayor dvayor bhinnakālatvāt. tathā hi śuktikārajatakāle 'nyadeśarajatakālo gataḥ. tataś ca kālabhedena deśabhedasyāvirodhāt kā bādhā.

22a S^3 records *ra* of *sarajato* in the right margin. 22d S^3 appears to have been corrected by a later hand at *bādhā*.

21d taddeśe] TDGJ$S^2S^3S^5$PRK$^{ed.}$; ddeśeva C 21d rajataṃ] TCDGJ$S^2S^{3p.c.}S^5$ PRK$^{ed.}$; rājataṃ $S^{3a.c.}$ 22a kāle] TDGJ$S^2S^3S^5$PRK$^{ed.}$; <?> (hypometric) C 22a sarajato] TDGJ$S^2S^{3p.c.}S^5$PRK$^{ed.}$; sarajo (hypometric) C, sajato $S^{3a.c.}$ 22b sa] CDGJ$S^2S^3S^5P^{p.c.}$RK$^{ed.}$; - T, se $P^{a.c.}$ 22b gatas] CDGJ$S^2S^3S^5$PRK$^{ed.}$; - - T 22b tadā] CDGJ$S^2S^3S^5$PRK$^{ed.}$; - - T 22d kā] TCDGJ$S^{2p.c.}S^3S^5$PRK$^{ed.}$; *om.* $S^{2a.c.}$ 22d bādhā] TCDGJ$S^2S^{3p.c.}S^{5p.c.}$PRK$^{ed.}$; bā (hypometric) $S^{3a.c.}S^{5a.c.}$ 22d °kālayoḥ] TDGJ$S^2S^3S^5$PRK$^{ed.}$; °layoḥ (hypometric) C

---

137 P's reading of *anyadeśam upalabdham* is corrected by a later hand. The same hand records an *akṣara*, perhaps *ra*, above the line at the point where P had initially and erroneously read *anyadeśaṃm upalabdham*. 139 It is possible that $P^{a.c.}$ read *vārghaka*°. The correction is added by a later hand. 139 It is possible that R reads *bādhaṃka*° for *bādhaka*°. 139 In S^3, *dvayor* is added in the left margin by what appears to be a later hand. 140 The reading in P of °*kālo* for °*kāle* is added by a later hand. 140 *kāle 'nyadeśarajata*° is added in the right margin of S^3. 141 In S^2, the mark used to record the various *e-kāras* at *kālabhedena deśabhedasya* resemble the diagonally written flag of *devanāgarī* and not the usual horizontal line of *śāradā*.

---

137 rajatam] $D^{p.c.}$GJ$S^2S^3S^5$PRK$^{ed.}$; rajataṃm $D^{a.c.}$ 137 anyadeśam upalabdham] DGJ$S^2S^3S^5P^{p.c.}$K$^{ed.}$; anyadeśaṃm upalabdham $P^{a.c.}$R 138 rajatāśrayo] *conj.*; sarajatāśrayo $D^{p.c.}$GJ$S^2S^3S^5$PRK$^{ed.}$, saṃrajatāśrayo $D^{a.c.}$ 138 deśo] DGJ$S^2S^3S^{5p.c.}$PRK$^{ed.}$; deśaṃ $S^{5a.c.}$ 138 °jñānakāle] DGJ$S^2S^3S^{5p.c.}$PRK$^{ed.}$; °jñāne kāle $S^{5a.c.}$ 139 bādhaka°] DGJ$S^2S^3S^5P^{p.c.}$RK$^{ed.}$; vārdhaka° $P^{a.c.}$ 140 bhinnakālatvāt] DGJ$S^{2p.c.}S^3S^5$PRK$^{ed.}$; bhinnakālāt $S^{2a.c.}$ 140 °kāle] DGJ$S^2S^3S^5P^{a.c.}$RK$^{ed.}$; °kālo $P^{p.c.}$ 140 °kālo gataḥ] D$S^2S^3S^5$K$^{ed.}$; °kālāgataḥ GJPR 141 kālabhedena] DGJS^2S^5PRK$^{ed.}$; kāle bhedena S^3

---

135 T folio 7r. Note that folio 7 is marked with the appropriate Arabic numeral, but this appears on the verso and not the recto side of the palm leaf. 136 D folio 155v. 138 S^5 folio 58v. 140 P folio 49. 140 S^2 folio 92r. 140 D folio 156r.

jñānāntareṇa jñānaṃ tadvirodhād atha bādhyate
na bādho bhinnakālatvāt prāktanasyāpy abhāvataḥ 23

atha tasminn eva vastuni rajatajñānaṃ śuktikājñānaṃ ceti virodhāc chuktikājñānena rajatajñānasya bādho nivṛttiḥ kriyate. tan na. ekavastuni yugapadanyathātvam ayuktam. krameṇa tu kṣīradadhnor na virodhaḥ prāktanasya dṛṣṭasya svarasato darśananivṛttyā nivṛtteḥ, nābhāvataḥ.

23a S^2 inserts *oṃ* prior to ŚD 4.23. The verse was initially left out of the reading of the manuscript following *jñānāntareṇa*—this was the result of an eye-skip to °*jñānaṃ śuktikājñānaṃ* in the beginning of the relevant passage of the *Vṛtti*—, but the remainder of the verse is supplied in what appears to be the writing of the scribe (though in a smaller hand) in the top margin of the folio. Also supplied there is the beginning of the *Vṛtti* up to the point of the eye-skip. 23a ŚD 4.23ab is omitted from C.

23a jñānāntareṇa] DGJ$S^2S^3S^5$PR$K^{ed.}$; jñāntareṇa (hypometric) T, *om.* C 23c bādho] TDGJ$S^2S^3S^5$PR$K^{ed.}$; bodho C 23d prāktanasyāpy] TDGJ$S^2S^3S^5$PR$K^{ed.}$; prāktanasyā (hypometric) C 23d abhāvataḥ] TDGJ$S^2S^3S^5$PR$K^{ed.}$; avyvataḥ C

---

145 S^3 could be interpreted to read *nan na* for *tan na.* 146 A gap appears between *da* and *dhnor* in S^3, for no readily apparent reason. 147 S^3 records *nā* of its variant reading of °*nivṛttānivṛttenābhāvataḥ* below the last line of the folio, as the scribe apparently left out the *akṣara* in question prior to beginning to copy the text on the next folio side. 147 G and J record *ata eva* prior to a dotted line that indicates a certain amount of the text is lost.

---

144 śuktikājñānaṃ] GJ$S^2S^3S^5K^{ed.}$; śuktijñānaṃ D, *om.* PR 146 °anyathātvam] DJ$S^2S^3S^5$PR$K^{ed.}$; °anyathātmatvam G 146 tu] DGJ$S^2S^3S^5K^{ed.}$; *om.* PR 146 virodhaḥ] DGJ$S^{2p.c.}S^3S^5$PR$K^{ed.}$; virodha $S^{2a.c.}$ 147 svarasato] D$G^{p.c.}$J$S^2S^3S^5$P$K^{ed.}$; svarasvato $G^{a.c.}$, svaramato R 147 °nivṛttyā nivṛtteḥ, nābhāvataḥ] $K^{ed.}$; °nivṛttyā nivṛttenābhāvataḥ DGJS^2S^5, °nivṛttānivṛttenābhāvataḥ S^3PR

---

145 J folio 60r. 146 D folio 156v. 146 G folio 63v. 147 S^3 folio 26r.

sahānavasthitir nāsti virodhaḥ prāgvināśataḥ
anyonyaparihāro vā jñānājñānātmakaḥ sthitaḥ 24

sahānavasthitir api virodho nāsti. na hi jñānaṃ kṣaṇikatvena prāgvinaṣṭam anyena nivartanīyam uṣṇena śītam iva viruddhaṃ bhavati rajataśuktikā jñānayoḥ. na cānyonyaparihārātmako virodho jñānājñānātmako

---

24a S^{3} records gaps following *atrā* and following *na* and *vā* in its reading of *atrānavasthitir* for *sahānavasthitir.* (S^{5} records the same gaps following *na* and *va,* as does D.) Note also that ŚD 4.24 is not highlighted in S^{3}, as is the scribe's practice when recording the other verses of the *mūla.*

24a sahānavasthitir] TCK$^{ed.}$; - - - - sthitir GJ, atrānavasthitir DS^{2}S^{3}S^{5}, ata eva sthiter P$^{p.c.}$, ata eva sthitir P$^{a.c.}$R 24b virodhaḥ] TDGJS^{2}S^{3}S^{5}PRK$^{ed.}$; virādhaḥ C 24b prāgvināśataḥ] CDGJS^{2}S^{3}S^{5}PK$^{ed.}$; prā<?> - - - T, prāgvināśitaḥ R 24d jñānājñānātmakaḥ] TDGJS$^{2p.c.}$S^{3}S^{5}PRK$^{ed.}$; jñānājñānātmi (hypometric) C, jñānājñānānātmakaḥ S$^{2a.c.}$

---

150 S^{5} records two pair of short vertical lines, appearing similar to quotation marks, at a point equidistant from the beginning of ŚD 4.24 and *hā* of *sahānavasthitir,* the first line of the corresponding passage of the *Vṛtti.* It is unclear what these marks indicate, though they appear to have been written in the hand of the scribe. 150 Cf. NB 3.74: *dvividho hi padārthānāṃ virodhaḥ;* and NB 3.75: *avikalakāraṇasya bhavato 'nyabhāve 'bhāvād virodhagatiḥ.* 150 The curved top of the *i-kāra* in *virodho* appears to be missing in J. 151 See NB 3.76: *śītoṣṇasparśavat.* 152 Cf. NB 3.77: *parasparaparihārasthitalakṣaṇatayā vā bhāvābhāvavat.*

---

150 sahānavasthitir] DS^{2}S^{3}S^{5}PRK$^{ed.}$; hāvanasthitir G, - - hāvanasthitir J 152 rajataśuktikājñānayoḥ. na cānyonyaparihārātmako virodho jñānājñānātmako] *em.*; rajataśuktijñānayoḥ. na cānyonyaparihārātmako virodho jñānājñānātmako DGJS^{3}S^{5}K$^{ed.}$; rajataśuktijñānayoḥ. na cānyonyaparihārātmako virodho jñānājñātmako S^{2}, rajataśuktijñānājñānātmako PR

---

152 D change of folio side. Note this next folio side should be counted as folio 157r., but the scribe leaves it out of the enumeration of pages, because it is mostly left blank after its reading of °*bhāvabhāvayo* for °*bhāvābhāvayo.* See the note at line 153 of the present edition. 152 S^{2} folio 92v. 152 R folio 40r. 152 S^{5} folio 59r.

bhāvābhāvayoḥ...

ajñānatve parijñāte tadā syāt svavirodhitā
ajñānatve svabhāvena virodhaḥ kena vāryate 25

25a ŚD 4.25 is omitted from D, G, J, S^2, S^3, S^5, P and R.

25a parijñāte] $TK^{ed.}$; parijñātvā C, *om.* DGJ$S^2S^3S^5$PR 25b syāt] $TK^{ed.}$; syā C, *om.* DGJ$S^2S^3S^5$PR 25b svavirodhitā] $TK^{ed.}$; suavirodhitā C, *om.* DGJ$S^2S^3S^5$PR 25c svabhāvena] $TK^{ed.}$; sa bhāvatve C, *om.* DGJ$S^2S^3S^5$PR

---

153 P and R record the absence of commentary following *bhāvābhāvayoḥ* with three long dashes (- - -) and a large gap in the readings of the manuscripts that takes up most of a line of text in both P and R. G does the same with a long series of dots, which extend to long dashes and take up the remainder of the line and an entire line following. The remainder of the side of the folio is left blank, as is the entirety of the following folio side, which nevertheless is numbered in G. The dotted lines continue for two lines of text on folio 64v. J also marks the absence of text with a series of dotted lines, one filling the remainder of the line at which the text breaks, and three additional lines spaced across the remainder of the side of the folio, which is otherwise left blank to the bottom of the side of the folio in question. S^3 also does the same, recording a dotted line to the end of the last line on which text appeared on the side of the folio in question, followed by a gap of six lines of text. S^2, in turn, records a series of dots to the end of the line of text in question, the first line of folio 93v. The remainder of this side of the folio is left blank. S^5 records seven short dashes and leaves the remainder of the side of the folio blank. (Only °*bhāvābhāvayo* appears on the entire side of the folio.) Finally, D records three short dashes following its reading of °*bhāvabhāvayo* for °*bhāvābhāvayo*, and leaves the remainder of the folio side blank. There is writing of only one line of text, plust two *akṣaras* on a second line of text, on the folio side, and the folio side is left out of the enumeration of pages recorded by the scribe.

---

153 bhāvābhāvayoḥ] GJ$S^2S^3S^5$PR$K^{ed.}$; bhāvabhāvayoḥ D

---

153 G folios 64r. and 64v. are left blank, following a mostly blank folio indicating the presence of lost passages of the text. Similarly, J folios 60v. and 61r. are simply missing from the enumeration of the pages found in this manuscript. The numbering of folios noted in this edition reflects these absences.

naivam atra svabhāvatve virodho bādhanātmakaḥ
sa vivekadṛśā jñeyo na svabhāvena kutracit 26
tathā sarvavikalpānāṃ satyarūpatvadarśanāt
garuḍādiśarīreṣu viṣabhūtāpahārataḥ 27
pratiṣṭhādevakarmādidhyānādiphalayogataḥ
satye 'pi na phalaṃ dṛṣṭaṃ kvacid rājñātisevite 28
tasmād avasthitaṃ sarvaṃ sattvaṃ cidvyaktiyogitā
yatra yatrāsti satyatvaṃ tatrāsti śivarūpatā 29
vyatireke na yujyeta vijñānaṃ hi ghaṭādiṣu
mūrtāmūrtadharmayogo ghaṭas tasya na gocaraḥ 30
amūrtā na ca vāṇūnām antar eva praveśitā
pratipattuḥ kathaṃ vetti ghaṭo 'yaṃ pratibhedataḥ 31

26a ŚD 4.26 is omitted from D, G, J, S^2, S^3, S^5, P and R. 27a ŚD 4.27 is omitted from D, G, J, S^2, S^3, S^5, P and R. 28a ŚD 4.28 is omitted from D, G, J, S^2, S^3, S^5, P and R. 29a ŚD 4.29 is omitted from D, G, J, S^2, S^3, S^5, P and R. 30a ŚD 4.30 is omitted from D, G, J, S^2, S^3, S^5, P and R. 30b A short vertical line, probably marking the end of the half-verse, is crossed out in C. 30c What appears to be what had been intended as a long *ī* following C's reading of *mūrttāmūrtter* for *mūrtāmūrta*° is crossed out. 31a ŚD 4.31 is omitted from D, G, J, S^2, S^3, S^5, P and R. 31c ŚD 4.31cd is omitted in C.

26b virodho] T$K^{ed.}$; virodhā C, *om.* DGJ$S^2S^3S^5$PR 26b bādhanātmakaḥ] $K^{ed.}$; bādhan - - kaḥ T, vā canātmakaḥ C, *om.* DGJ$S^2S^3S^5$PR 26c °dṛśā] T$K^{ed.}$; °daśā C, *om.* DGJ$S^2S^3S^5$PR 27a °vikalpānāṃ] T$K^{ed.}$; °vivekānāṃ C, *om.* DGJ$S^2S^3S^5$PR 27b satyarūpatvadarśanāt] C$K^{ed.}$; satyārūpatvadarśanāt T, *om.* DGJ$S^2S^3S^5$PR 27c °śarīreṣu] T$K^{ed.}$; °śarīrepu C, *om.* DGJ$S^2S^3S^5$PR 27d viṣabhūtāpahārataḥ] T$K^{ed.}$; viṣabhūtā ā - hātaḥ C, *om.* DGJ$S^2S^3S^5$PR 28c satye 'pi] $K^{ed.}$; satyena T, satye (hypometric) C, *om.* DGJ$S^2S^3S^5$PR 28c dṛṣṭaṃ] C$K^{ed.}$; dṛ - - T, *om.* DGJ$S^2S^3S^5$PR 28d rājñātisevite] *conj.*; rājño [']tisevitāt T, rajño visevitāt C, *om.* DGJ$S^2S^3S^5$PR, ajñānisevitāt $K^{ed.}$ 29a avasthitaṃ] T$K^{ed.}$; eva sthitaṃ C, *om.* DGJ$S^2S^3S^5$PR 29c asti satyatvaṃ] T; atabhra (hypometric) C, *om.* DGJ$S^2S^3S^5$PR, tatra tatra $K^{ed.}$ 29d tatrāsti] T; satyatvaṃ C$K^{ed.}$, *om.* DGJ$S^2S^3S^5$PR 29d śiva°] TC; viśva° $K^{ed.}$, *om.* DGJ$S^2S^3S^5$PR 30a vyatireke] $K^{ed.}$; vyatireko T, vyatiru (hypometric) C, *om.* DGJ$S^2S^3S^5$PR 30a na] T$K^{ed.}$; *om.* (hypometric) C, *om.* DGJ$S^2S^3S^5$PR 30a yujyeta] T$K^{ed.}$; jyeta (hypometric) C, *om.* DGJ$S^2S^3S^5$PR 30b ghaṭādiṣu] T$K^{ed.}$; phalāduṣu C, *om.* DGJ$S^2S^3S^5$PR 30c mūrtāmūrtadharmayogo] T$K^{ed.}$; mūrttāmūrtter madhe yogo C, *om.* DGJ$S^2S^3S^5$PR 30d gocaraḥ] C$K^{ed.}$; - <o/e?> caraḥ T, *om.* DGJ$S^2S^3S^5$PR 31a vāṇūnām] T$K^{ed.}$; mānūnam C, *om.* DGJ$S^2S^3S^5$PR 31b eva] T$K^{ed.}$; e (hypometric) C, *om.* DGJ$S^2S^3S^5$PR 31c vetti] T$K^{ed.}$; veti C, *om.* DGJ$S^2S^3S^5$PR 31d pratibhedataḥ] C$K^{ed.}$; pratibheditaḥ T, *om.* DGJ$S^2S^3S^5$PR mūrtāmūrtādibhir dharmair yogo yasya ghaṭādeḥ sa, tasya vijñānasya ghaṭātmano vyatiriktaḥ san na gocaro bhavitum arhati. tad uktam Īśvarapratyabhijñāyāṃ

prāg ivārtho 'prakāśaḥ syāt... (ĪPK 1.5.2)

ityādinā. na ca vā ghaṭādayaḥ paramāṇurūpatve 'mūrtāḥ. asarvagatadravyaparimāṇaṃ deśayogyatā vāpi hi mūrtiḥ. tatas teṣām aṇūnāṃ bodhamayasya śivarūpasya pratipattur antar eva praveśitvam abheda ity arthaḥ. anyathā sa

---

169 $K^{ed.}$ records in the errata that its reading of *ghaṭātmano* is the product of a correction. The reading *ante correctionem* in the errata is illegible, however, though it appears to be *ghatmatmano*. And yet, $K^{ed.}$ records the correct reading in the edition itself, what suggests that the error was caught prior to printing, even as the editor failed to remove the correction from the errata. 171 ĪPK 1.5.2 reads as follows: *prāg ivārtho 'prakāśaḥ syāt prakāśātmatayā vinā | na ca prakāśo bhinnaḥ syād ātmārthasya prakāśatā ||* 173 What appears to have been a partially-written *akṣara* is struck out prior to *ṇaṃ* of °*parimāṇaṃ* in J. 173 Cf. PDhSaṃ (p. 734): *mūrtir asarvagatadravyaparimāṇaṃ tadanuvidhāyinī ca kriyā sā cākāśādiṣu nāsti tasmān na teṣāṃ kriyāsambandho 'stiti.* 174 P marks its erroneous reading of *partipattar* for *pratipattur* with a mark, shaped like a small plus-sign (+), above the mis-recorded *akṣaras*.

---

168 mūrtāmūrtādibhir] $K^{ed.}$; dibhir $DGJS^2S^3S^5PR$ 168 dharmair] $DGJS^2S^3S^5K^{ed.}$; dharme P, dharmai R 168 vijñānasya] $DGJS^2S^3PRK^{ed.}$; vijñānam asya $S^{5p.c.}$, vijñānatmasya $S^{5a.c.}$ 169 san na gocaro] $DGJS^2S^3S^5K^{ed.}$; sarvagocaro PR 173 teṣām] $DGJS^2S^3S^5P^{p.c.}RK^{ed.}$; teṣāmm $P^{a.c.}$ 174 pratipattur] $DGJS^2S^3S^5K^{ed.}$; partipattar PR 174 antar eva] $GJS^{2a.c.}S^3S^5PRK^{ed.}$; anteva $DS^{2p.c.}$ 174 praveśitvam] $DGJS^2S^3S^5K^{ed.}$; praveśatvam PR

---

168 G folio 65r. 168 D folio 158r. Note that the copyist of D here has left out ŚD 4.25-31. On the absence of folio sides 157r. and 157v., see my note at the folio change of D to 158v., below. 168 S^2 folio 93r. 168 S^5 folio 59v. 168 J folio 61v. J records two full dashed lines at the top of the folio, clearly to indicate that text is missing from the manuscript. On the numbering of this manuscript folio, see the remark in the bottom register of notes at line 153. 174 D folio 158v. Note that the present enumeration of folio pages reflects what is recorded in D. There, folio 157r. and 158v. are not recorded in the manuscript's enumeration of verses. There is a folio side that should be counted as 157r., but because it only records a few *akṣaras* at the point where a part of the ŚDVṛ is lost (in the middle of its commentary on ŚD 4.24), the folio side is not counted in D's enumeration of verses. This is to say I here preserve the enumeration of folios as recorded in D.

175 pratipattā pravibhedāt kāraṇāt kathaṃ ghaṭo 'yam iti vetti na kathañcij jānīyād
ity arthaḥ.

> vinaikatvaṃ ca na bhavet kārakatvaṃ kadācana
> śaśaśṛṅgādike nāpi syād vibhaktyā samanvayaḥ 32
> sarvathābhāvaśabdasya nāsty abhāvātmakaṃ kvacit

180 ghaṭādeś ca yad etat svakāryakaraṇaṃ bhavadbhir iṣyate, tac cidekarūpatvaṃ
vinā na syāt. jaḍasya nirabhisaṃdheḥ karaṇāyogād ity etad

32b ĪPK 2.4.16 offers a parallel to what is said at ŚD 4.32ab: *ata eva vibhakt-
yarthaḥ pramātrekasamāśrayaḥ | kriyākārakabhāvākhyo yukto bhāvasamanvayaḥ
||* See also the corresponding passage of the ĪPKVṛ: *ekapramātṛsaṃlagnas tu
kriyākārakabhāvākhyo vibhaktyartho bhūmibījodakādīnāṃ samanvayo yukto na
tu śuṣko 'nyaḥ kāryakāraṇabhāvaḥ.* 33b C appears to cross out the reading
abhāvātmekaṃ for *abhāvātmakaṃ*, and the appearance of the final *aunsvāra* is
occluded by a blotch in the manuscript.

32a vinaikatvaṃ] TDGJS²S³S⁵PRK^{ed.}; vinekatvaṃ C   32a   ca
] TDGJS²S³S⁵PRK^{ed.}; *om.* (hypometric) C   32d   samanvayaḥ] CDGJS²S³S⁵
PRK^{ed.}; samanvaya - T   33a   sarvathābhāvaśabdasya] DGJS²S³S⁵PRK^{ed.};
- vathābhāvaśabdasya T, sarvathāsarvabhāvaśabdasya (hypermetric) C   33b
nāsty abhāvātmakaṃ] TCGJS²S³K^{ed.}; nāsya bhāvātmakaṃ DS⁵PR

---

175   P marks its erroneous reading of *pravibhedat* for *pravibhedāt* with a
mark, shaped like a small plus-sign (+), above the mis-recorded *akṣara*.   180
J corrects its reading to *bhavadbhir* by adding the missing *akṣara* (i.e.: *dbhi*)
in the right margin.   181   See ĪPK 2.4.14, where what is articulated by
jaḍasya nirabhisaṃdheḥ is also expressed, viz., that that which is insentient
cannot "expect" or have motivation toward another entity: *asmin satīdam astīti
kāryakāraṇatāpi yā | sāpy apekṣāvihīnānāṃ jaḍānāṃ nopapadyate ||* See, also,
the corresponding passage of Utpaladeva's *Vṛtti*: *asmin satīdaṃ bhavatīti niy-
ataṃ paurvāparyaṃ kṛttikārohiṇyudayayor akāryakāraṇayor apy astīti pūrvasya
sāmarthye parasya satteti syāt kāryakāraṇabhāvaḥ, tac cāpekṣārahitānāṃ jaḍānāṃ
na yuktam. etāvad etat syāt pūrvasya sāmarthyaṃ parasya sattā na caivaṃ kiñcid
uktaṃ syān na ca pūrvasya sāmarthyalakṣaṇaḥ svabhāvaḥ parasattārūpaḥ.* Cf.
Torella 1994: 183, fn. 26

---

175   pravibhedāt] DGJS²S³S⁵K^{ed.}; pravibhedat PR   175   ghaṭo
] S²K^{ed.}; paṭo DGJS³S⁵PR   175   iti] GJS²S³S⁵K^{ed.}; *om.* DPR   180
bhavadbhir] DGJ^{p.c.}S²S³S⁵PRK^{ed.}; bhavar J^{a.c.}   180   cidekarūpatvaṃ
] DG^{p.c.}JS²S³S⁵^{p.c.}PRK^{ed.}; cikaderūpatvaṃ G^{a.c.}, cidekatvarūpatvaṃ S⁵^{a.c.}

---

178   C folio 9v.   179   S² folio 93v.   180   D folio 159r.

apīśvarapratyabhijñāyām evoktam. tasmād yad arthakriyākāritvāt sat, tat sarvaṃ śivarūpam. yad apy atyantāsattvenābhimataṃ śaśaśṛṅgādi tatrārthe vartamānasya sarvathaivābhāvavācitvena matasya śabdasya vibhaktyā yogo na syāt. śaśaśṛṅgaṃ jñāyate 'bhidhīyate ceti kārakāśritatvād vibhaktīnām asataś ca kārakatvāyogāt kriyānimittatvāt kārakasya. tasmāt tatrāpi vibhaktiyogena kārakatve sati sattaiva śivatākhyā. vastutaś ca ghaṭo 'rthakriyām udakāharaṇādikāṃ karotīti yo 'yaṁ avabodhaḥ, sa eva tathāsvarūpo na tu tataḥ pṛthagbhūto ghaṭādis tathākārī siddhyatīti pratyabhijñāyām eva himālayo nāmāstīti vicāre

---

182 Reference here to the *Īśvarapratyabhijñā* could be to ĪPK 2.4.16. Cf. ŚD 5.16-17ab: *jānan kartāram ātmānaṃ ghaṭaḥ kuryāt svakāṃ kriyām | ajñāte svātmakartṛtve na ghaṭaḥ sampravartate || svakarmaṇi mamaitat tad ity ajñānān na ceṣṭanam |* 182 P seems to record an extraneous *s* that is disconnected from what follows it, this prior to the final *t* of *arthakriyākāritvāt.* 183 See also Kumārila's ŚV (*abhāva* section), verse 4: *śiraso 'vayavā nimnā vṛddhikāṭhinyavarjitāḥ | śaśaśṛṅgādirūpeṇa so 'tyantābhāva ucyate ||* The same term used in the ŚV (*atyantābhāva*) is also found in Bhaṭṭa Jayanta's NM, as well, this in the first *āhnika*, section on *abhāva*, around verses 208*ff.* See NM (vol. 1, p. 166, lines 7-8 of the Mysore edition): *sa ca dvividhaḥ — prāgabhāvaḥ, pradhvaṃsābhāvaś ceti. caturvidha ity anye — itaretarābhāvaḥ, atyantābhāvaḥ, tau ca dvāv iti...* Cf. verse 210ab: *sa evāvadhiśūnyatvād atyantābhāvatāṃ gataḥ |* 184 A faint mark appears to correct P's reading of *sa tasya* to *matasya.* 184 In J, a mark above *śa* of *śabdasya* possibly could be interpreted to record *e*, meaning the text could be understood erroneously to read *śebdasya.* 185 Cf. PDhSaṃ: *ṣaṇṇām api padārthānām astitvābhidheyatvajñeyatvāni.* 189 Kālidāsa, *Kumārasaṃbhava* 1ab: *asty uttarasyāṃ diśi devatātmā himālayo nāma nagādhirājaḥ |* 189 Cp. with ĪPKVṛ ad ĪPK 2.4.20: *jaḍasyāpy asti bhavatīty asyām api sattākriyāyāṃ bubhūṣāyogena svātantryābhāvād akartṛtvam, tena pramātaiva taṃ bhāvayati tena tena vā himācalādinā rūpeṇa sa bhavatīty atra paramārthaḥ.* See also my notes to the translation, where it is conjectured that reference here is in fact to the *Vivṛti.*

---

182 evoktam] DGJS^{3}S^{5}PRK$^{ed.}$; evektam S^{2} 184 matasya] DK$^{ed.}$; sa tasya GJS^{2}S^{3}PR; sa tasyaṃ S^{5} 185 kārakāśritatvād] DS^{2}S^{5}PRK$^{ed.}$; kārakārakāśritatvād GJS^{3} 185 vibhaktīnām] DGJS^{2}S^{5}PRK$^{ed.}$; vibhaktīnāṃm S^{3} 186 kārakatvāyogāt] DGJS^{2}S^{3}S^{5}P$^{p.c.}$ K$^{ed.}$; kārakātvāyogāt P$^{a.c.}$R 187 ca] DGS^{2}S^{3}S^{5}PRK$^{ed.}$; tu J 187 'rthakriyām] DGJS^{2}S$^{3p.c.}$S^{5}PRK$^{ed.}$; [']rthikriyām S$^{3a.c.}$ 189 pratyabhijñāyām] DGJS^{2}S^{5}PRK$^{ed.}$; prāyabhijñāyām S^{3}

---

182 G folio 65v. 183 J folio 62r. 184 S^{5} folio 60r. 185 S^{3} folio 26v. 185 D folio 159v. 187 S^{2} folio 94r. 188 R folio 40v. 189 P folio 50. 189 D folio 160r.

darśitam. abhāvo 'pi jñāyamāno bodhātmaiva tadātmakatvāc ca śivarūpa eva. tasmān nāsty abhāvātmakam aśivarūpaṃ kvacid api viśvamadhye.

ito 'pi sarvaśivatā sata utpattiyogataḥ 33
sa evāste purā tādṛkśaktirūpasvarūpakaḥ
sa eva kāryarūpeṇa bhagavān avakalpate 34

ito 'pi hetoḥ sarvaśivatā yasmād utpattimadbhāvajātaṃ sad evotpadyate tatsvabhāvasya kāryātmanaḥ prāg api viruddhāsattāsaṃsparśāyogāt. tad eva ca prāg api sad aṅkurarūpaṃ syāt, yadi sattāsatattvo 'ṅkuraḥ śaktirūpaḥ pūrvam āste punar aṅkurātmakakāryarūpeṇa bhavati.

34a It is not possible to know whether J reads *evāste* or *evaste* (though one strongly suspects the latter), because a piece of tape covers *va*, the last *akṣara* of the line. 34b The final *ka* of °*svarūpakaḥ* in P is written in such a manner as to suggest the scribe might have first recorded *ta* in its place.

33c ito] TDGJ$S^2S^3S^5K^{ed.}$; to (hypometric) C, yato PR 33d sata utpattiyogataḥ] DGJ$S^2S^3S^5$PR$K^{ed.}$; tata utpattiyogataḥ T, sadutpattiṃ ca yogataḥ C 34a sa] TDGJ$S^2S^3S^5$PR$K^{ed.}$; ya C 34a evāste] TCDG$S^2S^3S^5$PR$K^{ed.}$; e<?>ste J 34a tādṛk] TDGJ$S^2S^3S^5$PR $K^{ed.}$; dādṛśa C 34b °śaktirūpasvarūpakaḥ] DGJ$S^2S^3S^5$P$K^{ed.}$; °śaktirūpaṃ sarūpakaḥ T, °śaktiṣasvarūpakaḥ C, °<?>ktirūpasvarūpakaḥ R 34c kārya°] TDGJ$S^2S^3S^5$PR$K^{ed.}$; kāma° C 34d avakalpate] DGJ$S^2S^3S^5$PR$K^{ed.}$; akalpate (hypometric) T, eva kalpyate C

---

191 It is not possible to know whether J reads *nasty* or *nāsty* (judging by the spacing one suspects the latter), because a piece of tape covers *na*, the last *akṣara* of the line. 195 G records a gap following *sarvaśivatā*. J punctuates in the same place. 195 G records a gap following *sad evotpadyate*. 196 G seems to delete an *anusvāra* following it's reading of *viruddāsatta*° for *viruddhāsattā*°. 196 S^2 marks the presence of an *avagraha* that indicates one should understand the *sandhi* of *viruddhāsattā*° to conceal a reading of *viruddhā asattā*°.

---

190 jñāyamāno] DGJS^2S^5PR$K^{ed.}$; jñāno S^3 190 śivarūpa] *em.*; viśvarūpa DGJ$S^2S^3S^5$PR$K^{ed.}$ 191 nāsty] DG$S^2S^3S^5$PR$K^{ed.}$; <?>sty J 195 utpattimadbhāvajātaṃ] DG$S^2S^3S^5$PR$K^{ed.}$; utpattisadbhāvajātaṃ J 195 utpadyate] DGJ$S^2S^3S^5K^{ed.}$; utpadyeta PR 196 viruddhāsattā°] DJ$S^2S^3S^5$PR$K^{ed.}$; viruddhāsatta° G 196 °saṃsparśāyogāt] DGJS^2S^5PR$K^{ed.}$; °saṃsparśāyogā S^3 196 eva] $K^{ed.}$; evaṃ DGJ$S^2S^3S^5$PR 197 śaktirūpaḥ] DGJ$S^2S^3S^5K^{ed.}$; śivarūpaḥ PR

---

195 G folio 66r. 195 D folio 160v. 196 S^2 folio 94v. 196 J folio 62v. 198 S^5 folio 60v.

satkāryaṃ nopapannaṃ cet sataḥ kiṃ karaṇena yat
abhivyaktir athāsyātra kriyate sāpi kiṃ satī 35
kriyate hy asatī vātha satyāḥ kiṃ nopalabdhatā
vyaktyabhāvād athānantyam asatyā hānisaṃbhavaḥ 36
svayam evāśrite pakṣe tadvad vā vastv asad bhavet

atha yadi sadrūpaṃ kāryaṃ nopapannaṃ sataḥ karaṇaṃ viphalaṃ yasmāt. atha sataḥ svarūpaṃ na kriyate 'pi tu tasyābhivyaktis tad api na yuktaṃ, yataḥ

36a The erroneous reading of *votha* for *vātha* in T is oddly recorded. The short diphthong appears to have been written by the scribe who copied the manuscript, but it is recorded in a very small hand and appears as if appended to *vā*, showing thereby a crowding in the writing, as well.

35a satkāryaṃ nopapannaṃ] $DGJS^{2}S^{3}S^{5}PRK^{ed.}$; s - kāryaṃ nopapannaṃ T, satkāryeṇa kāryeṇa pattraṃ (hypermetric) C 35a cet] $TDGJS^{2}S^{3}S^{5}PRK^{ed.}$; cetha C 35b sataḥ] $TGJS^{2}S^{3}S^{5}PRK^{ed.}$; *om.* C, <?>taḥ D 35b karaṇena] $CDGJS^{2}S^{3}S^{5}PRK^{ed.}$; karaṇana T 35c abhivyaktir athāsyātra] $DGJS^{2}S^{3}S^{5}PRK^{ed.}$; abhivyarasathāsyātra T, abhivyaktimadhyānyatra C 35d satī] $TDGJS^{2}S^{3}S^{5}PRK^{ed.}$; sati C 36a asatī] $TDGJS^{2}S^{3}S^{5}PRK^{ed.}$; asati C 36a vātha] $CDGJS^{2}S^{3}S^{5}PRK^{ed.}$; votha T 36b satyāḥ] $TDGJS^{2}S^{3}S^{5}PRK^{ed.}$; sa (hypometric) C 36b upalabdhatā] $TDGJS^{2}S^{3}S^{5}PRK^{ed.}$; upaladhvikāṃ C 36c vyaktyabhāvād] $TDGJS^{2p.c.}S^{3}S^{5}PRK^{ed.}$; vṛktyabhāvād C, vyaktabhāvād $S^{2a.c.}$ 36c athānantyam] $DGJS^{2}S^{3}S^{5}K^{ed.}$; athāsat- yam C, athānantya TPR 36d asatyā] $CDGJS^{2}S^{3}S^{5}K^{ed.}$; asamatyā (hypermetric) T, satyā PR 36d hānisaṃbhavaḥ] $DGJS^{2p.c.}S^{3}S^{5}PRK^{ed.}$; hāni - gamaḥ T, hānisaṃgamaḥ C, hinisambhavaḥ $S^{2a.c.}$ 37b vastv asad bhavet] $DGJS^{2p.c.}S^{3}S^{5}K^{ed.}$; vastv asaṃbhavet T, vaskta saṃbhavet C, vastu saṃbhavet $S^{2a.c.}P$, vastv asaṃbhavet R

---

204 G records a gap following *nopapannaṃ*. 204 G records a gap following *viphalaṃ yasmāt*. 205 The scribe of S^{2} records everything from *tad api* to *tad abhivyakter apy abhivyaktiḥ* in the bottom margin in a smaller hand, having at first omitted the passage by an eye-skip. 205 G records a gap following *na yuktaṃ*. 205 Cf. NBhūṣ, p. 459: *kāryasyābhivyaktiḥ kāraṇena kriyata iti cet, sā yady asatī kriyate, tato 'sat kāryaṃ syāt. satī ced abhivyaktis tadavasthaṃ kārakānarthakyam. abhivyakter apy abhivyaktiḥ kriyata iti cet, sāpi satī syād asatī vety aparyavasānam.*

---

204 upapannaṃ] $DGJS^{2p.c.}S^{3}S^{5}P^{p.c.}RK^{ed.}$; upapanaṃ $P^{a.c.}$, nopannaṃ $S^{2a.c.}$
205 tu] $DGJS^{2}S^{3}S^{5}PR^{p.c.}K^{ed.}$; ta $R^{a.c.}$

---

200 D folio 161r.

sāpi kiṃ satī kriyetāthāsatī. tatra satī ced abhivyaktis tat kiṃ kriyate kimiti kāryasya nopalabdhatā. atha sattve 'py abhivyakter abhivyaktyabhāvāt kāryaṃ nopalabdham, tad abhivyakter apy abhivyaktiḥ kriyata iti tatrāpi pūrvoktāt pātād ānantyam anavasthā, tataś ca prakṛtakāryadarśanānirvṛttiḥ. athāsatī kriyate 'bhivyaktis tad asatyāḥ karaṇe svayam āśritapakṣahāniprasaṅgaḥ. anavasthāparihārārthaṃ vābhivyaktāv asatkaraṇāśrayaṇe 'bhivyaktivad vastv apy aṅkurādikam asad eva. satkāryam astu kim ardhajaratīyena.

---

206 G records a gap following *tat kiṃ kriyate.* 207 P and R record the absence of a passage of text following *atha* and prior to *sattve 'pi* with three dashes (- - -). G records the same with three dots, J with two dashes. Note, however, that no text is recorded as absent in K$^{ed.}$, nor in S^2, S^3, or S^5—all of which carry the same reading as do P and R. (Note also the absence of the first *akṣara* of *sattva* in G and J. Perhaps the marks noting missing text have survived in the course of transmission of the readings of a witness similar to G or J, even though nothing more than this single *akṣara* was missing.) 207 G omits *abhivyaktyabhāvāt kāryaṃ nopalabdham, tad abhivyakter apy* by an eye-skip. 208 G records a gap following *kriyata iti.* 209 P marks its erroneous reading of *patād* (for *pātād*) with a plus sign (+) above the initial vowel. 211 The reading of P for °*āśrayaṇe* is corrected by a later hand. 212 Note that I add punctuation following *asad eva*. It is absent from K$^{ed.}$. D and R, however, leave a gap following *asad eva*, suggesting the copyists also wished to punctuate there with a full stop.

---

206 yataḥ sā] DGJS^{2}S^{3}S^{5}K$^{ed.}$; ya tasmāt P$^{a.c.}$, sa tasmāt P$^{p.c.}$, ya tasmād R 206 kriyetātha] D$^{p.c.}$GJS^{2}S^{3}S^{5}PRK$^{ed.}$; kriyethā D$^{a.c.}$ 206 abhivyaktis] DGJS^{2}S^{5}PRK$^{ed.}$; abhivyakti S^3 206 kriyate] DGJS^{2}S^{3}S^{5}P$^{p.c.}$K$^{ed.}$; kriyato P$^{a.c.}$R 206 kimiti] GJS^{3}S^{5}K$^{ed.}$; kim api DS^{2}PR 207 sattve] DS^{2}S^{3}S^{5}PRK$^{ed.}$; ttve GJ 207 abhivyaktyabhāvāt] DJS^{2}S^{3}S^{5}PRK$^{ed.}$; *om.* G, abhivyaktrabhāvāt (Ratié) 207 kāryaṃ] DJS^{2}S^{3}S^{5}RK$^{ed.}$; *om.* G, kārya P 208 abhivyaktiḥ] DGJS^{2}S^{5}PRK$^{ed.}$; abhivyakti S^3 208 pūrvoktāt] DGJS^{2}S^{3}S^{5}K$^{ed.}$; pūrvoktān PR 209 pātād] DGJS^{2}S^{3}S^{5}K$^{ed.}$; patād PR 209 °darśanānirvṛttiḥ] DS$^{2a.c.}$S$^{5p.c.}$PRK$^{ed.}$; °darśanānivṛttiḥ GJS$^{2p.c.}$S^{3}S$^{5a.c.}$ 210 asatyāḥ] DGJS^{2}S^{5}K$^{ed.}$; asatyā PRS^3 211 asatkaraṇa°] DS^{2}S^{3}S^{5}PRK$^{ed.}$; asatkāraṇa° GJ 211 °āśrayaṇe] D$^{p.c.}$JS^{2}S^{5}P$^{p.c.}$K$^{ed.}$; °āśrayeṇe D$^{a.c.}$, °āśrayeṇa G, °āśriyaṇe S^3, °āśrayane P$^{a.c.}$R 211 'bhivyaktivad] DGJS^{2}S^{3}S^{5}RK$^{ed.}$; [']bhivyakti<?>t P 211 vastv apy] DGJS^{2}S^{3}S^{5}RK$^{ed.}$; vastu pi P 212 ardhajaratīyena] DGJS^{2}S^{3}S^{5}K$^{ed.}$; anujaratīyena PR

---

206 D folio 161v. 208 S^2 folio 95r. 209 G folio 66v. 211 R folio 41r. 211 D folio 162r. 211 J folio 63r.

naivaṃ yasmāt tāṃ vihāya sarvatrānyatra satkriyā 37
ity abhyupagamo 'smākaṃ naikenānyatra tulyatā
kalpyā vaiśeṣikāṇāṃ hi kartṛtaiveśvare sthitā 38
tadvan na kiṃ pṛthivyāder bauddhe jñānam avasthitam
svānyaprakāśakaṃ nānyat tadvad anyan na kiṃ bhavet 39
bāhyaṃ rūpādi jalpanti pramāṇaṃ codanaiva te
niyamād dharmaviṣaye tasmān naikena tulyatā 40

37c A footnote in $K^{ed.}$ (p. 162) suggests that one source examined for the KSTS edition (*kha*) records a variant of °*vaṃ ca*, but it is not clear for what this is a variant reading. 37c C erroneously records *tāṃ* twice. 38c In J, *pyā* of *kalpyā* is blotched, perhaps indicating that the scribe here made a correction to the text. 38c G records a vertical line following *vai* of *vaiśeṣikāṇāṃ*. 39a C marks the absence of two *akṣaras* following *ta* of *tadvad na* with a dash-mark and by leaving a space in its reading following the initial *akṣara*. 40a A footnote in $K^{ed.}$ (p. 163) suggests that one source examined for the KSTS edition reads *kalpanti*, and this may refer to the fact that D, one manuscript examined by Kaul, reads *kalpanti* at ŚD 4.40a, whereas $K^{ed.}$ (and several other manuscripts) read *jalpanti*. 40d Though the manuscript is here badly damaged, one can almost make out *tā* in T where $K^{ed.}$ and several mss. read *tulyatā*.

37c yasmāt] TDGJ$S^2S^3S^5$PR$K^{ed.}$; yasmā C 37d sarvatrānyatra] DGJ$S^2S^3S^5$PR$K^{ed.}$; sarvaṃ nānya (hypometric) T, sarvaṃ nānyatra C 38a ity] TDGJ$S^2S^3S^5$PR$K^{ed.}$; ito C 38a abhyupagamo 'smākaṃ] TDGJ$S^2S^3S^5$PR$K^{ed.}$; abhyupagamāsmākaṃ C 38b naikena] TDGJ$S^2S^3S^5$PR$K^{ed.}$; nekena C 38b tulyatā] TDGJ$S^2S^3S^5$PR$K^{ed.}$; tulyatāṃ C 38c kalpyā] TCDJ$S^2S^3S^5$PR$K^{ed.}$; kalpā G 38c vaiśeṣikāṇāṃ] DGJ$S^{2p.c.}S^3S^5$PR$K^{ed.}$; vaiśeṣikāṇā - T, veṣeśiṇāṃ (hypometric) C, vaiśeṣakānāṃ $S^{2a.c.}$ 38c hi] CDGJ$S^2S^3S^5$PR$K^{ed.}$; - T 38d kartṛtaiveśvare] DGJ$S^2S^3S^5K^{ed.}$; karttanaiveśvara T, kartṛtaiveśvarā C, kartṛtaivaśvare PR 39a tadvan na] TDGJ$S^2S^3S^5$PR$K^{ed.}$; ta (hypometric) C 39b bauddhe] DGJ$S^2S^3S^5$P$K^{ed.}$; boddhe T, jādve C, vāddhe R 39b avasthitam] CDGJ$S^2S^3S^5$PR$K^{ed.}$; avasthi<?>am T 39d anyan na] TCDGJS^3S^5PR$K^{ed.}$; anyatra S^2 39d bhavet] TDGJ$S^2S^3S^5$PR$K^{ed.}$; chivet C 40a bāhyaṃ rūpādi] DGJ$S^2S^3S^5$PR$K^{ed.}$; bāhyarūpādi TC 40a jalpanti] TCGJ$S^{2p.c.}$PR$K^{ed.}$; kalpanti D$S^{2a.c.}S^3S^5$ 40c niyamād] TDGJ$S^2S^3S^5$PR$K^{ed.}$; niyamādh C 40c °viṣaye] CDGJ$S^2S^3S^5$PR$K^{ed.}$; °viṣa - e T 40d tasmān] CDGJ$S^2S^3S^5$PR$K^{ed.}$; - - T 40d naikena] CDGJ$S^2S^3S^5$P$K^{ed.}$; - - - T, nekena R 40d tulyatā] DGJ$S^2S^3S^5$PR$K^{ed.}$; - t - l<?> - <?> T, tulyatāṃ C

---

213 S^5 folio 61r. 214 S^3 folio 27r. 216 D folio 162v. 218 S^2 folio 95v.

bahūnāṃ kalpanīyātra na ca vā vyatirekataḥ
vyaktiḥ sthitā padārthānāṃ ghaṭo vyakto 'bhidhīyate 41
tasmāt sa eva vyaktyātmā na vyakter vyatiriktatā

tvaduktam eva na yuktaṃ yasmāt tām abhivyaktiṃ varjayitvānyat sad eva kāryam ity asmākaṃ tāvad abhyupagamaḥ. na hi sarvatra darśane sarvair evārthais tulyair bhāvyam. tathā hi vaiśeṣikeṣv īśvara eva viśvakartā, na tu pṛthivyādi dravyam. bauddhadarśane jñānam eva svaparaprakāśakaṃ, na rūpādi. te jaiminīyā jalpanti codanaiva niyamena dharmaviṣaye pramāṇaṃ

41a T is damaged at *bahūnāṃ* but is nevertheless legible. 41b A mark indicating that the end of a passage of text has been reached is recorded in the right margin of D following *vyatirekataḥ* (what is corrected there from *vyatirekatāḥ*). 41c A blotch mark covering the bottom of the final *akṣara* of *vyaktisthitā*, the reading for *vyaktiḥ sthitā* in C, leads one to believe it is possible, though unlikely, that the manuscript there reads *vyaktisthicā*.

41a kalpanīyātra] TDGJ$S^2S^3S^5$PRK$^{ed.}$; kalpanīyatra C 41b vā] TCDGJ$S^2S^3S^5$PRK$^{ed.}$; sā *conj.* (Ratié) 41b vyatirekataḥ] TCD$^{p.c.}$GJ$S^2S^3S^5$ PRK$^{ed.}$; vyatirekatāḥ D$^{a.c.}$ 41c vyaktiḥ sthitā] TDGJ$S^2S^3S^5$PRK$^{ed.}$; vyaktisthitā C 42a sa eva] TDGJ$S^2S^3S^5$PRK$^{ed.}$; saiva C 42a vyaktyātmā] *conj.*; vyaktātmā TDGJ$S^2S^3S^5$PRK$^{ed.}$, vyaktyātā C

---

223 In J, *bhi* of *abhivyaktiṃ*, though slightly blotched, appears to be recorded correctly, but the scribe marks it with a small circle above the *akṣara* and again records *bhi* next to a corresponding small circle in the right margin. 224 P's reading of *sarvar* for *sarvair* is corrected by a later hand. 225 P's reading of *arthes* for *arthais* is corrected by a later hand. 225 D appears to have recorded *vaiśeṣikeṣveśvara* before writing over that reading with *vaiśeṣikeṣv īśvara*. 225 P marks its erroneous reading of *nṛta* for *na tu* with a small plus sign (+) above *nṛ*. 227 P marks its (correct) reading of *te* with a small plus sign (+) above the *akṣara* in question. 227 The *o* of *codanaiva* in S^3 is partially obscured due to the manner in which the scribe recorded it, making it possible to understand (wrongly, in my view) the manuscript there to read *cādanaiva*.

---

223 tvaduktam] DGJ$S^2S^3S^5$K$^{ed.}$; taduktam PR 224 sarvair] DGJ$S^2S^3S^5$P$^{p.c.}$RK$^{ed.}$; sarvar P$^{a.c.}$ 225 arthais] DGJ$S^2S^3S^5$P$^{p.c.}$RK$^{ed.}$; sarves P$^{a.c.}$ 225 vaiśeṣikeṣv] DGJ$S^2S^3S^5$PK$^{ed.}$; vaiśeṣikaṭ R 225 na tu] DGJ$S^2S^3S^5$K$^{ed.}$; nṛta PR 226 bauddha°] DG$S^2S^3S^5$PRK$^{ed.}$; bāddha° J 227 jaiminīyā] GJK$^{ed.}$; jaimineyā D$S^2S^3S^5$PR 227 codanaiva] DGJ$S^2S^3S^5$K$^{ed.}$; caidanaiva PR 227 niyamena] DGJ$S^2S^3S^{5p.c.}$PRK$^{ed.}$; *om.* $S^{5a.c.}$ 227 dharmaviṣaye] DGJ$S^{2p.c.}S^3S^5$PRK$^{ed.}$; dharcaviṣaye $S^{2a.c.}$

---

223 D folio 163r. 224 P folio 51. 225 G folio 67r. 227 J folio 63v. 227 S^2 folio 96r.

codanālakṣaṇo 'rtho dharmaḥ (MīSū 1.1.2)

iti, na tu pratyakṣādikam. tasmād bahūnām ekalakṣaṇānāṃ pramāṇānāṃ prameyāṇāṃ vā naikena bhinnalakṣaṇābhimatenānyasyāpi tulyatāpādanadoṣa udbhāvanīyaḥ. tena sarveṣām arthānāṃ satām eva kāryatā. tathāpy abhivyaktir asaty eva kāryā, yathā dharme na codanāvad anyāny api pramāṇāni, yathā neśvaradravyavat pṛthivyādidravyam api viśvakāraṇam. upapattir api cātrāsti, nābhyupagamamātram. tathābhivyaktis tāvan nārthād vyatirekeṇa sthitā tathānupalambhāt. abhedenaiva ca vyavahāraḥ. tathā hi ghaṭo vyakto 'bhidhīyate

---

228 P deletes what appears to be *ta* prior to *dharmaḥ*. 229 I cannot make out whether J records the long *ū* of *bahūnām*, this only due to the quality of the reproduction I have in my possession of the manuscript, which appears to be free of any physical damage. 229 S^{2} first leaves out *pramāṇānāṃ* but adds it in the right margin in a small hand that appears to be that of the scribe. Ratié 2014: 157, fn. 101 records *pramāṇāṃ* for *pramāṇānāṃ*, what is clearly a mere typographical error. 233 In S^{2}, *api* is partially illegible before *pi* is rewritten above the *akṣara* in question. 234 J's (correct) reading of *nābhyupagamamātram* is blotched rather severly at *ābhyu*, but is nevertheless legible. 235 See PV (*pratyakṣapariccheda*) 3.335: *darśanopādhirahitasyāgrahāt tadgrahe grahāt | darśanaṃ nīlanirbhāsaṃ nārtho bāhyo 'sti kevalam ||* 235 P and R record *ca vyavahāraḥ. tathā hi ghaṭo vyana* following *vyakto 'bhidhīyate vyaktyabhedena*. The penultimate syllable of this string (*vya* of the nonsensical *vyana*) is marked as erroneous with a small plus mark (+) above the *akṣara* in question.

---

228 codanālakṣaṇo] DS^{2}S^{3}S^{5}K$^{ed.}$; codalakṣaṇo GJ, niyamena PR 230 vā] GS$^{2p.c.}$PRK$^{ed.}$; <?>ā J, *om.* DS$^{2a.c.}$S^{3}S^{5} 230 °doṣa] D$^{p.c.}$GJS^{2}S^{3}S^{5}PRK$^{ed.}$; °doṣo D$^{a.c.}$ 231 udbhāvanīyaḥ] GJS^{2}S^{3}S^{5}P$^{p.c.}$RK$^{ed.}$; dbhāvanīyaḥ D, udbhāvanīyāḥ P$^{a.c.}$ 231 sarveṣām] DGJS^{3}S^{5}PRK$^{ed.}$; sarveṣāṃm S^{2} 231 satām] DGJS$^{2p.c.}$S^{3}S^{5}PRK$^{ed.}$; *om.* S$^{2a.c.}$ 232 asaty eva] *conj.* (Ratié); asatyaiva DGJS^{2}S^{3}S^{5}PRK$^{ed.}$ 232 dharme na] D$^{p.c.}$K$^{ed.}$; dharmeṇa D$^{a.c.}$GJS^{2}S^{3}S^{5}PR 234 abhyupagamamātram] DGJS$^{2p.c.}$S^{3}S^{5}PRK$^{ed.}$; abhyupagamātram S$^{2a.c.}$ 234 vyatirekeṇa] DGJS^{2}S^{3}S^{5}P$^{p.c.}$RK$^{ed.}$; vyaktirekeṇa P$^{a.c.}$ 235 tathā] DGJS^{2}S^{3}S^{5}RK$^{ed.}$; *om.* P 235 ca] DGJS^{2}S^{5}PRK$^{ed.}$; *om.* S^{3} 235 vyakto] DGJS^{2}S^{3}S^{5}K$^{ed.}$; vyana PR

---

229 D folio 163v. 230 S^{5} folio 61v. 233 D folio 164r. 234 R folio 41v.

vyaktyabhedena. tasmāt padārtha eva vyaktyātmā. sa ca san kriyate, na tu vyakter vyatiriktāyā asatyāḥ karaṇam.

dīpena kriyate vyaktir ghaṭādeḥ sata eva vā 42
yathā sataḥ kriyā vyaktir vyakteḥ sattve tathā kṛtiḥ
ekenāparatulyatvān na ca vāsata udbhavaḥ 43
kim āśritya pravartante tadabhāvasvarūpataḥ

naivaitad apūrvam. pradīpena hi ghaṭādeḥ sata evābhivyaktiḥ kriyata iti padārtha eva kriyate. tataś ca yathā sato ghaṭāder vyaktisaṃjñā kriyā tathā

42c In C, *vyakti* is crossed out prior to the correct reading (*kriyate*) found there. 43a $K^{ed.a.c.}$ records *kriyāvyaktir vyakte* (no hiatus between *kriyā* and *vyaktir*), while $K^{ed.p.c.}$ records the hiatus: *kriyā vyaktir vyakteḥ*. 43b It is damage to T at *kṛtiḥ* that renders the first *akṣara* illegible.

42c kriyate] CDGJ$S^2S^3S^5$PR$K^{ed.}$; kriya - e T 42c vyaktir] CDGJ$S^2S^3S^5$PR$K^{ed.}$; - - T 42d ghaṭādeḥ] CDGJ$S^2S^3S^5$PR$K^{ed.}$; - - - T 42d sata] DGJ$S^2S^3S^5$PR$K^{ed.}$; - - T, tata C 42d eva vā] CDGJ$S^2S^3S^5$PR$K^{ed.}$; - - - T 43a yathā] CDGJ$S^2S^3S^5$PR$K^{ed.}$; - - T 43a sataḥ] CDGJ$S^2S^3S^5K^{ed.}$; - t - T, sa tat° PR 43a kriyā] CDGJ$S^2S^3S^5$PR$K^{ed.}$; - iy - T 43a vyaktir] CDGJ$S^2S^3S^5$PR$K^{ed.}$; - ktir T 43b vyakteḥ] TCGJ$K^{ed.p.c.}$; vyakte D$S^2S^3S^5$PR$K^{ed.a.c.}$ 43b kṛtiḥ] CDGJ$S^2S^3S^5$PR$K^{ed.}$; <?>tiḥ T 43c °tulyatvān] TDGJS^2S^5PR$K^{ed.}$; °tulyatvā C, °tulyatān S^3 43d na ca vā] TDGJ$S^2S^3S^5$PR$K^{ed.}$; na cā vā C, na caiva *conj.* (Ratié) 44a pravartante] CDGJ$S^2S^3S^5$PR$K^{ed.}$; pravartteta T 44b tadabhāva°] TGJ$K^{ed.}$; tadabhā° (hypometric) C, bhedabhāva° D$S^2S^3S^5$PR

---

236 A footnote in $K^{ed.}$ (p. 163) suggests that one source examined for that edition (*kha*) offers a variant reading of *vyaktibhedena*. This probably serves to mark the reading of *vyaktibhedena* in D for *vyaktyabhedena* (which appears on line 2 of p. 164 of $K^{ed.}$, 26 lines down from the beginning of the section of text and commentary in question, if one includes two lines for the two notes recorded on p. 163 of the edition). 236 S^2 inserts *parārtha eva vyaktātmā* following its reading of *vyāktātmā* (for my conjectured reading of *vyaktyātmā*); the same is marked off as added text by the scribe.

---

236 vyaktyabhedena] GJ$S^{2p.c.}S^3S^5$PR$K^{ed.}$; vyaktibhedena D, vyaktabhedena $S^{2a.c.}$ 236 vyaktyātmā] *conj.*; vyaktātmā DGJS^3S^5PR$K^{ed.}$, vyaktātmāt S^2 236 sa ca san kriyate, na] D$S^5K^{ed.}$; sa ca sat kriyate na GJS^2S^3, sa ca satkriyena PR 237 vyatiriktāyā] DGJ$S^2S^3S^5$R$K^{ed.}$; vyaktiriktāyā P 237 karaṇam] GJP$K^{ed.}$; kāraṇam D$S^2S^3S^5$R 242 naivaitad] D$S^2S^3S^5$PR$K^{ed.}$; naiva naitad GJ 243 sato] $K^{ed.}$; yato DGJ$S^2S^3S^5$PR

---

236 S^2 folio 96v. 238 G folio 67v. 239 D folio 164v. 242 J folio 64r.

vyakter api padārtharūpāyāḥ satyā eva pradīpādinā kṛtiḥ, bījādinā vāṅkurarūpāyā iti sarvatra tulyaḥ satkāryavādaḥ. yataḥ padārthena satā kāryeṇa vyakter api tadabhinnāyās tulyatvam. vyaktiś ca prakāśamānatā prakāśātmatā, aṅkurāder anādinidhanasya sata eva citprakāśasya tena tenātmanāvasthānam ity abhivyaktivādinā satkāryavāda ukto bhavati. yadi cāsataḥ kāryasyotpattis tadā kārakāṇi kim āśritya kim uddiśya pravartante vyāpriyante, kāryakāraṇabhāvasya kriyākārakasaṃbandhamānatveneśvarapratyabhijñāyāṃ pravartanaṃ pākādyārambhe rūpam iva coditam. athavā kim uddiśya pravartante kasmin viṣaye teṣāṃ sāmarthyaṃ, viṣayābhāve sāmarthyasyānupapatter

---

244 The second syllable of *satyā* in P is blotched. Perhaps *v* was initially recorded for *t*. 244 S^2 deletes *satyā eva pradipāyāḥ* prior to *satyā eva pradīpādinā*. 246 P appears initially to have read *tadabhitāyās* for *tadabhinnāyās*. R, in turn, could be interpreted to read *tadabhittāyās* for *tadabhinnāyās*. 248 What is said here in the ŚDVṛ (lines 246-248) echoes ĪPK (and ĪPKVṛ ad) 2.4.16: *ata eva vibhaktyarthaḥ pramātrekasamāśrayaḥ | kriyākārakabhāvākhyo yukto bhāvasamanvayaḥ* || ĪPKVṛ: *ekapramātṛsaṃlagnas tu kriyākārakabhāvākhyo vibhaktyartho bhūmibījodakādīnāṃ samanvayo yukto na tu śuṣko 'nyaḥ kāryakāraṇabhāvaḥ*. 249 *ki* of *kim* is recorded in the right margin of P. 249 A footnote in K$^{ed.}$ (p. 165) suggests that one source examined for that edition (*kha*) reads *bheda*, but it is unclear for what this is a variant reading. 250 *ne* of °*tveneśvara*° is almost illegible in my reproduction of J. 251 A later hand crosses out an illegible pair of *akṣaras* and replaces them with *pava* above G's reading of *rūpa* for *rūpam iva*. *pava* is also recorded in a very small, later hand in J, above *rūpa*.

---

244 satyā] DGJS^{2}S^{3}S^{5}PK$^{ed.}$; savyā R 244 bījādinā] DGJS^{2}S^{3}S$^{5p.c.}$PRK$^{ed.}$; bījācīdinā S$^{5a.c.}$ 244 °rūpāyā] DGJS^{2}S^{5}PRK$^{ed.}$; °rūpāya S^3 245 satā] JS^{2}S^{3}S^{5}K$^{ed.}$; sataḥ DGPR 245 vyakter] DGJS^{2}S^{5}RK$^{ed.}$; vyaktir S^3, vyākter P 247 anādi°] DG$^{p.c.}$JS^{2}S^{3}S^{5}PRK$^{ed.}$; anāde° G$^{a.c.}$ 249 kārakāṇi] DGJS^{2}S$^{3p.c.}$S^{5}PRK$^{ed.}$; kāraṇakāṇi S$^{3a.c.}$ 249 pravartante] DGJS^{2}S^{3}S^{5}PK$^{ed.}$; pravartate R 249 vyāpriyante] K$^{ed.p.c.}$; vyākriyante DGJS^{2}S^{3}S^{5}PK$^{ed.a.c.}$, vyākriyate R 250 īśvarapratyabhijñāyāṃ] GJS^{2}S^{3}S^{5}PRK$^{ed.}$; īścarapratyabhijñāyāṃ D 251 pravartanaṃ] GJPRK$^{ed.}$; ravartanaṃ S$^{2p.c.}$, *om.* DS$^{2a.c.}$S^{3}S^5 251 pākādyārambhe] DGJS^{2}S^{3}S^{5}P$^{p.c.}$K$^{ed.}$; pakādyārambhe P$^{a.c.}$R 251 rūpam iva coditam] DS^{2}S^{3}S^{5}PRK$^{ed.}$; rūpacoditam GJ 252 anupapatter] DGJS^{3}S^{5}PRK$^{ed.}$; parārtha eva anupapapatter S^2

---

244 D folio 165r. 244 S^5 folio 62r. 245 S^2 folio 97r. 248 S^3 folio 27v. 248 D folio 165v. 250 G folio 68r. 252 D folio 166r. 252 S^2 folio 97v.

viṣayasāpekṣarūpatvāt tasya, viṣayasya ca kāryasya tadānīm abhāvasvarūpatvāt.

ghaṭāntaraṃ pūrvadṛṣṭam ākalayyātha ceṣṭanam 44
anyenānyasya kalanāsaṃbhavād aticitratā

atha kārakāṇāṃ ceṣṭanaṃ vyāpāraḥ sāmarthyaṃ vā pūrvotpannadṛṣṭāṅkurakalanena, tad ayuktaṃ bījādīnām acetanatvenākalanābhāvāt. yatrāpi sacetanaṃ kumbhakārādi kāraṇaṃ, tatrāpi pūrvaṃ ghaṭāntaraṃ yady ākalitaṃ syāt tat tadā kartavyasya ghaṭāntarasya kim āyātaṃ yena tat kriyate, tadarthasyāticitratānupapadyamānasyāpi bhāvād ity upahāsaḥ.

44c C might reasonably be interpreted to read °*daṣṭam* for °*dṛṣṭam*. 44d P appears correctly to read *ceṣṭanam*, but the initial *akṣara* is blotched and might have read *ve* for *ce*; a later hand records the correct reading below the line.

44c pūrvadṛṣṭam] CDGJ$S^2S^3S^5$PR$K^{ed.}$; pūrva - - T 44d ākalayyātha] CDGJ$S^2S^3S^5$PR$K^{ed.}$; - - - - T 44d ceṣṭanam] DGJ$S^2S^3S^5$PR$K^{ed.}$; - - - T, veṣṭanāṃ C 45a anyenānyasya] CDGJ$S^2S^3S^{5p.c.}$PR$K^{ed.}$; - - - - - T, anyenyānyasya $S^{5a.c.}$ 45a kalanā] CDGJS^2S^5PR$K^{ed.}$; - - <?>ā T, vā lanā S^3 45b aticitratā] $D^{p.c.}K^{ed.}$; iticitratā TC$D^{a.c.}$GJ$S^2S^3S^5$PR

---

253 A footnote in $K^{ed.}$ (p. 166) suggests that one source examined for that edition (*kha*) offers a variant reading of *sāpekṣa*, but it is unclear for what this is a variant reading. 257 A footnote in $K^{ed.}$ (p. 166) suggests that one source examined for that edition reads (what appears to be) *vādati*, but it is unclear for what this is a variant reading. 257 Two successive footnotes in $K^{ed.}$ (p. 166) suggest that one source examined for that edition (*kha*) reads *karaṇaṃ* and shows *tat* to have been omitted from that manuscript, but it is unclear where these variants appear in the text. 259 Where P reads *na syāt* for *syāt* it might have first read *ta syāt*. 260 S^3 could be interpreted to read *anupapayamānasya* for *anupapadyamānasya*.

---

253 viṣaya°] DJ$S^2S^3S^5$PR$K^{ed.}$; °viṣayā G 253 tadānīm] DGJ$S^2S^{3p.c.}S^5$PR$K^{ed.}$; tadānīṃm $S^{3a.c.}$ 256 kārakāṇāṃ] DGJ$S^2S^{3p.c.}S^5$PR$K^{ed.}$; kāraṇakā<?>ṇāṃ $S^{3a.c.}$ 256 pūrvotpanna°] DGJ$S^2S^3S^5P^{p.c.}$R$K^{ed.}$; pūrvotpānna° $P^{a.c.}$ 257 acetanatvena] DGJ$S^2S^3S^5K^{ed.}$; acetatvena PR 257 ākalanābhāvāt] D$S^2S^3S^5$PR$K^{ed.}$; kalābhāvāt GJ 258 kāraṇaṃ] $K^{ed.}$; karaṇaṃ DGJ$S^2S^3S^5$PR 259 syāt DGJ$S^2S^3S^5K^{ed.}$; na syāt P, ta syāt R 259 tat tadā] GJ$S^{2p.c.}$; tadā D$S^{2a.c.}S^3S^5$PR$K^{ed.}$ 259 ghaṭāntarasya] DGJ$S^2S^3S^5K^{ed.}$; paṭāntarasya PR 260 anupapadyamānasya] GJ$S^{2p.c.}S^3S^5$PR$K^{ed.}$; anupadyamānasya D$S^{2a.c.}$

---

254 T folio 7v. 254 J folio 64v. 255 R folio 42r. 255 P folio 52. 257 D folio 166v. 260 S^5 folio 62v.

aṅkuro jāyata iti na bhavet kārakātmatā 45
asattve kārakāṇāṃ hi samūho na bhavet tadā
karmākhyasya hy asatyatvāt tatsaṃbandho 'satā katham 46
tasmāt sa eva bhagavān svayam eva prakalpate
tathātathābhāvarūpaiḥ sann eva parameśvaraḥ 47

aṅkuro jāyate bījabhūmāv ity atrāsato 'ṅkurasya kāraṇatā kartṛtā na syāt, ghaṭaṃ vā karoti kumbhakāra ity asatā karmaṇā kārakāntarāṇāṃ kartur vā kaḥ saṃbandhaḥ, tat kathaṃ samūhaḥ kārakāṇāṃ, tataḥ kriyā notpadyeta.

45c A parallel to the present passage is found in ĪPVV ad ĪPK 2.4.2 (vol. 3, p. 186, lines 15-19): *aṅkurasya sato vāsato vā yat paridṛśyate sattvaṃ, tatra na bījasya śaktir nāṅkurasya. aṅkuro jāyata iti hy aṅkuravṛttānto 'nyasya bījasya kathaṃ śaktiḥ, aṅkuraś ca na kaścana tadā. tasmāt kriyāśaktyā bhāsyamānaṃ karmaiva kāryaṃ, bhāsayitā ca kartaiva kāraṇam.* 45c The reading of S^{3} at *jāyata* is corrected by a later hand. 45c T reads *iti*, but the top part of *ti* is broken off. 47a C records ŚD 4.50 prior to ŚD 4.47. 47a S^{5} might record an *anusvāra* above *e* of *eva bhagavān.*

45c aṅkuro] CDGJ$S^{2}S^{3}S^{5}$PR$K^{ed.}$; aṅku - o T 45c jāyata] TCD$S^{2}S^{3p.c.}S^{5}$PR$K^{ed.}$; [']tha yata GJ, jāta $S^{3a.c.}$ 45d na] TDGJ$S^{2}S^{3}S^{5}$PR$K^{ed.}$; sa C 45d kārakātmatā] TDGJ$S^{2}S^{3}S^{5}$PR$K^{ed.}$; kārakāṃ matāṃ C 46a kārakāṇāṃ] TDGJ$S^{2}S^{3}S^{5}$PR$K^{ed.}$; kāravmāṇāṃ C 46b samūho] TDGJ$S^{2}S^{3}S^{5}$PR$K^{ed.}$; samāho C 46b na] TDGJ$S^{2}S^{3}S^{5}$PR$K^{ed.}$; *om.* (hypometric) C 46b bhavet] TCDGJ$S^{2}S^{3}S^{5}$R$K^{ed.}$; bhave P 46c karmākhyasya] TCDGJ$S^{2}S^{3}S^{5}K^{ed.}$; kārmākhyasya PR 46c hy asatyatvāt] DGJ$S^{2}S^{3}S^{5}$PR$K^{ed.}$; svasatyatvāt T, hy āsatyatvāt C 46d tatsaṃbandho] DGJ$S^{2}S^{3}S^{5}$PR$K^{ed.}$; tat - - - T, asaṃbandho C 46d 'satā] DGJ$S^{2}S^{3}S^{5}$PR$K^{ed.}$; - - T, na tat C 46d katham] CDGJ$S^{2}S^{3}S^{5}$PR$K^{ed.}$; - - T 47a tasmāt] CDGJ$S^{2}S^{3}S^{5}$PR$K^{ed.}$; - - T 47a sa] CDGJ$S^{2}S^{3}S^{5}$PR$K^{ed.}$; - T

---

266 kāraṇatā kartṛtā] D$S^{2a.c.}S^{3}S^{5}$PR$K^{ed.}$; kāraṇakartṛtā GJ$S^{2p.c.}$ 267 asatā] DGJ$S^{2}S^{3}S^{5}$P$K^{ed.}$; asatyā R 267 karmaṇā] DGJ$S^{2p.c.}S^{3}S^{5}$PR$K^{ed.}$; karmani ca $S^{2a.c.}$ 267 kārakāntarāṇāṃ] DGJ$S^{2}S^{3}S^{5}K^{ed.}$; karakāntaraṇāṃ PR 267 kartur] DGJ$S^{2}S^{5}$PR$K^{ed.}$; kartu S^{3} 268 saṃbandhaḥ] DGJ$S^{2}S^{3}S^{5}P^{p.c.}$R$K^{ed.}$; saṃmbandhaḥ $P^{a.c.}$ 268 samūhaḥ] DGJ$S^{2}S^{5}$PR$K^{ed.}$; samūha S^{3} 268 notpadyeta] GJ$S^{2}S^{3}S^{5}K^{ed.}$; notpadyate DPR

---

262 S^{2} folio 98r. 262 D folio 167r. 264 G folio 68v. 268 D folio 167v.

tasmāc cidrūpaḥ parameśvaras tathātathābhāvarūpaiḥ svayam eva prakalpate bhavati. sa ca nityam eva sann iti katham asatkāryatāśaṅkā.

svayaṃ ca na prajāyeta kenānyena prajanyate
vyatiriktena kartrādyā yadi syus te tadātmakāḥ 48
tat tasya janmitā yuktā vyatiriktaiḥ kathaṃ bhavet

svayaṃ cāsattvād ghaṭādiḥ kathaṃ jāyeta jananakartā kathaṃ syād yadā, tadā kena sāmarthyenānyenāpi kumbhakārādinā katham asaj janmayogyatālakṣaṇasvabhāvarahitaṃ śaśaśṛṅgād aviśiṣṭaṃ janyeta. janayitā yady

---

48d S^2 deletes a mark below *syu*, though what was indicated by it remains unclear. 48d The manuscript of T is badly damaged at *tadātmakāḥ*, where a number of *akṣaras* are missing or partially missing due to fraying of the palm leaf, but the text is nevertheless partially legible. 49a C adds *ta* above the line in correcting its hypometric reading of *tasya* for *tat tasya*. The reading of *ta tasya* exemplifies the sort of degemination that is typical of this manuscript, even at points, such as this one, where *sandhi* necessitates the recording of the geminate consonant.

48b kenānyena] TCDGJ$S^2S^3S^5$R$K^{ed.}$; kiṃ nānyena P 48c vyatiriktena] TDGJ$S^2S^3S^5$PR$K^{ed.}$; vyatiriktana C 48c kartrādyā] TDGJ$S^2S^3S^5$PR$K^{ed.}$; kartāvyā C 48d syus] CDGJ$S^2S^3S^5$PR$K^{ed.}$; syu - T 48d te] CDJ$S^2S^3S^5$PR$K^{ed.}$; - e T, teḥ G 48d tadātmakāḥ] CDGJ$S^2S^3S^5$PR$K^{ed.}$; - <?><?>kāḥ T 49a tat tasya] TDGJ$S^2S^3S^5$PR$K^{ed.}$; ta tasya $C^{p.c.}$, tasya $C^{a.c.}$ 49a janmitā yuktā] TGJ$S^2S^3S^5$PR$K^{ed.}$; janyayuktā (hypometric) C, janmatā yuktā D 49b vyatiriktaiḥ] TDGJ$S^2S^3S^5$PR$K^{ed.}$; vyatirikte C 49b bhavet] TDGJ$S^2S^3S^5$PR$K^{ed.}$; bhaveta (hypermetric) C

---

270 It is possible that S^3 erroneously reads *nityaṃm* for *nityam*. 274 S^5 is blotched at *jā* of *jāyeta*, but the reading appears to be the correct one. 274 The reading of P (°*kartā*) has been corrected by a later hand. 276 The vertical line of the *i-kāra* of *janayitā* is missing in P. The *akṣara* in question is marked by a diagonal underline.

---

269 tathātathābhāvarūpaiḥ] GJ$K^{ed.}$; tathātathābhāvasvarūpaiḥ $S^{2p.c.}$, tathābhāvasvarūpaiḥ D$S^{2a.c.}S^3S^5$PR 270 sann] DGJ$S^2S^3S^5P^{p.c.}$R$K^{ed.}$; san $P^{a.c.}$ 270 katham] $D^{p.c.}K^{ed.}$; kathā $D^{a.c.}$GJ$S^2S^3S^5$PR 274 ghaṭādiḥ] DGJS^2S^5PR$K^{ed.}$; ghaṭādi S^3 274 jāyeta] DGJS^2S^5PR$K^{ed.}$; jāyate S^3 274 °kartā] DGJ$S^2S^3S^5P^{p.c.}$R$K^{ed.}$; °<?>rtā $P^{a.c.}$ 274 yadā] DGJ$S^2S^3S^5P^{p.c.}$R$K^{ed.}$; yudā $P^{a.c.}$ 275 asaj] DGJ$S^2S^3S^5$R$K^{ed.}$; sat P 276 °svabhāvarahitaṃ] $K^{ed.}$; °svabhāvabhāvarahita GJS^2, °svabhāvabhāvarahitaṃ DS^3S^5PR 276 śaśaśṛṅgād aviśiṣṭaṃ] D$G^{p.c.}J^{p.c.}S^{2p.c.}S^3S^5PRK^{ed.}$; śaśaśṛṅgādiviśiṣṭaṃ $G^{a.c.}$, śa<tha?>- śṛṅgād $J^{a.c.}$, śaśiśṛṅgād aviśiṣṭaṃ $S^{2a.c.}$

---

269 J folio 65r. 272 S^2 folio 98v. 274 D folio 168r.

api saṃs tathāpi tatsattā janyasya na kadācid bhavati vyatiriktatvāt, tatas tayāpi na tasya yogyatāpattiḥ. evaṃ hi sā janmayogyatāyāṃ vyāpriyeta yadi tayā tasya janmitā yujyeta yadi janayitā kartā sahakāriṇaś ca karaṇādirūpā janyātmakāḥ syuḥ. vyatiriktais tu sadbhir apy asataḥ kathaṃ janmitā bhavet.

janmakāle ghaṭābhāvāt saṃbandho naiva kārakaiḥ 49
nāsaṃbandhasya karaṇaṃ satkāryāc cet sa vidyate

49d Cf., e.g., MT 1.9.17: *anyathā kārakavrātapravṛttyanupapattitaḥ* | *śrutir ādānam arthaś ca vyapaitīty api tad dhatam* || See also MTT ad 1.9.17: *saty asadutpattyabhyupagame kārakavrātasyaiva pravṛttir nopapadyate. asato hi kāryasya vandhyāsutāder ivotpattaye kiṃ kila kārakāṇi kuryuḥ. kārakapravṛttyanupapatteś ca ghaṭādicikīrṣor mṛpiṇḍādy ānayetyādikā śrutiḥ, teṣāṃ ca kārakāṇām ādānaṃ grahaṇam, arthaś ca tadvyāpāralakṣaṇā kriyā vyapaiti vighaṭate. tasmiṃś ca vyapete sarvaceṣṭāvyāghātaḥ, pratyuta yuṣmatpakṣe jagadvyāhataṃ syāt.* 50a As noted above, C records ŚD 4.50 prior to ŚD 4.47. 50b The initial *akṣara* of *satkāryāc* is set high, almost above the line, as it were, in T. The reading is nevertheless correct.

49c °abhāvāt] TDGJ$S^2S^3S^5$PRK$^{ed.}$; °abhāt (hypometric) C 50a nāsaṃbandhasya] *em.*; nāsaṃnandhasya T, na saṃbaṃdhsya C, nāsaṃbaddhasya D$^{p.c.}$GJ$S^2S^{5p.c.}$P$^{p.c.}$K$^{ed.}$, nāsambaddha (hypometric) D$^{a.c.}$, na saṃbaddhasya $S^3S^{5a.c.}$, nāsaṃvaṃddhaṃsya P$^{a.c.}$R 50b satkāryāc] TD$^{a.c.}$GJ$S^2S^3S^5$K$^{ed.}$; satkāryaṃ C, satkāryac D$^{p.c.}$, satkāryāś PR

---

277 A footnote in K$^{ed.}$ (p. 168) suggests that *tathā* is omitted in one of the sources examined for that edition (*kha*). Presumably, this is the *tathā* of *yadyapi saṃs tathāpi*. The same note suggests that the same manuscript reads *utpadyate*, but it is unclear for what this is a variant. 277 P's reading of *bhavati* was corrected by a later hand. 278 S^2 records *gya* of *janmayogyatāyāṃ* in the left margin; the *akṣara* it replaces was deleted and is no longer legible. 280 One can understand S^5 to delete a final *anusvāra* following *janmitā*.

---

277 yady api] D$^{p.c.}$GJ$S^2S^3S^5$PRK$^{ed.}$; yady apya D$^{a.c.}$ 277 na] DGJ$S^2S^3S^5$RK$^{ed.}$; *om.* P 277 kadācid] GJ$S^2S^3S^5$PR; kācid DK$^{ed.}$ 277 bhavati] DGJ$S^2S^3S^5$P$^{p.c.}$K$^{ed.}$; bhavasi P$^{a.c.}$R 277 vyatiriktatvāt] DJ$S^2S^3S^5$PRK$^{ed.}$; vyaktiriktatvāt G 278 na tasya] D$^{p.c.}$GJ$S^{2p.c.}$PRK$^{ed.}$; *om.* D$^{a.c.}$$S^{2a.c.}S^3S^5$ 278 janmayogyatāyāṃ] DGJ$S^{2p.c.}S^3S^5$PRK$^{ed.}$; janmayo<?>tāyāṃ $S^{2a.c.}$ 279 janyātmakāḥ] DGJ$S^2S^3S^5$RK$^{ed.}$; janyatmakāḥ P$^{p.c.}$, jarnyatmakāḥ P$^{a.c.}$

---

277 S^5 folio 63r. 278 G folio 69r. 278 R folio 42v. 278 D folio 168v. 279 S^3 folio 28r. 281 S^2 folio 99r.

sann apy asāv asaṃvedyo vyañjakasyāpy abhāvataḥ 50
tasmāt svayaṃ svabhāvena bhāvair bhāvī bhaved bhavaḥ

ghaṭasya janyasya janmārambhakāle 'bhāvāt kumbhakāramṛtpiṇḍādibhir na saṃbandhaḥ. na cāvidyamānasaṃbandhasya karaṇaṃ pūrvam apy anyato 'pi vāprasaṅgāt. janyāsaṃbandhe 'pi tadapekṣayaiva janakānām eva sa sāmarthyasya viśeṣo yena teṣu satsu tasya viśiṣṭasyaiva sattā, na tu yasya kasyacid ity eṣo 'satkāryavāda īśvarapratyabhijñādau nirākṛtaḥ. atha sa

---

50d A small gap appears following *kasyā* in *vyañjakasyāpy* in S^2.

50c sann apy asāv] TCDJ$S^2S^3S^5$PR$K^{ed.}$; sann asyasāv G 50c asaṃvedyo] TDGJ$S^2S^3S^5$PR$K^{ed.}$; asaṃcevyā C 50d vyañjakasyāpy] DGJ$S^2S^3S^5$PR$K^{ed.}$; vya - kasyāpy T, vyaṃjakesyāpy C 51b bhāvair] TDGJ$S^2S^3S^5$PR$K^{ed.}$; bhāvai C

---

285 The corrected reading of P (of *janyasya* for *janasya*) was rendered by a later hand. 285 In J, *mā* of *janmārambhakāle* is heavily blotched but nevertheless legible. 285 The vertical line of the vowel *i* of °*mṛtpiṇḍa*° is omitted in P. 287 While $K^{ed.}$ records a hiatus following *vā* (= *vā prasaṅgāt*), I understand the text to read *aprasaṅgāt* and thus erase the hiatus. 288 S^2 appears to have first read *yeva* for *yena*. 288 In J, *sya* of *tasya* is written in a heavily blotched hand. 289 A later hand adds *kasya* in P, above the line. 289 S^2 adds *da* of *'satkāryavāda* in the bottom margin. 289 Reference here to *Īśvarapratyabhijñādi* likely refers to ĪPK 2.4.2: *jaḍasya tu na sā śaktiḥ sattā yad asataḥ sataḥ* | *kartṛkarmatvatattvaiva kāryakāraṇatā tataḥ* || Also to ĪPK 2.4.3-4: *yad asat tad asad yuktā nāsataḥ satsvarūpatā* | *sato 'pi na punaḥ sattālābhenārtho 'tha cocyate* || *kāryakāraṇatā loke sāntarvipariavartinaḥ* | *ubhayendriyavedyatvaṃ tasya kasyāpi śaktitaḥ* ||

---

285 janyasya] DGJ$S^2S^3S^5P^{p.c.}$R$K^{ed.}$; janasya $P^{a.c.}$ 286 karaṇaṃ] $S^{2p.c.}S^3S^5$PR$K^{ed.}$; kāraṇaṃ DGJ$S^{2a.c.}$ 286 apy] DGJ$S^2S^{3p.c.}S^5$PR$K^{ed.}$; api $S^{3a.c.}$ 287 °apekṣayaiva] DGJ$S^2S^3S^5$P$K^{ed.}$; °apekṣaiva R 288 satsu] DGJS^2S^5PR$K^{ed.}$; tatsu S^3 288 yasya] DJ$S^2S^3S^5$PR$K^{ed.}$; vasya G 289 kasyacid] DGJ$S^2S^3S^5P^{p.c.}K^{ed.}$; cid $P^{a.c.}$R 289 ity eṣo] D$S^2S^3S^5$PR$K^{ed.}$; y eṣo GJ 289 'satkāryavāda] DGJ$S^{2p.c.}S^5$PR$K^{ed.}$; [']satkāryavā $S^{2a.c.}$, 'satkāvāda S^3

---

284 J folio 65v. 284 D folior 169r. 289 D folio 169v. 289 P folio 53.

vidyate saṃbandhaḥ sataḥ kāryātmakatvāt kāraṇasya. tad api na, yataḥ sann apy asau janyo ghaṭādir artho 'saṃvedyo 'saṃvedyatvāc ca saṃbandhino 'prakhyatvena saṃbandhāgamanaṃ vyañjakatvaṃ ca kumbhakārāder ghaṭaṃ prati nāsti yataḥ sarvathā pratītyagocare vastuni vyañjako na bhavati. siddha evārthe vyañjako mato yathā ghaṭādau dīpaḥ. tato vyañjakasyāpy abhāvataḥ kathaṃ

---

290 Note the parallel with SK 9: *asadakaraṇād upādānagrahaṇāt sarvasambhavābhāvāt | śaktasya śakyakaraṇāt kāraṇabhāvāc ca sat kāryam || 9 ||* Note also that P's reading for *kāryātmakatvāt* is corrected by a later hand, which underlines the added *ka* in a faint horizontal stroke. 290 Cf. JM ad SK 9: *kāraṇabhāvāc ceti. kāraṇasya sattvād ity arthaḥ. yady asat kāryam utpadyate kim iti? kāraṇād eva na kāryasya bhāvo bhavati, bhavati ca. tasmāc chaktirūpeṇāvasthitam iti gamyate.* 291 In P's reading of *[']saṃbedyatā* for *'saṃvedyatvāc*, the final *tā* is written in an excessively large hand, perhaps covering over a prior reading of *tvā*. 292 S^4 records only part of ŚD 4. Five folio sides of it are available to me, beginning with folio 41r. The readings of S^4 begin here at °*der ghaṭaṃ prati nāsti...* 293 It is an apparently later hand that inserts *na* in small print following *sarvathā pratītyagocare* in G. The same appears, again in a very small hand, in J. 293 I propose that the present passage of the ŚDVṛ (*siddha evārthe vyañjako mato yathā ghaṭādau dīpaḥ*) offers a close paraphrase of PV (*svārthānumānapariccheda*) 1.263cd-264ab: *svajñānenānyadhīhetuḥ siddhe 'rthe vyañjako mataḥ* || 1.263 || *yathā dīpo 'nyathā vāpi ko viśeṣo 'sya kārakāt* | 294 A footnote in $K^{ed.}$ (p. 170) suggests that one source examined for that edition (*kha*) reads °*ko 'sato* for *[vyañja]ko mato*. It appears to me that this is a reference to the reading of D, and it signals the close similarity of *sa* and *ma* in *Śāradā* script. I understand D to read *mato*, as noted in the present edition. 294 S^3 deletes *ma* (or is it possibly *sa*?) prior to *mato*. S^2 deletes what appears to be *ma*, but could be *sa*, following *sa* of its reading of *sato* for *mato*. S^5 also deletes something, though what is not clear, prior to its reading of *mato*. Perhaps an *anusvāra* is deleted?

---

290 kāraṇasya] *em.*; kāryasya DGJ$S^2S^3S^5$PR$K^{ed.}$ 291 'saṃvedyatvāc] DGJ$S^2S^3S^5K^{ed.}$; [']saṃbedyatā P, [']saṃvedyatvā R 292 saṃbandhino 'prakhyatvena saṃbandhāgamanaṃ vyañjakatvaṃ ca] DGJ$S^2S^3S^5K^{ed.}$; *om.* PR 292 kumbhakārāder] DGJ$S^{2p.c.}S^3S^5$PR$K^{ed.}$; kumbhakārādīr $S^{2a.c.}$, - - - - der S^4 293 pratītyagocare] D$G^{a.c.}J^{a.c.}S^2S^3S^4S^5PRK^{ed.}$; pratītyagocare na $G^{p.c.}J^{p.c.}$ 294 arthe vyañjako] DGJ$S^2S^3S^5K^{ed.}$; arthavyañjako S^4PR 294 mato] DG$S^3S^4S^5K^{ed.}$; sato JS^2PR 294 ghaṭādau] DGJ$S^2S^3S^4S^5$P$K^{ed.}$; gheṭādau R 294 apy] GJ$S^{2p.c.}S^3S^5K^{ed.}$; *om.* DS^4PR, api $S^{2a.c.}$

---

290 S^2 folio 99v. 291 G folio 69v. 292 S^4 folio 41r. 294 D folio 170r. 294 S^5 folio 63v.

saṃbandhaḥ. evaṃ hi kāraṇaṃ kāryātmanā sat tadā bhaved yady avyatirekas tayoḥ syāt. sa ca pratyakṣaviruddhaḥ. tasmād aviruddhasarvabhāvaikabhāvaḥ svayaṃ bhava eva parameśvaras tathāvasthānasvabhāvena, nāpareṇa hetunā kāraṇena bhāvābhāvaiḥ saṃsāravartibhir bhāvī bhavaty abhīkṣṇaṃ tatsvabhāvatvāt. athavā nityaṃ bhāvasaṃbandhīti śivakāraṇatayā satkāryavādaḥ.

ito 'pi viddhi satkāryaṃ mṛtpiṇḍāt kiṃ ghaṭaḥ pṛthak 51

51d It is difficult to read *ghaṭaḥ* of D, due to damage to the manuscript. 51d S^4 records the final *k* of *pṛthak* in the right margin, having left it out of the original transcription.

51c 'pi] $TDGJS^2S^3S^4S^5PRK^{ed.}$; pa C 51c satkāryaṃ] $CDGJS^2S^3S^4S^5PRK^{ed.}$; sā kāryaṃ T 51d mṛtpiṇḍāt kiṃ] $TDGJS^2S^3S^4S^5PRK^{ed.}$; mṛtpiṇḍātmakaṃ C 51d ghaṭaḥ] $TDGJS^2S^3S^4S^5PRK^{ed.}$; *om.* (hypometric) C 51d pṛthak] $TDGJS^2S^3S^4S^5PRK^{ed.}$; prathak C

---

297 S^2, which was corrected from *parameśras* to *parameśvaras*, shows the added *va* subsequently to have been deleted, again. 297 A later hand redraws the *e* of *hetunā* in R in a thin line that appears as if written by a ball-point pen. The manuscript appears to have recorded the same prior to the correction, however, albeit in a faint hand. 299 P corrects its reading of *bhāva*° by recording the lengthening of the initial vowel in the right margin. 299 D is misfigured across the first three lines of folio 170v. It appears a thick streak of ink was drawn onto the page. The second line of the folio side shows a large gap left to avoid the long, vertical mark, but it also partially occludes *ti śi* of *sambandhīti śivakāraṇatayā*. The entire mark is colored in yellow, the convention used in D to correct errors.

---

295 sat tadā] $K^{ed.p.c.}$; sat tathā $DGJS^2S^3S^4S^5PRK^{ed.a.c.}$ 295 avyatirekas] $DJS^2S^3S^4S^5PRK^{ed.}$; arekas G 296 tayoḥ] $DGJS^2S^3S^4S^5K^{ed.}$; tayo PR 296 sa] $DGJS^2S^3S^4S^5PK^{ed.}$; ma R 296 ca] $DGJS^2S^3S^4S^5RK^{ed.}$; *om.* P 296 pratyakṣaviruddhaḥ] $DS^{2p.c.}S^3S^4S^{5p.c.}PRK^{ed.}$; pratyakṣavirukṣaḥ GJ, <?>tyakṣaviruddhaḥ $S^{2a.c.}$, viruddhaḥ $S^{5a.c.}$ 297 eva] $D^{p.c.}GJS^2S^3S^4S^5PRK^{ed.}$; *om.* $D^{a.c.}$ 297 parameśvaras] $DGJS^{2p.c.}S^3S^4S^5RK^{ed.}$; parameśras $S^{2a.c.}$, parameśvaraḥ $P^{p.c.}$, parameśvara $P^{a.c.}$ 297 tathāvasthāna°] $DGS^2S^3S^4S^5PRK^{ed.}$; tathā - <?>sthāna° J 297 nāpareṇa] $GJS^2S^3S^5RK^{ed.}$; vapareṇa $D^{p.c.}$, vāpareṇa $D^{a.c.}$, apareṇa S^4, nāṣareṇa P 298 kāraṇena] $DS^2S^3S^4S^5PRK^{ed.}$; karaṇena GJ 298 bhāvābhāvaiḥ] $DGJS^2S^3S^4S^5K^{ed.}$; bhāvābhāvai PR 299 bhāva°] $DGJS^2S^3S^4S^5P^{p.c.}RK^{ed.}$; bhava° $P^{a.c.}$

---

297 J folio 66r. 299 S^2 folio 100r. 299 D folio 170v.

apṛthag vā pṛthaktvena paṭādeḥ karaṇaṃ na kim
anupādānataiva syād apṛthaktve sa eva saḥ 52

ito 'pi śivātmatayārthānāṃ satkāryavādopapattiṃ jānīhi yato mṛtpiṇḍaghaṭayoḥ sadāsatkāryavāde 'pi kāryakāraṇatopapattiḥ. mṛtpiṇḍād dhi ghaṭasya pṛthaktve tathā cāsattve paṭaśaśaviṣāṇayor apy asattvāviśeṣāt karaṇaṃ syāt. na cāsti tat, asaty arthe padabandhasyānyaparihāreṇa kāryatvena svīkaraṇasya kartum

---

52b In S^5, *ḥ ka* of *paṭādeḥ karaṇaṃ* is heavily blotched and therefore rewritten in the margin. 52d S^2 fails to highlight ŚD 4.52cd to indicate that it is part of the *mūla* and not the commentary.

52a apṛthag vā] CDGJ$S^3S^4S^5$PRK$^{ed.}$; athavā (hypometric) T, apṛg vā (hypometric) S^2 52a pṛthaktvena] C; pṛthaddhe (hypometric) T, pṛthaktve tu DGJ$S^2S^3S^5$PRK$^{ed.}$, pṛthaktva tu S^4 52b paṭādeḥ] TCDGJ$S^2S^4S^5$PRK$^{ed.}$; paṭāde S^3 52b karaṇaṃ] TCDGJ$S^2S^3S^5$PK$^{ed.}$; kāraṇaṃ S^4R 52c anupādānataiva] DGJ$S^2S^3S^4S^5$PRK$^{ed.}$; anupādānataivā T, anupādāteva (hypometric) C 52d apṛthaktve] CDGJ$S^3S^4S^5$PRK$^{ed.}$; apṛth - ktv - na (hypermetric) T, apṛktve (hypometric) S^2

---

303 It appears that the reading of R was corrected from *nānīhi* to *jānīhi*, perhaps by a later hand. 303 The vertical line of *i* in *mṛtpiṇḍa*° of J is drawn over what appears to be a (thus deleted) *ta*. 304 The readings of D^a, of which only 12 folio sides are available (and commencing here with folio 171r.), begin only at *mṛtpiṇḍād dhi ghaṭasya* and run to the end of the extant commentary on the ŚD at 4.73cd-75. 304 D^a punctuates following its reading of *pṛthaktvena* for *pṛthaktve*. 306 A footnote in K$^{ed.}$ (p. 170) suggests that one source for that edition (*kha*) reads *parihāre*°, but it is unclear for what this is a variant. Kaul likely here refers to a reading of *anyaparihāreṇa* for the *anyāparihāreṇa* that appears in his edition and, it must be added, in D (which informed the KSTS edition of the ŚDVṛ).

---

303 upapattiṃ] DGJ$S^2S^3S^4S^5$P$^{p.c.}$RK$^{ed.}$; upipatiṃ P$^{a.c.}$ 304 kāryakāraṇatopapattiḥ] D$S^2S^3S^4S^5$PRK$^{ed.}$; kāryakāraṇatātpattiḥ G, kāryakāraṇatāpattiḥ J 304 pṛthaktve] DGJ$S^2S^3S^4S^5$PRK$^{ed.}$; pṛthaktvena D^a 305 ca] DD^aG$S^{2a.c.}S^3S^4S^5$PRK$^{ed.}$; *om.* J$S^{2p.c.}$ 305 apy] DGJ$S^2S^3S^4S^5$PRK$^{ed.}$; *om.* D^a 305 karaṇaṃ] DD^aGJ$S^2S^3S^5$PK$^{ed.}$; kāraṇaṃ S^4R 306 padabandhasya] DGJ$S^{2a.c.}S^3S^4S^5$PRK$^{ed.}$; paṇabandhanasya $D^{ap.c.}$, pa<?>bandhanasya $D^{aa.c.}$, padabandhanasya $S^{2p.c.}$ 306 °parihāreṇa] *em.*; °aparihāreṇa DD^aGJ$S^2S^3S^5$K$^{ed.}$, °apahāreṇa S^4PR

---

301 R folio 43r. 301 C folio 10r. 304 G folio 70r. 304 D folio 171r. 304 D^a folio 171r.

aśakyatvāt, tasya mṛtpiṇḍāder anupādānataiva syāt prakṛtirūpatā naiva syād ity arthaḥ. apṛthaktve mṛtpiṇḍa eva sa ghaṭaḥ, na tv apūrvaḥ. tataḥ prāg api piṇḍo ghaṭaḥ syāt.

nāmasaṃsthānabhedaś ced dhaste muṣṭyādyabheditā
sthitam eva hi satkāryam ata evāvināśitā 53
śivasya bhāvanāśe 'pi maulināśe 'pi hemavat

atha mṛtpiṇḍaghaṭayor nāmasanniveśabhedād bheda eva, tat kathaṃ satkāryam iti. tan na, nāmasaṃsthānamātra evātra bhedaḥ, na tu mṛdrūpatāyāṃ yathā haste muṣṭiprasṛtatādeḥ. atra hi hastatā tulyā dvayor api, tathā

53a S^{2} fails to highlight ŚD 4.53-54ab in yellow to indicate that it is part of the *mūla* and not the commentary. Red marks are smeared in the small gaps in the text prior to and following the passage in question, however. 53a The long *ā* of T's reading of °*ābhedaś* for °*abhedaś* is crowded into the manuscript, appearing slightly below the line in the hand of the copyist.

53a nāmasaṃsthānabhedaś] $CDD^{a}GJS^{2}S^{3}S^{4}S^{5}PRK^{ed.}$; nāmasaṃsthānābhedaś T 53b dhaste] $TDD^{a}S^{2}S^{3}S^{4}S^{5}PRK^{ed.}$; aste C, dhate GJ 53b muṣṭyādyabheditā] $DD^{a}GJS^{3}S^{4}S^{5}PRK^{ed.}$; muṣṭyādyabhedatā T, muṣṭyādibheditaḥ C, muṣṭyādibheditā S^{2} 53c satkāryam] $TCDD^{a}GJS^{2}S^{4}S^{5}PRK^{ed.}$; satkārya<?> S^{3}

307 S^{2} marks the need for a change at *dā* of *anupādānataiva*, but what is to be added is not apparent. Perhaps the long *ā* itself was inserted into the line, but no crowding of *akṣara*s suggests that this occurred: it does not appear to be a later addition to the reading. 307 S^{2} deletes *tvā* prior to *tā* of *prakṛtirūpatā*. 308 P reads *eva sa*, but the *sa* is blotched, and it is written in a manner that perhaps covers a prior reading of *sva*. 314 The final *akṣara* of °*mātram* in P's reading of °*mātram eva* for °*mātra eva* is recorded in such a way as to suggest the scribe might have initially recorded *e* there, rather than *m*.

307 prakṛtirūpatā naiva] $DGJS^{2}S^{3}S^{4}S^{5}PRK^{ed.}$; prakṛtirūpataiva na D^{a} 307 ity] $DD^{a}GJS^{2p.c.}S^{3}S^{4}S^{5}PRK^{ed.}$; iti $S^{2a.c.}$ 308 apṛthaktve] $DD^{a}GJS^{3}S^{4}S^{5}PRK^{ed.}$; apṛktve S^{2} 308 piṇḍo] $DD^{a}GJS^{2}S^{3}S^{4}S^{5}RK^{ed.}$; piṇḍe P 313 tat kathaṃ satkāryam] $D^{p.c.}D^{a}GJS^{2}S^{3}S^{4}S^{5}PRK^{ed.}$; tat kāryam $D^{a.c.}$ 314 °mātra] $DD^{a}GJS^{2}S^{3}S^{4}S^{5}RK^{ed.}$; °mātram P 315 tulyā] $DD^{a}GJS^{2}S^{3}S^{4}S^{5}P^{p.c.}RK^{ed.}$; telyā $P^{a.c.}$

307 S^{2} folio 100v. 309 D folio 171v. 311 S^{3} folio 28v. 311 S^{5} folio 64r. 313 J folio 66v. 315 S^{4} folio 41v.

sadrūpatānayoḥ. etac cātyantaprasiddham etadvyutpādanārthaṃ pradarśitaṃ. vastuto mṛd api paryālocyamānaśabdasparśāditanmātramayī jalādivilakṣaṇā yāvat traiguṇyatādavasthyam, tat tāvadavasthe 'pi yāni kāryāṇi mahadādīni pṛthivyantāni ghaṭādyantāni vā, tāni traiguṇyamātrarūpāṇi viśvasyaikatvāpatteḥ. tadadhikatve tv idaṃ śabdatanmātramayam ākāśaḥ, iyaṃ pṛthivī, ayaṃ ghaṭaḥ, ayaṃ paṭa iti vibhāgaḥ. vibhāgo 'pi ca tadabhedād vāstava eva. na ca prakāśamānasyāvastutā yujyate traiguṇyasyāpi tathā prāpteḥ. prakāśanaṃ ca pratīyamānatā pratyakṣeṇāstv anumānena vā, sarvathā sadrūpavattā syāt. evaṃ

---

317 D leaves a large gap between *paryālocya* and *mānaśabdasparśādi*°, as if there to punctuate with a full stop. 318 P's reading of *traiṣuṇyatāvadasthyam* for *traiguṇyatādavasthyam* is corrected to *traiguṇyatāvadasthyam* by a later hand. 318 A footnote in K$^{ed.}$ (p. 171) suggests that one source for that edition (*kha*) reads *[traiguṇyatādava]stham* for *[traiguṇyatādava]sthyam*. This apparently refers to the reading of D^{a}. 318 The reading of R at *tat tā* of *tat tāvadavasthe 'pi* is blotched, apparently from water damage to the manuscript, but is nevertheless legible. 320 P records a plus mark (+) above the final *akṣara* of *viśvasyaikatvāpatteḥ*, this mark often being used to flag incorrect readings in the manuscript. 320 Cf., e.g., SāṅKā 11: *triguṇam aviveki viṣayaḥ sāmānyam acetanaṃ prasavadharmi | vyaktaṃ tathā pradhānaṃ tadviparītas tathā ca pumān* || 320 A footnote in K$^{ed.}$ (p. 171) suggests a variant reading may be found in one source examined for that edition (*kha*), the reading being of *tadadhikatve*. This reading is not at variance with what is recorded in K$^{ed.}$, however, which also reads *tadadhikatve*. D also attests to the same.

---

316 etadvyutpādanārthaṃ] DD^{a}GJS^{2}S^{3}S^{4}S^{5}P$^{p.c.}$RK$^{ed.}$; etadyutpādanārthaṃ P$^{a.c.}$ 317 mṛd] D^{a}GJS^{2}S^{3}S^{4}S^{5}PRK$^{ed.}$; m<?>d D 317 paryālocya°] DD^{a}S^{2}S^{3}S^{4}S^{5}PRK$^{ed.}$; paṭālocya° GJ 318 traiguṇyatādavasthyam] GS^{4}K$^{ed.}$; traiguṇyatādavastham DJS^{2}S^{3}S^{5}, traiguṇyaṃ tāvadavasthaṃ D$^{a p.c.}$, traiguṇyaṃ tādavasthaṃ D$^{a a.c.}$, traiguṇyatāvadasthyam P$^{p.c.}$R, traiṣuṇyatāvadasthyam P$^{a.c.}$ 318 tat] DD^{a}GJS^{2}S^{3}S^{4}S^{5} P$^{p.c.}$RK$^{ed.}$; ta P$^{a.c.}$ 318 °avasthe] DD^{a}GJS^{3}S^{4}S^{5}PR K$^{ed.}$; °asthe S^{2} 319 traiguṇyamātrarūpāṇi] DGJS^{2}S^{3}S^{4}S^{5}PRK$^{ed.}$; traiguṇyarūpāṇi D^{a} 320 śabdatanmātramayam] DD$^{a p.c.}$GJS^{2}S^{3}S^{4}S$^{5 p.c.}$PRK$^{ed.}$; śabdatanmātraṃ mayam D$^{a a.c.}$, śabdatabdatanmātramayam S$^{5 a.c.}$ 320 ākāśaḥ] DGJS^{2}S^{3}S^{4}S^{5}PRK$^{ed.}$; ākāśaṃ D^{a} 322 avastutā] DD^{a}S^{2}S$^{3 p.c.}$S^{4}S^{5}PRK$^{ed.}$; vastutā GJS$^{3 a.c.}$ 322 prakāśanaṃ] DD^{a}GJS^{2}S^{3}S^{5}PK$^{ed.}$; prakāśamānaṃ S^{4}R

---

316 D folio 172r. 317 D^{a} folio 171v. 317 G folio 70v. 317 S^{2} folio 101r. 320 D folio 172v. 321 R folio 43v. 322 P folio 54.

ca mṛtpiṇḍo ’nya eva sati yasmin ghaṭo bhavati, ghaṭaś cāpy anyo, mṛd apy anyā, yā sarvamṛṇmayeṣv anugatā, ghaṭaś cānanugataḥ. na cānugatānanugatayor aikyaṃ ghaṭate, tataś ca paṭādeḥ karaṇaṃ na kim iti doṣaḥ. darpaṇavad viśvapratibimbayogi traiguṇyam ity abhyupagame ’pi yadvaśāt tathāpratibimbayogas tad eva kāraṇam, tatrāpi bhedābhedaparyālocanād anupapattir iti cinmayaśivarūpataiva sarvakāryāṇām īśvarapratyabhijñoktanyāyenety āha sthitam eva hi satkāryam iti. ata eva śivarūpatayā sattvād avināśitā. na hi śivasya svasaṃvidrūpasya sato vināśa itīśvarapratyabhijñāyām evaṃ coktam. maulināśe ’pi hemavad iti sarvalokānusāreṇa pūrvavan nidarśanam.

---

324 S^{2} deletes an illegible *akṣara* following *cāpy anyo*. 325 P’s reading of *cānugatānanugatayor* was corrected by a later hand. 326 See, e.g., SāṅKā 3: *mūlaprakṛtir avikṛtir mahadādayaḥ prakṛtivikṛtayaḥ sapta | ṣoḍaśakas tu vikāro na prakṛtir na vikṛtiḥ puruṣaḥ* || 327 What appears to be an imperfection in the paper manuscript allows the reading of *yadvaśāt* in S^{4} to appear to offer the erroneous reading of *yadvaśaḥt*. 329 See ĪPK 2.4.19: *na ca yuktaṃ jaḍasyaivaṃ bhedābhedavirodhataḥ | ābhāsabhedād ekatra cidātmani tu yujyate* || See also the *Vṛtti* thereon: *jaḍasyābhinnātmano bhedenāvasthiter virodhād ayuktam, svacche cidātmany ekasminn evam anekapratibimbadhāraṇenāvirodhād yujyate.* 330 The present is a quotation of ŚD 4.53c: *sthitam eva hi satkāryam.* 331 See, e.g., ĪPKVṛ ad ĪPK 2.4.3-4: *asataḥ satsvabhāvatā viruddhā sataś ca siddhā. siddhasyaivāntarbāhyāntaḥkaraṇadvayīvedyatāpādanam īśvareṇotpādanam.*

---

324 ’nya] DD^{a}G$^{p.c.}$JS^{2}S^{3}S^{4}S^{5}PRK$^{ed.}$; [’]nyo G$^{a.c.}$ 325 °mṛṇmayeṣv] DD^{a}GJS$^{2p.c.}$S^{3}S^{4}S^{5}PRK$^{ed.}$; °mṛnmayeṣv S$^{2a.c.}$ 325 anugatā] DGJS^{2}S^{3}S^{4}S^{5}PRK$^{ed.}$; an<?>gatā D^{a} 325 cānugatānanugatayor] DD^{a}GJS^{2}S^{3}S^{4}S^{5}P$^{p.c.}$RK$^{ed.}$; ghānugatānanugatayor P$^{a.c.}$ 326 aikyaṃ] DGJS^{2}S^{3}S^{4}S^{5}PRK$^{ed.}$; ekyaṃ D^{a} 327 traiguṇyam] DD^{a}GJS^{3}S^{4}S^{5}PRK$^{ed.}$; treguṇyam S^{2} 328 °paryālocanād anupapattir] DD^{a}S$^{2p.c.}$S^{3}S^{4}S^{5}PRK$^{ed.}$; °paryālocanānupapattir GJ, °paryālocanād anupattir S$^{2a.c.}$ 329 cinmaya°] DGJS^{2}S^{3}S^{4}S^{5}PRK$^{ed.}$; *om.* D^{a} 329 °rūpataiva] DD^{a}GJS^{3}S^{4}S^{5}PRK$^{ed.}$; °rūpa<?>iva S^{2} 329 sarvakāryāṇām] DD^{a}GJ$^{2p.c.}$S^{3}S^{4}S^{5}PRK$^{ed.}$; sarvaryāṇām S$^{2a.c.}$ 330 eva] DD^{a}GJS$^{2p.c.}$S^{3}S^{4}S^{5}PRK$^{ed.}$; ava S$^{2a.c.}$ 330 sattvād avināśitā] DD^{a}JS$^{2a.c.}$S^{3}S^{4}S^{5}PRK$^{ed.}$; sattvādivināśitā GS$^{2p.c.}$ 330 hi] D$^{p.c.}$D^{a}GJS^{2}S^{3}S^{4}S^{5}PRK$^{ed.}$; *om.* D$^{a.c.}$ 331 śivasya] DD^{a}GJS^{2}S^{3}S^{4}S^{5}K$^{ed.}$; viśvasya PR 331 itīśvarapratyabhijñāyām] GJS$^{2p.c.}$S^{3}S^{4}S^{5}PRK$^{ed.}$; itīśvarapratyabhijñām D, itītyevaṃ ceśvarapratyabhijñāyām D^{a}, itīśvarapratyabhijñāyāṃm S$^{2a.c.}$ 331 evaṃ] DS^{2}S^{3}S^{4}S^{5}PRK$^{ed.}$; *om.* D^{a}G, eva J 331 ca] DGJS^{2}S^{3}S^{4}S^{5}PRK$^{ed.}$; *om.* D^{a}

---

324 J folio 67r. 325 D folio 173r. 325 S^{2} folio 101v. 326 S^{5} folio 64v. 328 D^{a} folio 172r. 328 G folio 71r. 330 D folio 173v.

nāśaḥ kaṭakarūpeṇa sadbhāvaḥ kuṇḍalādinā 54
suvarṇatve 'pi na bhraṃśaḥ saṃsthāne 'pi vicāryatām

kaṭakakuṇḍalādilaukikanidarśanena saṃsthānamātrabheda uktaḥ. sa saṃsthāne 'pi bhedo vicāryatām.

tadvicāreṇa ca śivakāraṇatām eva paryavasānayann āha
kiṃ śivatvena tad vyāptam avyāptaṃ vābhidhīyatām 55
vyāpitve tadvināśitvam avyāptau syāt pradeśitā

55c It is possible that the erroneous reading of C of *kiṃ śīvatvena* for *kiṃ śivatvena* instead should be understood (again erroneously) to read *kiṃr śāvatvena.* 56a S^{2} does not highlight ŚD 4.56ab in yellow, as is the usual practice for marking verses of the *mūla*, but the end of the half-verse is marked off from the *Vṛtti* by a mark of red stain just prior to the beginning of the relevant passage of commentary. 56a S^{2} appears to correct a previous reading of *tadvināśitviṃ* to *tadvināśitvaṃ.* 56b S^{2} might delete a long *ī* of what would then read *dī* where it now properly reads *de* in *pradeśitā.*

54d sadbhāvaḥ] CDD^{a}GJS^{2}S^{3}S^{4}S^{5}PRK$^{ed.}$; sadbhā - T 54d kuṇḍalādinā] DD^{a}GJS^{2}S^{3}S^{4}S^{5}PRK$^{ed.}$; kuṇḍalādike TC 55a suvarṇatve 'pi] DD$^{a\,p.c.}$GJS^{2}S^{3}S^{4}S^{5}PRK$^{ed.}$; suvarṇatve (hypometric) T, suvarṇatvena C, suvarṇatve [']dhi D$^{a\,a.c.}$ 55b saṃsthāne] TDD^{a}GJS^{2}S^{3}S^{5}PRK$^{ed.}$; sasthāne CS^{4} 55c śivatvena] T$^{p.c.}$DD^{a}GJS^{2}S^{3}S^{4}S^{5}PRK$^{ed.}$; śi<?>tvena T$^{a.c.}$, śīvatvena C 55d abhidhīyatām] DD^{a}GJS^{2}S^{3}S^{4}S^{5}PRK$^{ed.}$; abhidhīyaṃtāṃ TC 56a vyāpitve] TDD^{a}GJS^{2}S^{3}S^{4}S^{5}PRK$^{ed.}$; tadvyāpitve C 56a tadvināśitvam] TDD^{a}GJS^{2}S^{3}S^{4}S^{5}PRK$^{ed.}$; tadviśitvam C 56b avyāptau] TDD^{a}GJS^{2}S^{3}S^{4}S^{5}PRK$^{ed.}$; adhyānhe C 56b syāt] TDD^{a}GJS^{2}S^{3}S^{4}S^{5}PRK$^{ed.}$; syā C 56b pradeśitā] TDD^{a}GJS^{2}S^{3}S^{5}PRK$^{ed.}$; prabhodhitaḥ C

---

335 P's variant reading for *saṃsthānamātrabheda uktaḥ* was corrected by a later hand. 335 A footnote in K$^{ed.}$ (p. 172) suggests one source consulted for that edition (*kha*) offers a variant reading of °*sānaya*° , but for what this is a variant is unclear. 336 A gap is recorded in D between *vicāryatām* and *tadvicāreṇa* to mark a full stop, but it is more narrow than what is usually recorded in the manuscript. The same may be said of D^{a}.

---

335 saṃsthānamātrabheda uktaḥ] DD^{a}GJS^{2}S^{3}S^{5}K$^{ed.}$; saṃsthānabhedamātra uktaḥ S^{4}R, saṃsthānabhedamātram uktam P$^{p.c.}$, saṃsthānabhedamātrayuktaḥ P$^{a.c.}$ 335 sa] DD^{a}S^{4}S^{5}; *om.* GJS^{2}S^{3}PRK$^{ed.}$ 336 saṃsthāne] DD^{a}GJS^{2}S^{3}S^{4}S^{5}K$^{ed.}$; svasaṃ - sthāne P, s<v?>asaṃsthāne R 336 bhedo] DD^{a}GS^{2}S^{3}S^{4}S^{5}PR K$^{ed.}$; bhodo J 337 ca] D^{a}GJS^{2}S^{3}S^{4}S^{5}PRK$^{ed.}$; *om.* D 337 śivakāraṇatām] DD^{a}GJS^{2}S^{3}S^{5}PRK$^{ed.}$; śikāraṇatām S^{4} 337 paryavasānayann] DD^{a}G$^{p.c.}$JS^{2}S^{3}S^{4}S^{5}PRK$^{ed.}$; paryanuvasānayann G$^{a.c.}$

---

333 S^{2} folio 102r. 335 D folio 174r. 335 S^{4} folio 42r. 335 J folio 67v.

mauliśivatvavyāptau maulivināśe śivavināśaḥ. śivāvyāptatve vā śivasya pradeśavṛttitā maulighaṭapaṭādisvarūpadeśaparihāreṇāvasthāne bhinnasvarūpadeśatvaṃ tataś cāvibhutvam iti saṃsthāna ubhayathābhidhīyamāno doṣaḥ.

naivaṃ yato hi bhāvānāṃ vināśe 'smāsu neṣṭatā 56
aṃśābhivyaktitā nāśo na nāśaḥ sarvalopitā

noktadoṣaḥ. yato bhāvānāṃ vināśe viṣaye neṣṭatāsmān prati, bhāvā na vināśino 'smābhir iṣyanta iti yāvat. asmaddarśane hi mauleḥ kaṭakotpādakāle 'ṃśasya hemamātrasyābhivyaktiḥ prāktanasya mauliparīṇāmakṣaṇasyeti nāśa ucyate na tu sarvāṃśādarśanam. tato na niranvayavināśadoṣaḥ, nāpy aṃśasya

---

56c yato] CDD^{a}GJS^{2}S^{3}S^{4}S^{5}PRK$^{ed.}$; - to T 56c bhāvānāṃ] DD^{a}GJS^{2}S^{3}S^{4}S^5 PRK$^{ed.}$; bhāvānā TC 56d vināśe] DD^{a}GJS^{2}S^{3}S^{4}S^{5}PRK$^{ed.}$; vināśo TC 56d neṣṭatā] TDD^{a}GJS^{2}S^{3}S^{4}S^{5}PRK$^{ed.}$; neṣṭatāṃ C 57a aṃśābhivyaktitā] DD^{a}GJS^{2}S^{3}S^{4}S^{5}PRK$^{ed.}$; aṃśo [']pi vyaktitā T, aṃśābhivyaktito C 57b na nāśaḥ] TCK$^{ed.p.c.}$; vināśaḥ DD^{a}GJS^{2}S^{3}S^{4}S^{5}PRK$^{ed.a.c.}$ 57b °lopitā] TDD^{a}GJS^{2}S^{3}S^{4}S^{5}PRK$^{ed.}$; °yogitā C

---

341 S^3 seems to record an *anusvāra* following *pradeśa* in *pradeśavṛttitā.* 342 G twice records *bhinnasvarūpadeśatvaṃ tataś cāvibhuktatvam iti.* 342 S^2 deletes an extraneous *anusvāra* following *avibhutva.* 348 S^4 writes *ṇa* of °*kṣaṇasyeti* into the right margin, indicating that it was perhaps at first left out of the recorded transcription. 349 On *niranvayavināśa* see PVV 413, 16-414, 1: *na hy asata utpattimattvaṃ sataś ca niranvayavināśo 'nityatvaṃ hetuḥ sāṃkhyasiddhaḥ. bauddhasya punar āgamāt siddhaḥ.*

---

340 °vināśe] DGJS^{2}S^{3}S^{4}S^{5}PRK$^{ed.}$; °nāśe D^a 340 śivāvyāptatve] DD$^{a p.c.}$GJS^{2}S^{3}PRK$^{ed.}$; śivatvavyāpatve D$^{a a.c.}$, śivavyāptatve S^{4}S^5 341 °ghaṭa°] DD^{a}GJS^{2}S^{4}S^{5}PRK$^{ed.}$; °ghaṭā° S^3 341 °svarūpa°] DGJS^{2}S^{3}S^{4}S^{5}PRK$^{ed.}$; °bhāva° D^a 342 °deśatvaṃ] DD$^{a p.c.}$GJS^{2}S^{3}S^{4}S^{5}PRK$^{ed.}$; °deśatve D$^{a a.c.}$ 342 avibhutvam] DD$^{a p.c.}$JS$^{2 a.c.}$S$^{3 p.c.}$S^{4}S^{5}PRK$^{ed.}$; avibhuktatvam D$^{a a.c.}$G, avibhuktam S$^{2 p.c.}$, avitvam S$^{3 a.c.}$ 346 noktadoṣaḥ] DD^{a}S^{2}S^{3}S^{4}S^{5}PRK$^{ed.}$; nokto doṣaḥ GJ 347 na vināśino] DD^{a}GJS^{2}S^{3}S^{4}S^{5}K$^{ed.}$; avināśino PR 347 mauleḥ] DD^{a}GJS^{2}S^{5}PRK$^{ed.}$; maule S^{3}S^4 348 'ṃśasya] DD^{a}GJS^{2}S^{3}S^{5}PRK$^{ed.}$; [']śasya S^4 349 °adarśanam] DD^{a}GJS^{2}S^{3}S^{4}S$^{5 p.c.}$PRK$^{ed.}$; °darśanam S$^{5 a.c.}$

---

340 D^a folio 172v. 341 G folio 71v. 341 D folio 174v. 341 S^3 folio 29r. 341 S^5 folio 65r. 342 R folio 44r. 344 S^2 folio 102v. 347 D folio 175r. 348 J folio 68r.

niranvayatānabhivyaktimātrasya nāśatvāt.

abhivyakter vināśitve tatrāpy ānantyam āpatet 57
indriyāṇām asāmarthyamātram atra vināśitā
asāv evānabhivyaktiḥ sa pracchannas tadā sthitaḥ 58

atha sthitānām evārthānāṃ yathābhivyaktimātrasyotpādas tathā vināśo 'pi tasyaiveti prāktanāṃśamātrasyānabhivyaktir vināśa ukta iti. etan na. yato yathābhivyakter apy asatyā utpattir uta satyā ity arthotpādoktadoṣo 'navasthā ca,

---

58a S^{5} appears to offer a correct reading of *asāmarthya*, but a later hand marks the presence of the long *ā* for clarity's sake. 58d C records *na* after a gap in the right margin at the end of the line, which ends with *sa pra°* of the manuscript's variant reading: *sa prachannatayā*. Could this be the *akṣara* missing from C's reading at ŚD 4.58b, where the manuscript's corrected reading offers *viśītā* for *vināśitā*?

57c abhivyakter] TDD^{a}GJS^{2}S^{5}PRK$^{ed.}$; abhivyakti C, abhivyakte S^{3}S^{4} 57d tatrāpi] TK$^{ed.p.c.}$; tathāpy CDD^{a}GJS^{2}S^{3}S^{4}S^{5}PRK$^{ed.a.c.}$ 57d ānantyam] TCDD^{a}GJS^{2}S$^{3p.c.}$S^{4}S^{5}PRK$^{ed.}$; ānanstyam S$^{3a.c.}$ 57d āpatet] TDD^{a}GJS^{2}S^{3}S^{4}S^{5} PRK$^{ed.}$; āpatṛl C 58a indriyāṇām] TDD^{a}GJS^{2}S^{3}S^{4}S^{5}PRK$^{ed.}$; indriyāṇāṃm C 58b °mātram] CDD^{a}GJS^{2}S^{3}S^{4}S^{5}PRK$^{ed.}$; - tram T 58b vināśitā] TDD^{a}GJS^{2}S^{3}S^{4}S^{5}PRK$^{ed.}$; viśītā (hypometric) C 58c evānabhivyaktiḥ] TDD^{a}GJS^{2}S^{3}S^{4}S^{5}PRK$^{ed.}$; evābhivyaktiḥ (hypometric) C 58d pracchannas tadā] TDD^{a}GJS^{2}S^{3}S^{4}S^{5}PRK$^{ed.}$; prachannatayā C 58d sthitaḥ] TDD^{a}GJS^{2}S$^{3p.c.}$S^{4}S^{5}PRK$^{ed.}$; sthitā C, sthitāḥ S$^{3a.c.}$

---

350 On *niranvayatā* see PVV 427, 9-12: *tatra ca niranvayaviruddhate kathite. tathā hy abhivyaktacaitanyadehalakṣaṇapuruṣena sadvitīyatvaṃ sādhyam. tena ca kuḍye 'nvayo na dṛṣṭa iti niranvayatā. ghaṭasya tu kuḍye 'nvayo dṛṣṭa iti tena sadvitīyatvasādhanāt viruddhatā syāt.* 354 In S^{3} *nā* of *sthitānām* is badly blotched but nevertheless legible. 354 S^{3} could be interpreted to read *evāthāṃnāṃ* for *evārthānāṃ*.

---

350 nāśatvāt] D^{a}GJS^{2}S^{3}S^{4}S^{5}PRK$^{ed.}$; nāśatvātvāt D 355 tasya] DGJS^{2}S^{3}S^{4}S^{5}PRK$^{ed.}$; arthasya D^{a} 355 prāktanāṃśa°] DD^{a}GJS^{2}S$^{3p.c.}$S^{5}PR K$^{ed.}$; prākta - nāṃsa° S$^{3a.c.}$, prāktānāṃśa° S^{4} 356 yathābhivyakter] DD^{a}GJS^{2}S^{3}S^{4}S$^{5p.c.}$PRK$^{ed.}$; yathābhivyaktir S$^{5a.c.}$ 356 asatyā utpattir] D^{a}S^{2}S^{3}S^{5}P$^{p.c.}$; asatya utpattir D, asatyotpattir GJK$^{ed.}$, asatyā tatpattir S^{4}, āsatyā utpattir P$^{a.c.}$R 356 satyā iti] DD^{a}; satyety GJS^{2}S^{3}S^{4}S^{5}PRK$^{ed.}$ 356 arthotpādoktadoṣo] DGJS^{2}S^{3}S^{4}S^{5}PRK$^{ed.}$; pūrvoktadoṣo D^{a}

---

352 D folio 175v. 353 G folio 72r. 353 S^{2} folio 103r. 355 D^{a} folio 173r. 355 P folio 55.

tathaivārthasya vināśo nopapannaḥ sato vināśāyogāt tathābhivyakter api. athābhivyaktir evābhivyakter vinaśyati, na sattā. tat tasyā apy abhivyaktyabhivyakter na sattā naśyati, api tv abhivyaktir ity ānantyaṃ syāt. athavābhivyakter vināśo 'pi kim asann utpadyate 'tha san. asattve satkāryavādahānir anupapattiś ca. sattve pūrvam eva vināśaḥ syāt. athābhivyaktir vināśasya kāraṇena kriyate, tat pūrvoktānavasthety ānantyam. evam asmaddarśana īśvarapratyabhijñoktanītyā

---

358 P records *śya* of its corrected reading of *naśyati* for *vinaśyati* in the right margin. 359 S^{4} omits *na sattā. tat tasyā apy abhivyaktyabhivyakter na sattā naśyati.* 361 K$^{ed.}$ does not punctuate after *kāraṇena kriyate*, but since *tat* marks the reply to the objection offered (itself signaled with *atha*), I here punctuate with a comma. 362 See, first of all, ĪPK 2.4.3-4, cited in the notes to the translation at line 289 of the edition, with the corresponding passage of the ĪPKVṛ cited in the notes to the translation at line 331. Cf. ĪPKVṛ ad ĪPK 1.8.8: *vikalpe ghaṭādyullekhaś cakṣurādyagocaro 'pi pṛthagābhāsād bāhya eva. ahaṃvimarśo hy antaratvam, idam iti tu bāhyatā. evaṃ ca ghaṭādīnām ubhayī bāhyatā bāhyāntaḥkaraṇadvayīvedyatā, sukhādes tv ekāntaḥkaraṇavedyataiva.* Finally, see ĪPK 2.2.2: *tatraikam āntaraṃ tattvaṃ tad evendriyavedyatām | saṃprāpyānekatāṃ yāti deśakālasvabhāvataḥ ||* Cf. ĪPKVṛ ad ĪPK 2.2.2: *abhinnam eva tattvam antarbahirābhāsabhedād ekānekam, bahirdeśakālasvabhāvabhedābhāsasaṃbhedamayaikaikasvalakṣaṇābhāsānām anekatvāt.*

---

357 tathaiva] DGJS^{2}S^{3}S^{4}S^{5}PRK$^{ed.}$; <?>thaiva D$^{ap.c.}$, tasyaiva D$^{aa.c.}$ 357 vināśo] D^{a}GJS^{2}S^{3}S^{4}S^{5}PRK$^{ed.}$; vivināśo D 357 tathābhivyakter] DD^{a}GJS$^{2p.c.}$S^{3}S^{4}S^{5}PRK$^{ed.}$; tathābhikter S$^{2a.c.}$ 358 evābhivyakter] DD^{a}GJS^{2}S^{4}S^{5}PRK$^{ed.}$; evābhivyakte S^{3} 358 vinaśyati] DD^{a}GJS^{2}S^{3}S^{5}K$^{ed.}$; naśyati S^{4}P$^{p.c.}$R, na<?>ti P$^{a.c.}$ 358 abhivyaktyabhivyakter] DD^{a}S^{2}S^{5}PRK$^{ed.}$; abhivyaktyābhivyakter GJ, abhivyaktyabhivyakte S^{3}, *om.* S^{4} 359 sattā] DD^{a}GJS^{2}S^{3}S^{5}P$^{p.c.}$RK$^{ed.}$; sutā P$^{a.c.}$, *om.* S^{4} 359 abhivyaktir] DD^{a}GJS^{3}S^{4}S^{5}PRK$^{ed.}$; abhiv<?>ktir S^{2} 360 'pi] DD^{a}GJS^{2}S^{3}S^{5}K$^{ed.}$; *om.* S^{4}PR 360 asann] DD^{a}GJS$^{2p.c.}$S^{3}S^{4}S^{5}PRK$^{ed.}$; ann S$^{2a.c.}$ 360 asattve] GJ, asatye DD^{a}S^{2}S^{3}S^{4}S^{5}PRK$^{ed.}$ 360 satkāryavādahānir] DD^{a}GJS^{2}S$^{3p.c.}$S^{4}S^{5}RK$^{ed.}$; satkāryavāda<?>nir S$^{3a.c.}$, satkārthavādahānir P 361 atha] DD^{a}GJS^{2}S^{3}S^{4}S^{5}RK$^{ed.}$; athavā P 361 abhivyaktir vināśasya] DD^{a}S$^{2p.c.}$S^{3}S^{4}S^{5}PRK$^{ed.}$; abhivyaktivināśasya GJ, abhivyaktar vināśasya S$^{2a.c.}$ 362 pūrvoktānavasthety] D$^{p.c.}$D^{a}GJS^{2}S^{3}S^{4}S^{5}PRK$^{ed.}$; pūrvoktānavasthyety D$^{a.c.}$ 362 °ukta°] D^{a}S^{4}PRK$^{ed.}$; °ādi° D, °udita° GJS^{2}S^{3}S^{5}

---

357 D folio 176r. 358 S^{5} folio 65v. 359 S^{4} folio 42v. 361 J folio 68v. 361 D folio 176v. 361 S^{2} folio 103v.

yathobhayendriyavedyatvaṃ śivābhedākhyātimayam arthānāṃ karaṇam, tathā vināśa ubhayendriyavedyatvābhāvaḥ śivābhedaḥ śivatvena pracchādanaṃ, tad evoktaṃ indriyāṇām asāmarthyaṁ tathāsāv evānabhivyaktiḥ, sa ghaṭādiḥ śivatayā pracchannas tadā sthita iti.

ito 'pi nāśo nāsty asya ghaṭasya karaṇāt punaḥ
nābhāvaprāptarūpasya karaṇaṃ yujyate punaḥ 59
tasmād bhāvavināśe 'pi śivatattvāvināśitā

59c ŚD 4.59cd is omitted from T. 59c A later hand adds the *visarga* to P's corrected reading of *nābhāvaḥ* for *nābhāva°*. 60b S^{2} is written in such a manner that one could understand it to have first read *yiva°* (or perhaps even *piva°*) for *śiva°*.

59a ito 'pi nāśo] TCDD^{a}GJS^{2}S^{3}S^{5}K$^{ed.}$; yato nāśe (hypometric) S^{4}, yato nāśe pi P, yato nāśo pi R 59c nābhāva°] DD$^{a\,p.c.}$GJS^{2}S^{3}S^{4}S^{5}P$^{a.c.}$RK$^{ed.}$; *om.* T, nābhāvaḥ CD$^{a\,a.c.}$P$^{p.c.}$ 59d karaṇaṃ] DD^{a}GJS^{2}S^{3}S^{4}S^{5}PRK$^{ed.}$; *om.* T, karaṃ (hypometric) C 59d punaḥ] CDD^{a}GJS^{2}S^{3}S^{5}PRK$^{ed.}$; *om.* T, puḥ (hypometric) S^{4} 60a bhāvavināśe] TDD^{a}GJS^{2}S^{3}S^{4}S^{5}PRK$^{ed.}$; bhāvaś cināśe C 60b °vināśitā] TDD^{a}GJS^{2}S^{3}S^{4}S^{5}PRK$^{ed.}$; °vināśitaḥ C

---

363 The *i* of *śivābheda°* is heavily blotched in S^{3}. 363 S^{2} records *da* above *dā* in its (correct) reading of *śivābhedākhyātimaya*. 367 A footnote in K$^{ed.}$ (p. 173) suggests that *ca* is omitted from the reading of one source examined for that edition (*kha*), but it is unclear to what Kaul refers with this note. It seems likely that this refers to the missing connective particle (*ca*) in D at *śaśaviṣāṇatām eva ca* (line 372 of the present edition), which appears on p. 174, line 1 of the KSTS edition.

---

363 °vedyatvaṃ] DD^{a}GJS$^{2\,p.c.}$S^{3}S^{4}S^{5}PRK$^{ed.}$; °vediyatvaṃ S$^{2\,a.c.}$ 363 śivābhedākhyātimayaṃ] DD^{a}GJS^{2}S^{3}S^{4}S^{5}P$^{a.c.}$RK$^{ed.}$; śivābhedākhyātimaya P$^{p.c.}$ 363 karaṇam] PK$^{ed.}$; kāraṇam DD^{a}GJS^{2}S^{3}S^{4}S^{5}R 364 vināśa] DD^{a}GJS^{2}S^{3}S^{4}S^{5}P$^{p.c.}$K$^{ed.}$; vināśi P$^{a.c.}$R 364 śivābhedaḥ] DD^{a}JS^{2}S^{4}S^{5}PRK$^{ed.}$; śibhedaḥ G, śivābheda S^{3} 365 indriyāṇām] DD^{a}GJS^{2}S^{3}S^{4}S^{5}K$^{ed.}$; indriyāṇāṃm PR 365 tathā] DD^{a}GJS^{2}S^{3}S^{5}K$^{ed.}$; *om.* S^{4}PR 365 anabhivyaktiḥ] DD$^{a\,p.c.}$GJS^{2}S^{3}S^{4}S^{5}PRK$^{ed.}$; anavyaktiḥ D$^{a\,a.c.}$ 365 ghaṭādiḥ śivatayā] DD^{a}GJS^{2}S^{3}S^{5}PRK$^{ed.}$; ghaṭādiśivatayā S^{4} 366 pracchannas] DD^{a}GJS$^{2\,p.c.}$S^{3}S^{4}S^{5}PRK$^{ed.}$; pracchanna S$^{2\,a.c.}$

---

363 R folio 44v. 364 G folio 72v. 366 D folio 177r.

ito 'pi hetor nāśo nāsty asya ghaṭādeḥ punaḥ karaṇāt. na hi yasya sarvathā śaśaviṣāṇatulyam abhāvaṃ prāptaṃ rūpaṃ tasyārthasya punaḥ sattā bhavet. nanu pūrvo 'nya eva ghaṭaḥ śaśaviṣāṇatām eva ca prāpto 'yaṃ cānya eva kriyate. tad etan nāsti. na hi ghaṭād anyo ghaṭaḥ syāt. mahattvalohitatvocchritatvādisāmānyāntarasaṃparke 'ntaravasthita evendriyavedyo 'bhedākhyātimayaḥ kriyata iti pūrvam uktam. tasmād uktakrameṇa bhāvānāṃ śivatattvanimajjanarūpeṇa tadabhedākhyātivināśe 'pi śivatattvāvināśitā. evam utpattivināśānyathānupapattyā sarvaśivatā vyavasthitā.

---

370 S^3 highlights *sya* in its (erroneous) variant reading, that of *ghaṭasyadeḥ* for *ghaṭādeḥ*. 370 S^3 records *rva* of *sarvathā* at the bottom of the folio, below the last line of text. 371 D^a adds *rūpaṃ* with a marginal note that reads: *rūpam iti śeṣaḥ*. 372 P records *śaśaviṣāṇatām* in a manner suggesting the scribe first there recorded an initial vowel *e* in place of the final *m*. 372 S^2 deletes an *akṣara* prior to *m eva* of *śaśaviṣāṇatām eva*. 373 S^5 deletes *eva* following *ghaṭād anyo ghaṭaḥ*. 373 $K^{ed.}$ does not punctuate following *anyo ghaṭaḥ syāt*, but I here add a full stop in order to clarify the syntax. 375 S^2 records *tasmād uktakrameṇa bhāvānāṃ śivatattvanimajjanarūpeṇa tadabhedākhyāti°* in the bottom margin, having first left it out of its rendering. The manuscript appears to have recorded a long *ā* following *uktam* prior to this correction. 376 D twice records *'bhedākhyātimayaḥ kriyata iti pūrvam uktam. tasmād uktakrameṇa bhāvānāṃ śivatattvanimajjanarūpeṇa*. This is caused by an eye-skip. Note that the folio change to 178r. occurs at the second instance of recording *tasmād ukta°*. D^a, in turn, twice records *abhedākhyātimayaḥ kriyata iti pūrvam uktaṃ*. 377 P records *sarva* of *sarvaśivatā* in the right margin.

---

370 nāśo] $DD^aJS^2S^3S^4S^5PRK^{ed.}$; nā G 370 nāsty] $DD^aGJS^2S^3S^4S^5RK^{ed.}$; nāś<?>y P 370 ghaṭādeḥ] $DD^aGJS^2S^4S^{5p.c.}PRK^{ed.}$; ghaṭasyadeḥ $S^3S^{5a.c.}$ 370 sarvathā] $DD^aGJS^2S^{3p.c.}S^4S^5PRK^{ed.}$; sathā $S^{3a.c.}$ 371 śaśaviṣāṇa°] $DD^aGJS^{2p.c.}S^3S^4S^5PRK^{ed.}$; śaśiviṣāṇa° $S^{2a.c.}$ 371 °tulyam] $DGJS^2S^3S^4S^5PRK^{ed.}$; °sadṛśam $D^{ap.c.}$, °sadṛśaṃm $D^{aa.c.}$ 371 rūpaṃ tasyārthasya] $DD^{ap.c.}S^{2a.c.}S^3S^4S^5PK^{ed.}$; tasyārthasya $D^{aa.c.}$, rūpāntarasyārthasya GJ, rūpaṃ rūpāntarasyārthasya $S^{2p.c.}$ 372 śaśaviṣāṇatām] $DD^aGJS^{2p.c.}S^3S^4S^5PRK^{ed.}$; śaśaviṣāṇatāṃm $S^{2a.c.}$ 372 ca] $D^aGJS^2S^3S^4S^5PRK^{ed.}$; *om.* D 374 °lohitatvocchritatva°] $DD^aS^2S^3S^4S^5PRK^{ed.}$; °lohitocchritatva° GJ 374 'ntaravasthita] $DD^aGJS^2S^4S^5PRK^{ed.}$; [']nratavasthita S^3 374 evendriya°] $DD^aS^2S^3S^4S^5PRK^{ed.}$; evaindriya° GJ 376 °tattva°] $DD^aGS^2S^3S^4S^5PRK^{ed.}$; °ttva° J 377 °anupapattyā] $DD^aGJS^3S^4S^5PRK^{ed.}$; °anupattyā S^2 377 sarvaśivatā] $DGJS^2S^3S^4S^5P^{p.c.}RK^{ed.}$; sarvaśivamayatā D^a, śivatā $P^{a.c.}$

---

370 D^a folio 173v. 371 S^2 folio 104r. 372 D folio 177v. 372 S^3 folio 29v. 373 S^5 folio 66r. 373 J folio 69r. 375 D folio 178r. 377 G folio 73r.

itaś ca sarvaśivatāvayavebhyo na kutracit 60
vyatireko 'vayavinas tad evedaṃ vicāryatām
bhinneṣv aikyam abhedaś ca yathā tatra vyavasthitaḥ 61
tathā tatra parijñeyaṃ patyuḥ sāmarthyam īdṛśam
abhinne bhedatā yena bhinneṣv apy asty abhedatā 62
yathāvayavagaṃ rūpaṃ tathā sarvapadārthagam

ito 'pi ca hetoḥ sarvaśivatā. avayavebhyo vyatirikto 'vayavī na kvacij jñāne cākṣuṣe mānase vāvabhāsate. yair api vyatirikto 'sau pratijñātas taiḥ pratītiḥ

62d The final *akṣara* in C's reading of *asti* for *asty* appears to have been added after the scribe first recorded *asi*. 62d C correctly records the present verse as ŚD 4.62, but seems to have corrected the enumeration from what appears to have previously read ŚD 4.64.

60c sarvaśivatā] $CDD^aGJS^2S^3S^4S^5PRK^{ed.}$; sarva - - tā T 61a vyatireko] $TDD^aGJS^2S^3S^4S^5PRK^{ed.}$; vyatire (hypometric) C 61a 'vayavinas] $TDD^aGJS^2S^3S^4S^5PRK^{ed.}$; 'vayavis (hypometric) C 61b evedaṃ] $TDD^aGJS^2S^3S^4S^5PRK^{ed.}$; avedaṃ C 61b vicāryatām] $TDD^aGJS^2S^3S^4S^5PRK^{ed.}$; vicāryataṃ C 61c bhinneṣv] $TDD^aGJS^2S^3S^4S^5PRK^{ed.}$; bhinnapy C 61c aikyam] $TCDD^aJS^2S^3S^4S^5PRK^{ed.}$; aikam G 61d tatra] $TDD^aGJS^2S^3S^4S^5PRK^{ed.}$; tatham C 61d vyavasthitaḥ] *conj.*; vyavasthitam $TDD^aGJS^2S^3S^4S^5PK^{ed.}$; avasthitaṃ C, vya<?>sthitam R 62b īdṛśam] $TDD^aGJS^2S^3S^4S^5PRK^{ed.}$; īdṛśyaṃ C 62c abhinne bhedatā] $DD^aGJS^2S^3S^4S^5PRK^{ed.}$; abhinnabhedatā TC 62c yena] $CDD^aGJS^2S^3S^4S^5PRK^{ed.}$; ye - T 62d bhinneṣv] $CDD^aGJS^2S^3S^4S^5PRK^{ed.}$; - nneṣv T 62d asty] $TDD^aGJS^2S^3S^4S^5PRK^{ed.}$; asti C 62d abhedatā] $TDD^aGJS^2S^3S^4S^5PRK^{ed.}$; bhedatā C 63b tathā] $DD^aGJS^2S^3S^4S^5PRK^{ed.}$; tadvat TC

---

384 R is apparently damaged by water and the *akṣaras* are blurred where it apparently reads *vyatiriktor* for *vyatirikto*. 385 G records the absence of some text between *vyatiri* and *kto* (together a correct reading), this by there recording two short dashes (- -).

---

384 avayavebhyo] $DD^aJS^2S^3S^4S^5PRK^{ed.}$; avayebhyo G 384 vyatirikto] $DD^aGJS^2S^3S^4S^5PK^{ed.}$; vyatiriktor R 384 'vayavī] $DD^aGJS^2S^3S^4S^5P^{p.c.}K^{ed.}$; veyavī $P^{a.c.}$ 385 'sau] $DD^aGJS^2S^3S^4S^5PK^{ed.}$; <?> R 385 pratītiḥ] $DD^aS^2S^{3p.c.}S^4S^5PRK^{ed.}$; pratīti $GJS^{3a.c.}$

---

380 S^2 folio 104v. 381 D folio 178v. 382 S^4 folio 43r. 384 P folio 56. 385 R folio 45r.

samavāyavaśād abhedenaiveṣyate. tac cedaṃ vicāryatām. yady api vitatāvabhāse 'vayavā bhinnā vyavasthitāḥ paramāṇumātre hy abhedini vaitatyābhāvāt tathāpy eka eva devadattasaṃjño 'rtho niḥsandhibandha ekaghano 'vabhātīti bhinneṣv evāvayaveṣv aikyaṃ bhāti. tatra yathaikyaṃ, tathā patyuḥ śivasya cinmayasya tatsāmarthyam īśvarapratyabhijñāyām uktaṃ yena sāmarthyenābhinne devadatte 'vayavabhedātmatā, avayaveṣu ca bhinneṣv ekaiva devadattatā

---

386 See, e.g., NS 2.1.32-36, esp. 2.1.34 (2.1.35 in Jha's translation): *sarvāgrahaṇam avayavasiddheḥ.* Cf. NSBh ad NS 2.1.34: *yady avayavī nāsti sarvasya grahaṇaṃ nopapadyate. kiṃ tat sarvam. dravyaguṇakarmasāmānyaviśeṣasamavāyāḥ. kathaṃ kṛtvā. paramāṇusamavasthānaṃ tāvad darśanaviṣayo na bhavaty atīndriyatvād aṇūnām, dravyāntarañ cāvayavibhūtaṃ darśanaviṣayo nāsti, darśanaviṣayasthāś ceme dravyādayo gṛhante te niradhiṣṭhānā na gṛhyeran. gṛhyante tu kumbho 'yaṃ śyāma eko mahān saṃyuktaḥ spandate 'sti mṛnmayaś ceti, santi ceme guṇādayo dharmā iti. tena sarvasya grahaṇāt paśyāmo 'sti dravyāntarabhūto 'vayavīti.* 386 P crosses out the horizontal stroke of the final *ta* of its (erroneous) reading of *vicāryatam* for *vicāryatām*. Perhaps the scribe, in haste, had first written or begun to write *vicāryate*? 388 A later hand adds *datta* to *devadattasaṃjño* in P, recording the addition just above the line. 390 See, e.g., ĪPK 2.1.8: *kintu nirmāṇaśaktiḥ sāpy evaṃviduṣa īśituḥ | tathā vijñātṛvijñeyabhedo yad avabhāsyate* || The corresponding passage of the ĪPKVṛ reads as follows: *evaṃ pūrṇatayā prakāśamānasyāpi parameśvarasya saiṣā sṛṣṭiśaktir yajjñātṛjñeyasvabhāvā bhāvāḥ svato 'nyonyaṃ ca vibhāgenāvasīyante, na ca tathāvasāyena tasya svarūpasthitis tirodhīyate.* 390 D leaves a space, signaling a full stop, following *īśvarapratyabhijñāyām uktaṃ*. D^{a} also marks with punctuation in the same place. 391 P and R omit *avayaveṣu ca bhinneṣv ekaiva devadattatā yujyate.*

---

386 tac] $DGJS^{2}S^{3}S^{4}S^{5}PRK^{ed.}$; tataś D^{a} 386 vicāryatām] $DD^{a}GJS^{2}S^{3}S^{5}K^{ed.}$; vicāryatam P, vicāryam S^{4}R 387 abhedini] $DD^{a}GJS^{2}S^{3}S^{5}PRK^{ed.}$; abhedani S^{4} 388 °datta°] $DD^{a}GJS^{2}S^{3}S^{5}P^{p.c.}K^{ed.}$; °deva° S^{4}, *om.* $P^{a.c.}$R 389 evāvayaveṣv] $DD^{a}GJS^{2}S^{3}S^{5}PRK^{ed.}$; evāyaveṣv S^{4} 390 cinmayasya] $GJK^{ed.}$; cinmātrasya $DD^{a}S^{2}S^{3}S^{4}S^{5}PR$ 391 devadatte] $DD^{a}GJS^{3}S^{4}S^{5}PRK^{ed.}$; devadatteva S^{2} 391 'vayavabhedātmatā] $DD^{a}JS^{3}S^{4}S^{5}PRK^{ed.}$; [']vayabhedātmatā GS^{2} 391 eva] $DD^{a}S^{2}S^{3}S^{4}S^{5}K^{ed.}$; *om.* GJPR 391 devadattatā] $DGJS^{2}S^{3}S^{5}PRK^{ed.}$; devadattatayā D^{a}, devadattā S^{4}

---

386 D^{a} folio 174r. 386 D folio 179r. 387 J folio 69v. 388 S^{5} folio 66v. 389 S^{2} folio 105r. 390 G folio 73v. 391 D folio 179v.

yujyate. yathāvayavabhedagatam ekaṃ rūpam, evaṃ trailokyavartiṣv api sarveṣv evārtheṣu gataṃ śivarūpam.

tad eva vyanakti

kva pāṇipādaṃ kva śiro yathaikyaṃ bhinnadeśagam 63
tadvat sarvapadārthānāṃ jagaty aikye sthitaḥ śivaḥ

avayavabhedasyāpy abhinnāvayavirūpatā śivarūpatayaiveti pratipāditam īśvarapratyabhijñāyām. evaṃ jagaty aikye śivarūpatopapādikā sthitā.

64b The hand in D^{a} that corrects by adding *śivaḥ* is the same as the one that records the marginal notes in that manuscript.

63d yathaikyaṃ] $TDD^{a}GJS^{2}S^{3}S^{4}S^{5}PRK^{ed.}$; yathaiśāṃ C 64b śivaḥ] $TCDD^{a\,p.c.}GJS^{2}S^{3}S^{4}S^{5}PRK^{ed.}$; *om.* $D^{a\,a.c.}$

---

392 $K^{ed.}$ punctuates with a comma following *yujyate*; I punctuate with a full stop. See my notes corresponding to the relevant passages of the translation for an explanation as to why I do so. 392 $K^{ed.}$ punctuates with a full stop following *ekaṃ rūpam*. I punctuate with a comma and understand what follows to gloss *tathā sarvapadārthagam* (ŚD 4.63b), the correlative clause connected syntactically to ŚD 4.63a: *yathāvayavagaṃ rūpaṃ*. See my notes corresponding to the relevant passages of the translation of the ŚD and ŚDVṛ for an explanation as to why I do so. 398 Accepting the reading of $K^{ed.\,p.c.}$ of *evaṃ* for *eva*, I punctuate following *īśvarapratyabhijñāyām* with a full stop, what is absent from $K^{ed.}$. 398 Cf. ĪPK (and ĪPKVṛ ad) 2.2.5: *jātidravyāvabhāsānāṃ bahir apy ekarūpatām | vyaktyekadeśabhedaṃ cāpy ālambante vikalpanāḥ* || ĪPKVṛ: *gāvaś caitra iti ca matayo bahir api gomātraikaghanapuruṣaviśeṣākārābhāsaikyaṃ svalakṣaṇāvayavābhāsabahutvaṃ ca parāmṛśanti.*

---

392 yathā] $K^{ed.\,p.c.}$; tathā ca $D^{a}GJS^{2}S^{3}S^{5}$, tathā $DS^{4}PRK^{ed.\,a.c.}$ 397 avayavabhedasyāpy] $DD^{a}GJS^{2}S^{3}S^{5}PRK^{ed.}$; avayabhedasyāpy S^{4} 397 abhinnāvayavirūpatā śivarūpatayaiveti] $GJS^{3}S^{5\,p.c.}K^{ed.}$; abhinnāvayavibhinnarūpatā śivarūpataiveti $DS^{2\,p.c.}$, abhinnāvayavirūpatā śivarūpataiveti D^{a}, abhinnāvayavarūpatā śivarūpatayaiveti $S^{2\,a.c.}$, abhinnāvayavibhinnarūpataiveti $S^{4}PR$, avayavibhinnarūpatā śivarūpatayaiveti $S^{5\,a.c.}$ 398 evaṃ] $K^{ed.\,p.c.}$; eva $DD^{a}GJS^{2}S^{3}S^{4}S^{5}PRK^{ed.\,a.c.}$

---

398 D folio 180r.

śabdāder grahaṇaṃ nāsti pūrvāparasahoditaiḥ 64
manasaḥ preraṇaṃ kasmāt prāgjñānena vinā sthitā
sarvaikatāta evātra tathā sauṣuptabodhanam 65
ghaṭate kathaṃ nimittasya prāgyogāyogacoditaiḥ
yoge jāgradavasthaiva tasmāt sarvaṃ śivātmakam 66

65c Damage to the manuscript makes it difficult to read *sa* of *sarva*° in T, but it is nevertheless legible. 65c A footnote in K$^{ed.}$ (p. 175) suggests that one source examined for that edition (*kha*) offers a variant reading of *pratijñātaḥ*. For what this is a variant is unclear. Perhaps it is somehow associated with *pratijñātas tais*, which appears on p. 174, line 16 of K$^{ed.}$, line 385 of the present edition, though in that case there would be no variant here recorded (unless what is meant is that *tais* is omitted(?)). 65c C records *na* in the right margin, following *evā* of *evātra*. While the manuscript does not appear to indicate as much, this could be the missing *akṣara* of C's reading (*post correctionem*) of *jñāne* for *jñānena* at ŚD 4.65b. 65d C appears to delete what would have read *tatho* for *tathā*. 66a ŚD 4.66a is hypermetric and does not conform to *śloka* metre.

64c śabdāder] C$^{p.c.}$DD^{a}GJS^{2}S^{3}S^{4}S^{5}PRK$^{ed.}$; śa<?>ā - e T, śabdader C$^{a.c.}$ 64c grahaṇaṃ] CDD^{a}GJS^{2}S^{3}S^{4}S^{5}PRK$^{ed.}$; - haṇaṃ T 65a preraṇaṃ] TCDD^{a}GJS^{2}S^{4}S^{5}PRK$^{ed.}$; preraṇe S^{3} 65a kasmāt] TDD^{a}GJS^{2}S^{3}S^{4}S^{5}PRK$^{ed.}$; tasmāt C 65b prāg°] DD^{a}GJS^{2}S^{3}S^{4}S^{5}PRK$^{ed.}$; tat TC 65b °jñānena] TDD^{a}GJS^{2}S^{3}S^{4}S^{5}PRK$^{ed.}$; jñāne (hypometric) C$^{p.c.}$; jñānau C$^{a.c.}$ 65b vinā sthitā] TDD^{a}GJK$^{ed.}$; vinā sthitaḥ C, avinā sthitā S^{2}S^{5}, avinā sthita S^{3}, avyavasthitā S^{4}PR 65c ekatāta] TDD^{a}GJS^{2}S^{3}S^{4}S^{5}PRK$^{ed.}$; ekatātāta (hypermetric) C 65d sauṣuptabodhanam] TDD^{a}GJS^{2}S^{3}S^{4}S^{5}PRK$^{ed.}$; śausavodhanaṃ (hypometric) C 66a ghaṭate] TDD^{a}GJS^{3}S^{4}S^{5}PRK$^{ed.}$; ghaṭe C, ghaṭetai S^{2} 66a kathaṃ] TCDD^{a}GJS^{2}S$^{3p.c.}$S^{4}S^{5}PRK$^{ed.}$; kithaṃ S$^{3a.c.}$ 66a nimittasya] CDD^{a}GJS^{2}S^{3}S^{4}S^{5}PRK$^{ed.}$; nimittasyā T 66b prāgyogāyogacoditaiḥ] DD^{a}GJS^{2}S^{3}S^{4}S^{5}PRK$^{ed.}$; prāgyog<e/o?> - coditaiḥ T, prāgyogavādhitaiḥ (hypometric) C 66c jāgradavasthaiva] CDD^{a}GJS^{2}S^{3}S^{4}S^{5}PRK$^{ed.}$; jāgradavastheva T 66d tasmāt] TDD^{a}GJS^{2}S^{3}S^{4}S^{5}PRK$^{ed.}$; tasmāta (missing *virāma*) C 66d sarvaṃ śivātmakam] TDD^{a}GJS^{2}S^{3}S^{4}S^{5}PRK$^{ed.}$; sarvaśivātmakaṃ C

---

399 S^{2} folio 105v. 402 J folio 70r. 402 D^{a} folio 174v. 402 T folio 8r.

ata eva cātra jagati sarvaikatā sthitā yataḥ śabdasparśarūpāder viṣayasya sarvasya pūrvāparasahotpannair jñānair vyatiriktatvāj jñānaṃ nāsti. tathā hi pūrvaṃ tāvaj jñānaṃ kathaṃ viṣayeṇa vinā syāt, paścāc ca sahāpi dvayoḥ svātmani sthitayoḥ kathaṃ grāhyagrāhakabhāvaḥ, arthābhisaṃdhijñānena ca vinā

---

404 S^2 records what appears to be *ṭī* above *ata* of *ata eva cātra.* Could this stand for *ṭīkā*, marking the passage as part of the commentary (despite it's properly being named the *Vṛtti* or *Padasaṅgati*)? For, S^2 also highlights *ata eva cātra jagati sarvaikatā sthitā yataḥ*, the manner in which is intimated in that manuscript that a passage (though this one is a part of the commentary and anyhow is unmetrical) should be counted as part of the *mūla.* 405 It is a later hand that corrects the reading in P of *pūrvāparasahotpannair.* 405 S^4 appears to mark *pa* of *pūrvāparasahotpannair* for correction, but the reading in the manuscript is correct as it stands. 405 S^5 ends with its reading of *pūrvāparasahotpannai* for *pūrvāparasahotpannair.* No marks indicate that any of the remaining text of the ŚD or ŚDVṛ are missing. D also ends with the same reading of *pūrvāparasahotpannai* for *pūrvāparasahotpannair,* this on folio 180v., which is left blank after the line-and-a-half of text it records is written (with the exception of the labeling of the folio side in the bottom left-hand corner of the folio side). 405 The readings of S^4, P and R end prior to *jñānaṃ nāsti.* There is no mark in the manuscripts suggesting the pasage here recorded is incomplete. One merely sees the text end following the reading of *vyatiriktatvā* for *vyatiriktatvāj* in all three manuscrupts, though P adds a double *daṇḍa* immediately following. There is no colophon or any other mark at the end of the manuscript of P apart from the double *daṇḍa,* and there is no mark at all in S^4. R ends with a colophon at the bottom of the last folio side of the manuscript. It reads: *prācīnapustakeṣu jīrṇatayai<?>vānevādarśo tas tadabhāvāvataḥ paraṃnati<?>itaṃ.* 405 A footnote in $K^{ed.}$ (p. 175) records a variant reading in one source that was examined for that edition (*kha*), that of *cinmātrasya.* With what this reading should be associated is unclear. Perhaps it is a variant for *cinmayasya,* which appears on p. 174, line 20 of the KSTS edition and on line 390 of the present edition. 406 G and J insert *mi* following *svātmani* and prior to *sthitayoḥ.* 407 S^2 records *vinā ca kasmād ātmanaḥ manasaḥ preraṇaṃ, tad bāhyārthagrahaṇārtham asti cet pūrvaṃ jñānaṃ kiṃ manaḥpreraṇena. na cābhisaṃdhijñānānena* in the bottom margin, having first left it out of the transcription.

---

405 pūrvāparasahotpannair] $D^aGJS^2S^3S^4P^{p.c.}RK^{ed.}$; pūrvāparasahotpannai DS^5, pūrvāparasahotpatair $P^{a.c.}$ 405 jñānair] $D^aGJS^2S^3K^{ed.}$; tair S^4PR 405 vyatiriktatvāj] $D^aGJS^2S^3K^{ed.}$; vyatiriktatvā S^4PR 407 grāhya°] $D^aGJS^{2p.c.}S^3K^{ed.}$; grāhi° $S^{2a.c.}$ 407 ca vinā] $D^aK^{ed.}$; vinā ca GJS^2S^3

---

404 D folio 180v. 405 G folio 74r. 406 S^3 folio 30r.

kasmād ātmanā manasaḥ preraṇaṃ, tad bāhyārthagrahaṇārtham astīti cet pūrvaṃ jñānaṃ kiṃ manaḥpreraṇena. na cābhisaṃdhijñānena bāhyo 'rtho jñātas tadarthaṃ manasaḥ preraṇaṃ na syāt. tasmāc cidrūpaśivaikye sarvadā saṃvedane sthite prakriyāmātram idaṃ niyatiśaktikṛtam īśvarapratyabhijñoktam abhedākhyātimayaṃ draṣṭavyam. tathā sauṣupte sthitasya prabodhanam uccaiḥśabdādisamuccāraṇena kathaṃ ghaṭetaikatāṃ vinā. tathā hy uccaiḥśabdādijñānaṃ prabodhanimittaṃ tasya ca prāg yogo 'tha na yoga iti codyaiḥ kathaṃ ghaṭanam, tathā hi prāk śabdādijñānena yoge jāgradavasthaiva syāt tasyās tathālakṣaṇatvāt, prāk śabdādijñānasya nimittasya tu virahe kathaṃ prabodhaḥ. tad etad eva syād vidyaikatve śivatvākhyātiprakriyāmātram etat syāt. tīvraśabdādikenājñātenāpy āvaraṇapreraṇe kṛte sauṣuptavinivṛttir iti ca paroktaṃ kutaḥ, pramāṇāt siddham iti ca na niścāyakaṃ katham.

sāmānyarūpatā vāsti sā cābhinnā viśeṣataḥ
bhinnābhinnātmakaḥ kvāpi padārthas tādṛg iṣyate 67

67c The *akṣara ma* of °*ātmakaṃ* in C is blotched but nevertheless legible.

67a vāsti] TD^{a}K$^{ed.}$; vyāptiḥ C, nāsti GJS^{2}S^{3} 67b cābhinnā] TD^{a}GJS^{2}S^{3}K$^{ed.}$; sābhinnā C 67c bhinnābhinnātmakaḥ] TD^{a}GJS^{2}S^{3}K$^{ed.}$; bhinnabhinnātmakaṃ C 67c kvāpi] TD^{a}GJS^{2}S^{3}K$^{ed.}$; vāpi C 67d padārthas] TCD^{a}S^{2}S^{3}K$^{ed.}$; pādārthas GJ

---

410 In S^{2}, *na* is added above the margin, having first been left out of the transcription. 416 In S^{2}, *ve* of the manuscript's reading of *abhāve tu* is heavily blotched but nevertheless legible.

---

408 ātmanā] GJS^{3}K$^{ed.}$; ātmanaḥ D^{a}S^{2} 408 preraṇaṃ] D^{a}GJS^{2}K$^{ed.}$; preraṇa S^{3} 408 astīti] *conj.*; asti D^{a}GJS^{2}S^{3}K$^{ed.}$ 409 abhisaṃdhijñānena] D^{a}GJS^{3}K$^{ed.}$; abhisaṃdhijñānānena S^{2} 410 jñātas] D^{a}GJS^{3}K$^{ed.}$; jñā<?>as S^{2} 412 abhedākhyātimayaṃ] S^{2}S^{3}; abhedābhidhāyimamayaṃ D^{a}GJ, abhedābhidhāyimayaṃ K$^{ed.}$ 415 prāk śabdādijñānena] GJS^{2}S^{3}K$^{ed.}$; prāk chabdādijñānena D^{a} 416 prāk śabdādijñānasya] GJS^{2}S^{3}K$^{ed.}$; prāk chabdādijñānasya D^{a} 416 tu virahe] D^{a}K$^{ed.}$; abhāve tu GJS^{2}S^{3} 417 eva] D^{a}S^{2}K$^{ed.}$; evaṃ GJS^{3} 417 vidyaikatve] D^{a}K$^{ed.}$; yady ekatve GJS^{3}, vidyekatve S^{2} 418 ajñātena] D^{a}GJS^{2}S^{3}; ajñānena K$^{ed.}$ 418 āvaraṇapreraṇe] D^{a}GJS^{2}S^{3}; āvaraṇe K$^{ed.}$ 418 iti ca] D^{a}K$^{ed.}$; aty api GJ, ity api S^{2}S^{3} 419 ca] D^{a}GJS^{3}K$^{ed.}$; *om.* S^{2} 419 niścāyakaṃ katham] *conj.*; niścāyakam D^{a}GJS^{2}S$^{3\,p.c.}$K$^{ed.}$, niścāya katham S$^{3\,a.c.}$

---

411 S^{2} folio 106r. 413 J folio 70v. 416 D^{a} folio 175r. 417 G folio 74v. 419 S^{2} folio 106v.

sāmānyarūpatā vā sarveṣāṃ śāvaleyādīnāṃ viśeṣāṇām aikyātmikāsti. sā cābhinnā tebhyo viśeṣebhyaḥ. bhinnābhinnātmako hi padārthaḥ sāṅkhyārhatādidarśane yathā pratīyate tādṛg vāstava iṣyate. sa ca tattvasyaikyaṃ vinā na syād iti vakṣyamāṇena saṃbandhaḥ.

bauddhasya cen na sāmānyam anumānaṃ nivartate
yathā suvarṇabhāṇḍeṣu na tathā hematāmrayoḥ 68
suvarṇam ānayety ukte śūnyatā kiṃ pratīyate
viśeṣasparśavirahāt kadācid api yujyate 69

68a Perhaps Somānanda here has PV (*pratyakṣapariccheda*) 3.30 in mind: *arthānāṃ yac ca sāmānyam anyavyāvṛttilakṣaṇam | yanniṣṭhās ta ime śabdā na rūpaṃ tasya kiṃcana* || Cf. PV (*pratyakṣapariccheda*) 3.43ab: *tasmāt samānatayaivāsmin sāmānye 'vastulakṣaṇam* | 68b A worm-hole occludes what might be the curved vertical stroke for the long *ā* of *anumānaṃ* in T. The spacing suggests that an additional mark should appear there, and a short trace of the top of an *ā* appears at the top left side of the hole of the folio. Could this damage possibly explain the genesis of the erroneous reading in C, which records *anumanaṃ*, precisely what T reads if one skips over the damaged part of the folio? 69a ŚD 4.69-71 are omitted from C, and the enumeration of verses found in that manuscript reflects that absence by counting ŚD 4.72 as ŚD 4.69, and so on, up to ŚD 4.96, where two additional half-verses are omitted, the numbering of the verses there reflecting those further omissions, as well. 69b What appears to be a tear in the manuscript obscures *ya* of *pratīyate* in S^{3}.

68a bauddhasya] TD^{a}GJS^{2}S^{3}K$^{ed.}$; bodhasya C 68a cen] TD^{a}GJS^{2}S^{3}K$^{ed.}$; cān C 68a sāmānyam] TD^{a}GJS^{2}S^{3}K$^{ed.}$; sāmānyamm C 68b anumānaṃ] D^{a}GJS^{2}S^{3}K$^{ed.}$; anum<?>naṃ T, anumanaṃ C 68b nivartate] CD^{a}GJS^{2}S^{3}K$^{ed.}$; ni - - - T 68d na] T$^{p.c.}$CD^{a}GJS^{2}S^{3}K$^{ed.}$; *om.* T$^{a.c.}$ 68d tathā] CD^{a}GJS^{2}S^{3}K$^{ed.}$; tatha T 68d hematāmrayoḥ] TD^{a}S^{2}K$^{ed.}$; haimatāmrayau C, haimatāmrayoḥ GJ, hematāmrayo S^{3} 69c °virahāt] D^{a}GJS^{2}S^{3}K$^{ed.}$; °viharāt T, *om.* C 69d kadācid] TD^{a}S^{2}S^{3}K$^{ed.}$; *om.* C, kadācir GJ

---

423 S^{2} deletes what appears to read *viśeṣataḥ* prior to *tebhyo viśeṣebhaḥ*.

---

422 śāvaleyādīnāṃ] D^{a}S^{2}K$^{ed.}$; śāvalīyādīnāṃ GJS^{3} 424 sa ca tattvasya] D^{a}GJK$^{ed.}$; sa cai<?><?>sya S^{2}, sa ca tasya S^{3} 424 aikyaṃ] D^{a}GJS$^{2p.c.}$S^{3}K$^{ed.}$; kyaṃ S$^{2a.c.}$ 424 vinā] D$^{ap.c.}$GJS^{2}S^{3}K$^{ed.}$; *om.* D$^{aa.c.}$

---

427 J folio 71r. 429 S^{2} folio 107r.

tattvasyaikyaṃ vinā na syād ekasyaiva viruddhatā
sāmānyena viśeṣeṇa katham ekasya yogitā 70

atha sāmānyaṃ bauddhasya nāsti, tad anumānaṃ sāmānyaviṣayam abhīṣṭaṃ hīyate. tathā sāmānyaṃ vinā yathā suvarṇam ānayety ukte sauvarṇakaṭakakeyūrādiṣv artheṣu pratītir na tathā hematāmrayoḥ, tāmrāsaṃsparśena hemna eva pratīteḥ, kaṭakakeyūrādiṣu tu na kasyacit parityāgaḥ. anyāpohasyāpi sāmānyatve 'bhyupagate kiṃ suvarṇam ānayeti śūnyatā prasajyapratiṣedharūpā pratīyate viśeṣasparśavirahād dhetoḥ, api tv asauvarṇavyāvṛttāḥ suvarṇapratyavamarśakāriṇaḥ ta ekatām āpādyamānā viśeṣā eveti kadācid

---

70a A footnote in K$^{ed.}$ (p. 176) records a variant reading in one source examined for that edition. The variant is *ajñānena*. It is unclear for what this is a variant reading. 70a T could be interpreted to read *tatvam aikyaṃ*, rather than *matvam aikyaṃ*, where G, J, and K$^{ed.}$ read *tattvasyaikyaṃ*. 70a The present verse is omitted from C. See the note on ŚD 4.69a, supra. 70b G records the final *akṣara* (*tā*) of *viruddhatā* in the right margin. It is the last *akṣara* of the given line of text. 70c What appears to be a tear in the manuscript obscures *śe* of *viśeṣeṇa* in S^3. 70d D^a records *yogitā* in the bottom margin at the very end of the folio side, the term being written in the scribe's own hand.

70a tattvasyaikyaṃ] D^{a}GJS^{3}K$^{ed.}$; matvam aikyaṃ T, *om.* C, tattvaisyaikyaṃ S$^{2p.c.}$, tattvaisyaktaṃ S$^{2a.c.}$ 70c sāmānyena] D^{a}GJS^{2}S^{3}K$^{ed.}$; s - mānyena T, *om.* C

---

434 S^2 appears to delete an *anusvāra* following *kaṭakake* of *sauvarṇakaṭakakeyūrādiṣv*. 438 In S^3, damage to the manuscript renders *va* of *pratyavamarśa*° nearly illegible.

---

432 bauddhasya] D^{a}GJS^{2}K$^{ed.}$; boddhasya S^3 432 tad] D$^{a\,a.c.}$GJS^{2}S^{3}K$^{ed.}$; tataḥ D$^{a\,p.c.}$ 432 anumānaṃ sāmānyaviṣayam] D^{a}GJS$^{2p.c.}$K$^{ed.}$; anumānaṃ viṣayam S$^{2a.c.}$, anumānaviṣayam S^3 433 hīyate] D^{a}GJS^{2}K$^{ed.}$; hīyeta S^3 434 °keyūrādiṣv] GJS^{2}S^{3}K$^{ed.}$; °kīyūrādiṣv D^a 434 pratītir] D^{a}GJS^{2}K$^{ed.}$; pratīti S^3 434 hematāmrayoḥ] D^{a}S^{2}S^{3}K$^{ed.}$; haimatāmrayoḥ GJ 435 kaṭakakeyūrādiṣu] GJS$^{2p.c.}$S^{3}K$^{ed.}$; kaṭakakīyūrādiṣu D^a, kaṭakakeyūrādi S$^{2a.c.}$ 437 °vyāvṛttāḥ] D^{a}G$^{p.c.}$JS^{3}K$^{ed.}$; °vyāvṛttyāḥ G$^{a.c.}$, °vyāvyarttāḥ S^2 438 suvarṇapratyavamarśakāriṇaḥ] D^{a}GJK$^{ed.}$; suvarṇapratyavimarśakāriṇaḥ S$^{2p.c.}$, suvarṇapratyivimarśakāriṇaḥ S$^{2a.c.}$, suvarṇapratyavamarśakāriṇa S^3 438 ekatām] D^{a}GJS^{2}K$^{ed.}$; ekaṃ tām S^3

---

431 G folio 75r. 431 D^a folio 175v. 434 S^3 folio 30v. 438 S^2 folio 107v.

api yujyata iti kākvā vyākhyeyam. na kadācid apy etad yujyate śūnyatāpi bhātīti. tad etac cittattvasya padārtheṣv aikyaṃ vinā na syād ekasyaivārthasya parasparaviruddhatvāt. acidrūpasya bāhyasyaitan na ghaṭate, tad vyanakti sāmānyenety abhedena, viśeṣeṇeti bhedena. cittattvasya punaḥ svacchandatvān naiva virodha ity uktaṃ pratyabhijñāyām eva.

ekatattvaṃ vinaitac ca vyavahāro na jāyate
śabdārthayor na saṃbandho bhinnayor bhinnadeśayoḥ 71
viruddharūpayor bhinnakaraṇagrāhyayor api

71a The verses are misnumbered in K$^{ed.}$ from here to the end of the chapter: K$^{ed.}$ erroneously marks both the present verse and the preceding one as ŚD 4.70, and the numbering of every verse from here to the end of the chapter reflects this error in K$^{ed.}$. 71a The present verse is omitted from C. See the note on ŚD 4.69a, supra. 71c D^{a} records its reading for *saṃbandho* over some discoloration in the manuscript paper, which might have been caused by smearing of ink in the course of attempting to correct the text.

71c saṃbandho] TCGJS^{2}S^{3}K$^{ed.}$; sam<?>ondho D^{a} 71d bhinnayor] TD^{a}GJS^{2}K$^{ed.}$; *om.* C, bhinnayo S^{3} 72b karaṇagrāhyayor] D^{a}S^{2}S^{3}K$^{ed.}$; karaṇagrāhya- y<e/o?> - r T, karaṇagyāhyayor C, kāraṇagrāhyayor GJ

---

439 Damage to the manuscript renders *apy e* of *apy etad* nearly illegible in S^{3}. 439 S^{2} deletes an *akṣara*, now illegible, prior to *śūnyatā*. 440 Cf., e.g., NM (*apohaśabdārthapakṣadūṣaṇam*), edition of Kataoka 2008: 19: *tathā hy apoho nāma vyāvṛttir abhāva ucyate. na cābhāvaḥ svatantratayā ghaṭādivad avagamyate.* 441 See NB 3.77: *parasparaparihārasthitalakṣaṇatayā vā bhāvābhāvavat*, which is also cited at ŚDVṛ ad ŚD 4.24. 443 J may have first read *verodha* for *virodha*. 443 See, esp., ĪPK 2.3.14: *guṇaiḥ śabdādibhir bhedo jātyādibhir abhinnatā | bhāvānām ittham ekatra pramātary upapadyate ||* See also the corresponding passage of the ĪPKVṛ: *bhāvānāṃ śabdarūpasaṃsthānādinā bhedākṣepo jātyādinā ca ekatākṣepo 'nubhūyamānaḥ pramātraikye ghaṭate. anyonyabhedavyavasthāpy anusaṃdhānāyattā.*

---

439 śūnyatāpi] K$^{ed.}$; śunyatā D^{a}GJS^{2}S^{3} 440 bhātīti] GJS^{3}K$^{ed.}$; avabhātīti D^{a}S^{2} 440 padārtheṣv] D^{a}JS^{2}S^{3}K$^{ed.}$; padārthaiṣv G 440 vinā] D$^{a\,p.c.}$GJS^{2}S^{3}K$^{ed.}$; *om.* D$^{a\,a.c.}$ 441 °viruddhatvāt] D^{a}K$^{ed.}$; °viruddhatvam GJS^{2}S^{3} 442 svacchandatvān] D^{a}GJS$^{2\,p.c.}$S^{3}K$^{ed.}$; svacchatvān S$^{2\,a.c.}$ 443 naiva] GJS^{2}S^{3}; na D^{a}K$^{ed.}$ 443 virodha] D^{a}GJS$^{2\,p.c.}$S^{3}K$^{ed.}$; vi<?>odha S$^{2\,a.c.}$

---

439 J folio 71v. 442 G folio 75v. 446 D^{a} folio 176r.

mukhe hi śabdo bhūmau ca vidyate ’rthaḥ kva saṃgamaḥ 72
amūrta eko mūrtaś ca dvitīyo yogitā katham

itaś caikatvaṃ, yata ekacittattvātmatāṃ vinā vyavahāro na jāyate. yataḥ śabdārthayor yo ’yam ekaparāmarśamayo vācyavācakalakṣaṇaḥ saṃbandhaḥ, sa kathaṃ bhinnatve bhinnadeśatve bhinnamūrtāmūrtatvādisvabhāvatve bhinnendriyagrāhyatve ca sati syāt, tad eva bhinnadeśatādi vyanakti mukhe hīti. yogitā saṃbandhitā sa caikaparāmarśo bhinnayor api satoḥ.

72c Compare ŚD 4.72cd with *Śābarabhāṣya* ad MīSū 1.5: *mukhe hi śabdam upalabhāmahe, bhūmāv artham. śabdo ’yaṃ na tv arthaḥ, artho ’yaṃ na śabda iti ca vyapadiśanti.* 72c T leaves a space for an additional *akṣara* where the manuscript should read *hi*, but does not.

72c mukhe hi śabdo] D^{a}GJS^{2}S^{3}K$^{ed.}$; mukhe śabdo (hypometric) T$^{p.c.}$, mukhe śabdā (hypometric) T$^{a.c.}$, mukhāśabdo (hypometric) C 72d vidyate] TD^{a}GJS^{2}S^{3}K$^{ed.}$; vidyateḥ C 72d ’rthaḥ] TD^{a}GJS^{2}S^{3}K$^{ed.}$; rtha C 73a ca] TD^{a}GJS^{2}S^{3}K$^{ed.}$; ceti (hypermetric) C 73b dvitīyo] TGJS^{2}S^{3}K$^{ed.}$; *om.* (hypometric) C, dvitīye D^{a} 73b yogitā] TCD$^{ap.c.}$GJS^{3}K$^{ed.}$; yogyatā D$^{aa.c.}$S^{2}

---

449 In J, *yataḥ śabdārthayor yo ’yam ekaparāmarśamayo* is mostly illegible, this due to damage to the manuscript.

---

449 ekacittattvātmatāṃ] S^{2}; ekacittvātmatāṃ D^{a}GJS^{3}K$^{ed.}$ 450 ekaparāmarśamayo] D^{a}K$^{ed.}$; ekaparāmarśatāmayo [’]py āsanam G, eka <?><?><?><?><?><?> J, ekaparāmarśatāmayo [’]dhyāsa nāmayor yo yaṃ ekaparāmarśamayo [’]dhyāso nāma S$^{2p.c.}$, ekaparāmarśayor yo yaṃ ekaparāmarśamayo [’]dhyāso nāma S$^{2a.c.}$, ekaparāmarśamayo [’]dhyāso nāma S^{3} 450 vācyavācakalakṣaṇaḥ saṃbandhaḥ] D^{a}GJS$^{2p.c.}$K$^{ed.}$; vācyavācalakṣaṇaḥ saṃbandhaḥ S$^{2a.c.}$, vācyavācakabhāvalakṣaṇasaṃbandhaḥ S$^{3p.c.}$, vācyavācakalakṣaṇa- saṃbandhaḥ S$^{3a.c.}$ 451 bhinnatve] GJS$^{2p.c.}$; cittattve D^{a}S$^{2a.c.}$K$^{ed.}$, ciktattve S^{3} 451 °mūrtāmūrta°] D^{a}JS^{2}S^{3}K$^{ed.}$; °mūrta° G

---

448 S^{2} folio 108r. 453 J folio 72r.

tathātmāder adṛṣṭasya tacchabdair yogitā katham 73
asataḥ śaśaśṛṅgādeḥ śaśaśabdādinānvayaḥ
ghaṭate jātucin naivam asatāṃ vyavahāryatā 74
śabdena cet tad evaṃ hi sarvasaṃsāranāśatā
asatyavyavahāreṇa tādṛg eva jagad bhavet 75

73c On *dṛṣṭārtha* and *adṛṣṭārtha* see, e.g., NS 1.1.7-8 (and NSBh ad 1.1.8): *āptopadeśaḥ śabdaḥ* (1.1.7). *sa dvividho dṛṣṭādṛṣṭārthatvāt* (1.1.8). NSBh ad 1.1.8: *yasyeha dṛśyate 'rthaḥ sa dṛṣṭārthaḥ. yasyāmutra pratīyate so 'dṛṣṭārthaḥ. evam ṛṣilaukikavākyānāṃ vibhāga iti. kimarthaṃ punar idam ucyate? sa na manyeta dṛṣṭārtha evāptopadeśaḥ pramāṇam, arthasyāvadhāraṇād iti, adṛṣṭārtho 'pi pramāṇam arthasyānumānād iti.* 74b Cf. VS (and Candrānanda's commentary ad) 7.2.18: *asati nāstīti ca prayogāt.* Candrānanda: *arthasaṃyoge sati śabdaḥ "asati" abhāve "nāsti" iti na prayujyeta. na hy asatā saṃyogaḥ.* 74b Damage to the manuscript renders the reading of S^3 nearly illegible at *bdā* of *śaśaśabdādinānvayaḥ*. 75a C appears to correct the numbering of this verse from ŚD 4.74 to ŚD 4.72. (Because C omits ŚD 4.69-71, the manuscript may be expected to count the present verse as ŚD 4.72.)

73c tathātmāder] TCGJ$S^3K^{ed.}$; tadātmāder D^aS^2 73d °chabdair] TD^aGJ$S^2S^3K^{ed.}$; °chabde C 73d yogitā] TCD^aGJ$S^3K^{ed.}$; yogyatā S^2 74a asataḥ] TD^aGJ$S^2S^3K^{ed.}$; aśataḥ C 74a śaśaśṛṅgādeḥ] TD^aGJ$S^2S^3K^{ed.}$; śaśaśṛṅgāde C 74b śaśaśabdādinā] T$D^aS^2S^3$; śaśabdādinā (hypometric) CGJ, śaśaśṛṅgādinā $K^{ed.}$ 74c ghaṭate] CD^aGJ$S^2S^3K^{ed.}$; gh - ṭate T 74c jātucin] TD^aGJ$S^2S^3K^{ed.}$; jotucin C 74d vyavahāryatā] D^aGJ$S^2S^3K^{ed.}$; vyavahāratāṃ T, tyapahāratā C 75b sarva°] TGJ$S^2S^3K^{ed.}$; sarvaṃ C, *om.* D^a 75b °saṃsāranāśatā] C$K^{ed.}$; °saṃsāranāśitā TGJS^2S^3, saṃsārasya vināśitā D^a 75c °vyavahāreṇa] TCD^aGJ$S^2K^{ed.}$; °vyavahār<?> S^3 75d tādṛg] TD^aGJ$S^2S^3K^{ed.}$; dṛg (hypometric) C

---

457 S^2 folio 108v. 457 G folio 76r. Note that this folio side is unlike all the other recto sides of G of the present *āhnika* in that it is not numbered. 458 C folio 10v.

apratyakṣasyātmādeḥ śaśaśṛṅgādeś cāsataḥ katham ātmādiśabdena śaśaśṛṅgādiśabdena ca khapuṣpasyāpi khapuṣpaśabdena yojanam. naivaṃ doṣaḥ, asatām eva hi śabdena vyavahāryatā śabdānām asadviṣayatvād yadi, tad evaṃ hi sarvasya saṃsārasya nāśaḥ prāpnoti. tad vyanakty asatyena śabdavyavahāreṇa tādṛśam asatyam eva jagad bhavet, jagataś ca pratibhāsamānaśabda...

---

459 S^3 notes the absence of text following *śaśaśṛṅgādeś ca* by recording a short dotted line there. 459 S^2 deletes two now-illegible *akṣaras* following *katha* of *katham*. 460 S^2 records *pra* of *prayojanam* in the left margin, as if the scribe added it shortly after recording the word in question without this *upasarga*. 461 The reading in D^a of *asadviṣayatvād* is blotched at *tvād* but is nevertheless legible. 462 The testimony of S^3 ends mid-word at *prāpno* of *prāpnoti*. No colophon or any other mark indicating the loss of text is here offered. The manuscript simply ends here, having reached the end of last line of text on the folio side in question. 463 S^2 omits *tad vyanakty asatyena śabdavyavahāreṇa*. 463 J could be understood to read *śābdavyavahāreṇa* for *śabdavyavahāreṇa*. 464 A later hand appears to have added *bda* of °*samānaśabda* in S^2. 464 The commentary from this point forward is lost in $K^{ed.}$. The commentary recorded in G and J also ends here, and both manuscripts note the loss of commentary by recording a series of short dashes on the remainder of the given line of the manuscript, as well as on two (in G) or four (in J) full lines, following. No colophon or additional notes or commentary are offered at the end of either G or J. D^a also ends here, with three dots recorded to indicate that further text is lost. No colophon is recorded for D^a, and the remainder of the folio side is left blank, and D^a does not record the folio number in the bottom left corner of this (verso) folio side, as is the copyist's normal practice. Finally, S^2 also ends here, leaving blank the remainder of the folio in question, excepting for 7 short dashes at the beginning of the next line of text. No additional marks or colophon are to be found at the end of this manuscript.

---

459 apratyakṣasya] $D^aK^{ed.}$; apratyakṣasya ca GJS^2S^3 459 °ātmādeḥ] $D^aGJS^2K^{ed.}$; °ātmāde S^3 459 cāsataḥ katham] $D^aGJS^2K^{ed.}$; ca - - - tyam S^3 460 khapuṣpasyāpi] $GJS^2S^{3p.c.}K^{ed.}$; khapuṣpasyāpi ca D^a, khapuṣpa<?>pi $S^{3a.c.}$ 460 khapuṣpaśabdena] $D^aGJK^{ed.}$; ca khapuṣpaśabdena $S^{2p.c.}S^3$, ca puṣpaśabdena $S^{2a.c.}$ 460 yojanam] $D^{ap.c.}JK^{ed.}$; prayojanīyaṃ $D^{aa.c.}$, prayojanam $GS^{2p.c.}$, prayojanīyaṃ $S^{2a.c.}$, yojanīyaṃ S^3 460 naivaṃ] $D^aS^2S^3K^{ed.}$; atha naivaṃ GJ 463 asatyam] $D^aGS^2K^{ed.}$; satyaṃ J 464 pratibhāsamānaśabda°] $D^aS^2K^{ed.}$; pratibhāsanaṃ śābda° GJ

---

463 D^a folio 176v.

tathābhinavajātasya tannāmnā saṃgamaḥ katham
tatsaṃgamasyāsatyatve yantravaśyādikaṃ katham 76
tasmād aikyena tattvasya sarvaṃ tad api yujyate
vyatiriktena śabdena mantreṇānatirekiṇā 77
kathaṃ na devadattasya yajñadattavad ākhyayā
atra saṃketitatvāc cet saṃketenātra kiṃ kṛtam 78
saṃyogaś cen na dūreṣu mūrtāmūrteṣu yujyate
śabdasyoccāritadhvaṃsān naṣṭānaṣṭadvaye na ca 79
vācyavācakarūpaś cet sa eva niyamaḥ kutaḥ
uktasya vācakatvaṃ hi vācyatvam aparasya tu 80
vācyavācakarūpatve vācyavācakatānvayaḥ
itaś cāsti jagaty aikyaṃ pratyakṣāgrahaṇād api 81
svalakṣaṇena yogitvād vyavahārasya sarvataḥ
loke cānupapatteś ca pramā vā vyavahāragā 82

76d C records the present verse number above the line. 77d On this dichotomy of speech, see, e.g., the *avataraṇikā* to TĀ 5.134: *na kevalaṃ vācyārthāvyatirekiṇo lokottarā māntrā varṇā evaṃ yāval laukikā api, ity āha*. See also the notes to the translation of the present passage of text. 78c Cf. PVSV ad PV 1.72cd: *yasya pratyāyanārthaṃ saṃketaḥ kriyate, abhinnasādhyān bhāvān atatsādhyebhyo bhedena jñātvā tatparihāreṇa pravarteteti*. 81b C appears to correct an erroneous reading of *vācyayācakatānvayaḥ* to the correct reading: *vācyavācakatānvayaḥ*. The transcription of this compound is offset into the left margin of C, suggesting the first *akṣara* (*vā*) may have been added by the scribe after noticing it to be missing. 81b Cp. with ŚV (*saṃbandhākṣepaparihāra*) v. 12: *svato naivāsti śaktatvaṃ vācyavācakayor mithaḥ* | *pratītiḥ samayāt puṃsāṃ bhaved akṣinikocavat* || 82b C appears to read *vyavyahārasya* for *vyavahārasya*, but it might also be interpreted to read *vavyahārasya*.

76a tathābhinavajātasya] K$^{ed.}$; tathābhivanavajātasya (hypermetric) T, tathā hi navajñātasya C 76b tan°] TK$^{ed.}$; jan° C 76c tatsaṃgamasyāsatyatve] CK$^{ed.}$; ta<?> - saṃgamasyāsatyatve T 76d katham] TK$^{ed.}$; thaṃ (hypometric) C 77a tattvasya] CK$^{ed.}$; natvasya T 77b tad] TK$^{ed.}$; d (hypometric) C 77c vyatiriktena] TK$^{ed.}$; kātiriktena C 77d mantreṇānatirekiṇā] K$^{ed.}$; mantramānātirekiṇaḥ T, mantraṇānātireṇā (hypometric) C 78c saṃketitatvāc] TK$^{ed.}$; saṃtatitatvāc C 79a cen] CK$^{ed.}$; can T 79b mūrtā°] TK$^{ed.}$; mūrtāmūrtā° (hypermetric) C 80a vācyavācakarūpaś cet] CK$^{ed.}$; vācyavācakarūpatve T 80b eva] TC; eṣa K$^{ed.}$ 80b kutaḥ] TK$^{ed.}$; kutā C 80c uktasya] C; yat tasya TK$^{ed.}$ 81c itaś] T$^{p.c.}$CK$^{ed.}$; ityaś T$^{a.c.}$ 81c cāsti] TK$^{ed.}$; cāti C 81d pratyakṣāgrahaṇād] TK$^{ed.}$; pratyakṣād grahaṇād C 82a yogitvād] K$^{ed.}$; ayogy - tvāt T, ayogyatvād C 82b vyavahārasya] TK$^{ed.}$; vyavyahārasya C 82c anupapatteś] TK$^{ed.}$; anupattiś (hypometric) C 82d vā vyavahāragā] *conj.*; ca vyavahāragā TK$^{ed.}$; vācyavahārataḥ C

bālamūkādivijñānasadṛśī kīdṛśī kriyā
savikalpasya yogitvād yathāvastu grahaḥ katham 83
tena jñeyam ekam eva vastu bhinne grahaḥ kutaḥ
tathānumānaṃ na bhaved dhūmāgnyor anvaye kvacit 84
apūrvayor gṛhīte 'pi tatkālaṃ gatayor dvayoḥ
agṛhīte na gṛhītaḥ saṃbandho 'gniḥ pratīyate 85
sāmānyam aviśeṣaṃ ced aviśeṣāt kutaḥ pramā
viśeṣasyāpy apūrvatvāt kathaṃ cāsti samanvayaḥ 86
sādṛśyād atha cen nāsti yāthātmyena samāgamaḥ
na ca vātrānumānatvaṃ dhūmataḥ kevalād bhavet 87

83a Cp. with ŚV (*pratyakṣapariccheda*) vv. 112-113: *asti hy ālocanājñānaṃ prathamaṃ nirvikalpakam | bālamūkādivijñānasadṛśaṃ śuddhavastujam || na viśeṣo na sāmānyaṃ tadānīm anubhūyate | tayor ādhārabhūtā tu vyaktir evāvasīyate* || 85b There is some damage to T that makes it difficult to see whether the *visarga* was left off of *dvayoḥ*. 86a Though badly frayed, it is possible that a *saṃyuktākṣara* partially appearing in T suggests the manuscript once showed *aviśeṣaṃ* ending instead with *ś*, presumably reading *aviśeṣaś*, though only the last *akṣara* (conjoined with *c* of *cet*, which follows) survives the fraying of the manuscript. 87a Though the *akṣaras* are half-missing in T, the manuscript appears correctly to read *atha* where C and Ked. do, as well.

83a °vijñāna°] CKed.; °vijñana° T 83b kīdṛśī] TKed.; vedṛśī C 83c yogitvād] Ked.; ayogyatvād T, ayogyatvad C 84a tena] TKed.; kena C 84a ekam] CKed.; ek - T 84a eva] CKed.; - T 84b vastu] CKed.; - s - T 84b bhinne grahaḥ] TKed.; bhinnagrahaḥ C 84b kutaḥ] TKed.; kuśaḥ C 84c tathānumānaṃ] CKed.; tathānubhamānaṃ (hypermetric) T 84d dhūmāgnyor] TKed.; bhūtognyor C 84d anvaye] CKed.; advaye T 85a apūrvayor] TKed.; apūrvayo C 85b tatkālaṃ gatayor] TKed.; ratkālagatayor C 85b dvayoḥ] Ked.; dvayo<?> T, thayoḥ C 85c na gṛhītaḥ] Ked.; nāgṛhīta T, nāgṛhīte C 85d saṃbandho] Ked.; saṃbandhena T, ti saṃbandho C 85d 'gniḥ] Ked.; ani T, [']gneḥ C 85d pratīyate] CKed.; pradīyate T 86a sāmānyam] Ked.; sā - - T, sāmānya C 86a aviśeṣaṃ] Ked.; - - - - T, tu viśeṣaṃ C 86a ced] CKed.; <?> - T 86b aviśeṣāt] CKed.; - - ś - t T 86b kutaḥ] CKed.; k - taḥ T 86c apūrvatvād] TC; apūrvatve Ked. 86d kathaṃ] Ked.; atha TC 87a sādṛśyād] CKed.; sādṛśye T 87b yāthātmyena] Ked.; yathātmyena T, yāthārthe (hypometric) C 87b samāgamaḥ] TKed.; samāgataḥ C 87d kevalād] TKed.; kevalaṃ C

tatsaṃbandhād athocyeta saṃbandhe dviṣṭhatā na ca
dviniṣṭhatvād ekataragrahaṇān nāpi tadgrahaḥ 88
dhūmadṛṣṭyātha kalpyeta vahnis tadyogitāpi ca
itaretaradoṣo 'tra durnivāraḥ prasajyate 89
yāvan na vahnikalanā na yogakalanā bhavet
yāvad vā yogakalanā na vahnikalanākṣamā 90

88b Cf. Dharmakīrti's SP 11ab: *dviṣṭho hi kaścit sambandho nāto' nyat tasya lakṣaṇam* | Cf. Prabhācandra ad SP 11: *na yena kenacid ekena sambandhāt seṣyate. kiṃ tarhi. sambandhalakṣaṇenaiveti cet tan na, dviṣṭho hi kaścit padārthaḥ sambandhaḥ, nāto 'rthadvayābhisambandhād anyat tasya lakṣaṇam yenāsya saṃkhyāder viśeṣo vyavasthāpyeta.* 88c See also ĪPK 1.2.11: *dviṣṭhasyānekarūpatvāt siddhasyānyānapekṣaṇāt* | *pāratantryādyayogāc ca tena kartāpi kalpitaḥ* || Cf. the corresponding passage of the IPKVṛ: *saṃbandho dviṣṭho na caikenātmanobhayatrāvasthitir yuktā na ca dvayoḥ siddhayor anyonyāpekṣātmā nāpi svātmamātraniṣṭhayoḥ pāratantryarūpaḥ saṃbandhaḥ. tato yathā jñātṛtvaṃ kalpitaṃ tathā kartṛtvam apīti katham ātmā sarveśvara iti.* 88d C records the numbering of the present verse above the line, clearly added after the scribe noticed its omission. 90b C records the negative particle, *na*, in the left margin. 90d C records the numbering of the present verse above the line, clearly added after the scribe noticed its omission.

88a tatsaṃbandhād] K$^{ed.}$; tatsa - - - T, tatatsaṃbaṃdhād (hypermetric) C 88b dviṣṭhatā na ca] K$^{ed.}$; - - - - - T, dviṣiatānya (hypometric) C 88c dviniṣṭhatvād] K$^{ed.}$; - - - - T, dviniṣṭatvād C 88c ekatara°] CK$^{ed.}$; - k <?> T 88d °grahaḥ] K$^{ed.}$; °grahaṃ T, °grahā C 89a °dṛṣṭyā] TK$^{ed.}$; °dṛśyā C 89b °yogitā] K$^{ed.}$; °yogatā T, °yogyatā C 89c itaretaradoṣo] K$^{ed.}$; itareratatadoṣo (hypermetric) T, itaretarayogo C 90a na] TK$^{ed.}$; ni C 90a vahnikalanā] TK$^{ed.}$; vahnikalanaṃ C 90b na] C$^{p.c.}$K$^{ed.}$; - T, *om.* C$^{a.c.}$ 90b yogakalanā] CK$^{ed.}$; - - - - - T 90b bhavet] CK$^{ed.}$; - - T 90c vā] TK$^{ed.}$; va C 90d °kṣamā] TK$^{ed.}$; °kṣamāsā (hypermetric) C

489 T folio 8v.

nāptavākyād athāstīha tatsatyatve 'dṛḍhā matiḥ
vārān śataṃ hi yo vaktā satyabhāṣī kadācana 91
so 'py anyathā pradarśyetākṣayato rāgadveṣayoḥ
pitrāder apy asatyatvaṃ tatrānyatra na niścayaḥ 92
tasmān na bhede bhāvānāṃ tadgrahādy api yujyate
kṣaṇabhaṅgaparāmarśād apy etad upapadyate 93
śaktāśaktavikalpair hi dīpajvālādyudāhṛtaiḥ
sthiratā nopapannā te pratyakṣenāpi ca sthitā 94
sthiratvaṃ kṣaṇikatvāc ca pramāṇāṃ cintayā sthitam
avisaṃvādirūpāc ca viruddhaṃ tat kathaṃ bhavet 95

91a Cf. NS 2.1.68: *mantrāyurvedaprāmāṇyavac ca tatprāmāṇyam āptaprāmāṇyāt*; ŚBh ad MīSū 1.1.5: *tathā ca codanālakṣaṇaḥ samyakpratyaya iti. pauruṣeye hi sati saṃbandhe yaḥ pratyayaḥ, tasya mithyābhāva āśaṅkyeta. parapratyayo hi tadā syāt.* 91b C erroneously elides the vowel of the initial syllable of *tat* with a *virāma*, this in the compound *tatsatyatve.* 92b T is damaged but partially legible at °*dveṣayoḥ*, where the last *akṣara*s that can be read are half-broken off due to the damage to the manuscript. 94a To record the long diphthong *au* in Grantha Malayalam, two added marks are needed, one preceding and the other following the *akṣara* to which the diphthong is to be attached. T records only the following one and not the one preceding the final *p* of *śaktāśāktavikalpau*, what is its reading for the place where $\mathrm{K}^{\mathrm{ed.}}$ records *śaktāśaktavikalpair.* 95a C corrects the numbering of the verse from what possibly was ŚD 4.94 to ŚD 4.92 (this latter enumeration being consistent with the fact that C omits ŚD 4.69-71). $\mathrm{K}^{\mathrm{ed.}}$ records the verse as ŚD 4.94, having counted ŚD 4.70 twice. (This could suggest that the scribe of C had the KSTS edition in hand when copying the text.) 95c Cf. PV 2.1ab: *pramāṇam avisaṃvādi jñānam arthakriyāsthitiḥ* |

91a nāpta°] T; nātha C, āpta° $\mathrm{K}^{\mathrm{ed.}}$ 91b matiḥ] C$\mathrm{K}^{\mathrm{ed.}}$; mati T 91c vārān śataṃ] T; vārāt kṛtaṃ C, na rājate $\mathrm{K}^{\mathrm{ed.}}$ 91c hi yo vaktā] T; dvayor vaktā *em.* (Chaturvedi), hi yo paktā C, hy ayovaktā $\mathrm{K}^{\mathrm{ed.}}$ 91d °bhāṣī] T$\mathrm{K}^{\mathrm{ed.}}$; <?>ṣī C 92a 'py] T$\mathrm{K}^{\mathrm{ed.}}$; vy C 92a pradarśyeta] $\mathrm{K}^{\mathrm{ed.}}$; pradṛśeta TC 92b °dveṣayoḥ] $\mathrm{K}^{\mathrm{ed.}}$; - e - yoḥ T, °śeṣayoḥ C 92c pitrāder] T$\mathrm{K}^{\mathrm{ed.}}$; pitrādev C 92c asatyatvaṃ] C$\mathrm{K}^{\mathrm{ed.}}$; amitratvam T 92d na] $\mathrm{K}^{\mathrm{ed.}}$; *om.* (hypometric) TC 93a tasmān] T$\mathrm{K}^{\mathrm{ed.}}$; tasmāṃn C 93a bhede bhāvānāṃ] T$\mathrm{K}^{\mathrm{ed.}}$; bhedabhāvānāṃ C 93b °grahādy api] C$\mathrm{K}^{\mathrm{ed.}}$; °grāhādyāpi T 93c kṣaṇa°] T$\mathrm{K}^{\mathrm{ed.}}$; kṣakṣaṇa (hypermetric) C 93d etad] C$\mathrm{K}^{\mathrm{ed.}}$; e (hypometric) T 94a śaktāśaktavikalpair] $\mathrm{K}^{\mathrm{ed.}}$; śaktāśāktavikalpau<?> T, śaktāsavikalpai (hypometric) C 94b °jvālādy°] $\mathrm{K}^{\mathrm{ed.}}$; °jvālād T, °tvālādy° C 94c sthiratā] C$\mathrm{K}^{\mathrm{ed.}}$; sthi - tā T 94c nopapannā te] T$\mathrm{K}^{\mathrm{ed.}}$; nopapanno ta C 94d ca sthitā] $\mathrm{K}^{\mathrm{ed.}}$; ca sthitaiḥ T, cāsthitaḥ C 95a kṣaṇikatvāc] *conj.*; kṣaṇikatvaṃ T$\mathrm{K}^{\mathrm{ed.}}$; kṣaṇitvaṃ (hypometric) C 95b pramāṇāṃ] T$\mathrm{K}^{\mathrm{ed.}}$; pramāṇād C 95b cintayā] $\mathrm{K}^{\mathrm{ed.}}$; citayām T, citayo C 95c avisaṃvādirūpāc ca] *conj.*; api saṃvādirūpāc ca T, atisaṃvādarūpā ca C, apy asaṃvādarūpaṃ ca $\mathrm{K}^{\mathrm{ed.}}$ 95d bhavet] T$\mathrm{K}^{\mathrm{ed.}}$; bhaveta (no *virāma*) C

yāvan na sarvabhāvānām ekatvena vyavasthitiḥ
pareṇa kṣaṇabhaṅgasya parāmarśāgamaḥ kutaḥ 96
tato 'py etac chivātmatvaṃ bhāvānām upapadyate
tathārthāvagatir vākyāt padād vā nopapadyate 97
kṣaṇikatvena śabdānām anabhivyaktito 'pi vā
sphoṭābhivyaṅgyapakṣe tu tatrāpi kramatā katham 98
nirbhāgatvāt sphoṭatattve sphoṭatattvātmakāt katham
ābhāsarūpavastūnāṃ śābdikānāṃ bhaved grahaḥ 99
tasmād evaṃvidhe 'rthe 'pi yuktatā syād ihaikyataḥ
tathātmecchāvaśān nākṣagrāme ceṣṭopapadyate 100
mūrtacodakavaikalyān manaś cet preritāsya no
ekatve punar īdṛk syāt sarvatraiva hi yuktatā 101

96c ŚD 4.96cd is omitted from C. ŚD 4.97cd is inserted in its place. 97a ŚD 4.97ab is omitted from both T and C. The pair of half-verses, ŚD 4.96ab and 4.97cd, is numbered ŚD 4.93 in C, reflecting the absence of ŚD 4.69-71, ŚD 4.96cd, and 4.97ab from the manuscript. The next verse, ŚD 4.98, is counted as ŚD 4.94 in C. The numbering of the verses reflects this discrepancy to ŚD 4.115, where a half-verse not found in K$^{ed.}$ is recorded in C. 99a It is possible that C's erroneous reading of *phoṭavatve* for *sphoṭatattve* should be interpreted to read (hypometrically) *phoṭaktve*. 100c T might record *ātmecśā* for *ātmecchā*°. 101a Cf. NS 1.1.12: *ghrāṇarasanacakṣustvakśrotrāṇīndriyāṇi bhūtebhyaḥ*.

96a yāvan] TK$^{ed.}$; yāvad C 96a na] TK$^{ed.}$; *om.* (hypometric) C 96b ekatvena] TK$^{ed.}$; ekatvenam C 96b vyavasthitiḥ] TK$^{ed.}$; avasthitaṃ C 97c tathārthāvagatir] K$^{ed.}$; ta - rthāvathatir T, tadarthāvagatir C 97c vākyāt] TK$^{ed.}$; vākyā C 97d padād vā] TK$^{ed.}$; sadāddha C 98b anabhivyaktito] K$^{ed.}$; anabhivyaktikobha (hypermetric) T, anabhivyaktite C 98d kramatā] TK$^{ed.}$; kramikā C 99a nirbhāgatvāt] TK$^{ed.}$; nibhāvatvā C 99a sphoṭatattve] TK$^{ed.}$; phoṭavatve C 99b sphoṭatattvātmakāt] K$^{ed.}$; sphoṭāttat - tmatā T, phoṭātatvātmakā C 99c ābhāsa°] TK$^{ed.}$; abhāva° C 99c °vastūnāṃ] K$^{ed.}$; °vastunāṃ TC 99d śābdikānāṃ] *conj.*; śabdikānāṃ TC, śābdikān no K$^{ed.}$ 100a 'pi] TK$^{ed.}$; ca C 100b yuktatā] TK$^{ed.}$; yuktā tā C 100b ihaikyataḥ] CK$^{ed.}$; ihoktikaḥ T 100c ātmecchā°] TK$^{ed.}$; ātmādhā° C 100c nākṣa°] TK$^{ed.}$; nokṣa° C 100d °grāme] TK$^{ed.}$; °me (hypometric) C 100d upapadyate] TK$^{ed.}$; upayujyate C 101a mūrtacodaka°] K$^{ed.}$; stutra - odaka° T, mārtamodaka° C 101a °vaikalyān] TK$^{ed.}$; °vaikalyyā C 101b manaś] CK$^{ed.}$; mānaś T 101b preritāsya] K$^{ed.\,p.c.}$; preryatātsya T, preryatāsya CK$^{ed.\,a.c.}$ 101c punar] TK$^{ed.}$; punad C 101c syāt] TK$^{ed.}$; sāt C

---

509 C folio 111r.

na cāpi bhede bhāvānāṃ grahaṇaṃ jñānam eva vā
saṃyogenopapadyeta yadi dṛṣṭyādinā bhavet 102
naivaṃ akṣārthasaṃyogamātrāt kiṃ boddhur udyamaḥ
saṃyoge 'nyasya sañjāte katham anyasya boddhṛtā 103
manaso bhinnakālatvāt smṛtijñānam athocyate
prārabdhaś cāsamāptaś ca vartamānaḥ kriyām anu 104
prakriyāmātram evaitad yataḥ pūrvāparātmatā
kriyāyāḥ kārakāṇāṃ hi kramo 'sty eva svakarmaṇi 105

102c See VS 3.1.13: *ātmendriyamano'rthasannikarṣād yan niṣpadyate tad anyat.* Cf. NS 1.1.4: *indriyārthasannikarṣotpannaṃ jñānam avyapadeśyam avyabhicāri vyavasāyātmakaṃ pratyakṣam.* 104a While I here accept *bhinnakālatvāt*, what is recorded in T and C, this over K$^{ed.}$'s reading of *'bhinnakālatvāt*, it must be remembered that these manuscripts regularly omit the *avagraha*, so in fact the reading selected amounts to a matter of interpreting the *sandhi*. 104a Cp. with VS 9.2.6: *ātmamanasoḥ saṃyogaviśeṣāt saṃskārāc ca smṛtiḥ.* 105c Cf. MBh, Edition of Kielhorn, vol. 1, p. 258: *kārakāṇāṃ pravṛttiviśeṣaḥ kriyā*; VP 3.8.4: *guṇabhūtair avayavaiḥ samūhaḥ kramajanmanām | buddhyā prakalpitābhedaḥ kriyeti vyapadiśyate*; ĪPKVṛ ad ĪPK 1.2.9: *kriyāpi pūrvāparībhūtāvayavaikā kārakavyāpārarūpā na yuktā kramikasyānekakālaspṛśaḥ svātmaikyāyogāt, nāpi kālakramavyāpī caikasvabhāvaś ca tasyā āśrayo yuktaḥ, kevalaṃ gamanapariṇāmādirūpā sā kriyā.*

102a na cāpi] CK$^{ed.}$; naivāpi T 102a bhede bhāvānāṃ] TK$^{ed.}$; bhedabhāvānāṃ C 102b grahaṇaṃ] TK$^{ed.}$; grahāṇāṃm C 102b jñānam] TK$^{ed.}$; *om.* C 102b eva vā] TK$^{ed.}$; eva vā gataṃ C 102c saṃyogenopapadyeta] K$^{ed.}$; saṃyogovopa - dy - ta T, saṃgo<?>opapadyeta C 103a naivam akṣārtha°] TK$^{ed.}$; nevakṣaprārtha° C 103b kiṃ] TK$^{ed.}$; kī C 103b boddhur udyamaḥ] TK$^{ed.}$; bodharūpyataḥ C 103c saṃyoge 'nyasya] K$^{ed.}$; saṃyogo [']nyasya T, saṃyogenādya C 103c sañjāte] TK$^{ed.}$; sañjāta C 103d anyasya] TK$^{ed.}$; anyanyasya (hypermetric) C 103d boddhṛtā] TK$^{ed.}$; bodhyatā C 104a manaso] TK$^{ed.}$; manāso C 104a bhinnakālatvāt] TC; 'bhinnakālatvāt K$^{ed.}$ 104b athocyate] K$^{ed.}$; atho - t - T, upapadyate (hypermetric) C 104d vartamānaḥ kriyām] TK$^{ed.}$; vartamānakriyām C 104d anu] TK$^{ed.}$; anuḥ C 105a °mātram] TK$^{ed.}$; °rūpam C 105a evaitad] K$^{ed.}$; evetad T, aite tad C 105b °ātmatā] TK$^{ed.}$; °ātmataḥ C 105c kārakāṇāṃ] CK$^{ed.}$; kārākāṇaṃ T 105d kramo] TK$^{ed.}$; tavākramo (hypermetric) C 105d 'sty eva] TK$^{ed.}$; sye C

yatra pūrvāparau śabdau kālaikyaṃ tatra yujyate
manasā nīyate tasya kiṃ padārthasvarūpatā 106
sāśakyā mūrtarūpatvād rūpaṃ cen na kathaṃ guṇaḥ
guṇino nīyate 'nyatra tṛṣārtaiś cākṛtiṃ prati 107
atha jñānaṃ na manasas taj jñānam upapadyate
karaṇatvāj jaḍatvāc ca tasya ced ātmanātra kim 108
karaṇe jñānasaṃbandhād bāhyārthe kiṃ na kalpyate
buddher guṇatvaṃ manasi prāpnuyād atha cetasā 109
evaṃvidho ghaṭo 'trāste ity ātmā pratibodhyate
tad evaṃ pūrvadṛṣṭasya varṇanāsadṛśaṃ bhavet 110
varṇanena ca caitanyam etāvan manaso yadi
svātmaśaktisamāveśād amūrtāveśatā katham 111

106a T again (as at ŚD 4.94a) records only the following symbol marking the long diphthongs of both *pūrvāparau* and *śabdau*, not the additional ones that would usually precede the *akṣaras* in question in the Malayalam script. 108c Cf. *Nyāyakandalī* p. 175, line 6: *manaś cetanaṃ na bhavati, karaṇatvād ghaṭādivad iti*. 111b In T, the mark following *s* of the final *o* of *manaso* is crowded into the line of text.

106a pūrvāparau] TK$^{ed.}$; pūrvāparā C 106a śabdau] TK$^{ed.}$; śabdā C 106b kālaikyaṃ] TK$^{ed.}$; kālaikyat C 106b tatra] CK$^{ed.}$; - - T 106b yujyate] CK$^{ed.}$; - jyate T 106c nīyate] TK$^{ed.}$; niyate C 106d °svarūpatā] TK$^{ed.}$; °svarūpataḥ C 107a sāśakyā mūrtarūpatvād] K$^{ed.}$; sā sāktā mūrttarūpatvād T, sāśaktyā mūrtirūpatvāt C 107b na] TK$^{ed.}$; *om.* (hypometric) C 107b kathaṃ] K$^{ed.}$; pṛthag TC 107b guṇaḥ] K$^{ed.}$; guṇaiḥ T, gṛṇaḥ C 107c guṇino] TK$^{ed.}$; guṇi (hypometric) C 107c nīyate] TK$^{ed.}$; niyate C 107d tṛṣārtaiś cākṛtiṃ] K$^{ed.}$; varttaiśā ca kṛtiṃ T, cārceṣāvādhṛtiṃ C 108a jñānaṃ] CK$^{ed.}$; jñāna - T 108a na manasas] K$^{ed.}$; - - - si T, na masita C 108b taj jñānam] TK$^{ed.}$; drajñānam C 108b upapadyate] TK$^{ed.}$; upadyate (hypometric) C 108c jaḍatvāc] TK$^{ed.}$; 'tvā (hypometric) C 108d ātmanātra kim] TK$^{ed.}$; ātmanārcākaṃ C 109a karaṇe] K$^{ed.}$; karaṇai T, kareṇa C 109b kalpyate] TK$^{ed.}$; payate C 109c buddher] TK$^{ed.}$; buddhe C 109c guṇatvaṃ] CK$^{ed.}$; guṇatva T 109c manasi] TK$^{ed.}$; mana (hypometric) C 109d cetasā] CK$^{ed.}$; - e - - T 110a evaṃvidho] K$^{ed.}$; - vaṃvidho T, evaṃ ghaṭo C 110a ghaṭo 'trāste] TK$^{ed.}$; vidhos trāste C 110b ātmā] TK$^{ed.}$; ā (hypometric) C 110c pūrvadṛṣṭasya] TK$^{ed.}$; pūrvadṛṣṭaṣṭasya (hypermetric) C 110d °asadṛśaṃ] TK$^{ed.}$; °asadarṣa C 110d bhavet] TK$^{ed.}$; bhaveta (no *virāma*) C 111a varṇanena] TK$^{ed.}$; varṇane (hypometric) C 111a caitanyam] TK$^{ed.}$; caitasyam C 111b manaso] TK$^{ed.}$; mānaso C 111c °samāveśād] TK$^{ed.}$; °svāveśād (hypometric) C

---

532 T folio 9r.

tena vā sampratīte 'rthe kriyate kiṃ tadātmanā
tatsvarūpātmasaṃyogaḥ na yogo bhinnadeśayoḥ 112
manasāveditārthasya taddeśitvam athocyate
varṇite yogitā kasya yadi vā tatsvarūpataḥ 113
saṃskaroti tadātmānam amūrte saṃskṛtiḥ katham
tadrūpam ātmany etad yenāśleṣo yadi cocyate 114
caitanyenāpy amūrtena miśratānyasya kīdṛśī
kiṃ svayaṃ tatprameyatvam asya ced atirekataḥ 115
manasā kiṃ kim akṣeṇa tena cet tatparamparā
evaṃ tad andhapāramparyatvarūpam idaṃ sphuṭam 116
kim ātmapreraṇenātra jñāte 'jñāte 'thavā bahiḥ
jñāte tu jñānarūpatvāt preraṇaṃ kena hetunā 117

115c C records the following half-verse as ŚD 4.115cd (marked there as ŚD 4.110, as opposed to 4.111, the latter of which we would expect given the omissions of ŚD 4.69-71, 4.96cd, and 4.97ab): *tadyāt prakriyāyā vātha jñānam asyopajvāyate.* This is clearly a corruption of what appears in T, which records the same half-verse in the same part of the text, as follows: *tayā prakriyayā vātha jñānam asyopajāyate.* 116a C records the present half-verse, together with the preceding half-verse (i.e., what is counted as ŚD 4.115cd in the present edition) as ŚD 4.112. This reflects the omission of ŚD 4.69-71, 4.96cd, and 4.97ab, as well as the addition of a half-verse that is not found in K$^{ed.}$ but is recorded following ŚD 4.115ab in C (and T). The numbering in C reflects as much from here to the end of the chapter.

112a vā sampratīte] K$^{ed.}$; v - praṇīte T, vā sampraṇīte C 112b kriyate] TK$^{ed.}$; kriyatet C 112c tatsvarūpātmasaṃyogaḥ] K$^{ed.}$; tatsvarūpotmasṃyogo T, tatsvarūpam asaṃyogo C 112d na yogo] TC; saṃyogo K$^{ed.}$ 112d bhinnadeśayoḥ] T; bhinnadeśyayoḥ C, 'bhinnadeśayoḥ K$^{ed.}$ 113a manasāveditārthasya] CK$^{ed.}$; manasā coditārthasya T 113b °deśitvam] K$^{ed.}$; °deśatvam TC 113d vā] TK$^{ed.}$; va C 114a saṃskaroti] K$^{ed.}$; saṃskāro - T, saṃsāroti C 114b amūrte saṃskṛtiḥ] TK$^{ed.}$; amūrtasaṃskṛtiḥ C 114b katham] TK$^{ed.}$; kathaḥ C 114c ātmany etad ye°] K$^{ed.}$; ātmacaitanye T, atātma caitanye (hypermetric) C 115a caitanyenāpy] TK$^{ed.}$; caitanyenātha C 115a amūrtena] TK$^{ed.}$; mūrtena C 115c tatprameyatvam] CK$^{ed.}$; tatprame - syatvam T 115d ced atirekataḥ] K$^{ed.}$; cetotiketaḥ T, ceto tirekataḥ C 116a manasā] TK$^{ed.}$; mānasā C 116b tat°] TK$^{ed.}$; *om.* (hypometric) C 116c tad andhapārampar°] TK$^{ed.}$; taraṃdhapāraṃ° (hypometric) C 116d °yatvarūpam] K$^{ed.}$; °yārtharūpam TC 116d sphuṭam] TK$^{ed.}$; phuṭam C 117a kim ātma°] K$^{ed.}$; athātma° T, akṣātma° C 117b bahiḥ] TK$^{ed.}$; bahi C 117c jñānarūpatvāt] TK$^{ed.}$; jñātarūpatvā C 117d preraṇaṃ] K$^{ed.}$; pre - - ṃ T, preraṇe C

ajñāte 'mutra yāhīti preryate kena mānasam
preryapreraṇatatkartṛdvayaikyād upapadyate 118
tasmāj jñeyaṃ samagraikyavastu śaivaṃ vyavasthitam
tathā smaraṇayogāc ca smaryate kiṃ tathāvidham 119
yādṛg dṛṣṭaṃ dṛṣṭatā syād athavā jñānam eva tat
dṛṣṭasmaraṇayor aikye sthite tad upapadyate 120
tathā sā pratyabhijñānāt sa evāyam iti sthitiḥ
yujyate katham atraiva jñānayoḥ kālabhinnayoḥ 121
dvayor aikyam anaikyaṃ vā tadaikyaṃ bhinnayoḥ katham

120a C records the absence of two *akṣaras* with two horizontal lines (- -) following its reading of *dṛṣṭaṃtā* for *dṛṣṭatā*. 120c There is crowding in the writing of the final syllable of *dṛṣṭasmaraṇayor* in T. Without the symbol that was crowded into the reading, the text would have here read *dṛṣṭasmaraṇayer*. 121b C records the omission of text with two horizontal lines (- -) following its reading of *pratyabhijñānā* for *pratyabhijñānāt*. 121b Cf. NS 3.1.7: *savyadṛṣṭasyetareṇa pratyabhijñānāt*.; see also the NSBh thereon: *pūrvāparayor vijñānayor ekaviṣaye pratisandhijñānaṃ pratyabhijñānam — tam evaitarhi paśyāmi yam ajñāsiṣam sa evāyam artha iti savyena cakṣuṣā dṛṣṭasyetareṇāpi cakṣuṣā pratyabhijñānād yam adrākṣaṃ tam evaitarhi paśyāmīti. indriyacaitanye tu nānyadṛṣṭam anyaḥ pratyabhijānātīti pratyabhijñānupapattiḥ. asti tv idaṃ pratyabhijñānaṃ tasmād indriyavyatiriktaś cetanaḥ*. 121c ŚD 4.121cd is omitted from T. 122a ŚD 4.122ab is omitted from T. 122a C records the omission of text with two horizontal lines (- -) following its reading of *tayor aikyam* for *dvayor aikyam*.

118a 'mutra] TK$^{ed.}$; matra C 118b kena] TK$^{ed.}$; kutra C 118b mānasam] TK$^{ed.}$; mānasaḥ C 118c °tatkartṛ°] TK$^{ed.}$; tartkṛ (hypometric) C 118d °dvayaikyād] K$^{ed.}$; °trayaikyād T, °traiyaikyā C 118d upapadyate] TK$^{ed.}$; pratipadyate C 119a jñeyaṃ] TK$^{ed.}$; jñāyaṃ C 119a samagraikya°] TK$^{ed.}$; samagraitya° C 119b vyavasthitam] K$^{ed.}$; samagra<?><?>itaṃ (hypermetric) T, vyavasthitaḥ C 119c smaraṇayogāc ca] K$^{ed.}$; - - - yogāc ca T, smaraṇayogo tra C 120a dṛṣṭatā] TK$^{ed.}$; dṛṣṭaṃtā C 120a syād] TK$^{ed.}$; *om.* C 120b athavā jñānam eva tat] TK$^{ed.}$; evāyam iti stitiḥ C 120c °smaraṇayor aikye] TK$^{ed.}$; °smaraṇayogo kyai C 120d sthite] TK$^{ed.}$; sthita C 120d tad] CK$^{ed.}$; d (hypometric) T 121a tathā] TK$^{ed.}$; yathā C 121a sā] K$^{ed.}$; syāt TC 121a pratyabhijñānāt] TK$^{ed.}$; pratyabhijñānā C 121b sa] TK$^{ed.}$; *om.* (hypometric) C 121b sthitiḥ] CK$^{ed.}$; sthi - T 121c katham] K$^{ed.}$; *om.* T, kam (hypometric) C 121c atraiva] K$^{ed.}$; *om.* T, atraivaṃ C 122a dvayor] K$^{ed.}$; *om.* T, tayor C 122a anaikyaṃ vā] K$^{ed.}$; *om.* T, *om.* (hypometric) C 122b °aikyaṃ] K$^{ed.}$; *om.* T, °aikyo C 122b bhinnayoḥ] K$^{ed.}$; *om.* T, bhinnayauḥ C 122b katham] K$^{ed.}$; *om.* T, kathaḥ C

---

555 C folio 11v.

anaikye na sa evāyam iti syād ghaṭadaṇḍayoḥ 122
tasmād aikyam iha spaṣṭaṃ saṃsāre samavasthitam
eṣaiva vārtā saṃyoge vasturūpatayā sthite 123
parasparena cāpy atra teṣāṃ rūpeṇa vānyathā
tasmāt samastabhāvānām aikyenaivāsti saṃgamaḥ 124
śivikodvāhakānāṃ ca nyāya eṣo 'nuvartatām
paracittaparijñānāt tasmāj jñeyaikyatā tataḥ 125
sārthasenāvanādyātma jagaty aikyaṃ sphuṭaṃ sthitam

iti śrīśivadṛṣṭāv anupapatticodanālakṣaṇaṃ caturtham āhnikaṃ sampūrṇam.

122c ŚD 4.122c (and part of 4.122d) is omitted from T. 122d T omits *iti syād* from its reading of ŚD 4.122d. 123a C records the omission of text with two horizontal lines (- -) following *tasmād aikyam.* 124d C inserts the following prior to its reading of ŚD 4.124d, and indicates that additional text should be inserted prior to this reading: *dyātmāthrdavede sphuṭaṃ sthitaḥ*. This closely echoes (with corruptions) ŚD 4.126b. C does not here alter its numbering of verses, however. 126a Cf. NS 2.1.36 (2.1.35 in Jha's translation): *senāvanavat grahaṇam iti cen nātīndriyatvād aṇūnām.* 126b C does not record ŚD 4.126b following ŚD 4.126a. It did record a *pāda* prior to ŚD 4.124d that echoes ŚD 4.126b, however, for which see the note, above, at ŚD 4.124d. 126b The colophon of C reads: *iti śrīśivadṛṣṭau caturtham āhnikaḥ*. The colophon of T reads: *iti caturtham āhnikaṃ.*

122d ghaṭadaṇḍayoḥ] TK$^{ed.}$; <?>ṭadaṃdayoḥ C 123a iha] TK$^{ed.}$; *om.* C 123c eṣaiva] TK$^{ed.}$; eśaiva C 124a cāpy] TK$^{ed.}$; cāky C 124b teṣāṃ] TK$^{ed.}$; sya (hypometric) C 124b vānyathā] TK$^{ed.}$; cānyathā C 124c samastabhāvānām] CK$^{ed.}$; sama - bhāvānām T$^{p.c.}$, sama - bhāvānābh T$^{a.c.}$ 124d asti] TK$^{ed.}$; *om.* (hypometric) C 125a ca] TK$^{ed.}$; nya C 125c paracittaparijñānāt] K$^{ed.}$; paracittāparijñānāt T, paracitāparajñātā C 125d tasmāj jñeyaikyatā] TK$^{ed.}$; tasmāt ajñeyaikyatā C 125d tataḥ] TK$^{ed.}$; taḥ C 126a sārthasenāvanādyātma] K$^{ed.}$; sārthasenā ca nādyātmā T, sāṃrthasonāvanā (hypometric) C 126b jagaty aikyaṃ] K$^{ed.}$; arthavad eva (hypermetric) T, *om.* C 126b sphuṭaṃ] K$^{ed.}$; sphu - T; *om.* C

{ BIBLIOGRAPHY }

Primary Sources (with Abbreviations)

Aṣṭādhyāyī (A) of Pāṇini. In George Cardona. 1997. *Pāṇini: His Work and Its Traditions. Vol. 1: Background and Introduction.* 2nd Edition. Delhi: Motilal Banarsidass. 607–731.

Chāndogyopaniṣad (ChUp). Ed. and trans. by Patrick Olivelle. 1998. *The Early Upaniṣads: Annotated Text and Translation.* New York: Oxford University Press.

Hetubindu (HB) of Dharmakīrti. Ed. by Ernst Steinkellner. 1967. *Dharmakīrti's Hetubindu, Teil I: Tibetischer Text und rekonstruierter Sanskrit-Text.* Vienna: Österreichische Akademie der Wissenschaften.

Īśvarapratyabhijñākārikā (ĪPK) of Utpaladeva. Ed. and trans. by Raffaele Torella. 1994. *The Īśvarapratyabhijñākārikā of Utpaladeva with the Author's Vṛtti: Critical Edition and Annotated Translation.* Rome: IsMEO.

Īśvarapratyabhijñākārikāvṛtti (ĪPKVṛ) of Utpaladeva. See *Īśvarapratyabhijñākārikā.*

Īśvarapratyabhijñāvimarśinī (ĪPV) of Abhinavagupta. Ed. by Mukund Rām Shāstrī. 1918–1921. *The Īśvarapratyabhijñā of Utpaladeva with the Vimarśinī by Abhinavagupta.* 2 vols. KSTS 22 and 33. Bombay: Nirnay Sagar Press.

Īśvarapratyabhijñāvivṛtivimarśinī (ĪPVV) of Abhinavagupta. Ed. by Pt. Madhusūdan Kaul Shāstrī. 1938, 1941, and 1943. *The Īśvarapratyabhijñā Vivṛtivimarśinī by Abhinavagupta.* 3 vols. KSTS 60, 62, and 65. Bombay: Nirnay Sagar Press.

Jayamaṅgalā (JM) of Śaṃkara. See *Sāṅkhyakārikā.*

Kiraṇatantra (KT). Ed. by Ti. Rā. Pañcāpageśaśivācārya and K. M. Subrahmaṇyaśāstrī. 1932. *Kiraṇatantra.* Śivāgamasiddhāntaparipālanasaṅgha 16. Devakōṭṭai.

Kiraṇatantra (KT). Ed. by M. P. Vivanti. 1975. *"Il Kiraṇāgama: Testo e traduzione del Vidyāpāda." Supplemento* n. 3 *agli Annali dell'Istituto Orientale di Napoli.* 35.2. Naples: Istituto Orientale di Napoli.

Kiraṇavṛtti (KVṛ) of Bhaṭṭa Rāmakaṇṭha. See Goodall 1998.

Kriyākālaguṇottara (KKGU). In Michael Slouber. 2016. *Early Tantric Medicine: Snakebite, Mantras and Healing in the Gāruḍa Tantras.* New York: Oxford University Press. 188–279.

Kumārasaṃbhava (KuSaṃ) of Kālidāsa. Ed. and trans. by M. R. Kale. [1917] 1995. *The Kumārasaṃbhava of Kālidāsa, Cantos I–VIII, Edited with the Commentary of Mallinātha, a Literal English Translation, Notes and Introduction.* Reprinted Edition. Delhi: Motilal Banarsidass.

Māṭharavṛtti (MāVṛ) of Māṭharācārya. See *Sāṅkhyakārikā.*

Vyākaraṇa-Mahābhāṣya (MaBhā) of Patañjali. [1880] 1985. Ed. by F. Kielhorn, rev. by K. V. Abhyankar. Pune: Bhandarkar Oriental Research Institute.

Mīmāṃsāsūtra (MīSū) of Jaimini. See *Śābarabhāṣya.*

Mṛgendratantra (MT). Ed. by Paṇḍit Madhusūdan Kaul Shāstrī. 1930. *The Śrī Mṛgendra Tantram (Vidyāpāda and Yogapāda), with the Commentary of Nārāyaṇakaṇṭha.* KSTS 50. Bombay: Nirnaya Sagar Press.

Mṛgendratantraṭīkā (MTṬ) of Nārāyaṇakaṇṭha. See *Mṛgendratantra.*

Nyāyabindu (NB) of Dharmakīrti. See *Nyāyabinduṭīkā.*

Nyāyabhūṣaṇa (NBh) of Bhāsarvajña. Ed. by Svāmī Yogīndrānanda. 1968. *Śrīmadācārya-bhāsarvajñapraṇītasya Nyāyasārasya Svopajñaṃ Vyākhyānaṃ Nyāyabhūṣaṇam.* Varanasi: Ṣaḍdarśana Prakāśana Granthamālā.

Nyāyabinduṭīkā (NBṬ) of Dharmottara. Ed. by Paṇḍita Dalsukhbhai Malvania. 1955. *Dharmottarapradīpa: Paṇḍita Durveka Miśra's Dharmottarapradīpa (Being a Sub-Commentary on Dharmottara's Nyayabindu-ṭīkā, A Commentary on Dharmakīrti's Nyaya-bindu).* Patna: Kashi Prasad Jayaswal Research Institute.

Nyāyakandalī (NK). See *Padārthadharmasaṅgraha.*

Nyāyamañjarī (NM) *of Jayantabhaṭṭa, with Editor's Nyāyasaurabha.* Ed. by K. S. Varadacharya. 1969–1983. 2 vols. Mysore: Oriental Research Institute.

Nyāyasūtra (NS). Ed. by A. Thakur. 1997. *Nyāyadarśana: Gautamīyanyāyadarśana with Bhāṣya of Vātsyāyana.* Delhi: Indian Council of Philosophical Research.

Nyāyasūtrabhāṣya (NSBh) of Vātsyāyana. See *Nyāyasūtra.*

Padārthadharmasaṅgraha (PDhS) of Praśastapāda. Ed. by V. P. Dvivedin. 1984. *Praśastapāda Bhāṣya (Padārthadharmasaṅgraha) with Commentary Nyāyakandalī of Śrīdhara.* Reprinted Edition [Banaras, 1895]. Delhi: Sri Satguru Publications.

Paramārthasāra (PS) of Abhinavagupta. Ed. by Jagadisha Chandra Chatterji. 1916. *The Paramārtha-Sāra by Abhinava Gupta, with the Commentary of Yogarāja.* KSTS 7. Srinagar, Kashmir: Kashmir Pratap Steam Press.

Paramārthasārasaṃgrahavivṛti (PSSaṃVi) of Yogarāja. See *Paramārthasāra.*

Pramāṇavārttika (PV) of Dharmakīrti. "Pramāṇavārttikam, by Ācārya Dharmakīrti." Ed. by Rāhula Sāṅkṛtyāyana. 1938–1940. *Journal of the Bihar and Orissa Research Society* 24–26. Appendices: 24: 1–136; 25: 137–480; and 26: 481–531 and 25–51.

Pramāṇavārttika (PV) of Dharmakīrti. Ed. by Raniero Gnoli. 1960. *The Pramāṇavārttikam of Dharmakīrti: The First Chapter with the Autocommentary.* Serie Orientale Roma 23. Rome: IsMEO.

Pramāṇavārttika(-alaṃkāra) (PVA) of Prajñākaragupta. Ed. by R. Sāṅkṛtyāyana. 1953. Patna: Kashi Prasad Jayaswal Research Institute.

Pramāṇavārttikasvopajñavṛtti (PVSV) of Dharmakīrti. Ed. by R. C. Pandeya. 1989. *Pramāṇavārttikavṛtti: Pramāṇavārttikam of Ācārya Dharmakīrti, with the Commentaries Svopajñavṛtti of the Author and Pramāṇavārttikavṛtti of Manorathanandin.* Delhi: Motilal Banarsidass.

Pramāṇavārttikavṛtti (PVV) of Manorathanandin. Ed. by R. C. Pandeya. 1989. *The Pramāṇavārttikam of Ācārya Dharmakīrti, with the Commentaries Svopajñavṛtti of the Author and Pramāṇavārttikavṛtti of Manorathanandin.* Delhi: Motilal Banarsidass.

Pramāṇaviniścaya (PVin) of Dharmakīrti. Ed. by Ernst Steinkellner. 2007. *Dharmakīrti's Pramāṇaviniścaya, Chapters 1 and 2.* Vienna and Beijing: China Tibetology Publishing House/Austrian Academy of Sciences Press, Beijing.

Śābarabhāṣya (ŚBh) of Śabarasvāmin. Ed. by E. Frauwallner. 1968. *Materialien zur ältesten Erkenntnislehre der Karmamīmāṃsā.* Wien: Verlag der Österreichischen Akademie der Wissenschaften.

Sāṅkhyakārikā (SāṅKā) of Īśvarakṛṣṇa. Ed. by Viṣṇu Prasād Śarmā [MV] and Satkāriśarmā Vaṅgīya [JM]. 1970. *Sāṁkhyakārikā of Śrīmad Īśvarakṛṣṇa with the Māṭharavṛtti of Māṭharācārya and the Jayamaṅgalā of Śrī Śaṅkara*. Chowkhamba Sanskrit Series 296 [work no. 56]. Varanasi: Chowkhamba Sanskrit Series Office.

Saṃbandhaparīkṣā (SP) of Dharmakīrti. Ed. and trans. by Erich Frauwallner. 1934. "Dharmakīrtis *Saṃbandhaparīkṣā*: Text und Übersetzung." *WZKM* 41: 261–300.

Saṃbandhasiddhi. See *Siddhitrayī*.

Siddhitrayī (ST) of Utpaladeva. Ed. by Pandit Madhusudan Kaul Shastri. 1921. *The Siddhitrayi and the Pratyabhijna-karika-vritti of Rajanaka Utpala Deva, Edited with Notes*. KSTS 34. Srinagar: Kashmir Pratap Steam Press.

Śivadṛṣṭi (ŚD) of Somānanda. Ed. by Madhusudan Kaul Shastri. 1934. *The Śivadṛṣṭi of Somānandanātha with the Vṛtti by Utpaladeva*. Kashmir Series of Texts and Studies 54. Pune: Aryabhushan Press.

Śivadṛṣṭivṛtti (ŚDVṛ) of Utpaladeva, a.k.a. the *Padasaṅgati*. See *Śivadṛṣṭi*.

Ślokavārttika (ŚV) of Kumārila. Ed. and rev. by Svāmī Dvārikādāsa Śāstrī. 1978. *Ślokavārttika of Śrī Kumārila Bhaṭṭa, with the Commentary Nyāyaratnākara of Śrī Pārthasārathi Miśra*. Varanasi: Tara Publications.

Ślokavārttikanyāyaratnākara (ŚVNRĀ) of Pārthasārathi MiŚra. See *Ślokavārttika*.

Tantrāloka (TĀ) of Abhinavagupta. Ed. by Mukund Rām Shāstrī (v. 1) and Madhusūdan Kaul Shāstrī (vv. 2–12). 1918–1938. *The Tantrāloka of Abhinava-Gupta, with Commentary by Rājānaka Jayaratha*. KSTS, nos. 23, 28, 30, 36, 35, 29, 41, 47, 59, 52, 57, 58. Allahabad and Bombay: Research Department of Jammu and Kashmir State.

Tantrālokaviveka (TĀV) of Jayaratha. See *Tantrāloka*.

Tantrasāra (TSā) of Abhinavagupta. Ed. by Mukund Rām Shāstrī. 1918. *The Tantrasāra of Abhinava Gupta*. KSTS 17. Bombay: Nirnay Sagar Press.

Tattvasaṅgraha (TS) of Śāntarakṣita. Ed. by Swami Dwarikadas Shastri. 1968. *The Tattvasaṅgraha of Ācārya Shāntarakṣita, with the Commentary "Pañjikā" of Shri Kamalashīla*. 2 vols. Bauddha Bharati Series 1. Varanasi: Bauddha Bhārati.

Tattvasaṅgrahapañjikā (TSP) of Kamalaśīla. See *Tattvasaṅgraha*.

Vaiśeṣikasūtra (VS) of Kaṇāda. Ed. by Muni Śrī Jambuvijayaji. 1961. *Vaiśeṣikasūtra of Kaṇāda, with the Commentary of Candrānanda*. Gaekwad's Oriental Series 136. Baroda: Oriental Institute.

Vaiśeṣikasūtravṛtti (VSVṛ) of Candrānanda. See *Vaiśeṣikasūtra*.

Vākyapadīya (VP) of *Bhartṛhari*. Ed. by W. Rau. 1977. *Bhratṛharis Vākyapadīya*. Abhandlungen für die Kunde des Morgenlandes 42. Wiesbaden: Komissionsverlag Frans Steiner.

Vākyapadīyavṛtti (VPVṛ) of Harivṛṣabha. Ed. by K. A. S. Iyer. 1966. *Vākyapadīya of Bhartṛhari with the Vṛtti and the Paddhati of Vṛṣabhadeva, Kāṇḍa I*. Deccan College Monograph Series 32. Pune: Deccan College.

Yuktidīpikā (YD) Commentary (Anonymous) on the SāṅKā. Ed. by A. Wezler and S. Motegi. 1998. *Yuktidīpikā: The Most Significant Commentary on the Sāṃkhyakārikā*. Vol. 1. Alt- und Neu-Indische Studien 44. Stuttgart: Franz Steiner Verlag.

Yogasūtra (YS) of Patañjali. Ed. by G. D. Śāstrī. 1989. *Sāṃkhyadarśana or Yogadarśana of Patañjali with the Scholium of Vyāsa and the Commentaries Tattva Vaiśāradī, Pātañjala Rahasya, Yogavārttika and Bhāsvatī of Vācaspati Miśra, Rāghavānanda Sarasvatī, Vijñāna

Bhikṣu and Hariharānandāraṇya. Second Edition. The Kashi Sanskrit Series 110. Varanasi: Chaukhamba Sanskrit Sansthan.

Secondary Sources

Akamatsu, Akihiko. 1999. "The Two Kinds of *anumāna* in Bhartṛhari's *Vākyapadīya*." *Journal of Indian Philosophy* 27.1: 17–22.

Aklujkar, Ashok. 1969. "Two Textual Studies of Bhartṛhari." *JAOS* 89.3: 547–563.

Aklujkar, Ashok. 1970. "The Philosophy of Bhartṛhari's *Trikāṇḍī*." Doctoral dissertation, Harvard University.

Alper, Harvey. 1971. "Abhinavagupta's Concept of Cognitive Power: A Translation of the *Jñānaśaktyāhnika* of the *Īśvarapratyabhijñāvimarśinī* with Commentary and Introduction." Doctoral dissertation, University of Pennsylvania.

Alper, Harvey. 1979. "Śiva and the Ubiquity of Consciousness: The Spaciousness of an Artful Yogi." *Journal of Indian Philosophy* 7.4: 345–407.

Apte, V. S. [1890] 1959. *The Practical Sanskrit-English Dictionary*. Revised and Enlarged Edition. Ed. by P. K. Gode and C. G. Karve. 3 Volumes. Poona: Prasad Prahashan.

Āraṇya, Hariharānanda, trans. [1963] 1983. *Patañjali: Yoga Philosophy of Patañjali Sūtra*. Albany: State University of New York Press.

Arnold, Dan. 2001a. "Of Intrinsic Validity: A Study on the Relevance of Pūrva Mīmāṃsā." *Philosophy East and West* 51.1: 26–53

Arnold, Dan. 2001b. "Intrinsic Validity Reconsidered: A Sympathetic Study of the Mīmāṃsaka Inversion of Buddhist Epistemology." *Journal of Indian Philosophy* 29.5–6: 589–675.

Arnold, Dan. 2005. *Buddhists, Brahmins, and Belief: Epistemology in South Asian Philosophy of Religion*. New York: Columbia University Press.

Arnold, Dan. 2006. "On Semantics and *Saṃketa*: Thoughts on a Neglected Problem with Buddhist *Apoha* Doctrine." *Journal of Indian Philosophy* 34.5: 415–478.

Arnold, Dan. 2008. "Buddhist Idealism, Epistemic and Otherwise: Thoughts on the Alternating Perspectives of Dharmakīrti." *Sophia* 47.1: 3–28.

Arnold, Dan. 2012. *Brains, Buddhas, and Believing: The Problem of Intentionality in Classical Buddhist and Cognitive-Scientific Philosophy of Mind*. New York: Columbia University Press.

Bandyopadhyay, Nandita. 1988. "The Conception of Contradiction in Indian Philosophy." *Journal of Indian Philosophy* 16.3: 225–246.

Bansat-Boudon, Lyne. 2014. "On Śaiva Terminology: Some Key Issues of Understanding." *Journal of Indian Philosophy* 42.1: 39–97.

Bansat-Boudon, Lyne, and Kamaleshadatta Tripathi. 2011. *An Introduction to Tantric Philosophy: The Paramārthasāra of Abhinavagupta with the Commentary of Yogarāja*. Routledge Studies in Tantric Traditions. London: Routledge.

Bäumer, Bettina and Raffaele Torella, Eds. 2016. *Utpaladeva, Philosopher of Recognition*. Shimla: Indian Institute of Advanced Study, and New Delhi: D. K. Printworld.

Bhate, Saroja, and Johannes Bronkhorst, Eds. 1994. *Bhartṛhari, Philosopher and Grammarian: Proceedings of the First International Conference on Bhartṛhari (University of Poona, January 6–8, 1992)*. 1st Edition. Delhi: Motilal Banarsidass.

Biardeau, Madeleine, Trans. 1958. *Sphoṭa Siddhi: La démonstration du sphoṭa, par Maṇḍana Miśra*. Pondicherry: Institut Français d'Indologie.

Biardeau, Madeleine. 1964a. *Théorie de la connaissance et philosophie de la parole dans le brahmanisme classique*. Paris and La Haye: Mouton & Co.

Biardeau, Madeleine, Trans. 1964b. *Vākyapadīya: Brahmakāṇḍa, avec la Vṛtti de Harivṛṣabha*. Paris: Éditions de Boccard.

Biardeau, Madeleine. 1969. *La Philosophie de Maṇḍana Miśra vue à partir de la Brahmasiddhi*. Publication of the École Française d'Extrême-Orient 76. Paris: École Française d'Extrême-Orient.

Bilimoria, Purushottama, and J. N. Mohanty, Eds. 1997. *Relativism, Suffering and Beyond: Essays in Memory of Bimal K. Matilal*. New Delhi: Oxford University Press.

Bronkhorst, Johannes. 1983. "God in Sāṃkhya." *WZKS* 27: 149–164.

Bronkhorst, Johannes. 1993. "Mysticisme et rationalité en Inde: Le cas du Vaiśeṣika." *Asiatische Studien/Études Asiatiques* 47.4: 559–569.

Bronkhorst, Johannes. 1996. "L'Inde classique et le dialogue des religions." *Asiatische Studien/Études Asiatiques* 50.4: 779–796.

Bronkhorst, Johannes. 2000. "The Last Reason for *satkāryavāda*." In R. Tsuchida and A. Wezler, Eds., *Harānandalaharī: Volume in Honour of Professor Minoru Hara on His Seventieth Birthday*. Reinbek: Dr. Inge Wezler Verlag für Orientalistische Fachpublikationen. 53–62.

Bronkhorst, Johannes, ed. 2007. *Mīmāṃsā and Vedānta: Interaction and Continuity*. Delhi: Motilal Banarsidass.

Bronkhorst, Johannes. 2011. *Language and Reality: On an Episode of Indian Thought*. Trans. from the French by M. S. Allen and R. Raghunathan. Leiden: Brill. [*Trans. of Langage et réalité: Sur un épisode de la pensée indienne*. Turnhout: Brepols, 1999.]

Bronkhorst, Johannes, and Yves Ramseier. 1994. *Word Index to the Praśastapādabhāṣya: A Complete Word Index to the Printed Editions of the Praśastapādabhāṣya*. Delhi: Motilal Banarsidass.

Cardona, George. 1974. Pāṇini's *kārakas*: Agency, Animation and Identity. *Journal of Indian Philosophy* 2: 231–306.

Carrithers, Micahel, Steven Collins, and Steven Lukes, Eds. 1985. *The Category of the Person: Anthropology, Philosophy, History*. Cambridge, England and New York: Cambridge University Press.

Chakrabarti, Kisor Kumar. 1975. "The Nyāya-Vaiśeṣika Theory of Universals." *Journal of Indian Philosophy* 3.3–4: 363–382.

Chakrabarti, Kisor Kumar. 1987. "The *svabhāvahetu* in Dharmakīrti's Logic." *Philosophy East and West* 37.4: 392–401.

Chaturvedi, Radheshyam, Trans. 1986. *The Śivadṛṣṭi of Śri Somānanda Nātha. [Hindi and Sanskrit]*. Varanasi: Varanaseya Sanskrit Saṅsthan.

Chemparathy, George. [1972] 2018. *An Indian Rational Theology: Introduction to Udayana's Nyāyakusumāñjali*. Reprinted Edition. Delhi: Motilal Banarsidass.

Chu, J. 2011. "Sanskrit Fragments of Dharmakīrti's *Santānāntarasiddhi*." In Krasser, et al., Eds., 2011: 33–42.

Coward, Harold G., and K. Kunjunni Raja, Eds. 1990. *Encyclopedia of Indian Philosophies. Vol. V: The Philosophy of the Grammarians*. Delhi: Motilal Banarsidass.

Dasgupta, Surendranath. [1922] 1991. *A History of Indian Philosophy*. 5 vols. Reprinted Edition. Delhi: Motilal Banarsidass.

Dravid, Raja Ram. [1972] 2001. *The Problems of Universals in Indian Philosophy*. Ed. Dr. Kanshi Ram. New Delhi: Motilal Banarsidass.

D'Sa, Francis Xavier. 1980. *Śabdaprāmāṇyam in Śabara and Kumārila: Towards a Study of the Mīmāṃsā Experience of Language*. De Nobili Research Library 7. Vienna: Institut für Indologie der Universität Wien.

Dunne, John D. 2004. *Foundations of Dharmakīrti's Philosophy*. Boston: Wisdom Publications.

Dunne, John D. 2006. "Realizing the Unreal: Dharmakīrti's Theory of Yogic Perception." *Journal of Indian Philosophy* 34: 497–519.

Dwivedi, R. C., Ed. [1994] 2016. *Studies in Mīmāṃsā: Dr. Mandan Mishra Felicitation Volume*. Reprinted Edition. Delhi: Motilal Banarsidass.

Edelglass, William, and Jay L. Garfield, Eds. 2009. *Buddhist Philosophy: Essential Readings*. Oxford: Oxford University Press.

Eltschinger, Vincent. 2007. *Penser l'autorité des Écritures: La polémique de Dharmakīrti contre la notion brahmanique orthodoxe d'un Veda sans auteur, Autour de Pramāṇavārttika I. 213–268 et Svavṛtti*. Vienna: Verlag der Österreichischen Akademie der Wissenschaften.

Eltschinger, Vincent. 2009a. "Ignorance, Epistemology and Soteriology, Part I." *Journal of the International Association of Buddhist Studies* 32.1–2: 39–83.

Eltschinger, Vincent. 2009b. "On the Career and the Cognition of Yogins." In Franco, Ed., 2009: 169–214.

Eltschinger, Vincent. 2010. "Dharmakīrti." *Revue Internationale de Philosophie* 64.253.3: 397–440.

Eltschinger, Vincent. 2014. *Buddhist Epistemology as Apologetics: Studies on the History, Self-Understanding and Dogmatic Foundations of Late Indian Buddhist Philosophy*. Vienna: Verlag der Österreichischen Akademie der Wissenschaften.

Eltschinger, Vincent, and Helmut Krasser, Eds. 2013. *Scriptural Authority, Reason and Action: Proceedings of a Panel at the 14th World Sanskrit Conference, Kyoto, September 1st–5th, 2009*. Vienna: Verlag der Österreichischen Akademie der Wissenschaften.

Eltschinger, Vincent, Helmut Krasser, and John Taber. 2012. *Can the Veda Speak? Dharmakīrti against Mīmāṃsā Exegetics and Vedic Authority: An Annotated Translation of PVSV 164, 24–176, 16*. Vienna: Verlag der Österreichischen Akademie der Wissenschaften.

Eltschinger, Vincent, and Isabelle Ratié. 2013. *Self, No-Self, and Salvation: Dharmakīrti's Critique of the Notions of Self and Person*. Vienna: Verlag der Österreichischen Akademie der Wissenschaften.

Eltschinger, Vincent, John Taber, Michael Torsten Much, and Isabelle Ratié. 2018. *Dharmakīrti's Theory of Exclusion (apoha), Part I: On Concealing, An Annotated Translation of Pramāṇavārttikasvavṛtti 24, 16–45, 20 (Pramāṇavārttika 1.40–91)*. Studia Philologica Buddhica 36. Tokyo: The International Institute for Buddhist Studies.

Faddegon, Barend. 1918. *The Vaiçeṣika-System Described with the Help of the Oldest Texts*. Amsterdam: Koninklijke Akademie van Wetenschappen. (Reprint: Liechtenstein: Saendig Reprint Verlag, 1969.)

Franco, Eli. 1991. "Whatever Happened to the Yuktidīpikā?" *WZKS* 35: 123–137.

Franco, Eli, Ed. 2009. *Yogic Perception, Meditation and Altered States of Consciousness*. Vienna: Verlag der Österreichischen Akademie der Wissenschaften.

Franco, Eli. 2011. "Perception of Yogis: Some Epistemological and Metaphysical Considerations." In Krasser, et al., Eds., 2011: 81–98.

Franco, Eli, and Miyako Notake. 2014. *Dharmakīrti on the Duality of the Object: Pramāṇavārttika* III.1–63. Leipziger Studien zu Kultur und Geschichte Süd- und Zentralasiens 5. Vienna and Berlin: Lit Verlag.

Franco, Eli, and Isabelle Ratié, Eds. 2016. *Around Abhinavagupta: Aspects of the Intellectual History of Kashmir from the 9th to the 11th Centuries (Proceedings of the International Conference held in Leipzig, 8-10/06/2013)*. Leipziger Studien zu Kultur und Geschichte Süd- und Zentralasiens 6. Berlin: Lit Verlag.

Frauwallner, Erich. 1932–1933. "Beiträge zur Apohalehre. I: Dharmakīrti; Übersetzung." *WZKM* 39: 247–285; 40: 51–94.

Frauwallner, Erich. 1935. "Beiträge zur Apohalehre: I; Dharmakīrti; Zusummenfassung." *Wiener Zeitschrift für die Kunde des Morgenlande* 42: 93–102.

Frauwallner, Erich. 1959. "Dignāga, sein Werk und seine Entwicklung." *WZKSO* 3: 83–164.

Frauwallner, Erich. 1962a. "Kumārila's *Bṛhaṭṭīkā*." *WZKSO* 6: 78–90.

Frauwallner, Erich. 1962b. *Aus der Philosophie der Śivaitischen Systeme*. Deutsche Akademie der Wissenschaften zu Berlin, Vorträge und Schriften 78. Berlin: Akademie-Verlag.

Geertz, Clifford. 2000. "Found in Translation: On the Social History of the Moral Imagination." In *Local Knowledge: Further Essays in Interpretive Anthropology*, by Clifford Geertz. 3rd Edition. New York: Basic Books. 36–54.

Gnoli, Raniero. 1957. "*Śivadṛṣṭi* by Somānanda: Translation and Commentary, Chapter I." *East and West* 8: 16–22.

Gnoli, Raniero. 1959. "*Vāc*: Il secondo capitolo della *Śivadṛṣṭi* di Somānanda." *Rivista degli Studi Orientali* 34.1–2: 55–75.

Goodall, Dominic. 1998. *Bhaṭṭa Rāmakaṇṭha's Commentary on the Kiraṇatantra. Vol. 1: Chapters 1–6; Critical Edition and Annotated Translation*. Pondicherry: Institut Français d'Indologie.

Goodall, Dominic. 2004. *The Parākhyatantra: A Scripture of the Śaiva Siddhānta; A Critical Edition and Annotated Translation*. Collection Indologie 98. Pondichéry: Institut Français de Pondichéry/École Française d'Extrême-Orient.

Goodall, Dominic, and André Padoux, Eds. 2007. *Mélanges tantriques à la mémoire d'Hélène Brunner*. Collection Indologie 106. Pondichéry: Institut Français de Pondichéry/École Française d'Extrême-Orient.

Goudriaan, Teun. 1978. *Māyā Divine and Human: A Study of Magic and Its Religious Foundations in Sanskrit Texts, with Particular Attention to a Fragment of Viṣṇu's Māyā Preserved in Bali*. Delhi: Motilal Banarsidass.

Grünendahl, Reinhold. 2001. *South Indian Scripts in Sanskrit Manuscripts and Prints: Grantha Tamil, Malayalam, Telugu, Kannada, Nandinagari*. Wiesbaden: Harrassowitz Verlag.

Halbfass, Wilhelm. 1980a. *Studies in Kumārila and Śaṅkara*. Reinbek: Verlag für Orientalistische Fachpublikationen.

Halbfass, Wilhelm. 1980b. "Karma, *Apūrva*, and 'Natural' Causes: Observations on the Growth and Limits of the Theory of *Sāṃsāra*." In Wendy Doniger O'Flaherty, Ed., *Karma and Rebirth in Classical Indian Traditions*. Berkeley and Los Angeles: University of California Press. 268–302.

Halbfass, Wilhelm. 1992. *On Being and What There Is: Classical Vaiśeṣika and the History of Indian Ontology*. Albany: State University of New York Press.

Hattori, Masaaki. 1968. *Dignāga: On Perception, Being the Pratyakṣapariccheda of Dignāga's Pramāṇasamuccaya*. Harvard Oriental Series 47. Cambridge, MA: Harvard University Press.

Hattori, Masaaki. 1997. "The Buddhist Theory Concerning the Truth and Falsity of Cognition." In Bilimoria and Mohanty, Eds., 1997: 361–371.

Hattori, Masaaki. 2000. "Dignāga's Theory of Meaning: An Annotated Translation of the *Pramāṇasamuccayavṛtti*, Chapter V: *Anyāpoha-parīkṣā* (I)." In Jonathan A. Silk, Ed., *Wisdom, Compassion, and the Search for Understanding: The Buddhist Studies Legacy of Gadjin M. Nagao*. Honolulu: University of Hawaii Press. 137–146.

Hattori, Masaaki. 2006a. "Introduction." In M. Hattori, Ed., "Word and Meaning in Indian Philosophy." Special issue, *Acta Asiatica (Bulletin of the Institute of Eastern Culture)* 90: iii–xii.

Hattori, Masaaki. 2006b. "The *Apoha* Theory as Referred to in the *Nyāyamañjarī*." In M. Hattori, Ed., "Word and Meaning in Indian Philosophy." Special issue, *Acta Asiatica (Bulletin of the Institute of Eastern Culture)* 90: 55–70.

Hayes, Richard. 1988. *Dignāga on the Interpreation of Signs*. Studies of Classical India 9. Dordrecht, Boston, and London: Kluwer Academic Publishers.

Houben, Jan E. M. 1994. "Liberation and Natural Philosophy in Early Vaiśeṣika: Some Methodological Problems." *Asiatische Studien/Études Asiatiques* 48.2: 711–748.

Hulin, Michel. 1978. *Le Principe de l'ego dans la pensée indienne classique: La notion d'Ahaṃkāra*. Publications de l'Institut de Civilisation Indienne 44. Paris: De Boccard.

Ingalls, Daniel, Ed. and Trans, and Jeffrey Moussaieff Masson and M. V. Patwardhan, Trans. 1990. *The Dhvanyāloka of Ānandavardhana with the Locana of Abhinavagupta*. Harvard Oriental Series 49. Cambridge, MA: Harvard University Press.

Iwata, Takashi. 2004. "The Negative Concomitance (*vyatireka*) in the Case of Inconclusive (*anaikāntika*) Reasons." In Katsura and Steinkellner, Eds., 2004: 91–134.

Iyer, K. A. S. 1964. "Bhartṛhari on *vyākaraṇa* as a Means of Attaining *mokṣa*." *Adyar Library Bulletin* 28: 112–132.

Iyer, K. A. S., Trans. 1965. *The Vākyapadīya of Bhartṛhari with the Vṛtti: Chapter I; English Translation*. Pune: Deccan College.

Iyer, K. A. S., Trans. 1966. *Sphoṭasiddhi of Maṇḍana Miśra: English Translation*. Poona : Deccan College Postgraduate and Research Institute.

Iyer, K. A. S., Trans. 1971. *The Vākyapadīya of Bhartṛhari: Chapter III, Part I; English Translation*. Pune: Deccan College.

Iyer, K. A. S., Trans. 1974. *The Vākyapadīya of Bhartṛhari: Chapter III, Part II; English Translation*. Pune: Deccan College.

Iyer, K. A. S., Trans. 1977. *The Vākyapadīya of Bhartṛhari: Kāṇḍa II, English Translation with Exegetical Notes*. Delhi: Motilal Banarsidass.

Iyer, K. A. S. [1969] 1992. *Bhartrhari: A Study of the Vākyapadīya in Light of the Ancient Commentaries*. 2nd Edition. Pune: Deccan College.

Iyer, K. A. S., and K. C. Pandey, Eds. 1986. *The Doctrine of Divine Recognition*. 3 Vols. 2nd Edition. Delhi: Motilal Banarsidass.

Jha, Ganganatha, Trans. 1907. *Çlokavārttika: Translated from the Original Sanskrit with Extracts from the Commentaries of Sucarita Miśra (the Kāśikā) and Pārtha Sārathi Miśra (the Nyāyaratnākara)*. Calcutta: Asiatic Society.

Jha, Ganganatha, Trans. [1933–1936] 1973–1974. *Śābara-Bhāṣya, Translated into English.* 3 Vols. Baroda: University of Baroda (Sadhana Press).

Jha, Ganganatha, Trans. 1937–1939. *The Tattvasaṅgraha of Shāntarakṣita, with the Commentary of Kamalashīla, Translated into English.* 2 Vols. Gaekwad Oriental Series 80 and 83. Baroda: Oriental Institute.

Jha, Ganganatha, Trans. 1939. *Gautama's Nyāyasūtras, with Vātsyāyana-Bhāṣya, Translated into English with His Own Revised Notes.* Poona Oriental Series 59. Poona: Oriental book Agency.

Jha, Ganganatha, Trans. [1915] 1982. *Padārthadharmasaṅgraha of Praśastapāda, With the Nyāyakandalī of Śrīdhara.* Chaukhambha Oriental Series 4. Varanasi and Delhi: Chaukhambha Orientalia.

Kajiyama, Yuichi. 1965. "Controversy between the Sākāra- and Nirākāra-vādins of the Yogācāra School: Some Materials." *Journal of Indian and Buddhist Studies (Indogaku Bukkyōgaku Kenkyū)* 14.1: 429–418.

Kataoka, Kei. 2008. "A Critical Edition of Bhaṭṭa Jayanta's *Nyāyamañjarī*: The Section on Kumārila's Refutation of the *Apoha* Theory." *The Memoirs of the Institute of Oriental Culture* 154: 636–594.

Kataoka, Kei. 2011. *Kumārila on Truth, Omniscience, and Killing. Vol. 1: A Critical Edition of Mīmāṃsā-Ślokavārttika ad 1.1.2 (Codanāsūtra). Vol. 2: An Annotated Translation of Mīmāṃsā-Ślokavārttika ad 1.1.2 (Codanāsūtra).* Vienna: Verlag der Österreichischen Akademie der Wissenschaften.

Katsura, Shōryū. 1984. "Dharmakīrti's Theory of Truth." *Journal of Indian Philosophy* 12.3: 215–235.

Katsura, Shōryū. 1991. "Dignāga and Dharmakīrti on Apoha." In E. Steinkellner, Ed., *Studies in the Buddhist Epistemological Tradition: Proceedings of the Second International Dharmakīrti Conference.* Vienna: Österreichische Akademie der Wissenschaften. 129–146.

Katsura, Shōryū. 1993. "On Perceptual Judgement." In Wagle and Watanabe, Eds., 1993: 66–75.

Katsura, Shōryū, ed. 1999. *Dharmakīrti's Thought and Its Impact on Indian and Tibetan Philosophy: Proceedings of the Third International Dharmakīrti Conference, Hiroshima,* November 4–6, 1997. Vienna: Verlag der Österreichischen Akademie der Wissenschaften.

Katsura Shōryū, and Ernst Steinkellner, eds. 2004. *The Role of the Example (dṛṣṭānta) in Classical Indian Logic.* Wiener Studien zur Tibetologie und Buddhismuskunde 58. Vienna: Arbeitskreis für Tibetische und Buddhistische Studien Universität Wien.

Kaul, Mrinal and Ashok Aklujkar, eds. 2008. *Linguistic Traditions of Kashmir: Essays in Memory of Paṇḍit Dinanath Yaksha.* New Delhi: D.K. Printworld in association with Harabhatta Shastri Indological Research Institute, Jammu.

Kawajiri, Yohei. 2016. "New Fragments of the *Īśvarapratyabhijñā-ṭīkā*." In Bäumer and Torella, Eds., 2016: 77–101.

Kellner, Birgit, et al., Eds. 2007. *Pramāṇakīrti: Papers Dedicated to Ernst Steinkellner on the Occasion of His 70th Birthday.* 2 Vols. Vienna: Arbeitskreis für Tibetische und Buddhistische Studien, Universität Wien.

Klaus, Konrad, and Jens-Uwe Hartmann, Eds. 2007. *Indica et Tibetica: Festschrift für Michael Hahn zum 65 Geburtstag von Freunden und Schülern überreicht.* Wiener Studien zur Tibetologie und Buddhismuskunde 66. Vienna: Arbeitskreis für Tibetische und Buddhistische Studien, Universität Wien.

Krasser, Helmut. 2001. "On Dharmakīrti's Understanding of *pramāṇabhūta* and His Definition of *pramāṇa*." *WZKS* 45: 173–199.

Krasser, Helmut, Horst Lasic, Eli Franco, and Birgit Kellner, Eds. 2011. *Religion and Logic in Buddhist Philosophical Analysis: Proceedings of the Fourth International Dharmakīrti Conference, Vienna, August 23–27, 2005*. Beiträge zur Kultur- und Geistesgeschichte Asiens 69. Vienna: Verlag der Österreichischen Akademie der Wissenschaften.

Kupetz, Steven J. 1972. "The Non-Dualistic Philosophy of Kashmir Śaivism: An Analysis of the Pratyabhijñā School." Doctoral dissertation, University of Minnesota.

Kuranishi, Kenichi. 2013. "*Yantras* in the Buddhist Tantras: *Yamāritantras* and Related Literature." In Nina Mirnig, Péter-Dániel Szántó, and Michael Williams, Eds., *Puṣpikā: Tracing Ancient India Through Texts and Traditions*. Vol. 1. Oxford and Oakville: Oxbow Books. 265–281.

Larson, Gerald James. 1969. *Classical Sāṃkhya: An Interpretation of Its History and Meaning*. Delhi: Motilal Banarsidass.

Larson, Gerald James, and Ram Shankar Bhattacharya, Eds. 1987. *The Encyclopedia of Indian Philosophies. Vol. 4: Sāṃkhya, A Dualist Tradition in Indian Philosophy*. Delhi: Motilal Banarsidass, and Princeton, NJ: Princeton University Press.

Larson, Gerald James, and Ram Shankar Bhattacharya, Eds. 2003. *The Encyclopedia of Indian Philosophies. Vol. 12: Yoga: India's Philosophy of Meditation*. Delhi: Motilal Banarsidass.

Lawrence, David Peter. 2009. "Proof of a Sentient Knower: Utpaladeva's *Ajaḍapramātṛsiddhi* with the *Vṛtti* of Harabhatta Shastri." *Journal of Indian Philosophy* 37.6: 627–653.

Lindtner, Christian. 1984. "Marginalia to Dharmakīrti's *Pramāṇaviniścaya* I-II." *WZKS* 28: 149–175.

Lindtner, Christian. 1991. "The Initial Verses of the *Prāmāṇasiddhi* Chapter in the *Pramāṇavārttika*." In Ernst Steinkellner, Ed., *Studies in the Buddhist Epistemological Tradition: Proceedings of the Second International Dharmakīrti Conference, Vienna, June 11–16, 1989*. Beiträge zur Kultur- und Geistesgeschichte Asiens 8. Wien: Verlag der Österreichischen Akademie der Wissenschaften. 155–159.

Lindtner, Christian. 1994. "Linking Up Bhartṛhari and the Bauddhas." In Bhate and Bronkhorst, Eds., 1994: 195–215.

Matilal, Bimal Krishna. 1985. *Logic, Language and Reality*. New Delhi: Motilal Banarsidass.

Matilal, Bimal Krishna. 1986. *Perception: An Essay on Classical Indian Theories of Knowledge*. New Delhi: Oxford University Press.

Matilal, Bimal Krishna. 1991a. *The World and the Word: India's Contribution to the Study of Language*. New Delhi: Motilal Banarsidass.

Matilal, Bimal Krishna. 1991b. "Dharmakīrti and the Universally Negative Inference." In Ernst Steinkellner, Ed., *Studies in Buddhist Epistemological Tradition: Proceedings of the Second International Dharmakīrti Conference, Vienna, June 11–16, 1989*. Vienna: Österreichische Akademie der Wissenschaften. 161–168.

Matilal, Bimal Krishna, and R. D. Evans, eds. 1986. *Buddhist Logic and Epistemology: Studies in the Buddhist Analysis of Inference and Language*. Studies of Classical India 7. Dordrecht: D. Reidel.

McCrea, Lawrence. 2013. "The Transformations of Mīmāṃsā in the Larger Context of Indian Philosophical Discourse." In Eli Franco, Ed., *Periodization and Historiography of Indian Philosophy.* Vienna: Institut für Südasien-, Tibet- und Buddhismus- kunde der Universität Wien. 127–144.

McCrea, Lawrence. 2016. "Abhinavagupta as Intellectual Historian of Buddhism." In Eli Franco and Isabelle Ratié, Eds., *Around Abhinavagupta: Aspects of Intellectual History of Kashmir from the Ninth to the Eleventh Century.* Leipziger Studien zu Kultur und Geschichte Süd- und Zentralasiens 6. Leipzig: Lit Verlag. 263–286.

Merkrebs, Allen Hillel. 1977. "The Concept of *adṛṣṭa* in Vaiśeṣika Philosophy as an Explanation for the Law of Karma." Doctoral dissertation, University of Michigan.

Mimaki, Katsumi. 1976. *La Réfutation Bouddhique De La Permanence Des Choses (Sthirasiddhidūṣaṇa) et la Preuve De La Momentanéité Des Choses (Kṣaṇabhaṅgasiddhi).* Paris: Institut de Civilisation Indienne.

Muller-Ortega, Paul. 1989. *The Triadic Heart of Śiva: Kaula Tantricism of Abhinavagupta in the Non-Dual Shaivism of Kashmir.* Albany: State University of New York Press.

Nagatomi, Masatoshi. 1957. "A Study of Dharmakīrti's *Pramāṇavārttika*: An English Translation and Annotation of the *Pramāṇavārttika*, Book I." Doctoral dissertation, Harvard University.

Nemec, John. 2009. "Translation and the Study of Indian Religions." *Journal of the American Academy of Religion* 77.4: 757–780.

Nemec, John. 2011. *The Ubiquitous Śiva: Somānanda's Śivadṛṣṭi and His Tantric Interlocutors.* New York: Oxford University Press.

Nemec, John. 2012. "The Two Pratyabhijñā Theories of Error." *Journal of Indian Philosophy* 40.2: 225–257.

Nemec, John. 2016. "Realism and the Pratyabhijñā: Influences on and Legacies of Somānanda's Conception of Materiality." In Eli Franco and Isabelle Ratié, Eds., *Around Abhinavagupta: Aspects of Intellectual History of Kashmir from the Ninth to the Eleventh Century.* Leipziger Studien zu Kultur und Geschichte Sud- und Zentralasiens 6. Leipzig: Lit Verlag. 339–371.

Nemec, John. 2017. "On the Contributions of the *Śivadṛṣṭi* of Somānanda to the Intellectual History of the Pratyabhijñā." *Annuaire de l'École Pratique des Hautes Études (EPHE), Section des Sciences Religieuses* 124: 15–23.

Nemec, John. 2018. "The Body and Consciousness in Early Pratyabhijñā Philosophy: *Amūrtatva* in Somānanda's *Śivadṛṣṭi*." In Bettina Bäumer and Hamsa Stainton, Eds., *Tantrapuṣpāñjali: Tantric Traditions and Philosophy of Kashmir, Studies in Memory of Pandit H. N. Chakravarty.* New Delhi: Indira Gandhi National Centre for the Arts and Aryan Books International. 215–225.

Nemec, John. 2019. "Somānanda on the Meaningfulness of Language." *Indo-Iranian Journal* 62.3: 227–268.

Nemec, John. Forthcoming. "Somānanda's Arguments against the Vedāntins."

Oberhammer, Gerhard. 1960. "The Authorship of the *Ṣaṣṭitantram*." *WZKSO* 4: 71–91.

Oberhammer, Gerhard, and Ernst Steinkellner, Eds. 1982. *Erich Frauwallner: Kleine Schriften.* Glasenapp-Stiftung 22. Wiesbaden: Franz Steiner Verlag.

Olivelle, Patrick. 1996. *Upaniṣads. Oxford World's Classics.* New York: Oxford University Press.

Pandey, K. C. 1954. *Bhāskarī. Vol. 3: An English Translation of the Īśvara Pratyabhijñā Vimarśinī in the Light of the Bhāskarī with an Outline of the History of Śaiva Philosophy.* Princess of Wales Saraswati Bhavana Texts 84. Lucknow: Superintendent Printing and Stationary, U. P. (India).

Pandey, K. C. [1963] 2000. *Abhinavagupta: An Historical and Philosophical Study.* 2nd Edition. Varanasi: Chowkhamba Sanskrit Series Office.

Pandey, K. C., and R. C. Dwivedi. 1986. *An Outline of the History of Śaiva Philosophy.* Delhi: Motilal Banarsidass.

Pandit, B. N. 1973. *Kaśmīra-Śaiva-Darśana [Hindi].* Jammu: Śrīraṇavīra Kendrīya Sanskṛt Vidyāpītha.

Pandit, B. N. 1977. *Aspects of Kashmir Śaivism.* Srinagar: Utpal Publications.

Pandit, B. N., Trans. 1991. *The Essence of the Exact Reality (Paramārthasāra of Abhinavagupta).* New Delhi: Munshiram Manoharlal.

Pandit, B. N. 1997. *Specific Principles of Kashmir Shaivism.* New Delhi: Munshiram Manoharlal.

Pind, Ole Holten. 2009. "Dignāga's Philosophy of Language Dignāga on *anyāpoha Pramāṇasamuccaya* V: Texts, Translation, and Annotation." Doctoral dissertation, University of Vienna.

Rastogi, Navjivan. 1977–1978. "Recognition in the Pratyabhijñā School: A Study in Epistemology." *Annals of the Bhandarkar Oriental Research Institute* 58–59: 841–861.

Rastogi, Navjivan. 1986. "Theory of Error According to Abhinavagupta." *Journal of Indian Philosophy* 14.1: 1–34.

Ratié, Isabelle. 2006. "La mémoire et le Soi dans l'*Īśvarapratyabhijñāvimarśinī* d'Abhinavagupta." *Indo-Iranian Journal* 49.1–2: 39–103.

Ratié, Isabelle. 2007. "Otherness in the Pratyabhijñā Philosophy." *Journal of Indian Philosophy* 35.4: 313–370.

Ratié, Isabelle. 2010a. "The Dreamer and the Yogin: On the Relationship between Buddhist and Śaiva Idealisms." *Bulletin of the School of Oriental and African Studies* 73.3: 437–478.

Ratié, Isabelle. 2010b. "A Five-Trunked, Four-Tusked Elephant Is Running in the Sky: How Free Is Imagination According to Utpaladeva and Abhinavagupta?" *Asiatische Studien/Études Asiatiques* 64.2: 341–385.

Ratié, Isabelle. 2011a. *Le Soi et l'Autre: Identité, différence et altérité dans la philosophie de la Pratyabhijñā.* Jerusalem Studies in Religion and Culture 13. Leiden and Boston: Brill.

Ratié, Isabelle. 2011b. "Can One Prove That Something Exists Beyond Consciousness? A Śaiva Criticism of the Sautrāntika Inference of External Objects." *Journal of Indian Philosophy* 39.4–5: 479–501.

Ratié, Isabelle. 2014a. "A Śaiva Interpretation of the *Satkāryavāda*: The Sāṃkhya Notion of *Abhivyakti* and Its Transformation in the Pratyabhijñā Treatise." *Journal of Indian Philosophy* 42.1: 127–172.

Ratié, Isabelle. 2014b. *Une critique bouddhique du Soi selon la Mīmāṃsā: Présentation, édition critique et traduction de la Mīmāṃsakaparikalpitātmaparīkṣā de Śāntarakṣita (Tattvasaṅgraha 222–284 et Pañjikā).* Wien: Verlag der Österreichischen Akademie der Wissenschaften.

Ratié, Isabelle. 2016. "Some Hitherto Unknown Fragments of Utpaladeva's *Vivṛti* (I): On the Buddhist Controversy over the Existence of Other Conscious Streams." In Bäumer and Torella, Eds., 2016: 224–256.

Reich, James D. 2016. "Meaning and Appearance: The Theology of Literary Emotions in Medieval Kashmir." Doctoral dissertation, Harvard University.

Sanderson, Alexis. 1985. "Purity and Power among the Brahmins of Kashmir." In S. Collins, M. Carrithers, and S. Lukes, Eds., *The Category of the Person: Anthropology, Philosophy and History*. Cambridge, England: Cambridge University Press. 190–216.

Sanderson, Alexis. 2006. "The Date of Sadyojyotis and Bṛhaspati." *Cracow Indological Studies* 8: 39–91.

Sanderson, Alexis. 2007. "The Śaiva Exegesis of Kashmir." In Dominic Goodall and André Padoux, Eds., *Mélanges tantriques à la mémoire d'Hélène Brunner/Tantric Studies in Memory of Hélène Brunner.* Collection Indologie 106. Pondicherry: Institut Français d'Indologie/École Française d'Extrème-Orient. 231–442, 551–582.

Sharma, Arvind. 2004. *Sleep as a State of Consciousness in Advaita Vedānta*. Albany, NY: SUNY Press.

Stcherbatsky, F. Th. [1930–1932] 1993. *Buddhist Logic*. 2 Vols. 1st Indian Edition. Delhi: Motilal Banarsidass.

Steinkellner, Ernst, Ed. 1991. *Studies in Buddhist Epistemological Tradition: Proceedings of the Second International Dharmakīrti Conference, Vienna, June 11–16, 1989*. Vienna: Österreichische Akademie der Wissenschaften.

Taber, John. 1986. "Utpaladeva's *Īśvarasiddhi*." *The Adyar Library Bulletin* 52, Golden Jubilee Volume: 106–137.

Taber, John. 1990. "The Mīmāṃsā Theory of Self-Recognition." *Philosophy East and West* 40.1: 35–57.

Taber, John. 1992a. "Further Observations on Kumārila's *Bṛhaṭṭīkā*." *Journal of Oriental Research, Madras* 56.62: 179–189.

Taber, John. 1992b. "What Did Kumārila Bhaṭṭa Mean by *Svataḥ Prāmāṇya*?" *Journal of the American Oriental Society* 112.2: 204–221.

Taber, John. 1994. "Kumārila's Refutation of the Dreaming Argument: The *Nirālambana-vāda-adhikaraṇa*. In Dwivedi, Ed., 1994: 27–52.

Taber, John. 2005. *A Hindu Critique of Buddhist Epistemology: Kumārila on Perception, The "Determination of Perception" Chapter of Kumārila Bhaṭṭa's Ślokavārttika*. Routledge Hindu Studies Series. London: Routledge.

Taber, John. 2007. "Kumārila the Vedāntin?" In Bronkhorst, Ed., 2007: 159–184.

Taber, John. 2010. "Kumārila's Buddhist." *Journal of Indian Philosophy* 38.3: 279–296.

Tarkatīrtha, Pandit Visvabandhu. 1992. "The Nyāya on the Meaning of Some Words." Trans. with explanatory notes by J. L. Shaw. *Journal of Indian Philosophy* 20.1: 41–88.

Tillemans, Tom J. F. 2000. *Dharmakīrti's Pramāṇavārttika: An Annotated Translation of the Fourth Chapter (Parārthānumāna). Vol. 1: (k. 1-148)*. Vienna: Verlag der Österreichischen Akademie der Wissenschaften.

Torella, Raffaele. 1992. "The Pratyabhijñā and the Logical-Epistemological School of Buddhism." In Teun Goudriaan, Ed., *Ritual and Speculation in Early Tantrism: Studies in Honor of André Padoux*. Albany: State University of New York Press. 327–346.

Torella, Raffaele. 1999. "Sāṃkhya as *Sāmānyaśāstra*." *Asiatische Studien/Études Asiatiques* 53: 553–562.

Torella, Raffaele. 2004. "How Is Verbal Signification Possible: Understanding Abhinav-agupta's Reply." *Journal of Indian Philosophy* 32.2–3: 173–188.

Torella, Raffaele. 2007a. "Studies on Utpaladeva's *Īśvarapratyabhijñā-vivṛti*: Part I; Anupalabdhi and Apoha in a Śaiva Garb." In Karin Preisendanz, Ed., *Expanding and Merging Horizons: Contributions to South Asian and Cross-Cultural Studies in Commemoration of Wilhelm Halbfass.* Vienna: Österreichishce Akademie der Wissenschaften. 473–490.

Torella, Raffaele. 2007b. "Studies in the *Īśvarapratyabhijñāvivṛti*: Part II; What Is Memory?" In Hartmann and Klaus, Eds., 2007: 539–564.

Torella, Raffaele. 2007c. "Studies on Utpaladeva's *Īśvarapratyabhijñāvivṛti*: Part III; Can a Cognition Become the Object of Another Cognition?" In Goodall and Padoux, Eds., 2007: 475–484.

Torella, Raffaele. 2007d. "Studies in Utpaladeva's *Īśvarapratyabhijñāvivṛti*: Part IV; Light of the Subject—Light of the Object." In Kellner, et al., Eds., 2007, vol. 2: 925–939.

Torella, Raffaele. 2008. "From an Adversary to the Main Ally: The Place of Bhartṛhari in the Kashmirian Śaiva Advaita." In M. Kaul and A. Aklujkar, Eds., *The Linguistic Traditions of Kashmir: Essays in Memory of Pandit Dinanath Yaksha.* Delhi: D. K. Printworld. 508–524.

Torella, Raffaele. 2012. "Studies in Utpaladeva's *Īśvarapratyabhijñā-vivṛti*: Part V; Self-awareness and Yogic Perception." In Voegeli, et al., Eds., 2012: 275–300.

Voegeli, François, Vincent Eltschinger, Danielle Feller, Maria Piera Candotti, Bogdan Diaconescu and Malhar Kulkarni, Eds. 2012. *Devadattīyam: Johannes Bronkhorst Felicitation Volume.* Welten Süd- und Zentralasiens/Worlds of South and Inner Asia/Mondes de l'Asie du Sud et de l'Asie centrale 5. Bern: Peter Lang.

Wagle, Narendra K., and Fumimaro Watanabe, Eds. 1993. *Studies on Buddhism in Honour of Prof. A .K. Warder.* Toronto: University of Toronto, Center for South Asian Studies.

Watanabe, Toshikazu. 2011. "Dharmakīrti's Criticism of *Anityatva* in the Sāṃkhya Theory." *Journal of Indian Philosophy* 39.4–5: 553–569.

Watson, Alex. 2006. *The Self's Awareness of Itself: Bhaṭṭa Rāmakaṇṭha's Arguments against the Buddhist Doctrine of No-Self.* Publications of the De Nobili Research Library 32. Vienna: De Nobili Research Library.

Wezler, Albrecht. 1983. "A Note on the Concept of *adṛṣṭa* as Used in the *Vaiśeṣikasūtra.*" In B. Datta, U. C. Sharma, and Nitin J. Vyas, Eds., *Aruṇa-Bhāratī: Professor A. N. Jani Felicitation Volume (Essays in Contemporary Indological Research).* Baroda: Viveka Publications. 35–58.

{ ALPHABETICAL INDEX OF THE HALF-VERSES OF ŚD 4 }

{ INDEX OF REFERENCES TO THE ĪPK AND ĪPKVṛ }

ĪPK (and ĪPKVṛ ad) Adhikāra 1

ĪPK (and ĪPKVṛ ad) Adhikāra 2

ĪPK (and ĪPKVṛ ad) Adhikāra 3

ĪPK (and ĪPKVṛ ad) Adhikāra 4

{ INDEX OF KEY AUTHORS, TERMS, AND TEXTUAL REFERENCES }

All references are to page numbers of the book. If a term appears in the footnotes of a page, the reference indicates as much with: n. (= "n[otes]."). No reference to the appearance of a given term in the notes is made on pages on which the same term appears in the main body of the text, nor is any indication given where a term appears multiple times on the same page. No variant readings from the critical edition are indexed, but only the Sanskrit text of the *Śivadṛṣṭi* and Utpaladeva's commentary, along with the accompanying notes, are indexed here below.